The Handbook of
Narrative Analysis

Blackwell Handbooks in Linguistics

This outstanding multi-volume series covers all the major subdisciplines within linguistics today to offer a comprehensive survey of linguistics as a whole.
To see the full list of titles available in the series please visit www.wiley.com/go/linguistics-handbooks

The Handbook of Narrative Analysis

Edited by

Anna De Fina and Alexandra Georgakopoulou

WILEY Blackwell

Registered Office
John Wiley & Sons, Inc., 111 River Street, Hoboken, NJ 07030, USA

Editorial Office
9600 Garsington Road, Oxford, OX4 2DQ, UK

For details of our global editorial offices, customer services, and more information about Wiley products visit us at www.wiley.com.

Wiley also publishes its books in a variety of electronic formats and by print-on-demand. Some content that appears in standard print versions of this book may not be available in other formats.

Library of Congress Cataloging-in-Publication data applied for

Paperback [9781119052142]

Cover image: Abstract painting by Clive Watts – Blue Curve. © clivewa/Shutterstock
Cover design: Wiley

Set in 10/12pt Palatino by SPi Global, Pondicherry, India

Contents

Transcription Conventions

emphasis (voice slightly raised)	**bold typeface** or *italic*
following volume noticeably lower	°
in-breath	·hhhh (by length)
out-breath	hhhh (by length)
intonation unity continues into next line	→
latching between utterances	=
laughter during speech	@
lengthening of preceding sound	: :: ::: :::: (by length)
loud	CAPS
marked rising intonation	↑
marked falling intonation	↓
material omitted	[...]
omission of morphemes	Ø
overlap	[
(P)	pause more than 3 seconds
(p)	pause 3 seconds or less
pause	(.) (..) (...) (....) (by length)
plosive aspiration (breathiness, laughter, crying)	(h)
silent interval, in seconds	(0.0)
speech faster	> <
speech slower	< >
transcriber's comment	(( )) or [ ]
truncation of word or syllable	-
uncertain transcription	( )

Abbreviations for Chapter 7, Wolof Transcriptions

-ADV	adverb
-aux.emph	auxiliary verb

-AUX.SUBJ	subject auxiliary verb
-CLSF	classifier stem
-CNTV	continuative suffix
-DIST	distal deictic stem
-FR	French
-NEG	negative stem
-PROX	proximal deictic stem
-PAST	past tense
-SG	singular
-SIT	situative infix

Symbols for Chapter 10 Figures

intonation continuing	,
intonation falling	.
intonation rising	?

Notes on Contributors

Gary Barkhuizen is Professor and Head of the School of Cultures, Languages and Linguistics at the University of Auckland, New Zealand. His teaching and research interests include language teacher education, applied sociolinguistics, and learner language. He is the editor of *Narrative Research in Applied Linguistics* (2013) and author (with Phil Benson and Alice Chik) of *Narrative Inquiry in Language Teaching and Learning Research* (2014).

Mike Baynham is Professor of TESOL at the University of Leeds, UK. His research interests include literacy, language, and migration as well as oral narrative. He is currently researching translanguaging in a superdiverse inner city neighborhood and LGBT issues in Adult ESOL. He is also developing a research focus on the theme of queer migrations.

Isolda E. Carranza is Full Professor of Linguistics at the National University of Córdoba, Argentina. She has chaired the Argentine chapter of the Latin American Association of Discourse Studies, reviews articles for major international journals, and serves as a scientific evaluator in university and government funding agencies. Her writings have appeared in *Pragmatics*, *Discourse & Society*, *Narrative Inquiry*, *Oralia*, and *Spanish in Context*, and in volumes published by John Benjamins, Erlbaum, Vervuert, and Routledge.

Anna De Fina is Professor of Italian Language and Linguistics at Georgetown University, USA. She is the author of *Identity in Narrative: A Study of Immigrant Discourse* (2003), and co-editor of many volumes, among which *Discourse and Identity* (2006) with M. Bamberg and D. Schiffrin. She has published widely on topics related to migrant and transnational communities, superdiversity, identities, and narrative.

Anna De Fina and Alexandra Georgakopoulou are longstanding collaborators on narrative research. In addition to this *Handbook*, they have co-authored *Analyzing Narrative: Discourse and Sociolinguistic Perspectives* (2012) and they are currently co-editing the *Handbook of Discourse Studies*. They are also (co)-editors (with Ruth Page) of 'Narrative, interaction and discourse'.

Arnulf Deppermann is head of the department of Pragmatics at the Institute for the German Language (IDS) and Professor of German Linguistics at the University of

Mannheim, Germany. His main areas of research include conversation analysis, multimodal interaction, positioning, grammatical constructions, semantics, and understanding in interaction.

Susan Ehrlich is Professor of Linguistics in the Department of Languages, Literatures and Linguistics, York University, Toronto, Canada. She works on the intersections of language, gender, and the law. Her books include *Representing Rape: Language and Sexual Consent* (2001); *"Why Do You Ask": The Function of Questions in Institutional Discourse* (2010, co-edited with Alice Freed); and *Coercion and Consent in the Legal Process* (forthcoming, co-edited with Diana Eades and Janet Ainsworth).

Mark Freeman is Professor and Chair of Psychology as well as Distinguished Professor of Ethics and Society at the College of the Holy Cross, USA. He is the author of works including *Rewriting the Self: History, Memory, Narrative* (1993), and *Hindsight: The Promise and Peril of Looking Backward* (2010), and also serves as editor for the Oxford University Press series "Explorations in Narrative Psychology."

Yiannis Gabriel is Professor of Organizational Theory at Bath University, UK and a Visiting Professor at the University of Lund, Sweden. Yiannis is known for his work in leadership, management learning, organizational storytelling, and the culture and politics of contemporary consumption. Recently he has researched leadership and patient care and the experiences of unemployed managers and professionals.

Alexandra Georgakopoulou is Professor of Discourse Analysis and Sociolinguistics, King's College, London, UK. She has developed small stories research, a paradigm for the analysis of everyday life stories and their role in the (re)formation of social relations of intimacy and in youth and gender identity politics. Her latest research is on the mobilization of small stories on social media as part of the ERC project, *'Life-writing of the moment: The sharing and updating self on social media'*.

Alexandra Georgakopoulou and Anna De Fina are longstanding collaborators on narrative research. In addition to this *Handbook*, they have co-authored *Analyzing Narrative: Discourse and Sociolinguistic Perspectives* (2012) and they are currently co-editing the *Handbook of Discourse Studies*. They are also (co)-editors (with Ruth Page) of *'Narrative, interaction and discourse'*.

Charles Goodwin uses video to investigate how language is built through interaction between speakers and hearers, grammar in context, cognition in the lived social world, gesture, gaze, and embodiment as interactively organized social practices, aphasia in discourse, language in the professions, and the ethnography of science.

Cynthia Gordon is Associate Professor of Communication and Rhetorical Studies at Syracuse University, USA. A member of the editorial boards of *Language in Society* and the *Journal of Language and Social Psychology*, she is also author of *Making Meanings, Creating Family: Intertextuality and Framing in Family Interaction* (2009).

Emily Heavey is a research associate at York St John University, UK. She completed her PhD at King's College London, researching narrative body constructions by people who have undergone amputations and mastectomies. Her research interests include narratives of illness, surgery, and the post-surgery body, narrative identity, sociologies of the body, patient experiences, and narrative medicine.

Matti Hyvärinen, PhD, is Professor of Sociology at the University of Tampere, Finland. Hyvärinen is the co-editor of the volumes *Beyond Narrative Coherence* (2010) and *The Travelling Concepts of Narrative* (2013), and the special issue "Narrative Knowing, Living, Telling" for *Partial Answers* (2008).

Catherine Kohler Riessman is a sociologist and Emerita Professor at Boston University, USA. Throughout her long career, she has studied and compared the narratives women and men develop to account for biographical disruptions, including divorce, infertility, and chronic illness in mid-life. She is the author of *Divorce Talk* (1990), *Narrative Analysis* (1993), and *Narrative Methods for the Human Sciences* (2008), as well as many journal articles and book chapters.

Michele Koven is Associate Professor of Communication at the University of Illinois at Urbana-Champaign, USA. She holds courtesy appointments in Anthropology, Global Studies, French, and the Center for Writing Studies. She is interested in how transnationally mobile people perform and infer cultural identities in a variety of discourse contexts. She is the author of *Selves in Two Languages* (2007) and numerous articles in major sociolinguistic journals.

Masahiko Minami is Professor at San Francisco State University, USA. He is also an Invited Professor at the National Institute for Japanese Language and Linguistics as well as Editor-in-Chief of the *Journal of Japanese Linguistics*. He received his doctorate from Harvard University. His recent works include *Telling Stories in Two Languages: Multiple Approaches to Understanding English-Japanese Bilingual Children's Narratives* (2011).

Ruth Page is a Reader at the University of Leicester, UK. Her research spans literary-critical and discourse-analytic research traditions, with a special focus on language and gender and narratives told in new media.

Sabina Perrino is affiliated with the University of Michigan, USA. She earned a PhD in Linguistic and Sociocultural Anthropology at the University of Pennsylvania. She has conducted fieldwork in Senegal and among Senegalese migrants in Italy. Her interests include narrative analysis, interaction, textuality, dialect revitalization, transnational migration, and poetics in political speeches.

Catherine R. Rhodes is a joint-PhD candidate in Education, Culture, and Society and Linguistic Anthropology at the University of Pennsylvania, USA. She has written on scale, narrative, processes of social identification, and the New Latino Diaspora.

She currently conducts research in the Yucatan, Mexico on the relationship between the production of scientific knowledge and models of indigenous personhood.

Amy Shuman is Professor of Folklore and Director of Disability Studies at The Ohio State University, USA. Her books include *Storytelling Rights: The Uses of Oral and Written Texts by Urban Adolescents* (1986); *Other People's Stories: Entitlement Claims and the Critique of Empathy* (2005); and *Rejecting Refugees: Political Asylum in the 21st Century* (2007, with Carol Bohmer). She is a core faculty member of Project Narrative at Ohio State University.

Stef Slembrouck is a Professor at Ghent University, Belgium. His research addresses communicative practices in institutional contexts, including the effects of globalization-affected multilingualism. Recent book publications include *Language Practices in Social Work: Categorization and Accountability in Child Welfare* (2006, with Christopher Hall and Srikant Sarangi) and *Globalization and Language Contact: Scale, Migration, and Communicative Practices* (2009, with James Collins and Mike Baynham).

Dorien Van De Mieroop is an assistant professor in Dutch linguistics at the Faculty of Arts of the University of Leuven, Belgium. Her research focuses on the discursive analysis of identity construction in interview narratives and in naturally occurring interactions. She has published articles in *Discourse & Society*, *Narrative Inquiry*, *Pragmatics*, etc.

Stanton Wortham is Judy and Howard Berkowitz Professor of Education at the Graduate School of Education, University of Pennsylvania, USA. He has written on classroom discourse and the linguistic anthropology of education, interactional positioning in media discourse and autobiographical narrative, and Mexican immigrant communities in the New Latino Diaspora. More information can be found at http://scholar.gse.upenn.edu/stantonw.

Introduction

ANNA DE FINA AND ALEXANDRA GEORGAKOPOULOU

Why a Handbook in Narrative Analysis?

About a decade ago, in our transatlantic exchanges, we discovered that we shared a common experience as teachers and scholars of narrative who worked within a linguistic framework: there was a frustrating lack of state-of-the-art resources that would bring together existing sociolinguistic and discourse/micro-analytic research on everyday conversational storytelling while also reflecting on the latest advances in this body of work and its wider contribution to the study of narrative. It is now a truism that narrative studies constitute a rich and varied field that has been shaped by numerous disciplinary traditions. Nonetheless, it is also a fact that certain traditions have been better represented than others. Narratology, traditionally involving the study of literary narrative, can boast several state-of-the-art collections, including, for example, the *Routledge Encyclopedia of Narrative Theory* (Herman, Jahn, and Ryan 2005). As a result, classical and post-classical narratological texts are well established and widely known. Narrative psychology is another illustrative case of an area with a more or less agreed-upon history of foundational texts in narrative (see, e.g., Sarbin 1986; Crossley 2000). In both these fields, the formation of a critical mass has been premised on the longstanding privileging of specific types of narrative: fiction in the former and life-stories elicited in research interviews in the latter. In a similar vein, the term "narrative inquiry," often employed as an umbrella term for studies of (non-literary) autobiographical narrative in the social sciences (e.g., Clandinin and Connelly 2000), has not traditionally included in its remit linguistically-minded research on stories told by ordinary people in diverse environments. The study of such stories is frequently described as "narrative analysis" and tends to be subsumed under broader linguistic fields, as the inclusion of chapters on narrative analysis in sociolinguistics, pragmatics, and discourse analysis handbooks (Wodak, Johnstone, and Kersville 2010; Tannen, Hamilton, and Schiffrin, in press) shows. However

The Handbook of Narrative Analysis, First Edition. Edited by Anna De Fina and Alexandra Georgakopoulou.
© 2015 John Wiley & Sons, Inc. Published 2019 by John Wiley & Sons, Inc.

undeniable the cross-fertilization of narrative analysis with a wide array of linguistic areas is, it is also important to recognize that there are specific concerns within narrative analysis that are on occasion better served with dedicated publications, forums, and other scholarly activities. This move toward a consolidation of a critical mass is not aimed at homogenizing narrative analysis or constructing a false consensus. On the contrary, our aim is to showcase the multiplicity of traditions and influences – both within and outside linguistics – in the current forms and practices of narrative analysis. So far, the discussions of narrative analysis always in connection with a "broader" area of linguistics may have inadvertently privileged specific works, such as Labov's admittedly foundational study of narrative within sociolinguistics, at the expense of the more comprehensive coverage that dedicated collections inevitably produce.

Our first joint endeavor toward bringing together seemingly disparate works on narrative analysis and celebrating the critical mass created by them was to produce an introductory overview, *Analyzing Narrative: Discourse and Sociolinguistic Perspectives* (De Fina and Georgakopoulou 2012). The present Handbook felt like the natural next step. For readers of *Analyzing Narrative*, it provides a deeper, multi-strand engagement with specific topics that our earlier volume could not have developed more fully, such as time and space, embodiment, reflexivity. At the same time, for readers of this Handbook, *Analyzing Narrative* can provide a back-to-the-basics experience of specific issues, particularly regarding micro-analytical aspects. Of course, the Handbook is meant as an independent resource, too – one that can serve as a point of departure for focused readings of foundational works, through the tasters that its chapters provide to a wide array of issues. In its entirety, the Handbook can also serve as a barometer of the latest advances, including the decisive move of narrative analysis to concerns traditionally viewed as typical of "narrative inquiry" – for instance, the construction of subjectivities and experientiality through stories, the intimate link between narrative and modes of self- and other-understanding, and the epistemological place of narrative research in the wide range of qualitative micro-perspectives on people's identities.

In the absence of a body of publications that have crystallized both the key foundational works and the current trends in narrative analysis, this Handbook is inevitably, even if not unquestionably, serving in the role of a collective output that has had to select and push to the forefront certain approaches and not others. We are very mindful as editors of creating biases of all sorts, and our efforts not to become too wedded to specific standpoints have led us to a thematic organization. By singling out themes and issues that seem to have preoccupied narrative scholars in general, and by teasing out some of the ways of studying those themes as they have developed within narrative analysis, we are offering a set of guidelines for analytical engagement rather than prescriptions for specific frameworks of analysis. That said, several of our chapters showcase modes of analytical engagement that are compatible with a view of stories not just as texts, amenable to a purely formal analysis, but as socioculturally shaped practices, interactionally drafted in specific local contexts. We will discuss this in more detail below.

From Narrative Analysis of Texts to the Analysis of Social Practices

The Handbook represents another step in advancing a shift from texts to practices in narrative studies that has been at the center of our work for the last decade (see De Fina and Georgakopoulou 2008). The practice-based "social interactional" approach to narratives that we have been proposing involves combining a focus on local interaction as a starting point for analysis with an understanding of the embedding of narratives within discursive and sociocultural contexts. In particular, we have argued (De Fina and Georgakopoulou 2008: 275–276) that this "new" turn in narrative analysis should revolve around:

(i)   a focus on interaction and the local level
(ii) an emphasis on the contextualizing power of narratives
(iii) a commitment to social theoretical concerns

Let us briefly discuss each of these points. As emphasized by conversation analysts (see Sacks 1992; Schegloff 1997), the study of narratives needs to pay close attention to the local level of interaction, where stories should be analyzed for the ways in which they develop and emerge within specific participation frameworks and for how they are enmeshed in local doings, rather than as finished products. Thus, understanding what participants do with narratives in the storytelling world and how they position themselves vis-à-vis each other in the process is a premise for capturing the why and how of story-world contents as well. Our approach, however, takes a further step beyond the local level of tellings and looks for links and articulations between different levels of context and different scales in order to explain how the telling of stories shapes and is shaped by ideologies, social relations, and social agendas in different communities, times, and spaces. Narratives are shaped by contexts, but they also create new contexts by mobilizing and articulating fresh understandings of the world, by altering power relations between peoples, by constituting new practices. This dynamicity of storytelling cannot be captured without studying the embedding and functioning of narrative practices within other practices. The third point above refers to a concern with de-essentializing narrative, particularly regarding its connections with identity. While recognizing that telling stories is a fundamental tool in the building of identities, we also stress the situated nature of identity construction processes. This commitment to social constructionism as an approach to identity emphasizes the emergent, situated, and negotiated nature of all identity claims in discourse (see Hall 2000) – an important measure for overcoming the shortcomings of a transparent and representational equation between studying narratives and studying "the self" that has dominated the field, particularly since the consolidation of the narrative turn in the social sciences.

The theoretical methodological concerns described above underlie the selection of contributions included in the Handbook and the dialogue among them. The chapters collected here can be seen as both introducing scholars to different areas of narrative research and exemplifying new ways of approaching them. The works presented also testify to the richness of recent reflection and theorization in the field. Some of the chapters represent emerging and thriving foci within sociolinguistics, such as work on social media, small stories research, stories across contexts, that can feed into and engage with both narrative inquiry and narratological approaches. Other chapters deal with areas traditionally shaped and influenced by narrative inquiry concerns and sensibilities, such as work on reflexivity, embodiment, story ownership, and chronotopic configurations. However, in addressing longstanding concerns, the authors adopt perspectives and methodologies that reflect the new focus on practices and interaction that we have described above.

A clear articulation between our theoretical-methodological foci and the work presented here can be found in the contributions that address genre and narrative. Authors (see, for example, Hyvärinen, Carranza) propose the study of genres not as a priori categories defined by formal characteristics, but as embedded in social action and as aligning with particular expectations about form, content, and development in specific communities of practices. Here, the thrust of the argument is that in order to capture the nature of narrative genres, it is necessary to analyze the community of practice that produced the discourse, the "ways of speaking" used by that community within particular language practices (and therefore the knowledge and expectations surrounding the use of genres), and finally the constraints and affordances of the contexts and media in which these genres are emerging.

A different angle on genres is offered by authors who investigate the embedding of narratives within institutional contexts, where the analysis focuses on the kinds of narrative genres employed within routine activities, their functions, and their relations with identity claims. A case in point is Gabriel's critical assessment of the ways in which stories shape the identities of organizations and contribute to disseminating and sharing knowledge. Such contributions illustrate how what defines genres is not a set of characteristics, but dynamic relations between participants in communities, texts, and practices.

As mentioned above, a focus on practices also implies a highlighting of issues of performance and interactional management in storytelling. Thus, contributors who examine stories in everyday life tend to adopt a dual focus on topics and story worlds on the one hand and participation frameworks and local interaction on the other, thus documenting the inseparability of the two. For example, Gordon's chapter on family stories builds on a tradition that regards narrative as a significant socialization tool (see Heath 1983; Ochs and Capps 2001), illustrating how knowledge and rules are shared and socialized not only in terms of contents transmitted but also in terms of instantiation of social roles. In this way, storytelling is incorporated into everyday activities such as meals, and it helps shape and foster community attachments and identities. Issues of co-tellership and participation are a central focus in most chapters in the volume (see, among others, Georgakopoulou, De Fina, Heavey, Page), as authors discuss the many ways in which stories are co-produced, co-evaluated, owned, or contested by participants.

Story ownership is another important theme on which different chapters offer reflections. This is not a new topic in narrative research, as proponents of the "narrative turn" (Bruner 1991; Mishler 1986) have advocated the role that stories play in finding and at times being given a voice in the case of silenced and marginalized subjects. But the equation between telling a story and being empowered has recently been the object of critique and rethinking. Following this trend, Shuman, for example, proposes an investigation of the types of claims that are put forth to justify, defend, or contest entitlement and story ownership, and she illustrates how these claims intertwine with institutional and non-institutional roles. This area also clearly exemplifies the embedding of storytelling in different contexts and practices, as local negotiations and contestations about rights to own and tell stories link them to broader societal stances about who can talk, what is tellable, and by whom.

Another issue that has traditionally occupied narrative turn researchers (see Mishler 1986) is reflexivity – "the hall of mirrors," as pointedly defined by Riessman. The topic has also been of great interest to sociolinguists, especially in regards to research interviewing (see De Fina and Perrino 2011). Again, connections between this issue and the focus of our volume are obvious: the moment that storytelling is studied from a practice-based, interactional perspective, the inevitable consequence is that reflexivity comes to the fore. Among the questions that authors address in this regard are the following: What is the role of the researcher within the storytelling and the research process? What kind of investments and relations tie researchers and subjects? How do such investments shape interpretation of data? How are reciprocal responsibilities managed? As Slembrouck notes in his chapter, a focus on reflexivity illustrates the difference between viewing stories as monologically-narrated answers to interviewers' questions and viewing them as the sequential unfolding of narrative across successive question-answer sequences.

A common thread linking various contributions to the volume and a corollary to the stress on reflexivity can be found in the view of storytelling as a meaning-making process not only for narrators in general, but also for researchers. Applications of this idea can be seen in the deliberate choice of stories as methodological tools to make sense of events and situations. See, for example, Barkhuizen's use of the term "narrative knowledging" as a form of understanding. Such a conception takes us far from the contemplative mood of claims from within the "narrative turn" about narrative being essential to identity, as it points to connections between narrative, knowledge, and action.

An important objective of the Handbook is to bring to the fore new directions and methodological advances in narrative analysis. One area that is witnessing a growing interest is that of storytelling in new/social media environments. Yet work on this topic within narrative studies has been slow to catch up with research in other disciplines (see Georgakopoulou 2013). Mediated contexts (as analyzed here by Georgakopoulou and Page) illustrate not only the emergence of new genres, but also the blending of old and new, the potential for more complex forms of participation and more diverse audience roles than we are accustomed to in face-to-face interaction, and the wide distribution and embedding of storytelling within different media and platforms. All of this in turn makes us aware of the ever-evolving nature of storytelling practices, the ability of narrators to exploit the affordances of different media, but also the limitations that different kinds of mediated environments impose on the types of stories that can be told and how they can be told.

Another longstanding concern that is being viewed in new conceptual and analytical ways within social interactional approaches to narrative is the role of time and space in narrative plots. As we discuss below, a reflection on these dimensions can take narrative analysts in different (and all equally important) directions, opening up the study of chains of narrative events, the investigation of how connections between space, time, and ideological stances can index wide chronotopic configurations, and finally, the discovery of how storytelling transforms spaces into lived and meaningful places. In the rest of this introduction we present an overview of the structure of the Handbook.

Overview

"Narrative foundations" are a natural starting point for the thematic organization in the Handbook; indeed, this is the theme of the chapters that form Part I. Regardless of the diversity of perspectives within narrative studies, there have been certain themes and ideas that have preoccupied scholars across the board: How do we organize and make sense of our experience with stories? What is the role of narrative in the understanding of self over time? How are stories shaped by culture and by norms of socialization into communicative practices? If there is such an intimate link between experience and stories, who has the right to tell whose stories, where, why, and how? All of these questions are bound up with governing ideas in the inception of the narrative turn about the primacy of narrative as a mode of thinking and communication. It is fair to say that assumptions of narrative primacy have filtered down to most perspectives on the study of narrative, but they have also met with critique. This has particularly been the case within narrative analytic positions that have been effective in problematizing essentialist takes on narrative by drawing attention to issues of context and interaction. But as Mark Freeman's chapter shows, the critique of these positions has also happened from within narrative inquiry.

Freeman goes through each counter-position to the primacy of narrative as a mode for self-understanding, arriving at a post-critique "verdict," very much informed by Ricoeur's ideas on narrative and time, that there is something specific and unique about self-understanding through narrative. This rests on the *retrospective* dimension, that is, "the fact that narratives always and necessarily entail looking backward, from some present moment, and seeing in the movement of events *episodes* that are part of some larger whole," normally referred to as the "plot." Freeman suggests that if this active and essentially poetic (in the sense of a creative putting together) dimension of meaning-making is integral to narrative, its study cannot be done (only) in a dispassionate data-gathering fashion: narrative researchers are inevitably "ethnographers and writers, better attuned to cultural context, better able to see how this context has been woven into the fabric of both living and telling, and, not least, better able to draw upon the poetic power of language in conveying the ambiguity, messiness, and potential beauty of people's lives.". The need for such researcher reflexivity and engagement is resonant in other chapters, too, as we will see when discussing chapters in Part III. So is the idea that specific language choices partake in the creation of emplotment and meaningful connections among characters, events, and assessments.

This idea has been lent contextual nuance from social interactional approaches to narrative, as we see throughout the Handbook. At the same time, Freeman's foundational assumptions about the intimate link between reflection, self-understanding, and a specific type of narrative, namely the life story, have also become the object of discussion and contention, as we see in Georgakopoulou's chapter. The variety and diversity of narrative activities documented in everyday life contexts warrant a rethinking of the retrospective dimension and reflection as somehow inherently connected with narrative meaning-making and even as pivotal constituents of it. At the same time, it is also imperative to explore what happens to these retrospective notions of plot in contexts that do not always allow for reflection, for example, in social media (see Georgakopoulou, Page). If the notion of plot is a fundamentally retrospective idea, can the plot be established through interactional and reading practices rather than residing in the teller alone? Is there evidence that narrativity – that is, the inclination to make spatiotemporal and events-based configurations of meaning – remains an important need outside of contexts that engender self-reflection?

Most views in Freeman's chapter presuppose a primacy within narrative primacy, namely that of the personal life story. It is this link between personal experience and storying that is taken up in Amy Shuman's chapter, which explores what is at stake in contests and questions about who owns a story and who is entitled to tell it or hear it. Drawing on contextualized work from a variety of cases, from adolescents' stories to judicial contexts and from asylum seekers' stories to the use of personal stories to advocate a social cause, Shuman shows how claiming or challenging ownership of a story or the entitlement to tell it "points beyond the stories themselves to issues of status, dignity, power, moral, and ethical relations among tellers and listeners." Shuman pays special attention to cases of "retellings" which "complicate (and undermine) the unstated rule that the person who suffered or experienced the event has the right to tell it." As we see in other chapters as well (e.g., Wortham and Rhodes, Ehrlich), every retelling is a dynamic act of recontextualization that produces new meanings and, in Shuman's case, new authority relations, too. As Shuman shows, the nature of the contexts of retelling (i.e., private or public) and the surrounding cultural conventions are crucial for issues of story ownership, entitlement, and disclosure of experience. A very important device in these contexts of retelling is that of reported speech (also see Wortham and Rhodes, Perrino, as well as throughout Part V). Shuman shows how the entitlement to tell somebody else's story is always linked with complex relationships of power, authority, and credibility on the one hand, and questions of what can be told and what remains unspeakable on the other hand. Shuman's discussion adds dimensions of complexity to the longstanding ideas about tellers' ownership of experience. It shows that our stories as a rule travel beyond us and that the exploration of these travels raises "questions that can be answered at different levels of analysis, from observations of actual interactions … to philosophical and ethical arguments about the obligations and/ or rights to speak on behalf of oneself or others."

Within the narrative turn, the close links between narrative and understanding have often been sought in narrative's versatility as a communication mode and its ability to perform functions other than just telling a story. The study of narrative as a mode of argumentation has been key to this inquiry, and this is what Isolda Carranza's chapter explores. Carranza's contribution is a vivid illustration of how longstanding concerns within narrative studies have been enriched by the analytical focus on stories in everyday contexts as socioculturally shaped practices. Carranza shows how the pivotal "moves" of argumentation through narrative – namely putting forth claims and backing them – are bound up with what "different demands" various social contexts impose "on the means and paths for arguing in favor of a position or for justifying a decision." She also scrutinizes the context-specificity of linguistic choices through which certain operations of claim-backing are done – for instance, explanations and justifications that suspend the narrative action, answers to "why" questions during the telling of a story, etc. A very important conclusion from Carranza's study, and one that warrants more exploration in the future, concerns the inverse relationship between narrativity and argumentation: explicit articulations of the teller's evaluative ideological stances through a story's telling reduce its narrativity in the sense that they detract from the conveying of experience. If "in any single argumentative-narrative text, argumentativity and narrativity cannot be equally dominant," as Carranza has it, how does this connect with Freeman's close association between emplotment and self-understanding and with Shuman's entitlement issues in the telling of somebody else's experience?

Masahiko Minami's chapter specifically singles out the cultural context, and in particular the values, beliefs, and socialization norms of a culture, in order to explore how they shape narrative styles. The starting point of the chapter is that the acquisition of culture-specific communicative competence plays a critical role in the process of language acquisition and the development of narrative discourse skills. The chapter takes as its case study adult learners' oral personal narratives in Japanese as their second language in order to examine how narrative skills develop as learners' language proficiency levels increase. Drawing on Labov's (1972) structural model, the study mainly focuses on the organization of narratives as well as their actual length as indicators of narrative socialization and change. Overall, in the examination of JSL learners' L2 narrative discourse patterns, the study revealed that L2 learners seem to develop different strategies from those used by native speakers (e.g., talking loquaciously), and that some of L2 learners' strategies may reflect the influence of L1 on their L2 narratives. Minami's chapter illustrates how specific choices in stories at different levels (grammatical, lexical, organizational) can be the outcome of the intersection between the cognitive and the sociocultural: in particular, he points to the speakers' "cognitive ability to integrate forms from different systems and to develop those options so as to meet different communicative goals and discourse functions, and the cultural recognition of what constitutes the favored options of a given speech community, adapted to varied communicative contexts and to different norms of usage."

From cognitive and sociocultural ways of learning how to tell a story in a specific language, we move in Gary Barkhuizen's chapter to how second and foreign language teachers and learners learn about themselves through engaging in narrative research. Barkhuizen fittingly chooses a processual term to describe these journeys of learning and self-reflection, namely "narrative knowledging." This refers to "the meaning making, learning, or knowledge construction that takes place during the narrative research activities of (co)constructing narratives, analyzing narratives, reporting the findings, and reading/watching/listening to research reports." In this case, as in other chapters (see Riessman), narrative research itself becomes a co-construction – a jointly accomplished process of understanding that goes beyond the restrictive dualism of teacher-student.

In this chapter, too, the advances made by contextualized narrative analytic work are shown and discussed against the background of a tradition of content-focused studies within narrative inquiry. Processes of knowledging are irreducibly situated in the interactional dynamics of narrative encounters, and ultimately the study of content cannot be divorced from attention to the stories' communicative "how." Barkhuizen makes the important point that the time is now ripe to take contextualized, researcher-reflexive narrative analyses to new methodological ventures, for example by employing mixed and multi-methods in the study of narrative, by drawing on innovative ways of reporting research findings, and by involving numerous stakeholders, including broader communities of scholars, in narrative research projects. Such ventures, while firmly placed in the anti-positivist, hermeneutic tradition of narrative inquiry, and at the original political edge of the narrative turn in general, are now being notably infused with key insights from social interactional studies of narrative. As such, they attest to an emerging synergy between narrative inquiry and narrative analysis, which is to be found in other chapters in this Handbook, too (e.g., Gabriel, Georgakopoulou).

Part II brings together contributions that delve into time and space relations in stories, following up on a recent trend in narrative studies that advocates the reevaluation of the significance of the dimension of space vis-à-vis the dimension of time, both in the story world and in the storytelling world. We have argued, together with other scholars (see Baynham 2003, De Fina 2003, Georgakopoulou 2003, Slembrouck 2003), that because of the longstanding privileging of time and chronological sequencing as the hallmark of narrative, little attention has been devoted to space as another structuring principle and point of reference for narrative action. We have also argued that time and space have often been regarded simply as "orientational" elements and as mere background information in classic treatments of narratives (e.g., Labov and Waletzky 1967), when in fact they can be a fundamental resource for the creation of plots. This line of inquiry is continued by Mike Baynham, who illustrates the constitutive role of orientation in storytelling and argues for the need to overcome Aristotelian notions of narrative as essentially defined by chronology and causality. Baynham claims that narrative analysis should move toward a "performative account of space/time relations in narrative" may fully recognize the relationships between the linguistic and the social. Thus, orientation choices are never neutral, but also configure some kind of positioning by the narrator. In his thorough review of recent work in this area, Baynham shows how space-time orientation elements can be used not only to structure the action, but also to index and convey different kind of identities.

In similar ways, Sabina Perrino takes up the idea of the interconnectedness of time, space, and history in the chronotopic configurations that underlie narratives. Like Baynham, she uses the Bakhtinian notion of chronotope as a tool to both study and unveil the interactionally grounded nature of stories. Perrino argues that while narratives are often presumed to be anchored in the past, storytellers in fact create much more complex temporal and spatial configurations by exploiting the complex relations between present and past, the context of the telling, and the context of the told. While many narrative analysts have recognized the existence of this important distinction between the "denotational" and "interactional" text, Perrino shows that the notion of "chronotopes" provides a useful tool to analyze how narrators dynamically exploit the relations between these two elements. Using examples from storytelling events in different languages and contexts, she demonstrates that tellers achieve different pragmatic effects through the manipulation of varied spatio-temporal alignments between the world of the story and the storytelling world. Thus, she illustrates that an analysis in terms of chronotopes allows for an interactional account of narrative practices capable of linking the story worlds evoked with the storytelling here-and-now through the study of narrators' and audiences' negotiations.

Another direction taken by recent research on time and space in narrative is represented by the inquiry into forms of interconnectedness between storytelling events and narrators across times and spaces. In this line of research, illustrated in Stanton Wortham and Catherine Rhodes's chapter, storytelling instances often belong to chains of related events that can take place not only across time but also in different media and among different participants. The authors argue that storytelling events should not be studied exclusively as discrete communicative instances, since " narratives are joined together in chains or trajectories, through discursive processes that link speech events to each other, such that signs and individuals move along chains of narrating events that occur in different spatiotemporal locations." The authors review linguistic devices such as voicing, reported speech, reference, and other intertextual strategies that demonstrate the interconnectedness between a specific event and other elements of the context that lie behind and around it. But they then go on to argue that narrative events cannot be fully understood without looking at the communicative chains into which they are inserted. Retelling and gossip are obvious cases in which narratives link different communicative moments, but narrative chains and linked trajectories can also explain how identities, ideological stances, and other forms of social representation are constituted, circulated, and stabilized across time and space in different communities.

Matti Hyvärinen extends the reflection from specific narrative structures related to time and space to the construct of genre, a wider configuration designed to capture different kinds of narrative organization, including spatiotemporal elements. In line with the authors of the other chapters in Part II, Hyvärinen advocates a "social" and "sociological" perspective in which genres are seen as expressions of particular social norms and expectations and are conceived in light of their historical development and emergence rather than as responses to sets of abstract categories. For example, when considering the case of illness narratives, Hyvärinen argues that certain well-known genres such as "the restitution narrative" are created, circulated, and promoted thanks to the role that they play not only in the communicative practices of individuals, but also in institutional practices that promote them in service of particular ends. In this way, the author draws our attention to the historical developments and trajectories of genres and subgenres, once again illustrating the embedding of storytelling in social action.

Part III presents chapters that focus on the interactional accomplishment of storytelling. This is an area that saw exponential growth in the late 1990s in connection with an increasing dissatisfaction with the Labovian (Labov 1972; Labov and Waletzky 1967) model among narrative analysts, particularly in sociolinguistics. The critique has mainly centered on the inability of the model to account for the interactional negotiations that surround storytelling, its erasure of the context in which narratives emerge, its rigid division of stories into grammatical units (clauses), and its contradictory mixing of syntactic and functional criteria in the definition of narrative (see, e.g., Ochs and Capps 2001; Schegloff 1997). Subsequent work on stories-in-interaction, carried out mainly, albeit not exclusively, by conversation analysts, has highlighted, among other phenomena, the importance of openings and closings as moments of negotiation among narrators and participants (Jefferson 1978), the role of the audience in shaping tellings (Goodwin 1986), the limits of a view of narrative as a monological affair, and the need to closely analyze co-construction, resistance, and opposition (for details, see De Fina and Georgakopoulou 2012, chapter 4). As a consequence, attention has shifted from stories as structural units to storytelling as accomplishing social action and from exclusive interest in interview narratives to the consideration of a wide gamut of stories.

The chapters in Part III point to further developments in this direction, showing how it is possible to expand on the work of conversation analysts both in terms of the contexts studied and in terms of the methodological consequences that derive from an interactional orientation. A case in point is Georgakopoulou's chapter, which presents a view of the important developments that have taken place since the beginnings of the "small stories" movement in the early 2000s, together with reflections on the extent and manner of interactional embedding of storytelling in both research-generated and non-research-generated contexts. At the same time, the micro-analytically documented notion of interaction is brought into a productive dialogue with the notion of researcher-researched co-construction, as we see, for example, in Riessman's chapter. The grouping of chapters in Part III has therefore been a conscious choice aimed at highlighting precisely the clear connections between small stories research and other types of interactionally oriented approaches to narrative, but also the latest interconnections between interaction and reflexivity, which attest to an emerging synergy between narrative analysis and narrative inquiry. As individual chapters argue, a focus on reflexivity can be a consequence of a close analysis of the embedding of narratives into communicative contexts. The outreach of small stories research to studies with a narrative inquiry focus provides further evidence for the increasing orchestration of epistemological with micro-analytical concerns.

Charles Goodwin's contribution, which opens Part III, demonstrates the richness of recent developments in interactionally oriented approaches to storytelling and represents an extension and further development of his foundational work on narratives in interaction. Indeed, his early research (see Goodwin 1986) was a fundamental step in the recognition of the significance of participation structures in the moment-by-moment deployment and management of stories in face-to-face encounters. Here Goodwin turns to the fundamental embeddedness of storytelling within human actions and human cultures. Drawing on examples of tellings taken from family conversation, peer group interaction, and professional contexts, Goodwin reflects on how narrators are able to build on each other's actions through the telling of stories, but also on how storytelling allows them to incorporate objects that are defining of their cultures and to construct, through joint participation and engagements, new understandings of the world around them. Building on his influential work on the narrative interactional dynamics in everyday multi-party conversational contexts, Goodwin also underscores the role of embodiment in narrative interaction and participation by showing how simple gestures and movements can allow individuals to contribute to storytelling events, even in cases in which they have lost part of their verbal abilities.

Catherine Kohler Riessman's thought-provoking chapter analyzes the rewards, contradictions, and conflicts that come with a turn to reflexivity in the study of narratives. She underscores how a qualitative, ethnographic, and context-sensitive orientation to narrative cannot avoid turning the mirror toward the researcher and the process of investigating a subject. There is a need for such a sustained turn, according to Riessman, in light of the continuing dominance of objectivist paradigms in the social sciences. Riessman describes different levels and possibilities for applying an inward, reflexive look onto the research process, from factoring in and understanding the researcher's own sensibilities, emotions, and needs, to reconsidering the impact of the political and social structures that surround and weigh on a research context, questions, and methodologies, to using the research process itself to illuminate deeper understandings of social phenomena. But the author also warns against the risks of self-indulgence and of looking too much into the mirror, which can turn the entire research process into an "autobiography" of sorts. The chapter illustrates the impact of the researcher's own ideologies on data interpretation through the revisiting of a narrative decades after the first analysis was produced.

Stef Slembrouck also takes up the theme of reflexivity, looking specifically at the role of researchers in interviews in which narratives are elicited or develop spontaneously. As in the case of Riessman's chapter, the picture that emerges from this analysis is a complex one. Zooming in on the research interview is a necessary move if one wants to understand how meanings are produced and circulated through storytelling and how participants use narratives to position themselves and each other. The analysis shows that participation in storytelling may alter the roles and relationships between interviewers and interviewees and allow them to co-construct arguments and evaluations. At the same time, though, since interview narratives are also used to investigate the interviewees' (re)presentations of themselves through their stories, an inevitable paradox emerges: on the one hand researchers know that they participate in the process of production and reception of stories, while on the other hand they also want to use the products of those processes as windows into understandings of the social world. Slembrouck invites narrative analysts to embrace this ambiguity and consider all its possible implications instead of trying to sweep it under the carpet.

Alexandra Georgakopoulou closes Part III with a chapter devoted to small stories research, an approach to narratives that has become well established in the field in the last decade. The intent of this contribution is to highlight synergies between this approach to the analysis of stories and other orientations to narratives as talk-in-interaction at the same time as presenting the new directions of research for which small stories have paved the way. Georgakopoulou shows how by problematizing a paradigm dominated by a preoccupation with canonical narrative realizations, small stories research has been able to capture the fleeting but also ubiquitous nature of everyday storytelling in contexts of increasing significance, such as social media environments. There, stories are told as ways of capturing and sharing the minutiae of everyday life, but they can also be taken as illustrations of the deep imbrications between communicative practices and the media in which they emerge. Investigating such contexts, according to Georgakopoulou, has also opened surprising new avenues for research giving rise to "creative applications and synergies outside of the immediate analytical concerns of a sociolinguistic study of narrative and identities," for example in narrative inquiry research into teaching and education (see Barkhuizen) and in clinical psychology.

The chapters that form Part IV clearly illustrate how a practice-based approach to narratives as described at the beginning of this introduction not only allows for a full grasp of the functioning of narratives in specific contexts of use, but also contributes to advancing the theoretical depth of narrative analysis. Indeed, all the authors embrace the idea that storytelling needs to be studied as embedded in the semiotic practices of different institutions and communities and that therefore the work that narrators and stories do in these different contexts can only be accounted for by taking a close look at the routines, knowledge base, and relations that participants share and negotiate within them. Such analysis requires a close study of the affordances of different media, the transformation and entextualization processes involved in the creation of narratives in specific contexts, and the power struggles to which telling stories contributes. Different chapters are concerned with different communities and environments, but they all share an orientation to storytelling as a process.

Yiannis Gabriel's chapter deals with the study of stories in organizations and the different ways in which narratives enter the processes of creating collective/official and individual identities and of making sense of different aspects of the social existence of institutions. The author shows how recent theorizations view storytelling as an essential part of the life of organizations, which are faced with the task of continuously creating stories that justify and explain their strategies and actions. Such stories are consequential for both the management of their public image and their internal cohesion. Gabriel makes the important point that in order to study the way stories are built and negotiated in different organizations, narrative analysts need to abandon predefined models of what stories are; rather, they must remain flexible and be prepared to look for participant-based criteria for adequacy.

Susan Ehrlich centers her chapter on narratives in legal environments, but she explicitly focuses on how stories participate in gendered inequalities as women's accounts of violence are retold in the legal system. Ehrlich delves into the institutional processes through which female victims of violence are deprived of their rights to tell their story as they want, as their tellings are manipulated in order to fit "institutionally specified forms" by institutionally powerful actors who employ their knowledge about procedures and regulations so as to transform stories into weapons against their adversaries. Entextualization processes and strategies play a central role in these transformations of everyday stories into "official" stories. In this case, the travels of a story and the new meanings that it acquires through its retelling in new contexts become a vehicle for the reaffirmation of institutionally shaped asymmetries. This is in line with Shuman's finding that once stories travel beyond the confines of the personal and are told on somebody's behalf, issues of authority and power become central in how they are told, by whom, and for what purposes. As stories get altered, certain voices are silenced and others dominate: as Ehrlich shows, women's voices are altered and silenced during courtroom proceedings and in the entextualization of their accounts as official documents. Ehrlich does not, however, subscribe to a monolithic and static view of power relations. Her carefully contextualized analysis shows the trial as a dynamic site of engagement, where it is also possible for the less powerful parties to produce counter-narratives and alternative stories.

Cynthia Gordon's chapter turns attention to storytelling in family contexts. In her overview of studies that have analyzed these environments, Gordon summarizes the many insights that have emerged on the varied functions of narratives as tools for socialization and sociability. In terms of socialization, both early and more recent studies have emphasized the fundamental role that storytelling as a shared activity has in encoding and circulating common assumptions about learning, knowledge building, moral codes and more general ideologies, and in providing an arena for the negotiation and consolidation of roles and hierarchies among family members. In terms of sociability, Gordon discusses how research has demonstrated the power of stories in creating a sense of shared identity, in making sense of family conflicts and histories, and in connecting members with one another. Finally, the author emphasizes that this kind of qualitative, participant-oriented research also throws light on new ways in which the family as a unit is being defined.

The last chapter in Part IV is devoted to narratives in new media environments, an area of growing importance and interest in narrative studies given the overwhelming presence of media in late modern life. Ruth Page's examination of stories in social media provides a fascinating view of the many ways in which storytelling practices change in those environments with respect to face-to-face communication, as well as a theoretical and methodological reflection on the implications of studying social media for narrative analysis. Page shows how different media offer different affordances and limitations to users, but how there are also some general trends: in social media, stories tend to be "small," heavily co-constructed and co-evaluated, and strongly oriented to recency. Thus, traditional models of storytelling centered on canonical stories and on chronological/causal ordering are ill-equipped to account for them. Page voices the need for models of narrative activity that are both multidimensional and capable of dealing with multimodality, another central feature of social media narratives.

The exploration of how individuals present and fashion their self through narrative has been at the heart of the narrative research project. In sociolinguistic approaches to stories, this explicit turn to identities has happened more recently and as part of the latest wave of language and identities research, which has broadly embraced interactional perspectives on identities. In the last part of this collection, Part V, we showcase a variety of studies of narrative identities that, despite any differences in analytical emphases and categories, are all informed by approaches to identities with an interactional focus. Anna De Fina's chapter provides a discussion of how such an interactional focus departs from biographical studies of narrative identity. Broadly speaking, the difference can be located in that biographical approaches "regard the life story and the individual narrator as the source of data and target of analysis, while interactional approaches center on the interactional process of storytelling as the focus of attention." In De Fina's discussion, as in all the other chapters in Part V, a prominent position in this interactional analysis of narrative identities is occupied by the scrutiny of processes of categorization of self and other, in local contexts of storytelling, that broadly subscribes to anti-essentialist, social constructionist approaches. Such categorization is recognized to be dynamic and shifting in the interactional management of a story, yet at the same time owing its import and recognizability by interlocutors to larger sociocultural processes that may be themselves indexed (implied) by the choice of specific linguistic devices.

As we see in other chapters, too (Deppermann, Koven, Van De Mieroop), the concept of Membership Categorization Devices has been key to the exploration of how identities are generated and negotiated at the local level of interaction. Another commonality in these chapters is that they present close, turn-by-turn analyses of how identities may be proposed, opposed, taken up, or modified by participants in conversational (be they everyday or interview) storytelling contexts. In this way, all identity work – whether explicit, as when specific social categorizations are made relevant, named and oriented to, or implicit, as when specific linguistic and other semiotic choices index specific social categories – is grounded in concrete contexts, and is presented as the outcome of micro-analysis rather than its presupposition.

Another analytical mode that brings the chapters together is the assumption that the duality of the story world and the telling situation open up possibilities for identity work both at the level of narrator and characters and at the level of storytellers as inter-locutors. The interconnections between potentially multiple roles involving the telling self and the told self have been a key aspect of how the concept of positioning has been operationalized for the analysis of narrative identities, as Arnulf Deppermann's chapter shows. The chapter provides a thorough overview of different analytical approaches to an influential and complex concept, paying special attention to how different interac-tional perspectives address the issue of the relationship between identities done in local storytelling contexts and larger D-discourses operating beyond these contexts. Another ongoing issue in the analysis of positioning concerns the ways in which the irreducibly biographical scope of identities that extend beyond a single storytelling event can be brought into the analysis and properly identified. Deppermann discusses the role of ethnographic approaches to this problem. The shift away from single, confined, and self-sufficient storytelling events to trajectories of stories across space and time is increasingly attempted as a means of enriching local interactional analyses, as we see in other chapters in this Handbook. At the same time, the growing recognition that micro-analyses of identity construction on the spot can and should be supplemented by a focus on more stable and continuous teller identities is also providing a focal point for a synergy between foundational narrative concerns, such as the ones we see in the chap-ters of Part I and in interactional narrative analyses more broadly.

Alongside the prime focus on the interactional construction of biographical/self-identities in stories sits the sociolinguistically infused interest in how identities of social and cultural groups are invoked in stories. This is the focus in Michele Koven's chapter, which draws on concepts well suited to capturing the dialogicality and relationality of self and other, such as Goffman's (1979) notion of footing and Bakhtin's (1981) notion of heteroglossia, to show how "cultural identities" are multivoiced constructions. As Koven shows, this multivoicedness results from participants' coordinated presentations, evaluations, and enactments of multiple images of selves and others, what Koven refers to as "'recognized figures of personhood', across here-and-now narrating and there-and-then narrated events." Through meticulous analysis, Koven shows the spatiotemporally bounded and embodied aspects of such figures of personhood (a theme also taken up by Heavey) and the interlocutors' turn-by-turn alignment or misalignment with them. The main concern for future studies here, too, is with how "particular figures and participants' alignments toward them 'travel' beyond the individual storytelling" and how "the identities salient to a particular individual or to a given group may appear to stabilize or become 'enregistered' across contexts, over space and time." As in other chapters in the Handbook, specific linguistic devices seem to play a key role in the construction of meaning-making through stories: reported speech is one of them. So is deixis of time and space.

A common thread between Koven's chapter and Dorien Van De Mieroop's chapter, which also deals with "collective" group-based identities, is the shift of focus away from analyst-identified categories and toward participant-identified differences. Van De Mieroop's analysis also supports the fleeting and locally occasioned nature of the invocations of such identities in local storytelling contexts. In particular, her analysis documents a shift from an interpersonal to an intergroup perspective on narrated incidents that makes the criteria of ethnicity and gender relevant in the construction of an ingroup-outgroup dichotomy. She also shows how both ingroup and outgroup variability can be strategically downplayed so that certain positions can be attributed to whole groups rather than individuals. The polarizing power of the ingroup vs. outgroup differentiation is an insight that can be found in social identity theory, but Van De Mieroop shows the importance of grounding such insights in local interactional purposes in communicative storytelling encounters.

The final chapter by Emily Heavey turns attention to the underrepresented yet vital phenomenon of the body as a topic in narrative and a resource for narration. Any face-to-face storytelling event is ultimately an embodied practice, but in the case of Heavey's discussion, the stories themselves are about the body and body crises, as in cases of illness and disability. Heavey labels this "narrative body construction," which she defines as "the process of constructing, performing, and making meaningful one's own body in the narratives one tells about it." Heavey's analysis shows how the plot and structure, event presentation and linguistic choices in cases of narrative body construction are integral parts of the here-and-now performative exchanges between the interlocutors in concrete contexts, ultimately affected by and reliant on the narrators' materially real bodies, which partake in the actual narration. The interrelationships between the narrated and the narrating worlds are important in Heavey's analysis, as we have seen in other chapters, too. A notable aspect regarding the embodiedness of the narrated experience, however, is that the body in the here-and-now can actually facilitate or constrain specific tellings. The body becomes a constitutive part of the story's contextualizing and contextualized function. Other chapters in the Handbook have made similar points about the constitutive role of social spaces and mediational resources within them in the telling of stories (e.g., Baynham, Page). In this way, these chapters document not only the multifaceted means by which identities are interactionally constructed in the course of a storytelling, but also the multifaceted nature of the narrative identities themselves, encompassing individual and relational histories, social and cultural groupings, and, last but not least, physical and material realities.

REFERENCES

Bakhtin, M.M. (1981). *The Dialogic Imagination: Four Essays*. Edited by M. Holquist. Translated by C. Emerson and M. Holquist. Austin: University of Texas Press.

Baynham, M. (2003). Narrative in space and time: Beyond "backdrop" accounts of narrative orientation. *Narrative Inquiry*, 13 (2), pp. 347–366.

Bruner, J. (1991). The narrative construction of reality. *Critical Inquiry*, 18, pp. 1–21.

Clandinin, J., and M. Connelly. (2000). *Narrative Inquiry: Experience and Story in*

Qualitative Research. San Francisco, CA: Jossey-Bass.

Crossley, M.L. (2000). *Introducing Narrative Psychology: Self, Trauma, and the Construction of Meaning*. Buckingham, UK: Open University Press.

De Fina, A. (2003). Crossing borders: Time, space and disorientation in narrative. *Narrative Inquiry*, 13 (2), pp. 1–25.

De Fina, A., and A. Georgakopoulou. (2008). Analysing narratives as practices. *Qualitative Research*, 8 (3), pp. 379–387.

De Fina, A., and A. Georgakopoulou. (2012). *Analyzing Narrative: Discourse and Sociolinguistic Perspectives*. Cambridge: Cambridge University Press.

De Fina, A., and S. Perrino (eds.). (2011). Narratives in Interviews, Interviews in Narrative Studies. Special Issue, *Language in Society*, 40.

Georgakopoulou, A. (2003). Plotting the "right place" and the "right time": Place and time as interactional resources in narratives. *Narrative Inquiry*, 13 (2), pp. 413–423.

Georgakopoulou, A. (2013). Narrative analysis and computer-mediated communication. In S. Herring, D. Stein, and T. Virtanen (eds.), *The Pragmatics of Computer-Mediated Communication*. Berlin: Mouton De Gruyter, pp. 695–716.

Goffman, E. (1979). Footing. *Semiotica*, 25, pp. 1–29.

Goodwin, C. (1986). Audience diversity, participation and interpretation. *Text*, 6 (3), pp. 283–316.

Hall, S. (2000). Who needs identity? In P. Du Gay, G. Evans, and P. Redman (eds.), *Identity: A Reader*. London: Sage Publications and the Open University, pp. 15–30.

Heath, S.B. (1983). *Ways with Words: Language, Life and Work in Communities and Classrooms*. Cambridge: Cambridge University Press.

Herman, D., M. Jahn, and M.-L. Ryan (eds.). (2005). *The Routledge Encyclopedia of Narrative Theory*. London: Routledge.

Jefferson, G. (1978). Sequential aspects of storytelling in conversation. In J. Shenkein (ed.), *Studies in the Organization of Conversational Interaction*. New York: Academic Press, pp. 219–248.

Labov, W. (1972). The transformation of experience in narrative syntax. In W. Labov, *Language in the Inner City: Studies in the Black English Vernacular*. Philadelphia: University of Pennsylvania Press, pp. 354–396.

Labov, W., and J. Waletzky. (1967). Narrative analysis: Oral versions of personal experience. In J. Helm (ed.), *Essays on the Verbal and Visual Arts*. Seattle: University of Washington Press, pp. 12–44.

Mishler, E.G. (1986). *Research Interviewing: Context and Narrative*. Cambridge, MA: Harvard University Press.

Ochs, E., and L. Capps. (2001). *Living Narrative: Creating Lives in Everyday Storytelling*. Cambridge, MA: Harvard University Press.

Sacks, H. (1992). *Harvey Sacks: Lectures on Conversation*. 2 vols. Edited by G. Jefferson. Oxford: Blackwell.

Sarbin, T.R. (ed.). (1986). *Narrative Psychology: The Storied Nature of Human Conduct*. New York: Praeger.

Schegloff, E.A. (1997). "Narrative analysis" thirty years later. In M. Bamberg (ed.), Oral Versions of Personal Experience: Three Decades of Narrative Analysis. Special Issue, *Journal of Narrative and Life History*, 7, pp. 97–106.

Slembrouck, S. (2003). What the map cuts up, the story cuts across. *Narrative Inquiry*, 13 (2), pp. 459–467.

Tannen, D., H. Hamilton, and D. Schiffrin (eds.). (in press). *Handbook of Discourse Analysis*. 2nd edn. Oxford: Wiley-Blackwell.

Wodak, R., B. Johnstone, and P. Kerswill (eds.). (2011). *The Sage Handbook of Sociolinguistics*. London: Sage.

Part I Narrative Foundations: Knowledge, Learning, and Experience

1 Narrative as a Mode of Understanding

Method, Theory, Praxis

MARK FREEMAN

1.1 Introduction

The remarkable growth of narrative inquiry over the course of recent decades is a cause for both celebration and caution. Outstanding work has been carried out across a wide range of fields, and the result has been an extraordinary surge of intellectual energy and momentum. Indeed, in the eyes of some, the "narrative turn" in the social sciences reflects nothing less than a paradigmatic shift in thinking about the human condition and how it is best explored. At the same time, there has emerged some concern about narrative inquiry overextending its reach and thereby losing some of its specificity and value as a tool for thinking. More troubling is the notion that the narrative turn may be little more than an intellectual fad, here today but more than likely gone tomorrow. Perhaps most troubling, however, is the possibility that the narrative turn, particularly as applied to the domain of self-understanding, is simply misconceived, serving to undermine the very efforts it was thought to support.

My primary aim in the present chapter is to respond to these criticisms and the larger issues they raise by offering a defense of narrative as a mode of understanding. Acknowledging that the narrative turn has numerous sources, I will focus mainly on those sources that have sought to provide a philosophical rationale for the movement at hand. Foremost among them is the work of the philosopher Paul Ricoeur, whose groundbreaking scholarship on narrative provided fertile ground for future research in the social sciences and beyond. Of special importance in this context was Ricoeur's exploration of the interrelationship of time and narrative, which, drawing on such varied fields as psychoanalysis, historiography, and literary theory, underscored the *necessity* of narrative understanding in comprehending certain fundamental features of the human realm (e.g., 1981b, 1984, 1985, 1988). Following Ricoeur in broad outline, this necessity is threefold: methodological, theoretical, and practical. In speaking of the methodological necessity of narrative understanding, I shall advance the deceptively simple idea that there is no more appropriate vehicle for studying human lives than

The Handbook of Narrative Analysis, First Edition. Edited by Anna De Fina and Alexandra Georgakopoulou.
© 2015 John Wiley & Sons, Inc. Published 2019 by John Wiley & Sons, Inc.

through narrative inquiry. In speaking of the theoretical necessity of narrative understanding, I shall examine the relationship between time and narrative, focusing especially on the phenomenon of hindsight, the process of looking backward over the terrain of the personal past. In speaking of the practical necessity of narrative understanding, finally, I shall attempt to show the myriad ways in which narrative is woven into the fabric of life itself. Highlighting this threefold necessity of narrative as a mode of understanding will serve to underscore the pivotal role of narrative analysis in exploring the human realm.

1.2   Narrative Mania

"Narrative," Roland Barthes wrote nearly 50 years ago, "starts with the very history of mankind" (1975: 237). From other quarters entirely, we have been told that man is essentially "a story-telling animal" (MacIntyre 1981: 201; see also Gottschall 2012). According to Paul Ricoeur, "The form of life to which narrative discourse belongs is our historical condition itself" (1981a: 285). Peter Brooks would seem to concur, especially with regard to the kinds of narratives found in the study of human lives, for "telling the self's story remains our indispensable thread in the labyrinth of temporality" (1985: 285). Given such pronouncements about narrative from such notable figures, it might be assumed that the "narrative turn" (or "turns," see Hyvärinen 2010) in the social and human sciences would be beyond dispute. Remarkably enough, this would seem to be so on three distinct fronts. Narrative can be, and often is, a *method*, a mode of inquiry into the human realm. In addition, the idea of narrative can be employed in the context of *theory* about some aspect of the human condition, for instance cognition or personal identity. Finally, it can be considered in the context of *practice*, that is, the various human "doings" that are part of everyday life. In view of this threefold utility and value, one might ask, how could the idea of narrative *not* be at the very center of the social and human sciences?

But of course things often don't turn out quite as one might expect. One reason, it seems, has to do with the very utility and value just referred to. Here, I am referring to what might be considered *narrative fatigue* due to overkill. None other than Peter Brooks makes this point loudly and clearly in a short article entitled "Stories abounding."

> The notion that narrative is part of a universal cognitive tool kit, which seemed in the mid-60s a radical discovery, is now one of the banalities of postmodernism. Scholars from many disciplines have come to recognize, in a phrase made popular by the psychologist Jerome Bruner, "the narrative construction of reality." We don't simply assemble facts into narratives; our sense of the way stories go together, how life is made meaningful as narrative, presides at our choice of facts as well, and the ways we present them. Our daily lives, our daydreams, our sense of self are all constructed as stories.

Barthes and company were therefore quite right about the ubiquity of narrative. Little did they know, however, just *how* ubiquitous the idea would become. Brooks goes on to refer to George W. Bush's (brief) inaugural address, which used the word "story" some ten times; to Ronald Reagan's clear understanding of the fact that "the concrete particulars of storytelling will always be more vivid than compilations of fact"; to pharmaceutical companies wanting us to know the story of their drugs; to the many public events – for instance, the death of Princess Diana – that cry out for "a reconstruction of its story, complete with plot outlines and diagrams and restagings"; and, not least, to countless academic discourses, including some of those "traditionally held to be governed by logic, syllogism, or mathematical formula" (2001).

Isn't all this a good thing, particularly for those of us wishing to carry the narrative torch forward? Shouldn't Brooks himself be pleased with just how far the idea has come?

> I suppose that literary critics interested in the workings of narrative and the pervasive presence of "narrativity" in culture ought to be content that our subject of study appears to have colonized large realms of discourse, both popular and academic. The problem, however, is that the very promiscuity of the idea of narrative may have rendered the concept useless. The proliferation and celebration of the concept of narrative haven't been matched by a concurrent spread of attention to its analysis. (2001)

Barthes and others, including Brooks, had issued a plea for narratology, for a "serious, disciplined study" of the many forms of storytelling, one that "would analyze their design and intention, how their narrative rhetoric seeks a certain result, an effect on the reader, a change in reality." Narratology, of course, remains alive and well. But it "has not penetrated into other disciplines – or into the public discourse" (Brooks 2001). We therefore have "promiscuity" but without the sort of rigorous, incisive analysis that narratology can provide. The implication: narrative as method has fallen short of the mark.

1.3   Narrative Excess

At around the same time Brooks was lamenting the too loose use of the idea of narrative, in academics and beyond, Crispin Sartwell was penning *End of Story: Toward an Annihilation of Language and History* (2000). Sartwell adduces numerous reasons for casting into question the narrative turn. If for Brooks wanton sex seemed an apt metaphor for thinking about narrative's overuse, Sartwell turns instead to death: "The discourses that grow out of the obsession with discourse," he writes, "occasionally bloat language into something really hideous, like a corpse that has floated two weeks in the East River." Indeed, he continues,

> Occasionally the position is so overstated that it is … baldly ridiculous: if the assertion is that the world is a text, or people are texts, the assertion asserts what I daresay no one can actually believe. Try believing it when you stub your toe; try believing it at the moment of orgasm; try believing it while you undergo chemotherapy; try believing it in the wilderness or, for that matter, in a traffic jam. (2000: 4)

Thus far, Sartwell has only referred to "discourse," linguistic articulation. But it is not only discourse that Sartwell is after, but *narrative* discourse; for it is precisely when discourse assumes narrative form that it becomes most pernicious. "Narrative," Sartwell continues, "has become a sort of philosophical panacea." It has been used "to explain the human experience of time" and "the personal existential project of constructing a coherent life out of the chaos of experience" and "human sociality" and has been considered "a central ethical category," even "a ground for ethical theory." Cutting across all of these functions is the idea of narrative as "a principle of or a strategy for organization. Narrative gives form, or displays form, or imposes form" (2000: 9). And in doing so, Sartwell goes on to suggest, it runs the risk of *de*forming those very persons, those very *lives*, it is thought to disclose.

Particularly problematic in this context is the idea – and alleged ideal – of narrative *coherence*. As Sartwell admits, he has tried to live his own life "with an extreme degree of coherence"; he has sought "to live it rationally" and to convince himself of having done so. At some point, however, he "came to experience the need to do that as a torture" and "wanted to learn to let the world be instead of trying to transform it into an instrument of my will" (2000: 16). On Sartwell's account, narratives, especially those that are in service of some teleologically driven life-project, can be excessively willful, domineering, controlling; they can become a kind of deadening prison, designed to tame and hold back, seclude us from the noisy clamor of experience. Speaking for himself, he wishes he could "play" more, move toward "deeper and longer forms of immersion." As he explains,

> The distance I purport to achieve in the narrative – when I think of myself as a character, think myself outside myself – is a distance from myself. I can take up more and more of my purported future, guide myself more and more ruthlessly, orient myself into the project more and more thoroughly, but then I lose a succession of present moments, and more and more of what I am all the while trying to render comprehensible escapes me. (2000: 66).

It's true: "All of us participate in the making of narratives." Indeed, as Sartwell acknowledges, "The lack of narrative is a kind of madness," or at least can be. "But too much narrative is also a kind of madness" (67).

In the end, Sartwell says, "to narrate an event is to divest it of its presence" (86), with the result that "Nothing is happening now. … What is happening today cannot be known until tomorrow, but the interpretation given tomorrow of today is indeterminate until the day after tomorrow, and so forth." This postponement, this endless deferral, saps the event itself of its being, its presence. "We live on the earth, not in history," Sartwell insists. Narrative, therefore, leads to the destruction of the very "pastness of the past" (87) through our will to interpret, and reinterpret, ever again. "I want to be able to *take shelter from my will* in the allowance of the present to lapse into the past, into a realm where it is no longer up to me what happened" (88). The challenge "is to hold onto and maybe affirm the fatality of the past," to recognize that "the past in reverse is inexorable" (89). Sartwell has more to say about all this, but I trust that his main message is clear enough: given the problems at hand, we would do well to stop telling and start living.

1.4   Narrative Illusion

But what does it actually mean to live? For many a narrativist, living and narrating are of a piece. Central to this thesis is the idea of "narrativity," which, broadly speaking, may be understood as that condition of being which is thought to precede the actual narratives we tell. Ricoeur, drawing on the Aristotelian notion of *phronesis*, or practical wisdom, thus speaks of "life as a story in its nascent state ... an *activity and a passion in search of a narrative*." Hence his decision "to grant to experience as such a virtual narrativity which stems, not from the projection of literature onto life, but which constitutes a genuine demand for narrative" (1991: 29). Indeed, "Without leaving the sphere of everyday experience, are we not inclined to see in a given chain of episodes in our own life something like *stories that have not yet been told, stories that demand to be told, stories that offer points of anchorage for the narrative?*" (30).

Galen Strawson provides a firm answer to this very question: *No.* Indeed, Strawson, in his well-known diatribe "Against narrativity" (2004), tells us that "it's just not true that there is only one good way for human beings to experience their being in time. There are deeply non-Narrative people and there are good ways to live that are deeply non-Narrative." Indeed, contra those who would assume otherwise, the two views under scrutiny – which Strawson calls the *psychological Narrativity thesis* and the *ethical Narrativity thesis,* respectively – "close down important avenues of thought, impoverish our grasp of ethical possibilities, needlessly and wrongly distress those who do not fit their model, and are potentially destructive in psychotherapeutic contexts" (2004: 429). No mincing words here!

Strawson goes on to offer a distinction between "Diachronic" and "Episodic" self-experience, the former referring to those who posit their own essentially continuous being in time (who are in turn likely to be "Narrative in their outlook on life"), the latter more inclined toward discontinuity (who are "likely to have no particular tendency to see their life in Narrative terms"). These two "styles" are "radically opposed" (430), which leads Strawson to assume that, rather than there being an intrinsic narrativity – understood as a dimension of being that is deemed to be part and parcel of the human condition as such – we are instead considering "a deep 'individual difference variable.'" Strawson writes,

> I have a past, like any human being, and I know perfectly well that I have a past. I have a respectable amount of factual knowledge about it, and I also remember some of my past experiences, "from the inside," as philosophers say. And yet I have absolutely no sense of my life as a narrative with form, or indeed as a narrative without form. Absolutely none. Nor do I have any great or special interest in my past. Nor do I have a great deal of concern for my future. (2004: 433)

Putting aside the fact that some of these statements are likely false, or at least falsely hyperbolic, Strawson wants to underscore the idea that he, as a self-professed Episodic, exists largely in the moment. Given this, he cannot help but ask "why on earth" others seem so dogged in their support of narrativity, especially in its ethical dimension. His answer is:

> I think that those who think in this way are motivated by a sense of their own importance or significance that is absent in other human beings. Many of them, connectedly, have religious commitments. They are wrapped up in forms of religious belief that are – like almost all religious belief – really all about self. (2004: 436–437)

This set of ideas could simply be considered silly if they weren't offensive. But they do bespeak a challenge, a radical challenge, to those of us for whom, *whatever* the reason, narrativity remains not only real but ethically and morally significant. Let me therefore set aside as best I can my own distaste for this particular portion of Strawson's argument and try to consider what's at the heart of his claims.

It may be, Strawson continues, that what philosophers like MacIntyre (1981) and Taylor (1989) are saying "is true for them, both psychologically and ethically. This may be the best ethical project that people like themselves can hope to engage in." His own conviction, however, "is that the best kind of lives almost never involve this kind of self-telling, and that we have here yet another deep divider of the human race" (2004: 437). Now, I am trying to be open-minded as I work through Strawson's argument. But notice what is now being said: those who engage in the kind of ethically tinged self-telling that MacIntyre and Taylor (among many others) engage in cannot possibly be living "the best kind of lives," for they are apparently too religiously self-preoccupied to do so. Who *does* live the best kind of lives? Presumably, those ostensibly humble Episodics who, like Strawson himself, never stop to ask what they have made of these lives. "Is there some burden on me to explain the popularity of the two theses [at hand], given that I think they're false? Hardly. Theorizing human beings tend to favour false views in matters of this kind," and the reason they/we do so is their/our tendency to "generalize from their own case with that special, fabulously misplaced confidence that people feel when, considering elements of their own that are existentially fundamental for them, they take it that they must also be fundamental for everyone else" (2004: 439). Narrativists are therefore religiously self-preoccupied in yet another sense for Strawson. In mistaking their own personal views for the gospel Truth, they seek to spread the good news with just that sort of cultish zeal which befalls those who imagine they have seen the light.

There is one additional sense, it would seem, in which there is a kind of "religious" commitment being made via the idea of narrativity. What the "Narrative attitude" entails is engaging "in some sort of construal of one's life. One must have some sort of relatively large-scale coherence-seeking, unity-seeking, pattern-seeking, or most generally *form-finding* tendency when it comes to one's apprehension of one's life, or relatively large-scale parts of one's life" (2004: 441). Strawson is speaking here of a kind of intelligent design, as it were, the assumption that spread throughout *difference*, the saccadic movement of one's life, is a measure of *identity*, form, continuity.

Could it be that the commitment to narrativity – at least in its "big story" form (e.g., Freeman 2006, 2011) – is the product of some sort of surreptitious religious longing? Perhaps. And if so, Strawson implies, we ought to be highly suspicious of it. For, while "the aspiration to explicit Narrative self-articulation is natural for some," even helpful, "in others it is highly unnatural and ruinous," and, "in general, a gross hindrance to self-understanding" (2004: 447). Why? As neurophysiological research seems to suggest, "the more you recall, retell, narrate yourself, the further you risk moving away from accurate self-understanding, from the truth of your being" (447). As Strawson points out, rightly in my view (see Freeman 2002, 2010), narrativity *need* not entail falsification and deception. Nor need it be in the service of portraying ourselves in a favorable light; some people revise their stories downward, as it were, rendering their lives and selves worse than what they actually were. These important qualifications notwithstanding, one's self-narrative is "an almost inevitably falsifying narrative" (448). How could it be that so many of us have built not only theories and the like but careers based on a phenomenon that is "almost inevitably falsifying" and that thereby takes us away from the very understanding we seek?

More generally, we can, and should, also ask: *Why* narrative? Are there *any* truly substantial reasons for taking the narrative turn? Or is this one great big bit of faddish foolishness? Is it possible that we will look at this particular juncture of intellectual life and be humbled by the sheer folly of our having once been duped into supposing that what we were doing had some small measure of validity and value? It is possible. But we will only be able to arrive at this judgment through narrative. This simple fact, I believe, holds at least part of the key to narrative's deep and long-lasting value as a mode of understanding.

1.5   Narrative as Method: Reading for Meaning

As I have argued in numerous works throughout the course of nearly three decades, at the core of the idea of narrative as a mode of understanding is its *retrospective* dimension, that is, the fact that narratives always and necessarily entail looking backward, from some present moment, and seeing in the movement of events *episodes* that are part of some larger whole (e.g., Freeman 1984, 1993, 1997, 2012). My own work tends to involve what I earlier referred to as "big stories," which I have described as "those narratives, often derived from interviews, clinical encounters, and other such interrogative venues, that entail a significant measure of reflection on either an event or experience, a significant portion of a life, or the whole of it" (Freeman 2006: 132). It is in these big stories that the retrospective dimension is most visible, for in one way or another, they involve discrete tellings, from some present moment, looking backward. But this dimension, I would argue, is also inherent in small stories (e.g., Bamberg 2006; Georgakopoulou 2006, and this volume, chapter 13) of the sort we find in conversational exchanges and the like. These latter stories are generally more inchoate and involve less synoptic constructing and configuring than big stories, but insofar as we can designate them as *stories*, which transpire in time and have something roughly akin to a beginning-middle-end structure, the retrospective dimension remains key.

Why is the retrospective dimension important in the context of thinking about narrative as method? Among the many possible answers to this question, one strikes me as painfully obvious. Bearing in mind the abstractness and aridity and depersonalized nature of much of contemporary psychology, it stands to reason that we might at times want to look at *people*, at the lives of real human beings, and there is no more sensible way of doing so than through the stories they tell, whether big, small, or in-between. As we all know at this point, this process is fraught with any number of potential problems, not the least of which include the kinds of distortions, illusions, and outright falsifications that Strawson and others have identified. For some critics, this fact in itself should suffice to disqualify narrative inquiry, of the big story variety especially, from serious consideration as method. But doing so would be foolish indeed. The reason is that when it comes to human *understanding* – whether of the individual person or of larger social units – there is no getting around the equally significant fact that we have to await the movement of time in order to make sense of what exactly has gone on.

This brings me all the way back to my initial musings about narrative way back when (Freeman 1984). At the time, the field in which I had been immersed – life-span developmental psychology – had been seen as being in a state of crisis (e.g., Gergen 1980). By all indications, there were as many discontinuities in people's lives as there were continuities (Neugarten 1969), predictability was notoriously difficult to come by, and the prospect of building a systematic science of the life-span was increasingly being cast into question. Gergen (1977) had even gone so far as to propose an "aleatoric" model of development, one that emphasized chance, accident, unintended consequences. This was an important move: rather than the more lawful, predictable, quasi-evolutionary unfolding that took place earlier in the developmental process (at least as it was conceived then), it appeared that different processes entirely were occurring in the adult years, ones that were decidedly more resistant to this sort of ordering. What had struck me then, however, was the idea that this ostensible discontinuity and randomness was tied to a fundamentally *prospective* lens. As I had put the matter at the time, "the notion of chance, being tied to expectation or lack thereof, is predicated upon an essentially forward-looking perspective, a kind of stochastic unraveling of events through time. But," I had added, "to the extent that sense can be made, that events in their unfolding can be understood – perhaps even explained – after the fact, there is frequently the conviction that what has transpired does indeed possess a certain order." As such, "it seems evident that a viable science of the life course must admit the necessity of adopting a fundamentally retrospective perspective for at least a portion of the questions it addresses – a willingness to entertain the possibilities of aposteriority" (1984: 2). In sum: "What calls for the recourse to narrative is the ineradicable asymmetry between the knowledge that derives from looking forward in time and that which comes from looking back" (14).

Three decades have passed and I still find myself returning to these ideas. Set against the still-pervasive tendency within the social sciences to seek lawful, predictive relations, narrative understanding embraces the *historical* nature of human reality, seeing in retrospection not an impediment to knowing but an inroad, a pathway into dimensions of *meaning* that cannot be had any other way. In looking backward, we not only want to know what happened when, as in historical chronicle, but how events and experiences might be related to one another, perhaps even assuming the form of a *plot*, a constellation of meaning that holds together, in some semblance of unity, the disparate threads of the past. Consider for a moment what happened in the wake of the bombings that took place in April 2013 at the Boston Marathon, which killed three people and maimed numerous others: fingers began pointing in any number of directions, operating on the presupposition that "we ought to have known," that is, that it ought to have been possible to identify the relevant "predictors" and prevent this terrible tragedy from happening. It may be so; given recent reports, it seems as though federal officials ought to have flagged one of the attackers for the local authorities. But even if they had done so, can we really assume that more eyes would have been on this would-be attacker that very day? What we are considering here is what might be called "bad" hindsight – as in the "20-20" idea, which essentially posits that we ought to have known then what we know now. Note too the collective, dialogical dimension of this sort of after-the-fact meaning-making, in this case, the turn toward blame serving to underscore the possible incompetence of those allegedly in charge. But there is also "good" hindsight, which looks backward in the hope of discerning connections that can only emerge after the fact.

In some ways, the perspective is a humble one. As history is unfolding, it may be virtually impossible to see what is going on. This seems to have been the case in Boston. Now that we know the outcome, however, we can see any number of factors – a trip to Russia, where one of the bombers may have become radicalized; a failed boxing career; a feeling of being an outsider, a stranger in a strange land – that, taken together, as narrative, may help to explain why this young man did what he did. I emphasize *may*: another feature of narrative understanding, particularly as it transpires in the study of human lives, is that it is irrevocably *interpretive*. Will we ever know for certain why this happened? Can we ever put together a definitive account? The answer is clearly *no*. Narrative understanding is interpretive through and through, and although we can certainly hope for *better* accounts – more comprehensive, deeper, more fully able to accommodate the known facts – there is no final point of arrival. This may be disturbing to some. But there is no getting around the fact that, in the realm of narrative, we are always and inevitably reading for meaning, knowing all the while that our accounts are destined to remain provisional.

Other features of narrative understanding may be disturbing as well, particularly to those seeking to build the kind of science that tends to be enshrined in psychology. Much narrative work is idiographic in orientation, focused on the individual life (or, as I somewhat dramatically put it a while back, "the living, loving, suffering, dying human being" [1997: 171]). It is also often qualitative rather than quantitative and seeks to take into account the cultural situatedness of human lives. What all this suggests is that portions of narrative inquiry are as close to literature as to science, at least as traditionally conceived, and that we ourselves need not only to be researchers, dispassionate data-gatherers, but ethnographers and writers, better attuned to cultural context, better able to see how this context has been woven into the fabric of both living and telling, and, not least, better able to draw upon the poetic power of language in conveying the ambiguity, messiness, and potential beauty of people's lives (see Riessman, this volume, chapter 11).

Can there be a better means of understanding human lives than through narrative? There are of course numerous other ways of defending the idea of narrative as method. But if we wished to formulate a response to Brooks's complaint about narrative's "promiscuity," it would nevertheless be something like the following: in exploring the realm of real-life human affairs, in academic psychology and well beyond, narrative is, arguably, the most natural and appropriate means available. This is most obviously so in the big story context, when we want to know about the movement of individuals' lives over some significant span of time. But the necessity of narrative is in no way limited to big stories (see Georgakopoulou, this volume, chapter 13). Its significance is not limited to matters of method, either. For narrative, it turns out, is of great and enduring theoretical significance as well.

1.6 Narrative as Theory: The Hermeneutics of Human Understanding

According to Sartwell (2000), you will recall, narrative is perhaps most problematic due to its ordering and function, its putative insistence on subjugating and taming experience, rendering it too coherent. He is quite right to call attention to this danger. For some – including, apparently, Sartwell himself – narratives can become veritable prisons, closing off entire regions of experience, in the name of order, sensibility, *meaning*. Narrative therapists and other such literary healers are well aware of this problem. Oftentimes, those with whom they work have come to find themselves inhabiting just these sorts of narrative prisons, the chains of the past, both real and imagined, dragging them ever down. As such, the challenge is to fashion new narratives, ones that will better allow them to get on in the world more freely. But then there is the Sartwell alternative, which, essentially, is to abandon narrative entirely – or at least to try. His call in this context is reminiscent of what my teacher would sometimes say in the mindfulness class I took a while back: "Let go of your story. … Let your thoughts float by, like clouds. Just observe what's there in front of you. And don't criticize or condemn it or try to make it better. It is what it is" (Freeman 2010: 7). I found this helpful. It is indeed perilously easy to get caught up in the tales we tell ourselves.

But I wasn't at all convinced that stories had to be seen in these constricting, claustrophobic terms. Perhaps more important for present purposes, however, was my lingering conviction that narrative, for all its potential troubles, was simply intrinsic to the process of understanding the human world. This was most obviously the case when considering *self*-understanding, but it was also the case, I believed, in understanding human action more generally. Paul Ricoeur's classic 1971 article "The model of the text: Meaningful action considered as a text" (in Ricoeur 1981a; see also Freeman 1985) was pivotal in this context. Something happens, and its consequences may reverberate into the future. But *how* it will do so will, of course, depend on what happens subsequently. It is for this reason, Ricoeur writes, that history may appear "as a play," but "with players who do not know the plot" (1981a: 207). As a corollary to this idea, he continues, it can be said that "a meaningful action is an action the *importance* of which goes 'beyond' its *relevance* to its initial situation. … An important action," therefore, "develops meanings which can be actualised or fulfilled in situations other than the one in which this action occurred" (1981a: 208).

It is precisely at this juncture that we can begin to see the seeds of Ricoeur's seminal work on narrative (e.g., 1981b, 1984, 1985, 1988). For, in speaking of action in this consequential way, he is essentially speaking of the way in which actions become *episodes*, integral parts of the evolving whole that is the narrative. It is against the backdrop of these ideas that he would eventually speak in more explicit terms of the aforementioned idea of plot, that is, "the intelligible unity that holds together circumstances, ends and means, initiatives, and unwanted consequences" (1983: 178). What is important to emphasize here is that this notion of plot is itself a fundamentally retrospective idea. We do not, and cannot, know the plot of a story ahead of time; it can only emerge during the course of reading, when we begin to discern the meaning and significance of what has come before. It is with this notion of plot in mind that Brooks refers to "the active quest of the reader for those shaping ends that, terminating the dynamic process of reading, promise to bestow meaning and significance on the beginning and the middle" (1985: 19). As such, he continues, "Perhaps we would do best to speak of the *anticipation of recollection* as our chief tool in making sense of narrative, the master trope of its strange logic" (23). We might also say that "we are able to read present moments … as endowed with narrative meaning only because we read them in anticipation of the structuring power of those endings that will retrospectively give them the order and significance of plot" (94). Along these lines, it may plausibly, if provocatively, be said that "All narrative may be in essence obituary" (95).

Let us look more carefully at the process Ricoeur and Brooks have outlined in their respective perspectives on narrative, focusing especially on the process of emplotment. In reading a work of literature, we frequently encounter a scene or event, or a series of them. We know that they will likely be playing a role of some sort in the story to come, but we do not know what quite yet. This very uncertainty and open-endedness ignites our desire as readers and beckons us to keep reading. As further details emerge, we may sketch out a preliminary sense of the whole, a sense of "what's going on," retaining it as a kind of hermeneutic schema. Depending on what happens subsequently – and, of course, on the genre of narrative in question – we may refine this schema further or revise it entirely. Episodes thus become situated in relation to this emerging whole, which in turn continues to evolve as a function of these same episodes. Reading may therefore be understood as a hermeneutic process of "tacking back and forth between part and whole," such that "meanings that had emerged earlier both contribute to, and are retroactively transfigured by, what occurs later" (Freeman 1997: 173). Along the lines being drawn, Ricoeur (e.g., 1981b, 1984) has spoken of the *episodic* and *configurational* dimensions of narrative, the former referring to the various events of which the narrative is comprised, the latter to the poetic process of seeing-together so as to discern in and through these events a pattern, a larger constellation of meaning.

This basic process applies not only to reading works of literature, but to reading – and, on some level, writing and *rewriting* – ourselves (Freeman 1993, 2010). Note that in framing the process at hand in these terms, we have underscored once more the *retrospective* aspect of narrative: to extract the plot of a story, whether in actual works of literature or in the quasi-literary works that are ourselves, requires looking backward and "recollecting" – in classical terms, gathering-together – the disparate episodes of the past. Such recollection, Ricoeur has suggested, "inverts the so-called natural order of time. By reading the end in the beginning and the beginning in the end, we learn also to read time itself backward, as the recapitulating of the initial conditions of a course of action in its terminal consequences" (1981b: 176). Ricoeur is making a larger point in offering these words as well – namely that *narrative time* is part and parcel of the distinctive mode of being we call "human" and that narrative itself is intrinsic to the process of human meaning-making (see especially Bruner 1987; also Brockmeier 1995, 2001).

There are dangers involved in this process, to be sure, and Sartwell and others have done well to warn us of them. We can become entrapped by our own stories, imprisoned by their seemingly immoveable hold upon us. We can be suffocated as well, so consumed by our need to tell that we fail to breathe the cool, clean air of just being in the moment. We can become fetishists of coherence, so doggedly insistent on our own unity and integrity that we gloss over the patent *in*coherence that characterizes much of our lives. We can extract plots when there really are none. All this is true. But none of it ought to lead us to assume that narrative is merely a control mechanism, foisted upon the flux in order to stem the tide of meaninglessness or to subdue recalcitrant experience. Does it make sense to consider *all* of human experience in terms of "discourse"? No, surely not; stubbing toes and having orgasms, etc. (Sartwell's examples) would seem to challenge the limits of such a perspective. But when it comes to the realm of meaning, there is no getting around the broadly hermeneutic dimension of understanding. And when it comes to understanding human lives, there is also no getting around the narrative form such understanding assumes. Some will lament this state of affairs; that much is clear. What they ultimately seem to be lamenting, however, is nothing less than being human.

1.7   Narrative as Praxis: From Big Stories to Small

But what about this idea of "being human"? In speaking as I just have, one might be led to assume that I am arguing that there is but one way, the narrative way, and that anyone who doesn't live this way is somehow *less* than human. It's no wonder that some might be offended at this (apparent) argument: set against the storied lives of narrativists, their own lives might appear to be woefully incomplete. But, Strawson has argued, they're not. And *because* they're not, the narrativity thesis must be wrong. Now, if all Strawson is ultimately saying is that we human beings vary in terms of how much explicit self-narrating we are inclined to do, there is hardly any need to contest his perspective. Clearly, however, he's after larger game. Unlike Sartwell, who confesses to still partaking of narrative and wishing he didn't or could do so less, Strawson suggests that, insofar as narrativity is a personality trait or some such character-specific predilection, it is not to be regarded as the universal characteristic it is frequently, and erroneously, thought to be. *Some* of us may be "storytelling animals." But others, apparently, are not – not unless they are asked by social scientists and the like to tell the stories of their lives.

On my reading, big stories, of the sort promoted by MacIntyre, Ricoeur, and Taylor, are Strawson's primary target. But given that he is arguing against narrativity more generally, I assume he wouldn't be entirely satisfied with small stories either, for they too are part of the bandwagon, the movement to enshrine narrative as some privileged inroad into the human realm. It is true that small story theorists are less inclined to "ontologize" than big story theorists; they are more likely to speak of narrative *practices*, "doings," not some existential sphere tied to the temporal structure of being. Be that as it may, strong claims are still being made, particularly about human identity (e.g., Bamberg 2011). And so Bamberg, Georgakopoulou, and other proponents of the small story approach would be fair game as well. Here, then, we can ask: Is there *any* basis for maintaining the narrativity thesis? Could it be that this bandwagon is so alluring, so positively seductive, that, despite its seemingly weak foundations, big story theorists, small story theorists, and everything in-between have been duped into hopping on board?

Let me be clear about what is, and what is not, being said in adhering to the idea of narrativity. There are unquestionably plenty of people who do not engage, or who do not engage regularly, in the kind of synoptic, stock-taking narrative reflection that I and many others have addressed. They may not *care* about the personal past, or their identity, or how they might better achieve "the good life." And even if they do care about these things, they may not care in an explicitly narrative way. This appears to be the case with Strawson himself. But the fact that he has no particular inclination to tell his story doesn't mean there is no story to tell. For, *others* – his would-be biographer, for instance – can jump in and tell this very story. It may not be easy, mind you (particularly if Strawson were to insist on keeping mum about the meaning of his life). But unless his life is little more than an utterly disconnected string of events, with no discernible shape whatsoever, a story can still be told. Following Ricoeur, there still remains a (quasi-)text; there still remain actions, some of which are clearly and obviously more important and relevant than others; and there still remains the fact that "the text's career escapes the finite horizon lived by its author" (1981a: 201). It is thus an "open work," as Ricoeur calls it, and can be read differently by different readers. Strawson's own intentions vis-à-vis the meaning (or lack thereof) of his life, therefore, are not determinative. So, while we may wish to respect his wishes for us to desist from telling a story he himself might disavow, we are certainly not bound to do so. The author's intention and the meaning of the text are quite separate matters.

Very well, then, Strawson might say: "Go ahead and tell your story, or my story, whichever; I can't stop you. But what do you make of the fact that not only other individuals but entire *cultures* might find this storytelling process quite alien to their own mode of meaning-making?" This is likely so, and much ink has been spilled in support of the idea. I have even spilled some myself in addressing the oft-cited difference between *mythical* time, which tends toward the circle, and *historical* time, which tends toward the line (Freeman 1998). Just as individuals vary with respect to their narrative practices, in other words, so do cultures. Now, once again, *we* could go ahead and try to tell *their* stories. This gets us into some hotter water, however, for if in fact their most fundamental modes of meaning-making are appreciably different than our own, it behooves us to be extremely cautious about doing so (see Crapanzano 1985). Can one tell a psychologically-informed "life story" of a person for whom the very categories in question are alien? *Should* one do so? More to the point for present purposes, we should also ask: Is it conceivable that there are entirely non-narrative cultures, ones whose existence is utterly and completely momentary, for instance, such that they have no sense at all of any sort of narrative trajectory? I haven't inspected all of them, so I can't say for sure. By all indications, however, the answer is "No." Not all cultures *tell* narratives the way we (most of us, anyway) are inclined to do. Nor are they necessarily interested in "history" or "life history" or any of the other large categories with which we reckon with the movement of our lives. But it is patently inconceivable that they would step out of narrativity altogether. In invoking the idea of narrativity, we do not necessarily invoke the further idea that it must assume the classical beginning-middle-end narrative form generally found in our own culture. But amidst the vast multiplicity of ways of speaking, of reckoning with time, and of organizing the meaning and movement of one's life, there still remains narrativity, that is, "a basic human inclination to see actions together, as temporal patterns, configurations of meaning, and to situate these configurations within larger wholes – whether myths, histories, or what have you – that serve ultimately to organize and make sense of temporal existence" (Freeman 1997: 175).

In offering this perspective, I join the ranks of those who see narrative not as some sort of fictive imposition on the (allegedly) chaotic flux of experience but as woven into the very fabric of experience. David Carr speaks cogently and compellingly to this very idea. As a student of the philosophy of history, his main interest is in big stories. But he is no less attentive to those smaller stories that are part of everyday life, wherever it may be found. According to Carr, "the flow of conscious life, like the temporal objects (events) we encounter around us, is lived as a complex of configurations whose phases figure as parts within larger wholes" (1986: 28). We must therefore "correct the view that structure in general and narrative structure in particular is imposed upon a human experience intrinsically devoid of it so that such structure is an artifice, something not 'natural' but forced, something which distorts or does violence to the true nature of human reality" (43). From Carr's perspective, then,

> the real difference between [narrative] "art" and "life" is not organization versus chaos, but rather the absence in life of that point of view which transforms events into a story by *telling* them. Narrative requires narration; and this activity is not just a recounting of events but a recounting informed by a certain kind of superior knowledge. (59)

The retrospective dimension of the endeavor is again central: "What is essential to the story-teller's position is the advantage of *real* hindsight, a real freedom from the constraint of the present assured by occupying a position after, above, or outside the events narrated" (60). At the same time, however, Carr continues, action itself – and conversation, of the sort we find in small stories – bears within it a measure of narrativity, which in turn suggests that "the retrospective view of the narrator, with its capacity for seeing the whole in all its irony, is not in irreconcilable opposition to the agent's view but is an extension and refinement of a viewpoint inherent in action itself" (61). If Carr is right,

> no elements enter our experience ... unstoried or unnarrativized. They can emerge as such only under a special analytical view. It is this latter, not the narrativization, which is "artificial" and runs so counter to the normal current of our experience that it requires a special effort. (68)

What Carr is suggesting here, rightly, is that what transpires moment to moment, in the course of ongoing life, is of a different narrative order than what goes on when we step out of this flow of experience to reflect upon or tell about our lives. As I have emphasized in my work on hindsight (Freeman 2010) especially, this sort of reflective pausing entails an element of *poiesis*, configurational meaning-making, that is less operative in the flux of the present moment. The point, in any case, is to see the difference at hand as one of degree. Following Ricoeur (1991), it is the difference between the "virtual" or incomplete narrativity that is part and parcel of ongoing experience and the actualized narrativity that emerges in the act of storytelling. We have thus come full circle, and are in a position to understand more clearly the aforementioned idea that, in the flow of ongoing experience, we find "something like stories that have not yet been told," the notion being that we are "entangled" in stories and that narrative proper is to be understood as a "secondary process" that is "grafted" onto this entanglement. The implication: "Recounting, following, understanding stories is then simply the continuation of these unspoken stories" (1991: 30).

There are exceptions to this state of affairs. There are, for instance, people without language and without a sense of the very ongoingness of experience. There are also people who have been brutally traumatized, whose very world has been so corrupted and reduced that they have been virtually exiled from the narrative order. And there are those like my mother, a 91-year-old woman with dementia, whose experience is at times so limited to the present moment, shorn of any connection to past or future, that it is difficult to see in her world any evidence of narrativity at all. At times like these, my mother is a true Episodic, providing ample testimony that there are indeed people, millions in fact, who fall outside the realm of narrativity. Or at least appear to: my mother's disturbance at her own sorry state still bespeaks the vestiges of narrativity, or perhaps more appropriately, of a kind of narrativity *in absentia*. We should remember these people before forging ahead too surely in our proclamations about the narrative fabric of life. But we should also remember that these same people are hardly to be seen as exemplary – except, of course, in one way: in showing what a life largely devoid of narrativity can be, they also show how integral it is to the practice of everyday life, at least before the ravages of disease set in.

To *choose* to live more in the moment, as Sartwell and others recommend, is one thing. I can also see the virtue of being so narratively carefree, in the manner of Strawson, that one needn't busy oneself with pondering the past or the future; one can just go on, this way or that, and enjoy the ride. But this very enjoyment is itself contingent on knowing who and what one is, on being located, in having an address, a home, a place in the world. Perhaps, following Brooks, those of us who carry the torch of narrative should ease up in spreading the good word and be a bit more cautious about colonizing the whole of reality. And perhaps, following Sartwell and Strawson, we should be more attentive to those momentary pleasures, and pains, that bring us outside the narrative order. Nevertheless, there can be no home, no place in the world, without the kind of existential rootedness that narrativity provides. I will be going to see my mother shortly. I hope she's out of the terror today and that my presence makes some sense to her, that she can recognize me and, in turn, become located. This is what will allow us to speak with one another, mother and son, living in a shared world, filled, albeit obscurely, with our own unspoken stories.

REFERENCES

Bamberg, M. (2006). Stories: Big or small: Why do we care? *Narrative Inquiry*, 16 (1), pp. 139–147.

Bamberg, M. (2011). Who am I? Narration and its contribution to self and identity. *Theory & Psychology*, 21 (1), pp. 3–24.

Barthes, R. (1975). An introduction to the structural analysis of narrative. *New Literary History*, 6 (2), pp. 237–272. (Originally published 1966.)

Brockmeier, J. (1995). The language of human temporality: Narrative schemes and cultural meanings of time. *Mind, Culture, and Activity*, 2, pp. 102–118.

Brockmeier, J. (2001). From the beginning to the end: Retrospective teleology in autobiography. In J. Brockmeier and D. Carbaugh (eds.), *Narrative and Identity: Studies in Autobiography, Self, and Culture*. Amsterdam: John Benjamins, pp. 246–280.

Brooks, P. (1985). *Reading for the Plot: Design and Intention in Narrative*. New York: Vintage.

Brooks, P. (2001). Stories abounding. *Chronicle of Higher Education*, 47 (28), p. B11.

Bruner, J. (1987). Life as narrative. *Social Research*, 54 (1), pp. 11–32.

Carr, D. (1986). *Time, Narrative, and History*. Bloomington: Indiana University Press.

Crapanzano, V. (1985). *Tuhami: Portrait of a Moroccan*. Chicago, IL: University of Chicago Press.

Freeman, M. (1984). History, narrative, and life-span developmental knowledge. *Human Development*, 27, pp. 1–19.

Freeman, M. (1985). Paul Ricoeur on interpretation: The mode of the text and the idea of development. *Human Development*, 28, pp. 295–312.

Freeman, M. (1993). *Rewriting the Self: History, Memory, Narrative*. London: Routledge.

Freeman, M. (1997). Why narrative? Hermeneutics, historical understanding, and the significance of stories. *Journal of Narrative and Life History*, 7, pp. 169–176.

Freeman, M. (1998). Mythical time, historical time, and the narrative fabric of the self. *Narrative Inquiry*, 8, pp. 27–50.

Freeman, M. (2002). The burden of truth: Psychoanalytic *poiesis* and narrative understanding. In W. Patterson (ed.), *Strategic Narrative: New Perspectives on the Power of Personal and Cultural Stories*. Lanham, MD: Lexington Books, pp. 9–27.

Freeman, M. (2006). Life "on holiday"? *Narrative Inquiry*, 16 (1), pp. 131–138.

Freeman, M. (2010). *Hindsight: The Promise and Peril of Looking Backward*. Oxford: Oxford University Press.

Freeman, M. (2011). Stories, big and small: Toward a synthesis. *Theory & Psychology*, 21, pp. 114–121.

Freeman, M. (2012). Self-observation theory in the narrative tradition: Rescuing the possibility of self-understanding. In J. Clegg (ed.), *Self-Observation in the Social Sciences*. Piscataway, NJ: Transaction, pp. 239–257.

Georgakopoulou, A. (2006). Thinking big with small narrative and identity analysis. *Narrative Inquiry*, 16, pp. 129–137.

Gergen, K.J. (1977). Stability, change, and chance in understanding human development. In N. Datan and H.W. Reese (eds.), *Life-Span Developmental Psychology: Dialectical Perspectives*. New York: Academic Press, pp. 135–157.

Gergen, K.J. (1980). The emerging crisis in life-span developmental psychology. In P.B. Baltes and O.G. Brim (eds.), *Life-Span Development and Behavior*, Vol. 3. New York: Academic Press, pp. 30–63.

Gottschall, J. (2012). *The Storytelling Animal: How Stories Make Us Human*. New York: Houghton Mifflin Harcourt.

Hyvärinen, M. (2010). Revisiting the narrative turns. *Life Writing*, 7 (1), pp. 69–82.

MacIntyre, A. (1981). *After Virtue: An Essay in Moral Theory*. Notre Dame, IN: University of Notre Dame Press.

Neugarten, B. (1969). Continuities and discontinuities of psychological issues into adult life. *Human Development*, 12, pp. 121–130.

Ricoeur, P. (1981a). *Hermeneutics and the Human Sciences*. Cambridge: Cambridge University Press.

Ricoeur, P. (1981b). Narrative time. In W.J.T. Mitchell (ed.), *On Narrative*. Chicago, IL: University of Chicago Press, pp. 165–186.

Ricoeur, P. (1983). On interpretation. In A. Montefiore (ed.), *Philosophy in France Today*. Cambridge: Cambridge University Press, pp. 175–197.

Ricoeur, P. (1984). *Time and Narrative*, Vol. 1. Chicago, IL: University of Chicago Press.

Ricoeur, P. (1985). *Time and Narrative*, Vol. 2. Chicago, IL: University of Chicago Press.

Ricoeur, P. (1988). *Time and Narrative*, Vol. 3. Chicago, IL: University of Chicago Press.

Ricoeur, P. (1991). Life in quest of narrative. In D. Wood (ed.), *On Paul Ricoeur: Narrative and Interpretation*. London: Routledge, pp. 20–33.

Sartwell, C. (2000). *End of Story: Toward an Annihilation of Language and History*. Albany, NY: SUNY Press.

Strawson, G. (2004). Against narrativity. *Ratio*, 17 (4), pp. 428–452.

Taylor, C. (1989). *Sources of the Self: The Making of the Modern Identity*. Cambridge, MA: Harvard University Press.

2 Story Ownership and Entitlement

AMY SHUMAN

2.1 Introduction

Much is at stake in contests and questions about who owns a story and who is entitled to tell it or hear it. Claiming ownership of a story, or challenging someone else's right to tell it, points beyond the stories themselves to issues of status, dignity, power, and moral and ethical relations between tellers and listeners. Story ownership is contested for different reasons and at different points of interaction, from disputes among people who know each other well to questions about the exploitive use of others' stories and the use of personal stories to advocate a social cause among people distantly connected to each other.

The rule for the junior high school girls I studied in an inner-city Philadelphia school was that no one can talk about anyone else, ever, and doing so was grounds for dispute, possibly (but rarely) leading to a physical fight (Shuman 1986, 1993). Transgressions included both the frequent reports about a girl's interest in a boy (and vice versa) and less frequent accounts of events of wider and more sustained newsworthy interest such as the story about a girl who was absent from school because she was pregnant. In the latter case, although many people *knew* about the girl's absence and pregnancy, only her close associates had the right to *tell* about it.

At the junior high school, accusations of transgressions, whether involving immediate or distant circles of tellers and listeners, were interestingly similar, although for adults in many communities, accusations about people inappropriately telling stories that don't belong to them differ depending on the import of the news, the use of the story, and the proximity of the tellers to the events. Betraying a confidence by telling a friend and spying on a neighbor and reporting to the secret service are both violations of rules about story ownership, but they have vastly different consequences. Exploring a great range of entitlement claims, from the intimate to the political, can provide understanding of the ways that people claim or assign authority and the ways they manage

The Handbook of Narrative Analysis, First Edition. Edited by Anna De Fina and Alexandra Georgakopoulou.
© 2015 John Wiley & Sons, Inc. Published 2019 by John Wiley & Sons, Inc.

the complexities of speaking for themselves, speaking for others, and relying on representative speakers to speak for them.

Many disputes about story ownership suggest that the person who suffered or experienced the event has the right to tell it. Gathered during the course of the author's fieldwork, the following story told by a middle-class Jewish American woman in her 80s is a classic example of the betrayal of a confidence. The teller, M, set up her story by recounting a conversation she had with her seven-year-old daughter in which the daughter asked if any of the mother's friends' parents had ever divorced; we learn later that this conversation included a betrayal of a confidence told 30 years earlier.

M recounted:

So when T was 7
she had two really good friends
And they were over at OUR house
And they were really upSET
because their fathers were leaving their house
Their parents were getting DIVORCED
I think they started to cry.
When they left
T asked
"Will our daddy do that?
Will our daddy not come home?"
I said no, your daddy ...
And then T asked,
"Did you ever have friends whose parents got divorced?"
And so I said,
"Yah my friend
when I was in high school
Uh my friend
uh S
S's uh
mother and father got divorced
And we were in high school"
And T said, "what happened
what **happened**"
I said,
"well it was during the war"

As if obligated to respond to her daughter's repeated and emphatic question, "what happened," the mother tells her about the divorce of her friend S's parents 30 years earlier. In framing the story as a response to a question, the mother attempts to establish a warrant for telling something she had been told as a secret. Further, she describes the conditions in which S told her the story in the first place as an explanation for an out-of-the-ordinary event, traveling to Nevada during the war. S's family was taking a trip during the war when travel was difficult, and S told M the secret to explain the otherwise unexplainable trip.

S told me she was going to go to Nevada
Nevada! from (**name of home city**).
It was like something like going to the **moon**.
People just didn't do that.
"Why are you going to Nevada?"
And she said,
"Well it's a secret"
She said
"my um mother and father are getting divorced"
I had never met her father
I'd known S all through high school
And she lived with her mother
And there was no father
And I **never** had asked her about it

The secret is revealed through the recounting of a conversation, embodied and reen-
acted through the use of constructed speech. At the end of this section of the narrative,
M says that she "never had asked her about" the absence of S's father. The disclosure of
the secret, then – from M's perspective – was not in response to a (possibly invasive)
question about the father, but rather was in response to the (perfectly reasonable)
question about why S was going far away. Within the context of a conversation with her
daughter 30 years later, the long-ago-told secret becomes a response to a reasonable (not
probing) question, just as the initial telling is framed as the response to a reasonable (not
probing) question. The rights to tell the story depend not only on the larger situational
context but also on the interactional context.

   This story contains many elements important for understanding story ownership,
especially (1) the betrayal of the confidence; (2) the report of the betrayal contextualized as
the response to a daughter's question; (3) the account of the original telling of the secret as
a response to a legitimate question about extraordinary events; (4) the use of reported
speech; and (5) shifts in the contexts of retelling. This story contains two additional elements that contribute to the negotiation of story ownership. First, the secret is about a
divorce, which was a stigmatizing experience at the time of the initial telling, between two
high school girls in the early 1940s. S did not want people to know that her parents were
getting divorced, and for S, this stigma continued; she did not tell either her husband or
her children. Second, the betrayal depends on a "small world" coincidence. M telling the
story to her seven-year old daughter, T, might not have constituted a betrayal. However,
when T was almost 40 years old, she met S's daughter. They did not grow up in the same
part of the country and did not meet until they were adults, in another part of the country.
As a part of learning about each other as new friends, they talked about their mothers, and
S's daughter was especially interested in hearing T's stories about their mothers.
T describes the conversation in which she told S's daughter the secret.

[She said] "I wish I had a cousin"
I said "maybe you do have a cousin"
She says "how could I have a cousin"
(I had had a mimosa)

on and on about not having a cousin
"because your father got divorced and why would he get divorced if he didn't want to remarry"
she was like "what **what what**
I'm in **shock**
What do you mean"
"Cause your mother's father got a divorce"
[...]
She's actually shaking and stuff
And I'm thinking oh my god what did I do

Although, chronologically, the events begin with the telling of the confidence, both the mother's and daughter's retrospective accounts of the various tellings begin not with the confidence itself but with the occasion on which it was retold in a temporally and geographically distant context as part of a mother-daughter conversation about shared experience. This recontextualization provides partial justification for retelling the confidence.

2.2   Story Ownership and Retellings

Retellings complicate (and undermine) the unstated rule that the person who suffered or experienced the event has the right to tell it. Each retelling creates a new context, and with these transformations ownership can be refigured, reclaimed, and/or contested.

As Erving Goffman (1974) pointed out, retellings can depend on the existence of new hearers, people who have not yet heard a story that is perhaps familiar to others present. The rights to retell a frequently told story can accrue not only to the person who suffered the experience, but also, or instead, to a designated performer. The designated performer is often, but not only, someone recognized as telling the story well, just as a designated singer can "own" a song familiar to other potential singers (though re-singings do not require new hearers [Posen 1988]). Instead, among familiars, one person might be (sometimes tacitly) identified as the designated teller, and others will yield the floor as long as that person is present. When stories reach a wider public, for example in reports of a scandal involving a public figure, the right to interpret, rather than the right to tell, a story can be contested (Bamberg 2010). The public telling of events carries responsibilities, whether concerns about further traumatizing victims, issues about the appropriation and exploitation of one person's tragedy for another person's inspiration, efforts to provide opportunities for powerless people to speak, or the obligation to tell. The act of narrating does not necessarily change the conditions of marginalization that underlie access to speaking for oneself or that assign some events to public and others to hidden status. On the contrary, giving voice to the voiceless can just as often reproduce the power relations underlying a group's or a speaker's status. Taking authorship for one's own story *can* shift authority relations, and in any case, contests about story ownership and entitlement place authority in the arena of a social drama where authority is maintained or renegotiated, whether among intimates or in public life. This potential maintenance or renegotiation of authority and the cultural conventions for disclosure is what is at stake in claims to story ownership.

Stories travel beyond the people whose experiences they describe. They travel among friends and family members and beyond, sometimes taking on new interpretations, often changing as they exchange hands. How, then, do people claim entitlement to stories? Who owns stories? Do they belong to the person whose experiences they describe? What happens when someone else, a witness, has a better vantage point to observe what happened? When stories are passed from one person to another, does ownership travel with the story? Who is entitled to speak on behalf of others? When we speak on behalf of others, are we depriving individuals of speaking for themselves? When we tell someone else's story, do we create the sense that this one story represents who they are? When we tell a story about an event, do we similarly constrain understanding? How are stories and retellings of stories part of cultural circulations? How are they part of the way we shape our identities as members of families, groups, or fellow travelers with similar experiences? And finally, how is the ownership of stories similar to the ownership of ideas, opinions, and other personal and cultural artifacts?

These questions can be answered at different levels of analysis, from observations of actual interactions in particular cultural contexts in which narrators claim or dispute the rights to tell a particular story, to philosophical and ethical arguments about the obligations and/or rights to speak on behalf of oneself or others. In social interactions, claims to own a story often depend on the genre of the story. People can claim a personal story because it describes their own experiences; narrators can claim a performance of a legend or cautionary tale as their story to tell based on prior occasions in which they have told it and thus claimed ownership of the performance of it. People may also claim ownership of a story because it has affected them, become a part of how they define themselves. Claiming ownership of a story often means claiming authority, whether the authority is an epistemological claim to know about what happened, or a hermeneutic/ legal/political/social claim to have the authority to interpret what happened.

In other words, understanding story ownership requires attention to the contexts in which one person is entitled to tell and to the conditions in which that entitlement is challenged. In everyday life, in politics, or in the media, challenges to entitlement are one means of monitoring and governing who can speak about what. These challenges also point to the dynamics of storytelling and narrative interpretation in which ownership and authority are constantly negotiated. Observing entitlement claims and/or challenges offers a view into the dynamics of narrative interaction and the complex relations between texts, contexts, and intertextuality. Just as stories themselves travel, disputes about who owns the stories can circulate far beyond the original tellers and listeners.

Methodologically, the study of narrative ownership begins with the idea that narrative is interactive (see Goodwin, this volume, chapter 10); it is about a relationship between tellers and hearers (and also, in some cases, the people described in the narrative). Ownership describes a relationship between speakers and listeners and between narrative and events; it is "territory shared by both addresser and addressee" (Volosinov 1973: 86). This territory is not always contested, but when it is, questions of ownership are implicated in every level of social discourse, from the designation and maintenance of family secrets, to efforts to prevent the disclosure of atrocities, to the questions of who speaks to whom, to what is experienced as unspeakable.

To explore these dimensions of story ownership, I begin with Harvey Sacks's socio-linguistic observations about entitlement, addressing some of the philosophical and ethical discussions. I then turn to what we can learn by observing the claims people make in social interaction, and finally I consider the larger significant issues raised by questions of narrative ownership.

2.3   Entitlement in Conversation

The concepts of entitlement and story ownership were introduced by Sacks in a series of lectures delivered at UC Irvine in 1970. The question of entitlement was a part of his exploration of how ordinary conversation works. Within that framework, the owner-ship of stories is part of how people organize their relations to each other and their knowledge about their experiences. Later, as Sacks's work was developed within sociolinguistics, ethnomethodology, and folklore studies, scholars expanded discus-sions of story ownership to include both the issues of authoritative discourse that had been analyzed by M.M. Bakhtin in the 1920s and contemporary issues in feminist and cultural studies about the rights, constraints, and obligations of people to speak on behalf of others. Speaking others' words or telling others' stories can be a way of claiming authority – the authority to represent, for example, or the authority that comes from insider knowledge. It can also be a way to claim that an idea, fact, or story is to be attributed not to oneself but to another, supposedly reputable or more credible, source. Several other discourses have bearing on questions of story ownership, especially when speaking for another reproduces power relations, as the fields of disability studies and subaltern studies demonstrate.

The concept of story ownership has implications for how tellers and listeners position themselves in a narrative (Bamberg 2006b). Sacks begins his discussion of entitlement in an account of the teller as witness. He points out that

> people sharply differentiate how they come to know things, and they make a point of making it known how they come to know something, where that distinction – what you saw and what you inferred from what you saw – is a used distinction. ... The "witness" position [allows] you to tell what you saw. (1992, vol. 2: 242)

It's clear that people who have "suffered an experience" are entitled to it, but the more interesting question Sacks asks is, "Does the recipient of a story come to own it in the way that the teller has owned it?" Importantly, Sacks describes the transfer of enti-tlement, of story ownership, in terms of affect. The new teller must establish a warrant for telling based on felt experience: "she doesn't just latch onto the experience of the first and borrow it for her own emotions" (1992, vol. 2: 244). Sacks offers a distinction between knowledge and "a stock of experiences." Basically, he argues,

> On the one hand, if you haven't had an experience, you aren't entitled to feelings, and on the other, if somebody tells you an experience you're not entitled to feel as they have, but on the third hand, if you've had an experience and now you're told a similar experience by

another, then you can make very big generalizations from it and feel more than you would have felt in either of the prior two cases. (1992, vol. 2: 246)

In other words, first-hand, second-hand, and third-hand experiences are narrated differently, received differently, and play out differently in terms of the "distributional character of experience" (1992, vol. 2: 246).

Sacks's work on entitlement has consequences for how we understand the concept of available narrative, or accounts that are recognized, whether by tellers or listeners, as credible and acceptable. In his statement, "It's a fact that entitlement to experiences are [sic] differentially available" (1992, vol. 2: 243), he refers to the idea that entitlement is both a matter of the teller's proximity to the event, whether as someone who suffered the experience or as a witness, and of the kinds of feelings one is entitled to have by virtue of those positions. Underlying these questions of position, availability, and entitlement is the observation that listeners and tellers conform their responses to expectations. Consistent with those expectations, "you borrow for a while that experience that's available, as compared to that you now invent the experience that you might be entitled to" (1992, vol. 2: 247). A narrator has to establish that a story is his/hers to tell. The mother in the betrayal of a confidence narrative above establishes the warrant to tell the story as a response to her daughter's question. Essentially, the daughter asked if her mother had a divorce-of-a-friend's-parents story, and the mother's response was yes. However, from the perspective of the friend who initially told the secret, the story was not the mother's to tell.

2.4   Story Ownership, Authoritative Discourse, and Reported Speech

Bakhtin's work unsettles the idea of ownership and instead begins with the idea that language itself is *always* borrowed. Bakhtin wrote,

> The word in language is always half someone else's. It becomes one's own only when the speaker populates it with their own intentions, their own accent, when they appropriate the word, adapting it to their own semantic and expressive intention. Prior to this appropriation, the word does not exist in a neutral and impersonal language. (1981: 293)

This quotation can be read two ways, both to point out that language is borrowed and to point out that people also make language their own. Narrative is one way of claiming language as one's own. Telling others' stories is a dimension of what Bakhtin described as authoritative discourse (1981: 342–343). Bakhtin viewed discourse as dialogic, as involving a tension between openness to interpretation and adherence to social relationships, expectations, and assumptions. Telling another person's story is an example of what Bakhtin referred to as heteroglossia, which he defined as "another's speech in another's language" (1981: 324). Heteroglossia produces double-voicedness: voices in dialogue with each other. Questions of story ownership point to the possibility of more than one voice, more than one speaker, and more than one meaning, sometimes in conflict with each other and in any case in dialogue with each other.

Reported speech complicates story ownership by inserting words that belong to someone else in a narrative. Both M and T use extensive reported speech in their narratives about the betrayal of the confidence. Reported speech also performs rather than merely describes an occasion in the past. By quoting what someone else says, and especially by relaying the telling of the confidence as a response to another's question, they reconfigure ownership of the story.

The use of reported speech is arguably one of the most persuasive claims to ownership. By quoting, a narrator claims not only his/her own authority but also the authority of the speaker quoted. As Niko Besnier demonstrates, reported speech has an affective component (1993: 163). Borrowing another's speech potentially not only borrows authority but also emotion, marking an experience as positive, negative, neutral, exciting, scary, etc.

Speaking for oneself does not necessarily imply originality, whether the originality of the text or the uniqueness of the self. Instead, the entangled speech of self and of others in narrative can be seen as a fundamentally dynamic element of narrative. Reported speech can be understood in this way. Deborah Tannen argues that "when speech uttered in one context is repeated in another, it is fundamentally changed even if 'reported' accurately," and that the more accurate term for this phenomenon is "constructed dialogue" (1989: 110). She points out,

> In many, perhaps most, cases, however, material represented as dialogue was never spoken by anyone else in a form resembling that constructed, if at all. Rather, casting ideas as dialogue rather than statements is a discourse strategy for framing information in a way that communicates effectively and creates involvement. (1989: 110)

The novelist Chimamanda Adichie (2009) takes the idea of the unmaking of the unique self, especially as a voice representing her culture, one step further. She argues against the notion of authentic cultural voice and expresses concern that if we hear only a single story about another person or country, we risk engaging in a critical misunderstanding. In pointing to the problem of the representability of any one voice, Adichie highlights some of the larger questions of representation underlying the concept of story ownership.

2.5 Speaking for Others: Problems of Representation

In feminist scholarship, the problem of entitlement has most often been connected to privilege. Privilege determines the position from which one speaks, and disparities in privilege provide one rationale for people to speak on behalf of others. Linda Alcoff articulates this perspective:

> The recognition that there is a problem in speaking for others has followed from the widespread acceptance of two claims. First, there has been a growing awareness that where an individual speaks from affects both the meaning and truth of what she says and thus she cannot assume an ability to transcend her location ... second ... that not

only is location epistemically salient but certain privileged locations are discursively dangerous. (1991–1992: 98–99)

Further, Alcoff argues, "The problem of representation underlies all cases of speaking for, whether I am speaking for myself or others" (101). Like many others, Alcoff points out that a neutral voice is not possible (105), but the lack of neutrality poses problems, in Alcoff's view, for truth and accountability. Alcoff recommends analyzing "the probable or actual effects of the words on the discursive and material context." Beyond examining a speaker's credentials or location and the arguments proposed, Alcoff proposes, "We must also look at where the speech goes and what it does there" (113). In other words, Alcoff recommends that speaking for others be understood in terms of interactive, rhetorical occasions. And yet, after espousing an approach to what she calls "discursive responsibility" (114), Alcoff returns to a position that maintains both the possibility of authorship and the idea that words are not necessarily tethered to context:

> We can de-privilege the "original" author and reconceptualize ideas as traversing (almost) freely in a discursive space, available from many locations and without a clearly identifiable originary track, and yet retain our sense that source remains relevant to effect. (115)

The question that remains is, who is in the position of conferring or denying privilege? Who is the arbiter? In essence, although beginning with questions of responsibility, Alcoff legitimizes what has become a popular position in feminism and cultural studies more widely, of seeing discourses as free-floating, untethered.

2.6   Speaking on Behalf of Another: Advocacy and Exploitation

Many of the feminist discussions about the problem of speaking for others are located in the academy, which has become an important site for considering the imbalances between privileged scholars writing about less privileged people's experiences. Anthropologists and folklorists have written about the ventriloquizing effects of the ethnographer who animates the voices of her subjects (Ritchie 1993). Susan Ritchie's point is that folkloristic and anthropological representations of the other might be a means of representing difference, but they are also located within political, historical constructions of what counts as a representation and how representations are used. Along those lines, Catherine Riessman, writing about research and reflexivity in chapter 11 in this volume, recommends attention to "the evolving research relationships that produced these accounts."

The problem of speaking on behalf of another invokes the two different meanings of representation, the poetic and the political. Gayatri Spivak refers to Gilles Deleuze's two senses of representation, "'speaking for,' as in politics, and representation as 're-presentation' as in art or philosophy" (1988: 275). Politically, representing someone else's interests as an advocate can be a crucial means for social change. Such advocacy can misrepresent those interests and/or can reproduce the conditions that require a stand-in. Poetically, representation is equally necessary and fraught. The representation is always vulnerable to the challenges that it is too accurate or not accurate enough.

All of these concerns arise in the Disability Rights Movement's adoption of the slogan, "Nothing About Us Without Us," which points to the problem of dependency implicit in being spoken for. People with disabilities are accustomed to being spoken for in medical, legal, and educational meetings about their conditions, as if their condition makes them invisible, incapable of speaking, or both. Speaking for oneself is a way to take back control ceded to, or claimed by, professionals or family members. Speaking is a way of producing one's own subjectivity; speaking is a claim to competence (Shuman 2011).

From the perspective of the Disability Rights Movement, advocates can make a difference, and their work is crucial as long as they do not also serve as an obstacle to direct participation by the person with the disability. Representations are a greater problem, whether in the form of the poster-child for an illness or the character with a limp in a work of literature, when they work to incite pity or sympathy, reproduce stigma, and create impenetrable distances between the palatable image and the repudiated person.

In the Disability Rights Movement, speaking on one's own behalf, telling one's own story, is a form of redress, a correction to a power imbalance. Personal stories of suffering countermand disability as metaphor. Reconfiguring and undercutting the power of metaphor and insisting on the personal story has played a significant role in the Disability Rights Movement.

2.7 Disclosure/Non-disclosure

The telling of narratives that deliberately disclose an experience otherwise kept secret can have significant consequences for maintaining or disrupting dominant paradigms and dominant narratives. For example, Betty Ford's disclosure of her breast cancer and her addiction called attention to, and in some cases changed, the stigma attached to both. Here, we can expand Sacks's observation, "stories organize the occasions they are in" (1992: 2:468), to include the role of story ownership in public discourses. Entitlement, in Sacks's conceptualization, refers to the right to have particular kinds of experiences, as well as to the right to tell about them and interpret them. Disclosure and non-disclosure are part of the regulation Sacks described as central to understanding narrative in conversation. In the narrative above, M discusses the secret of the divorce as part of a larger secrecy about divorce, something which had changed enough so that she was having a conversation about it with her daughter 30 years later. However, for S, the stigma and secrecy had not changed. It is not surprising that all of the disclosures, from the initial telling of the secret to the retellings, are replies to questions. As Michael Bamberg has observed, more formal interviews are also occasions for disclosure (2006a: 71).

Through disclosures, narrators reposition their own relationship to dominant ideologies and, in some cases, reconfigure the dominant ideologies also. In her study of deaf and hearing lesbian coming-out stories, Kathleen Wood argues, "If identities are socially constructed via language and surrounding ideologies, then ideologies are the nucleus around which people orient themselves in order to reveal recognizable and acceptable identities" (1999: 52). Coming-out stories are themselves regulated. Wood writes,

> Like all self-transformation stories, coming-out stories are rhetorical attempts to justify one's life, to realize acceptable selves by creating coherent identities. For a life story to be coherent, the justification of one's choices or experiences must be recognizable and acceptable. (1999: 47)

Coherence might be the ideal, but in reality, not all self-transformation stories are either recognized or accepted. Barbara Fox writes,

> Simply producing an utterance with a given level of authority, responsibility, or entitlement marked does not ensure that the recipients of that utterance will accept and ratify that level; as with all facets of conversation, such displays are open to all manner of challenge and resistance. (2001: 187)

2.8   Cultural Rules for Ownership and Tellability

Many communities have explicit, if unarticulated, rules about who can say what about whom and when. In some communities these implicit rules are communicated through family situations, while riding in the car or at the dinner table. As Alexandra Georgakopoulou (2002) points out, cultural notions of story ownership are often socialized in family contexts. Donald Brenneis (1996) describes how in Bhatgaon, a rural Fijian community, the stories told about people make them vulnerable to reputational damage. The genres of gossip and testimony play significant roles in disputes, and both require co-narration. Writing about how conflict-related narratives work, Brenneis observes,

> The two critical elements here are entitlement and authorship. One recurrent feature of the role of narratives over the course of a dispute is a transformation of entitlement to the experiences being represented. Privately held stories become more or less public; one's sole right to recount one's own activities or grievances is often lost. As long as only the disputing parties are considered entitled to tell their own stories, illicit uses such as gossip – while pleasurable – may become the topics of appropriately censorious narratives. When others gain legitimate access to such stories, however, personal experience becomes public record, serving as explanatory information, moral example of informal precedent. As such, these tales redefine one's relationship to others and one's moral and political stature. (1996: 48)

As an anthropologist, Brenneis served in the role of scribe, documenting the conventions for entitlement and authorship in Bhatgaon. Rarely are such rules codified and articulated as such within a community, but an exception can be found in the rules for gossip among Orthodox Jews. A distinguished rabbi, known as the Chofetz Chayim, born in 1839 in Eastern Europe, wrote about many Talmudic rules and gave particular attention to the laws of "evil speech" (*loshon hora*). His work has been adapted by Zelig Pliskin in an English version, *Guard Your Tongue*, a book on the shelves of many, if not most, English-speaking Orthodox Jews. Avoiding *loshon hora* (gossip and other talk about others) is of primary concern in these communities. For example, in the days of desk-top telephones, many Orthodox Jews placed a sticker under the receiver reminding them to avoid *loshon hora* while talking on the phone. *Loshon hora* refers more broadly to any derogatory speech. The Chofetz Chayim identifies several biblical sources of negative prohibitions, including "You shall not go about as a talebearer among your people" (Vayikra 19:16) and "You shall not utter a false report" (Shemot 23:1; Pliskin 1975: 14). He similarly identifies the positive commandments, including several obligations to remember, to teach, to honor, and the familiar "Love your neighbor as yourself" (Vayikra 19:18, Pliskin 1975: 21). *Guard Your Tongue* differentiates between acceptable and unacceptable talk about others.

> Certain statements are permissible when they are related in the presence of three people or more. Ambiguous statements that can be construed as either harmless or only slightly derogatory depend for their meaning on the way in which they are said – the tone of voice and gestures. If someone relates such a statement in the presence of three people, we may be sure that he will say it in a harmless manner. Such an assumption is based on the principle that when three people hear information about someone, we can surmise that it will be spread, and that the maligned person will eventually find out about it. (Pliskin 1975: 36)

The rules forbid any talk that will insult or demean someone or possibly cause someone embarrassment. The exceptions are few. For example, "You are generally forbidden to say about a particular craftsman that he is not competent at his trade. If, however, your sole intention is to save others from loss, it is permissible" (77). It is also forbidden to listen to others who say derogatory things. Most of the book comprises detailed descriptions of particular kinds of things, contexts, and interactions that are forbidden. A short section lists things one is obligated to say, for example, telling someone about a partnership that could be harmful (164) or informing one of the prospective marriage partners that the other has a physical deficiency or illness. In this case, the teller must be certain of the illness, must not exaggerate, and must not be motivated by dislike. Further, "If you feel that they will marry despite your advice you should refrain from mentioning the matter. Since nothing beneficial will emerge from your warning, it is forbidden" (176).

2.9   Questions of Belonging and Ownership

The idea that our experiences belong to us and that we demonstrate this belonging through storytelling is often claimed and rarely challenged. Robyn Fivush writes, "To a large extent, we are the stories we tell ourselves. As we narrate experienced events to ourselves, we simultaneously create structure and meaning in our lives" (2010: 88). Fivush is actually more interested in stories that *don't* get told and in how silences play a role in creating resistance narratives. "I argue that silence can lead to power through providing the space for the creation of narratives of resistance and healing" (89). Fivush describes two kinds of silence, imposed silence that "can lead to a loss of memory and a loss of part of the self" (92) and "silence as power ... the freedom *not* to speak, to be silent, the freedom to assume shared knowledge that comes from a position of power" (94). Arguing against normative life scripts, Fivish observes,

> Rather, it is those narratives that do not conform to the life script that define individual identity, stories that differentiate us from the norm, events that must be voiced; they must be explained, justified, understood, and this leads to narrative plot and tension. (96)

She asks "whether the deviation from the culturally dominant narrative can be heard when it is voiced" (96).

2.10   Credibility, Story Ownership, and Genre

Discussions of story ownership inevitably turn to the question of whether an eye-witness or participant in an occasion is a more credible reporter, able to recount events more accurately. The struggle between validity, accuracy, and the integrity of particular voices is measured in a variety of ways; each narrative genre configures the significance and measure of validity differently.

Controversies about Rigoberta Menchú's *testimonio*, her account of her experiences in the Guatemalan Civil War, are a good example. In response to accusations that not all of the events she described occurred as she described them, or that she was not present when she said she was, several anthropologists have argued that Menchú's work needs to be assessed according to the conventions of the genre of *testimonio*. In response to revelations about Menchú's presentation of herself, Mary Louise Pratt writes,

> These are standard aspects of *testimonio*, regularly recognized in readings (and teachings) of the text. To find fault with them is to misapprehend the genre. The logic of the *testimonio* dictates that the testimonial subject decides what to tell and how to tell it. (2001: 41)[1]

John Beverley further argues that the criticism of Menchú "re-subalterns Menchú's voice" (2008: 577). In the case of Menchú, Pratt and Beverley essentially argue that story ownership includes the right to choose one's own genre and that interpretation and assessment of validity should abide by the conventions of cultural genres.

Story ownership is also contested in critiques of the use of particular material in particular genres as inappropriate. For example, the film *Life is Beautiful* has been criticized for its use of humor in portraying events in the Holocaust. The film's director, Roberto Benigni, argued that the film was meant as a fable, presumably a plea for the film to be evaluated according to expectations of fables.

Sander Gilman frames his critique of *Life is Beautiful* within a discussion of portrayals of the horrors of the Shoah through laughter more generally. He asks,

> Why is it that, if humor does have a function in ameliorating the effects of the Shoah, we are so very uncomfortable imagining laughter in the context of the Shoah? Indeed, can there be anything funny about representing the Holocaust? (2000: 285)

His answer points in part to the role of positioning of the characters, including the comic, the victim, the aggressor, and the enemy.

> The comic is possible when imagining the Third Reich and the Nazis as the enemy. It is a means of assuring the viewer that the "victim" is smarter and more resilient than the aggressor. The victim must be in a position to win or at least survive the world of the Nazis. (2000: 286)[2]

Gilman cleverly shifts his discussion away from the question of whether Benigni, who is not Jewish, had the right to tell a personal, sometimes humorous, story about experiences in a concentration camp. As Gilman points out, in television, fiction, and other genres, humor has been used. The more interesting question, Gilman suggests, is how particular subjects, such as the Shoah, are accompanied by the particular obligations tellers and listeners have to each other.

These obligations include, but are not limited to, the (explicit or tacit) agreement not to tell (for example, to keep a confidence), the obligation to tell (for example, as a designated reporter of atrocities), and the obligation to bear witness to someone else's suffering. As Sacks pointed out in his earliest work, stories about suffering belong to the people who have suffered them. However, the victim of persecution is often not in a position to know what occurred and must then rely upon witnesses for facts (Shuman 2005: 36). Sometimes the witness is the perpetrator of the crime and is therefore the most untrustworthy of narrators. In any case, the witness – the position that prompts Sacks's inquiry – is in a compromised position. The Holocaust scholar Dori Laub has described the complex role of the witness who "bears witness."

> The victim's narrative – the very process of bearing witness to massive trauma – does indeed begin with someone who testifies to an absence, to an event that has not yet come into existence, in spite of the overwhelming and compelling nature of the reality of its occurrence. (Laub 1992: 57)

In the case of the Holocaust and other atrocities, tellers face potentially incredulous listeners; the events are too horrible to be believed. In fact persecutors are known to use the phrase "no one will believe you" to further terrorize their victims. Thus in addition to the question of who can tell stories of suffering are questions of who will listen and who will regard a teller as credible. Gilman observes that people whom he refers to as accidentally surviving are sometimes then obligated to tell the story of what happened (2000: 304). They are more than bearers of tradition; they are the bearers of stories that verge on the unspeakable.

2.11   The Obligation to Tell/Speak

The obligation to tell is the other side of concealed stories; as Ochs and Capps note in their discussion of the moral dimension of narrative interactions, "Each telling positions not only protagonists but also tellers as more or less moral persons" (2001: 283–284). They go on to say, "credibility is as essential as reportability for the success of a narrative" (284).

Some occasions produce an obligation to tell; for example, political asylum applicants attempting to prove that they have faced persecution in their homelands and have a "well-founded fear of return" often have only their narratives to document the atrocities they have suffered; the political asylum hearing obligates the telling of horrific details. The applicants describe their reluctance to describe these details as a reluctance to relive the horrors (Bohmer and Shuman 2007).

Sometimes the obligation to tell is in response to knowledge that has been obfuscated or concealed. In the introduction to his account of his experiences in Auschwitz, Primo Levi writes:

> The need to tell our story to "the rest," to make "the rest" participate in it, had taken on for us, before our liberation and after, the character of an immediate and violent impulse, to the point of competing with our other elementary needs. (1993/1958: 9)

In a stark and tragic version of the phenomenon of the obligation to tell, Letty Pogrebin describes her uncle Isaac, a "designated survivor" of his town, "instructed to do anything to stay alive and tell the story" (Smith 1997: 61). Survival required him to masquerade as a German, including sending his own wife and children to the gas chamber.

> The "designated survivor" arrived in America at about age forty, with prematurely white hair and a dead gaze within the sky-blue eyes that had helped save his life. As promised, he told his story to dozens of Jewish agencies and community leaders, and to groups of family and friends … For months he talked, speaking the unspeakable, describing a horror that American Jews had suspected but could not conceive, a monstrous tale that dwarfed the demonology of legend and gave me the nightmare I still dream to this day. And as he talked, Isaac seemed to grow older and older until one night a few months later, when he finished telling everything he knew, he died. (quoted in Smith 1997: 61–62)

2.12 Silence, the Unspeakable, and the Illegible

As scholars writing about the use of narrative in contested political situations have observed, claiming or contesting story ownership can be a means to assert or challenge power relations. Once a narrative moves beyond its original "occasions of production" (De Fina and Georgakopoulou 2012: 133), it can be transformed and recontextualized. In her work on legal discourse and especially rape cases, Susan Ehrlich (this volume, chapter 15) discusses the many possible consequences of retelling narratives in different contexts within the legal system. The question is, how have positions, voices, and narrators been rendered silent, and how does the effort to change these circumstances change the underlying power relations? Pierre Macherey writes:

> What is important in a work is what it does not say. This is not the same as the careless notation "what it refuses to say" … What the work *cannot say* is important, because there the elaboration of the utterance is acted out, in a sort of journey to silence. (1978: 87)

Macherey is writing about written texts rather than face-to-face conversations, in which the conditions of unspeakability are different, and the silences can be traced to social relationships and power dynamics. In her book *Using Women*, Nancy Campbell documents the Congressional Hearings on drug addiction in the 1950s, in which women who told narratives about being good mothers were not selected to testify. The legislators could only hear the narratives of women addicts unable to perform their responsibilities as mothers.

> Addiction provides a narrative by which significant numbers of women make sense of their lives and differentiate "their" story from that of countless others. For legislators, addiction provides an exemplary narrative that compels belief. (Campbell 2000: 50)

Gayatri Spivak revised her famous question, "Can the subaltern speak?" (to which she initially answered, "The subaltern cannot speak" (1999: 308) to ask "What is at stake when we insist that the subaltern speaks?" (309). As Spivak points out, one of the things at stake is privilege, a power dynamic not changed by giving voice to those without power. In this category, we can also consider censorship and contests about the rights of free speech, though these contests often assume the speaker's ownership of her narrative and instead the struggle centers on the context in which the story can be told.[3]

2.13   Conclusion

Claims about story ownership follow unstated, culturally specific rules about who has a right to tell about particular experiences and in what way, to whom. Research on story ownership begins with Harvey Sacks's observation that, at least in some communities, the idea that we own our own experiences can lead to challenges in which people claim that their stories have been taken from them or used inappropriately. Claiming the right to tell one's own experiences is a means of claiming authority; similarly, talking about others is a way of borrowing authority. These simple rules are rarely followed, in part because they are too simple; they oversimplify complex relationships of power, authority, and credibility, and they risk blurring complexities about how telling stories is always connected to questions of what can be told and what remains unspeakable. As the example of the story betrayal demonstrates, a subject once taboo for discussion (divorce) can become, for some of the participants, with some restrictions, available for telling. The idea of story ownership as a fundamental way in which we manage our relationship to our experiences is helpful for observing the powerful role that storytelling plays in negotiating social relationships. In addition to asking about tellability – the kinds of things people can or can't talk about, and the kinds of stories that travel beyond the people whose experiences they describe – it is important to ask about how narrative can be a means of sorting out our relations to each other, to our experiences, and to the larger social discourses that constrain and enable what we talk about, to whom, when, where, and to what purpose. Who is entitled to tell a particular story and what is the basis of that entitlement? What are the consequences of speaking on behalf of others? What responsibilities and obligations are involved? Although research in this area began with

Harvey Sacks's claim that we own our own experiences, the discussion of story owner-ship, whether in our conversations, in the media, or in scholarship, points to the fact that our stories travel beyond us. Studying story ownership inevitably helps to understand how we negotiate our relationships both with people we know well and with strangers.

NOTES

1   See Schiffrin's account of the significance of evaluation, rather than "the objective representa-tion of what happened," as the goal of narrative (2003: 553).
2   Entirely different rules apply to the genre of joking. Folklorist Alan Dundes observed, it is often acceptable for people to tell the same jokes in-group that would be regarded as racist or sexist when told by outsiders (Dundes 1985).
3   See, for example, Rae Terada's (2011) discussion of the Irvine Eleven.

REFERENCES

Adichie, C. (2009). The Danger of a Single Story. Filmed July 2009. TED video, 18:49. http://www.ted.com/talks/chimamanda_adichie_the_danger_of_a_single_story.html (accessed October 28, 2014).

Alcoff, L. (1991–1992). The problem of speaking for others. *Cultural Critique*, 20 (Winter), pp. 5–32.

Bakhtin, M.M. (1981). *The Dialogic Imagination: Four Essays*. Edited by M. Holquist. Austin: University of Texas Press.

Bamberg, M. (2006a). Biographic-narrative research, quo vadis? A critical review of "big stories" from the perspective of "small stories." In K. Milnes, C. Horrocks, N. Kelly, B. Roberts, and D. Robinson (eds.), *Narrative, Memory & Knowledge: Representations, Aesthetics, Contexts*. Huddersfield: University of Huddersfield, pp. 63–79.

Bamberg, Michael. (2006b). Stories: Big or small: Why do we care? *Narrative Inquiry*, 16 (1), pp. 139–147.

Bamberg, Michael. (2010). Blank check for biography? Openness and ingenuity in the management of the "who-am-I question" and what life stories actually may not be good for. In D. Schiffrin, A. De Fina, and A. Nylund (eds.), *Telling Stories: Language, Narrative, and Social Life*. Washington, DC: Georgetown University Press, pp. 109–121.

Besnier, N. (1993). Reported speech and affect on Nukulaelae Atoll. In J. Hill and J. Irvine (eds.), *Responsibility and Evidence in Oral Discourse*. Cambridge: Cambridge University Press, pp. 161–181.

Beverley, J. (2008). Testimonio, subalternity, and narrative authority. In S. Castro-Klaren (ed.), *A Companion to Latin American Literature and Culture*. Oxford: Blackwell, pp. 571–583.

Bohmer, C., and A. Shuman. (2007). *Rejecting Refugees: Political Asylum in the 21st Century*. London: Routledge.

Brenneis, D. (1996). Telling troubles: Narrative, conflict, and experience. In C. Briggs (ed.), *Disorderly Discourse: Narrative, Conflict, and Inequality*. Oxford: Oxford University Press, pp. 41–51.

Campbell, N. (2000). *Using Women: Gender, Drug Policy, and Social Justice*. New York: Routledge.

De Fina, A., and A. Georgakopoulou. (2012). *Analyzing Narrative: Discourse and Sociolinguistic Perspectives*. Cambridge: Cambridge University Press.

Dundes, A. (1985). The JAP and the JAM in American jokelore. *Journal of American Folklore*, 98 (390), pp. 456–475.

Fivush, R. (2010). Speaking silence: The social construction of silence in autobiographical and cultural narratives. *Memory*, 18 (2), pp. 88–98.

Fox, B.A. (2001). Authority, responsibility, and entitlement in English conversation. *Journal of Linguistic Anthropology*, 11 (2), pp. 167–192.

Georgakopoulou, A. (2006). The other side of the story: Towards a narrative analysis of narratives-in-interaction. *Discourse Studies*, 8 (2), pp. 235–257.

Georgakopoulou, A. (2002). Greek children and familiar narratives in family contexts: En route to cultural performances. In S. Blum-Kulka and C.E. Snow (eds.), *Talking to Adults: The Contribution of Multiparty Discourse to Language Acquisition*. Mahwah, NJ: Lawrence Erlbaum Associates, pp. 33–54.

Gilman, S.L. (2000). Is life beautiful? Can the Shoah be funny? Some thoughts on recent and older films. *Critical Inquiry*, 26 (2), pp. 279–308.

Goffman, E. (1974). *Frame Analysis: An Essay on the Organization of Experience*. New York: Harper and Row.

Laub, D. (1992). Bearing witness, or the vicissitudes of listening. In S. Felman and D. Laub (eds.), *Testimony: Crises of Witnessing in Literature, Psychoanalysis, and History*. New York: Taylor & Francis, pp. 57–74.

Labov, W. (1972). The transformation of experience in narrative syntax. In *Language in the Inner City: Studies in the Black English Vernacular*. Philadelphia: University of Pennsylvania Press, pp. 354–396.

Levi, P. (1993/1958). *Survival in Auschwitz*. Translated by Stuart Woolf. New York: Simon and Schuster.

Macherey, P. (1978). *A Theory of Literary Production*. London: Routledge & Kegan Paul.

Ochs, E., and L. Capps. (2001). *Living Narrative: Creating Lives in Everyday Storytelling*. Cambridge, MA: Harvard University Press.

Pliskin, Z. (1975). *Guard Your Tongue: A Practical Guide to the Laws of Loshon Hora, Based on Chofetz Chayim*. Brooklyn: Z. Pliskin.

Pogrebin, L. (1991). *Deborah, Golda, and Me: Being Female and Jewish in America*. New York: Crown Publishers.

Posen, I.S. (1988). *For Singing and Dancing and All Sorts of Fun*. Toronto: Deneau.

Pratt, M.L. (2001). I, Rigoberta Menchú and the "Culture Wars." In A. Arias (ed.), *The Rigoberta Menchú Controversy*. Minneapolis: University of Minnesota Press, pp. 29–49.

Ritchie, S. (1993). Ventriloquist folklore: Who speaks for representation? *Western Folklore*, 52 (2/4), pp. 365–378.

Sacks, H. (1992). *Lectures on Conversation*. 2 vols. Edited by G. Jefferson. Oxford: Basil Blackwell.

Schiffrin, D. (2003). "We knew that's it": Retelling the turning point of a narrative. *Discourse Studies*, 5 (4), pp. 535–561.

Shuman, A. (1986). *Storytelling Rights: The Uses of Oral and Written Texts among Urban Adolescents*. Cambridge: Cambridge University Press.

Shuman, A. (1993). "Get outa my face": Entitlement and authoritative discourse. In J.H. Hill and J.T. Irvine (eds.), *Responsibility and Evidence in Oral Discourse*. Cambridge: Cambridge University Press, pp. 136–160.

Shuman, A. (2005). *Other People's Stories: Entitlement Claims and the Critique of Empathy*. Urbana: University of Illinois Press.

Shuman, A. (2011). On the verge: Phenomenology and empathic unsettlement. *Journal of American Folklore*, 124 (493), pp. 147–174.

Smith, A.D. (1997). *Fires in the Mirror: Crown Heights, Brooklyn, and Other Identities*. Dramatists Play Service, Inc.

Spivak, G.C. (1988). Can the subaltern speak? In C. Nelson and L. Grossberg (eds.), *Marxism and the Interpretation of Culture*. Urbana: University of Illinois Press, pp. 271–313.

Spivak, G.C. (1999). *A Critique of Postcolonial Reason: Toward a History of the Vanishing Present*. Cambridge, MA: Harvard University Press.

Tannen, D. (1989). *Talking Voices: Repetition, Dialogue, and Imagery in Conversational Discourse*. Cambridge: Cambridge University Press.

Terada, R. (2011). Out of place: Free speech, disruption, and student protest. *Qui Parle: Critical Humanities and Social Sciences*, 20 (1), pp. 251–269.

Volosinov, V.N. (1973). *Marxism and the Philosophy of Language*. Translated by L. Matejka and I.R. Titunik. New York: Seminar Press. (Originally published 1929.)

Wood, K.M. (1999). Coherent identities amid heterosexist ideologies: Deaf and hearing lesbian coming-out stories. In M. Bucholz, A.C. Liang, and L.A. Sutton (eds.), *Reinventing Identities: The Gendered Self in Discourse*. Oxford: Oxford University Press, pp. 46–64.

3 Narrating and Arguing
From Plausibility to Local Moves

ISOLDA E. CARRANZA

3.1 Introduction

The present work aims to study storytelling as it takes place within socially recognizable genres and becomes an integral part of a social practice. These two characteristics are seen as intimately related if our starting point is the view of genre upheld in the linguistic anthropological tradition (e.g., Bauman 2001). Just as some aspects of the ways of narrating are typical of a genre (Carranza 2003, 2010), arguing, too, can be examined in relation to genre expectations and audience design, and within the discourse of a community of practice. The theoretical and methodological approach adopted here proposes to consider habitual discursive practices in the context of the cultural assumptions of a community so that the strength of shared beliefs comes to light. Within that framework, applying the concept of (narrative, argumentative or descriptive) "discourse mode" (e.g., Georgakopoulou and Goutsos 2000; Smith 2003) allows for the productive study of some research questions formulated in natural narratology, such as finding "the functional alignment of discourse modes within genres" (Fludernik 2000: 284), and the related question posed here: how narrating and arguing combine, alternate, or intersect. The search for the answers will be carried out on a single genre in a sociocultural practice.

On the other hand, the fields of poetics, rhetoric, and discourse studies have dealt with the concept of *doxa*, which has been used to denote common sense, commonsense knowledge and, in some lines of inquiry, collective social representations. At present, the value of doxa is recognized in that it can serve as the basis for persuasion and the social acceptance of opinions. Foundational work on literary narrative has always viewed verisimilitude and perceived narrative coherence as achieved on the basis of elements of doxa. It is useful to notice that doxa is related to what seems reasonable; in addition, it is a culturally specific social construction. As noted in discourse studies, "what we 'spontaneously' perceive as obvious is nothing but a cultural product" (Amossy 2002: 373). Moreover, analysis of narratives in social life confirms that

The Handbook of Narrative Analysis, First Edition. Edited by Anna De Fina and Alexandra Georgakopoulou.
© 2015 John Wiley & Sons, Inc. Published 2019 by John Wiley & Sons, Inc.

verisimilitude is related to normal expectations about events and the causal relations binding events to their consequences. Such insight is particularly useful here, since this chapter seeks to understand both the claim-backing that is part of the process of narrating or that is associated with a story, and adherence to those claims in the particular social practice where they take place. In order to offer a view of the range of argumentative phenomena we come across in and around stories, the discussion deals with those at the level of the entire narrative by focusing on the *reasoned solution to interpretation problems*, and those at the level of the local dialogic pair by focusing on *syllogistic moves*.

Most work on arguments in the discourse of a domain has been – and continues to be – based on written data. Examples include Bondi's (1999) work in the field of economics, Arnoux's (2012) exploration of three devices, "illustrative example," "case," and "scene," in the written discourse of psychoanalysis; Greco Morasso's (2014) application of the normative "strategic maneuvering" perspective to news articles; and Emediato's (2011) discussion of the "argumentative" quality, in the broadest sense, of headlines in news magazines. In contrast, O'Halloran's (2011) study is based on audio-recorded data from debates among reading groups as they discuss novels; it points out the shortcomings of normative theories, and, by applying quantitative research tools, locates "claims," "challenges," and "co-constructions" and documents the resulting problem-solving and lack of confrontation in the oral debates. None of these recent argumentation studies tap into the central role of genre and social practice as explanatory constructs, nor do they show an interest in the blends of argumentation with the narrative mode.

The view supported here is that argumentativity is a question of degree, and that manifestations of the argumentative mode of discourse can be examined both at the level of the genre and at the level of the textual surface. Furthermore, it will be shown that argumentation in non-interactional genres is far from monological. One major way that a proponent can defend a standpoint is by narrating. This is achieved, for example, by establishing a relation of either contrast or analogy between two tales (Carranza 1998a, 2001a), and this chapter will show that it can be carried out by exploiting a key narrative element, the chain of causality.

The rest of the chapter first traces conceptualizations that contribute to the issues formulated above, then delimits the phenomena in focus and the chosen kind of data. A sample text is introduced to illustrate the interplay between narrating and claim-backing. The discussion then offers an overview of what we know about the alternations and embeddings of narration and argumentation, and goes on to show that narratives are interrupted by strictly local claim-backing. Finally, the insights drawn from the empirical evidence are integrated and some issues for further inquiry are identified. (Readers will find compatible views and related discussions in Shuman's, Ehrlich's and Hyvärinen's contributions to this volume.)

3.2   Views on Everyday Argumentation and Reasoning

It needs to be noted that one non-technical meaning of the English word "argument" may be paraphrased as "a typically angry exchange or disagreement with somebody in a conflict," as in the common phrase "a heated argument." The technical and rhetorical sense of the term "argument," which is the one we are concerned with here, and which figures in the theoretical strands reviewed below, points rather to "evidence in support of a position." The heuristic approach adopted here will make use of "argumentative move," a term broad enough to include rebuttals, concessions, consequences, analogies, etc. Like the concept "conversational move" dating back to the 1970s, this one captures the dynamic, locally occasioned quality of a participant's contribution in emergent discursive performances before the addressee. Therefore, an "argumentative move" is a step in an ongoing argumentation. (On the other hand, the concept "argumentative schemes," which originated in informal logic and has applications in artificial intelligence, is not applicable in the linguistic anthropological perspective endorsed here.)

Various approaches to the study of argumentation in discourse have found their sources of inspiration in major works whose extraordinary influence went beyond their disciplinary territory and can only be briefly mentioned here. Thus, contemporary research in discourse analysis acknowledges, and to an extent integrates, some of Perelman's insights into rhetoric and Toulmin's work in the philosophy of practical reasoning. The concise review below touches upon how their legacy figures in today's intellectual landscape, particularly with regard to pragmadialectics, informal logic, discursive psychology, and French discourse analysis.

Perelman's New Rhetoric achieved the revival of rhetorical logic by proposing to seek what is reasonable and what arguments are relevant to issues in a dispute, by deconstructing and assessing arguments not in terms of formal validity, but of appropriateness, and by emphasizing the importance of the audience that would adhere to an argument, the universal audience being the ultimate standard (Perelman 1982). In this tradition, it was first pointed out that people may use *generally accepted* starting points to convince an audience of the acceptability of their position. Even in the legal field, we find that judges build arguments on generally accepted principles such as equity, fairness, good faith, freedom, etc., rather than just on legal principles such as a judge's jurisdiction, a single punishment for a single act, etc.

In ordinary language philosophy, on the other hand, Toulmin put forth a view of rationality as dependent on particular fields such as science, law, art, or ethics; therefore, acceptability of the argument and its content depends on its subject matter and on the audience to which it is addressed. This contextualized logic assessed arguments in terms of soundness. It schematized the anatomy of arguments by using the concepts of "data," "warrant," "backing," "reservation," and "conclusion." It is known as the "jurisprudential model," alluding to the emphasis on *social consensus* in a given area of practice (Hitchcock and Verheij 2006; Toulmin, Rieke, and Janik 1979).

In addition, a comprehensive research program anchored in pragmatics has been developing the integration of normative and descriptive interests in argumentation on the basis of an ideal model of critical discussion, which presupposes conditions for resolving differences of opinion (van Eemeren 2010; van Eemeren, Garssen, and Meuffels 2009; van Eemeren, Houtlosser, and Snoek Henkemans 2007). The pragmadialectal approach is concerned with the formal and content aspects of arguments and of responses to arguments. It proposes that the debate proceeds in clear stages. In this theory, the criteria of rationality are procedural. The concept of "strategic maneuvering" is used to acknowledge that the choice of argumentative moves, shared starting points, and justifications for starting points are all adapted to the arguers' rhetorical ends, and that speech events affect the moves that can be carried out. Along these lines, researchers have contrasted the conditions that exist in situations of adjudication, mediation, and negotiation. Collaborations with conversational analysts have helped to advance this theory by applying it to evaluate arguments in empirical data. Two aspects of this theory are useful to the task at hand in this chapter: it models (and reminds us of) the empirical fact that arguers may *anticipate* various forms of critical reactions; in addition, although it initially treated fallacies as violations of rules, it has developed a view of fallacious moves as situation-dependent: some cases are derailments, while others are a way to strike a balance between norms and goals, or, in other words, between reasonableness and effectiveness.

The field of informal logic (Walton and Macagno 2011) has made major contributions to describing the ways in which arguments can be weak, irrelevant, without enough information on the case, or fallacious. More importantly, informal logic has described the legitimate use in some contexts of arguments involving character attacks, appeals to pity, appeals to fear, etc. This type of pragmatic argumentation theory is designed to provide abstract schemes that model arguments; nevertheless, for the analytical task in this chapter, it is illuminating in one particular respect: it has shown that *common knowledge* about how sequences of actions and events can be expected to unfold can serve as the basis for evidence. Evidence of that kind supports the similarity premise in an argument from analogy (Walton 2012).

Neither van Eemeren's nor Walton's theory is meant to account for any of the following three aspects of argumentation: the emergence of new points of view in the course of a dispute, the online building of arguments, or their adaptation to local inter-actional contexts. All of these aspects are contemplated in another rhetorical approach, discursive psychology. In particular, Billig's line of research aimed to account for ordinary reasoning about social issues and emphasized that participants both state opinions and argue for the superiority of that position over others, constructing their views from common points of agreement that he termed *"commonplaces"* (e.g., Billig 1996). A very early example concerning stance-taking in public controversies demonstrates the application of these ideas. Working on interviews about "positive discrimination" and educational inequality in New Zealand, Potter and Wetherell (1989) document the taken-for-granted quality of meritocratic ideals and the "togetherness" repertoire. The *common sense* status of the togetherness repertoire makes it a powerful rhetorical resource for criticizing educational inequality. In addition, they find that a participant can vary his or her claims according to the details of the interpretative context. Current conversational analysis continues to draw fruitfully from the discursive psychological view of relevant accounts as intrinsically activity-bound and of contestation as invoking cultural and historical scripts (Mäkitalo 2003).

In view of the focus of this chapter, it is relevant to highlight the central role of the "third party" (Chabrol 2009; Charaudeau 2009; Plantin 1998, 2005). Distinctions have been elaborated between the actual social actors and the discourse roles (or textual sub-jects) of Proponent, Opponent, and the "Third Party" (Plantin 2002). These discourse roles have been applied not only in relation to the set "proposition" / "counterproposition" / "doubt" (Plantin 1996) but also to describe the relationships between a "discourse," a "counterdiscourse," and an "audience." The latter set has broad societal distribution, and analyses are typically carried out on political and media discourse. In "polemical discourse" – that is to say, discourse about a controversy and based on a confrontation between two parties – the proponent tries to persuade a "third party," which can be an implicit, ideal audience or an actual one. This has often been the way in which political discourse has been viewed. Two ways of understanding the role of third party will be relevant in dealing with the data in this chapter. On the one hand, at the level of the social occasion type, specific genres are characterized by participant roles with their relative social standing and interpersonal relationships, and they may include a decision-making or mediating "third" participant role. On the other hand, the concept of "third party" can be understood in a broad sense at the level of *socially shared* values and interdiscursivity, corresponding to circulating discourses in society.

The panorama outlined in the previous paragraphs, which is characterized by a considerable degree of mutual influence among the various strands, forms the background for any discourse analytical pursuit on argumentative manifestations in and around narrative. With this theoretical orientation in mind, a few notes on terminology are in order. The term "storyteller" will be applied here to refer to the social actor who has a situational role in a social encounter. In contrast, as in literary studies, the "narrator" has a textual existence as the narrating voice inscribed in the text. The narrator can be homodiegetic – a character in the story world, such as a narrator of personal experiences – or heterodiegetic, like the narrator of *The Iliad* who tells us about Ulysses but was not a participant in the recounted events. Thus a trial lawyer is a heterodiegetic narrator as well as a flesh-and-blood storyteller. The term "proponent" will denote the textual subject who argues and reasons to support the narrator's thesis, and "opponent" will be used to designate the subject who puts forth the contrary argument. These figures are not always coterminous with protagonist and antagonist, respectively, because there are cases in which a given character is the main agent and patient of the story actions (protagonist) while a different character voices the reasoned discourse which supports the thesis being defended (proponent). Finally, in order to refer to the material that is worked into a narrative – what the Russian formalists called "fabula" – the term "tale" will be preferred.

3.3 The Importance of the Discourse of a Sociocultural Practice

Various social contexts pose different demands on the means and paths for arguing in favor of a position or for justifying a decision. For instance, the variety of arguments and other realizations of the argumentative and narrative discourse modes in a judge's sentence or a higher tribunal's opinion differ from those in oral genres, such as an attorney's closing arguments in a criminal trial. In turn, the closing arguments of the prosecution and the defense have different typical characteristics basically stemming from their distinct communicative goals and the range of rhetorical licenses available to each, as well as due to the sequential order in which they are produced – that is, the defense following the prosecution.

The data that provide the examples in this chapter belong to the discourse of the everyday social practice of administering justice; as such, it emerges and circulates in a specific domain, but it cannot be characterized as discourse of a certain discipline or scientific field. The oral discourse produced in face-to-face verbal interactions within judicial speech events – for example, criminal trials or depositions before a clerk for the preparation of a file – can be considered forensic discourse or, as some authors prefer, courtroom discourse, but it is not the language that characterizes laws, constitutions, and books by legal specialists. Most of the ways of arguing and much of the content we are about to examine are not associated exclusively with experts' discourse – on the contrary, they are firmly anchored in the life-world, to use Habermas's term, and expressed in ordinary, lay language. The sample texts will illuminate aspects of claim-backing that are dependent on what constitutes common knowledge within the broader cultural community, that is to say, society at large. However, the tendencies in members' choices of strategies and resources contribute to delineating typical, habitual ways of combining narrating and backing a claim in a specific community of practice.

It should be noted that in polemic, dialectical argumentation, the voice of the opponent can be related to actual discourse by co-participants in the social encounter, or it can arise from a contrary viewpoint already in the common background shared by the audience and the proponent (Amossy 2010). Courtroom data has the advantage of displaying the actual standpoints put forward by all the sides in a dispute. For example, trials with more than one defendant and different defense attorneys for each of them give rise to defense closing arguments that may refute the standpoints of several adversaries.

The genre "closing argument" is inherently both narrative and argumentative due to its function in the speech event where it is instantiated and due to the communicative goals of the participants entitled as text-producers. Therefore, the texts that belong to this genre display an extremely rich variety of combinations and imbrications of narration and claim-backing as they naturally take place in the normal development of an everyday institutional encounter. They also provide the opportunity to deepen our understanding of a socially and culturally significant practice, justice administration, which draws from socially shared beliefs and assumptions. Defense closing arguments are the source of data chosen for this chapter because they are especially varied in discourse devices, rhetorical resources, and even logical-rhetorical operations that, if evaluated from the point of view of a logician's syntax, would appear to be fallacies (e.g., *ad hominem* arguments, which attribute negative qualities to the opponent instead of refuting his or her argument, and *ad misericordiam* arguments, which defend a position by appealing to the audience's compassion), but are relevant argumentative moves serving the goals and constraints in the production context (Carranza 2002). The data set consists of 20 closing arguments, each of an average duration of three hours; therefore, the empirical basis for the discussion is a large number of encompassing argumentative-narrative texts containing narratives of various kinds, from fully developed retrospective stories to low-narrativity narratives – that is, narratives of repeated or habitual actions as well as counterfactual and hypothetical narratives (Carranza 2001a).

Next, the discussion addresses relations between narration and claim-backing whose scopes lie at two ends of a continuum. At one end lies a complete, fully formed narrative that is in itself a means to argue in favor of a position; and at the other end lie the brief instances of local claim-backing that are embedded within a narrative. In between both levels of analysis there are various forms of the alternation between the narrative and the argumentative modes of discourse (e.g., mid-range analogies, argument from consequences and *reductio ad absurdum* regarding a narrative or its interpretation) which cannot be dealt with here.

3.4   Arguing by Narrating

Since much of the content of common sense is culturally specific, it is important to find out what can be invoked as doxa in a given social practice. Drawing from background assumptions and beliefs that are part of common sense is often not just the basis for premises and principles in the service of argumentation, but also the basis for narrative plausibility. The view adopted in this paper is that narrative plausibility, particularly concerning the world as we know it, derives from common sense.

This analytical focus is explored in a text containing sequences of events assigned to opposing narrators. The proponent's version of the tale portrays the protagonist – a female defendant accused of conspiring to commit murder – as a simple woman whose life experiences have always amounted to mere hard work. In view of that, the opponent's version of the final part of the tale is indefensible because it allegedly grants the protagonist enough sophistication to be able to mastermind a conspiracy to kill her husband by enlisting three experienced men to execute the plan.

The identifiable beginning of the text fragment from a closing statement is a quotative formula and a quote which the storyteller attributes to the renowned philosopher Sartre ("one is what one does and what others have made of one"). The lack of cohesion of this statement with preceding utterances anticipates that its orientation is cataphoric.

Example 1

  (1) Yo voy a citar a Sartre

  (2) "Uno es lo que hace y lo que han hecho de él". (..)

  (3) ¿qué es lo que hacía Marcia Segal.↓

  (4) y qué hicieron de Marcia Segal?↓

  (5) A los quince años **se puso** de novio.↓

  (6) Antes de cumplir los dieciocho, **se casó**. ↓

  (7) Vivía en un pequeño pueblo del interior. **Se vino** a Córdoba.↓

  (8) ¿Qué **hizo** al otro día de que se casara?↑ Trabajar en la panadería.↓

  (9) ¿Qué instrucción tenía? ((next utterance in lower volume)) Primaria.↓

(10) Qué es lo que hizo ((([equivalent to "ha hecho"])) toda su vida sino trabajar en la panadería.

(11) vendiendo el bollito.↓ el pan criollo.↓

(12) Uno es lo que hace. ((next utterance in lower volume)) Vender el pan criollo.↓

(13) Y lo que hicieron de ella. Escuela primaria, mamá, un hermano,↑

(1) I am going to quote Sartre

(2) "One is what one does and what others have made of one". (..)

(3) What did Marcia Segal do↓

(4) And what did [others] make of Marcia Segal?↓

(5) At fifteen **she dated.**↓

(6) Before eighteen, **she married.**↓

(7) She lived in a small town of the interior of the province. **She moved** to Cordoba.↓

(8) What did she **do** the day after she got married?↑ Work at the bakery.↓

(9) What level of schooling? ((next utterance in lower volume)) Elementary.↓

(10) What did she do (([equivalent to "has done"])) all her life but work at the bakery.

(11) Selling buns.↓ the local bread.↓

(12) One is what one does. ((next utterance in lower volume)) Sell the local bread.↓

(13) And what [people] made of her. Elementary school, mother, a brother,↑

The initial generalization is paralleled by two rhetorical questions about a concrete case set in the past time ("What did Marcia do?" and "What did [others] make of her?"). As is typical of questions, this one announces forthcoming content that must be taken as the relevant answer. The two-part structure of the initial dictum and of the rhetorical questions that mirror it open up a space for the development of a two-part ideational unit, which consists of a narrative of what Marcia "did" and what others "made of her". A chronologically ordered sequence of discrete past actions begins. Three of them are expressed by finite verbs ("dated," "married," "moved"), while the other two are expressed through the finite past-tense verb in the question "What did she do the day after she got married?" plus the infinitive in the answer ("work"). Therefore, this action is understood to mean the assertion "she worked". Lines 10–11 suggest "she has just been working all this time," portraying the protagonist's life as reduced to a single, continuous experience: work. The especially belittling, not idiomatic presence of the article in *el bollito* [lit. "the bun"] and *el pan criollo* [lit. "the creole bread"] is compatible with the idea of limited life experiences restricted to simple, prosaic things.

The second part of this narrative is brief because there is only one finite verb in "And what they made of her"), but this uninformative utterance is followed by an illuminating list of three nouns that give a succinct description of young Mercedes's life circumstances ("elementary school, mother, a brother"). Although level of schooling and a single-parent family structure can hardly be considered actions, the teller's choice is to present them as what other agents (and fate) did to the protagonist.

Key to the storytelling is the rhetorical effect of its rhythm up to this point. The chopped pace of the list of ordered actions and of the short question-answer pairs is compatible with the factuality of the narrative. This recurrent, marked prosodic pattern enhances the step-like quality of an uneventful life course moving through the expected stages. The representation of the opponent's narrative stands in stark contrast to the life trajectory just recounted.

Example 1 (continued)

(14) **Pero claro. parece** que **mágicamente,↑ adquirió** la capacidad de ser mafiosa

(15) porque para ser mafiosa también hay que tener capacidad.↓ organizativa.↓ creativa.↓

(16) relacioneØ.↓ audacia.↓

(17) Una mujer de estudio primario

(18) que lo único que sabe es vender bollitos de pan,↑

(19) **tuvo la capacidad** según la acusación

(20) ((next utterance in lower volume)) a la que voy a desmenuzar minuciosamente,↑

(21) **para convencer** a un veterano comisario como el que está aquí,

(22) ((next utterance in lower volume)) que no se ha mostrado como un inocente.

(23) a su ayudante el sargento Olmos,

(24) ((next utterance in lower volume)) que no me parece que fuera la madre Teresa.

(25) y a "Mandrake",

(26) ((next utterance in lower volume)) delincuente profesional asaltante de banco orgulloso.

(27) A todos los **convenció** Marcia Segal. ↓

(28) Bueno esto es otra **interpretación** que vamos a demostrar que es **absolutamente imposible**.

(14) **But of course. it seems** that she **magically,↑ got** the ability to be mafiosa

(15) Because to be mafiosa you also have to have organizational.↓ creative. ability.↓

(16) public relations.↓ audacity.↓

(17) A woman with primary education

(18) who knows only one thing sell buns,↑

(19) **had the ability** according to the accusation

(20) ((next utterance in lower volume)) which I'm going to analyze meticulously,↑

(21) **to convince** a veteran commissary like the one sitting here,

(22) ((next utterance in lower volume)) who hasn't come out as gullible.

(23) his assistant sergeant Olmos

(24) ((next utterance in lower volume)) who doesn't seem Mother Theresa to me.

(25) and "Mandrake,"

(26) ((next utterance in lower volume)) a professional delinquent proud bank robber.

(27) Marcia Segal **convinced** everybody.↓

(28) Well that is another **interpretation** that we will show to be **absolutely impossible**.

This continuation of the tale offers a view of the protagonist's adulthood. The combination *Pero claro* itself (adversative plus a reinforcing expression) announces the contrast and sets the ironic tone, but it is not a key to anticipating the scope of the contrast, which will encompass an entire narrative. The first evaluative clues are the evidential main clause *parece*, "it seems" and the adverb "magically." The allegedly questionable alternative tale consists of the following sequence of actions, "got" (*adquirió*, line 14) and *convinced. The latter is not uttered (its implicit character is signaled with an asterisk), but it is expressed first through the combination "had the ability ... to convince" (*tuvo la capacidad ... para convencer*, lines 19 and 21), equivalent in this context to three discrete actions: she convinced a commissary, she convinced a sergeant, and she convinced a thief. Then, this is expressed through the finite verb "convinced" in "convinced everybody" (*a todos los convenció*, line 26). The opponent's version is explicitly dismissed as "absolutely impossible" (*absolutamente imposible*, line 27) and called an "interpretation" (*interpretación*) as opposed to facts.

These coupled episodes demonstrate a basic argumentative relationship: opposition. What is presented as uncontestable facts is contrasted with their absurd follow-up sequence, thus "demonstrating" the latter's unlikeliness. With the opponent's alleged continuation of the narrative action, the event sequence does not hold together. As has been found for narratives of hypothetical events in an analogical or contrasting relation to factual narratives (see Carranza 1998a on Salvadoran immigrants' narratives, Carranza 2001a on courtroom narratives), here, too, narrating is a means to back up an argumentative position. The invocation of a "given" is clear. With an initial tongue-in-cheek tone, normal expectations about human behavior are invoked so that the event-string attributed to the opponent's tale is shown to be inconsistent and thus clearly flawed. Thus, attacking the *plausibility* of the opponent's alternative thread of actions strengthens the narrator's version of the past and the proponent's claim.

We know that narrative coherence is relative to the world created in the story. The diegetic world may be of a type where real-life logic does not hold, as is the case in dreams or in the possible or imagined worlds of fiction. However, when the diegetic world is a representation of actual past events, or when the argumentative position being defended pertains to the actual past, coherence and plausibility are intimately associated.

In addition, the case under examination points to the theoretical problem of knowledge in narratives. This is usually approached in terms of characters' or the first-person narrator's epistemological status, but a different issue comes to light here. This case shows that some of the facts can be known by the audience, not just by the narrator; however, the congruence arising from the connections imposed on the facts is newsworthy and tellable. That congruence is the core of the claim that is expected to be accepted and adopted by the audience.

We have seen that arguing by recounting a particular tale is one way of putting forward an argumentative position. The next section reviews alternative imbrications of narrative and argumentation.

3.5   Other Ways of Backing a Claim in, with, and across Narratives

Among the main ways in which narrating and arguing combine are those in which the expression of an argumentative position calls for some evidence to back it up and make it acceptable; in that case, the story provides the relevant support (i.e., the evidence). The claim, whose formulation may precede or follow the narrative text, is then the defended "story thesis" (Carranza 1996).

In a different combination, the presentation of past events itself is the center of controversy or leads to interpretations expressed in what is known as the "internal" and "external" evaluation of a story. The story-world situation helps establish the logical system that allows the narrator, in the embedding argumentative-narrative text as a whole or in the story proper, to reason from the propositions it contains. Since opinions, interpretations of experience, and evaluative statements require accounting for, reasoned discourse is often produced. Consequently, the dramaturgy created in a story can be the site for some arguments that unfold in the voices of characters (Carranza 1998b, 1999), others that are developed in the narrator's voice, and still others that extend across the limits of the story (Carranza 1997). Fully developed arguments, whether incorporated as direct represented discourse or verbalized thought, are typically the proponent-protagonist's rather than the antagonist's; and this story-world argumentation is inherently addressed to multiple addressees: the opponent in the story world, the interlocutor in the storytelling situation, and indirect targets beyond the interaction in progress (Carranza 1999).

In addition, narrating can have an explanatory function. In this regard, De Fina has studied "narrative accounts" and defines them as "recapitulations of past events reconstructed as responses to an explicit or implied 'why' or 'how' question by an interlocutor" (De Fina 2009: 240). The umbrella term of "claim-backing" denotes a variety of discourse tasks, from arguing (in a restricted sense of the term) to explaining and justifying. Claim-backing may concern past events, as when a particular past action gets accounted for by means of a narratorial commentary. It may concern the interpretation of past events by either narrators or characters; in other words, what gets accounted for is an evaluation. It may even consist in metadiscursive justifications of the storytelling itself, as will be shown in the next section.

3.6 A Local Mechanism for the Effective Presentation of Claims

Rhetorical questions are a pervasive mechanism of oral discourse, especially oral discourse that is public, and they recurrently crop up in the development of a story. Zooming in on local manifestations of argumentation, we can find that the basic question-answer structure is a mold often applied to express the argumentative position in the answer slot (Carranza 2001b) and is characteristic of political speeches, religious sermons (Carranza 2012) and trial lawyers' closing arguments (Pascual 2006). As we know, declaratives containing a finite, material process verb advance the narrative action, while negative clauses and questions do not. Questions suspend the progress of the narrative action and have a focusing effect because they underscore the content that resolves the polarity in a Yes-No question or satisfies the unknown element expressed in a Wh-question.

When rhetorical question use is overabundant, the oral performance of the text and the storyline itself seem choppy and halting. The answers to some rhetorical questions are explicit, while others are left implicit and are easily retrieved from the co-text and the interactional history. The question-answer exchange can be used simply to present new content immediately afterward, as in "What did he do next? He went to his mom's"; but the interest of rhetorical questions for our present purpose lies in the fact that a question opens up a space for the relevant answer, which is strategically used to express the proponent's voice, and in the fact that it can bring into sharp focus an element from the story world, as will be shown in this section.

Because a question involves the audience as a potential addressee and engages actual interlocutors in a quest for the answer, the content that is indicated as the relevant second pair-part acquires the appearance of a "shared" answer and, indeed, the only possible one. This key property accounts for the tendency to choose the answer slot to present or imply a *claim*. In every case in my corpus, the second part of the question-answer pair expresses the content that the text-producer seeks to have the addressee adhere to. The two examples that follow illustrate explicit answers. It is important to keep in mind that the storytellers who produced the data have not witnessed the events being recounted and that even if certain actions can be taken to be facts, their interpretation must be put forward for the audience to endorse it.

Example 2
(Defense attorney Ortiz)
¿quién **se benefició** con la muerte de Hugo? (..) VamoØ a seguir (.) ¿Quién **se benefició**? (.) A Marcia Segal le han rematado hoy hasta los muebles de la casa, (.) ¿Quién tiene un auto importado, viaja a Europa, dirige la empresa? **Oscar Corro**.

Who **benefited** from Hugo's death? (..) Let's go on (.) Who **benefited**? (.) Marcia Segal had even the house furniture seized by creditors, (.) Who has an imported car, travels to Europe, conducts the firm? **Oscar Corro**.

The explicit answer to all the questions in (2) is the name of a man who, in this attorney's view, should be brought to court. Thus, by implication, the female defendant has not profited from the murder, nor was she the perpetrator. Such is the idea which the audience is induced to accept. In the next example, when the utterances in (3) were produced, the text-producer had been describing how, in the course of a single fight, a man hit the victim with an object and another man stabbed him. The question delimits the core of what is "in dispute" at this point of the development of the argumentation. Its finite verb unambiguously indicates the past time of the action.

Example 3
(Defense attorney Gutiérrez)
¿Quién **causó** la muerte de Claudio? Fueron **los dos**.

Who **caused** Claudio's death? **Both of them** did.

The audience of this storytelling is called upon to accept the idea that the two perpetrators are equally responsible and that the result originated from the combined aggression, not just from the hitting, nor from the stabbing alone. Space precludes a detailed analysis of the story and the development of its argumentative direction here, but this case makes apparent that embedded in narrative discourse is a fleeting surface realization of the argumentative mode of discourse where the claim is the storyteller's interpretation of the past events.

Implicit answers are exemplified by the next case, (4) below, taken from a story involving three characters: the victim, the perpetrator, and the perpetrator's boss, Salas. The extended co-text allows for the interpretation of the finite verb as a Historical Present with a perfect (i.e., non-durative) past time reference. Square brackets in the examples below indicate the propositional content of the implied answers.

Example 4
(Defense attorney Mazza)
   ¿La acción de Salas ((omitted modifiers)) **trae** ((Historical Present)) como consecuencia la muerte de uno de los comensales a manos de otro? ["No"]

   Does Salas's action ((omitted modifiers)) **bring** ((Historical Present)) as a consequence the death of one of the people dining together by another one? ["No"]

Here the text-producer, who is Salas's defense attorney, seems engaged in making sense of the tale. In the context of his closing argument, this polarity question leads to what appears to be the single logical answer: "No." It is inevitably evoked by the audience. The absence of its formulation highlights its obviousness.

Questions are also applied to attack the tale as told by the counterpart. In the final stages of a criminal trial, the audience first listens to the prosecutor's closing argument and then the defense's; therefore, the defense attorney uses that opportunity to undermine the prosecutor's version of past events. However, the narrator-proponent's responses to an opponent are not unique to this genre. Stories from various situational contexts contain refutations of another version of the tale or an alternative interpretation of an event by an (actual or represented) opponent. The latter is illustrated in (5) and (6), which include explicit answers. It should also be noted that refutations through answers to rhetorical questions are performed in the narrator's, not the protagonist's, voice, as both of the following examples show.

Example 5
(Defense attorney Ortiz)
   ¿Cuáles son los motivos que tenía Bessone? (.) **Ninguno**.

   What are the motives that Bessone had? (.) **None**.

Example 6
(Defense attorney Gómez)
   ¿De dónde **surge** ((Historical Present)) esa disparidad de fuerzas ((between two groups in a fight))? Esta defensa ((this noun phrase refers to the "I" of the speaker)) **no** puede descubrir.

   Where **does** ((Historical Present)) that disparity of strength ((between two groups in a fight)) **come** from? This defense ((this noun phrase refers to the "I" of the speaker)) is **not** able to figure it out.

In the course of a narrative, these challenges to the adversary's evaluation of past events can also be left implicit, as in (7) and (8).

Example 7
(Defense attorney Ortiz)
     ¿De qué ocultamiento me hablan? ¿Qué? ¿**Tenía** que sacar en el diario que cobraba el seguro? ["No, no tenía que hacer saber a todos que recibiría dinero."] ["Luego, no ocultó el hecho de que recibiría dinero."]

     What hiding are they talking about? What? **Did** she **have to** announce in the papers that she would cash the insurance? ["No, she did not have to let everybody know that she would get money."] ["Then she did not hide the fact that she would receive money."]

The defense's advantage of speaking after the accusers creates opportunities to refute them and establishing intertextual relations with their closing argument. Thus, the lexical item chosen by the opponent, *ocultamiento* "hiding," is retained in (7) but the idea is bluntly dismissed with *¿De qué me hablan?* "What are you talking about?" The finite verb in the past tense, "Did she have to," unambiguously indicates the disputed narrative element. Most importantly, derived from the implicit answer is an additional inferable proposition with which the rebuttal is achieved. Likewise, in the next example, the proponent answers an opponent back with a challenging question that starts with the common, fixed expression "will someone tell me?"

Example 8
(Defense attorney Ortiz)
     Si no había armas, ¿me quieren decir de dónde **salió** el revólver que es la base fundamental de la acusación?↑ ["Sí había armas"]

     If there weren't any guns, will someone tell me where the revolver which is the fundamental basis of the accusation **came** from? ↑ ["There were indeed guns"]

We have seen that the rhetorical question may concern the proponent's story, as in examples (2) to (4), or it may concern the opponent's story, as in examples (5) to (8). It has also been amply shown that the question always announces content that is put forth by the proponent, and when that content is not explicitly manifested, it is derived by implication from the co-text and the context. If we consider that one storyteller is competing with another to have her version or interpretation prevail, the "third party" concept is applicable to the questions' addressee. Given that the direct addressee of the questions can be a posited or textually created audience in addition to the actual audience, multiple roles are inscribed in the text – among them that of the audience and that of the proponent who summons the audience. These "fictitious" exchanges are useful to present new content or to express a logical chain. In more general terms, they are useful to move the text forward. Our next step is to notice the way rhetorical questions initiated with "Why" function as narratorial comment.

3.7   The Special Case of "Why"

Questions also take part in kinds of claim-backing that do not involve presenting a conclusion as derived from evidence, but consist in explaining or justifying. This section deals with explaining and justifying that stop the narrative action. In the course of a story, immediately after reference to a state or an event in the diegetic world, a why-question may be asked about it. The question-answer mechanism is used as a means for ensuring comprehension of the plot or, more precisely, for presenting the narrator's version and interpretation of the past events or states as well-grounded. Answers to why-questions are always explicit. The example below shows that what needs to be accounted for is the "uncertain" quality attributed to a promised insurance payment, and the question creates the conditional relevance for the explanation.

Example 9
(Defense attorney Ortiz)
   ¿**por qué era incierta** la promesa? (.) en primer lugar porque no había hecho el seguro ella ni sabía cuál era la póliza, (.) no estaba pagada según Badra (.) y en segundo lugar, había que hacer un juicio para cobrarlo.

   Why was the promise **uncertain**? (.) first because the insurance had not been contracted by her nor did she know what the policy was, (.) according to Badra it ((the policy)) hadn't been paid for (.) and secondly, a lawsuit had to be started to be able to cash it.

The focus of the why-question can be the story or the storytelling because the why-question creates the opportunity for a justification of the tale and of the way it is being told. Like "uncertain" in (9), in the next example the quality of being "important" gets backed up. In (10) the narrative element which gets evaluated as "important" is the fact that a character saw two bags, and this attribution needs justifying. The present tense of the finite verb in the question "Why is this important?" is indicative of the omniscient outsider's perspective on the story events. The narrator's standpoint is later specified with the utterance "it is a clue" [to the fact that they may be the victim's bags].

Example 10
(Defense attorney Alba)
   Montes nos **dice** ((Historical Present)) que la boleta la **hizo** en el capot y que en el asiento de atrás del auto **vio** dos bolsos.
   vio dos bolsos en el asien- en el asiento trasero.
   ¿**Por qué** es **importante**? Porque la señora cuando **va** ((Historical Present)) de viaje, **lleva** ((Historical Present)) dos bolsos. Eso **dice** ((Historical Present)) su hermana Elena quien la **ayudó** a preparar los dos bolsos.
   yo no puedo decir que sean **los mismos** bolsos, pero es un **indicio**.

   Montes **tells** ((Historical Present)) us that he **wrote** the receipt on the car hood and that on seat in the back he **saw** two bags.

he **saw** two bags (.) on the back s- on the back seat.

Why is it **important**? Because when the woman **goes** ((Historical Present)) on this trip, she **takes** ((Historical Present)) two bags. So her sister Elena says ((Historical Present)) who **helped** her pack the two bags.

I cannot guarantee that they are **the same** bags, but it is a **clue**.

It is clear that the claim-backing in (10) is not meant to support the view that a certain sequence of events took place, but rather to support the way the past events are interpreted. In the examples below, the storyteller becomes salient due to the first-person singular verb morphology of the finite verb in the question, *reconstruyo* "reconstruct" in (11) and *digo* "say" in (12). Such inscription in the textual surface of the participant as animator and performer is an indication of the focus on the telling. In (11) and (12) below, the storyteller assumes full responsibility as a decision-making agent.

Example 11
(Defense attorney Vera)
    Y ¿por qué lo **reconstruyo así** al hecho?

    And why do **I** reconstruct the event **like that**?

Example 12
(Defense attorney Mazza)
    Traverso **se encuentra** ((Historical Present)) con Álvarez de manera casual ¿Por qué **digo casual**?

    Traverso **runs into** ((Historical Present)) Álvarez by coincidence ¿Why do **I** say **by coincidence**?

We have seen questions that express the storyteller's voice. Unlike Yes-No and other Wh-questions, those with *why* do not serve as a platform to launch a claim as the conclusion in a logical argument. The claim expressed in the proposition accompanied by a *why*-question announces an explanation or justification with which all other alternative versions of the tale are dismissed. In (11), the ensuing justification annuls the soundness of reconstructing the event in a different way; and in (12), the justification makes it unacceptable to say that Traverso meets Álvarez deliberately.

In this section, we have seen that explanations of narrative elements and justifications for the storytelling are useful means for presenting the story version as grounded on solid, reasoned bases. The location of the particular closing argument in the sequence of closing arguments is not the sole factor shaping the emergence of claim-backing and what can safely be left implicit. The value granted to reason and reasoned discourse is also a key factor underlying the production of explanations of events or justifications for the narrators' evaluations of narrative elements. The proliferation of rhetorical questions is accounted for by the social expectation that those discursive tasks be performed. The genre under observation and the public discourse to which that genre is related are part of the sociocultural practice of administering justice, whose basis in reason and reasonability are explicitly laid out in laws, dogmatic works, jurisprudence, and legal training in law schools.

3.8   Conclusions

The exploration of this chapter's topic started off from the theoretical-methodological decision to observe naturally occurring narratives produced by participants in the normal performance of their social roles and in the service of their own goals, not the researcher's, and from the decision to define genre as the level on which they can be accounted for (Carranza 2012). On that basis, progress can be made in understanding how narratives are produced and received, given the specific social and discursive conventions enforced by the genre and the social occasion.

The search for ways in which narrating and claim-backing interpenetrate has led to the examination of significant manifestations – on the one hand, the *dispute over interpretation of the past*, and on the other, the *presentation of a local claim* that suspends the narrative in progress. The former has been shown in a sample text that features the interplay of two factors: The causal connection between the initial and the final episodes is deliberately absent, and the adversary's section of the tale is overtly evaluated and, in this case, rejected. These two facts reduce narrativity because they detract from the "transfer of experience" and increase argumentativity because they make apparent the evaluative ideological stance. This evidence supports the general contention I posit here: that, notwithstanding the potential for interrelations between them, in any single argumentative-narrative text, argumentativity and narrativity cannot be equally dominant.

Secondly, insights from the analysis of rhetorical questions enable us to address the double fact that they can be found in narratives and are particularly abundant in a specific genre. Three central aspects of rhetorical questions seem to account for that. They offer a two-part structure into which ideational material is organized. This is the reason why they can be used to advance the narrative action or to introduce an argumentative move. They also induce the target audience to satisfy the relevance conditions created through them by anticipating a certain answer. Finally, they allow for planning opportunities in the process of discourse production.

The surface manifestations of the narrative and argumentative modes of discourse we have reviewed in a single genre are ultimately related to underlying assumptions and values circulating in the domain of a given social practice. The domain of criminal justice administration is characterized by assumptions about historical truth – for example, that it can be proved through evidence – and about the valid applications of reason and rationality required to convince judges and jurors that something is true. The discourse production and interpretation processes in progress during its emblematic speech event, the trial, are governed by those basic assumptions; they constrain the activity of narrating and condition the preference for as well as the receivers' familiarity with ways of drawing on narrative plausibility and exploiting the question-answer format. At the same time, however, ways of reasoning and arguing in the defense closing argument follow common, ordinary, everyday paths and build on doxa. Discourse by co-participants did not indicate a rejection of this mix of habitual ways of narrating within a specialized community of practice and generalized knowledge to defend a claim. To conclude, more research is desirable on the balance of common sense and expert knowledge and their expression through narrativity and argumentativity in a consequential social practice – such work has the potential to further our comprehension of both narratological and social issues.

REFERENCES

Amossy, R. (2002). Introduction to the study of doxa. *Poetics Today*, (23) 3, pp. 369–394.

Amossy, R. (2010). The functions of polemical discourse in the public sphere. In M. Smith and B. Warnick (eds.), *The Responsibilities of Rhetoric*. Long Grove, IL: Waveland Press, pp. 52–61.

Arnoux, E.N. de. (2012). Potencialidades y limitaciones de los dispositivos argumentativos que articulan materiales clínicos y reflexión teórica en los escritos del campo psicoanalítico. *Cogency. Journal of Reasoning and Argumentation*, 4 (2), pp. 47–75.

Bauman, R. (2001). The ethnography of genre in a Mexican market: Form, function, variation. In P. Eckert and J. Rickford (eds.), *Style and Sociolinguistic Variation*. Cambridge: Cambridge University Press, pp. 57–77.

Billig, M. (1996). *Arguing and Thinking: A Rhetorical Approach to Social Psychology*. Revised edition. Cambridge: Cambridge University Press.

Bondi, M. (1999). *English Across Genres: Language Variation in the Discourse of Economics*. Modena: Edizioni Il Fiorino.

Carranza, I.E. (1996). Argumentation and ideological outlook in storytelling. PhD dissertation. Georgetown University.

Carranza, I.E. (1997). Argumentar narrando. *Revista Versión*, 7, pp. 57–69.

Carranza, I.E. (1998a). Low-narrativity narratives and argumentation. *Narrative Inquiry*, 8 (2), pp. 287–317.

Carranza, I.E. (1998b). Autoridad retórica y conversación. *Diálogos Hispánicos*, 22, pp. 25–50.

Carranza, I.E. (1999). Winning the battle in private discourse: Rhetorical-logical operations in storytelling. *Discourse & Society*, 10 (4), pp. 509–541.

Carranza, I.E. (2001a). Narrativas de responsabilidad penal. In *6th International Conference of the Latin American Association of Discourse Studies*. Recife: Universidade Estadual do Pernambuco Press, pp. 344–357.

Carranza, I.E. (2001b). Argumentar, explicar y justificar con preguntas retóricas. *Revista Iberoamericana sobre Discurso y Sociedad*, 3 (2), pp. 61–83.

Carranza, I.E. (2002). Juicio oral y público: La atribución. In *International Conference Argumentation: Linguistics, Rhetoric, Logic, Pedagogy, in Honor of Oswald Ducrot*. Buenos Aires: Buenos Aires University Press, pp. 1047–1052.

Carranza, I.E. (2003). Genre and institution: Narrative temporality in final arguments. *Narrative Inquiry*, 13 (1), pp. 41–69.

Carranza, I.E. (2010). Truth and authorship in textual trajectories. In D. Schiffrin, A. De Fina, and A. Nylund (eds.), *Telling Stories: Language, Narrative, and Social Life*. Washington, DC: Georgetown University Press, pp. 173–181.

Carranza, I.E. (2012). Los géneros en la vida social: La perspectiva fundada en las prácticas sociales. In M. Shiro, P. Charaudeau, and L. Granato (eds.), *Los géneros discursivos desde múltiples perspectivas: Teorías y análisis*. Madrid/Frankfurt: Iberoamericana Vervuert, pp. 97–120.

Chabrol, C. (2009). El tercero del discurso como metaenunciador autorizado en el espacio de interdiscursividad ideológica. In R.G. Montes and P. Charaudeau (eds.), *El "tercero": Fondo y figura de las personas del discurso*. Puebla, Mexico: BUAP Press.

Charaudeau, P. (2009). Tercero ¿dónde estás? A propósito del tercero del discurso. In R.G. Montes and P. Charaudeau (eds.), *El "tercero": Fondo y figura de las personas del discurso*. Puebla, Mexico: BUAP Press.

De Fina, A. (2009). Narratives in interviews: The case of accounts. *Narrative Inquiry*, 19 (2), pp. 233–258.

Eemeren, F.H. van. (2010). *Strategic Maneuvering in Argumentative Discourse: Extending the Pragma-Dialectical Theory of Argumentation*. Amsterdam: John Benjamins.

Eemeren, F.H. van, B. Garssen, and B. Meuffels. (2009). *Fallacies and Judgments of Reasonableness*. Dordrecht: Springer.

Eemeren, F.H. van, P. Houtlosser, and A.F. Snoeck Henkemans. (2007). *Argumentative Indicators: A Pragma-Dialectical Study*. Dordrecht: Springer.

Emediato, W. (2011). L'argumentation dans le discours d'information médiatique. *Argumentation et Analyse du Discours*, 7, pp. 1–19.

Fludernik, M. (2000). Genres, text-types, or discourse modes? Narrative modalities and generic categorization. *Style*, 34 (1), pp. 274–292.

Georgakopoulou, A., and D. Goutsos. (2000). Revisiting discourse boundaries: The narrative and non-narrative modes. *Text*, 20 (1), pp. 63–82.

Greco Morasso, S. (2014). Contextual frames and their argumentative implications: A case study in media argumentation. *Discourse Studies*, 14 (2), pp. 197–216.

Hitchcock, D.I., and B. Verheij (eds.). (2006). *Arguing on the Toulmin Model: New Essays in Argument Analysis and Evaluation*. Dordrecht: Springer.

Mäkitalo, A. (2003). Accounting practices as situated knowing: Dilemmas and dynamics in institutional categorization. *Discourse Studies*, 5 (4), pp. 495–516.

O'Halloran, K. (2011). Investigating argumentation in reading groups: Combining manual qualitative coding and automated corpus analysis tools. *Applied Linguistics*, 32 (2), pp. 172–196.

Pascual, E. (2006). Questions in legal monologues: Fictive interaction as argumentative strategy in a murder trial. *Text & Talk*, (26) 3, pp. 383–402.

Perelman, C. (1982/1977). *The Realm of Rhetoric*. Notre Dame, IN: University of Notre Dame Press.

Plantin, C. (1996). Le trilogue argumentatif: Présentation du modèle, analyse de cas. *Langue française*, 112, pp. 9–30.

Plantin, C. (1998). L'interaction argumentative. In *Dialoganalyse VI. Proceedings of the 6th Conference on Dialogue Analysis*. Tübingen: Max Niemeyer Verlag, pp. 151–159.

Plantin, C. (2002). Des les polémistes à les polémiqueurs. In M. Murat, G. Declercq, and J. Dangel (eds.), *La parole polémique*. Paris: Champion, pp. 377–408.

Plantin, C. (2005). *L'argumentation: Histoire, théories, perspectives*. Paris: PUF.

Potter, J., and M. Wetherell. (1989). Fragmented ideologies: Accounts of educational failure and positive discrimination. *Text*, 9 (2), pp. 175–190.

Smith, C.S. (2003). *Modes of Discourse: The Local Structure of Texts*. Cambridge: Cambridge University Press.

Toulmin, S., R. Rieke, and A. Janik. (1979). *An Introduction to Reasoning*. New York: Macmillan.

Walton, D. (2012). Story similarity in arguments from analogy. *Informal Logic*, 32 (2), pp. 190–218.

Walton, D., and F. Macagno. (2011). Burdens of persuasion and proof in everyday argumentation. In *Proceedings of the Seventh International Conference of the International Society for the Study of Argumentation*. Amsterdam: SicSat, pp. 1940–1950.

4 Narrative, Cognition, and Socialization

MASAHIKO MINAMI

4.1 Introduction

Language can be thought of as not only a manifestation but also a product of culture. One of the major issues in developmental psychology in general and language development in particular is: "Which plays a more critical role, heredity or environment?" People have asked this question for years (e.g., Jensen 1969). Imagine, for instance, Japanese-American toddlers who are genetically Japanese but being raised in an American cultural environment. If hereditary factors are the predominant determinant of human behavior, Japanese-American toddlers should behave like Japanese. If, on the other hand, environmental factors play a more critical role, the young children should be more like Americans. Conducting this line of research, Caudill and Frost (1974) found that Japanese-American infants behaved more like American infants than infants from other cultural backgrounds. The finding in this early cross-cultural research on development not only suggests that environmental factors are the crucial determinants of individual behaviors, but also emphasizes the primary role of culture in driving parenting behaviors that result in changes in infants and young children. The implication is that culture provides the structure and environment for parents, particularly mothers, to influence their children in culturally appropriate ways. This applies to language development as well. As Snow and Ferguson (1977) suggest, parents play a far more important role in their children's language acquisition than simply modeling the language and providing input for the so-called language acquisition device.

The issue, in reality, is not so simple. Culture consists of many complicated factors. Consider, for instance, US society, which sociologists have long described as a melting pot in which a variety of cultural experiences and backgrounds merge into something entirely new. According to Matsumoto (2000: 24), culture can be defined as:

> a dynamic system of rules, explicit and implicit, established by groups in order to ensure their survival, involving attitudes, values, beliefs, norms, and behaviors, shared by a group

The Handbook of Narrative Analysis, First Edition. Edited by Anna De Fina and Alexandra Georgakopoulou.
© 2015 John Wiley & Sons, Inc. Published 2019 by John Wiley & Sons, Inc.

but harbored differently by each specific unit within the group, communicated across generations, relatively stable but with the potential to change across time.

Because values, beliefs, and norms, for instance, are cognitive products, we can view culture as being cognitive. In other words, cultures are nothing but knowledge/cognitive representations translated into certain norms, opinions, attitudes, values, and beliefs (Matsumoto and Juang 2008).

The aforementioned definition also illustrates the nature of cultural psychology, the central tenet of which rests on the "constructivist" conception of meaning, stipulating that social interactions are culturally constrained. In different cultures, children's lives are shaped in different ways according to their parents' models and expectations of what the children's development should be. According to specific cultural norms, distinct goals and plans for child development are implemented in a wide variety of ways. We call this process socialization or sometimes enculturation, the process by which children learn and internalize the rules and patterns of the society in which they live. As socialization or enculturation agents, parents, especially mothers, in each culture socialize their children differently. Through the process of socialization, children engage in cultural learning; they acquire the ability to recognize and interpret the variety of activities that take place in their socioculturally specific environments. Consequently, children growing up in different cultures have particular experiences through which they develop diverse expectations, preferences, and even beliefs.

Needless to say, culture has a pervasive influence on the language we use – the words as well as the rules by which words are put together in order to construct meaningful phrases, sentences, and, more globally, narrative discourse. Indeed, everyone everywhere speaks in narrative discourse, and in personal narratives in particular. We all have stories to tell. Wherever we go, we find narratives serving such important functions as mediating interpersonal relationships, enabling self-presentation, and making sense of experiences. Deeply embedded within this universality, however, are starkly culture-specific or even language-specific narrative styles. It is even possible to encounter individuals from other cultures with speech styles that we find difficult to understand, even though we may "know" their language. This is because the more socialized or enculturated we become, the more we have a tendency to view the world through our own cultural filters. In other words, these filters are like lenses that allow us to perceive the world in a specific way. As we grow, we add layers to these filters, and, by the time we become adults, we share similar filters with others in the society/culture in which we live. In this way, cognition, socialization, and narrative have close relationships with one another through culture as a medium. (For further information on narrative and culture, see Koven in this volume, chapter 20.)

4.2   L2 Narrative Development

With the aforementioned cultural issues as a backdrop, this chapter addresses problems related to narrative, cognition, and culture within the framework of foreign- or second-language (L2) narrative discourse. To begin with, narrative is generally defined as the manner of talking about a series of logically and chronologically related events (Ervin-Tripp and Küntay 1997; Labov 1972). Narrative, in fact, includes a variety of discourse genres – not only fictional storytelling and scripts, but also personal anecdotes. As discussed earlier, while narratives are common in the way all people communicate, it is important to remember that not all cultures construct narratives in the same way.

Research on language socialization has indeed identified the ways in which mothers attempt to familiarize their children with culture-specific patterns of communicative styles; in some cultures, mothers even directly model culturally valued narrative styles (Ochs and Schieffelin 1984). As Hymes (1974) stressed, from early childhood on, children in different cultural settings learn the appropriate social use of their language, as well as its grammar and vocabulary. While the basic narrative structure is more or less similar across different languages, the specific content of narratives frequently exhibits culture-specific patterns. Those culture-specific differences attest to the results of language socialization, reflecting the values and beliefs of the culture in which the narrator was born and raised. With respect to conversational scaffolding, Japanese mothers, for instance, request fewer descriptions and give fewer evaluations in their narrative discourse with their children, whereas North American mothers tend to employ more information-oriented speech with their children (Minami and McCabe 1995). The types of information contained in narratives reflect what mothers want to promote in their child-rearing practices, particularly through language socialization processes. Cross-cultural differences become evident through the comparison of narrative discourse across different languages. The acquisition of culture-specific communicative competence hence plays a critical role in the process of language acquisition and the development of narrative discourse skills.

Through research such as that carried out by Minami and McCabe (1995), cross-cultural, cross-linguistic research has addressed the culture- and language-specific nature of narratives. Extending this line of thought to L2 narratives, learning to imitate culturally specific narrative styles seems an appropriate goal in the acquisition of L2 skills. From the analysis of such styles, we may uncover the techniques needed for L2 learners to acquire the means by which to encode their own perspectives and emotions in the target language appropriately.

To date, however, with some exceptions, few studies have extensively examined narratives in the context of L2 acquisition. Our knowledge about the culture-specific elements in narratives is limited, with the result that in many classrooms little attention is given to the style and structure of narrative discourse (note that "style" in this chapter refers to the way in which something is stated, expressed, or performed). Even though L2 learners' difficulties conveying their messages, emotions in particular, in the target language may relate closely to their use of unique narrative styles (including first-language [L1] interference-like narrative styles) in their oral discourse, foreign language teaching is often limited to grammar and vocabulary. Language instructors may have good reason to emphasize grammatical accuracy (or, more globally, grammatical competence) in their classrooms, but discourse-level problems often seem to go unnoticed in the course of language instruction. To include this important element of language acquisition, narrative styles should be studied empirically and revealed through narrative discourse analysis. (For further information on narrative in L2 teaching environments, see Barkhuizen in this volume, chapter 5.)

4.3   Content-based Narrative Analyses: Labovian Methodology

One piece of research relevant to the present study is the seminal study conducted by Labov (1972), the sociolinguist who pioneered the study of oral personal narratives through the examination of the interface between cultural and linguistic issues. Labov shifted a paradigm from isolated linguistic form (i.e., syntax or the grammatical sentences of a language) to linguistic form in human context, and his analysis of the sequential use of language (i.e., narrative discourse) played a key role in this shift. Specifically, Labov studied the structure of African American Vernacular English (AAVE) narratives. To demonstrate that nonstandard dialects are highly structured systems, Labov took a unique approach. In interviewing inner-city youth, he used the so-called "danger-of-death" prompts, such as "Were you ever in a situation where you thought you were in serious danger of being killed?" (Labov 1972: 363), to elicit narratives. And he described how narrators incorporate life-threatening events into their personal histories.

Labov (1972: 359–360) defined narrative technically as "one method of recapitulating past experience by matching a verbal sequence of clauses to the sequence of events which (it is inferred) actually occurred." Following Labov and Waletzky's (1967) argument, the smallest unit of linguistic expression that defines the function of narrative should be the independent, temporally ordered clause, because a temporal sequence of such narrative clauses constitutes the backbone of a narrative. Labov (1972) proposed that a fully formed oral narrative consists of a six-part structure: abstracts (summaries of the whole narrative at its outset), orientations (statements that provide the setting or context of a narrative), complicating actions (specific events), evaluations (statements that tell the listener what to think about a person, place, thing, event, or, more globally, the entire experience described in a narrative), resolutions (what finally happened), and codas (formalized endings of a narrative). Labov claimed that stories of personal experience provide the simplest but most fundamental narrative structures. His analysis presented the linguistic techniques and devices employed to evaluate experience within the speaker's particular cultural norms, such as those of AAVE, and examined the basic structure of narrative within a particular culture. Overall, Labov's major contribution to the field was that he identified a delimited set of recurrent patterns. Although his analysis suggests that structural components in story/narrative are universal, it also stresses that some linguistic variables fall under the influence of sociocultural variation, including not simply the local sociolinguistic environment but also the wider cultural setting.

According to Labov (1972), the narrator relies on affective expression as a primary means of conveying the relational significance of narrative events. Telling a story, furthermore, involves many factors, some of which add diverse cultural flavors to the narrative. People from different sociocultural backgrounds, for example, might encode their own perspectives and emotions in distinct ways. African American children may tell a narrative consisting of a series of implicitly associated personal anecdotes (Michaels 1991). And Hawaiian children may present "talk stories," rambling personal narratives enhanced with humor, jokes, and teasing in the form of joint performance, or cooperative production of responses by two or more speakers (Au 1993). These examples illustrate the importance of considering cultural differences in the ways in which individuals are socialized, and, as a result, structure their oral personal narratives.

Discourse strategies include, either consciously or unconsciously, plans to solve potential problems in order to reach a particular communication goal. This is not limited to native speakers. When L2 learners communicate in their target language, they use a variety of discourse strategies to make communication successful. An example of this is code switching (the practice of moving back and forth between two or more languages, or language varieties/dialects), which involves stretches of discourse ranging from single words to whole phrases and even complete turns. Another discourse strategy draws on prosodic resources, such as a rising intonation that attempts to elicit help from the interlocutor indirectly by implying lack of confidence in a needed L2 item. In the case of bilinguals, we must also take into consideration whether narratives are told in the narrator's L1 or L2. Using a wordless picture book, Kang (2003) explored how oral English narratives told by adult Korean English-as-a-foreign-language (EFL) learners differ from those told by native speakers of English. Kang (2006) further investigated culturally preferred written narrative styles and their effects on L2 narrative styles. What Kang has brought to light is the strong influence of L1 discourse strategies (e.g., heavily relying on the use of culturally preferred narrative structural elements and evaluative devices, which individuals have acquired as a result of socialization/enculturation) on English narratives produced by EFL learners. The claim made by Kang is that Korean cultural strategies are more prominent in Korean English learners' English narrative discourse than the preferred narrative discourse style of the target language and culture. We realize here that cognition is socially situated in the interface between individuals' L1 culture and the target L2 culture, and that narratives can be viewed as socially constructed tools of reasoning.

Yet it is true that only a few studies have dealt with narratives spoken by persons acquiring an L2, and also that very little narrative research has been conducted on L2 learners using Labov's technique. Designed to address some of the gaps in the literature, the present study, which follows the analytical procedure elaborated by Labov (1972), examines adult Japanese-as-a-second-language (JSL) learners' oral personal narratives in order to track the nature of the development of their narrative abilities and to determine whether adult JSL learners cognitively become able to utilize appropriate discourse strategies for producing native-speaker-like narratives as their language proficiency levels increase. While the goals of this study are multiple, its main objective is to make a start toward understanding the relationship between the L2 learning process (e.g., vocabulary development) and the acquisition of effective narrative ability. The study specifically examines the following key questions: Absent specific instruction in narrative techniques, (1) do the structures of narratives told by JSL learners change as their Japanese skills develop? (2) do the structures of narratives told by JSL learners approach the structure of narratives told by native speakers?

The above questions, which are deeply associated with the end result of language socialization, address not only whether but also how the L2 learner's storytelling ability (i.e., narrative performance) develops. The first question examines the proficiency levels (verbal ability) of L2 learners and addresses the relationship between their level of proficiency and the structure of their narratives. The second question examines whether, as L2 speakers' proficiency levels increase, their narrative structure becomes similar to that of native Japanese speakers. The second, and broader, question obviously includes the issue of whether there exist similarities or differences in the narratives of L2 learners compared with native Japanese speakers, children and adults. Note here that the background of this question derives from the assumption of culture-specific narrative styles as the result of language socialization (discussed earlier in this chapter). For example, brevity is considered a characteristic feature of Japanese discourse, and it thus seems natural that not only young Japanese children but also Japanese adults tend to provide succinct narratives when compared to narratives told by their English-speaking counterparts. This is because, if one hypothesizes that human development is continuous, early interactional patterns (such as using a concise communication style) seem to contribute to interactional differences in later years (such as continuing to use a concise communication style) (Minami 2002). Conversely, one might be able to claim that differences in narrative discourse skills in later years – or even differences in adult individuals building relationships with others – can be traced back to this early age period.

4.4   Method

4.4.1   Participants

Thirty-two English-speaking adults (21 males and 11 females, $M = 29$ years and 7 months) participated in this study. English is the mother tongue of all the participants, and they had studied Japanese as a second or foreign language through classroom instruction. The average length of studying Japanese (which included individual tutoring and/or independent or self-study) was 3 years and 3 months. Also included in the study were 20 middle-class preschoolers in Japan (10 boys and 10 girls, $M = 4$ years and 9 months) and their mothers. We elicited natural, unmonitored, informal speech by using the so-called danger-of-death or scary event story that was originally developed in Labov's (1972) sociolinguistic research. JSL learners as well as a control group of native Japanese speakers (Japanese mothers, hereafter described as adult native speakers, and their children) were asked to talk about past experiences. Specifically, JSL learners talked about early childhood memories and injury-related stories of their choosing. On the other hand, adult native speakers talked about an early childhood memory, whereas Japanese children talked about an injury-related experience.

4.4.2   Task, procedure, and materials

4.4.2.1   Evaluation of oral personal narratives produced by JSL learners   The JSL learners were categorized into two different levels, intermediate and advanced, by four native Japanese speakers who rated the learners' level of proficiency in Japanese. Each of the four trained raters independently listened to the tape-recorded narratives told by each of the JSL learners. The narratives had been edited onto a single audiotape in random order so as to preserve the anonymity of the speakers. The raters indicated how advanced each JSL learner was with regard to the following three categories: (1) grammatical aspects (whether or not the subject made frequent grammatical errors); (2) oral fluency (pronunciation, accent, and speed); and (3) story content (whether the story was easy to follow, clearly understandable, and interesting). Note that these evaluation measures will reflect socially accepted behavior in the raters' native culture.

4.4.3   *Transcription and coding categories*

Native Japanese speakers who were trained for the task transcribed the gathered narrative data verbatim. Transcripts were then formatted following the guidelines of *Codes for the Human Analysis of Transcripts* (CHAT), so that they were readable by the computer program *Computerized Language Analysis* (CLAN) (MacWhinney 2000; MacWhinney and Snow 1985, 1990). All the narrative data were transcribed in accordance with the coding rules previously developed for monologic narrative data (i.e., monologues) in Japanese (Minami 2002). Just as the data collection method followed the Labovian technique, the coding scheme employed for this analysis also followed Labovian methodology (Labov 1997), focusing on the content of each clause in the personal narrative.

Note that reported speech (i.e., talk that generally reproduces the speech of a character) was added to the analysis. Reported speech – quotations of words spoken in the form of direct speech, indirect speech, or even a summary description of a speech event – is an important category because it is considered a linguistically marked recounting of a past speech event. For instance, reported speech serves a variety of functions; it is used to express some kind of evaluation of an exact quotation, but it can be used as a means of conveying something more creative than factual as well (Ely and McCabe 1993). In other words, reported speech as indirect discourse holds significance because the specific narrative feature of evaluation is not only embedded in the continuous acts of description that constitute a narrative, but it is also inserted in the second-order evaluations provided by reported speech (Gwyn 2000).

Labov's (1972) six-fold characterization of overall narrative is nothing but the cognitive representation of reality imposed by narrative structure on our experience of the world and on how we evaluate that experience. Recall that Bruner (1986) viewed narrative structure as analogous to landscape painting consisting of two major landscapes: the landscape of action and the landscape of consciousness. The narrator "paints" the latter to show "how the world is perceived or felt by various members of the cast of characters, each from their own perspective" (Feldman et al. 1990: 2). Reported speech sets us thinking about narrative not simply as a form of text, but also as a mode of thought, or a cognitive representation constrained by a culture.

Examples of the important narrative components (which were elicited in both injury-related experiences and early childhood memories told by JSL learners and coded according to the earlier described coding categories) are shown below. Note that complicating action, which corresponds to foreground information (Hopper 1979; Hopper and Thompson 1980), refers to the parts of the narrative that relate a sequence of events with respect to a timeline and thus constitutes the "narrative skeleton" of restricted narrative clauses. On the other hand, orientation and evaluation form background information.

(1) Abstract (an optional précis of the story)
kekkoo hidoi kega attan desu ga …
(I) got injured pretty badly …
(2) Orientation (the time, the place, those involved in the story)
kodomo no toki ni …
When (I) was a child …
(3) Complicating action (Then what happened?)
sono torakutaa no hoo e chikazuite itte …
(I) went closer to that tractor …
(4) Evaluation (So what?)
taishita koto ja nakatta keredomo …
(It) was nothing serious but …
(5) Reported Speech (references to past speech)
"isha ga 'chotto X-ray ton' nakya ikenai" tte.
"The doctor said, 'You have to have an X-ray.'"
(6) Coda (formalized endings of a narrative)
ja, sore dake desu.
Well, that's it.

4.4.4   Coding reliability

Two individuals coded nine full transcripts independently. For the main categories of the JSL learners' narratives, Cohen's kappa was .89; Cohen's kappa statistics for the two subcategories of the narrative coding were .77 and .94, respectively. Except for one, which is still in the "substantial" agreement range, all estimates of reliability fall into the range of "almost perfect" agreement (Bakeman and Gottman 1997; Landis and Koch 1977). The coders discussed disagreements until resolution was achieved.

4.5   Results

The narrative components (i.e., complicating actions, orientations, evaluations, append-ages consisting of abstracts and codas, and reported speech) used by the two different levels of JSL learners were compared with those used by two groups of native Japanese speakers, children and adults. Not only were raw frequencies counted, but the propor-tional frequency was also calculated by dividing each narrative category by the total number of incidences.

4.5.1   A comparison of Japanese children and adults learning Japanese (injury-related stories)

4.5.1.1   Narrative length and vocabulary   Two measures of length were derived: (1) word count (i.e., the total number of words in the narrative) and (2) clause count (i.e., a clause was considered to be a subject-predicate proposition). Table 4.1 shows the means and standard deviations of the total number of words, the total number of different words,

Table 4.1   Means and standard deviations of total number of words, total number of different words, type-token ratio, total number of clauses in monologic narrative production (injury stories).

	Japanese Children (n = 20)		Intermediate JSL Learners (n = 17)		Advanced JSL Learners (n = 15)		
	M	SD	M	SD	M	SD	F value
Number of words	75.75	39.50	145.06	85.62	396.40	390.24	10.05****
Number of different words	37.60	15.47	68.65	30.39	164.87	118.18	16.55****
Type-token ratio	0.53	0.09	0.54	0.14	0.47	0.09	1.80
Number of clauses	10.80	3.68	21.41	10.13	64.20	52.11	16.06****

****$p < .0001$.

the type-token ratio (a measure of lexical diversity computed by dividing the number of different words used by the total number of words used in the narrative [Templin 1957]), and the total number of clauses. A series of one-way analyses of variance (ANOVA) was conducted in order to evaluate the differences between the three groups, namely, native Japanese-speaking children, intermediate JSL learners, and advanced JSL learners.

One-way ANOVAs were conducted in order to evaluate the differences between the three groups. As for the total number of words, the ANOVA was significant, $F(2, 49) = 10.05$, $p < .0001$. Follow-up tests were conducted. The standard deviations among the three groups ranged from 39.50 to 390.24, indicating that the variances (the standard deviation squared) are significantly different from each other, $F(2, 49) = 6.95$, $p < .002$, and thus post hoc comparisons were conducted with the use of the Dunnett's C test, a test that does not assume equal variances among the three groups. There was a significant difference in means between the children and either of the JSL learners' groups. While the advanced learners produced a much larger average number of words than the intermediate learners, due to wide variation no statistically significant difference was observed between the two levels of JSL learners. Thus, regardless of the proficiency level, even if they are L2 learners, adult speakers are more loquacious than native Japanese-speaking children.

As for the total number of different words, the ANOVA was significant, $F(2, 49) = 16.55$, $p < .0001$. Because the standard deviations among the three groups ranged from 15.47 to 118.18, we chose not to assume that the variances were homogeneous, and thus conducted the Dunnett's C test. There was a significant difference in means between the children and each of the two JSL learners' groups. Likewise, there was a significant difference between the two levels of JSL learners: the advanced learners produced the largest variety of words, followed by the intermediate JSL learners, and then by the children. Thus, regardless of the proficiency level, even if they are L2 learners, adult speakers are more capable of using a varied vocabulary than native Japanese-speaking children. The degree of variety in word production depends on L2 learners' level of language proficiency.

As for the total number of clauses, the ANOVA was also significant, $F(2, 49) = 16.06$, $p < .0001$. Because the test of homogeneity was significant, $F(2, 49) = 10.81$, $p < .0001$, we conducted the Dunnett's C test, which revealed a significant difference in means between the children and either of the JSL learners' groups. There was also a significant difference between the two levels of JSL learners. Thus, the advanced learners produced the longest narratives, followed by the intermediate JSL learners, and finally by the children. On the other hand, the type-token ratio revealed no difference between the three groups, $F(2, 49) = 1.80$, *ns*. As their L2 skills advanced, JSL learners lengthened their narratives and, accordingly, they used an increasingly wide variety of vocabulary. Comparison of intermediate and advanced learners and Japanese children predictably revealed that more advanced JSL learners tended to construct longer narratives using more words in greater variety and thus provided more information in their narratives. It may sound like an exaggeration, but the advantage afforded by cognitive maturation supersedes linguistic disadvantage. However, when it comes to vocabulary variation calculated by the type-token ratio, which is obtained by dividing the total number of different words by the total number of words (Templin 1957), no difference reached statistical significance between either group of the L2 learners and Japanese children.

4.5.1.2 Narrative components One-way multivariate analyses of variance (MANOVA) were conducted in order to evaluate differences among the three groups (native Japanese-speaking children, advanced JSL learners, and intermediate JSL learners) on the five dependent variables, (1) appendages, (2) orientations, (3) complicating actions, (4) evaluations, and (5) reported speech. Note that of the earlier described six components, abstracts (summaries of the whole narrative that appear at its outset) and codas (endings of a narrative) were put together as appendages primarily because their frequencies were low and because, as Peterson and McCabe (1983) explain, they can be included in the composite category. Table 4.2 presents these results.

With regard to raw frequencies, there was a significant multivariate effect of the group, Wilks's lambda = .49, approximate $F(10, 90) = 3.88$, $p < .0001$. Analysis of variances (ANOVA) on each dependent variable was conducted as a follow-up to the MANOVA. While the ANOVA on appendages was non-significant, the ANOVAs on the other variables were all significant (see Table 4.2). Post hoc analyses to the univariate ANOVA consisted of pairwise comparisons employed to find which narrative components most strongly affected narrative style. However, because Levene's test indicated that, except for appendages, the equal variance could not be assumed between the groups, the Dunnett's C test was used for pairwise comparisons.

The ANOVA on evaluations was significant, $F(2, 49) = 13.96$, $p < .0001$. Post hoc analyses revealed that the advanced JSL learners' group provided significantly more evaluations than the native Japanese-speaking children's group, and that the intermediate learners' group also provided significantly more evaluations than the children's group, but that there was no difference between the two levels of learners.

Table 4.2 Mean frequencies and percentages (standard deviations) of narrative components (injury stories).

	Japanese Children (n = 20)		Intermediate JSL Learners (n = 17)		Advanced JSL Learners (n = 15)		
	M	SD	M	SD	M	SD	F value
Appendages							
Frequencies	0.65	0.99	1.24	1.72	1.60	1.55	2.00
Percentages	4.61%	6.71	6.08%	7.63	2.99%	2.81	0.98
Orientations							
Frequencies	2.70	1.84	5.47	3.26	13.93	15.18	8.00***
Percentages	20.37%	11.14	24.96%	10.47	21.36%	8.16	1.00
Complicating actions							
Frequencies	5.30	2.18	5.41	2.81	16.87	18.26	7.10**
Percentages	42.81%	19.57	25.68%	10.11	24.84%	8.17	9.43****
Evaluations							
Frequencies	4.20	3.69	9.71	5.57	30.13	26.72	13.96****
Percentages	30.00%	18.33	41.61%	14.82	45.28%	7.78	5.23*
Reported Speech							
Frequencies	0.40	0.88	0.59	1.37	3.47	3.23	12.22****
Percentages	2.20%	4.83	1.67%	3.63	5.53%	4.73	3.53†

†$p < .04$. *$p < .01$. **$p < .002$. ***$p < .001$. ****$p < .0001$.
Note: Each ANOVA was tested at the .01 level (.05 divided by five variables).

The ANOVA on reported speech was also significant, $F(2, 49) = 12.22$, $p < .0001$. Post hoc analyses revealed that the advanced JSL learners' group provided significantly more reported speech than the children's group, but that there was no difference between the two levels of learners, and also that there was no difference between the intermediate learners' group and the children's group.

Proportions were also used because they correct for differences in number and allow us to see the relative emphasis on each component of narration. In terms of proportions, there was a significant multivariate effect of the group, Wilks's lambda = .63, approximate $F(8, 92) = 3.05$, $p = .004$. Follow-up analyses of variance (ANOVA) were conducted, then followed by Fisher's LSD test (for complicating actions) and Dunnett's C method (for evaluations), depending on whether equal variances are assumed.

The ANOVA on complicating actions was significant, $F(2, 49) = 9.43$, $p < .0001$. Post hoc pairwise comparisons revealed that the children's group provided proportionately more complicating actions than either of the adult JSL learners, as Figure 4.1 indicates, but there was no difference between the two levels of L2 learners. This result indicates that when controlling for narrative length, complicating actions (i.e., foreground information) occupy large portions of children's narratives, whereas adults, even if they are L2 learners, provide other narrative components in addition to complicating actions.

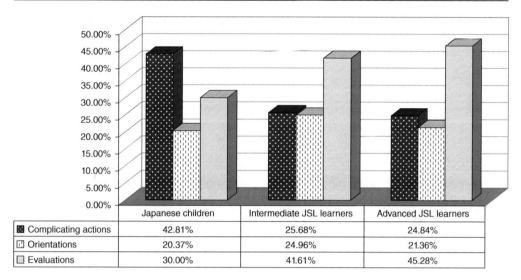

	Japanese children	Intermediate JSL learners	Advanced JSL learners
Complicating actions	42.81%	25.68%	24.84%
Orientations	20.37%	24.96%	21.36%
Evaluations	30.00%	41.61%	45.28%

Figure 4.1 Distribution of the three major narrative components: a comparison of Japanese children and JSL learners' monologic narratives (injury-related stories).

In contrast, advanced JSL learners' evaluations occupy a significantly larger portion of the narrative in comparison with native Japanese-speaking children's use of evaluations. The ANOVA on evaluations was also significant, $F(2, 49) = 5.23, p = .009$. Post hoc analyses revealed that the advanced L2 learners' group produced significantly more evaluations than the children's group, whereas no differences were observed between the two levels of the L2 learners and between the intermediate L2 learners' group and the children's group. In other words, as their L2 skills advanced, JSL learners provide proportionately less foreground information (i.e., complicating actions) and, instead, they increasingly provide more background information (i.e., evaluations).

In summary, adult L2 speakers, despite their apparent disadvantage in telling narratives in the target language, provided more evaluations as background information (in terms of both raw and proportional frequencies) than native Japanese-speaking children, whereas native Japanese-speaking children provided proportionately more complicating actions (i.e., foreground information) than adult L2 speakers. Thus, because adults are capable of conveying emotion from one language to another, which is a challenging task, we may claim that cognition overrides language deficits.

4.5.2 A comparison of adult native speakers and adults learning Japanese (early childhood memories)

4.5.2.1 Narrative length and vocabulary Table 4.3 shows the means and standard deviations of the total number of words, the total number of different words, the type-token ratio, and the total number of clauses. A series of one-way analyses of variance (ANOVA)

Table 4.3   Means and standard deviations of total number of words, total number of different words, type-token ratio, total number of clauses in monologic narrative production (early childhood memories).

	Intermediate JSL Learners ($n=17$)		Advanced JSL Learners ($n=15$)		Adult Native Speakers ($n=20$)		
	M	SD	M	SD	M	SD	F value
Number of words	126.24	85.77	303.20	225.06	384.35	175.28	10.89****
Number of different words	64.29	33.84	133.53	74.09	126.55	39.91	9.60****
Type-token ratio	0.58	0.14	0.51	0.11	0.36	0.09	16.20****
Number of clauses	23.35	17.63	46.27	31.34	37.85	16.96	4.41**

**p<.02. ****p<.0001.

was conducted in order to evaluate the differences between the three groups, namely, intermediate JSL learners, advanced JSL learners, and adult native speakers of Japanese.

As for the total number of words, the ANOVA was significant, $F(2, 49) = 10.89$, $p<.0001$. Follow-up tests were conducted. The fact that the standard deviations among the three groups ranged from 85.77 to 225.06 indicated that the variances (the standard deviations squared) are different from each other. The test of homogeneity of variance was significant, $F(2, 49) = 5.51$, $p=.007$; thus post hoc comparisons were conducted with the use of the Dunnett's C test. There was a significant difference in means between the two different levels of JSL learners. Likewise, there was a significant difference between the native Japanese speakers and the intermediate JSL learners. However, no difference reached statistical significance between the native Japanese speakers and the advanced JSL learners.

As for the total number of different words, the ANOVA was also significant, $F(2, 49) = 9.60$, $p<.0001$. Because the standard deviations among the three groups ranged from 33.84 to 74.09, we chose not to assume that the variances were homogenous. The test of homogeneity was significant, $F(2, 49) = 5.97$, $p=.005$, and we thus conducted the Dunnett's C test. There was a significant difference in means between the advanced JSL learners and the intermediate JSL learners, as well as a significant difference between the native Japanese speakers and the intermediate JSL learners. But no difference was observed between the native Japanese speakers and the advanced JSL learners. In terms of the total number of words and the total number of different words, therefore, advanced L2 learners had reached the native speaker's level of production.

As for the type-token ratio, the ANOVA was significant, $F(2, 49) = 16.20$, $p<.0001$. The test of homogeneity was non-significant, $F(2\ 49) = 1.77$, *ns*. We conducted post hoc comparisons using Fisher's least significant difference (LSD) test. Native Japanese speakers' type-token ratio was significantly lower than either of the JSL learners. Finally, as for the total number of clauses, the ANOVA was significant, $F(2, 49) = 4.41$, $p = .017$. The test of homogeneity was significant, $F(2, 49) = 5.94$, $p = .005$, and the Dunnett's C test revealed that the differences between the three groups were non-significant.

To summarize, the results indicated the following: (1) Predictably, vocabulary size was found to be a major factor in distinguishing L2 narrative proficiency levels. While the difference did not reach statistical significance, the advanced JSL learners constructed the longest narratives and, compared to the intermediate JSL group, used more words and a greater variety of words. (2) However, no statistically significant differences were observed between native Japanese speakers and the advanced JSL learners in either the length of narratives (measured by both the total number of words and the total number of clauses) or the number of different words. (3) Native Japanese speakers used a lower type-token ratio than either of the two different levels of JSL learners. Native speakers employed strategies, such as producing more clauses while repeating the same vocabulary, but L2 learners had not necessarily acquired such strategies.

4.5.2.2 Narrative components MANOVAs were conducted for the five dependent variables, (1) appendages, (2) orientations, (3) complicating actions, (4) evaluations, and (5) reported speech. With respect to raw frequencies, there was a significant multivariate effect of the group, Wilks's lambda = .54, approximate $F(10, 90) = 3.26$, $p < .001$. This effect was largely attributable to significant effects on complicating actions, $F(2, 49) = 8.53$, $p = .001$, and orientations, $F(2, 49) = 6.98$, $p = .002$, and a marginal effect on evaluations, $F(2, 49) = 4.56$, $p = .015$. (Note that follow-up ANOVAs were conducted at the .01 level, i.e., .05 divided by five variables.) Because the variances among the three groups ranged widely for these three narrative components, we chose not to assume that the variances were homogeneous and thus conducted post hoc comparisons using the Dunnett's C test. There was a significant difference in orientations between the native Japanese speakers ($M = 15.00$, $SD = 9.71$) and the intermediate JSL learners ($M = 6.88$, $SD = 3.94$). Interestingly, however, the post hoc tests revealed no statistically significant differences between advanced JSL learners and native Japanese speakers in any narrative component.

In terms of proportions, as illustrated in Figure 4.2, the overall multivariate test did not approach statistical significance, Wilks's lambda = .83, approximate $F(8, 92) = 1.12$, *ns*, and thus no further analyses were conducted. These results indicate that when controlling for narrative length, no differences reached statistical significance in terms of narrative structure (e.g., portions of complicating actions, orientations, and evaluations).

To sum up, comparisons of raw frequencies revealed that adult native speakers provided more background information (i.e., orientation) than did intermediate learners. Interestingly, however, there were no significant differences observed in any other narrative components – not only between advanced JSL learners and adult native Japanese speakers, but also between intermediate JSL learners and adult native Japanese speakers.

Comparisons of proportional frequencies revealed that the narrative patterning among the three groups did not differ greatly from one another. Although the narratives

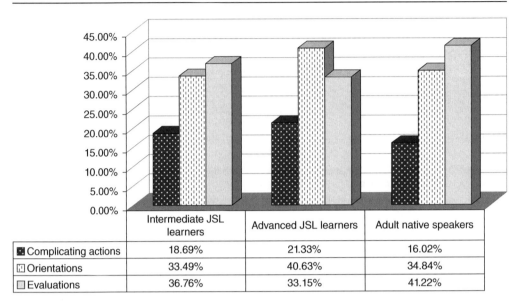

	Intermediate JSL learners	Advanced JSL learners	Adult native speakers
■ Complicating actions	18.69%	21.33%	16.02%
⬚ Orientations	33.49%	40.63%	34.84%
☐ Evaluations	36.76%	33.15%	41.22%

Figure 4.2   Distribution of the three major narrative components: a comparison of L1 adults' and JSL learners' monologic narratives (early childhood memories).

produced by intermediate JSL learners were shorter and used a smaller vocabulary, the narrative components (and thus the overall narrative structure) in their narratives did not differ greatly even from those of adult native speakers of Japanese. These results are different from those obtained by the comparison of JSL learners with children; children provided proportionally more foreground information but proportionally less background information (i.e., evaluation). What is also noteworthy is that, as their language skills advance, JSL learners tend to produce longer narratives using more words in greater variety, but are inclined to talk somewhat excessively when judged by native Japanese speakers' norms. The observed similarities and excesses provide evidence not only for the universal or quasi-universal model of well-constructed, globally organized narratives, but also for the fully developed use of language within a particular culture.

4.6   Overall Discussion

There are many ways to tell a story, and this chapter has addressed some of the many factors that play a role in developing narrative skills in both L1 and L2. The study mainly investigated adult JSL learners' oral personal narratives in order to examine how their narratives develop and whether they begin to produce native-speaker-like narratives as their language proficiency levels increase. The study specifically examined narratives told in Japanese by adult JSL learners with a particular focus on narrative length and structural characteristics.

First, the results of both cross-level (i.e., intermediate and advanced) and cross-group (i.e., native and non-native) comparisons have demonstrated that although all of the language learners involved in this study had sufficient command of the language to tell personal narratives using the target language, vocabulary size was one of the most important predictors for distinguishing L2 proficiency levels.

Second, a comparison of intermediate and advanced learners predictably revealed that more advanced JSL learners tended to construct longer narratives using more words in greater variety and thus provided more information in their narratives. While this result may be predictable, comparisons of narratives told by JSL learners with those produced by native Japanese speakers – children and adults – have revealed that JSL learners did not necessarily follow the native-style narrative patterns even as their language skills developed. For instance, adult native speakers lengthened their narratives with repeated use of the same vocabulary. Type-token ratios indicate the total number of different words over the total number of words. High type-token ratios indicate a varied vocabulary per words produced; low ratios indicate a less varied vocabulary. To mirror adult native speakers who use repetition of the same vocabulary, one would expect that the type-token ratio would decease as JSL learners progress from intermediate to advanced. The only marginal decrease in the type-token ratio found for advanced JSL learners in comparison to intermediate JSL learners, however, seems to suggest that language development for L2 learners is not progressing in the direction that would mimic or reflect language use patterns of adult native speakers. Overall, in the examination of JSL learners' L2 narrative discourse patterns, the study revealed that L2 learners seem to develop different strategies from those used by native speakers (e.g., talking loquaciously), and that some of L2 learners' strategies may reflect the influence of L1 on their L2 narratives.

Recall that foreground information refers to the parts of the narrative that relate a sequence of events with respect to a timeline and thus belongs to the skeletal structure of the narrative. In contrast, background information refers to supportive elements of narrative, including orientations, which present static descriptions of the scene, and evaluations, which describe or assess the agent's motives. In L1 narrative development, there exists a relationship between an individual's age and the amount of background information he or she adds to the narrative; compared to adults, young children tend to emphasize a temporal sequence of action with less emphasis on non-sequential information (Berman and Slobin 1994). This chapter has, in a sense, revealed mixed results in terms of the relationship between the level of narrative skill and the amount of non-sequential information. Initial comparisons using raw frequencies indicated that, in L2 acquisition, the relationship holds between an individual's narrative skill and the amount of background information (i.e., orientation) he or she adds to the narrative. Comparisons of proportional frequencies, however, revealed somewhat different patterns. What initially appeared to be a difference between intermediate and advanced L2 learners did not appear so when proportional frequencies were examined. In other words, the relationship between "the better an individual's narrative skill becomes" and "the more non-sequential, background information he or she adds to the narrative" holds true simply because advanced learners produce longer narratives.

The results of this study were, at least in part, also confirmed by the comparison of narratives told by L2 learners and native Japanese-speaking children. In L1 studies, it is well known that younger children may employ fewer expressive options during narrative constructions because they cannot (1) conceive of the full range of encodable perspectives from a cognitive point of view, (2) fully assess the listener's perspective from a communicative point of view, and (3) apply the full range of formal devices from a linguistic point of view (Berman and Slobin 1994; Minami 2002). The developmental patterns described above were supported by the results obtained through the analysis of narrative components used by adult JSL learners and native Japanese-speaking children. Thus, even though their L2 skills are limited, cognitively more mature adult L2 learners are capable of producing narratives that include both foreground and background information.

What is particularly interesting is that advanced JSL learners produced fairly long narratives, even according to the native Japanese standard. That is, a comparison of the narratives told by JSL learners with those produced by native Japanese speakers revealed that even JSL learners with more highly developed L2 language skills did not necessarily follow the native-style narrative patterns. The results of the study seem to imply either the existence of U-shaped patterns of behavioral growth (i.e., the overuse of available devices at a certain point in language development, see Kellerman 1985), or the strong influence of L1 discourse strategies on L2 narratives, or a combination of both. In other words, if the existence of U-shaped patterns of behavioral growth holds true, then, our interpretation would be that L2 learners' overuse of certain narrative strategies (i.e., lengthening a narrative) occurs in the developmental process because they might believe that a long narrative satisfies one of the requirements for a good narrative. Yet the possibility of the putative transfer of L1 narrative patterns should also be taken into consideration. If this is the case, telling a long narrative could be the norm in L2 learners' first language (L1) as well as a reflection of socially accepted behavior in their native culture.

Cazden (1988) claims that while narratives are a universal meaning-making strategy, there is no one way of transforming experience into a story. This trend in thinking is also advanced by Bruner (1990), who argues that meaning creation is tightly yoked to a specific style of cultural representation. Culture as cognitive representations presents further complex issues in an L2. As Stavans (2003: 153) puts it, "The adult bilingual is a narrator with one set of experiences that are subject to expression in either of two linguistic systems, each of which may be constrained by a different storytelling culture." According to Berman (2004), language proficiency involves a complex configuration of interrelated types of knowledge: (1) linguistic command of the full range of expressive options, both grammatical and lexical, available in the target language, (2) the cognitive ability to integrate forms from different systems of grammar, and to develop those options to meet different communicative goals and discourse functions, and (3) cultural recognition of what constitutes the favored options in a given speech community, adapted to varied communicative contexts and to different norms of usage. The current chapter has answered lexical issues. As can be seen in advanced JSL learners' increasing awareness of the importance of contextualizing background information, the chapter also dealt with cognitive issues. And the chapter here addresses possible cultural issues. As Vygotsky (1978) suggested, social experience (narrators' experiences in their L1 society, in this case) possibly shapes certain kinds of interpretive processes (e.g., narrators' conceptualization of what the desirable amount of narrative should be). A question still remains, however. Have the advanced JSL learners failed to produce the preferred narrative style of the target culture? Or have the advanced JSL learners deviated from the native adult Japanese speakers' narrative discourse norms? Regardless of the reason, the answer seems to be "yes," at least from the perspective of a native Japanese speaker; the judgment of whether the narrator narrates too much is culturally relative.

Clearly, many questions remain to be answered. In addition to the questions posed above, we do not know whether similar narrative structures (e.g., complicating actions, orientations, and evaluations) not only across different L2 levels but also across different native language groups reflect a universal or quasi-universal model of well-constructed, globally organized narratives (i.e., universal human "nature" of considering what a good narrative is all about), or whether similar narrative structures are the result of learning or having learned a particular language, in this case, Japanese. Issues of universality may be controversial or questionable, and if the latter is the case, the results obtained in this study would imply a reflection of some kind of "nurture," such as a language learner's acquisition of culture-specific patterns as a result of being immersed in the target language and culture, or even Whorfianism (Whorf 1956), which hypothesizes that the particular language one speaks affects the manner in which one perceives and thinks about the world; the linguistic relativity hypothesis itself is a manifestation of culture's deep relationship with cognition. Yet this is simply a matter of conjecture. Despite such potential limitations, however, this chapter, which has discussed issues related to cognition and socialization in the context of L2 narratives, has shed light on some important phenomena in narrative that until now have only been discussed with anecdotes and personal experiences.

4.7   Conclusion and Future Perspectives

Finally, the real challenge may be how we can preserve an individual's cultural communication style and yet enable the speaker to use a narrative style that is expected in the culture where the target language is spoken. This challenge is particularly poignant when two cultures are, in one way or another, contradictory with respect to views toward communication values or styles, as is exemplified by the value of being concise in Japanese culture whereas elaboration is appreciated in North American culture (Minami 2002). Narrative competence derives from a cognitive schema that is shared across mature speakers. It requires knowledge of core plot components – or what Labov (1972) termed referential elements – and devices for evaluation, so that narrators can alternate foreground information and background information for sophisticated elaboration. Content-based narrative analyses, to which Labovian methodology (Labov 1972, 1997) belongs, offer important predictions for the development of narrative abilities in both L1 and L2. In the past, research on L2 narrative production has revealed not only the role of the language learners' L2 proficiency and familiarity with the narrative discourse norms of the target language, but also the influences of L1 narrative conventions on an L2 (e.g., Kang 2003). This means that, in their L2 narrative production, language learners who have not yet developed adequate L2 skills will be obliged to rely on their L1 skills and discourse strategies. In fact, recent research on L2 learners' narratives (e.g., Minami 2009) has revealed the use of heavily L1-influenced strategies in their L2 narrative production.

In conclusion, little has been known about bilinguals or L2 leaners whose two languages are typologically distant. This chapter has endeavored to fill this gap by identifying potential relationships between cognitive maturation and linguistic disadvantage through the comparison of the narrative abilities of native Japanese-speaking children and adults and JSL learners. Of course, this line of investigation may not capture the entire picture of narrative competence and its production, and may need to examine narratives from different perspectives. Some recent studies (e.g., Kang 2012; Minami 2011) attempt to provide in-depth analyses of narratives produced by bilinguals of typologically distant languages in the context of both L1 acquisition and L2 acquisition simultaneously. These studies furthermore connect the story-related narrative quality (associated with the narrative structure and evaluations seen in Labovian methodology and in this chapter) and the language-related quality (directly concerned with the appropriate use of linguistic devices that contribute to the overall discourse cohesion) of narrative discourse. In other words, cohesion describes the linguistic relationships among clauses in a narrative, such as how the surface linguistic elements of a text are linked to one another. While cohesion devices such as connectives may at times indicate relatively mechanical links at a local level, coherence means whether or not the text makes sense at a global level. What is important is that both cohesion and coherence serve as the twin engines of narrative. Thus, paying attention not only to the narrative content/structure but also to the appropriate use of linguistic devices holds significance for further facilitating the line of research described in this chapter.

REFERENCES

Au, K.H. (1993). *Literacy Instruction in Multicultural Settings.* Fort Worth, TX: Harcourt Brace Jovanovich College Publishers.

Bakeman, R., and J.M. Gottman. (1997). *Observing Interaction: An Introduction to Sequential Analysis.* 2nd edn. Cambridge: Cambridge University Press.

Berman, R.A. (2004). Between emergence and mastery: The long developmental route of language acquisition. In R.A. Berman (ed.), *Language Development Across Childhood and Adolescence (Trends in Language Acquisition Research).* Amsterdam: John Benjamins, pp. 9–34.

Berman, R.A., and D.I. Slobin. (1994). *Relating Events in Narrative: A Crosslinguistic Developmental Study.* Hillsdale, NJ: Lawrence Erlbaum Associates.

Bruner, J. (1986). *Actual Minds, Possible Worlds.* Cambridge, MA: Harvard University Press.

Bruner, J. (1990). *Acts of Meaning.* Cambridge, MA: Harvard University Press.

Caudill, W., and L. Frost. (1974). A comparison of maternal care and infant behavior in Japanese-American and American families. In W. Lebra (ed.), *Mental Health Research in Asia and the Pacific,* vol. 2. Honolulu: East-West Center Press, pp. 25–48.

Cazden, C.B. (1988). *Classroom Discourse.* Portsmouth, NH: Heinemann.

Ely, R., and A. McCabe. (1993). Remembered voices. *Journal of Child Language,* 20 (3), pp. 671–696.

Ervin-Tripp, S.M., and A. Küntay. (1997). The occasioning and structure of conversational stories. In T. Givón (ed.), *Conversation*. Amsterdam: John Benjamins, pp. 133–166.

Feldman, C.F., J. Bruner, B. Renderer, and S. Spitzer. (1990). Narrative comprehension. In B.K. Britton and A.D. Pellegrini (eds.), *Narrative Thought and Narrative Language*. Hillsdale, NJ: Lawrence Erlbaum Associates, pp. 1–78.

Gwyn, R. (2000). "Really unreal": Narrative evaluation and the objectification of experience. *Narrative Inquiry*, 10 (2), pp. 313–340.

Hopper, P.J. (1979). Some observations on the typology of focus and aspect in narrative language. *Studies in Language*, 3 (1), pp. 37–64.

Hopper, P.J., and S.A. Thompson. (1980). Transitivity in grammar and discourse. *Language*, 56 (2), pp. 251–299.

Hymes, D. (1974). *Foundations in Sociolinguistics: An Ethnographic Approach*. Philadelphia: University of Pennsylvania Press.

Jensen, A.R. (1969). How much can we boost IQ and scholastic achievement? *Harvard Educational Review*, 39 (1), pp. 1–123.

Kang, J.Y. (2003). On the ability to tell good stories in another language: Analysis of Korean EFL learners' oral "frog story" narratives. *Narrative Inquiry*, 13 (1), pp. 127–149.

Kang, J.Y. (2006). A discourse analysis of Korean EFL learners' written narratives. *Narrative Inquiry*, 16 (2), pp. 379–407.

Kang, J.Y. (2012). How do narrative and language skills relate to each other? Investigation of young Korean EFL learners' oral narratives. *Narrative Inquiry*, 16 (2), pp. 307–331.

Kellerman, E. (1985). If first you do succeed. In S. Gass and C. Madden (eds.), *Input in Second Language Acquisition*. Rowley, MA: Newbury House, pp. 345–353.

Labov, W. (1972). *Language in the Inner City: Studies in the Black English Vernacular*. Philadelphia: University of Pennsylvania Press.

Labov, W. (1997). Some further steps in narrative analysis. *Journal of Narrative and Life History*, 7 (1–4), pp. 395–415.

Labov, W., and J. Waletzky. (1967). Narrative analysis: Oral versions of personal experience. In J. Helm (ed.), *Essays on the Verbal and Visual Arts*. Seattle: University of Washington Press, pp. 12–44.

Landis, J.R., and G.G. Koch. (1977). The measurement of observer agreement for categorical data. *Biometrics*, 33 (1), pp. 159–174.

MacWhinney, B. (2000). *The CHILDES Project, Volume I: Tools for Analyzing Talk*. 3rd edn. Mahwah, NJ: Lawrence Erlbaum Associates.

MacWhinney, B., and C.E. Snow. (1985). The Child Language Data Exchange System. *Child Language*, 12 (2), pp. 271–296.

MacWhinney, B., and C.E. Snow. (1990). The Child Language Data Exchange System: An update. *Child Language*, 17(2), pp. 457–472.

Matsumoto, D. (2000). *Culture and Psychology: People Around the World*. 2nd edn. Belmont, CA: Wadsworth/Thomson Learning.

Matsumoto, D., and L. Juang. (2008). *Culture and Psychology*. 4th edn. Belmont, CA: Thomson Higher Education.

Michaels, S. (1991). The dismantling of narrative. In A. McCabe and C. Peterson (eds.), *Developing Narrative Structure*. Hillsdale, NJ: Lawrence Erlbaum Associates, pp. 303–351.

Minami, M. (2002). *Culture-Specific Language Styles: The Development of Oral Narrative and Literacy*. Clevedon, UK: Multilingual Matters.

Minami, M. (2009). An analysis of narrative communication strategies used by Japanese-as-a-foreign-language learners. *Journal of Japanese Linguistics*, 25, pp. 1–15.

Minami, M. (2011). *Telling Stories in Two Languages: Multiple Approaches to Understanding English-Japanese Bilingual Children's Narratives*. Charlotte, NC: Information Age Publishing.

Minami, M., and A. McCabe. (1995). Rice balls and bear hunts: Japanese and North American family narrative patterns. *Journal of Child Language*, 22 (3), pp. 423–445.

Ochs, E., and B.B. Schieffelin. (1984). Language acquisition and socialization: Three developmental stories. In R. Schweder and

R. LeVine (eds.), *Culture Theory: Essays on Mind, Self and Emotion*. Cambridge: Cambridge University Press, pp. 276–320.

Peterson, C., and A. McCabe. (1983). *Developmental Psycholinguistics: Three Ways of Looking at a Child's Narrative*. New York: Plenum.

Snow, C.E., and C.A. Ferguson (eds.). (1977). *Talking to Children: Language Input and Acquisition*. Cambridge: Cambridge University Press.

Stavans, A. (2003). Bilinguals as narrators: A comparison of bilingual and monolingual Hebrew and English narratives. *Narrative Inquiry*, 13 (1), pp. 151–191.

Templin, M.C. (1957). *Certain Language Skills in Children*. Minneapolis: University of Minnesota Press.

Vygotsky, L.S. (1978). *Mind in Society: The Development of Higher Psychological Processes*. Cambridge, MA: Harvard University Press.

Whorf, B.L. (1956). *Language, Thought, and Reality: Selected Writings*. Edited by J.B. Carroll. Cambridge, MA: MIT Press.

5 Narrative Knowledging in Second Language Teaching and Learning Contexts

GARY BARKHUIZEN

5.1 Introduction

In this chapter I identify a number of contexts in which language teachers and learners engage in narrative research. These contexts reflect who the participants are, what their roles are in the research process, and the nature of the research. I focus specifically on research that has been carried out in second and foreign language educational contexts such as classrooms, schools, and professional development programs. I describe illustrative studies from each of the contexts and in doing so pay particular attention to the types of data the researchers collected and the methods they used to analyze their data. Some of the studies are autobiographical while others are biographical, often involving multiple participants. I use the concept of *narrative knowledging* (Barkhuizen 2011) to frame the description of the various research contexts. Briefly, narrative knowledging refers to the meaning-making, learning, and knowledge construction that takes place at all stages of a narrative research project, from the conception of the research project to the consumption of the research report.

In the field of second language teaching and learning, analytical approaches generally reflect those that have come before or are current in other fields, particularly general education, literacy studies, and sociolinguistics. Until fairly recently the focus on content (what the narratives are about) has been most conspicuous in the field (Vásquez 2011). Early diary studies in the 1970s and early 1980s, for example, aimed to describe the social and psychological experiences of language learners. At the time, cross-sectional research focusing on *group* characteristics dominated the field of second language acquisition (Schumann and Schumann 1977), and diary studies were seen to be an antidote. In-depth, longitudinal case studies of *individual* experiences provided introspective accounts of language learning in context. Studies of language learning histories produced similar descriptions of learners' learning careers (Benson 2011) – when they learned a language, how, and why. With regard to teachers, analyses of teacher reflective journals, for example, revealed rich details of their professional development, particularly

The Handbook of Narrative Analysis, First Edition. Edited by Anna De Fina and Alexandra Georgakopoulou.
© 2015 John Wiley & Sons, Inc. Published 2019 by John Wiley & Sons, Inc.

the sense they made of their own teaching practices. Following developments in research on teacher cognitions, whereby teachers were seen to be thinking individuals rather than mere technicians (Borg 2003), these studies focused on teachers' beliefs and emotions and their learning from their own perspective.

Pavlenko (2007) appealed to researchers in applied linguistics to go beyond the investigation of content only, arguing provocatively that content analysis isn't analysis at all. She urged researchers to pay attention also to the form of narratives (what she calls textual reality) and the context of their construction, particularly the wider socio-political contexts in which they take their shape. In the conclusion to her discussion of narrative contextual analysis she says:

> Narrative analysis in sociolinguistic studies has to consider larger historical, political, social, and economic circumstances that shape the narratives and are reflected in them, language ideologies and discourses that have currency in narrators' communities and with regard to which they position themselves, and, last but not least, the setting where particular versions of narrative experience are produced and the audience they are produced for. (Pavlenko 2007: 176–177)

Many of the illustrative studies in this chapter have heeded Pavlenko's call. More recent ones, for example, have exhibited analytical interest in the discursive performance and practice of narrative, the visual and multimodal representation of participants' experiences, and the local and macro contexts in which those experiences are lived and narrated. And researchers' analytical methods reflect these interests. The chapter includes studies that do indeed focus on content, but it is inevitable that even these take into consideration to some extent the contextual contributions to the construction, content, and form of the narrative analyzed. Together, the studies in this chapter represent a broad scope of narrative research practice in second language teaching and learning.

5.2   Narrative Knowledging

Narrative knowledging is "the meaning making, learning, or knowledge construction that takes place during the narrative research activities of (co)constructing narratives, analyzing narratives, reporting the findings, and reading/watching/listening to research reports" (Barkhuizen 2011: 395). As this definition implies, different participants engage in narrative knowledging at various mutually informing stages of the research process, including (co)narrators (which could include the researcher), researchers, and consumers of research reports. Figure 5.1 shows an (inevitably simplistic) breakdown of these stages and the participants involved in narrative knowledging at each stage.

Narrative knowledging is an activity (hence the verb *knowledging*). It is a cognitive activity. Making sense of and reshaping an experience through narrating, analyzing narratives, reporting narrative research, and consuming research findings are cognitive activities. Narrative knowledging is something that we do, and in the process we *understand* that experience – we generate knowledge (Doyle 1997; Elbaz-Luwisch 2007). However, this knowledge is not constant. When narrators retell stories of particular

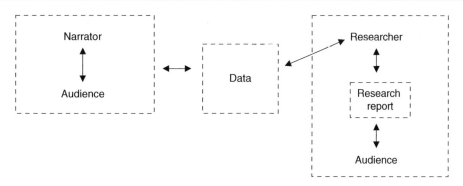

Figure 5.1   Stages and participants in narrative knowledging. Adapted with permission from TESOL International Association.

experiences, they may understand these experiences differently each time; researchers' interpretations of their narrative data may also change as they revisit and reflect further on their data, even after they have been fixed in research reports (see Bell 2011); and consumers of research, each time they read, listen to, watch, or reflect on research reports, shift understandings of the reported experiences. The concept of narrative knowledging, therefore, recognizes the active, fluid nature of meaning-making, and aims to avoid conceptions of narrative knowledge as stable, permanent, and unchallengeable. Narrative knowledging is also a social activity, of course. Narratives are discursively constructed with others in particular spatiotemporal contexts and, after analysis by researchers, are presented to an audience for (re)interpretation.

The various narrative knowledging "components" are not as static as depicted in Figure 5.1. In autobiographical studies, for example, the narrator (as research participant) and audience (see the left-hand box in Figure 5.1) may be the same person, both learner/ teacher and researcher (who would then also be the "researcher" in the right-hand box). Of course, they may not be the same person – the researcher (as audience/ researcher in the left-hand box) may engage with other research participants (teachers or learners). The audience in the left-hand box may, however, not be the researcher at all – for instance if a researcher analyzed data generated during a conversation between two research participants (the narrator and the audience). These various combinations, as well as others, are captured in the research contexts described in the following sections, each of which presents a number of illustrative studies. But first, I provide a brief overview of the key analytical approaches employed by researchers in the illustrative studies.

5.3   Analytical Approaches

5.3.1   *Thematic content analysis*

The content of narratives refers to *what* they are about, what was told, and why, when, where, and by whom. Thematic analysis focuses on the content of the experiences of the narrators and their reflections on these by searching for themes in the narrative data.

These themes are often grouped into larger categories for the purposes of further inter-pretation and discussion. The context in which the stories are told (i.e., the storytelling context) and the contexts of the told events and experiences are incorporated into the analysis to varying extents by the analysts.

5.3.2   Small story analysis

Small stories are snippets of often mundane talk in conversations (and sometimes in interviews) which tell of past, current, imagined, or hypothetical events, as opposed to "big" narratives like life histories and those compiled from multiple interviews and other ethnographic data collected over an extended period of time (Bamberg and Georgakopoulou 2008; Vásquez 2011; see Deppermann in this volume, chapter 19). A small story is like a "strip of discourse activity" (Bamberg and Georgakopoulou 2008: 380) in which narrators (co-)construct a sense of who they are, their identities. The analysis of small stories therefore involves analyzing in fine-grained detail the narratives-in-interaction using methods typically associated with conversation analysis. (Small stories are discussed in detail by Georgakopoulou in this volume, chapter 13.)

5.3.3   Positioning analysis

Davies and Harré (1990: 48) define positioning as a discursive practice "whereby selves are located in conversations as observably and intersubjectively coherent participants in jointly produced story lines." Positioning *analysis* therefore aims to unravel how people position themselves through their co-constructed talk-in-interaction performance. It focuses both on what the talk is about – what they are telling about – and on how they do the telling. In other words, positioning analysis makes "the interactive site of story-*telling* the empirical ground, where identities come into existence and are interactively displayed" (Bamberg 2004: 36). The storyteller's interactive engagement in the story's construction is thus central to the positioning analytical process.

5.3.4   Analysis of narratives and narrative analysis

Polkinghorne (1995) makes a distinction between *analysis of narratives* and *narrative analysis* corresponding to the two ways of knowing (i.e., two kinds of cognition or ways of organizing experience) described by Bruner (1986). One of these Bruner called paradig-matic cognition, which entails "classifying a particular instance as belonging to a category or concept" (Polkinghorne 1995: 9). Analyses of narrative content (Polkinghorne's analysis of narratives) follow the procedures of coding for themes, categorizing these and looking for patterns of association among them (see *thematic analysis* above). Many of the studies in this chapter that utilized a form of content analysis followed similar procedures. Bruner's second way of knowing, narrative cognition, organizes experience temporally, seeking explications "that are context sensitive and particular" (Bruner 2006: 116). What Polkinghorne's narrative analysis does is configure the various bits of data content into a coherent whole – in other words, the outcome of researcher narrative knowledging is a story.

5.4   Learners – Autobiographical Research

In autobiographical accounts of language learning, learners write about their learning experiences as research participants, and they themselves are the researchers. They construct and analyze their data and report the findings. They are therefore responsible for and involved in nearly all narrative knowledging processes. Data are typically written in such autobiographies, though more recently they have taken on multimodal forms. Two examples are provided here. The first is traditional learner diary studies, which are autobiographical, introspective documents that record the experiences of language learning from the learner's perspective. Very much like personal diaries, they consist of a series of entries written over an extended period of time. Diary studies are useful for researchers who aim to explore and understand affective factors, learning strategies, and the learners' own perceptions of their language learning through information that is recorded while learners are actually engaged in the process of learning. They make accessible data unobservable by other methods (Faerch and Kasper 1987), providing a rich, detailed picture of learning, particularly the social and cognitive dimensions of learners from their particular point of view.

Classic diary studies include those by Schumann and Schumann (1977) and Bailey (1980). Schumann and Schumann conducted longitudinal case studies to explore their own personal social-psychological experiences of learning Arabic and Persian both inside and outside language classrooms. They were interested in examining individual learning experiences as opposed to group profiles, a practice which was more common in second language acquisition research at the time. They discovered a number of *personal* variables (which interact with social, psychological, and cognitive variables) that affect second language acquisition. Bailey kept a journal while learning French in a formal university-level course. Like Schumann and Schumann, her focus in writing and thematically analyzing (see Riessman 2008) the journal entries was on personal experiences of learning, in particular her affective responses to learning in a classroom situation. In concluding her study, she suggested that introspective analyses of journals "hold considerable promise both as a research tool and as an aid to self-awareness" (1980: 65). In a later publication (Bailey 1983) she again reported the findings of her diary study, but this time provided considerable theoretical and empirical context in relation to both topic (anxiety in second language learning) and method (the use of diary studies as a research tool). She noted a number of potential benefits and limitations regarding the latter.

Maintaining the diary study tradition, Casanave (2012) more recently reports on research that focuses on her informal Japanese learning efforts over an eight-year period while living and teaching in Japan. She frames the analysis within an ecological perspective, taking into account "the idiosyncratic and fluctuating nature of motivation due to daily contextual, personal, and emotional factors that interacted in unpredictable ways" (2012: 642). In her report, an example of "writing as analysis" (Benson 2013), her *researcher* voice is specially highlighted, the diachronic processes of the research procedures are described in detail, and the findings are presented chronologically. In other words, it includes a number of interconnecting temporal threads, specifically, the story of the research process, the stories of Japanese learning and use told in the diary data, and Casanave's representation of her story (what she says about her story and about how she tells it in the article). In both Casanave's study and the classical diary studies, it is the same person (as narrator and researcher) who is involved in narrative knowledging throughout the mutually informing processes of data construction (writing the diaries), data analysis (thematically analyzing their contents), and the preparation of the research report (which is itself analysis).

5.5   Learners – Biographical Research

In biographical studies, language learners tell about their learning experiences as participants in research projects in which they are not the (primary) researchers. Biographical accounts of language learning are enormously varied, using a wide range of data-collection methods and approaches to analysis. From young learners to the middle-aged, participants are associated with both informal learning situations and more formal learning institutions. In some cases the narrative data are the product of a course activity or assignment, which are then used by a researcher (typically the instructor) for research purposes.

One such example is the study by Murphey, Chen, and Chen (2004). They were interested in first-year university students' social constructions of their identities as English learners. They wanted to discover if and how they invested in their learning and also in their imagined communities. Data for the project consisted of learners' first-person narratives of their learning, specifically their language learning histories (LLHs), which are retrospective accounts of past learning. The learners in Murphey et al.'s study came from universities in Japan and Taiwan. Writing the LLHs was a course assignment, and thus written mainly for the eyes of their teacher, although they were also shared with fellow students. Students were required to write a 750-word paper about their language learning history from when they began to learn English to the present time and also about their thoughts on future learning. Instructions included suggestions for content that might be covered in the LLHs. A thematic analysis of the LLHs revealed varying "degrees of identification or non-identification and investments with imagined communities" (2004: 86).

Kouritzin's (2000) study also involved participants who were enrolled in formal language classes, but the data she collected were not part of any planned course work and derived from oral interviews rather than written. She conducted qualitative life history interviews with adult immigrant mothers in Canada in order to investigate their access to ESL classes. She began the interviews by asking participants to tell in their own words their stories about learning English and about their family's experiences of immigration and settlement, including their children's education in Canada. The interviews were conducted in English because Kouritzin believed that the use of a translator would diminish the quality of the interviews. After analyzing the interviews thematically, she retells the stories of five women in order to illustrate three major influences constraining their access to ESL classes: time constraints, their ambivalence toward learning English, and contradictions between adopted Canadian cultural practices and their own cultural traditions. Similarly, Menard-Warwick (2007) addressed how her adult, female, immigrant participants respond to the second language learning expectations their communities and families place on them. Life history interviews were conducted in Spanish with two focal participants and these, too, were coded thematically. Menard-Warwick used extensive narrative data to illustrate how the gender ideologies and practices of the participants' communities mediate their learning.

Holmes and Marra (2011) focused their interest on narratives constructed during the social activity of small talk in the workplace. The four participants in their illustrative data were professional migrants enrolled in a Workplace Communication Skills course in New Zealand. The course aimed to teach socio-pragmatic knowledge and awareness of how to use English appropriately in the workplace. After a period of time in the classroom, participants do an internship in a workplace setting. In their study, the researchers present and analyze numerous workplace narratives, which, they argue, are often overlooked as discourse resources in the workplace, dismissed as distracting or superfluous. Instead, they show that the workplace narratives that the migrants co-construct with their workmates (in the form of small stories embedded in workplace discourse) are significant sites for professional identity construction and for the building of good relationships. The researchers in this study are not directly involved in the construction of the workplace narratives. Their narrative knowledging occurs in their role as researchers at the analysis stage. Simpson's (2011) study also makes connections between life outside and inside classrooms. He conducted a positioning analysis (Bamberg 1997) of a small story recorded during interaction between himself and a student in an adult ESL classroom in the UK. So, as a researcher, he was actually involved in the co-construction of the conversational data. Simpson shows how aspects of students' life stories outside the classroom are brought into the classroom by negotiating discursive space, consequently bringing with them identity positions that are typically under-explored in classrooms.

5.6   Teachers – Autobiographical Research

In this research context, teachers and teacher educators investigate their own practice, usually for professional development purposes. Many of the published reports take on the form of personal reflections, typically written accounts of their thoughts and feelings about a particular topic (e.g., planning classroom tasks, managing time effectively) or their practice generally. Others include systematic analyses of these reflective accounts; that is, they take on more of an empirical orientation. A number of collections have appeared over the past 10–20 years focusing on a range of topics relating to the professional lives and identities of language educators. Casanave and Schecter's (1997) book, for example, is a collection of stories and reflections written by language educators from diverse backgrounds and working contexts. Each contribution is a personal narrative, and the book overall presents a study of personal issues in language education. The authors in Braine's (1999) volume are all non-native speakers of English. They are located in diverse geographical areas and have various language backgrounds. Their accounts of personal experience address sociopolitical issues in their working lives. In Johnson and Golombek's (2002) collection of language teachers' narrative inquiries, the authors present stories of their understanding of their teaching practice and professional development experiences – specifically how they know what they know. A final example is Curtis and Romney's (2006) book in which contributors describe and reflect on critical events in their lives as TESOL professionals of color, considering particularly how these events had a bearing on their teaching practice. The autobiographies, therefore, deal explicitly with themes of race and ethnicity.

Canagarajah (2012) presents his story of professionalization as a periphery professional in TESOL through means of an analytic autoethnography (Anderson 2006). Canagarajah explains that in an autoethnographic approach, writing functions not only as a means of disseminating knowledge and experience, it is a central activity for generating, recording, and analyzing data. In writing his narrative he engages explicitly with the situatedness of his experiences, acknowledging that "knowledge is based on one's location and identities" (2012: 260). Adopting the communities of practice (Wenger 1998) orientation to scaffold his story, he makes the case, tentatively, for brokering and boundary crossing in the TESOL global community in order for peripheral teachers to negotiate a voice within the community, or "constellation of practices" (274).

O'Móchain's (2006) narrative account of an English as a foreign language course he taught is also an example of "writing as analysis." The setting of his narrative was a content-based English course at a Christian women's college in Japan. O'Móchain describes the college environment as strongly heteronormative, and his aim in the course was to find "a context-appropriate way of exploring gender and sexuality issues" and, in particular, to develop "a teaching strategy that would focus on queer lives in the local context" (2006: 51). His published article is constructed as a narrative telling his experience of teaching the course. It includes illustrative narrative materials that were actually used in the course. O'Móchain concludes that the teaching strategy he adopted was effective in that several students "showed a readiness to challenge the dominance of heteronormative paradigms" (64).

Like O'Móchain, Norton and Early (2011) were active researcher participants in the construction of the narrative data they analyzed. As already mentioned, narratives are constructed in particular interactional contexts, and storytellers constantly pay attention to the local (and wider sociocultural) contexts in which the stories are told, including the identities of participating co-narrators. Consequently, as De Fina (2011: 28) says, "storytelling activities and story types both reflect and shape relations among participants based, among other factors, on their local management of situational and portable identities." When the co-constructors are researchers, the storytelling that participants engage in inevitably follows a somewhat different trajectory. Norton and Early interrogate the negotiation of researcher identity in the midst of a narrative inquiry in which they as university researchers (and teacher educators) collaborate with teachers on a project to promote digital literacy in a poorly resourced rural school in Uganda – circumstances fraught with potentially inequitable power relationships. Their content analysis of the small stories co-constructed on site reveals a number of researcher identities, including researcher as international guest, teacher, teacher educator, and collaborative team member. Their narrative knowledge also reveals how they sought to transform the power differentials between themselves and the teachers and to encourage the teachers' investment in the collaborative project, thereby making "visible the complex ways in which researcher identity impacts research" (2011: 436).

5.7   Teachers – Biographical Research – Professional Development

Much biographical research on language teaching and teachers involves researchers recruiting teachers as research participants while the teachers are participating in professional development activities, either pre-service teacher training programs or in-service further study programs (usually at the graduate level). In such contexts language teachers construct narratives for professional development, usually for a course activity or assignment. The narratives, the data for the studies, typically take the form of reflective journals or written autobiographies in which they reflect on their own teaching and language learning experiences (past or present) and relate these to the content of the course they are taking. However, the outcomes of their reflections are used by researchers (usually their instructors) for further narrative knowledging as part of independent research projects. For example, Pavlenko's (2003) study aimed to discover ways in which English teachers enrolled in a TESOL program imagine their linguistic and professional memberships. Discursive positioning analysis was used to examine 30 linguistic autobiographies. As well as a content analysis, particular attention was paid to lexical choices and use of verbs to signal positioning within particular imagined groups. Pavlenko concluded that imagination can be productively exploited in critical pedagogy. Another example is Park's (2012) study. She investigated the identity transformations of students enrolled in a TESOL program at a US university. A thematic analysis was carried out on three sets of data: electronic autobiographies (email exchanges) prior to the TESOL program; e-journals maintained during the program; and individual interviews with the five participants over a six-month period. The experiences of one Chinese student, Xia, are discussed and interpreted in relation to seven snapshots (short excerpts of data).

Working with two students enrolled in a graduate course in South Africa, one an in-service teacher with 20 years' experience and the other a pre-service teacher with no classroom experience, Barkhuizen (2008) demonstrates a narrative inquiry approach to exploring teaching context for the purposes of professional development. The teachers wrote personal journals about their past and imagined language teaching experiences and had regular conversations about these with Barkhuizen, who was the class instructor. A thematic analysis of the journal entries revealed that three interconnected levels of story, or narrative context, were significant in the teachers' lives. On one level, story (with a small s) is personal and constructed in the teachers' immediate contexts; it "embodies the inner thoughts, emotions, ideas and theories of teachers, as well as the many social interactions in which they take part during their teaching practice" (2008: 225). The second level of Story (with a capital S) spreads out wider than the immediate psychological and interpersonal social context of the teachers. Here they have less power or agency in their practice – for example, prescribed syllabuses or a school's language-in-education policy. The third level of STORY (in capital letters) refers to the broader sociopolitical context, such as national language policies and state-wide curriculum and assessment practices. Teachers practice their professional lives, claims Barkhuizen, within the space constructed by the intersection of these different levels.

Taking a Vygotskian sociocultural theoretical perspective, Johnson and Golombek (2011) claim that written products such as teacher journals – and particularly the teachers' analyses of these – function as mediational tools for narrative knowledging. They argue that through narrative inquiry teachers not only make sense of their experiences but also make worthwhile changes to their teaching practices. The "transformative power of narrative" (2011: 486) therefore lies in narrative's functioning as a mediational tool for fostering teachers' professional development. Johnson and Golombek illustrate how this happens by analyzing (re-storying) two published teacher-authored narrative inquiries (see Johnson and Golombek 2002). The original teacher-authored products and their re-storied accounts in Johnson and Golombek's (2011) article are made available through their publication to other practitioners and to researchers. Johnson and Golombek suggest that this extends the transformative power of narrative as a tool for narrative knowledging to the wider professional landscape of second language teacher education, and they present examples of how this is currently taking place in contexts at both the center and the periphery.

5.8   Teachers – Biographical Research – Not Professional Development

In this narrative research context, language teachers (pre-service and in-service) construct narrative data about their teaching for a researcher. Although constructing the narratives may have some professional development value for the teachers, the purpose of doing so is empirical and not specifically for professional development, whether part of formal teacher education programs or not. Data can take the form of reflective diaries and journals, interviews, narrative frames, and collaborative conversations and discussions, often in combination. Following are examples of studies which exemplify these data types and compatible methods of analysis.

Tsui (2007) draws on Wenger's (1998) social theory of identity formation to examine the lived experience of Minfang, a college English foreign language (EFL) teacher in China. The data covered a six-year period of his teaching life, and consisted of written reflective diaries and lengthy face-to-face storytelling sessions. The first conversation took place at a conference where Tsui and Minfang met. For the next six months, Minfang shared his personal diaries with Tsui. She read them regularly and responded to his reflections, thus setting up a storytelling dialogue. Further intensive conversations took place four times for about four hours each over a week at the end of the six months. The construction of Minfang's multiple identities, particularly a communicative language teaching (CLT) teacher identity, were explored within the contexts of his institutional and personal lived experiences. To do this, all data were first arranged chronologically, then the identity conflicts Minfang experienced were categorized and examined, and finally Wenger's identification and negotiability of meanings framework was applied for further analysis.

Simon-Maeda (2004) conducted in-depth, open-ended life history interviews with nine female EFL teachers working in higher education contexts in Japan. She was interested in how the participants constructed their identities and contested oppressive forces within the sociocultural and ideological contexts of their workplaces. She analyzed the interview data thematically using the qualitative data analysis software program called NVivo. Simon-Maeda discusses the interface of gender and three themes that "contributed to narrativized perceptions of becoming and being a female teacher in a sometimes hostile traditional environment" (2004: 411): teachers' personal biographies, their ways of dealing with conflicts in the workplace, and their attitudes toward students and professional practices. Xu and Liu (2009) were also interested in college-level EFL teaching, this time examining the assessment knowledge and practices of one female teacher in China, Betty, in the midst of assessment reform. Drawing on the narrative inquiry work of Connelly and Clandinin (2006) in general education, Xu and Liu analyzed interview data (which they configured into three stories), personal communications with Betty about her teaching and learning experiences, and her personal records (e.g., assessment plans, evaluation sheets). Their aim was to explore tensions between the secret stories of assessment that Betty actually lived, and the sacred, prescribed stories told by those in authority.

Barkhuizen and Wette (2008) used a very different approach to explore college English teaching in China. While teaching in a professional development program in Beijing, they took the opportunity to learn about this particular teaching context by designing a series of what they called *narrative frames* to gather information from the participating teachers about their working lives. A narrative frame is a written story template consisting of a series of incomplete sentences and blank spaces of varying lengths. It is structured as a story in skeletal form. The aim is for participants to produce a coherent story by filling in the spaces according to their own experiences and their reflections on these in the process of narrative knowledging. Frames

> provide guidance and support in terms of both the structure and content of what is to be written. From the researcher's perspective the frames ensure that the content will be more or less what is expected (and required to address the research aims) and that it will be delivered in narrative form. (Barkhuizen and Wette 2008: 376)

In designing the frames, the researchers drew on the oft-quoted claim that a story has a beginning, a middle, and an end, and, where appropriate, they incorporated into the frames Labov's (1972) narrative elements, particularly orientation and evaluation. Both thematic and quantitative (frequency counts and ranking of the themes) analyses were carried out on the 83 completed frames (see Barkhuizen 2009; Wette and Barkhuizen 2009). Although the use of narrative frames as data-collection instruments has several limitations, the procedure enabled the researchers to gain knowledge of and entry into an unfamiliar teaching and learning environment (see also Barkhuizen 2014; Barnard and Nguyen 2010; and Macalister 2012, who used frames with language learners).

Rugen (2010) used Bamberg's (1997) positioning analysis to examine naturally occurring conversational narratives (or small stories) of pre-service teachers of English in an outside-classroom university context in Japan. He was particularly interested in the relevance of ratifications for the emergent social identities of those participants offering the ratifications. In a later example of this type of analysis, Rugen (2013) again used positioning analysis to examine a small story constructed by the Japanese pre-service teachers. The story was part of a larger ethnographic data-set collected over a period of 10 months. In this analysis he was interested in illuminating the unstable processes of identity construction, evident in talk-in-interaction, in the processes of learning to become a language teacher. Rugen's analytical attention to the discursive construction of conversational narratives has also been applied to interview data. Barkhuizen (2010), for example, conducted a positioning analysis of a small story embedded in an interview with a migrant pre-service teacher from the Pacific Island of Tonga who was studying in New Zealand to become an English teacher. He extended the usual procedures associated with positioning analysis to include analysis of data beyond the small story text, such as written autobiographical narratives and his informal conversations with the teacher. Through this process, Barkhuizen found that the teacher had discursively positioned herself and had been positioned as migrant, language teacher, activist/mediator, and investor/capitalizer. Baynham (2011) too looked at interviews. He examined the relationship between the notion of "stance" and discursive positioning, focusing particularly on the role of narrative performance in interview data with ESOL teachers. He identified different narrative types in the data and related these to performance. He concluded that the research interview is indeed a "dynamically co-constructed speech genre rather than … a neutral locus for gathering data" (2011: 63).

5.9   Teachers and Learners – Biographical Research

The final context to be discussed is narrative research involving both teachers and learners as participants in the same project. This can be interpreted in two ways: (1) the participants are both learners and teachers, and (2) the teachers and learners are different participants. But neither the teachers nor the learners are the researchers. Some innovative research approaches have been used in this context. Chik and Breidbach (2011), for example, explore the use of multimedia language learning histories (LLHs) for intercultural exchange between Hong Kong university English majors and pre-service English language student teachers in Germany. Their study aimed to facilitate dialogue among the students and to promote reflection on their language learning development. Chik and Breidbach used online platforms and Web 2.0 tools to facilitate the sharing of their LLHs. The Hong Kong students first posted their multimedia LLHs on a project wiki site, and the German students uploaded their text-based LLHs. They then exchanged their comments on the LLHs through the wiki site. A second cohort of students followed the same procedures, and then, following the initiative of the Hong Kong students, a Facebook group and two Skype meetings were set up to replace the wiki exchange. The researchers identified a number of significant challenges associated with sharing the LLHs in this way, especially in terms of interactivity and multimodality. For example, the Hong Kong students were eager to share LLHs and interact through more personal social media channels, but this suggestion was only welcomed by some of the German participants.

Finnish researchers Kalaja, Dufva, and Alanen (2013), have produced some novel work using visual images or narratives, particularly drawings of human figures, to explore the language learning experiences of EFL student teachers. In these analyses, then, the participants are student teachers reflecting on their language learning histories. The researchers report on a number of their studies drawing on data collected as part of a longitudinal project launched in 2005. In the study focusing on student teachers reflecting on their learning, the participants were asked to draw a portrait of themselves as an EFL learner – they were provided with an A4 sheet of paper bearing the pre-printed title "Self-portrait" and a caption reading, "This is what I look like as an EFL learner." In addition they were asked to write an interpretation of their drawing in a few sentences on the reverse side of the page. The drawings were then analyzed for content, focusing on the learner (e.g., what they looked like and what they were doing), any other people, and objects, which the researchers interpreted as mediational means used by the learners for learning (e.g., books representing reading, a CD player representing listening). Menezes (2008) was also interested in the language learning experiences of English teachers, specifically to explore the complexity of second language acquisition. She collected and analyzed multimedia LLHs written by the teachers. The LLHs contained written text as well as visual components and hyperlinks to web-based audio clips. Menezes suggests that while "multimedia portray much more information than each individual medium does" (2008: 201), it is the interactions among different media that promote narrative knowledging on behalf of both the participants and the researcher.

Benson (2013) reports on a narrative case study of the experiences of a Hong Kong university student during study abroad in the UK. It focuses on second language identity and how this is influenced by the experience. Using interview data and multi-modal blogs written by the student while overseas, Benson constructs and then retells the student's story of second language identity development. Drawing on the work of Polkinghorne (1995), particularly his distinction between analysis of narratives and narrative analysis, he makes the case for leaving much of the interpretation of the story up to readers of the report.

Focusing on classroom narratives, Nelson (2011) suggests incorporating crafted narratives of classroom life into research on language teaching and learning. Here she means narratives that are "deliberately styled in arts-based forms" (465), such as poems and plays, and which are meant to be evocative and aesthetically engaging. These could be in written, multimodal, or performance modes. In 1996, Canagarajah pointed out that "narratives are gaining prominence in research publications because they represent holistically the local knowledge of the communities studied" (1996: 327). Nelson agrees, but feels that narrative authors are not doing a satisfactory job. She recalls feeling disappointment when reading the conclusion of "yet another self-focussed text." She says why:

> … too much detail, too little depth; too much angst, not enough insight; too much about what happened, not enough about what it all might mean – especially for readers in other locales. Some autobiographic narratives seem strangely generic; on the bland side; sometimes the tone seems aimlessly confessional or self-consciously clever; sometimes the accompanying analysis seems sketchy, failing to come together into a focused scholarly argument. (Nelson 2011: 465)

Nelson's inspiration for considering the inclusion of crafted narratives in language education research was not only the disappointment she felt with the quality of the narrative reports she encountered, however; she also questioned the epistemological purpose of her own narrative reporting, especially within a context of shifting conceptions of knowledge. Nelson proposes that crafted classroom-life narratives within a critical narrative studies framework will contribute to the democratization of knowledge work – for teachers, learners, researchers and readers – by making what is reported more accessible, relevant, and inclusive (i.e., critical narrative knowledging). In a later publication (Nelson 2013) she describes in detail the analytical procedures she uses for dramatizing narrative data; specifically, transforming into playscripts data collected from classroom observations, focus-group interviews, and individual teacher and learner interviews.

5.10   Conclusion

This chapter has presented an array of studies in the field of second language teaching and learning in educational contexts. They have been organized into six research contexts, reflecting who the participants are in the studies, their role in narrative knowledging, and the nature of the studies' research designs and processes. Together the studies indicate a wide range of narrative research approaches, in terms of the types of data collected, the methods of analysis, the approaches to reporting research findings, and indeed theoretical and epistemological perspectives on narrative. This diversity reflects the rather eclectic way researchers have drawn on narrative practices in other disciplines, and it is probably safe to say that any field-specific paradigm in narrative research on language teaching and learning is still a long way off.

We would expect, therefore, the processes and outcomes of *narrative knowledging* to also be variable. For example, language teachers and learners might primarily play one role (e.g., research participant) or multiple roles (e.g., participant *and* researcher), as we saw in studies by Tsui (2007) and Canagarajah (2012), respectively. Researchers might be intimately involved (as audience) in the co-construction of small story data (e.g., Rugen 2013), or passive collectors of data generated without their direct participation (e.g., Holmes and Marra 2011). The studies reviewed in this chapter have also illustrated multiple approaches to analysis and reporting, including thematic content analysis (e.g., Kouritzen 2000), positioning analysis (Barkhuizen 2010), small story analysis (e.g., Early and Norton 2013), writing as analysis (Benson 2013), and the production of drama playscripts (Nelson 2013). Finally, narrative knowledging might occur within formal classroom or professional development contexts as learners and teachers go about their language learning (e.g., Bailey 1980) and teacher education (e.g., Johnson and Golombek 2011), or it may be quite separate from these formal contexts (e.g., Casanave 2012). Clearly, then, all aspects of narrative knowledging, fluid in itself by definition, are variable in language teaching and learning research, and, particularly recently, are constantly under systematic reflection and development by narrative researchers.

A number of trends, however, have begun to emerge which perhaps signal the direction in which these researchers are moving. To conclude this chapter, I present four aspects of narrative research which I believe will advance these trends in the field:

5.10.1 Teacher narrative research

There is growing interest in and support for language teachers engaging in research to explore their own experiences in classrooms and schools (Borg 2013; O'Mochain 2006). The aim is for teachers to better understand these experiences in order to develop a sense of agency in their working lives. Narrative forms of action and practitioner research are suitable means for doing so. And then disseminating inquiry findings through appropriate reporting channels will extend narrative knowledging to the wider professional community of second language teacher education

5.10.2 Mixed methodologies

There has been little experimentation with using multiple or mixed narrative methods of analysis within the same research project, at least as evident in published reports. Examples of these mixed methodologies can be found in Early and Norton (2013) and Barkhuizen (2013). Early and Norton analyzed small stories (see Georgakopoulou in this volume, chapter 13) both discursively and for their content. Barkhuizen thematically analyzed four short extracts or small stories (about 10 lines each) selected from across a series of interviews with a migrant in New Zealand to tell the participant's big story – a broad telling of his life relevant to the research focus. He then analyzed in much more detail, using discursive positioning analysis, one longer small story to investigate further the findings from the more general big story analysis. The thematic analysis of the content in the four short stories and the positioning analysis of the co-constructed interaction in the longer small story worked together to produce a systematic account of the migrant's experiences.

5.10.3 Narrative reporting

Ely (2007: 571) says simply about narrative reporting, "There are numerous ways for us to report." In addition to the approaches presented in this chapter, which range from fairly conventional social science formats to heavily contextualized, diachronic diary studies, Ely suggests alternative rhetorical forms more appropriate for presenting the findings of narrative inquiry, such as poetry, stories, and playscripts such as those developed by Nelson (2013). Reporting in innovative ways, however, does present some challenges. For instance, not all audiences will appreciate deviations from anticipated, traditional forms, for instance examiners of research dissertations or reviewers of manuscripts submitted to research journals. Nevertheless, over recent years there has been some movement toward a more inclusive approach to research reporting, as evident in a number of high-profile scholarly journals in the field.

5.10.4   *Researcher subjectivity*

Canagarajah (1996: 324) reminds us that during any research project "the subjectivity of the researchers – with their complex values, ideologies, and experiences – shapes the research activity and findings." However, we tend to hear little about the researchers in the reports – who they are, what positions they take on the topics and participants they investigate, their ideological stances, and their detailed experiences of the unfolding research processes. Research, especially narrative research, is seldom unproblematic, as researchers deal with personal decisions, practical matters and ethical issues. Narrative reporting has the potential to weave these experiences into descriptions of the theoretical background, methodological approaches and findings of a study. Casanave's (2012) diary study of her informal Japanese learning experiences while living and teaching in Japan and Canagarajah's (2012) autoethnography of his development as a TESOL professional are excellent examples of how this can be achieved.

To conclude, I offer a final comment, not so much about narrative research practice as about meta-level discussions on the place of narrative research in second language teaching and learning. It is perhaps an appropriate time in the evolution of narrative research in the field to consider issues that have to do with the status of narrative studies relative to other types of research, researcher perceptions of narrative research, and challenges to advocating for narrative research. Such discussions can take place both locally within programs and institutions, and more globally within broader communities of scholars represented by, for example, dissertation committees, professional associations, conference organizing committees, and journal editors. These discussions might lead to an awareness of the nature and practices of narrative research in the field, with possible consequences for legitimization, and they might make very interesting research stories themselves.

REFERENCES

Anderson, L. (2006). Analytic autoethnography. *Journal of Contemporary Ethnography*, 35, pp. 373–395.

Bailey, K.M. (1980). An introspective analysis of an individual's language learning experience. In R. Scarcella and S. Krashen (eds.), *Research in Second Language Acquisition: Selected Papers of the Los Angeles Second Language Research Forum*. Rowley, MA: Newbury House, pp. 58–65.

Bailey, K.M. (1983). Competitiveness and anxiety in adult second language learning: Looking *at* and *through* the diary studies. In H.W. Seliger and M.H. Long (eds.), *Classroom Oriented Research in Second Language Acquisition*. Rowley, MA: Newbury House, pp. 67–103.

Bamberg, M. (1997). Positioning between structure and performance. *Journal of Narrative and Life History*, 7 (1–4), pp. 335–342.

Bamberg, M. (2004). Positioning with Davie Hogan: Stories, tellings, and identities. In C. Daiute and C. Lightfoot (eds.), *Narrative Analysis: Studying the Development of Individuals in Society*. Thousand Oaks, CA: Sage, pp. 135–157.

Bamberg, M., and A. Georgakopoulou. (2008). Small stories as a new perspective in narrative and identity analysis. *Text and Talk*, 28 (3), pp. 377–396.

Barkhuizen, G. (2008). A narrative approach to exploring context in language teaching. *English Language Teaching Journal*, 62 (3), pp. 231–239.

Barkhuizen, G. (2009). Topics, aims, and constraints in English teacher research: A Chinese case study. *TESOL Quarterly*, 43 (1), pp. 113–125.

Barkhuizen, G. (2010). An extended positioning analysis of a pre-service teacher's *better life* small story. *Applied Linguistics*, 31 (2), pp. 282–300.

Barkhuizen, G. (2011). Narrative knowledging in TESOL. *TESOL Quarterly*, 45 (3), pp. 391–414.

Barkhuizen, G. (2013). Maintenance, identity and social inclusion narratives of an Afrikaans speaker living in New Zealand. *International Journal of the Sociology of Language*, 222, pp. 77–100.

Barkhuizen, G. (2014). Revisiting narrative frames: An instrument for investigating language teaching and learning. *System*, 47, pp. 12–27.

Barkhuizen, G., and R. Wette. (2008). Narrative frames for investigating the experiences of language teachers. *System*, 36 (3), pp. 372–387.

Barnard, R., and G.V. Nguyen. (2010). Task-based language teaching (TBLT): A Vietnamese case study using narrative frames to elicit teacher's beliefs. *Language Education in Asia*, 1, pp. 77–86.

Baynham, M. (2011). Stance, positioning, and alignment in narratives of professional experience. *Language in Society*, 40, pp. 63–74.

Bell, J.S. (2011). Reporting and publishing narrative inquiry in TESOL: Challenges and rewards. *TESOL Quarterly*, 45 (3), pp. 575–584.

Benson, P. (2011). Language learning careers as a unit of analysis in narrative research. *TESOL Quarterly*, 45 (3), pp. 545–553.

Benson, P. (2013). Narrative writing as method: Second language identity development in study abroad. In G. Barkhuizen (ed.), *Narrative Research in Applied Linguistics*. Cambridge: Cambridge University Press, pp. 244–263.

Borg, S. (2003). Teacher cognition in language teaching: A review of research on what language teachers think, know, believe and do. *Language Teaching*, 36, pp. 81–109.

Borg, S. (2013). *Teacher Research in Language Teaching: A Critical Analysis*. Cambridge: Cambridge University Press.

Braine, G. (ed.). (1999). *Non-Native Educators in English Language Teaching*. Mahwah, NJ: Lawrence Erlbaum.

Bruner, J. (1986). *Actual Minds, Possible Worlds*. Cambridge, MA: Harvard University Press.

Bruner, J.S. (2006). *In Search of Pedagogy Volume II: The Selected Works of Jerome S. Bruner*. London: Routledge.

Canagarajah, S. (1996). From critical research practice to critical research reporting. *TESOL Quarterly*, 30 (2), pp. 321–331.

Canagarajah, A.S. (2012). Teacher development in a global profession: An autoethnography. *TESOL Quarterly*, 46 (2), pp. 258–279.

Casanave, C.P. (2012). Diary of a dabbler: Ecological influences on an EFL teacher's efforts to study Japanese informally. *TESOL Quarterly*, 46 (4), pp. 642–670.

Casanave, C., and S. Schecter (eds.). (1997). *On Becoming a Language Educator*. Mahwah, NJ: Lawrence Erlbaum.

Chik, A., and S. Breidbach. (2011). Online language learning histories exchange: Hong Kong and German perspectives. *TESOL Quarterly*, 45 (3), pp. 553–564.

Connelly, F.M., and D.J. Clandinin. (2006). Narrative inquiry. In J.L. Green, G. Camilli, and P.B. Elmore (eds.), *Complementary Methods for Research in Education*. Mahwah, NJ: Lawrence Erlbaum, pp. 477–487.

Curtis, A., and M. Romney (eds.). (2006). *Color, Race, and English Language Teaching: Shades of Meaning*. Mahwah, NJ: Lawrence Erlbaum.

Davies, B., and R. Harré. (1990). Positioning: The discursive production of selves. *Journal for the Theory of Social Behaviour*, 20, pp. 43–63.

De Fina, A. (2011). Researcher and informant roles in narrative interactions: Constructions of belonging and foreign-ness. *Language in Society*, 40, pp. 27–38.

Doyle, W. (1997). Heard any really good stories lately? A critique of the critics of narrative in educational research. *Teaching and Teacher Education*, 13 (1), pp. 93–99.

Early, M., and B. Norton. (2013). Narrative inquiry in second language teacher education in rural Uganda. In G. Barkhuizen (ed.), *Narrative Research in Applied Linguistics*. Cambridge: Cambridge University Press, pp. 132–151.

Elbaz-Luwisch, F. (2007). Studying teachers' lives and experiences: Narrative inquiry into K-12 teaching. In D.J. Clandinin (ed.), *Handbook of Narrative Inquiry: Mapping a Methodology*. Thousand Oaks, CA: Sage, pp. 357–382.

Ely, M. (2007). In-forming re-presentations. In D.J. Clandinin (ed.), *Handbook of Narrative Inquiry: Mapping a Methodology*. Thousand Oaks, CA: Sage, pp. 567–598.

Faerch, C., and G. Kasper. (1987). *Introspection in Second Language Research*. Clevedon, UK: Multilingual Matters.

Holmes, J., and M. Marra. (2011). Harnessing storytelling as a sociopragmatic skill: Applying narrative research to workplace English courses. *TESOL Quarterly*, 45 (3), pp. 510–534.

Johnson, K.E., and P.R. Golombek (eds.). (2002). *Teachers' Narrative Inquiry as Professional Development*. Cambridge: Cambridge University Press.

Johnson, K.E., and P.R. Golombek. (2011). The transformative power of narrative in second language teacher education. *TESOL Quarterly*, 45 (3), pp. 486–509.

Kalaja, P., H. Dufva, and R. Alanen. (2013). Experimenting with visual narratives. In G. Barkhuizen (ed.), *Narrative Research in Applied Linguistics*. Cambridge: Cambridge University Press, pp. 105–131.

Kouritzin, S. (2000). Immigrant mothers redefine access to ESL classes: Contradiction and ambivalence. *Journal of Multilingual and Multicultural Development*, 21 (1), pp. 14–32.

Labov, W. (1972). *Language in the Inner City: Studies in the Black Vernacular*. Philadelphia: University of Pennsylvania Press.

Macalister, J. (2012). Narrative frames and needs analysis. *System*, 40 (1), pp. 120–128.

Menard-Warwick, J. (2007). "Because she made the beds. Every day." Social positioning, classroom discourse, and language learning. *Applied Linguistics*, 29 (2), pp. 267–289.

Menezes, V. (2008). Multimedia language learning histories. In P. Kalaja, V. Menezes, and A.M.F. Barcelos (eds.), *Narratives of Learning and Teaching EFL*. Basingstoke, UK: Palgrave Macmillan, pp. 199–213.

Murphey, T., J. Chen, and L.-C. Chen. (2004). Learners' constructions of identities and imagined communities. In P. Benson and D. Nunan (eds.), *Learners' Stories: Difference and Diversity in Language Learning*. Cambridge: Cambridge University Press, pp. 83–100.

Nelson, C.D. (2011). Narratives of classroom life: Changing conceptions of knowledge. *TESOL Quarterly*, 45 (3), pp. 463–485.

Nelson, C.D. (2013). From transcript to playscript: Dramatizing narrative research. In G. Barkhuizen (ed.), *Narrative Research in Applied Linguistics*. Cambridge: Cambridge University Press, pp. 220–243.

Norton, B., and M. Early. (2011). Researcher identity, narrative inquiry, and language teaching research. *TESOL Quarterly*, 45 (3), pp. 415–439.

O'Móchain, R. (2006). Discussing gender and sexuality in a context-appropriate way: Queer narratives in an EFL college classroom in Japan. *Journal of Language, Identity, and Education*, 5 (1), pp. 51–66.

Park, G. (2012). "I am never afraid of being recognized as an NNES": One teacher's journey in claiming and embracing her non-native-speaker identity. *TESOL Quarterly*, 46 (1), pp. 127–151.

Pavlenko, A. (2003). "I never knew I was a bilingual": Reimagining teacher identities in TESOL. *Journal of Language, Identity, and Education*, 2 (4), pp. 251–268.

Pavlenko, A. (2007). Autobiographic narratives as data in applied linguistics. *Applied Linguistics*, 28 (2), pp. 163–188.

Polkinghorne, D.E. (1995). Narrative configuration in qualitative analysis. *Qualitative Studies in Education*, 8 (1), pp. 5–23.

Riessman, C.K. (2008). *Narrative Methods for the Human Sciences*. Los Angeles, CA: Sage.

Rugen, B.D. (2010). The relevance of narrative

ratifications in talk-in-interaction for Japanese pre-service teachers of English. *Narrative Inquiry*, 20 (1), pp. 62–81.

Rugen, B. (2013). Language learner, language teacher: Negotiating identity positions in conversational narratives. In G. Barkhuizen (ed.), *Narrative Research in Applied Linguistics*. Cambridge: Cambridge University Press, pp. 199–217.

Schumann, F.E., and J.H. Schumann. (1977). Diary of a language learner: An introspective study of second language learning. In H.D. Brown, R.H. Crymes, and C.A. Yorio (eds.), *On TESOL '77: Teaching and Learning English as a Second Language: Trends in Research and Practice*. Washington, DC: TESOL, pp. 241–249.

Simon-Maeda, A. (2004). The complex construction of professional identities: Female EFL educators in Japan speak out. *TESOL Quarterly*, 38 (3), pp. 405–436.

Simpson, J. (2011). Telling tales: Discursive space and narratives in ESOL classrooms. *Linguistics and Education*, 22 (1), pp. 10–22.

Tsui, A. (2007). Complexities of identity formation: A narrative inquiry of an EFL teacher. *TESOL Quarterly*, 41 (4), pp. 657–680.

Vásquez, C. (2011). TESOL, teacher identity, and the need for "small story" research. *TESOL Quarterly*, 45 (3), pp. 535–545.

Wenger, E. (1998). *Communities of Practice: Learning, Meaning and Identity*. Cambridge: Cambridge University Press.

Wette, R., and G. Barkhuizen. (2009). Teaching the book and educating the person: Challenges for university English language teachers in China. *Asia Pacific Journal of Education*, 29 (2), pp. 195–212.

Xu, Y., and Y. Liu. (2009). Teacher assessment knowledge and practice: A narrative inquiry of a Chinese college EFL teacher's experience. *TESOL Quarterly*, 43 (3), pp. 493–513.

Part II Time-Space Organization

6 Narrative and Space/Time

MIKE BAYNHAM

Every story is a travel story – a spatial practice (de Certeau 1988: 115)

6.1 Introduction

As contributions to this volume demonstrate, narrative is a well-studied genre, with traditions that go back to Aristotle in rhetoric and over a century in modernist literary and folklore studies. From the early twentieth century, narrative was repeatedly thematized in literary theory (e.g., Bakhtin 1981, Genette 1980), folklore studies (for example Propp's 1968 *Morphology of the Folktale*), and semiotics (as Barthes 1977 suggests). The study of oral narrative is more recent, however, primarily because it required advances in audio recording combined with corresponding developments in linguistics that engaged with discourse. The latter only really developed in the course of the 1960s. The affordances of these technologies make it a routine possibility to record and transcribe long stretches of speech for analytic attention in ways that were simply not possible in the past. Nowadays of course, as Page's chapter in this volume demonstrates, the affordances of new digital media have the potential to further reshape the possibilities of narrative. The seminal paper on oral narrative is of course Labov and Waletzky (1967), proposing a model of narrative which was developed and refined by Labov in later publications (Labov 1972, most notably); and it is in relation to this work that much of the later research on narrative in linguistics – even that which consciously sees itself as post-Labovian – orients itself. The post-Labovian work, well represented in this volume, moves away from the canonical narrative of personal experience told in the course of an interview to examine narrative in a range of contexts including not just fully performed narratives, but also what Bamberg and Georgakopoulou (2008) term "small stories," iterative stories, hypothetical stories

The Handbook of Narrative Analysis, First Edition. Edited by Anna De Fina and Alexandra Georgakopoulou.
© 2015 John Wiley & Sons, Inc. Published 2019 by John Wiley & Sons, Inc.

(what if?), stories suggesting a family of narrative genres rather than a single genre. This insight is prefigured by Roland Barthes when he writes:

> Narrative is first and foremost a prodigious variety of genres, themselves distributed among different substances ... able to be carried by articulated language, spoken or written, fixed or moving images, gestures, and the ordered mixing of all these substances, narrative is present in myth, legend, fable, tale, novella, epic, history, tragedy, drama, comedy, mime, painting (think of Carpaccio's St Ursula), stained glass windows, cinema, comics, news items, conversation. (Barthes 1977: 79)

He captures a diversity that current narrative analysis takes for granted and which is indeed supplemented nowadays by other forms of modal proliferation in the variety of online media with their narrative affordances.

6.2   From Backdrop to Constitutive Accounts of Space/ Time Orientation in Narrative

It is tempting therefore to imagine that there is no more to be said about narrative, that it is a well-understood genre, and that there are simply no more discoveries to be made. In this chapter, I want to suggest that, while the analysis of narrative is indeed well-trodden ground, there remain unexplored, unexamined aspects of narrative as a result of particular theoretical biases that have been current and unquestioned since the time of Aristotle. This is seen for example in the continuing prevalence of *temporality* and *causality* in the definitions of narrative, which indeed dates from Aristotle's *Poetics*. Labov's influential analysis of oral narrative, for example, is essentially Aristotelean in origin, placing temporality along with action sequence squarely at the heart of narrative, with spatial orientation somewhat out of focus, part of the scene setting. Arguably, however, this is a product not just of the Aristotelean rhetorical traditions, and the later Renaissance developments of Castelvetro and others which solidified the looser maxims of Aristotle, but also of the type of data itself: the fight stories, which form the basis of his analysis, in a sense observe the unities of Aristotelean time and space just as much as Racine's *Phèdre* does. The fight stories are told more or less in the neighborhood settings in which the original fights took place. In other words they enact, among other things, a settled sense of place not unlike that which is part of the originary assumptions of sociolinguistics, as I have pointed out in Baynham (2012), where I examine the intersection of time and space in the presuppositions of sociolinguistics as a discipline. We shall see in this chapter how stories that are centrally about mobility and displacement – where mobility in space effectively is the story – problematize and require us to expand this narrative orientation. Such definitions ignore or downplay the constitutive, indeed performative, role of space and spatialization practices in narrative, limiting it to a kind of backdrop or stage-setting for the action which unfolds in time. The interaction of temporality and causality in traditional literary definitions of narrative is exemplified in E.M. Forster's well-known maxim that "The King died and then the Queen died" is not a narrative, but "The King died and then the Queen died of grief " is (Forster 1927).

Literary accounts (cf. Chatman 1978, Prince 2003) have typically set up a distinction between story time (the time of the events recounted) and discourse time (the time in which they are narrated). This approach is represented in literary accounts of narrative in the work of Genette (1980), whose treatment of temporality distinguishes categories of "order" (the order in which events occur), "duration" (how long or short the events are in their narrative portrayal, whether stretched or compressed in story time or discourse time), and frequency (how often narrative events occur, singly or iteratively). In linguistic terms, these last two categories correspond with the verbal category aspect, again demonstrating how fundamentally traditional conceptualizations of narrative are bound up with notions of time. Of course in literary narrative, acknowledged or not, space remains a central organizer whether from the perspective of story or discourse. In Proust's *À la recherche du temps perdu*, for example, an iconic treatment of time and memory is also an iconic treatment of place. Place is centrally at issue in the book, with movement in and around the familiar spaces of the narrator's childhood – organized, for example, around walks in Combray which go "du côté de chez Swann" or "du côté de chez Guermantes." Bridgeman provides an overview of contemporary treatments of time and space in narrative theory, suggesting ways in which the narrative analyst can account for the movements, stases, and aporia of narrator and actants in space and time:

> Time has always played an important role in theories of narrative, given that we tend to think of stories as sequences of events. Space has often been set in opposition to time, associated with static description which slows up and intrudes into the narration of dynamic events. However this opposition fails to recognize how far time and space are bound up with each other, as Bakhtin has shown. (Bridgeman 2007: 53)

As Bridgeman points out, the interconnectedness of time and space in both story and discourse is effectively captured by Bakhtin's notion of the chronotope, discussed and made available for the analysis of oral narrative by Perrino (see chapter 7 in this volume). The significance of space as a topic is also made clear in the work of philosophers such as Bachelard, for example in his luminous *Poetics of Space* (1994), whose potential contribution to our understanding of space and spatialization practices in oral narrative is great and currently underexploited, as Michael Murphy (2010) demonstrates in his study of the narratives of undocumented migrant women in France. Other theoretical work on space/time which can contribute to narrative analysis and is as yet undeveloped is Turner's concept of liminality:

> Liminality is a theoretical construct, developed by the sociologist Turner (1969) in his work on ritual to characterize circumstances of "in-between-ness", "neither one thing nor the other". The class is literally situated in an in-between space, in a kind of anteroom where everyone must be able to pass through freely. The liminality of the physical space is echoed in the "in-between-ness" of the asylum seekers' life situation, in a kind of in-between space before the decision to grant refugee status is decided. In this case the liminality can become a way of life … decisions can be indefinitely prolonged over as much as five years. The class seems to be characterized by an attitude of "carry on as if", despite the fact that a student's life in this country could be abruptly terminated by a decision not to allow asylum. (Baynham 2012: 123)

As can be seen, the in-between-ness of liminality can be experienced in both time and space and in a way exemplifies the interconnectedness of the two that Bakhtin's chronotope points us toward.

Arguments for the centrality of space in oral narrative have been made in Baynham and De Fina (2005) and in a series of papers published in the journal *Narrative Inquiry* (Baynham 2003; De Fina 2003; Georgakopoulou 2003), and I will draw on the arguments from these papers here, along with the commentary on them provided by Stef Slembrouck (2003).

In my contribution to this discussion, I argued that sociolinguistic studies of narrative have been characterized by "backdrop" accounts of space/time orientation, and drawing on the work of Harvey (1989), Giddens (1981), and of course de Certeau (1988), I suggested that it is necessary to move to a more constitutive and, as I would put it now, performative account of space/time relations in narrative. As I have discussed in relation to the idea of a performative sociolinguistics which rethinks/reworks the relationship between language and context:

> If the focus of correlational sociolinguistics is on the establishment of links between linguistic items (sounds or words), typically taken atomistically, one by one, and social phenomena, the shift in performative sociolinguistics is to a relationship between the linguistic and the social which is dynamically enacted or performative, in the sense that Butler (1990) has made current. It involves a focus on holistic analysis of interactions, texts, events and practices. ... The narrative construction of the fieldworker's move into the field, the crossing of a threshold into someone else's space, the strange that becomes familiar, destabilizes cartographic certainties. It is this step that Labov's fieldworkers are taking willy nilly, even if recuperated into the positivist frame by means of the Observer's Paradox. So, in this third moment, sociolinguistic space becomes an environment that is inhabited, made over through identity work. It is, for example, an "ordinary" corner of Philadelphia as the fieldworkers take hold of and make it over, thus transforming it through their research activity into a consciously theorized sociolinguistic space. (Baynham 2012: 119–120)

The narrative of sociolinguistic fieldwork, making over and appropriating space in time, exemplifies the connection between space/time, performativity, narrative action, and identity work.

This intricate, constitutive/performative relationship between space/time orientation and narrative action is well expressed by Giddens: "We can only grasp time and space in terms of the relations of things and events: they *are* the modes in which relations between objects and events are expressed" (1981: 31).

Additionally, as Harvey and cultural geography more generally show us, space/time orientation, though often treated as a neutral, taken-for-granted reality, is in truth anything but that: "Spatial and temporal practices are never neutral in social affairs. They always express some kind of class or other social content and are more often than not the focus of intense social struggle" (Harvey 1989: 239). So as the cultural geographer Blunt puts it, space has reentered our thinking on the social world in a way that can no longer be ignored or downplayed:

> More than ever before, scholars working in other disciplines in the humanities are thinking and writing in explicitly spatial terms, most notably in terms of multiple geographies and

the multiple and contested spaces of identity, which are often articulated through spatial images such as mobility, location, borderlands, exile and home. (Blunt 2003: 75–76)

Based on such arguments, I proposed a move in narrative analysis from backdrop to constitutive accounts of space/time orientation in narrative, suggesting the key research questions about narrative orientation do not ask:

- How are narratives oriented in space and time?

but rather:

- How are spaces and times, understood as semiotic resources, involved in the construction of narrative?
- How can space/time orientation be understood as constitutive of narrative action?
- What does space/time orientation contribute to the identity work involved in narrative?

In a sense, the project is to realize the programmatic statement of de Certeau (1988) that every story is a travel story, a spatial practice. Nowhere is this more obvious than in migration stories, where displacement and mobility in time/space *constitute* the narrative action.

This theme was developed in an edited collection by Anna De Fina and myself (Baynham and De Fina 2005) entitled *Dislocations/Relocations: Narratives of Displacement*. The papers collected in that volume all took narratives of mobility and displacement as their theme, whether they are the narratives of Zinacantec migrants in Oregon (Haviland 2005), asylum seekers in Belgium (Maryns 2005), or West Germans moving East after the reunification of Germany (Liebscher and Dailey-O'Cain 2005). Nor does dislocation and displacement have to take place across international borders. The oral histories analyzed by McCormick (2005) document poignantly the internal displacement caused by the racially driven resettlement policies of the apartheid system in South Africa. So is space/time only thematized in narratives of mobility and displacement? The answer, of course, is no, as is demonstrated in Georgakopoulou's (2007) work on the narratives of a group of young female friends in a small-town community in Arcadia, southern Greece. As de Certeau says, every story is a spatial practice.

6.3   Narratives of Border Crossing

De Fina (2003) examines narratives of border crossing told by undocumented Mexican immigrants to the United States, the so called *mojarras* or wetbacks. In these narratives, temporal and spatial disorientation is central to the unfolding of the narrative plot. Far from being a static backdrop to the action, De Fina shows how "orientation in the story world is often treated as a central point of concern in the interactional world," with narrators producing orientation devices that are vague and problematic and thus drawing on their interlocutors for help, and interlocutors correspondingly becoming engaged in the clarification of orientation details. Through these negotiations, align-ments are built between interactants, revealing shared and unshared aspects of experi-ence. De Fina also suggests that the types of orientation elements and devices used can be related to the degree of control the narrators experience over their lives. Putting your life in the hands of a "coyote" who will take you over the border is indeed a giving up of control. These stories are fundamentally about the temporal/spatial dis-orientation of displacement across the border; thus an unproblematic sense of when and where becomes a topic for narrative co-construction (De Fina 2005: 372). De Fina also shows how orientations in space/time accumulate through repetition and become sedimented over time as a form of habitus – common ways of talking about space/time that become part of speakers' common language:

> This is clearly the case with talk about the border, a highly symbolic space in the retelling of immigration experience for Mexicans. The border is always represented as an imaginary line which exists in order to be crossed.(De Fina 2003: 380)

This joint construction of orientation against a background of shared understandings sedimented over years and innumerable crossings is exemplified in the following data extract between L (Leo), A (the researcher), and I (research assistant):

(01) L: y en eso llegamos al primer pueblito que se lla:ma (.)

(02)   es adonde llega (.) lo lo como se llama Rosv- Rosvi-

(03) A: Qué es eso California?

(04) L: No.

(05) I: No es Tejas=

(06) L: =Es Tejas, el valle de Tejas.

(07) A: Uh.

(08) L: Es un pueblo adelante de Donald.

(09) A: Uhu.

(10) L: Llegamos a ese pueblillo

(11)   y luego pus íbamos a entrar al pueblillo

(12)   en eso nos vio un hispano

(13)   dice "ustedes son mojarras verdad?"

Translation

(01) L: and then we arrived in the first small village which is called (.)

(02)   it's where it comes (.) the the what is it called Rosv- Rosvi-

(03) A: What is that California?

(04) L: No.

(05) I: No it's Texas=

(06) L: =It's Texas, the valley of Texas.

(07) A: Uh.

(08) L: It is a village after Donald.

(09) A: Uhu.

(10) L: We arrived in this village

(11) and then we were going to enter this village

(12) and at that moment a Hispanic came

(13) he says "you are wetbacks right?"

(De Fina 2003: 386)

This extract illustrates the joint negotiation of orientation between participants, as the vagueness of the narrator's orientation translates into an appeal for help. In the following extract from De Fina's data, we see how the sedimentation of shared understanding can be drawn on interactionally:

(01) L: Si así fue y de allí estuvimos en Reynosa

(02) y allí fue donde le brincamos para acá.

(03) A: Uhu.

(04) L: Por la, por el monte.

(05) A: No por el río?

(06) No hay río allá? Es que –

(07) L: Si hay río,

(08) A: Es que yo la geografía no me la sé muy bien.

(09) L: Si hay río

(10) pero este nosotros pasamos por una compuerta,

Translation

(01) L: Yes it was like that and from there we went to Reynosa

(02) and there was where we jumped here.

(03) A: Uhu.

(04) L: Through the, through the mountain.

(05) A: Not through the river?

(06) There is no river there? It's that –

(07) L: Yes there is a river,

(08) A: It's that I don't know geography very well.

(09) L: Yes there is a river.

(10) but we came through a gate.

(De Fina 2003: 376–377)

As De Fina points out, Leo's description of crossing through the mountains runs contrary to her expectation of a river crossing, thus triggering the negotiation of meaning in lines 05–09. The prototypical crossing is across the Rio Grande, hence the term *mojarras* or wetbacks, not through the mountains. The interviewer, A, downplays her intervention (line 08) by suggesting she is not strong in geography. Orientation here is intimately caught up in the storyline, but also in the interactional relationships between the interlocutors. This is very different in texture from the orientation as backdrop to the action. De Fina's analysis points up the interactional achievement of orientation and the imbrications of space/time orientation in the event structure of the crossing stories. There is a sedimentation of shared knowledge and repeatedly used terms such as *brincar*, "to jump" to characterize the process of crossing. Disorientation as a narrative motif highlights the venturing into unknown territory, putting oneself in the hands of others:

Sergio

(01) ahí nos quedamos en una traila un día no tres dias ahí,

(02) en una traila donde le digo que el coyote nos dejó (unclear)

(03) y sin dinero y sin nada,

(04) todo ahi (pelándonos) de hambre no?

(05) hasta que luego llegó el coyote como a las cinco de la mañana cuatro por ahí

(06) y nos dio a otros,

(07) nos dio con otros coyotes para que nos fuéramos a dormir en- allí donde nos dejaron.

Translation
Sergio

(01) there we stayed in a trailer one day no three days there,

(02) in a trailer where I tell you that the coyote left us (unclear)

(03) and without money and without anything,

(04) all there (dying) of hunger right?

(05) until the coyote came like at five in the morning four about then

(06) and gave us to other,

(07) gave us to other coyotes so that we went to sleep in- there where they left us.

(De Fina 2003: 378)

As De Fina (2003: 379–380) explains: "Narrators as real life characters were brought into the country by 'coyotes', left for days without information on where they were going, sometimes abandoned by the smugglers who fled in order to avoid being caught, transported by unknown people to different, mysterious, locations." She notes a pervasive vagueness of orientation combined with linguistic indicators of lack of agency and loss of control in which "they" do things to "us":

- Nos rebotaron (they rejected us)
- Nos dejaron (they left us)
- Nos metieron (they put us)
- Llegaron por nosotros y ya nos llevaron (they came for us and took us)

In discussing the symbolic construction of the border as a line that can be jumped, De Fina points out how this

> becomes another important positioning device, since narrators choose to construct their place in the story world relative to their current position as speakers, or to their position at the time of the crossing. Thus the description of either side as *here* or *there* shifts according to the narrators' presentation of self, which can either be identical to the story world character, or be looking at the story world character from the here and now. (2003: 380–381)

De Fina's analysis gives us a sense of the narrator's orientation strategies, which are apt to accomplish more than one purpose simultaneously, on one hand positioning interlocutors in relation to each other while on the other hand evoking people and events dynamically in place and time.

6.4   Deictic Transposition in Migration Narratives

Fine-grained strategic deployment of such deictic categories as "here" and "there" in narrative is a focus for Haviland's 2005 paper. Here again Haviland's research subjects, Zinacantecs in Oregon, are people who have crossed and recrossed borders over many years. Using the concept of deictic transposition (Haviland 1996), Haviland documents how his subjects use indexical shifts in Zinacantec Tzotzil between here/there depending on location (in the home village or el Norte) in order to produce subtle expressive and interpersonal effects, positioning the narrator in relation to his interlocutors who may be present with him in Oregon or at the other end of a telephone back in the home village in Chiapas, Mexico. In the following discussion, Haviland illustrates the deictic affordances offered by long-distance telephone conversation:

> It appears that in Zinacantec Tzotzil, in recent years when long distance communication – for example by letter or telephone – has produced situations in which the deictic centres of speakers and hearers are geographically separated, one convention has developed in which a directional element attached to a verb of speaking reflects the *recipient's* perspective. Although the speaker , located in Chiapas in the following extract, refers with the deictic *li'* "here" to his own location, the directional "tal" attached to the verbs of speakers represents a perspective in which the words will be "coming" in the direction of the recipients, in this case in Oregon. (2005: 108)

Haviland then illustrates this with a transcript example of "I send you a greeting":

(04) li'on ta jobel
       Here I am in San Cristobal

(06) li' ta sna li. Jch'uk tot jorje
       Here I am in the house of my godfather George

(09) k'elavil. xun
       Look, Juan –

(10) li' chakalbee
       Here I am telling you

(11) chajtakbe tal jun chabanuk
       I send you (coming) a greeting

So the speaker's strategy is to switch between the deictic coordinates of the place (San Cristobal) where he is speaking from (i.e., lines 4, 6, 10) and take the deictic coordinates in Oregon of the recipient (line 11). Haviland later shows how one of his subjects, Mamal, after a decade in the United States, expresses his ambivalence about his location – and hence his relationship with his interlocutors – through deictic switching:

"I would be here [in the village] were it not for ..."

(82) tik'u cha 'al kalojbeik- lakalbeik komel ava'iik
      As I told you (when I left there)

(83) ti k'alal ti litale
      When I came

(84) ta ox tzk'an chisut tal lavi jabile
      I had wanted to return here again during this year

(85) ti manchuk li x'elan k'usi jpase
      If it were not for what happened to me [a back injury at work]

(86) i: ti manchuk i x'elan ijpase
      And if it weren't for what happened to me

(87) lital ox yech
      I would have come as planned

(88) lital ox ta . jtob xchi'uk vaxakib li. Li novyembre
      I was going to come on the 28th of November

(89) li'on xa yechuke
      I should be here now

(Haviland 2005: 124–125)

In lines 82 and 83 Mamal's utterances orient to the deictic coordinates of his current location (Oregon), but from line 84 onward, the orientation is to the deictic coordinates of his interlocutors in Chiapas. This switch indexically signals a sense of being together in the same space, saying something about the interpersonal relations of closeness that he is trying to evoke despite distances in time and space and presumably also in human closeness.

6.5   Migration from West to East in Post-Unification Germany

Looking below the surface of spatial deixis is productive for understanding the constitutive nature of spatialization practices in narrative, as we see in Liebscher and Dailey-O'Cain's work on narratives of West German migrants to former East Germany. Liebscher and Dailey-O'Cain quote a narrative recounted in the summer of 2000 by Walter, who had migrated to East Germany in 1994 after receiving a job offer. He has an East German partner. Here he talks about the process of getting a telephone:

"Getting a telephone"

(01) W: das war schon ne (.) tolle wohnung
            that was a really (.) great apartment

(02)   aber (...) was ja wirklich kurios war (.) als ich damals hinkam
            But (...) what was really strange was (.) when I arrived back then

(03)   (.) august (..) vierenneunzig? (..) da fragt ich so den (.)
          (.) august (..) ninety-four? (..) I asked the (.)
(Liebscher and Dailey O'Cain 2005: 65)

The analysis turns on the narrator's choice of time/space orientation, *damals* ("back then") and *hinkam* ("arrived"). *Damals* indexes the historicity of the narrative (back then) while *hinkam* is a combination of the directional adverb *hin*, meaning "toward" and the motion verb *kommen*, "to come." In using *kommen*, the researchers point out,

> the speaker positions himself at the place of arrival in East Germany, looking back to the point of departure. Using the adverb "hin", however, the speaker indexes the opposite direction and positions himself at the place of departure in western Germany, looking towards the place of arrival. … The combination of "hin"and "kommen" is pragmatically awkward, since the speaker cannot be in both places at the same time. Since place of arrival and place of departure for the speaker are in former eastern and western Germany respectively, the combination indexes his migrant identity as "in-between." (Liebscher and Dailey O'Cain 2005: 67)

In our discussion of the data from De Fina, Haviland, and Liebscher and Dailey O'Cain, we have seen how space/time orientation is part of the repertoire of the narrator to be strategically deployed in order to signal complex and subtle social meanings. Drawing on the work of scholars such as Dubois (2007) and Jaffe (2009), these can also be understood in terms of stance, positioning and alignment, all theoretical constructs which themselves have a spatial dimension. By his deictic choices, Mamal is positioning himself in relation to those he has left behind in his home village, aligning himself with them in evoking the common here and now of the village. By his choice of adverbs and verb of motion, Walter positions himself as in-between, leaving from there and arriving here. Once again in these narratives of border crossing we see that space/time orientation, far from being a background, is in fact what constitutes the story. But perhaps those stories that are spatial practices are simply those whose plot-lines involve mobility and the crossing of borders? I will explore the question of space/time orientation further through a consideration of the research of Georgakopoulou (2003), who investigated the narrative practices of a female affinity group in Arcadia, Southern Greece.

6.6   Socio-symbolic Meanings of Space/Time in Narrative

This is how Georgakopoulou characterizes the setting for her research and the space/time relations involved:

> … the participants live in a small provincial town which has historically been a "closed community": situated in a mountainous area and with no easy access to beaches, this is by no means a tourist destination. Similarly its residents are by and large people who were born and brought up there. The participants have spent all their lives in the town in question.

Over the period of their regular socializing, space (in its interactions with time, as will be argued) has become an integral part of their interactional history and memory, filled with shared socio-symbolic meanings. (2003: 416–417)

Georgakopoulou then goes on to describe how these socio-symbolic spatial meanings are called upon in the joint construction of stories among members of the friendship group. The focus on interactional history and memory is a significant dimension here, made possible by the ethnographic study of the friendship group over time. In this fixed, apparently rather sedentary context, we see in process the accumulation and sedimentation of shared meanings that De Fina pointed out in relation to the border. As I have suggested, this process has parallels with Bourdieu's idea of the formation of habitus. Even within the confines of small-town social life, there is no lack of movement, mobility, and differentiation to be encountered, as Georgakopoulou demonstrates:

Within the town's topography, the most important places for participants are those that are centered around socializing: cafeterias, bars, pubs, and other such, so called "hang outs"(*stekia*), which almost unexceptionally attract people at the age group of 15–30, with a concentration of 18–24 year olds. (2003: 417)

Unsurprisingly, the narratives of the friendship group index the space/time coordinates of their favorite hangouts, drawing on shared socio-symbolic meanings to orient their narratives. Georgakopoulou strongly emphasizes the interaction between space and time in narrative orientation in the analysis of a narrative informed by the socio-symbolic affordances of two hang-outs; Roma, a safe outdoor cafe visible from the street and active in the early evening; and Kallisto, a late-night drinking spot with an apparently wilder reputation:

Place affordances invoke in subtle and implicit ways time affordances too. Roma is an early evening hang-out, while Kallisto is a night hang-out. As a result and on the basis of what transpired in the group's ethnographic interviews, it is more permissible and acceptable for a young woman to chat to somebody who hangs-out in the former than to approach people hanging-out, or worse, working, as is the case of the man in question, in the latter. (2003: 422)

This shared socio-symbolic knowledge is drawn upon in the group's narratives. Here, members Tonia and Vivi are discussing potential encounters with Dan, a possible man for Vivi:

T: No Vivi let me tell you something
      listen (.) Nick was sitting at Roma all alone all alone
      hheh an' **he** was having his orangina all alone all alone
      but Dan works in Kallisto
      and he is not all alone all alone
      and he drinks alcohol
      so you ca:n't go and talk to him like that (.) can you?
V: Only when he's not too busy (..) like late at night

                                        (Georgakopoulou 2003: 428)

When Tonia presents the contrasting scenarios of a docile Orangina at Roma in early evening or a wild reputation-risking encounter late at night at the bar called Kallisto, she is drawing on shared socio-symbolic knowledge which is crucial not just to the stage-setting of the action, but to the action itself; and the implication of potential harm to Vivi's reputation is consequential to the group's ongoing identity work around gender. In her monograph on the data, Georgakopoulou persuasively demonstrates how these heterosexual teenage girls are doing identity work around gender issues, constructing their identities through telling and retelling key episodes in their shared history, sketching out hypothetical narratives. What is significant here is how the analysis brings in time and history, showing how both interact with space in the shaping of these narratives.

This is not to suggest that time and history are absent from the other narrative data we have so far examined. Far from it. Walter, after all, like the other subjects in the study, is moving east after the reunification of Germany, and the specification of dates in the narrative excerpt we examined (*vierenneunzig* "ninety-four") is highly significant. The *mojarras* bumping toward the border in someone's trailer are caught up in a historical process of significant proportions, as indeed are the Zinacantecs in Haviland's study. The emphasis in the early part of this chapter has been on space and spatialization practices in narrative, but I have also consistently talked about space/time throughout in order to emphasize the interaction of both. The virtue of Georgakopoulou's study is that it affords a temporal/historical perspective on a small scale: We can see the accumulation of shared experience in a friendship group and the way it is drawn on and reinterpreted in new situations.

6.7   Scale and Space/Time Orientation in Narrative

Another factor worth bearing in mind about the analysis so far is that the construction of space has been relatively intimate and small-scale, even in the contexts of dislocation and border crossing. When Mamal phones home he is connecting his Oregon lifeworld with that of his Chiapas lifeworld. The teenage girls in Georgakopoulou's study seem primarily concerned with the immediate, face-to-face aspects of their environment. However, work on the sociolinguistics of scale tells us that it is not just the intimate face-to-face characteristics of interaction that are implicated in the construction of the social world, but larger-scale formations which influence and shape interactions, while in turn interactions enact and perpetuate large-scale phenomena. The notion of scale is after all a spatial one, though we will persist in thinking about these issues in terms of space/time to emphasize the impossibility of unpicking the two. So in the next section of this chapter, I will ask what scale relations can contribute to our understanding of spatialization practices in narrative.

An issue that has recently been of concern to sociolinguistics (cf., e.g., Blommaert, Collins, and Slembrouck 2005; Collins, Slembrouck, and Baynham 2009) has been how to make a connection between large social processes and the micro focus on interaction in social life. Analysts wish to take account of the fact that, while interaction is contingent and locally produced, it is influenced and shaped by these large social processes.

The case for what is in effect a retheorizing of sociolinguistic space, turning from the interactional and the local to incorporate wider social formations including the global, is made in a number of papers by Blommaert, Slembrouck, Collins, and others:

> Based on urban neighbourhood ethnography, Blommaert, Collins & Slembrouck (2005) embarked on a theoretical exercise aimed at creating a more profiled place for socio-spatial features in sociolinguistic analysis. We argued that space is an agentive force in sociolinguistic processes, notably in the assessment of competences, and we also argued that human social environments needed to be seen as polycentric and stratified, where people continuously need to observe "norms" – orders of indexicality – that are attached to a multitude of centres of authority, local as well as translocal, momentary as well as lasting. (Blommaert 2006: 3)

The notion of scale (local, regional, national, transnational, global), derived from geography, has been enlisted to engage with the layered and hierarchical way that the local and translocal shapes and influences interaction: "Spatial and temporal scales … offer a connection between macro-conditions and micro-processes" (Blommaert et al. 2005). Here we see the emphasis on the socio-spatial that we have already noted in the work of De Fina, Haviland, and Liebscher and Dailey O'Cain, but combined with the temporal as argued above. To reiterate, both the *mojarras* bumping their way to the border and the Zinacantecs in Oregon are implicated in large-scale transnational and global processes and economic imbalances, which create labor needs and migration flows with their push and pull factors. The Rio Grande is not just a river; it is also a border, invoking scales that are at once national, transnational, and, in terms of the migration patterns, regional. Walter's narrative of getting a telephone in the former East Germany indexes that country's history both pre- and post-unification:

W: ja aber (..) die (.)   [infrastructure
     Yeah but (..) the (.)   *[infrastructure*
JD: [da sah nichts mehr so viel nach DDR
                                 [nothing really looked like East Germany
     aus (..) vierrundneun   [zig
     anymore either (..) ninety *[four*
W: [na jaaa (.) aber die soziale
                                 [I don't know (.) but the social
     infrastruktur mitten in der city da gabs ja nur ganz wenige
     infrastructure downtown there were only a few
     kneipen wo man hingehen konnte (.)
     bars you could go to

                         (Liebscher and Dailey O'Cain 2005: 73)

So here an argument emerges between Walter and the interviewer about how much the eastern Germany of 1994 still resembled the former German Democratic Republic (DDR). Walter is assuming a greater continuity than the interviewer, who challenges him. I am reminded of Harvey's remark quoted above that spatial and temporal practices are never neutral in human affairs and more often than not involve some kind of struggle. This is an example of how a feature of scale can operate in spatial and temporal dimensions on levels that are national as well as transnational: the back story is of two historically divided countries with a heavily policed border becoming one. So one way to take on the issue of scale in narrative analysis is to expand and become sensitive to the notion of what counts as spatio-temporal orientation, to recognize the regimes and orders of indexicality that are being brought into play both to construct and to draw on shared knowledge of the sort that I have described above. We also need to bear in mind Harvey's advice as a methodological preliminary: these spatio-temporal practices are almost always sites of struggle. We must remain sensitive to this in our analysis.

Writing of ways of linking the micro-social to the macro-social, Blommaert describes:

> the jump from one scale to another: from the individual to the collective, the temporally situated to the trans-temporal, the unique to the common, the token to the type, the specific to the general. And the connection between such scales is indexical: it resides in the ways in which unique instances of communication can be captured, indexically, as "framed", understandable communication, as pointing towards socially and culturally ordered norms, genres, traditions, expectations – phenomena of a higher scale-level. The capacity to achieve understanding in communication is the capacity to lift momentary instances of interaction to the level of common meanings, and the two directions of indexicality (presupposing – the retrieval of available meanings – and entailing – the production of new meanings; Silverstein 2006: 14) are at the heart of such processes. (2006: 4)

In this sense, the identity work that Georgakopoulou finds her young female subjects engaged in – which we have seen turns frequently on the right and wrong place and time for something – is a work of producing the gendered self, indexing widely shared social norms about the right/wrong ways for girls to behave.

6.8 Scale and Indexicality in Narratives of Migration

In Baynham (2009), I asked what scale theory can bring to narrative analysis, using examples from my research on narratives told by Moroccan migrants to the United Kingdom in the 1960s and 1970s. Here Mr R Talks about his arrival in London and first experiences in the West End restaurant world:

Mr R/ then he drop me in Green Park is another company same company name Hatches

I/ yeah

Mr R/ club night e was open from seven till four o'clock a disco well I find that place first then the Spanish bloke I remember he come in with the car I f- he's English then he talk to me in Spanish then I feel very happy

I/ yeah

Mr R/ cos you know I find somebody that speak my language then he drive me with the car in the restaurant then I don't like it I feel very horrible is a bloke from Lebanon he speak to me in Arabic ah habibi tfaddal qsa qahwa and he give me that coffee s very different taste of the Moroccan

(Baynham 2009: 141)

This excerpt is interesting in terms of the sociolinguistic space which it indexes, drawing not only on English, but also Spanish and varieties of Arabic (Moroccan, Lebanese). In fact the native language for Mr R is not Lebanese Arabic, but rather Spanish, a legacy of the colonial period during which Larache, Mr R's hometown, was under Spanish control. "My language" in this context is the language of colonialism rather than another variety of Arabic, which he imitated disparagingly, suggesting perhaps that it is as unhomely as the Lebanese coffee. The interpretative frame for this narrative involves a sense of the twentieth-century history of Morocco and its linguistic legacy as well as the dialect continuum of Arabic.

In the next extract, ML recounts an argument with his father, who doesn't want him to migrate to Europe, arguing that such a move would take him out of the Muslim world and into the non-Muslim world, which might turn him into a *kaffar*, "unbeliever." Again what is indexically presupposed in this extract is the scalar division of the world on religious grounds into Muslim and non-Muslim.

I/   so what did he say when you left

ML/   well I left and he say I going to England or going to France I no want to still here that what I thinking

I/   yeah and what did your father think about

ML/   he say you no muslim

I/   yeah

ML/   you go any place is no muslim yes he said to me you no muslim

I/   yeah

ML/   you maybe kaffar (= unbeliever)

(Baynham 2009: 142)

In the following extract M.B. is describing how his coming to independence as a young man capable of earning his own living coincided with Morocco's independence in 1957. The narrative indexically invokes the end of colonialism, the king of Morocco's recognition by world powers, and the beginning of national independence. The parallel created between his own independence as a young man and that of Morocco as a country shows another way in which a phenomenon of scale can be brought in as it were as a rhetorical trope, creating a metaphorical linkage between his own independence and that of his country.

M.B./   so yeah when they left that time they left er I remember nineteen fifty s-seven they was the last time when I we saw the Spanish government ruling our country and er when they left Mohammed the Fifth he you know he was the king at that time well recognized official by the world wide he was a king and the country was ruled and that our kingdom

I/   yeah

M.B./   so by that time when we took independence I was already working

(Baynham 2009: 143)

Finally, this example from an account by Mrs T of how she first arrived in England creates what I have called a zero degree of scale. In contrast with Mr R, who uses dates and historical events to anchor his narrative and indeed weaves them into his own story, Mrs T resists the calendar, collapsing story time with discourse time and time with space, orienting the day recounted in her narrative with this day on which she is recounting it: it was any old day, just like today. This collapsing of time and space is a powerful story telling device for making the past present, but viewed from a perspective of scale, it is an interesting refusal to engage with the large scale and to orient within the human life world.

Mrs T/   when me come back here I can't speak English very well because I'm I speak Spanish last day
       is finished the eh contrato **just one day like today** when me come here in the airport

(Baynham 2009: 144)

6.9   Space/Time in Language Classrooms

I will conclude these arguments about the constitutive role of spatial and temporal practices in narrative by looking at some data from a small, relatively settled world – that of the language classroom. The data are drawn from a dataset of 40 interviews conducted with ESOL teachers, collected as part of a larger study into adult ESOL classrooms in the United Kingdom (Baynham et al. 2006). The primary focus of the interviews was not on eliciting narrative, but nevertheless there was a pervasive deployment of narrative, at least in Georgakopoulou and Bamberg's "small narrative" sense (Bamberg and Georgakopoulou 2008; see also Georgakopoulou, this volume, chapter 13), as the interviewees responded to the invitation to display their professional practices to the interviewer. The interviewers involved in the study were either practicing ESOL teachers or researchers who had been ESOL teachers at earlier stages in their careers. How, then, do these arguments about space/time play out in such contexts? Here, L, the teacher, is talking to J, the researcher:

L: mm the problem for them is it's a community class because it's like an introduction to studying. And normally when students (.) they start often in the community and when they're starting to feel confident and start attending regularly they start begging to come to the college.

J: mm

L: then they feel that's real study. So they don't really approach this as real study because they don't see themselves in an educational institution.

(Baynham 2011: 66)

Spatial segregation is immediately apparent as a theme in this narrative. The distinction is made between the community class, which is held in a community setting (e.g., in a health center, a library, a community center, often with a crèche) to provide for students with commitments that make mainstream graded progress difficult;

and the college, which offers courses with graded progression toward vocational and academic courses and work. (For a fuller discussion of the spatial dimensions of such classes, including in terms of liminality, see Baynham and Simpson 2010.) So to make sense of the framing of this narrative, it is important to understand the relationship between the community class and the college course as one of periphery to center. Somehow for the students, the community class doesn't feel like "real study," perhaps because it isn't so insulated from everyday life. So the point of this narrative extract turns on space (central/peripheral) and, crucially, how it is perceived by participants.

L: But you know but today considering how little support they had in terms of human support they'd learnt a lot of study skills to refer to bits of paper and write. So you know

M: yeah they were all doing that.

L: yeah and I actually- And they were helping each other. And I mean really really technically they needed more help but I was actually surprised at how they were helping each other. And at one point for example Maurier got up from my group and asked if she could go and get Hal from the other group to help her. And that's that's that's really- And at one point I thought Oh God Kumar and Singha were sitting there doing nothing. When I went over there they seemed to be actually conferring they weren't doing nothing. So they've learnt a lot in all sorts of ways. How to use their resources. The resources that I've given them to lean on. I think they've learnt a lot.

(Baynham 2011: 67)

This data extract takes us inside the classroom. It is interesting to unpack what the extract is telling us about spatial practices in the classroom and the corresponding roles of participants, teacher, and students. The students, it seems, are in groups ("Maurier got up from my group and asked if she could get Hal from the other group to help her"). They are engaged in some activity that doesn't directly involve the teacher. What is the teacher doing? She is circulating, monitoring what is going on ("And at one point I thought Oh God Kumar and Singha were sitting there doing nothing"); she goes over to discover that "they seemed to be actually conferring they weren't doing nothing." So this is a class based on activities which students undertake in groups. After setting up the activity, the teacher circulates as a resource and monitor, worrying whether the interactional freedom afforded by the current format will leave students idle. So this small excerpt of classroom narrative has given us plenty of movement in space and, in its own way, plenty of action and drama.

But what about issues of scale? When I use such narratives or extracts of classroom interaction for discussion with TESOL Masters students, I often ask them to articulate what ideas about teaching and learning are being performed here. I don't have space in the current chapter to discuss this in detail, but suffice it to say that these ideas might include the notion that students learn effectively through doing activities rather than listening to a teacher speak, and that at times a teacher can be usefully employed in supporting and monitoring learning as well as in imparting knowledge. What are being indexed here are deeply held ideological positions about learning and teaching which have implications for the spatio-temporal organizations of classrooms and which are in themselves controversial. Indeed, they are a potential focus for the intense social struggle that Harvey talks of; for example, as in the United Kingdom at present, a government or political interest group may argue that progressive methods are failing children, and the conflict between the ideological positions of "progressive" teachers and a government committed to a "back to basics" agenda becomes heightened. Such ideological conflicts are indexed in narrative, and scale as a theoretical construct provides us with a sensitive tool to register what is indexed in a given context.

6.10   Conclusion

In this chapter I have argued for a constitutive, indeed performative role for space/time orientation in narrative, showing that it is not enough to think of space/time orientation as a backdrop for the action, but rather that it frequently – perhaps always – *is* the action. Lurking behind these ideas are Aristotelean notions of narrative action and setting that have over centuries uncritically informed our ideas. It is relatively easy to demonstrate how a backdrop account of orientation is inadequate to account for the role of space/time orientation in narrative. Bakhtin's notion of the chronotope points us to a more performative notion of the role of time/space in narrative, which can be seen in effect as displacing the Aristotelean backdrop account. From a performative perspective, orientation in time and space is the action, and this action in narrative is characteristically doing identity work. I have also tried to show that this is true not just in narratives of mobility and dislocation, but also in the narratives told in relation to relatively settled and stable contexts such as Georgakopoulou's Arcadian town and the ESOL classroom. Social theorists such as de Certeau and Giddens can enrich our understanding of the dynamics of space/time, as can concepts like Turner's liminality and the rich and provocative work of Bachelard, an underused resource. Complementing this reorientation, I have also shown how conceptualizing space/time in sociolinguistics through scale theory can enrich our understanding of the space/time orientation in narrative, taking it beyond the here and now of the moment of telling to encompass an awareness of how subtly or crudely large-scale social formations inform and shape the stories we tell each other.

REFERENCES

Bachelard, G. (1994). *The Poetics of Space*. Boston, MA: Beacon Press.

Bakhtin, M. (1981). *The Dialogic Imagination: Four Essays*. Edited by M. Holquist. Translated by C. Emerson and M. Holquist. Austin: University of Texas Press.

Bamberg, M., and A. Georgakopoulou. (2008). Small stories as a new perspective in narrative and identity analysis. *Text & Talk*, 28 (3), pp. 377–396.

Barthes, R. (1977). *Image – Music – Text*. Translated by Stephen Heath. London: Fontana.

Baynham, M. (2003). Narrative in space and time: Beyond "backdrop" accounts of narrative orientation. *Narrative Inquiry*, 13 (2), pp. 347–366.

Baynham, M. (2009). "Just one day like today": Scale and the analysis of space/ time orientation in narratives of displacement. In J. Collins, S. Slembrouck, and M. Baynham (eds.), *Globalization and Language in Contact: Scale, Migration and Communicative Practices*. London: Continuum, pp. 130–147.

Baynham, M. (2011). Stance, positioning, and alignment in narratives of professional experience. *Language in Society*, 40, 63–74.

Baynham, M. (2012). Cultural geography and the re-theorization of sociolinguistic space. In S. Gardner and M. Martin-Jones (eds.), *Multilingualism, Discourse and Ethnography*. New York: Routledge, pp. 114–130.

Baynham, M., and A. De Fina (eds.). (2005). *Dislocations/Relocations: Narratives of Displacement*. Manchester: St Jerome Publishing.

Baynham, M., and J. Simpson. (2010). Onwards and upwards: Space, placement, and liminality in adult ESOL classes. *TESOL Quarterly*, 44 (3), pp. 420–440.

Baynham, M., C. Roberts, M. Cooke, J. Simpson, et al. (2006). *Effective Teaching and Learning in ESOL*. London: NRDC.

Blommaert, J. (2006). *Discourse*. Cambridge: Cambridge University Press.

Blommaert, J., J. Collins, and S. Slembrouck. (2005). Spaces of multilingualism. *Language and Communication*, 24, pp. 197–216.

Blunt, A. (2003). Geography and the humanities tradition. In S. Holloway, S.P. Rice, and G. Valentine (eds.), *Key Concepts in Geography*. London: Sage, pp. 73–91.

Bridgeman, T. (2007). Time and space. In D. Herman (ed.), *The Cambridge Companion to Narrative*. Cambridge: Cambridge University Press, pp. 52–65.

Butler, J. (1990). *Gender Trouble: Feminism and the Subversion of Identity*. New York: Routledge.

Chatman, S. (1978). *Story and Discourse*. Ithaca, NY: Cornell University Press.

Collins, J., S. Slembrouck, and M. Baynham (eds.). (2009). *Globalization and Language in Contact*. London: Continuum.

de Certeau, M. (1988). *The Practice of Everyday Life*. Berkeley: University of California Press.

De Fina, A. (2003). Crossing borders: Time, space, and disorientation in narrative. *Narrative Inquiry*, 13 (2), pp. 367–391.

Dubois, J. (2007). The stance triangle. In R. Engelbretson (ed.), *Stancetaking in Discourse: Subjectivity, Evaluation, Interaction*. Amsterdam: John Benjamins, pp. 139–182.

Forster, E.M. (1927). *Aspects of the Novel*. London: Edward Arnold.

Genette, G. (1980). *Narrative Discourse*. Oxford: Blackwell.

Georgakopoulou, A. (2003). Plotting the "right place" and the "right time": Place and time as an interactional resource in narrative. *Narrative Inquiry*, 13 (2), pp. 413–432.

Georgakopoulou, A. (2007). *Small Stories, Interaction and Identities*. Amsterdam: John Benjamins.

Giddens, A. (1981). *A Contemporary Critique of Historical Materialism, Vol. 1: Power, Property and the State*. London: Macmillan.

Harvey, D. (1989). *The Condition of Postmodernity: An Inquiry into the Origins of Cultural Change*. Oxford: Blackwell.

Haviland, J. (1996). Projections, transpositions and relativity. In J. Gumperz and S. Levinson (eds.), *Re-thinking Linguistic Relativity*. Cambridge: Cambridge University Press, pp. 271–323.

Haviland, J. (2005). Dreams of blood: Zinacantecs in Oregon. In M. Baynham and A. De Fina (eds.), *Dislocations/Relocations: Narratives of Displacement*. Manchester: St Jerome Publishing, pp. 91–127.

Jaffe, A. (2009). *Stance: Sociolinguistic Perspectives*. Oxford: Oxford University Press.

Labov, W. (1972). *Language in the Inner City: Studies in the Black English Vernacular*. Oxford: Blackwell.

Labov, W., and J. Waletzky. (1967). Narrative Analysis. In J. Helm (ed.), *Essays on the Verbal and Visual Arts*. Seattle: University of Washington Press, pp. 12–44.

Liebscher, G., and J. Dailey-O'Cain. (2005). West Germans moving east: Place, political space and positioning in conversational narratives. In M. Baynham and A. De Fina (eds.), *Dislocations/Relocations: Narratives of Displacement*. Manchester: St Jerome Publishing, pp. 61–85.

Maryns, K. (2005). Displacement in asylum seekers' narratives. In M. Baynham and A. De Fina (eds.), *Dislocations/ Relocations: Narratives of Displacement*. Manchester: St Jerome Publishing, pp. 174–196.

McCormick, K. (2005). Working with webs: Narrative constructions of forced removal and relocation. In M. Baynham and A. De Fina (eds.), *Dislocations/Relocations: Narratives of Displacement*. Manchester: St Jerome Publishing, pp. 144–169.

Murphy, M.F. (2010). La mise en récit des espaces et des relations identitaires de trois femmes "sans papiers" en France. Unpublished doctoral thesis, Paris, Sorbonne.

Prince, G. (2003). *A Dictionary of Narratology*. Lincoln: University of Nebraska Press.

Propp, V. (1968). *Morphology of the Folktale*. Austin: University of Texas Press.

Slembrouck, S. (2003). What the map cuts up, the story cuts across: Commentary on papers by M. Baynham, A. De Fina, A. Galasinska & A. Georgakopoulou. *Narrative Inquiry*, 13 (2), pp. 459–467.

Turner, V. (1969). *The Ritual Process*. London: Routledge and Kegan Paul.

7 Chronotopes

Time and Space in Oral Narrative

SABINA PERRINO

7.1 Introduction

Narratives are renowned for their capacity to transport storytellers and audiences in both time and space. Both literary narratives and real-time oral narratives have been a fertile site for the analysis of spatial and temporal effects partly for this reason. While oral narratives are often presumed to be deictically framed as "past" by default, narrators create more complex and varied temporalization effects in actual interaction, often combining these effects with spatialization, such that time and space are fused. This chapter considers Mikhail Bakhtin's (1981) notion of "chronotope" (literally, "time-space") as one approach to these interactional effects. Bakhtin unveiled the chronotope in literary narratives in order to talk about the inseparability of time and space, and this notion has been lately revived and applied across the social sciences, including in research on language use rather than only on literary texts (Agha 2007a, 2007b; Dick 2010; Perrino 2007; Silverstein 2005).

In this chapter, I extend Bakhtin's notion of literary chronotopes to the empirical analysis of real-time oral narratives in discursive interaction. I explore how this Bakhtinian notion is useful for the way it draws together distinct effects, rather than having us look only at temporalization, for example. I also suggest that this notion can be adapted so that it is not only compatible with a view on narrative as an interactional achievement, but also can help us better appreciate the ongoing construction of the relationship between story and storytelling event. Narrators often use spatio-temporal deictic expressions and other discursive resources to frame the events described in the story as a distinct there-and-then universe of narrated actions and agents, not to be confused with the here-and-now storytelling event (Perrino 2005, 2007; Wortham 2001). Using Bakhtin's terms, one can describe the two events – the story and the storytelling event – as belonging to separate "chronotopes." Though this may be the default expectation when people tell stories, narrators in practice often align the two chronotopes of story and storytelling event in other, marked ways, including through the use of certain metaphoric or, more broadly, tropic forms of alignment (Agha 2007b; Perrino 2005, 2007). For various kinds of rhetorical and interactional effects, one may create, for

The Handbook of Narrative Analysis, First Edition. Edited by Anna De Fina and Alexandra Georgakopoulou.
© 2015 John Wiley & Sons, Inc. Published 2019 by John Wiley & Sons, Inc.

example, various tropes of "coevalness" (Silverstein 2005), where one narrates the past as if it were co-occurring in the present. Tropes of coevalness include the familiar, so-called "historical present" in oral narrative, where narrators shift into non-past deixis for events that are otherwise framed as, or presumed to be, "past" (Schiffrin 1981; Wolfson 1982). In other words, through the use of the historical present – Jespersen's "dramatic present" (1924: 258) – narrators conflate the past with the present and thus the past event can become part of the present interaction. In such cases the time-spaces of story and storytelling event are collapsed, as if they were part of the same spatio-temporal setting. As I explain below, very often the fusion of the story with the storytelling event coincides with a communicative act such as a self-presentation that the storyteller tries to project in the interaction.

This chapter illustrates some basic variation in cross-chronotope alignment using a corpus of oral narrative data in Wolof (the vehicular language of Senegal, West Africa), French, and Italian, collected during linguistic anthropological fieldwork in Senegal and Italy.[1] These alignments serve various interactional functions and can, and often do, shift over the course of discursive interaction in ways that deserve study. In addition to coeval alignments like that of the "historical present," narrators sometimes even use coeval cross-chronotope alignment in an attempt to transport addressees "into" their stories. A particularly vivid case of this phenomenon is drawn from oral narrative data from Senegal. Here, Senegalese narrators often address co-present audience members as if they were characters in the narrated story, engaging in a particular phenomenon that I call "participant transposition," or what some of my Senegalese informants meta-discursively referred to in French as *démarche participative* (literally, "participatory move") (Perrino 2005, 2007, 2011).

In sum, this chapter will analyze and discuss these and similar cases that allow us to see cross-chronotope alignment as something that narrators themselves regulate over the course of their storytelling. After first outlining the Bakhtinian notion of chronotope as he applied it to literary works, I will note recent research on narrative in sociolinguistics and linguistic anthropology that examines the linguistic construction of space and time and that has sometimes been informed by Bakhtin's notion of chronotope. I will illustrate how the notion of chronotope can be usefully extended to the study of real-time oral narratives and will develop the notion of cross-chronotope alignment in oral narratives by illustrating some types of alignment in different contexts and languages (Italian, Wolof, and French). Through my analysis, I will show that chronotopes are useful for unveiling subtle interactional tensions that can develop between storyteller and audience members. I will also demonstrate that chronotopes can be employed by storytellers to manipulate and alter the interactional text, the very sense of what is happening.

7.2   Bakhtin's Chronotope in Literature and Beyond

Bakhtin's chronotope concept has been extended from literature to cinema, art criticism, and, as noted, to the empirical study of language use. "We will give the name *chronotope* (literally 'time space')," wrote Bakhtin, "to the intrinsic connectedness of temporal and spatial relationships that are artistically expressed in literature" (1981: 84–85). Originally, Bakhtin used this notion to study literary works, written narratives in particular (Bakhtin 1981; Todorov 1981). The chronotope was a way to draw attention to the inseparability of space and time, and the way the entanglement of the two are constructed in different literary materials and genres. In his words:

> In literature and art itself, temporal and spatial determinations are inseparable from one another, and always colored by emotions and values. Abstract thought can, of course, think time and space as separate entities and conceive them as things apart from the emotions and values that attach to them. But *living* artistic perception (which also of course involves thought, but not abstract thought) makes no such divisions and permits no such segmentation. It seizes on the chronotope in all its wholeness and fullness. Art and literature are shot through with chronotopic values of varying degree and scope. (Bakhtin 1981: 243; emphasis in original)

Bakhtin analyzes some generic literary chronotopes such as the chronotope of "the encounter," which he also defines as a "real-life chronotope of meeting" where the time, the place, and the rank of the person met are fundamental to the kind of event being narrated. In this case, the where-and-when is not separate, in the sense that in any encounter or meeting the "temporal marker" is inseparable from the "spatial marker." Bakhtin emphasizes how chronotopes are central to the narrative genres, since

> [t]he chronotope is the place where the knots of narrative are tied and untied. It can be said without qualification that to them belongs the meaning that shapes narrative. ... Time becomes, in effect, palpable and visible; the chronotope makes narrative events concrete, makes them take on flesh, causes blood to flow in their veins. An event can be communicated, it becomes information, one can give precise data on the place and time of its occurrence. (Bakhtin 1981: 434)

Other types of chronotopes are the chronotope of "the road" (which, in literature, is linked to the chronotope of meeting, since several encounters happen on the road at a precise time and, of course, location); the chronotope of "the castle" (from the Gothic or black novels of seventeenth-century England, in which castles played an important role in terms of the historical past, being the places where important historical figures lived), the chronotope of cafés and salons (found especially in the French novels by Stendhal and Balzac, where salons and parlors were important places of literary and political encounters), and the chronotope of threshold and crisis, which is metaphorical in literature, and charged with emotions and values. In Dostoyevsky's novels, for example, the threshold (and related chronotopes such as the stairs, front hall, and corridors) are usually places where action leads to crisis: "In this chronotope, time is essentially instantaneous; it is as if it has no duration and falls out of the normal course of biographical time" (1981: 433).

Bakhtin's notion of literary chronotopes has been extended to the empirical analysis of time-space framing found in real-time oral narratives. Since the narrative turn in the 1980s, narrative methods and analyses have become more prominent across most disciplines in the social sciences (De Fina and Georgakopoulou 2012), and of special importance is the recognition that one needs to study oral narrative in its context, considering both the story and the storytelling event. Researchers have long used narratives told in interview contexts, but, as has been increasingly appreciated (De Fina 2009; De Fina and Perrino 2011), one cannot study these stories by only focusing on the narrative's literal content – the denotational text, such as information about what characters exist and what events occur. Rather, the narrative's denotational text needs to be studied in relation to the flow of the interaction itself, the interactional text (Bauman 1986; De Fina 2009; De Fina and Perrino 2011; Perrino 2011; Silverstein 1997; Wortham 1994, 2000, 2001, 2006;). Stories thus emerge dynamically in interaction between interviewer and interviewee, and as Wortham (2001) in particular has shown, participants often play an active role in regulating and controlling this interplay.

7.2.1   Time and space in narrative studies

Sociolinguists and linguistic anthropologists have looked in depth at time and space in different types of narratives, sometimes as if these strands were "knotted" together (reminiscent of the Bakhtinian chronotope), but more often as separate dimensions of stories. Temporality in narrative, in particular, has received a considerable amount of attention. In their work on life stories, for instance, Keller-Cohen and Gordon (2003) explore how interviewees use metaphors in their stories about courtroom experiences. More specifically, the researchers analyze the courtroom "trial" metaphor not only as a way to interpret past events, but also to construct the storyteller's coherent narrative and thus to confirm her identity in the here-and-now storytelling event, thus considering the interactional text in the analysis. The "trial" metaphor ties together spatial and temporal threads so that storytellers are able to regulate their interplay in a way similar to the Bakhtinian chronotope. In a study of actual courtroom discourse, Carranza (2003) conducted ethnographic observation of a criminal court in Argentina and explored the narrative temporalities in a trial's closing arguments. Carranza shows that while the final argument formally consists of a series of past narrated events, the fact that they are continuously reported in the present speech event through direct reported speech, along with other temporalization effects, makes those past events part of the here-and-now interaction of the court trial. Working on illness narratives by people affected by Chronic Fatigue Syndrome in Sweden, Bülow and Hydén (2003) demonstrate how temporalities are shaped differently (and with different meanings) during the here-and-now interview event. Drawing on the work of historians Morson (1994) and Bernstein (1994), Bülow and Hydén introduce the notion of "shadows of time" as a way to analyze the multiple temporalities emerging in illness narratives and the sense of responsibility that the storytellers might have in delivering their stories about suffering and disease. Time becomes a "discursive tool" to analyze illness and identity as they unfold in interviewees' narratives, a tool that the authors name *"temporalizing"* (Bülow and Hydén 2003: 74, emphasis in original). Focusing more on the intricate relationship between past and present, Chang (2003) investigates the narrative elicitation strategies that Mandarin Chinese-speaking mothers use with their children across different spans of time. The analysis revealed that there was no systematic change in maternal interactive strategies or in the amount of narrative information provided to the children over time.

Research on space in narrative and in discourse more generally has a diverse literature. Barbara Johnstone's (2010) work on "language and geographical space" describes how sociolinguistics has started to refer to human and discursive geography. For example, storytellers often evoke particular places and ways of speaking in their stories, and dialects are typically attributed to particular towns or places (Johnstone 2010: 11; see also Basso 1988). Similarly, Taylor (2003) explores space more than time in interview narratives with women living in the southeast of England. It is through narratives of place of residence that storytellers construct multiple identities, Taylor shows. Space is often fundamental to identity formation in multilingual contexts (Blommaert, Collins, and Slembrouck 2005). While conducting their fieldwork in a single immigrant neighborhood in Ghent (Belgium), and not focusing exclusively on oral narratives, Blommaert and colleagues view space in relation to scaling processes since "movements across space involve movements across scales of social structure having indexical value and thus providing meaning to individual, situated acts" (2005: 199–200). Spatially, these multilingual environments are "polycentric" in nature, since individuals continuously refer to a myriad of different centers. In other words, a spatial and scalar perspective is well motivated for the study of multilingualism as well as transnationalism, given the interplay between "centers" and "peripheries" (Blommaert et al. 2005: 201; Heller 2003; Vigouroux 2008). Though also not focused on narratives, Scollon and Scollon (2003) extend the notion of space (and of time as well, but in a secondary way) through geo-semiotics, a framework that integrates multiple semiotic resources, including the built environment, and that seeks to explain social meanings "in reference to the material world of users of signs" (2003: 4).

While issues of time and space have been widely explored as separate topics, scholars have started to look at them in conjunction as well – although this research is still in its beginnings and remains primarily experimental in nature. While the existing literature in this area is not exclusively focused on narrative studies, it is worth mentioning experiments looking at space and time together, sometimes through an explicit Bakhtinian framing, sometimes not. Of special importance are the studies of Hanks (1990) and Haviland (1996) on spatio-temporal "transposition," which focused on shifts in the deictic center or "origo" (Bühler 1990), and work more generally on the deictic "field" (Hanks 2005), which some have treated as an analogy to Bakhtin's chronotope (Lempert and Perrino 2007). Lempert (2007), for example, looks at the diagrammatic relationship between past and present deictic fields constructed through Tibetan speech styles, while Wirtz (2007) examines the collapse of past and present in Cuban Santería's ritual speech. Other scholars investigate the cross-chronotope alignment of space and time (Agha 2007b; Davidson 2007; Parmentier 2007; Perrino 2007), the "chronotopic landscapes of environmental racism" (Blanton 2011), the use of minor and major chronotopes in the Northern English Sheep Counting system (Anderson 2011), as well as the analysis of chronotopes in classroom settings (Bloome and Katz 1997). Finally, Silverstein redefines Bakhtin's notion in these terms: "the temporally (hence, chrono-) and spatially (hence, -tope) particular envelope in the narrated universe of social space-time in which and through which, in emplotment, narrative characters move" (2005: 6). Though this is narrower than what Bakhtin intended, this makes the notion particularly productive for oral narrative and a rich field for potential research exploration. From this brief mention of recent work in linguistic anthropology and in sociolinguistics, it would seem that a chronotopic analysis of sociocultural phenomena can not only help analysts unveil the subtle dynamics of narrative in interaction, as I illustrate further below, but it can also uncover situations that would be otherwise unclear or hidden, such as "environmental racism" (Blanton 2011), student dynamics in the classroom (Bloome and Katz 1997; Wortham 2001), or, more broadly, overarching linguistic ideologies (Irvine 2004).

7.3   Enacting Cross-Chronotope Alignment in Oral Narratives

In what follows, I extend Bakhtin's notion of literary chronotopes to the empirical analysis of real-time oral narratives in discursive environments. In particular, I investigate how this notion is useful for the way it draws together distinct pragmatic effects, revealing how time and space coalesce in creative and strategic ways. Through a corpus of oral narratives that I collected both in Senegal and in Italy during fieldwork, I demonstrate that this adaptation is not only useful and compatible with a view on narrative as an interactional achievement, but can help narrative scholars better appreciate the ongoing co-construction of the interplay between story and storytelling event.

As noted, Bakhtin's notion of literary chronotopes has been adapted by some for the study not just of oral narratives in discourse, where the story is studied as an isolated text, but also, and especially, for the interplay between story and storytelling event. Though not concerned with the event of narration per se, Bakhtin himself wrote of the dialogic interrelationship of chronotopes:

> Chronotopes are mutually inclusive, they co-exist, they may be interwoven with, replace or oppose one another, contradict one another or find themselves in ever more complex interrelationships … The general characteristic of these interactions is that they are dialogical (in the broadest sense of the word). (1981: 252)

In addition, Bakhtin states that the chronotope provides not only the internal structure, map, and configuration of the narrative, but also a link between the narrative content and the social, cultural, and historical context of the narrating action. It is thus easy to extend his notion beyond the realm of the story itself and into the storytelling event, which can be considered its own time-space or "chronotope." In oral narratives, narrators try to align story and storytelling event through the manipulation of linguistic resources for expressing time and space. In what follows, I focus on the way speakers use language to anchor stories in time and space as they narrate, and on the way this anchoring is subject to the narrator's manipulation.

Narratives of personal experience may be typically understood as "past" by default, so that the expectation is that the speaker will use spatio-temporal deixis and other linguistic resources to frame the narrative as there-and-then, not to be confused with the here-and-now storytelling event. In this way, the narrated event and the narrating event are treated as two separate chronotopes, yet these can be brought into alignment by

narrators in various ways, a process Agha (2007b) terms "cross-chronotope alignment."
As he writes:

> Chronotopic representations enlarge the "historical present" of their audiences by creating
> chronotopic displacements and cross-chronotope alignments between persons here-and-
> now and persons altogether elsewhere, transposing selves across discrete zones of cultural
> spacetime through communicative practices that have immediate consequences for how
> social actors in the public sphere are mobilized to think, feel and act. (Agha 2007b: 324)

These two narrative chronotopes – story and storytelling event – have been described
and theorized by several scholars. Jakobson (1957), for example, distinguished "narrated
event" from "narrating event," while some linguistic anthropologists have reconceptual-
ized this as a divide between "denotational text" and "interactional text" (Silverstein and
Urban 1996; Wortham 1994, 2001). But this distinction is not limited to cases of "narrative"
in the more narrow sociolinguistic sense of the term. As Silverstein (1997) clarifies,
"denotational text" refers to coherence in terms of reference and predication about states
of affairs, while "interactional text" refers to the coherence that the interaction itself is
felt to have, in terms of role inhabitance and actions performed (for more on this distinction, see also Agha 2007a; Perrino 2002; Wortham 2001). In what is perhaps a default
cross-chronotope alignment found in storytelling, the event of narration involves what
Chafe termed a "displaced mode" (1994: 196) in which the narrated event and the narrating event are sharply separated. The narrated event is placed in the "past" with respect
to the present interaction (Perrino 2005: 349). In other words, the two events belong to
separate chronotopes, with no confusion between the two. The notion of chronotope can
thus be very productive in narrative analysis, since it motivates the empirical study of
different types of alignment between story and event, because, as Silverstein (2005)
notes, there are many cases in which the two chronotopes do not have clear boundaries
or are deliberately blurred. Some of these cases yield situations of "coeval" alignment
(2005: 17–18) in which the two narrative chronotopes (narrated event and narrating
event) overlap both temporally and spatially, so that "past" and "present" seem to converge. Through this convergence, storytellers can influence or alter the dynamics of the
storytelling event.

Although it is not typically framed in Bakhtinian terms, one of the most well-known
strategies of coeval cross-chronotope alignment is the "historical present" of narrative,
where speakers shift into non-past deixis for events that are otherwise framed as, or
assumed to be, past. However, the so-called historical present is only one very general
way to describe how storytellers align the chronotope of the story and the chronotope
of the here-and-now storytelling event as "coeval" (Silverstein 2005). This blurring of
the boundaries between chronotopes can be accomplished with many different resources
and methods, and there are varieties of coeval alignment that go even further than the
historical present; some go so far as to transport participants in the here-and-now "into"
stories, even though these stories are understood to have occurred in the past. I have
explored this kind of dramatic movement into stories in my earlier work on Senegalese
narrative practices (Perrino 2005, 2007), and I will touch on them again in the last section
of this chapter.

It is very useful to track shifts of alignment when analyzing oral narratives in order to see how narrators manage the relationship between representation and interaction, between narrated event and narrating event. This method of analysis can reveal alignment strategies in oral narratives of various kinds, and to illustrate this I will draw on stories from diverse contexts, from Italy and Senegal in particular. These cases are meant to broaden the phenomena of coeval alignment beyond the special case of the "historical present," and they illustrate, more generally, the methodological utility of mapping chronotopes in oral narrative. By looking at chronotopic alignments across narratives, researchers can gain a better sense of how the storytelling event can be altered or manipulated by storytellers.

7.4 From "Displaced" to "Coeval" Alignment in Italian Oral Narratives

As noted earlier, the default expectation for a story is that it be deictically anchored as there-and-then. This is the case for the following short story, which is told with a consistent "displaced," non-coeval alignment. The story is a joke which was delivered during an Italian national political gathering and which contains a fictional self-narrative. This sort of joke telling constitutes a genre called *barzelletta* in Italian,[2] and it seems to be common in political rallies and oratory. Former Italian Prime Minister Silvio Berlusconi was known for using *barzellette* before and after his meetings, and even during parliamentary sessions. After a political speech in Naples on May 13, 2011, Berlusconi launched into a *barzelletta* about a trip he took in which he met, in his words, "a very beautiful blond girl" absorbed in reading a book. Here is how he told this story to the Italian audience at the political meeting:

Original Italian	**English Translation**[3]
(1) ho viaggiato su un aereo normale	I traveled on a normal airplane [i.e., not a government one]
(2) dovevo andare fuori Italia	I had to go outside Italy
(3) salgo sull'aereo e c'è una bellissima ragazza	I get on the plane and there is a very beautiful girl
(4) "Gianni [addressing the man near him], dovevi vederla"	"Gianni [addressing the man near him], you should have seen her"
(5) una bellissima ragazza bionda	a very beautiful blond girl
(6) che leggeva intensamente un libro	who was intensely reading a book
(7) poltrona libera vicino a lei	[the] seat [was] vacant next to her
(8) mi sono fiondato [laughter from audience]	I catapulted myself into it [laughter from audience]
(9) e ho cercato di cominciare una conversazione	and I tried to start a conversation
(10) niente da fare	she wasn't going to [have one]
(11) leggeva	she was reading
(12) allora a un certo punto proprio anche forte ho detto	so at a certain opportune moment quite loudly I said

(13)   "signorina, ma lei legge con una intensità straordinaria"
(14)   di che cosa parla questo libro?"
(15)   e lei mi ha guardato e soavemente mi ha detto
(16)   "parla dell'amore"
(17)   "ah"
(18)   "E che cosa le ha insegnato di così importante
(19)   vista la sua straordinaria attenzione?"
(20)   "mi ha insegnato due cose fondamentali:
(21)   che gli amanti sessualmente più potenti sono gli arabi
(22)   e quelli più sentimentalmente forti
(23)   quelli più romantici sono i napoletani"

(24)   e allora io le ho dato la mano e le ho detto:

(25)   "signorina permetta che mi presenti: Mohammed Esposito"

"Young lady, but you read with an extraordinary intensity"
what's the book about?"
and she looked at me and sweetly she said to me
"it's about love"
"ah"
"And what has it taught you that's so important
given your extraordinary attention?"
"it has taught me two fundamental things:
that the most sexually potent lovers are the Arabs
and that the most sentimentally strong and most romantic ones are the Neapolitans"
and at that point I gave her my hand and I told her
"Young lady, let me introduce myself: Mohammed Esposito"

In this short *barzelletta* told as a first-person narrative, Berlusconi recounted an imaginary trip he had to take on a regular plane (not a governmental one). When Berlusconi entered the plane, he saw a beautiful blonde woman reading a book. The seat near her was vacant and so he naturally sat near her. But she ignored him and continued to read intently. He asked her why she was reading so intently, and she responded that she was reading a book about love. Berlusconi, curious, asked her what the book had taught her, and she said that the book taught her two fundamental facts: (1) that the most sexually potent lovers are Arabs, and (2) that the most romantically devoted ones are the Neapolitans. In the end, Berlusconi extended his hand to introduce himself to her and uttered "Mohammed Esposito," Esposito being a typical Neapolitan last name. In this short story, the chronotopes are kept distinct and distant, since Berlusconi uses a clear structure of direct report with the verb of speaking in the past, or *passato prossimo* ("ha detto" [she said], "ho detto" [I said], see lines 12, 15, and 24). There is just one case of use of historical present at line 3, when he says "salgo sull'aereo e c'è una bellissima ragazza" ("I get on the plane and there is a very beautiful girl"). The short story is almost entirely in what Chafe (1994) terms a "displaced" or "displaced-retrospective" perspective, or what I will call a displaced cross-chronotope alignment.

The above example features a mostly displaced alignment in which the two events are kept separate. I use this example[4] as a reference point for the cases I illustrate next, where non-"past" framing is more prevalent. Tropes of coeval cross-chronotope alignment include, as noted earlier, the historical present in oral narrative, where speakers shift into non-past deixis for events that are otherwise framed as, or presumed to be, past. By juxtaposing seemingly non-congruent temporalization effects – effects that do not seem consistent with one another – speakers can invite hearers to align the spatio-temporal chronotope of the narrated event with the here-and-now narrating event in different ways.

My second example is taken from a narrative produced by a schoolteacher in her late 40s who lives in a small town in the Veneto region of Italy. Her narrative involves alternations between displaced and coeval alignments, as we shall see. My interview with her, which lasted nearly an hour, focused on the issue of how Italian hospitals and hospital personnel were reacting to new waves of immigrants in Italy. At a certain point, when she was talking about the relationship between Italian doctors and immigrant patients, she launched into three personal narratives. In one narrative, this storyteller recounted an experience she had with a neurologist. Her father had been previously hospitalized for a possible brain tumor. After the doctors performed a CAT-scan on him, she went to the neurology department to learn about her father's diagnosis, and there she met the department's director. At the beginning of her story, the narrated and narrating events are kept separate through a displaced cross-chronotope alignment. That is, it is as if the narrator is standing back and recounting this past event; the past does not seem to overlap with the present. However, the schoolteacher initiates a shift in alignment in the following lines.

T: Teacher

S: Interviewer

Original Italian		**English Translation**
(1)	T: ehmm	ehmm
(2)	io- eh	I- uh
(3)	c'era mio padre ricoverato	there was my father [who was] hospitalized
(4)	che aveva un tumore al cervello	who had a tumor in his brain
(5)	e io ero andata	and I had gone
(6)	il giorno dopo	the day after
(7)	che gli avevano fatto la TAC	they had performed the CAT on him
(8)	per sapere	to know
(9)	di quale:-	of wha:t-
(10)	quale era il problema di cui era affetto	what was the problem by which he was affected
(11)	e:h e	u:h and
(12)	avevo mio figlio	I had my son
(13)	Giovanni a casa	Giovanni at home
(14)	con mia sorella e	with my sister and
(15)	io non lo potevo lasciare mio figlio	I couldn't leave him my son
(16)	quindi è stata uhm	so she [my sister] was uhm
(17)	S: sì	yes
(18)	T: mia sorella	my sister
(19)	era in grado di fare determinate manovre	was able to take certain steps
(20)	pe:::rché|	be:::cause
(21)	S: per lui	for him
(22)	T: lui	him
(23)	eh	eh

(24) e:h però:: io naturalmente ero venuta via col cuore in mano=	u:h bu::t I of course had gone away with [my] heart in [my] hand=
(25) S: =eh	=eh
(26) T: perciò ero-	so I was-
(27) mordevo anche un po' il freno	I was also a bit in a rush
(28) guardavo l'orologio	I was looking at [my] watch
(29) ero ansiosa e preoccupata sia	I was anxious and worried both
(30) per mio figlio sia per mio padre perché non sapevo-	for my son and for my father because I didn't know-
(31) e questo medico::::	and this docto::::r
(32) al quale io ho chiesto	to whom I asked
(33) "scusi professore	"sorry professor
(34) ma lei" dico	but do you" I say
(35) "pensa di poterci:: eh spiegare quanto prima	"think [you] can:: uh explain to us as soon as possible
(36) sa ho dei problemi	you know I have some problems
(37) avrei dei problemi	[that] I would have some problems
(38) posso anche spiegarle"	I can also explain [them] to you"
(39) "qua problemi ne abbiamo tutti"	"here we all have problems"
(40) mi ha risposto mi ha inveito	he replied to me, he railed at me
(41) ha inveito contro di me	he railed against me
(42) nel corridoio dicendo che lì:	in the corridor saying that there:
(43) lì lavoravano non è che::	there they were working [it] is not tha::t
(44) stessero lì a grattarsi i cosiddetti	they were standing there scratching their you-know-whats

The narrator started telling her story in a displaced cross-chronotope alignment, by using the three past tenses in Italian, the *imperfetto* (imperfect), the *trapassato prossimo* (past perfect), and the *passato prossimo* (simple past) in several turns. While past framing continued with the past tense of the verb *chiedere* ("to ask"), *ho chiesto* ("I asked") in line 32, a shift into the historical present occurred in line 34, when the schoolteacher used the non-past verb of speaking *dico* ("I say") as a matrix clause verb in a direct report. The tropic reading of coeval alignment is a form of deictic transposition in which the narrator is addressing the doctor as if he were metaphorically present in, and part of, the here-and-now interaction.

After this moment, the schoolteacher did not return to past-tense framing at line 40. Instead, she produced a continuous stretch of direct reported speech without any matrix reporting clauses to mark this discourse as reported speech and hence with no opportunities to use the historical present. This narrative includes a long stretch of direct reports without matrix clauses (which belong to the narrating event), which arguably helps blur the boundaries between past and present, especially since it occurs after an instance of historical present. The doctor finally gave a response to the schoolteacher (line 39), which greatly disconcerted her. In short, the storyteller moved back and forth throughout this portion of her narrative. After this stretch of reported speech, she shifted back to a displaced cross-chronotope alignment in line 40, creating a sharp separation between narrated and narrating event. The schoolteacher, in a sense, "returned" to the present interview (Perrino 2007, 2011).

7.5 Participant Transposition through Coeval Alignment in Senegalese Oral Narrative

Thus far I have illustrated some basic variability of cross-chronotope alignment from "displaced" to "coeval," including shifts between the two. These shifts depend on shifts in the use of deictic resources, notably tense, over turns of talk. I now turn to an example of another case in which Senegalese narrators draw interlocutors "into" their stories through a form of coeval alignment that may be called "participant transposition" (Perrino 2005, 2007). "Participant transposition" in Senegalese oral narrative has parallels with recent linguistic anthropological research, especially with Wortham's (1994, 2001) work on "participant examples" in US classrooms. In Wortham's cases, classroom teachers recruit interactants (students, in his case) to play particular roles in a story. More specifically, Wortham shows how participant examples can create "doubled" roles, where a person plays a role both in the story and in the storytelling event, thus drawing both events into the same chronotopic frame. Similarly, in Senegalese narratives, storytellers "move" their addressees into their stories, and this movement alters the coherence of the interaction-in-progress. The boundaries between the narrated event and the narrating event are blurred, and this blurring helps transform participants into characters of the past story – even when they didn't play any actual role in these past events.

In this way, encounters with narratives can involve a strong sense of "movement" into the narrated event. Focusing on written narratives, for example, Gerrig (1993: 2) observes two recurrent metaphors: "readers are often described as *being transported* by a narrative by virtue of *performing* that narrative" (emphasis in original). Segal (1995: 15) similarly writes that "[r]eaders get inside of stories and vicariously experience them." Gerrig, Segal, and others (see Duchan, Bruder, and Hewitt 1995) study this sense of "being transported" as an underlying cognitive process. More specifically, using a "deictic shift theory," Segal analyzes the movement into a story where the origo, the zero-point of deictic reckoning (Bühler 1990), is transposed from the storytelling to the story itself (see also Zubin and Hewitt 1995). Since scholars like Segal (1995) privilege novels and focus on the solitary reader, they do not investigate this kind of transposition in interactional storytelling events or how this transport can influence the social action between interactants (Becker and Quasthoff 2005: 2; Ochs and Capps 2001).

The Senegalese oral narrative practice that I analyze here is widespread among Senegalese storytellers and cuts across discourse genres. This specific narrative practice has also received metadiscursive attention, since several of my Senegalese informants called it by the French term *démarche participative* ("participatory move") during my playback sessions with them. In interviews with a Senegalese informant and research assistant of mine, for example, he used the verbs "transpose" and "transport" to gloss *démarche participative*: "la démarche participative, pour te faire rentrer dans ce contexte-là. C'est comme si je t'avais transposée, transportée dans mon histoire-là" ("the participatory move [is done] in order to make you enter that context. It is as if I had transposed [or] transported you inside my own story"). In terms of its stereotypic pragmatic effects in interaction, my informant suggested that participant transposition has "purely pedagogical" functions (*purement pédagogique*), in the sense that it serves only to illustrate and exemplify the denotational content of the original story or discourse, "re-presenting" it for an audience in terms that are more accessible and experientially immediate (Perrino 2005).

The following narrative excerpt exemplifies this. In June 2000, I conducted an interview in Dakar (Senegal) with a Senegalese informant of mine. The interview was conducted in Wolof and French, a language combination typical for Dakar. I had been conducting research on Senegalese ethnomedicine at the time, and I asked him if he would share some illness stories of his with me. Among the many stories he shared with me, one concerned a dramatic case of dysentery. It was the longest narrative of that corpus, lasting slightly over 37 minutes, and he used participant transposition four times in his telling. My informant recounted how he had once paid a visit to his older brother, but when he returned home, he urgently needed to go to the bathroom, where he experienced a severe case of diarrhea. After his father gave him some medication, he went to sleep without eating dinner. When he awoke, he ran to the bathroom again, but this time there was blood in his stool. He narrated that his diarrhea with blood continued for three months with a frequency of five episodes daily. Here are some examples of participant transposition in which I (Sabina) become a witness of this disease of his in his past story.

P[s]   **Line 1: Wolof E[n]**
       Line 2: Interlinear Gloss
       Line 3: English Translation[5]

I = informant
S = interviewer

I: 21   = juróomi yoon gis nga   ritmu boobu
        five   time see you-AUX.SUBJ-PAST rhythm that-CLSF-SG-DIST
        = five times, do you see what kind of rhythm [I had] there?

    22   (1.4) "oh Sabina excuse-moi   maa   ngiy   dem toilette"
             "oh Sabina excuse-me-FR I-AUX.SUBJ here-SIT go   bathroom"
         (1.4) "oh Sabina, excuse me, I am going to the bathroom"

    23   (1.3) donc dem naa   même pa::s
             SO-FR go   I-AUX.SUBJ-PAST even not-FR
         (1.3) so, I didn't even [have the time to really] go::

    24   (1.6) deux   minutes   pare naa::
             two   minutes-FR finish I-AUX.SUBJ-PAST
         (1.6) [after] two minutes I:: was finished

    25   (.) ma   ñëw   toog
            I-AUX.SUBJ come-back squat
         (.) I go back squatting

S: 26   [clears throat] =

I: 27   = mu   waxtaan waxtaan waxtaan ncee::h
        he-AUX.SUBJ   talk   talk   talk   neeeh
        = he talks, talks, talks neee::h

28   "Sabina,   excuse-moi" (1.1) um?
     "Sabina,   excuse-me"   um? [French]
     "Sabina, excuse me" (1.1) um?

29   (1.4) man   dem naa   dem naa   dem naa
          I-AUX.EMPH go I-AUX.SUBJ-PAST   go I-AUX.SUBJ-PAST   go I-AUX.SUBJ-PAST
     (1.4) I really went, I went, I went

30   finalement (.) man   dematuma   toilette
     finally-FR   I-AUX.EMPH   go-I-AUX.SUBJ-NEG bathroom
     finally (.) I stop going to the bathroom

Immediately before the start of participant transposition at line 1, my informant asked me whether I had really understood what his past self underwent: "do you realize what kind of rhythm [I had]?" (in Wolof, *"gis nga ritmu boobu?"*). In his question to me, he used past-tense deictic anchoring together with the Wolof spatial-deictic distal demonstrative *boobu*, which put his question in a "displaced-retrospective" perspective; it is "retrospective" because it is also deictically framed as "past" (Perrino 2005: 352). The narrated event being denoted is hence framed as occurring in a chronotope distinct from the here-and-now space-time. Thus far, the trope of cross-chronotope coevalness has not occurred yet. In line 22, however, the storyteller shifted perspective. In his direct report of his past self's speech at line 22, he recruited me, "Sabina," to the role of addressee, hence initiating participant transposition and implementing the trope of coevalness. I suddenly became a "witness" who saw the terrible "rhythm" (in Wolof, *ritmu*) of his diarrhea in the past. Given the framing from the previous line, it is as if I was transported into his specific biographical past. After a brief return to the past, the storyteller initiated participant transposition, recruiting me once again to the role of witness at line 28. This brief sequence illustrates rapid shifts in cross-chronotope alignment that produce a sense of "transposition" and transport between the storytelling event and the story.

What triggered this extreme case of cross-chronotope alignment? In order to answer this question, I will now consider what transpired interactionally between the Senegalese storyteller and the interviewer (myself) earlier in the interaction. As I mentioned above, immediately before this case of participant transposition, at line 1, the storyteller asked me whether I understood what his past self had undergone, that is, "do you realize what kind of rhythm [I had]?" (*"gis nga ritmu boobu?"*).[6] Moving back to previous lines in his story, there is a moment when I asked him a question about his narrative that could have been taken as an insult to his telling. The storyteller had been characterizing his past self as someone suffering from a severe illness, someone who was shocked by the blood that presumably had rushed out of him.

I: 9   ma:::   xëy   ci   ëllëg   sa
        I-AUX.SUBJ wake-up in-CLSF-SG-PROX morning the-CLSF-SG-DIST
        I::: wake up the next morning

    10 (1.6) ma   dem encore   (.) ci   wanak   ba
             I-AUX.SUBJ go   again-FR   in-CLSF-SG-PROX bathroom the-CLSF-SG-DIST
             (1.6) I go again (.) to the bathroom

    11 (1.3) waaye   cette   fois-ci (2.1) u:::h   dërët la   doon   génne
             but   this   time-here-FR uh:::   blood it-AUX.SUBJ PAST-CNTV come-out
             (1.3) but this time (2.1) u:::h blood was coming out

    12 (2.4) à la place des   toilettes (1.5) je sortais   du   sang
             at the place of-the feces   I   come-out of-the blood [French]
             (2.4) instead of feces (1.5), I had blood

S: 13   (2.0) mmmm =
            mmmm
            (2.0) mmmm =

I: 14   = dama   doon   génne   dërët
        I-AUX.EMPH PAST CNTV come-out blood
        = blood was coming out [of] me
                                [
S: 15   à   la- au li- (.) au lieu de la diarrhée
                               at the- instead- instead of the diarrhea [French]
                               at the- instead- (.) instead of the diarrhea

    16   (.) il y   avait même le   sang =
                               it there had   also the blood [French]
                               (.) There was blood too =

I: 17   = il y   avait le sang
        it there had   the blood [French]
        = there was blood
                               [
S: 18   oh: mm hm (1.1) dërët bu   bari?
                               oh: mm hm   blood the-CLSF-SG-DIST much?
                               oh: mm hm (1.1) a lot of blood?

I: 19   tuuti   dërët =
        a-little-ADV   blood
        a little blood =

S: 20   = tuuti =
          a-little-ADV
        = a little [blood] =

The storyteller used several cases of repetition to claim that blood appeared in his stool.
At line 14, for example, he claimed that "blood was coming out" (*"dama doon génne dërët"*),

the Wolof particle *doon* marking the continuative aspect in the past, thus suggesting that the process of blood "coming out" occurred over a period of time. This aspectual marking suggests that the blood was more like a continuous stream rather than a few drops. The storyteller also suggested a sense of shock and urgency in this self-representation during his storytelling. He graphically characterized his past self as someone suffering from a severe illness, someone who saw a lot of blood coming out of his body. However, my questions about this characterization of his past self might have been the cause of his reactions. At lines 15 and 16, I overlapped with him and suggested that the blood in his stool was not as abundant as he had implied. I further suggested that there was blood in addition to diarrhea, not blood *instead* of diarrhea. At line 18, then, I asked him whether there was "a lot of blood?" (in Wolof, *dërët bu bari?*), which could have been seen as a suggestion that he may have been exaggerating. My remarks could have been interpreted as questioning his characterization of his past self as someone who survived a severe illness, by insinuating that, as a narrator, he was hyperbolic. It is revealing that immediately after my remarks, the storyteller responded by saying "it [the diarrhea] attacked me" (in Wolof, "*mu attake ma*"), emphasizing, again, the gravity of his past disease. It is in this context that he went into graphic details about the frequency, the nature, and the consistency of his diarrhea. Finally, he asked me: "Do you realize what kind of rhythm [I had]?" (in Wolof, "*gis nga ritmu boobu?*"). This last question leaves open the possibility that I might *not* have realized the severity of his illness, indeed. It is exactly at this precise moment that the storyteller engaged in the participant transposition that I discussed above. Through this participant transposition, therefore, he went so far as to transform me into a friend who witnessed the terrible disease he underwent. By making me into a witness in the denotational text, the participant transposition makes the implicit counter-claim that the storyteller had made interactionally just prior to the participant transposition – namely, that he was *not* a hyperbolic narrator, as I had implied.

This case illustrates how shifts in cross-chronotope alignment – in particular, a trope of coevalness – are used not only to alter the interactional text but to also make the story more credible and convincing (for a more detailed analysis of this and other cases, see Perrino 2005, 2007). Through participant transposition, the Senegalese storyteller can manipulate the storytelling event, making the story more tangible, more vivid, and thus more believable for the audience. In a way, this narrative strategy is similar to what Schiffrin (1990) called "self-lamination," an argumentative device used in storytelling to make stories more convincing to audience members. Furthermore, narratives' topics may constitute an important interactional resource, as storytellers might become empowered by telling stories about social suffering, trauma, and illness. While this needs more investigation, it is thus possible that traumatic topics in oral narratives use coeval alignment and perhaps even participant transposition more than other genres.

7.6 Conclusion

While the Bakhtinian chronotope emerged from work on literary narratives, it can be adapted for the empirical study of oral narrative and its spatio-temporalization effects. In addition to exploring how the spatial and temporal dimensions of a narrative are constituted, especially through deictic resources, we can also explore cross-chronotope alignment, namely, how the time-space of the narrative is complexly anchored to the time-space of the event of narration itself – which is its own chronotope.

In the cases I analyzed in this chapter, I illustrated some forms of variation in the relationship between story and storytelling chronotopes, from a sharp differentiation between the two to a gradient overlapping until they reach moments in which they seem inseparable, their confluence total, as in the Senegalese case of participant transposition. The first short joking narrative showed basic cases of consistent displaced alignment and coeval alignment, respectively, with the storyteller (the former Italian Prime Minister) framing his fictional story as there and then. The second narrative, produced by a schoolteacher in Northern Italy, is mainly told with displaced alignment but features shifts into coeval alignment. In the last, more extreme case, as noted, the Senegalese storyteller collapses the two chronotopes in order to move me into his biographical past through participant transposition. By transposing the audience member – in this case, me – into his narrated event, he has me participate and witness his terrible disease in order to fully appreciate what he was going through at that particular moment of his life. In doing so, the storyteller also tries to alter the course of the current interaction between the interviewer and himself due to a previous interactional tension between the two speech participants. While non-past, coeval alignments may seem to be the exception to the rule – the rule being past, displaced alignment – they are in fact common in storytelling, and their complexities need more scholarly attention. The familiar notion of "historical present" does not capture the range of variation in coeval alignments in chronotopes, neither in terms of how coevalness is achieved linguistically, nor in terms of what pragmatic effects can be achieved by means of such shifts. The inadequacy of this notion can be seen especially by comparing familiar kinds of shifts into non-past, which I illustrated with the Italian material and with the extraordinary case of "participant transposition" in Senegalese oral narrative. Adaptation of Bakhtin's chronotope to the relation between story and storytelling event can open up the complexities of their relationship to sociolinguistic study.

NOTES

1   The data used in this chapter were collected during linguistic anthropological fieldwork that I conducted in Senegal (West Africa) and Northern Italy between 2000 and 2012. The chapter is based on data that I collected in Senegal during pre-dissertation research in the summer of 2000 and of 2001, which was funded by the Department of Anthropology of the University of Pennsylvania, and during dissertation fieldwork conducted in 2002–2004 and funded by a Wenner-Gren Dissertation Fieldwork Grant (# 6957), and a Penfield Scholarship in Diplomacy, International Affairs, and *Belles Lettres*. In this chapter, I use both pseudonyms and real names (only for speakers who agreed to have their name published). My special thanks go to my Italian and Senegalese informants. Without their numerous stories, this chapter could have never been written. I particularly thank Anna De Fina and Alexandra Georgakopoulou for

inviting me to contribute to this volume and for their astute comments and insightful guidance in several drafts of this chapter. I wish to thank Gregory Kohler and Michael Lempert for their editorial feedback. I alone am responsible for any remaining mistakes.

2 In Italy, *barzellette* are short funny stories that are usually told after a meal with friends or with relatives, especially when there are many participants at the table. One or two participants who are "good" *barzellette* tellers stand up and tell the jokes (this can go on for hours). There are always people who know how to engage in the telling of these stories, while the other participants just listen and have fun. *Barzellette* are mostly of a sexual or a political nature, and involve several stereotyped characters, such as the Southerners (for the northern regions) and the Northerners (for the southern regions). Reflecting the recent influence of *Lega Nord* and *Veneto Stato*, two extremist and separatist political parties in Italy, these *barzellette* can also be used to mock migrants, especially Africans, Northern Africans, Indians, and Muslims more generally. In my corpus, I looked at *barzellette* told during dinners, at stand-up comedy-like performances during folkloristic events in towns, during political speeches, and on television.

3 In this chapter, all translations are mine unless otherwise stated.

4 The fact that Berlusconi was the teller of this short story has no bearing on my argument about past framing in oral narratives.

5 This transcript has a different format with respect to the previous ones since an interlinear gloss is needed to better show the different uses of past tense in the Wolof language.

6 In my Senegalese narrative corpus with this informant and with others, these types of questions often happen right before a case of participant transposition.

REFERENCES

Agha, A. (2007a). *Language and Social Relations*. Cambridge: Cambridge University Press.

Agha, A. (2007b). Recombinant selves in mass mediated spacetime. *Language and Communication*, 27, pp. 320–335.

Anderson, D.N. (2011). Major and minor chronotopes in a specialized counting system. *Journal of Linguistic Anthropology*, 21 (1), pp. 124–141.

Bakhtin, M.M. (1981). *The Dialogic Imagination*. Translated by C. Emerson and M. Holquist. Edited by M. Holquist. Austin: University of Texas Press.

Basso, K.H. (1988). "Speaking with names": Language and landscape among the Western Apache. *Cultural Anthropology*, 3 (2), pp. 99–130.

Bauman, R. (1986). *Story, Performance, and Event: Contextual Studies of Oral Narrative*. Cambridge: Cambridge University Press.

Becker, T., and U.M. Quasthoff. (2005). Introduction: Different dimensions in the field of narrative interaction. In U.M.

Quasthoff and T. Becker (eds.), *Narrative Interaction*. Amsterdam: John Benjamins, pp. 1–11.

Bernstein, M.A. (1994). *Foregone Conclusions*. Berkeley: University of California Press.

Blanton, R. (2011). Chronotopic landscapes of environmental racism. *Journal of Linguistic Anthropology*, 21 (S1), pp. E76–E93.

Blommaert, J., J. Collins, and S. Slembrouck. (2005). Spaces of multilingualism. *Language & Communication*, 25 (3), pp. 197–216.

Bloome, D., and L. Katz. (1997). Literacy as practice and classroom chronotopes. *Reading & Writing Quarterly: Overcoming Learning Difficulties*, 13 (3), pp. 205–225.

Bühler, K. (1990). *Theory of Language: The Representational Function of Language*. Edited by A. Eschbach. Amsterdam: John Benjamins.

Bülow, P.H., and L.-C. Hydén. (2003). In dialogue with time: Identity and illness in narratives about chronic fatigue. *Narrative Inquiry*, 13 (1), pp. 71–97.

Carranza, I.E. (2003). Genre and institution: Narrative temporality in final arguments. *Narrative Inquiry*, 13 (1), pp. 41–69.

Chafe, W.L. (1994). *Discourse, Consciousness, and Time: The Flow and Displacement of Conscious Experience in Speaking and Writing.* Chicago, IL: University of Chicago Press.

Chang, C. (2003). Talking about the past: How do Chinese mothers elicit narratives from their young children across time? *Narrative Inquiry*, 13 (1), pp. 99–126.

Davidson, D. (2007). East spaces in west times: Deictic reference and political self-positioning in a post-socialist East German chronotope. *Language and Communication*, 27 (3), pp. 212–226.

De Fina, A. (2009). Narratives in interview – The case of accounts: For an interactional approach to narrative genres. *Narrative Inquiry*, 19 (2), pp. 233–258.

De Fina, A., and A. Georgakopoulou. (2012). *Analyzing Narrative: Discourse and Sociolinguistic Perspectives.* Cambridge: Cambridge University Press.

De Fina, A., and S. Perrino. (2011). Introduction: Interviews vs. "natural" contexts: A false dilemma. *Language in Society*, 40 (1), pp. 1–11.

Dick, H.P. (2010). Imagined lives and modernist chronotopes in Mexican nonmigrant discourse. *American Ethnologist*, 37 (2), pp. 275–290.

Duchan, J.F., G.A. Bruder, and L.E. Hewitt (eds.). (1995). *Deixis in Narrative: A Cognitive Science Perspective.* Hillsdale, NJ: Lawrence Erlbaum Associates.

Gerrig, R.J. (1993). *Experiencing Narrative Worlds: On the Psychological Activities of Reading.* New Haven, CT: Yale University Press.

Hanks, W.F. (1990). *Referential Practice: Language and Lived Space among the Maya.* Chicago, IL: University of Chicago Press.

Hanks, W.F. (2005). Explorations in the deictic field. *Current Anthropology*, 46 (2), pp. 191–220.

Haviland, J.B. (1996). Projections, transpositions, and relativity. In J.J. Gumperz and S.C. Levinson (eds.), *Rethinking Linguistic Relativity*. Cambridge: Cambridge University Press, pp. 271–323.

Heller, M. (2003). Globalization, the new economy, and the commodification of language and identity. *Journal of Sociolinguistics*, 7 (4), pp. 473–492.

Irvine, J.T. (2004). Say when: Temporalities in language ideology. *Journal of Linguistic Anthropology*, 14 (1), pp. 99–109.

Jakobson, R. (1957/1990). Shifters and verbal categories. In *On Language: Roman Jakobson*. Edited by L.R. Waugh and M. Monville-Burston. Cambridge, MA: Harvard University Press, pp. 386–392.

Jespersen, O. (1924). *The Philosophy of Grammar*. New York: Henry Holt and Company.

Johnstone, B. (2010). Language and geographical space. In P. Auer and J.E. Schmidt (eds.), *Language and Space: An International Handbook of Linguistic Variation*. Berlin: Walter de Gruyter, pp. 1–17.

Keller-Cohen, D., and C. Gordon. (2003). "On trial": Metaphor in telling the life story. *Narrative Inquiry*, 13 (1), pp. 1–40.

Lempert, M. (2007). Conspicuously past: Distressed discourse and diagrammatic embedding in a Tibetan represented speech style. *Language and Communication*, 27 (3), pp. 258–271.

Lempert, M., and S. Perrino. (2007). Introduction: Entextualization and the ends of temporality. *Language and Communication*, 27 (3), pp. 205–211.

Morson, G.S. (1994). *Narrative and Freedom: The Shadows of Time*. New Haven, CT: Yale University Press.

Ochs, E., and L. Capps. (2001). *Living Narrative*. Cambridge, MA: Harvard University Press.

Parmentier, R.J. (2007). It's about time: On the semiotics of temporality. *Language & Communication*, 27 (3), pp. 272–277.

Perrino, S. (2002). Intimate hierarchies and Qur'anic saliva (*Tëfli*): Textuality in a Senegalese ethnomedical encounter. *Journal of Linguistic Anthropology*, 12 (2), pp. 225–259.

Perrino, S. (2005). Participant transposition in Senegalese oral narrative. *Narrative Inquiry*, 15 (2), pp. 345–375.

Perrino, S. (2007). Cross-chronotope alignment in Senegalese oral narrative. *Language and Communication*, 27 (3), pp. 227–244.

Perrino, S. (2011). Chronotopes of story and storytelling event in interviews. *Language in Society*, 40, pp. 91–103.

Schiffrin, D. (1981). Tense variation in narrative. *Language*, 57 (1), pp. 45–62.

Schiffrin, D. (1990). The management of a co-operative self during agreement: The role of opinions and stories. In A.D. Grimshaw (ed.), *Conflict Talk: Sociolinguistic Investigations of Arguments in Conversations*. Cambridge: Cambridge University Press, pp. 241–259.

Scollon, R., and S.B.K. Scollon. (2003). *Discourses in Place: Language in the Material World*. London: Routledge.

Segal, E.M. (1995). Narrative comprehension and the role of deictic shift theory. In J.F. Duchan, G.A. Bruder, and L.E. Hewitt (eds.), *Deixis in Narrative: A Cognitive Science Perspective*. Hillsdale, NJ: Lawrence Erlbaum Associates, pp. 3–17.

Silverstein, M. (1997). The improvisational performance of culture in realtime discursive practice. In R.K. Sawyer (ed.), *Creativity in Performance*. Greenwich, CT: Ablex Publishing, pp. 265–312.

Silverstein, M. (2005). Axes of evals: Token versus type interdiscursivity. *Journal of Linguistic Anthropology*, 15 (1), pp. 6–22.

Silverstein, M., and G. Urban. (1996). The natural history of discourse. In M. Silverstein and G. Urban (eds.), *Natural Histories of Discourse*. Chicago, IL: University of Chicago Press, pp. 1–17.

Taylor, S. (2003). A place for the future? Residence and continuity in women's narratives of their lives. *Narrative Inquiry*, 13 (1), pp. 193–215.

Todorov, T. (1981). *Introduction to Poetics*. Vol. 1. Translated by R. Howard. Minneapolis: University of Minnesota Press.

Vigouroux, C. (2008). From Africa to Africa: Globalization, migration and language vitality. In C. Vigouroux and S. Mufwene (eds.), *Globalization and Language Vitality: Perspectives from Africa*. London: Continuum, pp. 229–254.

Wirtz, K. (2007). Enregistered memory and Afro-Cuban historicity in Santería's ritual speech. *Language and Communication*, 27 (3), pp. 245–257.

Wolfson, N. (1982). *CHP: The Conversational Historical Present in American English Narrative*. Cinnaminson, NJ: Foris Publications.

Wortham, S.E.F. (1994). *Acting Out Participant Examples in the Classroom*. Amsterdam: John Benjamins.

Wortham, S.E.F. (2000). Interactional positioning and narrative self-construction. *Narrative Inquiry*, 10 (1), pp. 157–184.

Wortham, S.E.F. (2001). *Narratives in Action*. New York: Teachers College, Columbia University.

Wortham, S.E.F. (2006). *Learning Identity*. Cambridge: Cambridge University Press.

Zubin, D.A., and L.E. Hewitt. (1995). The deictic center: A theory of deixis in narrative. In J.F. Duchan, G.A. Bruder, and L.E. Hewitt (eds.), *Deixis in Narrative: A Cognitive Science Perspective*. Hillsdale, NJ: Lawrence Erlbaum Associates, pp. 129–155.

8 Narratives Across Speech Events

STANTON WORTHAM AND
CATHERINE R. RHODES

8.1 Introduction

Most approaches to narrative and discourse analysis focus on the speech event. Some work analyzes individual events of narration (e.g., Jefferson 1978; Schegloff 1997; Wortham 2001). Other work studies recurring narrative events, analyzing the typical structures and functions of some type of narrative event (e.g., Labov 1972; Ochs 1994; Polanyi 1981). Even work that explores "intertextuality" usually examines multiple events in order to analyze the meaning of individual events or recurring types of events. Much of this work has made important contributions to our understandings of narrative and social life. In this chapter we propose another unit for narrative analysis, in addition to individual events and types of narrating events: chains of linked events, which together form a trajectory across which important functions of narrative are accomplished. Our approach does not replace the useful analysis of discrete events and narrative types. We build on this other research and argue that attention to chains of narrative speech events can also be productive.

Recent theoretical work has described how discourse connects across speech events, how signs and individuals travel across trajectories, and how events link to each other at various scales (Agha 2007; Agha and Wortham 2005; Blommaert 2007). This work has shown how the appropriate unit of analysis for many important social processes goes beyond discrete speech events and how linked speech events are essential to social life. Social identities, for example, have often been understood as characteristic positionings or representations that recur in individual speech events. It has become clear, however, that social identification depends on trajectories as individuals move across events (Wortham 2006). Such trajectories involve more than macro-level context and go beyond the instantiation of widely circulating social types. They are instead a unit of analysis in between the "macro" and the "micro" (Wortham 2012) – a trajectory of contingent, linked events that together accomplish some social function.

The Handbook of Narrative Analysis, First Edition. Edited by Anna De Fina and Alexandra Georgakopoulou.
© 2015 John Wiley & Sons, Inc. Published 2019 by John Wiley & Sons, Inc.

As Hymes (1962) describes, a single speech event involves a sender communicating a message to a receiver, on some topic, through some channel (like speech), in some code (like English), in some spatio-temporal location. We follow Hymes and many others in arguing that even analyses of discrete speech events depend on information about other events, models, and stances outside of the focal event itself. But we also make an additional argument: narratives are joined together in chains or trajectories, through discursive processes that link speech events to each other, such that signs and individuals move along chains of narrating events that occur in different spatio-temporal locations. In recent years, more sophisticated ways of analyzing how discourse moves across linked speech events have become available (Agha and Wortham 2005), and in this chapter we apply such an account to narrative discourse.

We focus on chains of linked narratives, through which cultural models, personal identities, and other social phenomena are established as a linked trajectory of narrating events takes shape. We combine insights from narrative analysis with contemporary work on discourse across speech events to construct an approach to analyzing narratives across events. In the first half of the chapter, before going on to describe how narratives can form trajectories across events, we describe various ways in which traditional speech-event-focused accounts of narrative depend on information from other events. We review research on the familiar fact that both referential and evaluative meanings in narrative necessarily presuppose resources beyond the speech event. In the second half of the chapter, we go on to discuss how narratives can form chains of narrating events, describing various ways in which narratives circulate across events through retellings, gossip, evaluative positioning, and canonical narratives.

8.2   How Narratives Presuppose Other Events

Like all discursive events, narratives are only intelligible insofar as participants or analysts presuppose ideas, models, and positionings from outside the speech event – at several levels. Participants inevitably presuppose phonological and lexicogrammatical regularities established across many events of language use in order to interpret a linguistic code. As Putnam (1975) argues, referential meaning depends in part on prototypes and stereotypes established prior to and presupposed in any event of language use. Bakhtin (1981) shows how language use is "dialogic," responding to prior and anticipated utterances and incorporating "voices" established in a speech community. Thus evaluative functions of narrative also depend on knowledge of or alignment with social types established elsewhere and presupposed in the focal speech event.

This section reviews research on various ways in which the intelligibility of narrative discourse depends on resources beyond the speech event. This dependence is well known, but reviewing work on narrative from this point of view reveals some interesting features. It is also important to distinguish this indexical presupposition of ideas, models, and positionings beyond the speech event from the chains of linked narrating events described in the following section. In this section we review work on referential intertextuality, reported speech, voicing and evaluation.

8.2.1   Reference

Narrative discourse refers to and describes characters and events. Reference and predication depend on information from outside the speech event. Deictic forms, for example, depend for their referential value on knowledge about the event of speaking and beyond. What counts as "there," "then," and "they" depends on models most often established in prior discourse. Various researchers have explored how the referential value of narratives depends on resources beyond the event of narration, some focusing on deictics and others on different vehicles for reference and predication.

Mertz (1996) analyzes American legal narratives. In her account of how *Brown v. Board of Education* overturned *Plessy v. Ferguson*, she shows that speakers used deictics to position *Plessy* as a presupposed interlocutor for *Brown*. This allowed the lawyers arguing *Brown* not just to challenge the claims made by *Plessy*, but also to challenge the case itself – which they showed to be of a different era and thus no longer relevant to the present day circumstances of *Brown*. They accomplished this by simultaneously creating distance and connection between the two cases – "taking opinions that address the same problem out of their historical contexts and juxtaposing them to create a continuing story about the development of legal doctrine" (Mertz 1996: 141–142) and at the same time positioning *Plessy* as a case from a different era. The deictics positioned one case in the past and the other in the present – using *now* and *then* – while at the same time establishing them as part of a larger, timeless discourse. This allowed the lawyers to show how the past case was simultaneously relevant and not relevant, metonymically using the aspects of the case that most served their argument.

Hanks (1990) analyzes how deictic reference works in shamanic ritual narrative speech, bringing three fundamental "natural attitude" assumptions into question: that deixis is concrete, subjective, and isolable (5–6). Against these assumptions, Hanks argues that deictic reference, at least among the Maya, is not egocentric but "sociocentric … grounded on the relation between interlocutors" (7). He explains how, for the Maya, space "always involves a combination of schematic prefabricated knowledge and the emergent awareness of one's own location relative to a context" (349). Shared understandings of social space and practice establish continuity beyond individual encounters and are woven into the broader social context of life for the Maya, such that narrative uses of deictics can only be interpreted by presupposing knowledge from beyond the speech event.

8.2.2   Reported speech

As Bauman (1986) argues, stories are "forms of discourse in which the concern with and use of other people's words takes on a special heightened quality, in which these words become especially prominent as the 'object of interpretation, discussion, evaluation, rebuttal, support, further development and so on'" (54). To achieve these effects, narrative discourse often represents others' words in various ways: directly quoting another, indirectly reporting what another said, or speaking in a way that sounds like a recognizable other. We will discuss the last of these under the title "voicing" in the following section. The direct or indirect representation of others' speech presupposes another speech event beyond the narrating event (i.e., the event in which the original speech took place). Various analyses have explored how narratives presuppose other events in this way.

Haviland (2005) shows how reported speech can help establish the social identification of an individual over time. In the case he describes, one speaker characterizes himself by quoting others' words; after enough repetition these quoted descriptions sediment, and he inhabits the role that he has established primarily through reported speech. This process both presupposes the prior speech events being quoted, which took place over several decades, and also relies on shared evaluations of the social values communicated by the quoted words.

In the law school classroom, Mertz (2007) shows that reported speech is often used to construct legal personae in building legal arguments. Reported speech need not quote an actual prior utterance. Instead, it is "frequently fictional or imputed," quoting a hypothetical speaker or using words not actually said in order to characterize a certain social position (2007: 102). Mertz argues that quoted speech can illustrate a quoted character's emotional stance on an issue, or serve as a means for "gauging, or … constructing the authenticity of [his/her] statement" (2007: 104). In either case, the quoted speech presupposes the other event in which the original speech occurred and the social types being indexed as people who have spoken that way in prior events.

Brookes (2005) shows that quoted "speech" does not need to be speech at all. She describes quotable gestures, or "gestures that can be recalled and glossed independently of speech" (2044–2045), which she argues can do the work of conveying and shaping event-based identities in narrative and other discourse. The quotability of gestures lies in the wide circulation of the cultural models upon which they rely. For example, Brookes describes a widely known gesture used among Black urban South African "male youth between the ages of 18 and 25 years, particularly in conjunction with a male youth argot sometimes referred to as *Iscamtho*" (2047). "The Drinking Gesture" can function "independently of speech … as a component of a message in combination with other quotable gestures, or it may communicate a complete message on its own, the meaning depending on context" (2048). Beyond the act of drinking, the Drinking Gesture can also communicate information about the quality of the action – for example, the frequency or speed of the gesture can communicate "the amount of drinking or alcohol" (2048). When such a gesture co-occurs with narrative speech, it communicates information about narrated events and narrator evaluations only as it presupposes the types of prior events in which it typically occurs.

8.2.3 *Voicing*

A voice is an identifiable social type, indexed by one or more signs. Bakhtin (1981) describes how narrative discourse often centers around the voices assigned to characters. Through voicing, the narrator identifies narrated characters as recognizable types of people. As described elsewhere (Wortham 2001), voices are assigned through various types of cues. Evaluative indexicals, for instance, are signs habitually associated with some social type. The word "groovy," for example, would only be used (unironically) by certain types of people. When a narrator associates such a sign with some character, s/he often both voices (characterizes) the person as some social type and evaluates that type (as, for example, out of date). Evaluative indexicals, and the other cues used to assign voices, presuppose information from outside the speech event, information about the types of events in which the sign has typically occurred.

Hill (1995) analyzes how a narrator uses various devices to establish heterogeneous voices in her story. She also shows how choice of linguistic code can voice cultural evaluations of practices – for example, how discourses about business and profit are better carried out in Spanish, rather than in Mexicano, because the colonial language is associated with the state and the public sphere. While a shift in linguistic code, register, or even genre can signal a change in voice in this way, Tannen (1989) shows how a variety of paralinguistic features, such as intonation and prosody, can also establish different voices. The success of these features in conveying something about the character being voiced relies upon culturally presupposed knowledge about how linguistic and paralinguistic features are typically used – that is, how they have been used in other events the speaker has experienced.

Wortham and Locher (1996) describe how newscasters voice the characters they describe in their news reports using metapragmatic framing, evaluative indexicals, and other types of cues. Metapragmatic framing devices include "verbs of speaking," which characterize speakers and speech events. It voices a character differently, for instance, to say that s/he "whined," as opposed to saying that s/he "asked" (Silverstein 2003). Wortham and Locher analyze US network news coverage of Presidential elections, showing how apparently neutral news coverage can assign highly presupposing voices to candidates. One of their examples traces how a Spanish language network describes the Iran-Contra affair as an *"escándalo"* (scandal) and associates US President George H.W. Bush with it. This term "starts to suggest a voice for Bush, as a morally suspect politician who has gotten himself in trouble" (1996: 569). The newscaster goes on to use the verb *"contradecir"* (to contradict) in evaluating Bush's version of the story, saying that "new evidence contradicts what Bush has said" (569). Wortham and Locher trace how such cues accumulate into a highly presupposing voice being assigned to Bush, as he is associated with the types of people such terms are habitually used to describe.

8.2.4   Evaluation

In addition to voicing characters as recognizable social types, narrators also inevitably adopt their own positions on those voices (Bakhtin 1981; Wortham 2001). This is part of what Labov and Waletzky (1967) refer to as "evaluation," but it is not just a cognitive process. In addition to expressing attitudes toward the types of people represented in their stories, narrators also position themselves interactionally with respect to social types and with respect to other participants in the event of speaking. Narrators rely upon grammatical, stylistic, and other narrative devices to communicate these evaluations. Evaluation presupposes knowledge of groups, alignments, and social stances from beyond the speech event.

Ehrlich (this volume, chapter 15) shows how models of women's sexual behavior influence evaluations of narrated characters' actions. She describes how lawyers present a rape victim's sexual interest in her accused perpetrator as allegedly "inconsistent with her claim that she was a victim of rape" (section 15.2.2). Lawyers tap into jury members' presupposed models and evaluations of sex, violence, and gendered behavior in order to undermine the alleged victim's testimony. In this case, patriarchal ideologies from beyond the narrating event play an essential role in narrators' evaluations of their protagonists.

Briggs (1996) shows how deictics in narrative discourse can help accomplish evaluation by highlighting ideological and stylistic aspects. Analyzing Warao dispute mediation, he shows how narrators use temporal and person deictics (e.g., equivalents of English "now," "then," "not yet," as well as "us" and "them"), plus metapragmatic discourse markers (e.g., explicit accounts of what is happening in a speech event, such as "I am just speaking my mind"), to establish the authority of their narratives. In Warao mediation, the central actor's use of deictics and metapragmatic markers often characterizes the speech as falling into the "counseling" genre, distinguishing it from more everyday speech and granting it added authority, because, in the Warao social hierarchy, "[government] officials ... can counsel all members of their community, husbands can counsel wives, and parents can counsel children" (Briggs 1996: 329). Briggs also shows how one narrator employs a shift from temporal to person deixis in order to establish an alternative interpretation to events her husband has just reported, ultimately establishing superior authority for her account. Both of these strategies require knowledge of other events for interlocutors to understand the evaluation of narrated characters that is being accomplished. They need to know how Warao typically speak, and they need to know about specific events being referred to, in order to understand how narrated characters and co-participants are being evaluated.

8.3   Chains of Narrating Events

Any adequate account of narrative discourse must acknowledge that narratives are only intelligible when listeners presuppose information from other speech events, in at least the four ways enumerated in the last section. As Agha and Wortham (2005) argue, narrative and other types of discourse *also* often involve a more specific type of dependence on other speech events. Sometimes the appropriate unit of analysis extends beyond discrete events to linked chains of speech events across which language change, social identification, and other social processes occur (Agha 2007). Silverstein (2005) calls this a distinction between "intertextuality" and "interdiscursivity." Intertextuality is "a structural principle of textuality that remains constant or recognizable across discursive events," while interdiscursivity describes how ways of talking can establish chains of speech events, "a relationship of event to event [that] is projected from the position ... of some particular event in respect of one or more others" (Silverstein 2005: 7). Agha (2005) uses the term "inter-event semiosis" for the latter type of process. Whichever term we use, the claim is that many discursive phenomena can only be understood if we study linked chains of speech events, across which linguistic forms, narrated objects, evaluative stances, and other non-referential phenomena move. In this section we describe how narrative meaning can depend on inter-event chains.

This claim does not compete with the claim in the last section: it is *both* true that any discrete event of narration can only be understood by presupposing information, models, and stances from beyond that event *and* that many functions of narrative discourse are best understood in terms of cross-event chains. This section reviews work illustrating the latter claim. Our focus on cross-event chains does not imply that event-focused analyses have no value. For some research questions and some narratives, a focus on discrete events – in addition to their presupposition of information, models, and stances from beyond the speech event – is adequate. Furthermore, many insights developed through prior analyses of discrete speech events are essential to our own and others' work analyzing chains of narrative events. We draw attention to another productive unit of analysis for understanding narratives and the social processes that they facilitate, pointing out a new object of investigation that builds on and can complement work on discrete events.

Agha (2007) gives a comprehensive account of how speech events are linked into "speech chains" – trajectories or pathways that accomplish various social processes. Agha writes, "The links of the chain are speech events in which social persons occupy roles such as 'sender' and 'receiver' of messages, and the [sign] being transmitted occurs as part of the linguistic message exchanged by the occupants of these roles" (2007: 66). In the case of naming, for example, Agha draws on Kripke (1972) to describe how names can only refer if one presupposes a chain of events in which that name has been used, extending back to the baptismal event in which the individual was first named. He extends this account to reference more generally and to other functions of language use. A speaker can only use language to signal a referent if s/he has already been "introduced to [it] … in a prior speech event" in which s/he occupied the role of receiver (2007: 66). Speech chains are thus formed through links across "a historical series of speech events connected together by the permutation of individuals across speech-act roles" (2007: 67). Speech events are linked as signs are used such that they presuppose earlier links in the chain.

The evaluation carried by an evaluative indexical term, for example, moves across a speech chain as the hearer in one event uses the form with that presupposition in a subsequent event. Across many such events, sets of signs become associated with certain social types and evaluations – a process Agha (2007) calls "enregisterment." For example, Mehan (1996) analyzes how a student becomes "learning disabled." The student is not labeled with an existing social typification, in one or more events, simply connecting a stable "macro" category with the individual. Instead, across a series of linked events the student gradually becomes associated with aspects of the stereotype "learning disabled," and the stereotype is contextualized in the local situation. Across a series of institutionally mandated forms and meetings, characterizations of the student, his family, and relevant educators emerge as subsequent events presuppose and modify descriptions and evaluations made in earlier events along the chain. Early in the chain, for example, the teacher makes notes on student performance, as she does for all students in the class, but over time her notes on the focal student start to include descriptions of non-normative behavior. These notes then serve as the basis for a memo to administrators, and parts of the notes enter into bureaucratic documents prepared by the school psychologist. The meaning of the teacher's behavioral observations shifts as these are recontextualized in subsequent events, moving from administrators' notes to communications with parents, formal assessment meetings, and psychological evaluations. The chain of relevant events takes place across months, with the social fact of a "learning disability" established across the trajectory.

In this section we apply the concept of speech chains to narrative discourse in particular, showing how narrating events participate in different kinds of chains. A narrative that describes actual events inevitably participates in a speech chain that has at least two events, because it links the event being narrated to the event of narration. Generally, more than two events are linked, because there is more than one narrated event and/or the narrated event itself presupposes prior events along some relevant trajectory. The chains of events thus created can serve various functions, and we review several in this section.

Narrated content is not the only object through which two or more events can be linked. Various types of signs, models or social positions can link events in a chain. A linguistic form – a phonological regularity, grammatical category, or lexical item – can recur across events and serve as the principle of linkage, as in the spread of a regional accent (Agha 2007) or the elimination of a grammatical category (Silverstein 1984), due to differential valuing of the forms and associated groups of people. A biographical individual can serve as the principle of linkage, as descriptions of that person recur and sometimes shift across events (Wortham 2006). In the subsections below, we review research that explores how narratives can be linked into chains of events in several different ways: through retellings, in which partial or entire narrated events are repeated across events; through gossip; through linkages of evaluative positions enacted in narrative discourse; and through the establishment of canonical narratives.

8.3.1   Retellings

For decades, analysts of narrative have studied retellings in which narrators repeat stories with similar characters and narrated events across more than one speech event. These retellings are often verbal art forms, with performances of the same story in different venues or for different groups. Such retellings create chains of narrating events, because they repeat narrated content and perhaps other features across events. The resulting chain of narrating events can accomplish various functions.

Bauman (1986) argues that each new telling of a narrative is embedded in its particular context, and he argues that the narrated and narrating events cannot be separated because they are bound together in "the indissoluble unity of text" (7). He also shows how narrative retellings vary in structure and form depending upon various factors. For example, he argues that "when quoted speech is the focus of the narrative and a particular utterance is the very point of it, the text is formally more constrained and less susceptible to change from one telling to the next" (75). Yet, while the text itself may be more structurally constrained, retelling a story can still serve to cast the reported text in a new light. Rekeying or reframing, Bauman argues, is one of the primary functions of retellings. Bauman thus shows how chains of retellings inevitably involve transformation in content and form, and how retellings can accomplish various functions in context.

Ehrlich (this volume, chapter 15) shows how "in the legal system as a whole, narratives 'travel' (Blommaert 2005: 78) or shift across contexts" (section 15.1). As stories circulate beyond their "original contexts of production," they "are modified so that they conform to institutionally-privileged genres and/or categories that are intelligible to the legal system" (section 15.4). These modifications have real consequences for women's lives. In the case Ehrlich describes, as narratives travel beyond their original events of production, they "authorized a definition of violence against women that is more consistent with stranger violence than with intimate partner violence" (section 15.3.1), despite that fact that most of the women's testimonies upon which this definition was built involved intimate partner violence. Further down the chains, the same stories are used to undermine prosecutions of intimate partner violence in courts of law.

The elements of a story preserved in a retelling vary. It can be the repetition of a single word, a phrase, stretches of a story, themes, content, tone, rhetorical style, or even an entire story. Analysts have described many functions of such repetition. Stivers (2004) analyzes speakers' repetitions of their own words, showing how such repetition can evaluate an interlocutor's prior talk negatively. Schegloff (1997) argues that the immediate repetition of another speaker's words can "initiate a repair" or serve to register receipt and direct the conversation toward the next action. Repetition of words can also be used as a strategy for keeping the floor during a conversation (Rieger 2003).

Slobin (1996) shows how bilinguals' narratives vary as they are retold across their languages, focusing his analysis on verbs of motion that propel the central actions in a story. He argues, for example, that, "Spanish ... stories devote less attention to movement and ground ... than do English versions" (6). He shows that the features of a given language "'train' the speakers ... in the development of a particular rhetorical style," one that may remain intact across dialects, discourse types, and genres (14). Such cross-language differences influence bilingual speakers' perceptions of and behaviors with respect to time and human action. As he follows stories across languages, he traces the consistencies and discontinuities created by different grammatical systems.

Polanyi (1981) explores what counts as a retelling and argues that narrated content and evaluative stance are both important. She shows how narrators draw upon recognizable "scripts" or "abstract semantic representation[s] of the expected events which make up the prototypical instance of a familiar experience" (330). Polanyi argues that

> in order to be considered multiple versions of the same story, the specific happenings in the various tellings must occur in structurally identical positions in the controlling script, and the general point to be inferred from the violations of expectation(s) in the tellings must be the same. (1981: 332)

Thus she argues that a chain of retellings only counts as the "same" story when both referential and evaluative aspects are preserved.

Sansom (1982) describes how voices are preserved across retellings. Characterizations can be the central feature that constitutes a chain of retellings. He also explores who is authorized to retell a given story. In his analysis of stories of sickness in an aboriginal community, the sick person is not allowed to tell his or her own story. Instead, caregivers must do so. Through public tellings of these stories, identities are constituted both for the sick and for those who care for them, as voices are established and held constant across the various events of narration.

Norrick (1997) shows how narrative retellings "[foster] group rapport, ... [ratify] group membership, and ... [convey] group values" (199). The stories he examines are already known to participants, allowing him to focus on the interpersonal work accomplished through narration and not the communication of propositional content. Norrick shows how co-narration in these retellings communicates, evaluates, and ratifies values, aligning participants with those values and establishing their membership within the family. The chains of retellings thus depend on and hold together a community of narrators and characters.

8.3.2 *Gossip*

Gossip involves the repeated narration of certain characters and events for a specific purpose: to characterize particular individuals, teasing or stigmatizing them, and perhaps to establish social boundaries or solidarities. Thus gossip involves the repetition of narrated content, but it also involves the repetition of voicing for characters and an evaluation of those characters. Gossip speech chains involve linked events that involve a package of narrated events, voicing and evaluation. The resulting chains can do important social work, as various analyses have shown.

Goodwin (1980) analyzes interactions in which gossip is repeated and social relationships are thereby maintained or transformed among urban American youth. She shows how a group of African American girls use gossip and other talk in order to create social organization, focusing on "he-said-she-said" events in which a narrator embeds events of speaking within each other in order to accuse someone of inappropriate talk. Goodwin analyzes prosodic, syntactic, and interactional features of gossip, focusing on the embedding of reported speech. Her account shows how these embedded quotations can evaluate others and create social alignments central to the peer group.

In Fiji, Brenneis (1984) shows how gossip (*talanoa*), which "must be about the less-than-worthy doings of absent others" (493) relies on "reference to larger sociopolitical features of community life in which gossip clearly plays an important role" (288). He explores the non-referential aspects of gossip, which are centrally involved in the constitution of community. While *talanoa* is referential in that it is about people and events, "it is a very opaque kind of referentiality," for "generally participants in *talanoa* sessions must come to them with some understanding of what is being discussed" (494). Brenneis shows that *talanoa* narratives are distinct from most kinds of gossip in other communities in that they rarely or only obliquely identify the main character and never announce why the story is being told. These features limit the culpability of speakers who gossip, for it is of great import in this community that *talanoa* not cause "irreparable damage" (496). Narrators only gossip with trustworthy interlocutors, relying on the "relative opacity of *talanoa* texts and the system of indirect reference sustained through the *bole* construction [the third-person singular present form of the verb 'to speak']" (494). Brenneis analyzes how "the stylistic and organizational features of *talanoa* allow ... a kind of conversational duet," one which creates "a remarkable degree of stylistic convergence on the part of the speakers," and he shows how this convergence establishes "the shared qualities and social identities of the speakers" (496).

Haviland (1977) shows how genealogical knowledge is key to understanding Zinacanteco gossip. He describes how "long sequences of identifying formulas" (52) form the foundation on which gossip is circulated. The number of schemata that recur are limited, however: "To establish a pathway the storyteller need only show kinship relations between the person he has in mind and a well-identified person" (52). This knowledge, Haviland argues, is distributed across individuals in the community, and in order to decipher gossip they must "tap the shared knowledge that people had of others throughout the *municipio*" (52). To understand identifying sequences in Zinacanteco gossip, one must not only understand kinship pathways but also individuals' "cargo careers, and their past transgressions" (53). The chain of gossip narratives is thus woven into and partly constitutes the relational background of the community.

8.3.3   *Evaluative positions*

Narrators inevitably evaluate their characters and aspects of the social context (Bakhtin 1981). As described above, evaluations are only accomplished as listeners draw on presupposed information about other events, models, and stances from beyond the narrating event. The evaluative functions of a narrative also often presuppose cross-event chains. For example, the voicing and evaluation of a social group in a characteristic way presupposes other events in which that group, and perhaps others, have been thus positioned. Larger processes of social identification and evaluation of groups take place across a chain of narrating events, as types of people are established and characterized. Narratives participate in these processes, as narrating events link to other events that establish an emergent evaluation for individuals or groups. The linked events that give rise to emergent evaluations need not be confined to the past. As Georgakopoulou points out in this volume (chapter 13), "breaking news" draws on currently unfolding happenings to form links in an evaluative narrative chain.

Bucholtz et al. (2012) study university science classrooms, analyzing how two female lab students marginalize a male lab student and the shifting gender roles negotiated across the classroom events in which this occurs. Despite the fact that the male student's academic performance is generally comparable to their own, they successfully position him as an "incompetent chemistry student" (159). They are able to do this by drawing upon prior narrating events in the classroom and on more widely circulating models of scientific behavior. The authors show how, over a chain of events that lasts an academic semester, "interlocutors' stance taking, participation, and other practices of intersubjective positioning gradually crystallize into more stable identities" (171). They show how these processes happen through the use of linguistic tools such as pronouns and other grammatical strategies for creating alignment with more widely circulating, presupposed values.

Hill (1995) writes about Don Gabriel, a man said to be the last speaker of Mexicano in his village, showing how he presupposes historically emergent processes of group formation and evaluation in his narrative. Hill explores in detail how Don Gabriel switches between Mexicano and Spanish while telling his story. She argues that

Mexicano speakers live in two opposed worlds – the more traditional world of "peasant communitarian values" and the Westernized world of "danger and business-for-profit" (111). Mexicano is associated with the former and Spanish with the latter. Switching between these two codes, Don Gabriel creates a "moral geography" and positively evaluates the more traditional world. To speak about something like the topic of murder, "Don Gabriel must invoke the ugly lexicon of dealings for profit, which for Mexicano speakers is drawn entirely from Spanish" (108). Thus Don Gabriel presupposes "contradictory ideologies," represented in "conflicting ways of speaking ... across a complex of 'voices' through which he constructs a narrative about the murder of his son" (98). Don Gabriel switches codes (Spanish and Mexicano) when he talks about different geographical spaces in his story – in town or outside of town, for example. In setting up the "moral geography" of the story, Don Gabriel makes use of multiple voices across languages to encode his ideological position with respect to the activities he describes, and these voices have been constituted through the establishment of specific registers associated with language and colonialism, across chains of events in which the languages and associated spaces have been characterized.

While Hill (1995) describes the role of code-switching in evaluative voicing, in the analysis mentioned earlier, Mehan (1996) shows the evaluative function of labeling. While analyzing how a student comes to be identified as "learning disabled," Mehan describes a process of stabilization across linked speech events through which a student becomes associated with an evaluative label. When such labels are institutionalized, their circulation expands and they draw upon institutional authority (such as the specialized scientific knowledge of psychology). This authority is created in chains across institutional contexts as "discourse from one setting in the sequence of events in the referral process generates the given text used for discussion in the next session" (258). The text-artifacts (e.g., the referral form filled out by a teacher) produced during this process become "decentered and de-'voiced'," detached from their original users and the transactions of their production (259). Mehan describes how this process relies upon expert registers that are used to construct the categories and ascribe them to students. Social actors' varying control of these categories affects their ability to negotiate their own or their children's emergent voices, as trajectories of evaluation become more rigid over time and it becomes more difficult to alter the momentum toward an essentializing diagnosis.

Briggs (2003) analyzes how the creation of audiences can be accomplished through the evaluation of discourses. In his discussion of a public health campaign about cholera in Venezuela, Briggs shows how "the public" that the campaign sought to address was not the public interpellated by the campaign. Because the discourse was highly medicalized, it was not accessible to the general public. The discourses of "media coverage and public health information" were nonetheless "aimed at the public and [allegedly] accessible to everyone," and so the public was cast as being culpable for not assimilating information and using it to prevent the spread of cholera (307). The public to whom the discourse was directed was thus projected as a principal in the discourse, without having authored or animated any part of it. Briggs draws on Warner (2002), who argues that, "although [the producers of public discourse] see themselves as speaking to 'the public,' a defined and knowable population, audiences for public discourse are produced by the circulation and reception of the discourse and the material underpinnings that shape these practices" (Briggs 2003: 289). Only by analyzing the larger chains presupposed by medicalized, bureaucratic, and popular discourses can we see how the public was constituted and characterized in this instance.

In our own work, we have shown how two types of narrative move across an American town that has recently received many Mexican immigrants. We call one type of story "payday mugging narratives," which describe an undocumented immigrant being mugged on payday after he cashes his check (Wortham et al. 2011). The other stories are accounts of the town's history, in which residents talk about the town's past and future trajectories given the recent arrival of Mexican immigrants (Wortham and Rhodes 2012). Both types of stories voice Mexicans (e.g., as passive and easily victimized or as aggressively defending their rights, as temporary sojourners just here to make money or as the latest in a long line of immigrants on the road to assimilation). Both types of stories draw on models of Mexican immigrant identity that circulate widely in the United States but are "inflected by more local considerations" (Wortham and Rhodes 2012: 85). As such, the stories rely on chains of other events in which models of Mexican immigrant identity have been circulated in national media and through local channels.

Our analysis documents local chains across which these narratives move in the town. We follow payday mugging stories as they are told across narrators, describing trajectories of narration from original narrated events (e.g., a mugging) through police reports, newspaper articles, friends and family, then out into the larger community. As the stories move across groups, they change in systematic ways. Young male Mexican narrators, for instance, characterize victims of payday muggings as less passive than Anglo or female Mexican narrators do. Black narrators voice the perpetrators of payday muggings differently than everyone else, distinguishing between different types of black residents. In our other project we compare narratives of town history from two different phases in the development of the immigrant community: about a decade ago, when Mexicans were more transient; and today, when the model Mexican resident is part of an intact young family with children. We show how Anglo residents have changed their narratives of Mexicans' likely future in the town, from seeing them as temporary sojourners to expecting more permanent residence and assimilation from them, while most adult Mexicans continue to narrate a future return to Mexico. Both of these studies document the shifting evaluation of Mexican immigrants through narrative discourse, as chains of narrating events form and change direction over time. Narratives are a powerful means of evaluating individuals and groups, and such evaluation is often accomplished through trajectories of narration across events.

8.3.4   *Canonical narratives*

Sometimes narratives become canonical, emblematic of a group or central to rituals of group formation. As we have seen above, quoted speech, voicing, and other common features of narrative discourse facilitate the characterization and evaluation of individuals and social types. When a canonical narrative becomes established and available for wide circulation, that narrative can be a crucial factor in holding together a social group, as in some ritual events (Janowitz 1985; Silverstein 1993, 1996), or in identifying in-group and out-group members.

Lempert and Silverstein (2012) argue that when individuals make sense of a narrated event, they "come to understand such incidents by invoking such structures of analogic associations as are already in circulation about the figurated characters, automatically bringing them to bear on what must have been going on in the reported event" (224). They suggest that there are recognizable genres and canonical examples upon which people draw to make stories interpretable: "Reporting a prior event, in print journalism or elsewhere, is never merely a report, never a passive, disinterested relay of narrated event in the past to addressees in the present" (200). The reliance on canonical narrative types – both genre and models of personhood – is essential to make sense of narratives in cultural context. Various analysts have explored how canonical narratives are produced in practice.

Lempert and Silverstein (2012) examine narrative accounts of an interaction between reporter Helen Thomas and President Richard Nixon at a White House news conference over 40 years ago. While the primary focus of this event was a bill signing, the interaction between Thomas and Nixon after the official event became a news item. In this interaction, Nixon chided Thomas for wearing pants (not a dress) to the White House. He suggests that, since pants do not cost less than dresses, she should change her clothes. Newspaper reports of the interaction between Thomas and Nixon circulated widely.

> This news story, then, is a report of an event within a ritual event that anthropologists – and psychiatric personnel – immediately recognize. It is an instance of ad hominem – or ad feminam – ritual degradation of the female reporter at the hands of the male president of the United States, a show ritual before an audience of the president's peers and the reporter's peers itself embedded within a larger show ritual for the American people: the signing of a bill … (Lempert and Silverstein 2012: 217).

The ideological topics exemplified in the interaction – women's rights, couched in a conversation about women's fashion – indexed topics that were widely circulating at the time the article was published. This is a ritual reinscription of a familiar type of social positioning between a powerful man and a less powerful woman. Lempert and Silverstein show how narratives of this event become one canonical instantiation of that larger social type, an important link in a chain of events that established something about gender at a time when "women's liberation" was salient.

Janowitz (1985) analyzes a similar phenomenon in written discourse, describing the interaction between narrative form and function in the citation of rabbinical texts: "As rituals become ossified, traditional forms, their linguistic component tends to lose a degree of propositional or semantic meaning. Ironically, however, this loss seems to imply an increase in pragmatic, socially effective, or creative value of ritual texts" (155). Janowitz analyzes a text that consists of a conversation between a rabbinical teacher and a student. The teacher and student read the text. The student's lines are questions asked of the teacher. The teacher's lines respond to the student, describing the next step the student must take on his journey of ascension to the uppermost heaven. The recitation of the text is an explicit primary performative (cf. Austin 1962/1975), in which social facts are created through the utterance of words. By reading this text, "the very discussion of the process effects the ascent because of the implicit theory of language and the particular forms and their arrangements found in the text" (Janowitz 1985: 159). As a ritual text, the semantic content and ritual meaning combine in the act of reading the text, allowing it to "communicate … about the transformation of ascent, while at the same time enacting it" (173). The canonical text thus plays a central role in the ritual enactment of basic cultural categories, as that text circulates into contemporary pedagogical encounters.

8.4   Conclusions

Narratives are typically studied as discrete events, either in themselves or as instances of recurring types of narratives. Such work is often illuminating. In both these types of narrative analysis, analysts must acknowledge the importance of other events – many of them not contiguous with the focal event. As argued in the first half of the chapter, and as established by much prior work, we cannot understand a narrative without knowledge of other events beyond the narrating event, because both the referential and evaluative functions of narrative discourse depend on information, models, and positionings from other events for their intelligibility.

In this chapter we argue for a second sense in which narrative analysis must go beyond the speech event. Sometimes the relevant unit of analysis for a social process is a chain or trajectory of events that together constitute social identity, group membership, social characterization, and the like. Analyses of narrative must sometimes go beyond studying discrete events, and beyond studying recurring types of events, to study chains of narrating events, because important functions of narrative discourse sometimes take shape only across such chains. Sometimes the action of establishing a social group or characterizing an individual can only be understood and empirically explored if we trace a chain of events. The crucial social work does not occur within the boundaries of one event, but instead emerges as actions across linked events accumulate to accomplish the focal process. We must move beyond the artificial constraint of "speech events" as a central analytic category if we hope to investigate such processes empirically.

The research reviewed in the second half of this chapter illustrates how analysts can study chains of narrating events across which group formation, social identification, and other social regularities emerge. Wortham and Reyes (2015) describe concretely how to do such narrative analysis. Discourse analysis beyond the speech event requires an analyst to analyze the structure and function of discrete events, and also to do three additional things: identify linked events, showing which events are in fact linked in a trajectory that accomplishes some social function; delineate the discursive patterns through which cross-event patterns are created; and trace the shape of cross-event trajectories, identifying what social pattern is in fact established. Adding a focus on cross-event trajectories to traditional work on discrete and recurring types of narrating events will show how narrative is an even more productive site of social activity than previously envisioned.

REFERENCES

Agha, A. (2005). Voice, footing, enregisterment. *Journal of Linguistic Anthropology*, 15, pp. 38–59.

Agha, A. (2007). *Language and Social Relations*. Cambridge: Cambridge University Press.

Agha, A., and S. Wortham (eds.). (2005). Discourse across speech events: Intertextuality and interdiscursivity in social life. Special issue of the *Journal of Linguistic Anthropology*, 15 (1).

Austin, J.L. (1962/1975). *How to Do Things with Words*. 2nd edn. Edited by J.O. Urmson and M. Sbisà. Cambridge, MA: Harvard University Press.

Bakhtin, M. (1981). *The Dialogic Imagination: Four Essays*. Edited by M. Holquist. Translated by C. Emerson and M. Holquist. Austin: University of Texas Press.

Bauman, R. (1986). *Story, Performance, and Event*. Cambridge: Cambridge University Press.

Blommaert, J. (2005). *Discourse: A Critical Introduction*. Cambridge: Cambridge University Press.

Blommaert, J. (2007). On scope and depth in linguistic ethnography. *Journal of Sociolinguistics*, 11, pp. 682–688.

Brenneis, D. (1984). Grog and gossip in Bhatgaon. *American Ethnologist*, 11, pp. 487–506.

Briggs, C. (1996). Conflict, language ideologies, and privileged arenas of discursive authority in Warao dispute mediations. In C. Briggs (ed.), *Disorderly Discourse: Narrative, Conflict, and Inequality*. Oxford: Oxford University Press, pp. 204–242.

Briggs, C. (2003). Why nation-states and journalists can't teach people to be healthy: Power and pragmatic miscalculation in public discourses on health. *Medical Anthropology Quarterly*, 17, pp. 287–321.

Brookes, H. (2005). What gestures do: Some communicative functions of quotable gestures in conversations among Black urban South Africans. *Journal of Pragmatics*, 37, pp. 2044–2085.

Bucholtz, M., B. Barnwell, E. Skapoulli, and J.J. Lee. (2012). Itineraries of identity in undergraduate science. *Anthropology & Education Quarterly*, 43, pp. 157–172.

Goodwin, M. (1980). He-said-she-said: Formal cultural procedures for the construction of a gossip dispute activity. *American Ethnologist*, 7, pp. 674–695.

Hanks, W. (1990). *Referential Practice: Language and Lived Space among the Maya*. Chicago, IL: University of Chicago Press.

Haviland, J. (1977). *Gossip, Reputation and Knowledge in Zinacantan*. Chicago, IL: University of Chicago Press.

Haviland, J. (2005). "Whorish old man" and "one (animal) gentleman." *Journal of Linguistic Anthropology*, 15, pp. 81–94.

Hill, J. (1995). The voices of Don Gabriel. In B. Mannheim and T. Tedlock (eds.), *The Dialogic Emergence of Culture*. Urbana: University of Illinois Press, pp. 97–147.

Hymes, D. (1962). The ethnography of speaking. In T. Gladwin and W.C. Sturtevant (eds.), *Anthropology and Human Behavior*. Washington, DC: The Anthropology Society of Washington, pp. 13–53.

Janowitz, N. (1985). Parallelism and framing devices in a late antique ascent text. In E. Mertz and R. Parmentier (eds.), *Semiotic Mediation*. New York: Academic Press, pp. 155–175.

Jefferson, G. (1978). Sequential aspects of storytelling in conversation. In J. Schenkein (ed.), *Studies in the Organization of Conversational Interaction*. New York: Academic Press, pp. 219–248.

Kripke, S. (1972). Naming and necessity. In D. Davidson and G. Harman (eds.), *Semantics of Natural Language*. Dordrecht: D. Reidel, pp. 252–355.

Labov, W. (1972). *Language in the Inner City: Studies in the Black English Vernacular*.

Philadelphia: University of Pennsylvania Press.

Labov, W., and J. Waletzky. (1967). Narrative analysis: Oral versions of personal experience. In J. Helm (ed.), *Essays on the Verbal and Visual Arts*. Seattle: University of Washington Press for the AES, pp. 12–44.

Lempert, M., and M. Silverstein. (2012). *Creatures of Politics: Media, Message, and the American Presidency*. Bloomington: Indiana University Press.

Mehan, H. (1996). The construction of an LD student: A case study in the politics of representation. In M. Silverstein and G. Urban (eds.), *Natural Histories of Discourse*. Chicago, IL: University of Chicago Press, pp. 253–276.

Mertz, E. (1996). Consensus and dissent in U.S. legal opinions: Narrative structure and social voices. In C. Briggs (ed.), *Disorderly Discourse: Narrative, Conflict, and Inequality*. Oxford: Oxford University Press, pp. 135–157.

Mertz, E. (2007). *The Language of Law School*. Oxford: Oxford University Press.

Norrick, N. (1997). Twice-told tales: Collaborative narration of familiar stories. *Language in Society*, 26, pp. 199–220.

Ochs, E. (1994). Stories that step into the future. In D. Biber and E. Finegan (eds.), *Perspectives on Register: Situating Language Variation in Sociolinguistics*. Oxford: Oxford University Press, pp. 106–135.

Polanyi, L. (1981). Telling the same story twice. *Text & Talk*, 1, pp. 315–336.

Putnam, H. (1975). *Mind, Language and Reality: Philosophical Papers*. Vol. 2. Cambridge: Cambridge University Press.

Rieger, C. (2003). Repetitions as self-repair strategies in English and German conversations. *Journal of Pragmatics*, 35, pp. 47–69.

Sansom, B. (1982). The sick who do not speak. In D. Parkin (ed.), *Semantic Anthropology*. London: Academic Press, pp. 183–195.

Schegloff, E. (1997). Practices and actions: Boundary cases of other-initiated repair. *Discourse Processes*, 23, pp. 499–545.

Silverstein, M. (1984). The "value" of objectual language. Paper presented at a symposium of the American Anthropology Association, Denver, CO.

Silverstein, M. (1993). Metapragmatic discourse and metapragmatic function. In J. Lucy (ed.), *Reflexive Language: Reported Speech and Metapragmatics*. Cambridge: Cambridge University Press, pp. 33–58.

Silverstein, M. (1996). The secret life of texts. In G. Urban (ed.), *Natural Histories of Discourse*. Chicago, IL: University of Chicago Press, pp. 81–105.

Silverstein, M. (2003). Indexical order and the dialectics of sociolinguistic life. *Language & Communication*, 23, pp. 193–229.

Silverstein, M. (2005). Axes of evals. *Journal of Linguistic Anthropology*, 15 (1), pp. 6–22.

Slobin, D. (1996). Two ways to travel: Verbs of motion in English and Spanish. In M.S. Shibatani and S.A. Thompson (eds.), *Grammatical Constructions: Their Form and Meaning*. Oxford: Clarendon Press, pp. 195–220.

Stivers, T. (2004). "No no no" and other types of multiple sayings in social interaction. *Human Communication Research*, 30, pp. 260–293.

Tannen, D. (1989). *Talking Voices: Repetition, Dialogue, and Imagery in Conversational Discourse*. Cambridge: Cambridge University Press.

Warner, M. (2002). Publics and counterpublics. *Public Culture*, 14 (1), pp. 49–90.

Wortham, S. (2001). *Narratives in Action: A Strategy for Research and Analysis*. New York: Teachers College Press.

Wortham, S. (2006). *Learning Identity: The Joint Emergence of Social Identification and Academic Learning*. Cambridge: Cambridge University Press.

Wortham, S. (2012). Beyond macro and micro in the linguistic anthropology of education. *Anthropology & Education Quarterly*, 43, pp. 128–137.

Wortham, S., and M. Locher. (1996). Voicing on the news. *Text*, 16, pp. 557–585.

Wortham, S., and A. Reyes. (2015). *Discourse Analysis Beyond the Speech Event*. New York: Routledge.

Wortham, S., and C. Rhodes. (2012). The production of relevant scales: Social identification of migrants during rapid demographic change in one American town. *Applied Linguistics Review*, 3, pp. 75–99.

Wortham, S., E. Allard, K. Lee, and K. Mortimer. (2011). Racialization in payday mugging narratives. *Journal of Linguistic Anthropology*, 21, pp. E56–E75.

9   Analyzing Narrative Genres

MATTI HYVÄRINEN

9.1   Introduction

Genre is one of those key concepts that narrative theorists freely use but only seldom theorize. As a result, narrative genres are understood in vastly different ways within different (sub)disciplines and research traditions. In the social research of narratives, the consideration of genres has not yet become a standard part of narrative analysis. This chapter argues, however, that genre could be a vital concept in the mediation between individual storytelling and the broader societal conditioning of narration through the study of how narrators and receivers activate narrative conventions. The chapter begins by tracing key ideas of recent genre theory. Next, the chapter discusses the social research on narrative and traces the ways in which genre has been used methodologically in narrative analysis. The purpose of the chapter is to present genre analysis as a relevant perspective in the study of the social aspects of narration.[1]

Genre and genre theories have lately inspired a wide range of research from literary theory (Frow 2006; Herman 2002; Pyrhönen 2007), linguistics (Swales 1990; Ventola 2006), sociolinguistics (Rampton 2006; De Fina 2009), anthropology (Hanks 1987), New Rhetorics (Miller 1984; Devitt 2004), sociology (Squire 1999, 2012), linguistic anthropology (Bauman 2001), media studies (Lacey 2000), political communication (Cap and Okulska 2013), and oral history (Tonkin 1992; Chamberlain and Thompson 1998). Within this gamut of disciplines and approaches, no standard theory or consensus about genre prevails. Originally, genre theories started as attempts at classifying texts and narratives, whereas there now prevails "a *distrust* of classification" (Swales 1990: 44). Another dilemma already resides in the volatile focus of genre; one can theorize about genres of literature, text, discourse, narrative, or action, and find in each case different categories of genre. In the case of narrative, oral narrative as such may be understood as a genre (Lee et al. 2004: 39; Martin and Rose 2008); the number of narrative genres may be limited to the four or five classical types (tragedy, comedy, romance, and irony/satire), as in neoclassical theory (Frye 1990; White 1973; Hogan 2003); or, finally, narrative may

The Handbook of Narrative Analysis, First Edition. Edited by Anna De Fina and Alexandra Georgakopoulou.
© 2015 John Wiley & Sons, Inc. Published 2019 by John Wiley & Sons, Inc.

be seen "first and foremost [as] a prodigious variety of genres" (Barthes 1977: 79). Before considering the particular issue of *narrative* genres, therefore, this chapter discusses recent ideas in literary, linguistic, and rhetorical genre theories. The purpose of this detour is to elicit the most useful distinctions and methodological contributions of genre theory to be later applied in the analysis of everyday social genres of narrative.

9.2   Genres and Modes

Genre theories go back to the Platonic discourse on the arts in ancient Greece. In his *Republic*, Plato (speaking as Socrates) suggests that "everything that is said by poets and storytellers" is "a narration" (*diegesis*) (Frow 2006: 55). This narration takes place either through "pure narration," when only the poet is speaking, or with the help of "imitation" (*mimesis*), or as a mixture of these two. Drama is an example of imitation, while epic relied more heavily on narration. In practice, Plato's famous Allegory of the Cave, like many other of his didactic narratives, draws on both of these modes of representation (Frow 2006: 55–58). Aristotle saw that these categories exist empirically only in a mixed form and "thus divided [the world of verbal art] between two major representational modes: authorial speech which tells us about human actions, and the speech of characters who act" (Frow 2006: 57).

Genette (1992) compellingly argues that Plato and Aristotle are discussing narrative and dramatic *modes of enunciation* rather than *genres* in making the previous distinctions. Aristotle cross-tabulates these modes by the quality of the described characters and actions (i.e., as superior or inferior), and ends up with his genres of tragedy (dramatic and superior), comedy (dramatic and inferior), epic (narrative and superior), and parody (narrative and inferior) (Genette 1992: 12–14). These categories of "comedy" and "tragedy" quite apparently made sense to both the ancient audiences and writers and, hence, provided shared frames of expectation in the institutional contexts of writing, performing, and attending dramas.

Over the next 2000 years, the list of potential literary genres extended far beyond unambiguous categorical arrangements. How to fit such new genres as the novel, *Bildungsroman*, film, or detective story into the old system of distinctions? According to Genette (1992: 72–74), the source of ambiguity derives from mixing the "logical order" of modes of enunciation with the historical and contingent formation of genres.

Genette (1992: 72–74) argues that the Platonic, Aristotelian, and subsequent modes are based on a logical order, while genres are historical and contingent formations. Genres can be understood as historically evolving narrative classes that orient tellers, receivers, and industries (such as the film industry or publishing houses). Modes are best understood as aspects, styles of enunciation, used in adjectival form, to characterize both genres and various social situations. A coming-out story, as a narrative genre, can consequently be told in a tragic, comedic, or satiric mode. In a similar way, one could talk about a *dramatic* milieu, meeting, or discussion. Frow (2006: 66) presents a compelling but not exhaustive list of potential modes, such as heroic, tragic, lyric, elegiac, satiric, romantic, and so on. Frow characterizes the distinction between genres and modes as follows: "The modes start their life as genres but over time take on a more general force which is detached from particular structural embodiments" (65). My proposal is to renounce this condition of origin in the study of everyday narration. The distinction between the abstract and logical categories of enunciation (modes) and the historically evolving, contingent genres is thus relevant in even more numerous cases than Frow suggests.

9.3   Theoretical and Historical Genres

A similar, yet not completely identical, distinction has been made between historical and theoretical genres. The most crucial aspect of this distinction resides in the obvious fact that the term "genre" can now refer to at least two entirely differently theorized and grounded entities. Instead of seeking a new synthesis between these perspectives, this chapter deliberately chooses the approach of historical genres and discusses the constitution of its theory within such disciplines as literature, linguistic anthropology, sociolinguistics, and New Rhetorics. The reason behind this choice is not to discard the theoretical aspects, but simply to narrow slightly the confusing use of concepts.

Historical genres, writes Todorov (1973: 13–14), "result from an observation [in the meaning of inductive analysis] of literary reality," while theoretical genres "result from a deduction of a theoretical order." Tellingly, Todorov's first example of "theoretical genre" comes from Plato's distinction between different narrative voices. Todorov thus uses the term "theoretical genres" partly for cases which Genette theorizes as modes. Nevertheless, Todorov privileges the theoretical genres and assumes the objective of developing a system of genres, while at the same time criticizing previous proposals (e.g., Frye 1990) for their lack of consistency.

A distantly similar distinction has been made between the *emic* and *etic* views in cultural anthropology. The "native's" point of view is called emic, whereas the categories drawn from the researcher's theory are etic. When applied to genres, this distinction foregrounds the pragmatic role of genre. Do standard language users, as members of a culture, know and in particular contexts activate some genres and genre differences, and if so, to what effects? If the answer is positive, we are discussing historical and emic genres; if negative, theoretical and etic ones. Swales (1990: 54) articulates a moderately emic position with respect to genres by maintaining that "[a] discourse community's nomenclature for genres is an important source of insight." However, the questions posed by the proponents of the historical approach to genres extend even beyond the *discourse* community, thus foregrounding the *social practices* in which the genres under analysis are embedded (e.g., Bauman 1986; Hanks 1987; Rampton 2006; Devitt 2004; De Fina and Georgakopoulou 2008).

Prince (1990) aptly notes that historical genres have typically been characterized by using highly miscellaneous criteria. However, all categories of natural language, including genres, are more or less fuzzy by nature, argues Virtanen (1992: 296). Such observations have encouraged cognitively oriented narratologists to explore a *prototypical* approach to genres (Herman 2002, 2008, 2009). The prototypical approach rejects the idea of clear classifications into different genres. It suggests that belonging to a genre is not a yes or no question; rather, it is a question of more or less. Therefore, instances of genres are best recognizable near the core of the prototype, whereas the most marginal cases may merge into other genres. Similarly, Swales (1990: 49) contrasts "the *definitional* approach and the *family resemblance* approach" to genres. Herman (2002) specifies this idea of family resemblance with the idea of "preference structure." For example, the genre of the "coming-out story" obviously *prefers* the use of first-person narration while second-arily accepting the use of second or third persons (see also Kearns 2005: 203–204).

The distinction between social and artistic genres is itself fuzzy in a number of ways. Smith and Watson (2001: 183–207), for example, introduce 52 "genres of life writing" by compiling a list of literary and oral, theoretical (e.g., autopathography, genealogy), and historical genres (e.g., diary, slave narrative, travel narrative). Trauma narrative and slave narrative function as social genres, while of course including highly artistic versions. Bauman (1986: 6) crosses generic boundaries by particularly focusing on the *artistic* genres of oral story-telling, such as "tall tales, stories of coonhounds and dog traders, local anecdotes, and stories about practical jokes." In the present chapter, social genres of narrative primarily refer to genres that are historical (i.e., emergent and mutable) and function as *frames of orientation* for the language users themselves, within certain social practices (cf. Bauman 2001; Hanks 1987; Rampton 2006; Devitt 2004). In some cases, users are able to identify the genres being used, but particularly when it comes to emergent genres, the criterion of naming may be too exclusive. During the trajectory of a genre, the naming and the accepted use of its name may be rather distinctive moments to be traced in empirical analysis. The joke, the life story, and the obituary are examples of genres that users easily recognize.

Hanks tries to find a subtle middle position between theoretical and historical genres:

> In a purely formal approach, genres consist of regular groupings of thematic, stylistic, and compositional elements. Generic types differ by the features of historiographer configurations by which they are defined, irrespective of the historical conditions under which the types come to exist and of the social values attached to them in a given context. (1987: 670)

Within this category of genres (or modes, as I propose), one could include Labov and Waletzky's (1997) proposal of oral narrative, as well as many of its supplements, such as "habitual narrative" (Riessman 1993), and many of the story types suggested by Martin and Rose (2008). Hanks, however, continues with a second version, writing that genres can also be understood "as the *historically specific conventions* and ideals according to which authors compose discourse and audiences receive it" (670). He suggests that these historical "genres consist of *orienting frameworks*, interpretive procedures, and sets of expectations that are not part of discourse structure, but of the ways actors relate to and use language" (670, italics added). His choice between genre options is not either/or; rather, his approach "incorporates formal features, but locates genre primarily in relation to action in this second, historically specific way" (670; see also Bauman 1975).

Rampton (2006: 128) follows this latter lead in his study about language use at schools, proposing that "genre is a set of *conventionalized expectations* that members of a social group or network use to shape and construe the communicative activity that they are engaged in." He further specifies that these expectations not only "include a sense of the *likely tasks on hand"* but also "the *roles and relationships* typically involved, the ways the activity can be organized, and the kinds of resources suited to carrying it out" (italics added). Of course, the distinction between historical and theoretical genres also concerns fuzziness and prototypicality. For one thing, theoretical terms can be and sometimes are adopted into popular use (Smith and Watson 2001); and for another, the "likely task at hand" can be understood on very different levels of abstraction.

9.4   Archetypal Genres

Neoclassical genre theory offers a striking account of theoretical genres. "What we are calling Neoclassical approaches to genre utilize a theoretical, trans-historical set of categories (or taxonomies) in order to classify literary texts," write Bawarshi and Reiff (2010: 15). The classic work in this tradition, Frye (1990), identifies "four archetypal mythos: comedy, romance, tragedy, and irony/satire" (Bawarshi and Reiff 2010: 16). Neoclassical approaches invest more in classification than in the emergence and modification of genres. Quite in tune with the argument of this chapter, Bawarshi and Reiff note that "the main critique of such approaches has been the way they universalize the ideological character of genres rather than seeing genres as emerging from and responding to socio-historically situated exigencies" (16).

Despite the claim Bawarshi and Reiff (2010: 15) make, the use of neoclassical models was not limited to literary texts. The historiographer Hayden White (1973) introduced the idea of classifying historiographical plotlines according to Frye's categories. Neoclassical classifications also inspired several social scientists in the early days of the narrative turn. Different versions of this theory are recognizable in Gergen and Gergen (1986), Murray (1989), Bruner (1987, 1996), Plummer (2001: 188), and Jacobs (2000). The basic approach is to collect and classify generically different life-story narratives and draw some social and ideological conclusions with the help of this frame. Both Frye and White draw the heavy ideological connotations of these categories from their ancient context without any compelling argument about the continuity of the forms and their implications. For example, White writes that romance "is a drama of the triumph of good over evil, of virtue over vice, of light over darkness, and of the ultimate transcendence of man over the world in which he was imprisoned by the Fall" (1973: 9).

Equally speculative connotations are attached to comedy, tragedy, and irony. What does this "ultimate transcendence of man over the world in which he was imprisoned by the Fall" have to do with ordinary, everyday narration, and how could this attribute be documented in empirical research?

A thought experiment may help us to consider the way the neoclassical categories can or cannot be used in everyday talk and ordinary self-representation. It is easy to imagine such everyday expressions as "This was the romance/tragedy of my life." The reference, however, is not to narrative discourse but to accounted-for life events. Life-story narrators seldom if ever resort to such expressions as, "I will now tell my story as a comedy/romance." Ordinary speakers hardly ever consciously orient themselves with the help of the neoclassical terminology in presenting their experiences and lives. Instead they can and do use the resources of any number of possible modes in various combinations, including tragic and comic, in their narration. Here we encounter the problem of how language users relate to genres. As White (1978: 67) puts it,

> I have suggested that historians interpret their materials in two ways: by the *choice of a plot structure*, which gives to their narratives a recognizable form, and by the choice of a paradigm of explanation. (italics added)

Within this formalist understanding, the narrator's role is to "choose" a preexisting plot from the list of neoclassical plotlines, and impose it on the narrative material. Within this theory, texts belong to particular genres, and these genres endow the texts with overall ideological content. Derrida (1981) famously gives a far more active role to individual writers in shaping genres. Texts do not simply belong to genres; instead, they refer to and participate in several genres, and writers modify genres by actively blending generic elements. The origin of genres, accordingly, is in the existing genres (Todorov 1990: 15). What matters, primarily, is the interaction between genres and language users in particular contexts.

9.5   Primary and Secondary Genres

Genre is no longer, at least primarily, an issue of taxonomy. Todorov (1973: 5) articulates the dilemma in saying that "we may already accept the idea that genres exist at different levels of generality, and that the content of the notion is defined by the point of view we have chosen." Originally, the idea of distinguishing between "primary (simple) and secondary (complex) speech genres" dates back to Bakhtin (1986: 60–62). Among the primary genres, Bakhtin mentions "genres of greetings, farewells, congratulations, all kinds of wishes [and] information about health" (79), while secondary genres comprise "novels, drama, all kinds of scientific research, major genres of commentary" (62).

The rationale behind Bakhtin's distinction is not the need for categorization; instead, it is informed by the layered embeddedness of genres within genres. McNeill recounts the following joke in an article that examines death notices:

> The story goes that when Mr McIntyre died, his wife called the local newspaper to place a death announcement. All she wished to say was, "McIntyre died". The newspaper agent said, "Well, ma'm, we do have a five word minimum, so you can add three more words for the same price." Mrs McIntyre thought for a minute, then replied, "OK, put 'McIntyre died. Boat for sale.'" (McNeill 2004: 151)

This short joke includes a surprising combination of colliding genres: the death notice, the commercial advert, and the business negotiation. As a result, the whole joke is about the incommensurability of the juxtaposed genres, and the inadequacy of Mrs McIntyre's reaction within the action frame of grieving the death of one's spouse.

Empirically, a pure category of primary genres can hardly be said to exist, due to this self-reflective aspect of all genres. Yet Bakhtin's notion foregrounds the relevance of the study in the emergent and volatile oral narrative genres that take place within the practice of talk-in-interaction. In a study of the conversational storytelling and small stories of young Greek women, Georgakopoulou (2007, and this volume, chapter 13) found such narrative genres as *breaking news, projections,* and *shared stories. Projections* are particularly interesting because they help the speakers co-construct what they will do in the future, rather than account for past experience, as Labov and Waletzky (1997) presumed narratives to do.

9.6   Genre as Text vs. Action

Literary scholars traditionally understand genres as genres of *text*, thus describing such examples as novel, detective novel, and feminist detective novel as possible genres (Pyrhönen 2007). The neoclassical genre theories likewise focus on texts, finding instances of genres in literature, historiography, and life stories. Bruner (1996: 135–136) explicitly locates genres in texts and their reception.

The attempts at situating genres socially, however, have led the theories in New Rhetorics to highlight social action rather than text or mere language use. While socio-linguists characteristically focus on *narration* in social context, as, for example Linde (2009), Georgakopoulou (2007), and De Fina (2009) do, theories of the New Rhetorics effectively situate the genre itself within the *sphere of social action.* Miller (1984: 151) argues that "a rhetorically sound definition of genre must be centered not on the sub-stance or the form of discourse but on the action it is used to accomplish." In Miller's theory, recurrent situations and social contexts both generate and define genres. Similarly, Ventola (2006: 97) argues that "our culture consists of a multitude of genres of social action"; "which have a recognizable linguistic and non-linguistic structure."

Devitt (2004) also connects genres and recurrent action within communities, collectives, or networks. "Genre sets help the community to cohere and define itself," she argues (56). Genres, therefore, are by no means marginal side-effects within the life of communities; rather, they orient and structure the action itself: "To say that genre is social action is to say that people take action through their conceptions of genres" (64). Devitt's analysis of the genres used by American tax accountants situates the different uses of language tightly within an institutional context (66–87). However, Devitt and other rhetorical genre theorists rarely offer plausible examples of narrative genres within institutional contexts.

Do narrative genres, therefore, always have a coherence-generating institutional frame? Institutions and communities sponsor a multitude of narrative genres, yet many of the more primary genres seem to remain ambiguous. For example, *gossiping, rumor,* and the exchange of "information about health" (Bakhtin 1986: 79) recur in polymorphous ways in many institutional and informal contexts. Institutional settings support particular types of jokes; yet the joke itself easily traverses institutional and contextual borders. In various everyday uses, narrative does not typically figure in the form of pure, complete, or finished genres, but is intermingled with forms of conversation, query, and description (Ochs and Capps 2001; Georgakopoulou 2007).

Langellier and Peterson (2004) analyze everyday family narration as an activity that binds and reinvents family belonging. Even family storytelling comprises recurring genres, they suggest. Within the research context of Franco-American culture, one example of a genre of family narration was the *courtship story*, which, in a typical case, "lays a family's groundwork and cements its foundation. A staple of family storytelling, courtship stories narrate origins, a family genesis, how grandparents, parents, and stepparents met" (61–62). Family genealogies and joint memories are not available as preformed stories; instead they require constant and shared "content-ordering" by different family members in order to be activated. Genres – birth stories, stories of success and failure – are forms that support such content-ordering. The authors emphasize the predictability of the motifs and the romantic plotline of the courtship stories without reducing them to the category of romance. In ordering content," Langellier and Peterson maintain, "families alter genres to fit their lives and rework genealogy in their own interests. Genres and genealogy enable families to more easily order content, but these narrative structures do not successfully discipline family storytelling" (67).

9.7   Genre in Systemic-Functional Linguistics and English for Special Purposes

Systemic-Functional linguistics (SFL) establishes one of the major inspirations behind the recent interest in genre studies (e.g., Halliday 1978; Bawarshi and Reiff 2010: 29–37). Michael Halliday, arguably the most prominent figure in the field of SFL, understands language as a meaning potential and thus investigates the uses of language for different purposes. The meaningful use of language requires choices between potential options, and the resulting maps of choices build what is called the "systemic" aspect on the theory. "Functional," in turn, refers to the interest in the language use in particular contexts, that is, what language does and what is done with and through it.

Halliday himself does not actively employ the terminology of genre, preferring instead to theorize the "registers" of language, and as Heikkinen (2013: 8) observes, "there is no consensus on the concept of genre of language use within the SF theory." In discussing the various contexts of language use, Halliday points out three separate elements constituting this *register*: "first, what is actually taking place; secondly, who is taking part; and thirdly, what part the language is playing" (1978: 31). Later, he names the first aspect as the *field*, the second as the *tenor*, and the third as the *mode* of language. Registers, understood in this manner, remarkably resemble the genres discussed in rhetorical genre theory. "A register is," Halliday specifies, "what you are speaking (at the time) determined by what you are doing (nature of social activity being engaged in), and expressing diversity of social process (social division of labour)" (1978: 35). Halliday unambiguously emphasizes the corresponding *social activity*, not exclusively what is done within language. This comes very close to what could be called a sociological understanding of genre.

More than Halliday himself, the writers from the Sydney school have explicitly theorized narrative and genre. Martin and Rose (2008) indeed generate an original theory of story genres, building principally on their reading of the Labovian theory of oral narrative, with particular emphasis on the formal elements described in Labov's proposal. The Labovian "stages," Abstract – Orientation – Complication – Evaluation – Resolution – Coda (Labov 1972: 363), of course represent the most distinctive formalist element of the theory; nevertheless, for Martin and Rose, these very stages define nothing less than *the genre of narrative* (2008: 67–73). "Narrative," in their terminology, is a particular sub-category of "story," more precisely a story containing an explicit complication and its resolution. Other genres include such variants as "recount" (which presents a record of experience without complicating departure from expectations), "anecdote" (which describes a remarkable event and the reaction to it), "exemplum" (which consists of an incidence and its interpretation), and "observation" (which corresponds to a description of an event with a comment) (52).

As a resource for nuanced narrative analysis, Martin and Rose's examination of different story types is of great help. A great many stories do not fit the strict form of the Labovian model, and different "modes of enunciation" inform the different positionings in terms of both the storyworld and the task at hand (cf. Fludernik 1996: 71). The idiosyncratic choice of terminology and the narrowing down of narrative to one particular case of story are of little help in facilitating communication with the rest of narrative studies, however. An additional problem derives from the unproblematized theoretical perspective to genre. In this perspective, genre seems to be something that needs to be taught to the language users, not a frame orienting language-users in action and talk (Martin and Rose 2008: 1, 7).

Swales (1990) made genre analysis relevant within the linguistic school English for Special Purposes (ESP). Swales argues that while textual analysis is a necessary part of genre analysis, "textual knowledge remains generally insufficient for a full account of genre" (6). For Swales, genres are embedded within goal-oriented "discourse communities" (24–27), and should be understood in terms of "communicative purposes and social action" (45). Swales emphasizes the discourse community's "nomenclatures for genres" as a relevant inspiration, without directly identifying or naming genres. He also uses the interesting concept of pre-genre, claiming that, for example, "ordinary conversation" and "ordinary narrative" are forms of telling too broad and general to be proper genres (58–59).

9.8 Narrative as a Text Type

Swales apparently thinks that narrative itself is a poor candidate for a genre because of its huge flexibility in terms of communicative purposes and discursive communities. The outer limits of narrative itself have been discussed on the level of text-type theory (Chatman 1990; Fludernik 2000; Herman 2008, 2009; Linde 1993; Virtanen 1992; Werlich 1976). Text type theorists disagree vigorously about the classification of text types, yet all of them tend to distinguish "narrative" from other types – for example, "description," "exposition," "argumentation," and "instruction" (Wehrlich 1976).

Historically, literary narratologists have been more interested in defining narrative than social scientists or linguists (Richardson 2000 and Tammi 2006 provide informative summaries). In social research, narrative was for a long time understood as a metaphor (Hyvärinen 2013: 26–29), or scholars simply maintained that "we all know what story means." Prince (1982: 4) epitomizes the structuralist, textual strategy by writing that narrative is "the representation of at least two real or fictive events or situations in a time sequence, neither of which presupposes or entails the other." Smith (1981) expresses a more communication-oriented version; according to her, narrative discourse could be understood "as verbal acts consisting of someone telling someone else that something happened" (228). In this literary definition, the distribution of roles between the "teller" and "recipient" is clear, and does not invite the perspective of collaboration.

In sociolinguistics, Labov and Waletzky's (1997) pivotal definition and structural model of oral narrative has the same effect as Smith's definition: it presents oral narrative as the product of a single narrator, detached from talk-in-interaction (De Fina and Georgakopoulou 2008). As they say, they "have defined narrative informally as one method of recapitulating past experience by matching a verbal sequence of clauses to the sequence of events that actually occurred" (Labov and Waletzky 1997: 12). This much-used definition narrows down the generic variety of narrative much more radically than the minimal literary definitions. It excludes, for example, complex and layered narratives (e.g., life story), present and *prospective* narration (Georgakopoulou 2007, and this volume, chapter 13), as well as invented stories.

The essential lesson to be learned from the previous discussion is that the definitions of narrative should not be genre-specific or genre-discriminating (see Hyvärinen 2012). Riessman (2008: 5) clearly has this point in mind when she criticizes "the very restrictive definition of social linguistics." Mentioning Labov (1992), she maintains that "here narrative refers to a discrete unit of discourse, an extended answer by a research participant to a single question." Riessman (1993) highlights the need to broaden Labov's model of oral narrative:

> When we hear stories, for instance, we expect protagonists, inciting conditions, and culminating events. But not all narratives … take this form. Some other genres include *habitual narratives* (when events happen over and over and consequently there is no peak in the action), *hypothetical narratives* (which depict events that did not happen), and *topic-centred narratives* (snapshots of past events that are linked thematically). (1993: 18, italics added)

Riessman contributes to the Labovian narrative in important ways, yet it might be more apposite to speak about narrative *modes of enunciation* than genres, for the obvious reason that none of these variations of narration are ultimately connected to particular situated action or communicative purpose but seem to be equally available for narrators in different contexts. An illness narrative, for example, can be partly presented in the form of habitual or hypothetical narrative. A *news story* might be an example of a topic-centered narrative genre that indeed evokes a sequence of events but that nevertheless presents the events in thematic order of importance, typically beginning with the key surprise already in the title.

9.9   Illness Narrative as a Suggested Genre

Genre does not yet constitute a systematic and theoretically solid perspective in narrative studies. More precisely, the kind of action-oriented, contextual approach to historical genres developed in literary (Frow 2006), rhetorical (Devitt 2004; Bawarshi and Reiff

2010), anthropological (Hanks 1987), and sociolinguistic studies (Rampton 2006) is illustrated in only a few prominent examples in narrative studies. Therefore, I suggest the rereading of some well-known narrative studies from the perspective of genre, even in cases where the terminology is not yet used (or used not in the sense suggested here) by the authors themselves. My list of suggested genre studies comprises, for example, Frank's (1995) *The Wounded Storyteller*, Plummer's (1995) *Telling Sexual Stories*, Linde's (2009) *Working the Past*, and Gubrium and Holstein's (2009) studies on narrative environments. In particular, I try out the sociological idea of illness narrative as a genre. Currently, the proposed genre is present in books, magazines, research interviews, and family stories, to mention a few variations. It has a temporal trajectory and writers and speakers who want to resist and modify the genre, and it obviously has an extensive nomenclature in the use of patients, doctors, and family members.

For example, the three basic types of illness narratives that Frank (1995) identifies – restitution, chaos, and quest narratives – are well-known categories in the research literature. Rather than submitting to the temptation to universalize these categories, it could be more productive to look at their institutional contexts. Frank, in fact, tries to locate these "types" in their most typical contexts, claiming, for example, that the restitution story, "whether told by television commercials, sociology, or medicine, is the culturally preferred narrative" (1995: 83). In brochures and advertisements, medical institutions are portrayed as cheering up real and potential patients, establishing an action environment in which the restitution narrative can grow and flourish. Patient organizations and media, in turn, constitute the most typical environment for quest narratives.

As Langellier and Peterson (2004) point out, illness narratives did not abound before the second half of the twentieth century. By explicitly adopting the terminology of genre, the authors claim that after 1950, "in ensemble with several other kinds of survival stories, the illness narrative emerged, proliferated, and evolved to a genre of storytelling" (189). In genre analysis, the compelling analytical goal is seldom the naming and characterizing of the top-level genre (e.g., novel, illness narrative); rather, the aim is to understand the range and patterning of its subgenres. The emergence of such subgenres typically include one or a few successful *narratives of disclosure* (again a potential genre) distributed through media, a wave of followers iterating the original models, and finally self-conscious attempts at transgressing the dominant modes of narration.

Langellier and Petersen choose *breast cancer narratives*, a subgenre of illness narrative, as their focus of study. Their analysis of the subgenre is especially fruitful for several reasons. The authors do not simply chart the studied subgenre; they also display its trajectory with inner tensions – that is, they exhibit it as a genuinely historical category. As late as the mid-1990s, Park-Fuller (1995: 60) was able to ponder the scarcity of breast cancer stories. In discussing the inner variation and tensions of the recent subgenre, Langellier and Peterson mobilize the language of modes as an analytic tool. They discuss the problematic oscillation between comedic and tragic plots or victim/victor scenarios suggested in popular culture (Park-Fuller 1995). Nevertheless, the authors' point is not to divide the subgenre into mode-based categories but to demonstrate the narrator's continuous struggle with culturally sanctioned closures and plotlines. Finally, their genre-oriented reading examines breast cancer stories as they move from books and newspapers to oral storytelling. However contextual narrative genres may be, one of their particular characteristics seems to be this fluid intermedial border-crossing. "Stories do not exist in isolation, and it is impossible to prevent a story from being appropriatcd, reinterpreted, and recategorized" (Shuman 2005: 19).

Squire (1999, 2012) analyzes *HIV-narratives* from the perspective of genre in order to resist the tendency "to take people's accounts of their relations to HIV as data about their subjective states" (1999: 112). Squire (1999) analyzes HIV interviews in relation to the *coming-out genre*. Squire (2004) additionally discusses a category of South African HIV stories in relation to the *religious genre of conversion*. In differing national contexts, the genre of HIV narratives may therefore participate in several genres rather than being a self-evident subgenre of illness narratives.

9.10   From Institutional Contexts to Genres

Plummer (1995) expresses a wish for a "formal sociology of stories." His purpose in analyzing sexual stories is to "push away from the dominant interest in stories simply as texts awaiting analysis and instead to see stories as *social action embedded in social worlds*" (17, italics original). This aim clearly corresponds to the outlined perspective on narrative genres, and sexual stories from *rape narratives* to *gay narratives*, constitute important narrative genres. Gubrium and Holstein (2009) have studied narration in particular institutional contexts, demonstrating how ways of telling about illness, recovery, and care differ from institution to institution, and from one care system to another. Their concept of "narrative environment" (123–198) and their discussion of how these environments can control possible ways of narration come theoretically and empirically close to genre analysis. Their prime example, the comparison between recovery ideas in AA and SSG (Secular Sobriety Groups) narratives, could serve as a textbook case for a sociological genre analysis. In a similar way, Linde's (2009) sociolinguistic investigation into the institutional storytelling within the Midwest insurance company found several stories (*foundation narrative, paradigmatic [career] narrative*) that could easily be translated as local narrative genres.

In Canada, potential refugees, who must apply for mandatory status as a *political* refugee in order to immigrate into the country, have to present their personal stories before a judge. However, the asylum seekers have plenty of time and opportunities beforehand to hear about the process and stories that have succeeded. This institutional setting, paradoxically, seems to sponsor certain kinds of stories, while the judges, in contrast, become increasingly cautious about stories that are too canonical (Barsky 2000). Within the broader genre of autobiography, the short autobiography written by psychoanalyst candidates as an entry test for training might be a valid example of an institutionally supported narrative genre, as well as the therapy narratives the candidates later write as a part of their training (Lauslahti Graves 1996).

In the case of typical folkloristic narratives, the distance to institutional setting may appear much greater. Cashman (2008) has investigated the genre of *character anecdote* in Northern Ireland. "Reliant as it may be on other genres, the local character anecdote is most useful in meditating on present identity and recent change" (26). However, some characters become so popular in stories that the various stories about them end up challenging the whole idea of "character," as when the same person is host to contrasting characters (218–219). The genre of character anecdote can be understood as a strong moral tool within a local, oral culture, particularly prior to the recent media revolutions.

9.11   Conclusions

This chapter has built on the attempt to make a systematic distinction between two different forms of narrative typicality – the theoretically based *narrative modes*, and the historically constituted *narrative genres*. The intent has not been to diminish the relevance of narrative modes of enunciation (from *tragic* to *hypothetical* modes) for narrative analysis, but to generate more theoretical coherence in the study of narrative genres.

The suggested perspective on narrative genres is emphatically social and sociological in the sense that narratives are not, primarily and exclusively, interpreted as *expressions* of individual experiences; rather, they always arise within the frame of social and institutional action at hand, and in relation to the socially, historically, and institutionally sanctioned and discouraged conventions of narration. The genre perspective encourages research into *narrative realities* (Gubrium and Holstein 2009), understanding that "genres consist of orienting frameworks, interpretive procedures, and sets of expectations that are not part of discourse structure, but of the ways actors relate to and use language" (Hanks 1987: 670). Genres characteristically orient and motivate social action.

The genre approach is sensitive to the historical emergence, models, adaptation, and intermedial transformations of ways of telling particular stories. Davis (2002), for example, locates and analyzes the first consequential display of a sexual-abuse survivor account, and the social conditions that made the uncovering possible. The *coming-out genre* conditions all kinds of new sexual stories (Plummer 1995), as well as such illness narratives as cancer narrative, HIV narratives, and depression narrative. Such new social phenomena as *downshifting* (a way of life which aims at the simultaneous reduction of the amount of consumption and work) are often supported and maintained by the emergence of the corresponding narrative genre.

In the analysis of individual narratives, the principal question no longer addresses the "belonging" to a genre. A more fruitful question arguably concerns the genres and subgenres the narrator is drawing on or deviating from (constructing, thus, possibly a counter-narrative to the genre). As a research orientation, genre analysis does not focus on the categorization of story collections, but endeavors to find, describe, and analyze particular narrative genres diachronically, from the emergence to solidification, addressing variations and possible ruptures. However, genres (studied in sociolinguistics and sociology, for example) are not located on the same level of generality and thus do not constitute exclusive systems or trees; instead narrators are able to draw from different genres from different levels of generality. Nevertheless, one criterion for the success of the genre approach depends on narrative scholars' ability to locate and name socially and culturally relevant narrative genres more systematically.

NOTE

1   An earlier, Finnish-language version of this chapter was published in V. Heikkinen, P. Lauerma, M. Lounela, U. Tiililä, and E. Voutilainen (eds.). (2012). *Genreanalyysi: tekstilajitutkimuksen käsikirja* [Genre analysis: a handbook of genre research]. Helsinki: Gaudeamus, pp. 392–410.

REFERENCES

Bakhtin, M.M. (1986). *Speech Genres and Other Late Essays*. Edited by C. Emerson and M. Holquist. Translated by V.W. McGee. Austin: University of Texas Press.

Barsky, R. F. (2000). *Arguing and Justifying: Assessing the Convention Refugees' Choice of Motive, Moment and Host Country*. Aldershot, UK: Ashgate.

Barthes, R. (1977). Introduction to the structural analysis of narrative. In R. Barthes, *Image – Music – Text*. Translated and edited by S. Heath. New York: Hill and Wang, pp. 79–124.

Bauman, R. (1986). *Story, Performance, and Event*. Cambridge: Cambridge University Press.

Bauman, R. (2001). Verbal art as performance. In A. Duranti (ed.), *Linguistic Anthropology*. Oxford: Blackwell, pp. 165–188. Original version (1975) published in *American Anthropologist*, 77, pp. 290–311.

Bawarshi, A.S., and M.J. Reiff. (2010). *Genre: An Introduction to History, Theory, Research, and Pedagogy*. West Lafayette, IN: Parlor Press.

Bruner, J. (1987). Life as narrative. *Social Research*, 54 (1), pp. 11–32.

Bruner, J. (1996). *The Culture of Education*. Cambridge, MA: Harvard University Press.

Cap, P., and U. Okulska. (2013). *Analyzing Genres in Political Communication*. Amsterdam: John Benjamins.

Cashman, R. (2008). *Storytelling on the Northern Irish Border*. Bloomington: Indiana University Press.

Chamberlain, M., and P. Thompson. (1998). Introduction: Genre and narrative in life stories. In M. Chamberlain and P. Thompson (eds.), *Narrative and Genre*. London: Routledge, pp. 1–22.

Chatman, S. (1990). *Coming to Terms: The Rhetoric of Narrative in Fiction and Film*. Ithaca, NY: Cornell University Press.

Davis, J.E. (2002). Social movements and strategic narratives: Creating the sexual abuse survivor account. In W. Patterson (ed.), *Strategic Narrative: New Perspectives on the Power of Personal and Cultural Stories*. Lanham, MD: Lexington Books, pp. 107–125.

De Fina, A. (2009). Narratives in interviews: The case of accounts. *Narrative Inquiry*, 19 (2), pp. 233–258.

De Fina, A., and A. Georgakopoulou. (2008). Analysing narratives as practices. *Qualitative Research*, 8 (3), pp. 379–387.

Derrida, J. (1981). The law of genre. In W.J.T. Mitchell (ed.), *On Narrative*. Chicago, IL: University of Chicago Press, pp. 51–77.

Devitt, A.J. (2004). *Writing Genres*. Carbondale: Southern Illinois University Press.

Fludernik, M. (1996). *Towards a 'Natural' Narratology*. London: Routledge.

Fludernik, M. (2000). Genres, text types, or discourse modes? Narrative modalities and generic categorization. *Style*, 34 (1), pp. 274–292.

Frank, A.W. (1995). *The Wounded Storyteller: Body, Illness, and Ethics*. Chicago, IL: University of Chicago Press.

Frow, J. (2006). *Genre*. London: Routledge.

Frye, N. (1990/1957). *Anatomy of Criticism*. Princeton, NJ: Princeton University Press.

Genette, G. (1992/1979). *The Architext: An Introduction*. Translated by J.E. Lewin. Berkeley: University of California Press.

Georgakopoulou, A. (2007). *Small Stories, Interaction and Identities*. Amsterdam: John Benjamins.

Gergen, K.J., and M.M. Gergen. (1986). Narrative form and the construction of psychological science. In T.R. Sarbin (ed.), *Narrative Psychology: The Storied Nature of Human Conduct*. New York: Praeger, pp. 22–44.

Gubrium, J.F., and J.A. Holstein. (2009). *Analyzing Narrative Realities*. Los Angeles, CA: Sage.

Halliday, M. (1978). *Language as Social Semiotic: The Social Interpretation of Language and Leaning*. London: Arnold.

Hanks, W.F. (1987). Discourse genres in a theory of practice. *American Ethnologist*, 14 (4), pp. 668–692.

Heikkinen, V. (2013). Linguistic genre analysis, intertextuality, and ideology. Unpublished manuscript.

Herman, D. (2002). *Story Logic: Problems and Possibilities of Narrative*. Lincoln: University of Nebraska Press.

Herman, D. (2008). Description, narrative, and explanation: Text-type categories and the cognitive foundations of discourse competence. *Poetics Today*, 29 (3), pp. 437–472.

Herman, D. (2009). *Basic Elements of Narrative*. Oxford: Wiley-Blackwell.

Hogan, P.C. (2003). *The Mind and Its Stories: Narrative Universals and Human Emotion*. Cambridge: Cambridge University Press.

Hyvärinen, M. (2012). Prototypes, genres, and concepts: Travelling with narratives. *Narrative Works: Issues, Investigations, & Interventions*, 2 (1), pp. 10–32.

Hyvärinen, M. (2013). Travelling metaphors, transforming concepts. In M. Hyvärinen, M. Hatavara, and L.-C. Hydén (eds.), *The Travelling Concepts of Narrative*. Amsterdam: John Benjamins, pp. 13–41.

Jacobs, R.N. (2000). Narrative, civil society and public culture. In M. Andrews, S.D. Sclater, C. Squire, and A. Treacher (eds.), *Lines of Narrative: Psychosocial Perspectives*. London: Routledge, pp. 18–35.

Kearns, M. (2005). Genre theory in narrative studies. In D. Herman, M. Jahn, and M.-L. Ryan (eds.), *Routledge Encyclopedia of Narrative Theory*. London: Routledge, pp. 201–205.

Labov, W. (1972). *Language in the Inner City: Studies in the Black English Vernacular*. Oxford: Basil Blackwell.

Labov, W., and J. Waletzky. (1997/1967). Narrative analysis: Oral versions of personal experience. *Journal of Narrative and Life History*, 7, pp. 3–38.

Lacey, N. (2000). *Narrative and Genre: Key Concepts in Media Studies*. New York: Palgrave Macmillan.

Langellier, K.M., and E.E. Peterson. (2004). *Storytelling in Daily Life*. Philadelphia, PA: Temple University Press.

Lauslahti Graves, P. (1996). Narrating a psychoanalytic case study. In R.E. Josselson (ed.), *Ethics and Process in the Narrative Study of Lives*. Thousand Oaks, CA: Sage, pp. 72–79.

Lee, C.D., E. Rosenfeld, R. Mendenhall, A. Rivers, and B. Tynes. (2004). Cultural modelling as a frame for narrative analysis. In C. Daiute and C. Lightfoot (eds.), *Narrative Analysis: Studying the Development of Individuals in Society*. Thousand Oaks, CA: Sage, pp. 39–62.

Linde, C. (1993). *Life Stories: The Creation of Coherence*. Oxford: Oxford University Press.

Linde, C. (2009). *Working the Past: Narrative and Institutional Memory*. Oxford: Oxford University Press.

Martin, J.R., and D. Rose. (2008). *Genre Relations: Mapping Culture*. London: Equinox.

McNeill, L. (2004). Generic subjects: Reading Canadian death notices as life writing. *Life Writing*, 1 (2), pp. 151–166.

Miller, C.R. (1984). Genre as social action. *Quarterly Journal of Speech*, 70, pp. 151–167.

Murray, K. (1989). The construction of identity in the narratives of romance and comedy. In J. Shotter and K.J. Gergen (eds.), *Texts of Identity*. London: Sage, pp. 176–205.

Ochs, E., and L. Capps. (2001). *Living Narrative: Creating Lives in Everyday Storytelling*. Cambridge, MA: Harvard University Press.

Park-Fuller, L.M. (1995). Narration and narrativization of a cancer story: Composing and performing *A Clean Breast of It*. *Text and Performance Quarterly*, 20, pp. 60–67.

Plummer, K. (1995). *Telling Sexual Stories: Power, Change and Social Worlds*. London: Routledge.

Plummer, K. (2001). *Documents of Life 2: An Invitation to a Critical Humanism*. London: Sage.

Prince, G. (1982). *Narratology: The Form and Functioning of Narrative*. Berlin: Mouton.

Prince, G. (1990). On narrative studies and narrative genres. *Poetics Today*, 11 (2), pp. 271–282.

Pyrhönen, H. (2007). Genre. In D. Herman (ed.), *The Cambridge Companion to Narrative*. Cambridge: Cambridge University Press, pp. 109–123.

Rampton, B. (2006). *Language in Late Modernity*. Cambridge: Cambridge University Press.

Richardson, B. (2000). Recent concepts of narrative and the narratives of narrative theory. *Style*, 34 (2), pp. 168–175.

Riessman, C.K. (1990). *Divorce Talk: Women and Men Make Sense of Personal Relationships*. New Brunswick, NJ: Rutgers University Press.

Riessman, C.K. (1993). *Narrative Analysis*. Newbury Park, CA: Sage.

Riessman, C.K. (2008). *Narrative Methods for the Human Sciences*. London: Sage.

Shuman, A. (2005). *Other People's Stories: Entitlement Claims and the Critique of Empathy*. Urbana: University of Illinois Press.

Smith, B.H. (1981). Narrative versions, narrative theories. In W.J.T. Mitchell (ed.), *On Narrative*. Chicago, IL: University of Chicago Press, pp. 209–232.

Smith, S., and J. Watson. (2001). *Reading Autobiography: A Guide for Interpreting Life Narratives*. Minneapolis: University of Minnesota Press.

Squire, C. (1999). "Neighbors who might become friends": Selves, genres, and citizenship in narratives of HIV. *The Sociological Quarterly*, 40 (1), pp. 109–137.

Squire, C. (2004). Narrative genres. In C. Seale, G. Gobo, J.F. Gubrium, and D. Silverman (eds.), *Qualitative Research Practice*. London: Sage, pp. 116–118.

Squire, C. (2012). Narratives, connections and social change. *Narrative Inquiry*, 22 (1), pp. 50–68.

Swales, J.M. (1990). *Genre Analysis: English in Academic and Research Settings*. Cambridge: Cambridge University Press.

Tammi, P. (2006). Against narrative: A boring story. *Partial Answers*, 4, (2), pp. 19–40.

Todorov, T. (1973). *The Fantastic: A Structural Approach to a Literary Genre*. Translated by R. Howard. Ithaca, NY: Cornell University Press.

Todorov, T. (1990/1978). *Genres in Discourse*. Translated by C. Porter. Cambridge: Cambridge University Press.

Tonkin, E. (1992). *Narrating Our Pasts: The Social Construction of Oral History*. Cambridge: Cambridge University Press.

Ventola, E. (2006). Genre systeemis-funktionaalisessa kielitieteessä: Esimerkkinä asiointitilanteet [Genre in systemic-functional language theory: Service encounters as an example]. In A. Mäntynen, S. Shore, and A. Solin (eds.), *Genre – tekstilaji*. Helsinki: Suomalaisen Kirjallisuuden Seura, pp. 96–121.

Virtanen, T. (1992). Issues of text typology: Narrative – a "basic" type of text? *Text*, 12, pp. 293–310.

Werlich, E. (1976). *A Text Grammar of English*. Heidelberg: Quelle & Meyer.

White, H. (1973). *Metahistory: The Historical Imagination in Nineteenth-Century Europe*. Baltimore, MD: Johns Hopkins University Press.

White, H. (1978). *Tropics of Discourse: Essays in Cultural Criticism*. Baltimore, MD: Johns Hopkins University Press.

Part III   Narrative Interaction

10 Narrative as Talk-in-Interaction

CHARLES GOODWIN

10.1 Introduction

Interaction between tellers and a range of different kinds of hearers (including participants who are characters in the stories being told) is deeply consequential to the organization of narrative. To demonstrate, rather than merely claim this, requires looking closely at concrete examples, and restricts the range of phenomena that can be covered.[1]

I will focus on (1) the interactive organization of story prefaces; (2) Goffman's deconstruction of the speaker; (3) how different kinds of present participants, such as the story's principal character, make crucial, visible contributions to the interactive field that constitute a telling even when they do not speak; (4) the pervasive importance for interactive narrative of building action by re-using with transformation materials provided by others in their earlier talk, such as types of characters and situations; (5) the visible cognitive life of the hearer; (6) participation as temporally unfolding, action-constitutive understanding; (7) building social and political organization through interactive narrative; (8) families of stories that extend across particular tellings and participants to build larger courses of action; (9) the interactive organization of narrative in aphasia: how a man with a three-word vocabulary is able to produce complex narrative by mobilizing resources provided by others; and (10) how communities, such as scientific professions, use quite particular kinds of narratives to build new members with the professional vision required to see and act upon the world in just the ways that define the expertise and activities of that community.

10.2 Story Prefaces

The following was told during a dinner in which Ann and Don were guests of Beth and John. In her story (Figure 10.1) Ann recounts what she formulates as a horrible gaffe made by her husband Don. He asked the owners of a brand new house: "Did they make

---

The Handbook of Narrative Analysis, First Edition. Edited by Anna De Fina and Alexandra Georgakopoulou.
© 2015 John Wiley & Sons, Inc. Published 2019 by John Wiley & Sons, Inc.

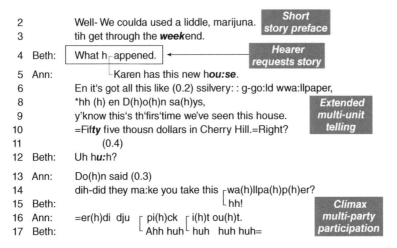

Figure 10.1   A story told in conversation (Goodwin 1984). Reprinted by permission of Cambridge University Press.

you take this wallpaper or did you pick it out" (lines 13–16). More detailed analysis of this story can be found in Goodwin (1984, 2007b).[2]

Ann's story has a distinctive shape. Her extended telling, which begins in line 5, is preceded by a short two-part sequence. In lines 2–3 she announces the availability of a story, without actually telling it. In line 4, her principal addressee, Beth, explicitly asks to hear the story. Sacks (1992a: 10–11, 18; 1974) noted not only that stories structured like this occur pervasively in conversation, but that the distinctive shape found here provides a systematic way of dealing with crucial contingencies faced by a potential storyteller in conversation. Typically, a speaker in conversation is entitled to only one turn constructional unit, such as a complete clause, before speaker transition becomes relevant. At the end of that unit others are provided a place where they might claim the floor. Being restricted to producing only a single turn constructional unit poses consequential problems for someone trying to tell a story, since stories typically take multiple units, as indeed this one does beginning at line 5. By first producing a story preface that announces the availability of a story, and then getting an addressee explicitly to display that they are prepared to listen to an extended telling (e.g., Beth's "what happened" in line 4), speaker and recipient explicitly provide for the systematic occurrence of a multi-unit turn. The shape found in the story thus constitutes a specific adaptation to the tasks posed by telling a story within interaction.

Note that this story does not have the canonical narrative structure described by Labov and Waletzky (1968), in that it does not begin with an abstract. Labov's methods for assembling a collection of stories, in which the researcher asked the teller to describe a highly charged event, put the teller in the position of having the rights to an extended floor at the very beginning of his or her talk. The task of securing permission for an extended telling thus did not arise because of the interactive structure of the talk in which Labov's narratives were produced. Both the stories analyzed by Sacks (1992b), and those brilliantly collected by Labov (whose interview methods were shaped in part by his need to obtain very high quality audio recordings for his ground-breaking analysis of vernacular language structure), display in the internal organization of their structure adaptation to the interactive contingencies that make possible their telling.

Several other features of the story will be briefly noted. The body of the narrative begins with what I will call background segments in lines 5–6, which set the scene for the story: the house they are seeing for the first time is new and expensive, and it has "ssilvery:: g-go:ld wwa:llpaper" which the teller subtly evaluates as garish with her prosody. In line 13, when the speaker reports what her husband said, the climax of the story is entered. Note that this part of the story has a different interactive organization from the parts leading up to it, in that recipients participate in the talk by actively displaying appreciation of the story. Finally, lines 8–10 constitute what I will call a parenthesis. In line 8 the teller enters the climax by marking that she is about to quote what her husband said. However, in line 9, she instead provides further background information, such as the price of the house and the fact that this is the first time the teller and her husband have visited it. This specific background information provides the teller with resources for prospectively structuring recipients' immediate, appropriate understanding of the quote that constitutes the climax of the story. A prototypical social scene is established: guests admiring their hosts' new possessions. This event, with its expectations about proper conduct, renders what Don said transparently visible as a salient faux pas.

10.3 Goffman's Deconstruction of the Speaker

Who is speaking in lines 14–16 in Figure 10.1? The voice being heard is a female one: Ann's. However, she is reporting something said by someone else: her husband. Goffman (1981) argued that the apparently simple notion of the *speaker* in fact encompasses within its boundaries a number of quite distinct entities, including (1) the sounding box or animator, the party actually producing speech (e.g., a press spokesman for the president), here Ann; (2) the author, the party who actually assembles the words being spoken (e.g, a presidential speechwriter); (3) the principal, the party responsible for the talk being spoken (e.g., the president, or in this case Don); and (4) the figure, the protagonist or character in the scene being animated by the voice of the current speaker, here Don (see Figure 10.2).

Because of this lamination of different kinds of entities within a single strip of reported speech, it would not be appropriate to enclose lines 14–16 within quotation marks. The laughter that peppers this talk belongs to the animator, Ann, and is not to be heard as part of the talk Don produced in the reported scene. As demonstrated powerfully by Volosinov (1973), such evaluative inflection is central to the organization of all reported speech, and to narrative more generally (Goodwin 2007b; Labov 1972).

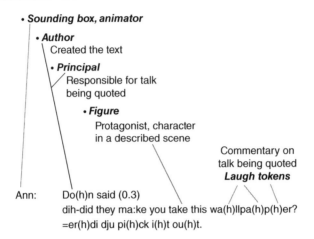

Figure 10.2   Goffman's deconstruction of the speaker (Goodwin 2007b). Reprinted by permission of Cambridge University Press.

Figure 10.3   Principal character's face intricately matches speaker's laugh (Goodwin 2007b). Reprinted by permission of Cambridge University Press.

10.4   A Silent Though Visible Principal Character

Goffman noted that within everyday interaction, the characters depicted within stories are frequently present during their telling. Don, the principal character in Ann's story in Figure 10.1, is seated at the table with her, but never says a word throughout the telling (though he does provide a subsequent second-story in which he counters her version of the events). Most analysis of narrative focuses exclusively on phenomena found within the stream of speech. Within such a framework, Don – and nonspeaking participants in general – are excluded from analysis. However, when a video of the telling is examined it is found that Don actively participates in the telling through the way in which he organizes his visible body. As the teller slowly escalates her laughter through lines 14–16 of Figure 10.1, the principal character's face matches this with visual laughter that tracks the speaker's vocal laughter syllable by syllable in exquisite detail, moving from a slight laugh at the end of line 14 to animated head movements by the end of line 16 (Figure 10.3).

In essence the laugh that occurs here is being performed simultaneously by two separate bodies, vocally by the speaker, and visually by the principal character whose actions are being depicted.

10.5   Building Action by Performing Structure-Preserving Transformations on a Public Substrate

Don's visible laughs cannot be understood or analyzed by studying his body in isolation. Instead, his escalating laugh constitutes a set of quite precise operations on the emerging structure of the teller's talk. The resources that provide for the intelligibility of what he is doing are distributed across multiple participants and diverse semiotic materials: the talk and vocal laughter of the speaker and the changing displays visible in Don's face. Don builds action by performing systematic operations on a public substrate: the emerging talk of the story. His operations preserve structure provided by the original substrate: both the laughter as an activity and the event that makes such laughter relevant. However, rather than simply copying or repeating that structure, Don transforms it by changing vocal laughter into silent facial displays. The action that occurs here is cooperative: one party contributes to the action in progress, or builds new action, by performing systematic operations on a structure provided by another. Building action cooperatively by performing structure-preserving transformations on resources provided by others is a quite general practice and deeply implicated in the organization of human action (Goodwin 2012). When such processes are used to build subsequent action by decomposing and reusing, with transformation, structure provided by the talk of others, they constitute a setting for the organization of grammar as public interactive practice. Figure 10.4 provides a simple example.

1   Tony: Why don't you get out my yard.
2   Chopper: Why don't you ⏜***make me***⏝ get out the yard.

Figure 10.4   Structure-preserving transformations on a public substrate that decompose and reuse prior structure with modification (Goodwin 2012). Reprinted by permission of Elsevier.

Chopper builds a powerful counter, one that uses Tony's own words against him, by decomposing the grammatical structure of Tony's utterance into separate parts, and then transforming its meaning by inserting something new between these parts, the challenging "make me."

10.6   The Visible Cognitive Life of the Hearer

The precision with which Don calibrates his visible body with the moment-by-moment emergence of story-relevant structure within the speaker's talk is not accidental. Line 13, "Do(h)n said," projects that he is about to be placed on stage as an animated figure in the speaker's telling. Moreover, the laugh token that occurs here projects that he will be depicted in a quite specific way, as someone whose actions can be aligned to with laughter. As the teller speaks line 13, Don, who had been looking to his side, moves his head back next to the speaker while looking slightly downward, almost like an actor standing in the wings in preparation for going on stage. The way in which he organizes his body is consistent with the possibility that he is performing a situated analysis of the emerging structure of the story. He is not simply listening to the story. As its principal character, he can recognize that his alignment to the events being told can be inspected at very specific points within it, such as when the faux pas he committed is revealed. Rather than simply waiting for that to be said, he uses line 13 to project its upcoming arrival so that he can act simultaneously with the teller. In Ann's story the phrase projecting the quote "Do(h)n said" occurs not only in line 13 but also in line 8. As can be seen in Figure 10.5, here too Don moves his face into a position where he is ready to come on stage.

However, at that point, instead of producing what Don said, Ann begins her parenthesis providing additional background information. As soon as this happens Don moves his head away, displaying interest in a bowl of soup that is being passed. His ongoing analysis of the emerging structure of the story, and specifically how different kinds of story elements make relevant different forms of participation in it, is visible in how he organizes his body so as to adapt to changing structural features and forms of cooperative participation as the story unfolds.

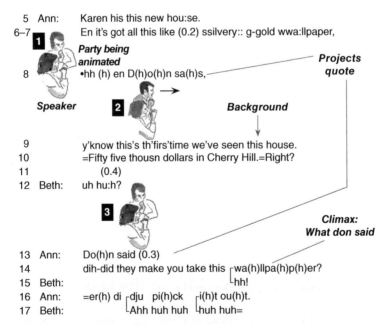

Figure 10.5   Participation and analysis by principal character (Goodwin 2007b). Reprinted by permission of Cambridge University Press.

10.7 Temporally Unfolding Participation Central to the Organization of Interactive Narrative

Human beings are able to build action by bringing together semiotic materials with quite different properties, such as talk with its language structure and the visible organization of embodied participation, into contextual configurations where mutual elaboration of these resources creates a whole that goes beyond what is provided by any of its parts in isolation (Goodwin 2000, 2012). Thus the speaker and the principal character (as well as other, structurally different kinds of participants such as the addressed recipient) can simultaneously contribute different kinds of materials (language structure in the talk of the speaker and relevant embodied displays by the principal character) to build as situated social practice a single action in concert with each other.

Within interaction stories do not reside entirely, or even primarily, within the stream of speech. Instead, a telling creates an interactive field that assigns those present to different positions (e.g., teller, principal character, addressed recipient, etc.). To build the story together each must analyze how they have been placed – specifically the story-relevant identity they now occupy, what forms of action are possible and relevant from that position, and precisely when in the visible unfolding organization of the story those actions should occur (e.g., structurally different components of the story, such as background and climax sections, each provide for alternative forms of participation within it).

The categories proposed in Goffman (1981) for the differentiation of structurally different kinds of hearers as well as speakers led to important subsequent research by linguistic anthropologists on participation that revealed a host of structurally different kinds of participants who could be implicated in the organization of talk (Irvine 1996; Levinson 1988). However, Don's visible action and analysis within the story being told about him by his wife suggest an alternative framework for the study of both participation and the interactive field that links different kinds of participants together as they work together within a narrative field. Rather than focusing primarily on a typology of categories, participation can be analyzed as a temporally unfolding process through which separate parties demonstrate to each other their ongoing understanding of the events they are engaged in by building actions that contribute to the further progression of these very same events (Goodwin 2007b: 24–25). Participation goes beyond the structure of talk to encompass the practices used by rich, feeling bodies to perform relevant operations on a public substrate provided by others. As demonstrated concisely by Don, participants inhabit each other's actions.

Such issues are also relevant to the interactive organization of understanding within narrative. It is frequently claimed that the place where understanding in conversation is demonstrated is in a subsequent turn (Levinson 2012). However, participants' simultaneous actions upon a story may be quite different from how the story is understood in the turn that responds to it (C. Goodwin and M.H. Goodwin 1987). More generally, a range of different kinds of participants are displaying through the organization of both their talk and their bodies detailed understanding of, and co-participation in, the emerging structure of the story. Such visible, action-relevant, ongoing analysis is constitutive of what a narrative is: a field of action built collaboratively by structurally different actors using a variety of semiotic resources within face-to-face interaction.

10.8   Building Social and Political Organization through Interactive Narrative

Marjorie Harness Goodwin recorded for a year and a half the talk and daily activities of preadolescent African American children, who had organized themselves into girls' and boys' peer groups (Goodwin 1982, 1990: M.H. Goodwin and C. Goodwin 1987). This enabled her to focus on narratives the children produced for each other as part of the process of building their local social and political organization. As action within interaction, the children's narratives were designed for specific addressees; responses to them were built from a particular position within the interactive field created by the narrative, with an orientation toward the construction of relevant future action.

Social scientists at least since Piaget have claimed that girls' social organization is intrinsically less complex than that of boys. For example boys were argued to engage in complex, competitive games like football, while the games of girls, such as hopscotch, were depicted as simple (Lever 1978). By way of contrast, Goodwin found the girls' social organization was in many respects more complex than that of boys, and also far more painful because it was based on exclusion and coalitions within triads. One powerful example of this is found in the gossip dispute activity that the girls called He-Said-She-Said (Goodwin 1982, 1990). Using utterances of the form "X said that you said that I said" one girl accuses another of having offended her by talking about her behind her back. Figure 10.6 provides an example.

He-Said-She-Said accusations are organized as concise formal narratives that position speaker and addressee in the present within relevant social identities – accuser and defendant – by providing a history of events in the past that warrants the current charge against the defendant. In essence these accusations use a repetitive formal language pattern to both state a charge and provide the evidence for it. Because of the way

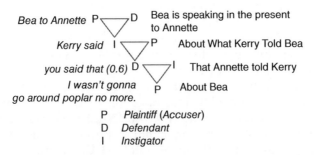

Figure 10.6   He-Said-She-Said accusations (Goodwin and Goodwin 2004). Reprinted by permission of John Wiley & Sons, Inc.

in which the narrative structure of these accusations initiates a vernacular legal process, abbreviations for Plaintiff and Defendant are used to diagram how different participants move systematically through the history of past events used to build the accusation.

During the confrontation the most vivid participants are the Accuser and Defendant, and indeed He-Said-She-Said confrontations are forms of high drama for the entire girls' community. However, the key player in this process is not one of the two focal protagonists, but instead the third party depicted in the accusation, the girl who set the dispute in motion by telling the current accuser what the defendant said about her. Since the girls call someone who does this an Instigator, the letter I is used to mark her position in the diagram in Figure 10.6.

The Instigator brings about the confrontation by telling the girl who will become the Accuser stories with a quite specific character and event structure (Goodwin 1982). The girl who will be the Defendant, and who is absent during the telling of an instigating story, is depicted as telling the Instigator disparaging things about the current addressee, the future Accuser. The addressee is placed simultaneously both as a character in the narrative who is being evaluated in a specific way by another character, and as a current participant occupying a specific position within the interactive field created by the telling. This positioning enables her to perform particular kinds of operations on the story in progress. In Figure 10.7 Bea, the Instigator, is talking to both Julia and Florence. In Lines 5–8 she reports that an absent party, Terry (the future Defendant), described Julia as "*actin a:ll stupid.*" In lines 9 and 13 Julia transforms the Instigator's "you" into

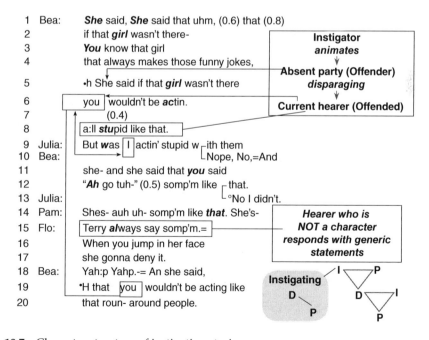

Figure 10.7   Character structure of instigating stories.

"I" as she disputes what she as a character in the story is reported to have done. This particular kind of structure-preserving operation on the story (reuse of the same focal character and type of event) is only available to someone being depicted as a character. Thus in lines 15–17 Florence, who is not being portrayed in the story, uses generic denunciations ("Terry *always* say somp'm") to negatively evaluate Terry, instead of making promises to confront, or transforming what was said in ways that are relevant to her own character. Florence's generic response receives only the most minimal acknowledgement at the beginning of line 18, as Bea immediately returns her instigating story to how her focal addressee, Julia, has been attacked by Terry. The internal organization of the story structures what counts as a proper addressee to it, and this has detailed consequences for the grammatical and modal choices used to build responses by different kinds of hearers.

Bea's continuing pursuit, with further examples of what Terry said about Julia, strongly suggests that a mere denial (line 13) is inadequate. As can be seen in line 63 of Figure 10.8, the response being sought to these stories is a promise to challenge the offender ("I'm a tell her about herself today"). When such a statement is made, the addressee who has been attacked behind her back assumes a new public identity, that of someone who has promised to confront the person who wronged her. At this moment an impending He-Said-She-Said confrontation is created as a visible, public event (see Figure 10.9 below).

Promising to confront the person who wronged her is, however, fraught with consequences for the future accuser. She will be described as "moling out" if she fails to carry through with her promise. The interactive organization of the instigating story displays a sensitivity to this. In lines 41–48 the Instigator depicts a social and political environment supportive of strong action by portraying both the Instigator's own stance toward each of the protagonists, and an alliance of multiple parties who supported the

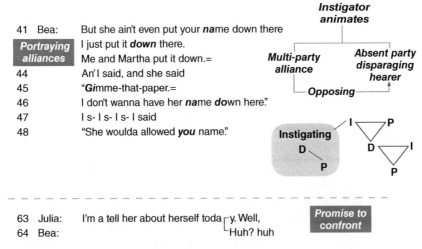

Figure 10.8   Depicting alliances and promising to confront.

current addressee and opposed the future defendant. The stories told by the Instigator are thus both organized internally in terms of characters and events depicted in ways that are structured by the larger activity they are designed to accomplish, and work to transform in consequential ways the identities of its recipients. When responded to with a promise to confront, instigating stories have an ontological power in that they create and position specific participants within consequential, politically charged social identities, and initiate the activity that these identities inhabit.

10.8.1 Cooperative transformation zones

The interactive process of telling instigating stories is organized as a cooperative transformation zone on a number of different levels. The Instigator builds a narrative substrate that not only includes the current addressee as a character, but which invites particular kinds of transformative next actions as a response. When the party depicted as having been wronged promises to confront, her identity is publicly transformed in a way that allows others to inspect and evaluate her character within the framework of a specific projected future course of action. Simultaneously this initiates a particular kind of event – a He-Said-She-Said – that the entire community can follow with rapt anticipation (see Figure 10.9). The organization of the diverse stories through which this occurs will now be briefly described.

10.9   A Family of Interactively Organized Stories

The instigating stories used to initiate the chain of action that will culminate in a confrontation are but one particular kind of interactive story implicated in the organization of a He-Said-She-Said dispute (Goodwin and Goodwin 2004). Instigating creates a landscape of stories that extend far beyond the current interaction.

As can be seen in Figure 10.9, after securing a promise to confront, the Instigator goes and reports to others in the community what happened. These stories have their own distinctive organization. For example, though most of the talk during the confrontation was produced by the Instigator, the stories reporting that process minimize her role and focus on both the Accuser's promise to confront, and what can be expected to happen next. Indeed, though Labov's initial model of narrative focused on the description of events in the past, the stories that occur here include *future hypothetical* stories about what can be expected to happen during the confrontation, what the Accuser will say, and how her opponent will defend herself. Goodwin found that stories that shape the future were as consequential for the building of relevant social organization as those that reported events from the past. All of this occurs within a state of high affective valence. As one of the girls says in lines 1–2 of Figure 10.9, "Can't wait t'see this *A::ction:n.*" For her part the Accuser talks to her friends about what the offender said about her. Consistent with Sacks's analysis of how second stories are built through particular kinds of structure-preserving character transformations (1992b), her recipients produce their own stories about how the offender attacked them. In preparation for the confrontation the Accuser uses stories animating the offender attacking herself to harvest a set of parallel stories

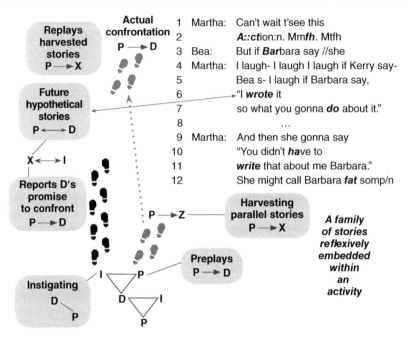

Figure 10.9   Building consequential events, social organization, and actors through interactive narrative (footprints of Instigator on left, Accuser on right).

from others. During the confrontation these will be recycled and thrown in the Defendant's face as further evidence for a general consensus about her flawed character.

The interactive organization of these stories also demonstrates the importance of fieldwork that focuses on how members of an endogenous community build stories for each other, rather than what they report to an outsider. The stories are designed specifically for an addressee who occupies a particular social position, and the responses that party makes – for example promising to confront – emerge from inhabiting that specific position, and would not be available to a neutral observer.

As noted by Goodwin and Goodwin (2004: 236–237), what one finds here is a collection of stories that can be systematically compared and contrasted in terms of structure and organization (e.g., specific arrangements of characters and actions). The classical typologies of scholars from Propp (1968) to Lévi-Strauss (1963) were based upon narratives extracted from their local circumstances of production. Here, however, differences in the structure of related stories that emerge in alternative positions in this process – including types of characters, relationships between them, temporal organization, precipitating events, and the ordering of events into larger sequences – are intimately linked to the ways in which the stories constitute relevant social action. Members of a community talking to one another (not to an outside ethnographer) use interactive narrative to participate in consequential courses of action. What one is dealing with is not a linguistic text, but cognitively sophisticated actors using language to build the consequential events that make up their life world.

10.10 A Powerful Storyteller Who Can't Speak

A clear demonstration of the interactive organization of narrative can be found in the actions of Chil, a man left with a three-word vocabulary – "yes," "no," and "and" – after a stroke. Though Chil was completely unable to produce the syntactically rich complex speech that is so central both to narrative and to the laminated speakers of Goffman (1981) and Volosinov (1973), he remained a powerful speaker in conversation. He led others to provide the words he needed to say what he wanted to say by intervening in the unfolding structure of their complex talk (Goodwin 1995, 2003a, 2003b; Wilkinson in press). Thus, as a response to what someone else has just said, "no" indexically incorporates into its own organization the grammatically and semantically rich talk being disagreed with (Goodwin 2010), while taking up an oppositional stance toward what was just said.

As a speaker, Chil is distributed across multiple utterances and actors as he appropriates the rich language structure of others for his own purposes. A very simple example occurred in the midst of a dispute with his son Chuck on an outdoor deck overlooking a canyon (Figure 10.10). Chuck had ordered Chil a hospital bed that Chil did not want. Immediately after Chuck says "It's a question of where to pu:t it" Chil produces a sequence of nonsense syllables that convey powerful stance through highly expressive prosody, while using his hand to animate an object being tossed into the canyon in front of them. The strong laughter this action receives clearly demonstrates that Chil has gesturally reused with transformation the structure provided by Chuck's utterance to vividly create a mini-narrative depicting the bed he does not want being tossed away.

```
1  Chuck:   Uh:, So- uh

2            It's a question of where to pu:t it.

3            (I    really thought)

4  Chil:     Yeah duh da   Heh huh yi dee dee Daaa
```

((General laughter))

Figure 10.10 Using gesture: incorporating the talk of others to build a vivid, oppositional future story.

```
50  Helen:   En the picture over the be-uh
                the crib fell ⌐on ( )
51  Candy:               ⌐Oh my: ⌐goodness
52  Chil:                ⌐No : .
```

```
53              (0.7)
54  Linda:   Fell?
55              (0.5)
56  Chil:    No⌐:.
57  Chuck:     ⌐started to fall?
58              (0.2)
59  Chil:    Ye : s.
60  Chuck:   En you stopped it?
61  Chil:    ⌐No
62  Chuck:   ⌐or you moved it
```

Figure 10.11 A Storyteller who can't speak (Goodwin 2004). Reprinted by permission of John Wiley & Sons, Inc.

Chil's interactive abilities to lead others to produce relevant language which he can transform for his own purposes allows him to tell a complex story about an event that happened almost 60 years in the past (Goodwin 2004).

After Chil's wife tells a story about an earthquake that occurred when they lived as newlyweds in California, Chil uses gesture and limited talk to indicate that he has a tied second story, another earthquake story, to tell (Figure 10.11). With a gesture over his head (later revealed to indicate a picture that almost fell on their sleeping baby) Chil leads his wife to recall and begin to describe this event. Throughout her telling he used his face and body not only to redirect her talk, but also to orient to the story's hearers as a co-speaker himself, and to solicit specific forms of participation from them. In line 52 he uses *No*: to disagree with what his wife has just said. Typically disagreements such as this include an account explicating why what was said is being treated as wrong. Though Chil can't produce the words necessary for such an account, he does attend to the relevance of this structure by producing a gesture, lifting his hand over his head as he says "No" and then turning his gaze first to Helen and then to Linda. This gesture in this sequential position (i.e., in a place where an account for the disagreement is relevant) is heard as an attempt to convey an alternative to what Helen described. In essence he constructs a multi-modal utterance, one part through talk (the word "No") and the other through sequentially positioned gesture. His action leads immediately to a series of guesses by Linda and Chuck as to what Chil might actually want to say (lines 54, 57, 60, 62–65), and it is through Chil's answers to these guesses that the rest of the story gets told (Goodwin 2004).

Chil was so skilled at using the interactive organization of talk to become a powerful speaker that his wife sometimes complained that her voice got lost, though frequently it was she who was providing both the words and the memory he needed to act as a storyteller.

10.11 Building Both Knowing Actors and the Discursive Objects to be Known through Interactive Narrative

Knowledge is lodged within communities. Geologists are expected to be able to recognize, map, and work appropriately with relevant structures in the earth; surgeons must recognize and operate appropriately on particular anatomical structures within the dense environment provided by a living human body; archaeologists must be able to see in the faint color differences within a patch of dirt the traces of ancient human structures. As a consequence of the inherent, open-ended, accumulative organization of human culture and knowledge, all communities are faced with the task of building (1) the objects of knowledge that animate their activities, and (2) actors who can be trusted to recognize, know, and work appropriately with those objects (Goodwin 2012), e.g., the professional vision (Goodwin 1994) that defines a competent member of the community. A particular kind of interactive narrative is central to the way in which this knowledge is organized as public practice, and new members are shaped into knowing entities whose cognitive skills and work can be trusted.

Figure 10.12 provides an example of work at an archaeological field school. Ann is a senior archaeologist while Sue is a beginning graduate student. She has been given the task of outlining the shape of a post mold visible as color patterning in the dirt she is excavating.

Unlike Labov's formulation of narrative as the telling of a past event, or M.H. Goodwin's future stories, here narrative activity is focused on what can be seen in the present. A specific color pattern in the dirt that both participants are intently scrutinizing, described in line 10 as a "stripe," is progressively reformulated into different kinds of discursive objects (e.g., in line 13 the stripe becomes a "plow scar"), a process that culminates when the student is told how to use what she can see in the present to see actions in the past: the movement of a plow. Narratives tied to the structure of what can be seen at the present moment are both common in vernacular settings (e.g., an announcer's description of unfolding action at a sports event), and crucial in many professional settings (Murphy 2011). Consider for example the descriptions during grand rounds by doctors in training as they report to their supervisor what they see in the patient's body, and what this might mean diagnostically, or the description of a landscape by a young geology student at a field school. The interactive organization of such narratives is central to their power as pedagogical devices that can publicly structure what newcomers to the profession are expected to know. Thus, the senior competent member can both see the world being described, such as the features in the dirt being worked with here, and, through the newcomer's narrative, assess what the newcomer has seen in that environment.

Rather than being organized within the world of talk alone, such narratives are deeply tied to both the interaction between the participants, and the material world they are operating on together. Consider line 6 in Figure 10.12, "En then we got to our problem area." Until this point, Ann, the professor, has been favorably assessing the line that Sue, the student, is drawing to outline the post mold they are working with. As she says "problem area," Ann points toward it in such a way that Sue is forced to pull her hand

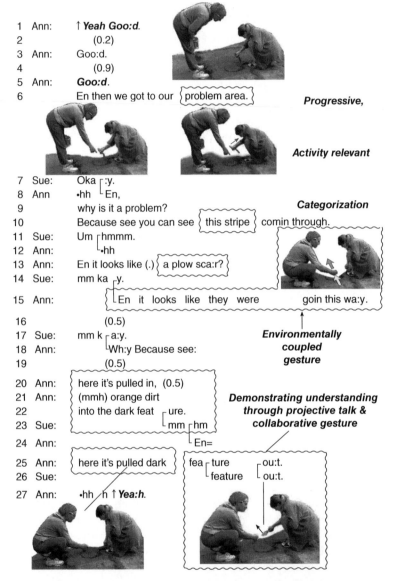

Figure 10.12   Constituting knowing actors and what they are expected to know through interactive narrative (Goodwin 2003c). Reprinted by Permission of Taylor & Francis.

back and stop outlining. Indeed, this is the activity-relevant meaning of "problem area": Sue should stop drawing because the outline of the feature she is trying to trace has become obscured.

Much like the prospective indexicals (Goodwin 1996) in story prefaces that announce the presence and evaluation of something without yet specifying what that is, the expression "problem" sets an agenda for further explication. In lines 10 and 13 Ann progressively reformulates the "problem area" first as "this stripe" – thus clarifying precisely what shape in the dirt should be focused on to understand what will be said next – and then as "a plow scar" (Goodwin 2003c). The addressee of this emerging narrative description is thus expected not only to listen to what was said, but to use that talk to appropriately see and construe the phenomena in the environment that the talk is formulating. This is made particularly clear in line 15 when Ann proposes that it is possible to see the direction of the plow. As she says this she performs an environmentally coupled gesture (Goodwin 2007a), a movement of her hands that is tied simultaneously to the description in her talk, and to the phenomena in the dirt that she is describing. As Sue listens she looks intently toward this conjunction of moving hand and dirt. A quite complex lamination of different semiotic fields, including specific phenomena in the dirt, selective attention to particular parts of each other's bodies, and formulation through language of what is being seen, is occurring during line 15. Rather than waiting to respond sequentially to what Ann has said, Sue is simultaneously inhabiting the action in progress, organizing her own body and perceptual activity so as to put herself in a position to properly understand what she is being told by appropriately scrutinizing the dirt being described.

Moreover, such narratives frequently have a forensic component, as in Figure 10.12. Instead of listening to a description of a past event, participants systematically reconstruct the now invisible processes that created what can be seen in the present.[3] In lines 20–23 Ann describes how the color patterning in the dirt reveals the direction that the plow moved, a form of professional vision (Goodwin 1994) that enables a skilled archaeologist to read events in the past from the patterns visible in a patch of dirt.

Though Sue is being told this, that does not mean that she could actually look at dirt and recognize such events on her own. How can her appropriate understanding be demonstrated, rather than simply claimed? As Ann continues her description in line 25 Sue overlaps with her own anticipatory projection of what Ann is about to say. By not waiting, and simply repeating what she just heard, Sue demonstrates her own independent knowledge of what Ann is telling her. However, the phenomenal domain that the participants are attending to as consequential for their work is not restricted to the stream of speech. Sue must be able to find on her own in the dirt the work-relevant categories, such as "feature," rendered in the talk through narrative description. As Sue performs her overlap she simultaneously points with her trowel to the visible structure in the dirt that provides the crucial evidence for the reconstruction of how the ancient plow moved. Once again subsequent action that demonstrates understanding in fine detail is built through structure-preserving transformations on existing public substrates, here both the immediately prior talk and the patterning of the dirt that is the focus of their attention.

Such forensic reconstruction is true as well for many narratives told in ordinary conversation. Thus, in analyzing a story about a car wreck, Sacks (1992a: 233) notes that the teller didn't actually see the accident, but only its aftermath: twisted, wrecked cars. Instead of telling a story about the aftermath, "she tells the story of an accident; work involving, e.g. that she constructs how the accident could have happened – that one car hit a car and then another car hit that one." This is thus a regular practice repetitively implicated in the organization of narrative. Interaction such as that seen in Figure 10.12 is of particular interest because one can systematically investigate the accountable organization of the practices required for such reconstruction – that is, the work a participant must do to transform what can be seen in the world into an appropriate narrative.

Interactive narrative, as a central locus for endogenous, world-revealing pedagogy, thus provides crucial resources for shaping simultaneously and reflexively both the discursive objects that animate the discourse of a particular community, such as the traces of earlier human activity that can be seen in a patch of dirt, and the actors, here competent archaeologists, who must be trusted to identify and work with such phenomena as skilled, cognitively rich members.

10.12   Conclusion

Central to the organization of narrative as talk-in-interaction is the way in which participants build responses to a narrative by performing structure-preserving transformations on a public substrate produced by someone else. Both the second stories analyzed by Sacks (1992a: 3–8, 21–26, 249–259) and the interactive sequence that emerges from the story being told in Figure 10.1 provide clear, simple examples of this. Don, the principal character in the story being told, uses his visible body to participate syllable by syllable in the teller's emerging laughter that proposes a stance toward what he did. His actions preserve the laughter, and demonstrate understanding of both the emerging structure of the language in progress and the alignment being proposed, while changing that laughter from a vocal to a visible embodied display. The interlocutors of Chil, the man with aphasia, use rich language structure to make public their understanding of what he is trying to tell them through his gesture and other actions (Goodwin 2007b). By transforming his nonlinguistic actions in this way, they make it possible for him to tell a complex story about events 50 years in the past, despite being restricted to a three-word vocabulary (Goodwin 2004). The girl in Figure 10.8 being told that someone has been disparaging her behind her back demonstrates her understanding of what such an instigating story means by promising to confront its principal character. The archaeologists transform the color patterns they see in the dirt they are excavating into work-relevant discursive objects, such as disturbances, features, and plow scars, by using narrative to depict the processes in the past that led to the creation of what they are now seeing. Within this process, the new student demonstrates her comprehension of what her professor is showing her through both anticipatory overlap and an environmentally coupled gesture that displays her independent understanding of how the dirt being narrated is to be construed.

Central to human knowledge and social organization is its accumulative diversity – the way in which members of different societies, and even professions within a society, construe the world around them in specific ways that are relevant to the distinctive interests of their particular community. All human societies are thus faced with the task of populating the worlds they inhabit with both the discursive objects that animate the discourse of their community, such as archaeological features, offensive actions, anatomical structure, a history of consequential, tellable events from the past, etc.; and epistemically accountable, skilled actors who can be trusted not only to recognize relevant objects (e.g., a disturbance obscuring an archaeological feature), but to work with them in just the ways that further develop the activities central to the community, for example responding to a particular kind of story by promising to confront its principal character. Participants demonstrate understanding by using with transformation the materials provided by their interlocutors and predecessors. Moreover, as demonstrated most simply by the principal character's embodied laughter in Figure 10.1, this process encompasses not only talk, but also relevant embodied action as a form of visible, public understanding. It thus provides a matrix within which both the linguistically organized, categorical knowledge of a profession such as archaeology or surgery can be publicly established, and its requisite embodied skills, such as ways of using a trowel as an archaeologist or a knife as a surgeon (Koschmann et al. 2011), can be constituted as accountable, public practice. Because of the way in which it organizes understanding as unfolding public practice, something visible to the participants themselves within the activities they are pursuing together, narrative within talk in interaction is central to the process through which communities construct endogenous life worlds inhabited by skilled, cognitively rich members.

There are also methodological implications for the work reviewed here. In interaction a story is designed in fine detail for its addressee. Though M.H. Goodwin was present as an ethnographer during the telling of the linked He-Said-She-Said stories, they could not have been told to her since she did not occupy one of the relevant social positions that were organizing the events constituted through the telling. Similarly, I was present during the recording of the archaeology narratives, but was not a young archaeologist trying to develop the ability to see the dirt in the excavation so that I could properly map it, and thus did not face the task of demonstrating proper understanding in a move subsequent to the story, or of acquiring competent membership. Those able to work with Chil to collaboratively help him tell his story shared a lifetime of experience with him. While recognizing the most important work on narrative that has been accomplished through interviews, and their genuine integrity as forms of discourse in their own terms (De Fina and Perrino 2011), I would like to argue strongly that there is also an important place for fieldwork designed to recover how participants within endogenous communities build stories for each other as a central part of the process through which they construct the events that are central to their lives (Ochs and Taylor 1995).

A considerable amount of very important research has highlighted the power of narrative to construct the self, indeed a complex fluid self (Bamberg, De Fina, and Schiffrin 2008; Bruner 1991; Ochs and Capps 2001). The investigation of narrative within interaction puts an equal focus on its unique capacity to construct and shape others. Indeed, the phenomena briefly investigated here have revealed two quite different kinds of addressees. First, there are rich, emotionally charged actors, such as the girls being hurt on hearing about the stories being told about them, Chil's vivid actions as he provides his interlocutors with the materials they are to transform into his story, Don participating in his own degradation as the terrible comment he made to his hosts is told to everyone present, etc. However, in the narratives of archaeologists focusing on events such as the movement of a plow, particular actors become so attenuated as to be made almost invisible. Indeed, in the narratives about past events used by geologists to understand the present (the movements of glaciers, etc.), human actors entirely disappear. Despite these differences, both of these kinds of narratives provide central resources for the consequential transformation of their addressees. Thus, the girl who learns about the offenses committed against her through the instigating stories can be transformed into an accuser, creating a dramatic event that mobilizes the anticipation of the entire girls' community. By performing the transformative operations made relevant by the environmentally coupled narratives they hear, newcomers to a profession such as archaeology are progressively transformed into competent members of that profession, actors who possess the shared understanding and skills required to see and act upon the world in the precise ways that enable the work of their community. The process of participating in the interactive field created by a narrative – performing transformative operations on it that display understanding and build appropriate, consequential subsequent action – simultaneously transforms those who perform such operations. Narratives in interaction provide central human practices for building actors with rich, though specific, locally relevant attributes, consequential discursive objects, and endogenous communities.

NOTES

1   I am deeply indebted to Marjorie Harness Goodwin and Numa Markee for insightful comments on an earlier version of this paper.
2   Talk is transcribed using the system developed by Gail Jefferson (Sacks, Schegloff, and Jefferson, 1974: 731–733).
3   See Murphy (2011) for a most relevant analysis of brief, interactive narratives that argue about how what is being seen in the present, in his case architectural diagrams, will shape the activities of participants in the future as they inhabit the spaces envisioned by the diagrams.

REFERENCES

Bamberg, M., A. De Fina, and D. Schiffrin (eds.). (2008). *Selves and Identities in Narratives and Discourse*. Amsterdam: John Benjamins.

Bruner, J. (1991). The narrative construction of reality. *Critical Inquiry*, 18 (1), pp. 1–21.

De Fina, A., and S. Perrino. (2011). Introduction: Interviews vs. "natural" contexts: A false dilemma. *Language in Society*, 40 (1), pp. 1–11.

Goffman, E. (1981). Footing. In E. Goffman (ed.), *Forms of Talk*. Philadelphia: University of Pennsylvania Press, pp. 124–159.

Goodwin, C. (1984). Notes on story structure and the organization of participation. In M. Atkinson and J. Heritage (eds.), *Structures of Social Action*. Cambridge: Cambridge University Press, pp. 225–246.

Goodwin, C. (1994). Professional vision. *American Anthropologist*, 96 (3), pp. 606–633.

Goodwin, C. (1995). Co-Constructing meaning in conversations with an aphasic man. *Research on Language and Social Interaction*, 28 (3), pp. 233–260.

Goodwin, C. (1996). Transparent vision. In E. Ochs, E.A. Schegloff, and S. Thompson (eds.), *Interaction and Grammar*.

Cambridge: Cambridge University Press, pp. 370–404.

Goodwin, C. (2000). Action and embodiment within situated human interaction. *Journal of Pragmatics*, 32, pp. 1489–1522.

Goodwin, C. (ed.). (2003a). *Conversation and Brain Damage*. Oxford: Oxford University Press.

Goodwin, C. (2003b). Conversational frameworks for the accomplishment of meaning in aphasia. In C. Goodwin (ed.), *Conversation and Brain Damage*. Oxford: Oxford University Press, pp. 90–116.

Goodwin, C. (2003c). Pointing as situated practice. In S. Kita (ed.), *Pointing: Where Language, Culture, and Cognition Meet*. Hillsdale, NJ: Lawrence Erlbaum Associates, pp. 217–241.

Goodwin, C. (2004). A competent speaker who can't speak: The social life of aphasia. *Journal of Linguistic Anthropology*, 14 (2), pp. 151–170.

Goodwin, C. (2007a). Environmentally coupled gestures. In S. Duncan, J. Cassell, and E. Levy (eds.), *Gesture and the Dynamic Dimension of Language*. Amsterdam: John Benjamins, pp. 195–212.

Goodwin, C. (2007b). Interactive footing. In E. Holt and R. Clift (eds.), *Reporting Talk: Reported Speech in Interaction*. Cambridge: Cambridge University Press, pp. 16–46.

Goodwin, C. (2010). Constructing meaning through prosody in aphasia. In D. Barth-Weingarten, E. Reber, and M. Selting (eds.), *Prosody in Interaction*. Amsterdam: John Benjamins, pp. 373–394.

Goodwin, C. (2012). The co-operative, transformative organization of human action and knowledge. *Journal of Pragmatics*, 46 (1), pp. 8–23.

Goodwin, C., and M.H. Goodwin. (1987). Concurrent operations on talk: Notes on the interactive organization of assessments. *IPrA Papers in Pragmatics*, 1 (1), pp. 1–52.

Goodwin, C., and M. Goodwin. (2004). Participation. In A. Duranti (ed.), *A Companion to Linguistic Anthropology*. Oxford: Basil Blackwell, pp. 222–243.

Goodwin, M.H. (1982). "Instigating": Storytelling as social process. *American Ethnologist*, 9, pp. 799–819.

Goodwin, M.H. (1990). *He Said She Said: Talk as Social Organization among Black Children*. Bloomington: Indiana University Press.

Goodwin, M.H., and C. Goodwin. (1987). Children's arguing. In S. Philips, S. Steele, and C. Tanz (eds.), *Language, Gender, and Sex in Comparative Perspective*. Cambridge: Cambridge University Press, pp. 200–248.

Irvine, J.T. (1996). Shadow conversations: The indeterminacy of participant roles. In M. Silverstein and G. Urban (eds.), *Natural Histories of Discourse*. Chicago, IL: University of Chicago Press, pp. 131–159.

Koschmann, T., C. LeBaron, C. Goodwin, and P. Feltovich. (2011). "Can you see the cystic artery yet?" A simple matter of trust. *Journal of Pragmatics*, 43 (2), pp. 521–541.

Labov, W. (1972). The transformation of experience in narrative syntax. In *Language in the Inner City: Studies in the Black English Vernacular*. Philadelphia: University of Pennsylvania Press, pp. 354–396.

Labov, W., and J. Waletzky. (1968). Narrative analysis. In W. Labov et al. (ed.), *A Study of the Non-Standard English of Negro and Puerto Rican Speakers in New York City*. Report authored at Columbia University for US Department of Health, pp. 286–338.

Lever, J.R. (1978). Sex differences in the complexity of children's play and games. *American Sociological Review*, 43, pp. 471–483.

Lévi-Strauss, C. (1963). *Structural Anthropology*. New York: Basic Books.

Levinson, S. (1988). Putting linguistics on a proper footing: Explorations in Goffman's concepts of participation. In A. Wootton and P. Drew (eds.), *Erving Goffman: Exploring the Interaction Order*. Boston, MA: Northeastern University Press, pp. 161–227.

Levinson, S.C. (2012). Action formation and ascription. In J. Sidnell and T. Stivers (eds.), *The Handbook of Conversation Analysis*. Oxford: Wiley-Blackwell, pp. 103–130.

Murphy, K. (2011). Building stories: The embodied narration of what might come to pass. In J. Streeck, C. Goodwin, and C.D. Lebaron (eds.), *Embodied Interaction: Language and Body in the Material World*. Cambridge: Cambridge University Press, pp. 243–253.

Ochs, E., and L. Capps. (2001). *Living Narrative: Creating Lives in Everyday Storytelling*. Cambridge, MA: Harvard University Press.

Ochs, E., and C. Taylor. (1995). The "father knows best" dynamic in dinnertime narratives. In K. Hall and M. Bucholtz (eds.), *Gender Articulated: Language and the Socially Constructed Self*. New York: Routledge, pp. 97–119.

Propp, V. (1968). *The Morphology of the Folktale*. 2nd edn. Translated by T. Scott. Austin: University of Texas Press.

Sacks, H. (1974). An analysis of the course of a joke's telling in conversation. In R. Bauman and J. Sherzer (eds.), *Explorations in the Ethnography of Speaking*. Cambridge: Cambridge University Press, pp. 337–353.

Sacks, H. (1992a). *Lectures on Conversation*. Vol. 2. Edited by G. Jefferson. Oxford: Basil Blackwell.

Sacks, H. (1992b). Second stories. In G. Jefferson (ed.), *Lectures on Conversation*, Vol. 2. Oxford: Basil Blackwell, pp. 764–772.

Sacks, H., E.A. Schegloff, and G. Jefferson. (1974). A simplest systematics for the organization of turn-taking for conversation. *Language*, 50, pp. 696–735.

Volosinov, V.N. (1973). *Marxism and the Philosophy of Language*. Cambridge, MA: Harvard University Press.

Wilkinson, R. (in press). Aphasia: Conversation analysis. In M. Perkins and S. Howard (eds.), *Case Studies in Clinical Linguistics*. London: Whurr Publishers.

11   Entering the Hall of Mirrors
Reflexivity and Narrative Research

CATHERINE KOHLER RIESSMAN

11.1   Introduction

When asked to contribute an essay on narrative and reflexivity, I was extremely reluctant. I had decided not to contribute any more chapters to handbooks, feeling the volumes had assumed too weighty a place in the methodological literature, crowding out other valuable ways of knowing about the research process. Chapters typically review topics in neat disembodied packages, rarely tied to the biography of the investigator, or the social and political conditions of a study or its setting – the very opposite of reflexivity in practice. Always emergent, reflexivity is closely tied to the phenomenon and our unfolding understanding of it during fieldwork and writing. I was also reluctant because I knew the field of narrative research, but I had never immersed myself in the reflexivity literature. While always stressing its value in my teaching, it is not how I've conceptualized my research. The editors apparently thought otherwise about what I'd been up to – an insight that intrigued and eventually engaged me. Is that what I have been doing? It might be instructive to read the literature, and rethink my own work in relation to it.

I finally agreed to write "a review article on Reflexivity in Narrative Research and use selections of my past work to show how I've attempted to include my current positionality in 'revisiting' narrative segments collected long ago."[1] Writing the paper took me in unanticipated directions: I slowly realized I needed to write my intellectual biography and politics into the text to embody aspects of the reflexive stance I was writing about. I had to experiment with my writing style, weaving together personal, political, and academic identities. I also began to read, asking some basic questions: what does "reflexivity" mean in social research? Where did the concept come from, and who are the central figures in the social sciences writing about and practicing reflexivity? Is there a continuum with "weaker" and "stronger" versions, or are there multiple modes – different ways of working reflexively depending on the purpose of a project? When did I first encounter the ideas? Has my work over the years reflected the various modes?

The Handbook of Narrative Analysis, First Edition. Edited by Anna De Fina and Alexandra Georgakopoulou.
© 2015 John Wiley & Sons, Inc. Published 2019 by John Wiley & Sons, Inc.

11.2   The Disparate Meanings of Reflexivity

Narrative researchers, like poets, describe moments in lives in their texts; like poets, they deal in facsimiles of the thing itself.

> Description is revelation. It is not
> The thing described, nor false facsimile,
>
> It is an artificial thing that exists,
> In its own seeming, plainly visible,
>
> Yet not too closely the double of our lives,
> Intenser than any actual life could be …
>   (Wallace Stevens 1990: 344)

How we take account of our role in the production is the analytic task, generally subsumed under the term "reflexivity." The word is ambiguous; it means different things in different scholarly traditions – "an elusive slippery gathering of sometimes disparate and contradictory ideas" (Doyle 2013: 253). Like the concept of narrative itself, definitions and boundaries are fluid. An old idea in philosophy, meanings have migrated over the last decades into anthropology and sociology, feminist studies, and into the practicing professions, converging in the busy intersection of narrative research. Checking out the recent literature, I found a resurgence of interest in reflexivity in several research journals and edited collections (cf. Bishop and Shepherd 2011; Burawoy 2003; Doyle 2013; Finlay 2012; Hertz 1997; Andrews, Squire, and Tamboukou 2013), including a discussion of "weak" vs. "strong" versions, but I could find little explicit reference to the concept in narrative journals. This is surprising, given that one mode is intrinsic to studies of talk-in-interaction.

To fully understand its historical development in the social sciences, I go back in time and begin with Myerhoff and Ruby's definition: reflexivity is "the capacity of any system of signification to turn back upon itself, to make itself its own object by referring to itself: subject and object fuse" (1982: 2). The authors borrow a communication transmission model to make a distinction between producer, process, and product, which I loosely adopt as a starting point – it provided a useful organizing device for the essay – but which I then broaden because of problems with the definition.[2] However imperfect, detailed knowledge about all three elements of reflexivity is essential for a fuller understanding of the making of any piece of research – the "backstage" of our scholarly performances (Goffman 1959).

The *producer* is the creator of the sign, the sender of the message. In interview studies – my primary focus in this paper – the term can refer to a participant's utterances, biographical information, and other signs, culminating in the emergent narratives embedded in a conversation. However, it is also possible to think of the investigator as producer of the sign, or message – another mirror in the infinite regress that characterizes reflexivity. (This approach has captured the imagination of many contemporary scholars, reviewed below).

Process, according to Myerhoff and Ruby (1982: 5), is "the means, methods, channel, mode, code, and the like, whereby a message is shaped, encoded and sent." For scholars in narrative studies, this component refers to our epistemological assumptions and methodological thinking – everything from our philosophical standpoint to choice of study design, evolving relationships with participants, how we compose our transcriptions, and on through the theories that guide interpretation. The *product* is what the receiver gets, the text, our scholarly productions – analysis of participants' narratives, for example. Extending this aspect, the mirror can shift to participants' responses to what we have done, and toward the responses of other audiences, bringing reflexivity full circle.

Although these clear divisions are useful for clarity, like all homogeneous categories they oversimplify; sharp boundaries blur in real life. Producer, process, and product are deeply interconnected. Nevertheless Myerhoff and Ruby argue for the relevance of each:

> being reflexive means the producer [the investigator here] deliberately, intentionally, reveals to an audience the underlying epistemological assumptions that caused the formulation of a set of questions in a particular way, the seeking of answers to those questions in a particular way, and finally the presentation of the findings in a particular way. (1982: 5)

Consistent with the social constructionist perspective, reflexivity exposes the constitutive nature of research: the inseparability of observer, observation, and interpretation.

One mode of reflexivity involves revisiting one's past work and turning it into the object of inquiry – a path many have followed, including me. Inevitably in these cases, personal narrative and reflexivity are joined. Over the last several decades scholars have modeled reflexivity in narrative work in a variety of ways, either by elaborating a single component fully – producer, process, or product – or by braiding them together throughout a study in their thinking and writing so that the "the audience assumes the producer, process, and product are a coherent whole" (Myerhoff and Ruby 1982: 6).

11.3   Beginnings: Personal and Anthropological

I first began to venture into the hall of mirrors that is reflexivity during second wave feminism, inspired by qualitative researchers who were beginning to question the pretense of the absent investigator in social science writing – what philosophers call "the view from nowhere" (Nagel 1986). As Susan Krieger (1991: 1) observes, the self of the social scientific investigator was viewed as "a contaminant … something to be separated out, neutralized, minimized, standardized and controlled," even though investigators must use themselves to know a phenomenon. Early feminist sociologists who challenged this view were foundational for many of us (Oakley 1980; Reinharz 1984; Smith 1987; Stacey 1988; Stanley and Wise 1983), and there was a similar movement in psychology, a central strand of which centered on intersubjectivity. We wanted to see the author behind a text, the human interactions that produced data, even in surveys. Critical scholars wanted to unveil the power relations embedded in scholarly work. Others stressed the partiality of any investigator's view – our limited capacity to represent self and Other. There were small moves that had big effects: we began to write in the first person, rather than referring to ourselves as "the investigator." We began to study topics relevant to women's lives by focusing on women's perspectives and experiences. We began to experiment with form in our writing, moving away from the hygienic report of "findings" – the taken-for-granted genre in social science writing. Experimental writing continues to be regarded with suspicion because standards for critique and discussion are "slippery" (DeVault 1997), even as the move has liberated investigators who can begin to include themselves as sentient beings with politics in their scholarly writing. Thinking about the thinking that runs through a research project and making that explicit is, of course, essential to reflexivity.

Anthropologists, for a variety of reasons, were way ahead of sociologists and psychologists, for they led the interpretive turn away from a positivist science – no detached standpoint exists for investigators in the human sciences (Geertz 1973; Rabinow and Sullivan 1979; Turner and Bruner 1986). A sentinel event in the reflexive turn was a day-long symposium at the American Anthropological Association's annual meeting in 1978, entitled "Portrayal of Self, Profession, and Culture: Reflexive Perspectives in Anthropology," which later gave rise to Ruby's (1982) edited volume. Participants included major anthropologists outside the objectivist ethnographic tradition who brought themselves into their work during the 1970s (Rabinow 1977; Turner 1980). Here and elsewhere, anthropologists realized the significance of storytelling, long before most other scholars did. At the time I read the anthropologists' work with admiration, but it seemed a long way from what I had been trained to do in social work research and medical sociology, and from the sociolinguistic focus I was developing during a post-doctoral fellowship (1986–1989) with Elliot Mishler. The work of several women anthropologists, however, left a strong mark, although it would take me years to find ways of folding their imaginative thinking and writing into my own research practice. Reading Jean Briggs's "Kapluna Daughter" (Briggs 1970) demonstrated how illuminating it is to tell a compelling story about a research project, especially one that makes visible the fieldworker's missteps along the way. I learned that errors and mistakes – interactions with particular participants that don't go according to plan – can sometimes be the most instructive, pushing knowledge about a phenomenon in new directions.

My first publication in the narrative field, "When Gender Is Not Enough" (Riessman 1987) analyzed an interview interaction that went awry because the woman interviewer expected a canonical, temporally organized divorce story, but got instead a long, associative episodic narrative, better suited to the marital experience of the Latina participant: back and forth migration from Puerto Rico to the United States interspersed with moments of conflict in the couple's families about women's proper place. The transcript of the long narrative segment included the speech of both interviewer and interviewee, including interruptions, false starts, break-offs, and other lexical utterances of both women (and I had to fight with the journal editor to get the transcript included!). Although I didn't think of reflexivity as I was writing the piece, I now see the work did take account of the interviewer's role in the production of narrative, and the resulting misunderstanding – one mode of reflexivity. By reanalyzing a long interactive segment that wasn't temporally organized, I began a focused interest in narrative form – *how* a story is told interactionally, over and beyond *what* is said, and how the organization offers a key to meaning and understanding, or misunderstanding. What a personal narrative is trying to accomplish, its purpose or function in the inter- actional context, shapes its form. The story is only one of several narrative forms avail- able to speakers in conversation (De Fina 2003; Polanyi 1989). In everyday usage, of course, story and narrative are often used interchangeably – a practice we often adopt to speak to broad audiences.

Educational researchers took up issues of narrative structure and interaction very early because they witnessed how different modes of children's storytelling in class- rooms had profound effects, often disadvantaging children of color (Cazden 2001; Gee 1985; Michaels 1981). The work had a major influence on my thinking and subsequent scholarship, proving especially relevant to interpreting interview narratives that contained interactional "trouble" (for a recent example, see Riessman 2012). I have never thought that the several case studies dealing with miscommunications were indicative of a reflexive turn, although they did shift the mirror away from narrative content and toward the dynamics of production and reception. Is critical self-aware- ness as one is doing the work a necessary condition for reflexivity? Thinking about, rather than simply revealing biographical facts about ourselves as producers of knowledge, is certainly necessary.

Barbara Myerhoff writes about her (dissertation) fieldwork in the mid 1960s: "I had an extreme sense of being a stranger … more a nonperson to the [Huichol] Indians [of northern Mexico] than they were to me." Relationships, "though strong and deep," were not symmetrical. "Enforced thought about how we saw each other ensued, though a term to call what we meant to each other never did appear" (Myerhoff and Ruby 1982: 32–33). Not only do these brief phrases locate the producer of the ethnography, they also hint at the politics constraining field relationships (the process) and the white Western ethnographer's limited capacity to construct "truthful portrayals" of an Other (Ortner 1996: 190). Crafting the dissertation ten years later into a book (Myerhoff 1974) – the product – pushed reflexivity further, thanks to a gifted editor, whose prodding the anthropologist later described:

> She deleted all the impersonal forms, the third person, the passive voice, the editorial "we," and insisted on responsibility. "How did you know this?" "Who saw that?" "What was seen?" "Who is 'one'"? Her insistence on an active and personal voice was extremely difficult but eventually invaluable. By requiring me to insert myself and my verified observations *into* the manuscript, the editor was requiring the methodological rigor that we are simultaneously trained to value and avoid. After this bout with the editor, I found I had written a book that I trusted more, that was clearer and more reliable (and, I think, more readable as well), and I had received a lesson in anthropological methods better than many I had been offered in the course of my formal training. (Myerhoff and Ruby 1982: 33)

Myerhoff's subsequent (and tragically last) fieldwork was among her own ethnic people: a group of elderly Eastern European Jews in a senior center in Venice, California. The ethnographic product – *Number Our Days* – braids the three strands of reflexivity together into a single work, arguably representing the first example of this process by a scholar (Myerhoff 1978). Experimenting with the form the "product" would take, she produced, in addition to the written ethnography, an award-winning film and play, accomplished collaboratively with performance artists. The performance pieces made her academic analysis recognizable to wide audiences. The genius of the work is widely appreciated and I won't summarize it here but emphasize, instead, that readers get detailed knowledge about the three essential components of reflexivity: the personal narratives and life stories of elders (the producers), the investigator's thinking and actions as her relationships with them evolved (the process) and, lastly, her interpretive understanding about the meanings of the life stories for the elder community (the product). Redirecting the mirror, readers also view relevant aspects of the biography of the investigator as knowledge producer. Myerhoff places herself as an observable character in her representations of conversations with participants and in the evolution of her "findings" about them. As she later wrote, "I found myself doing a complex enterprise that involved ceaseless evaluation of the effects of membership on my conclusions" (Myerhoff and Ruby, 1982: 33). Her persona – a specific, identifiable, thinking, feeling, and gendered ethnic participant observer – is deeply embedded in the ethnography, and she makes this persona visible in her writing. For many narrative scholars, a central problem with the book is her editing of participants' utterances – the power she assumes over their words. The anthropologist infiltrates the conversations in ways readers can never evaluate; subjects and investigator fuse, creating what she later called the third voice: "neither the voice of the informant nor the voice of the interviewer, but the voice of their collaboration" (Myerhoff as quoted in Kaminsky 1992: 7). Although she didn't know the work of Bakhtin (1981), her statement anticipates his dialogic perspective, as well as contemporary theory about talk-in-interaction in narrative studies (De Fina and Georgakopoulou 2008).

Finding a way to incorporate the various components of reflexivity into a narrative project is a huge challenge for investigators today, as it was for Myerhoff, I suspect. Like many of us, she used the essay form to reflect back on her prior work, including the ethnographic process of producing the book, film, and play. The reconstructed nature of the reflections led inevitably to personal storytelling. The essays were collected and published posthumously (Myerhoff 1992); in one written in 1984 that remained unfinished at the time of her early death, she adjusts the mirror to reflect on herself as the producer of *Number Our Days*. She questions the power relations embedded in customary research practices, such as assigning pseudonyms to protect anonymity, even when the practice went against the vehement wishes of participants: they wanted *their* names attached to *their* life stories. Anticipating issues that were to erupt in anthropology – "My subjects wanted the last word on how they should be understood, and I had decided to reserve that for myself" (Myerhoff 1992: 282) – she acknowledges her power and authority but does not question the ethical and political issues obscured in the neat producer/process/ product distinction that she had put forward earlier. Anticipating dialogism – also absent from the distinction – she writes about how some of the elders and members of an audience responded critically to the play. She discusses the decision "to include myself overtly as part of the story I was telling … That the observer is a part of all she witnesses has long been a truism … The decision to include myself was immensely liberating" (Myerhoff 1992: 294). She echoes the Wallace Stevens poem I cited earlier in the chapter:

> A new creation is constituted when two points of view are engaged in examining a life. The new creation has its own integrity but should not be mistaken for the spontaneous, unframed life-as-lived person who existed before the interview began … there are only choices, no faithful copies. (Myerhoff 1992: 291, 296)

11.4 Reflexivity in an Appendix

If anthropologists led the reflexive turn, how were other social scientists taking account of the effect of their presence on their research? A historically old and familiar way sociologists have attempted to incorporate a degree of reflexivity into a study is with an appendix written in a narrative style. I followed this traditional path in my first book (Riessman 1990) with a detailed methodological appendix describing the study design, sampling, and interview schedule, written in the first person but also in the distant objective voice of traditional social science writing. I broke this frame briefly to recount the epistemological transformation that occurred in the long intense interviews, and later during the coding process:

> I could no longer view the interviewees as objects, from whom data could be extracted and analyzed separate from the contexts in which they were created. I saw active and imaginative subjects, women and men who reflected on themselves and the gendered world of marriage … I began to see divorce as an interpretive process, not as a series of stages. I became intrigued with the imaginative enterprise itself – how individuals, through talk, construct meaning out of loss, and how gender is meaningful in this interpretive work. The subjects had changed the investigator and, thus, the research. (Riessman 1990: 227)

However brief and sketchy, there is a reflexive move here: the research was inseparable from the particular investigator, her observations, engagement with the data, and interpretation of them. By intentionally revealing a transformation in thinking, the reader gets a glimpse into the person and process that produced the scholarly product.

Ethnographers in sociology and anthropology for decades had placed themselves in appendices, or reserved personal disclosure for introductory remarks, postscripts, private diaries or subsequent writings. Twelve years after the 1943 publication of his classic ethnography, *Street Corner Society*, William Foote Whyte added a lengthy appendix detailing the many missteps in his fieldwork and evolving relationships with informants; he added to the appendix in subsequent editions. Here, in the fourth edition, White reflects on the writing practices of the earlier era:

> It seems as if the academic world had imposed a conspiracy of silence regarding the personal experiences of field workers … It was impossible to find realistic accounts that revealed the errors and confusions and the personal involvements that a field worker must experience. I decided [in the appendix] to do my bit to fill this gap. (Whyte 1993: 358)

In this mode of reflexivity, disclosure and reflection are separated from the substance of the work.

However limited the appendix may be as the only place for a reflexive stance, I do remember vividly the sense of liberation and freedom when writing mine. Readers also engage easily with narratives of investigators about how they do their work. The chapter poured out of me, in contrast to my writing struggles producing other chapters – even those in which I included, in narrative extracts, my verbal utterances as interviewer/ questioner. I knew that I was an active collaborator in the construction of the data – emergent narratives about participants' divorces. Influenced by scholars in sociolinguistics, I knew my lexical and non-lexical cues mattered. But did my experience in the interviews matter?

11.5   Reflexivity and the Conversational Context

Elliot Mishler uncovered for a generation of researchers the co-construction process: how the "personal" narratives produced in interview conversations are the outcome of a social interaction between speaker and listener/questioner (Mishler 1984, 1986; also see Bell 1988; Paget 1983). Earlier in a landmark essay, "Meaning in Context: Is There Any Other Kind?" (Mishler 1979), he anticipates what is the cornerstone of reflexivity – the contexts surrounding any piece of data. While interviewing and analyzing divorce stories, I had witnessed how powerfully the conversational context, evolving research relationship, physical setting, and broad cultural ideologies had shaped – even sometimes determined – what a particular participant divulged to me. I wrote these observations in my field notes, and took the knowledge under advisement as I wrote up my findings, but how could I include my thinking during an individual interview, without undermining the general argument I was making about 104 participants – the sample as a whole? I felt my experience as the interviewer/analyst did not belong in the center of the book – my continuing preference, although this mode of reflexivity proliferates in contemporary times.

At the other extreme are writings of the early narrative scholars in sociolinguistics in the 1960s and 1970s who provided scant attention to context even in their descriptions of methods (process), which were rarely written in the first person. Sociologists had recognized for years that "interviewer characteristics" mattered, and Labov does take account of the racial backgrounds of the research team in his seminal book *Language in the Inner City* (1972): "white researchers ... who are primarily linguists and outsiders to the vernacular culture, and black researchers ... who know the culture of the inner city as full participants and share a deep understanding of it, but who remain relative outsiders to linguistic theory" (xiv). The diverse membership of the team clearly made the research politically possible in the Harlem community. Addressing readers directly in the book's introduction, Labov acknowledges the racial politics of his project:

> Given the current state of black-white relations in the United States, the reader should certainly want to know how any report on the black English vernacular was prepared: who did the talking and who did the listening, who were the investigators, where did they work ... (1972: xviii).

Yet, in spite of this statement about race, power, and context, the particular narratives that were produced in dynamic exchanges – presumably with the black team members – were treated as free-standing units, detachable from any "local business" of previous talk and action (De Fina and Georgakopouou 2008) and, certainly, from the racialized communities in which the conversations took place. In Labov's chapter 9, based on his earlier work with Waletsky, we read what we assume are interviewers' verbatim questions that prompted the classic tales of violent incidents, but we never see the evolving research relationships that produced these accounts, nor the non-lexical cues that may have encouraged extended replies. Yet there is more information on the field context in Labov's work than in the abstracted speech samples that populated other sociolinguistic and conversation analysis writings of the time.

11.6   Contemporary Modes of Self-Reflexivity

Many scholars in the contemporary period turn the mirror on themselves. Autoethnography in sociology is one such move, echoed in a variety of work that gives prominence to the researcher's personal experience narrative (Ellis and Bochner 2000; Davies 2012). By emphasizing subjectivity, investigators' emotional responses in difficult situations have found a place in scholarly writing. A "self-indulgent" criticism – oversubjectivization tending toward narcissism – has been voiced by some, including, ironically, several who were pivotal in the reflexive turn in anthropology (Rosaldo 1989). Feminist scholars have countered the self-indulgent critique but, as Doyle (2013: 253) adds, the researcher's emotions and personal experiences "must be thought about and analyzed, and the analysis used purposefully in the research process." Research must do more than feature the self of the investigator in an evocative autoethnography.

One feminist sociologist argues that "we have not written ourselves in [to our research] nearly enough" (Presser 2005: 2067). "We should include as data the context of the interview, including the resources [and power relations] that allow the interview to take place at all" (2069). Working as a criminologist interviewing violent offenders, Presser discusses the social control procedures inherent in the male prison setting and her gendered position in that setting; jointly they influence the men's enactments of masculinity in interviews. By presenting her verbatim exchanges with the men, she allows readers to see the texture of interaction that produced particular accounts of violence and their inseparability from the gender and race relations of the conversations. Research interviews become "a site of gender activity" and power negotiation (2071). Speaking directly to narrative scholars (but apparently unaware of our prior work on the topic), Presser writes:

> The researcher's goal is not to emancipate *the* authentic story of the narrator – none exists – but rather to expose as much as she can of the relations that influence the construction of the story that is told. (2005: 2087)

She posits that a "strong reflexivity" would interrogate the institutional and political processes and social structures that contextualize a study, compared with a "weak reflexivity" that simply writes the investigator's background, evolving thinking and emotions into the research report (also see Wasserfall 1993 on this distinction). I return to institutional and political dimensions below.

For narrative scholars, one issue with self-reflexivity is what the investigator's personal disclosure does for a narrative analysis – that is, how it contributes to a larger methodological and substantive project (DeVault 1997). Years ago, Myerhoff and Ruby (1982: 24) put it bluntly: "excessive concern with either the producer or the process will obviously cause the focus of the product to turn inward; total attention to the producers creates autobiography, not ethnography." More recently, Doyle warns of forms of reflexivity that "overemphasize researchers' experience … eclipsing experiences of the research participant" (Doyle 2013: 253). Yet paradoxically, it may be necessary sometimes to explore the self before one can thoughtfully understand the phenomenon one is studying, as Krieger notes in reflecting on her research in a lesbian community (1991). In my view, the contemporary move to personal writing represents a significant corrective to the distant objectivist/realist tales that populated sociology and anthropology for too long, but considerable skill and discipline is needed. Self-reflexivity should work in the service of better understanding the phenomena at hand.

Looking back over my work, I see that I began to experiment more purposefully over time with ways to include myself as the observer/knowledge producer. The move still remained cordoned off from the "findings" of the study (the product), but there was a definite shift. It was stimulated during research I conducted in South India,[3] perhaps because I was crossing geopolitical borders and doing extended fieldwork for the first time. Influenced by the anthropologists (noted above) who had moved away from objectivism decades earlier, I was forced to confront an issue that sociology had not prepared me for: I was seen as the Other in India, and not because of my skin color. Looking now at my writing in 2000 (see excerpt below, from one of the first papers published from the study), note how I document my methods in a long personal narrative that includes a degree of self-knowledge, personal disclosure, and epistemological awareness. Although I didn't consciously realize it at the time, living and working in India forced self-reflexivity into my research practice.

I traveled to India in 1993 intending to study the meaning and management of infertility. In the [Fulbright] proposal, I wrote as a distant observer who would "collect data" and "produce findings." This positioning, in part, was for an imagined audience of grant reviewers, but it also reflected my distance from the topic and the field. As an outsider – a white Western woman with grown children, studying South Asian women who wanted to conceive – I hoped to give voice[4] to their invisible concerns in a country dominated by a discourse of popular control.

The subcontinent of India and its southern coast (Kerala) where I lived and worked from 1993 to 1994, dissolved distance. Traveling on crowded trains, I even began to question my topic: "India has too many people," I wrote in my field notes, "why am I studying infertility?" But fieldwork drew me into the topic, especially interviewing women (together with my Malayali research assistant, Liza) in a busy infertility clinic of a government hospital or in their homes in towns and villages ... For a time I lived in a fishing village and assisted in wedding preparation, working alongside childless women I had formally interviewed. Witnessing them in everyday life decentered my earlier notions of their subordination ...

I learned about dominant definitions of family from repeated questions about my own. "How many children do you have? Why aren't they married? Where is your husband?" (I was divorced at the time). From strangers on trains and others who asked about my personal life, I learned firsthand about compulsory motherhood, marriage, and stigma. Ironically, I lived in an apartment complex called Choice Gardens, but I felt stigmatized by my Indian neighbors' negative responses to my family status. Like a divorced woman, a married woman who is childless in India exists at the margins, in a liminal space – socially betwixt and between. With these insights, the interviews focused with increasing intensity on how women construct lives when they are not mothers and the social support others do (or do not) provide. (Riessman 2000: 114–115)

Rather than providing an objective description of my methods, the personal narrative communicates a shift in both topic and interest. My preconceived medicalized category – infertility – gave way to a social understanding: my participants were childless. Not sharing this identity, I disclose how I was able to find a common humanity with the women through my own experiences living and traveling in India. Going beyond empathy and imaginative identification, it was our shared "deviant" family structures – we were both questioned every day and negatively evaluated – that provided theoretical insight about what I came to see as compulsory marriage and motherhood. Interviews then explored the ingenious ways women resisted the mandate, including the questioning on trains that they were subjected to also. Paradoxically, in a country dominated by colonial policies of population control, childless women were cast as the Other. The focus of the research shifted to the ways married women subverted the motherhood mandate to recover their dignity. In sum, my emotions and positionality in the South Indian context became a major source of knowledge about the phenomenon I was studying.

In the excerpt, as in all narrative, there is an inevitable "'after the factness', a looking backward" (Freeman 2010: 185; see also this volume, chapter 1), compounded in this case (and always) because investigators can only write reflexively after some fieldwork (Bishop and Shepherd 2011). Like all narrative, mine was reconstructed, a selection, distillation, and reworking of personal experiences – a facsimile of real facts that unfolded over time. The numerous letters I wrote from Choice Gardens to friends, family, and my mentor, Elliot Mishler, contained other facts, observations, and experiences, including my extreme social isolation and loneliness. I chose not to share these in published papers, for I (still) don't see their relevance. My daily reflections were akin to private diaries and memos routinely written during fieldwork. As Myerhoff and Ruby (1982: 6) say, we must be sufficiently self-aware to know what aspects of self are necessary to reveal in the process of reporting, so that an audience is able to "understand both the process employed and the resulting product." Practicing the ideal form of self-reflexivity requires critical awareness of what *not* to include.

11.7   Moving Beyond the Self

So far I have drawn heavily on Myerhoff and Ruby's definition of reflexivity and the three aspects they identify, while also hinting at some limitations. I now complicate the argument by introducing another definition used in the contemporary feminist literature that calls for awareness of self-in-sociopolitical context. Helen Callaway writes:

> Often condemned as apolitical, reflexivity, on the contrary can be seen as opening the way to a more radical consciousness of self in facing the political dimensions of fieldwork and constructing knowledge. Other factors intersecting with gender – such as nationality, race, ethnicity, class, and age – also affect the anthropologist's field interactions and textual strategies. Reflexivity becomes a continuing mode of self-analysis and political awareness. (1992: 33)

This expansive definition extends Presser's critique (noted above) that we have not written ourselves into our research nearly enough. Rather than scholars simply revealing how their personal identities and evolving thinking shaped their narrative projects, the thrust in the second definition emphasizes how these identities intersect with the institutional, material, and geopolitical aspects of the investigator's position (Nagar and Geiger 2007) that, in turn, made the research possible in the first place.[5] If positionality is to become more than "a recitation of one's personal characteristics, or a textual strategy" (Larner 1995: 177), a stronger reflexivity reflects on the political dimensions of the entire research enterprise. For investigators working in the participatory action research tradition, there is an additional component: having a *critical commitment* to the participants (Martín-Baró 1996). The goal of greater social justice is central to this mode of reflexivity.

The most expansive formulation of the political dimension is provided by Linda Tuhiwai Smith (2012). The challenge is to "decolonize our minds" (23) by adopting "a more critical understanding of the underlying assumptions, motivations and values which inform research practices" (20). She takes on the politics of academic writing – "a form of selecting, arranging, and presenting knowledge [that] privileges sets of texts, views about the history of an idea," what counts as significant, and other aspects – all of which render the perspectives of the indigenous invisible (36). In a word, the academic style of discourse is "never innocent." Instead, political reflexivity necessitates some self-criticism "of the widely shared values and interests that constitute one's own institutionally shaped research assumptions" (Harding 1992: 569). The form involves interrogating how "our projects rest on taken for granted problems, categories, concepts and theories that are themselves created by systems of power, privilege, and patterns of inequality" (Luttrell 2010: 4).

Many contemporary scholars – particularly feminist and postcolonial critics – have taken up the challenges of a political mode of reflexivity. Rosalind Gill (2010) traces the punishing effects of the neoliberal university on the speeded-up lives of women academics, as communicated in their long narrative emails to one another. Wendy Luttrell (2003, 2013) has critically examined how different categories of persons – immigrant children or pregnant teens – get made into problem populations in schools; she contrasts these constructions with the narratives of the stigmatized groups themselves – their perceptions and experiences of home and school. Susan Bell (2009) traces through the stories of individual women how their embodied knowledge animated and politicized the women's health movement, eventually influencing medical knowledge and practice. Ken Plummer (1995) analyzes how political movements over time have shaped the stories of gays, lesbians, and other sexualized groups. Modernist tales of desire and danger, recovery, and freedom have replaced the secret and repressive tales of old. Molly Andrews (2007, 2013) examines personal narratives of activists in four countries. She places them in their shifting social and political contexts, weaving her own life story into the trajectories of the activists.

Here is a final look at a piece of my own narrative work where I seem to have combined aspects of reflexivity in the first definition with some of the political dimensions in the second. I look back on a case study that I had published years earlier and interpret it very differently (Riessman 2002).

Originally, I analyzed a long narrative that had developed in a conversation with a white North American working-class woman ("Tessa"), whom I had interviewed in the early 1980s. She described repeated sexual assaults by her husband and the difficulty divorcing him on those grounds. (The narrative and my original analysis of it are lengthy and can't be reproduced here, but see Riessman 1990: 80–95). I emphasized my role in co-producing the narrative with Tessa, both in micro aspects of the interaction, and interpretively with our collaborative meaning-making. Together, we developed the account of a victorious survivor – Tessa fought against victimization and got her husband to leave. Closely examining the contributions of both participants to the exchange – lexical and non-lexical – I could demonstrate how the narrative's structure and its message were jointly accomplished. As reviewed above and reiterated by De Fina and Georgakapoulou (2008: 382): "the researcher is very much part of the narrative telling" (also see Mishler 1986; Paget 1983) – the mode of reflexivity that is built into many narrative studies.

Twelve years later I turned the mirror onto my earlier published analysis, this time interrogating broader dimensions and extending my reflexive gaze. I examined additional interactions with Tessa, my field notes, memories of our research relationship, and important documents I had seen since the interview – Tessa's diary and drawings. Thus the data were much more extensive. Also critical for the reflexive turn were political events: since my original analysis, marital rape had become a crime in all 50 US states. Feminist theory and gender politics had also seen major advances. I took all these changes into account in a reanalysis. "Doing Justice" – the title of the paper – involved attending much more closely to the harsh circumstances of Tessa's life, including her treatment by the US criminal justice system in the 1980s and its casual response to sexual violence against women.

(01) Cathy: Would you state in your own words what were the main causes of your separation, as you see it?

(02) Tessa: (P) um the biggest the biggest thing in my mind was the fact that I had been raped three times by him (C: mmhmm)

(03)   but at that time it didn't, it wasn't *legal* in a probate court (C: mm-hmm)

(04)   you you couldn't get a divorce on those grounds
(05)   but that was my biggest (p) (C: uhhuh) complaint (C: uhhuh)
(06)   total disrespect for me (C: uhhuh) (P) (C: mmhmm)
(07) Cathy: Can you tell me a little bit more about that? I know it's hard to talk about.

                                                                (Riessman 2002: 195)

The transcript above displays the opening segment of my interaction with Tessa that invited a long narrative. Much could be said about the brief excerpt, which serves as an abstract and invitation for the emergent interactive narrative about violence that followed. Domination and devaluation of wives by husbands had been a recurring theme in women's divorce stories (Riessman 1990), but the sexual violence Tessa described was the most extreme we'd heard. Structurally, the narrative can be divided into three parts, each focusing on a different time in the marriage. The first part described graphically what happened "when it was time to go to bed." Tessa shifts topics in the second part and moves back in time – anticipating my puzzlement but without my asking directly – to explain why she married in the first place, the poverty and hunger the family endured, and how "dependent" and "powerless" she felt ("just like I was when I was raped"). In a third part, prompted by my question about "what made the difference" and her decision to leave, Tessa recounts specific moments of her violence and rage ("I don't *ever* want to feel that again, never"). She described an unsuccessful effort to obtain a restraining order and threatening to call the police. She ends the narrative with a triumphant coda: "he did leave reluctantly … but he did leave." "Women's courage and strength was the moral message I wanted my readers to take away from my [original] interpretive translation" (Riessman, 2002: 200).

Going beyond the co-production aspect, experiences I disclosed in the reanalysis add layers of reflexivity. I was implicated in the research relationship in a deeply personal way. The interview conversation had been extremely difficult because of events in my early life. I hinted as much, acknowledging how hard it had been to listen to the brutal violence Tessa described, but chose not to say more. I acknowledged that I had initiated a subsequent visit with Tessa at a local bar/restaurant where she asked about my divorce and current life. She positioned me in a class context with repeated questions about the elite college where I taught. Vast disparities in our material circumstances, life chances, and coping resources divided us. Despite many commonalities, my institutional and material advantage – which had made the research possible in the first place – was a barrier to any kind of friendship. I began to question whether the research relationship benefited Tessa at all.

Going beyond greater self-reflexivity and class analysis, my reinterpretation placed the personal narrative in the social world at the time of our conversations: the injustice of criminal justice in the 1980s and the conditions producing Tessa's economic dependence on a man. The victim was assumed to be guilty until proved innocent. Rape was "the natural entitlement of the man inside marriage … Most legislation until very recently denied the possibility of rape in marriage – thereby clearly reinforcing the view that a woman has no right to consent to sex in marriage" (Plummer 1995: 65, 72). The understanding of rape began to assume a fundamentally different form in the 1970s as women began to talk and write about their experiences: "the story becomes one of power and gender rather than sex and desire" (Plummer 1995: 67). It took several decades for state laws to reflect these changes.

Reading Tessa's diary (she had given it to me to copy) and looking at her drawings forced me to confront a level of violence in the family that further complicated the victim-to-survivor narrative we had constructed together during the interview. A language of violence infused her poetry. I began to notice moments in the transcript that I had minimized in my earlier analysis: Tessa's violence toward her husband and, I strongly suspect, her son (both children were placed in foster care, only her daughter was returned home). One of her drawings, titled "It's Empty," shows a teddy bear looking up at the viewer. Below the drawing Tessa had written "the baby's gone. He's not home. He dosn't sleep here anymore. His mommy still cries at night." At the top, Tessa wrote a dedication: "To ____ my son, my first love." That drawing moved me greatly, and I wrote reflectively in response (Riessman 2002: 202–203).

Shifts in feminist theory since the original analysis were more subtle than legal changes, but no less significant. The original paper was shaped by the victim discourse of the 1980s. By 2002 it was no longer as strong in feminism as scholars were deconstructing binary categories. These theoretical shifts, coupled with material Tessa had shared elsewhere in the interview and what I saw in her diary and drawings, forced me to rethink my earlier heroic portrayal. As I wrote in 2002 about the earlier analysis, "To position Tessa differently [in the 1980s] would have forced me to think more deeply, and complexly, about victimization, including complicity" (203). I could no longer hold onto binary thinking (victim vs. survivor, abuser vs. abused) in interpreting the narrative. Some might read the later analysis as less sympathetic to the woman, but I think it is simply more layered and complex – perhaps an instance of "compassionate objectivity" (Turner 1978). I historicized the narrative event, locating it in time and place: personally, theoretically, politically, and institutionally.

For narrative scholars generally, turning the mirror on one's previous work can reveal the historical situatedness of our interpretations – the academic, theoretical, political, disciplinary, and, "yes, autobiographical imperatives that draw us to certain interpretations and not others" (Riessman 2002: 210). It is often easier to locate one's distorting assumptions and blind spots after some time has passed. As Sandra Harding (1992: 585) notes about science, a claim "must always be held open to revision on the basis of future possibly disconfirming empirical observations or … revisions in the conceptual frameworks of the sciences." Reflexivity here is in the service of a stronger objectivity.

11.8   Conclusion: Multiple Reflexivities

Reflexivity involves entering a hall of mirrors that illuminates a social phenomenon from many angles. Although there is no single form, adding something personal as a rhetorical flourish is not sufficient. The task is to account for our situated selves in a scholarly product, thereby lending the research credibility and validity.

I have presented various definitions and modes of reflexivity that are particularly relevant to research in the social sciences, providing examples of the ways narrative scholars (myself included) have inscribed themselves into the phenomenon they are describing. Some are tied to the inevitable co-construction of data, others to one's personal biography and circumstances; some are tied to one's political positioning as the researcher, others involve revisiting one's earlier work, and so on. These are all quite different ways of working reflexively and bespeak very different purposes; readers might even question whether all should be located under the umbrellas of reflexivity. I think that different modes are suited to different projects, rather than advocating a hierarchy that values political modes over other ones in every instance. Perhaps this essay can become a point of departure for conversations about this issue.

The many detailed studies of interview interaction in our narrative journals are essential contributions to our understanding of reflexivity, even if the concept is rarely invoked and objectivist assumptions are often embedded. Returning to the poem that opened my chapter, narrative researchers create the object – "the artificial thing" – in the interviews and transcripts we interpret, thereby creating meaning for others. Put differently, the questioner/listener/analyst is implicated in the narrative accounts that get produced precisely because we position subjects with our questions and comments and we, in turn, are positioned by participants as audiences for and co-producers of the emergent narratives. "Together we produce an account ... we forge it interactionally" (Paget 1983: 80). If the product is never innocent, the challenge is to account responsibly for our presence as well as the influence of "ghostly audiences" and other contextual influences.

More attention is needed on the influence of the setting where a study is situated. Many of us interview in institutional settings – disability and welfare offices, hospitals, schools, and other more or less coercive environments – regulated by the state or other powerful bodies. How has the setting influenced what we, as well as what participants, can do and say? How does the setting insinuate its way into the texture of interaction? What about the resources we bring to the encounters, compared to those our participants may call on in these settings?

Although a "transparent reflexivity" (Rose 1997) may never be possible, surely we can do better. For example, in narrative work with interviews, one place to begin might be how we represent ourselves in our transcripts and analysis. In what I call dialogic/performance analysis (Riessman 2008: 137), the utterances of all participants in an interaction are presented and interpreted; the research relationship becomes "an unfolding dialogue that includes the voice of the investigator who speculates openly about the meaning of a participant's utterance." In ethnographic studies, we can "probe how we are in relation with the contexts we study and with our informants, understanding that we are all multiple in those relations" (Fine 1998: 135); the investigator adopts an active voice to interrogate her role in producing knowledge about others. The goal of such reflexive questioning is greater rigor; that is, to generate research that is more trustworthy – the kind of objectivity suited to the narrative enterprise. The subjectivity of the investigator does not stand in the way, nor does it belong at the center; rather it is one object among many. A stronger objectivity (Harding 1992), not objectivism, is what disciplined reflexivity encourages.

NOTES

1   Deepest thanks to Marj DeVault and Wendy Luttrell, who aided the development of my ideas in this paper, and to Mark Freeman for an incisive critique. The editors provided useful and supportive criticism, many others supplied references, and Glenn Pasanen provided scrupulous editing.

2   Mark Kaminsky (1992) criticizes Myerhoff and Ruby's use of producer/process/product distinction as a one-way model of transmission that assumes a passive consumer. It cannot accommodate ideas of co-production or Bakhtin's "immanent reader" – the "(imaginary) auditor in relation to whom the author positions herself and orients her discourse" (Kaminsky 1992: 85). The "other" remains at the margin and the dialogic process is ignored. Ironically, Myerhoff's practice of reflexivity in her empirical work gives considerable space to the imagined "other," even if she failed to develop a theory of discourse in her essays. I get into some of these issues later in my essay.

3   My thanks to the Indo-US Subcommission on Education and Culture, Council for International Exchange of Scholars that provided financial support for the fieldwork.

4   Although this was a common language practice at the time, I now regret my word choice here.

5   I thought long and hard about my political positioning during the research in India, wondering whether I should be doing the work at all. In 1993/4, I couldn't locate a South Indian scholar involved in social research on infertility or childlessness in women, although there was considerable medical research. In the intervening years, the topic has been taken up by social researchers in India. My invaluable Malayali research assistant, Liza, was invited to co-author papers, but her marriage was being arranged and she declined. Her perspective occupies a prominent place in one paper, and our collaboration influenced my thinking throughout. My deepest thanks to her.

REFERENCES

Andrews, M. (2007). *Shaping History: Narratives of Political Change*. Cambridge: Cambridge University Press.

Andrews, M. (2013). Never the last word: Revisiting data. In M. Andrews, C. Squire, and M. Tamboukou (eds.), *Doing Narrative Research in the Social Sciences*. 2nd edn. London: Sage, pp. 205–222.

Andrews, M., C. Squire, and M. Tamboukou (eds.). (2013). *Doing Narrative Research in the Social Sciences*. 2nd edn. London: Sage.

Bakhtin, M.M. (1981). *The Dialogic Imagination: Four Essays*. Translated by C. Emerson and M. Holquist. Austin: University of Texas Press.

Bell, S.E. (1988). Becoming a political woman: The reconstruction and interpretation of experience through stories. In A.D. Todd and S. Fisher (eds.), *Gender and Discourse: The Power of Talk*. Norwood, NJ: Ablex, pp. 97–123.

Bell, S.E. (2009). *DES Daughters: Embodied Knowledge and the Transformation of Women's Health Politics*. Philadelphia, PA: Temple University Press.

Bishop, E.C., and M.L. Shepherd. (2011). Ethical reflections: Examining reflexivity through the narrative paradigm. *Qualitative Health Research*, 21 (9), pp. 1283–1294.

Briggs, J. (1970). *Never in Anger*. Cambridge, MA: Harvard University Press.

Burawoy, M. (2003). Revisits: An outline of a theory of reflexive ethnography. *American Sociological Review*, 68, pp. 645–679.

Callaway, H. (1992). Ethnography and experience: Gender implications in fieldwork and texts. In J. Okely and H. Callaway (eds.), *Anthropology and Autobiography*. New York: Routledge, Chapman & Hall.

Cazden, C.B. (2001). *Classroom Discourse: The Language of Teaching and Learning*. 2nd edn. Portsmouth, NH: Heinemann.

Davies, P. (2012). "Me," "me," "me": The use of the first person in academic writing and some reflections on subjective analyses of personal experiences. *Sociology*, 46 (4), pp. 744–752.

De Fina, A. (2003). *Identity in Narrative: A Study of Immigrant Discourse*. Amsterdam: John Benjamins.

De Fina, A., and A. Georgakopoulou. (2008). Analyzing narratives as practices. *Qualitative Research*, 8 (3), pp. 379–387.

DeVault, M.L. (1997). Personal writing in social science: Issues of production and interpretation. In R. Hertz (ed.), *Reflexivity & Voice*. Thousand Oaks, CA: Sage, pp. 216–228.

Doyle, S. (2013). Reflexivity and the capacity to think. *Qualitative Health Research*, 23 (2), pp. 248–255.

Ellis, C., and A.P. Bochner. (2000). Autoethnography, personal narrative, and reflexivity: Researcher as subject. In N. Denzin and Y.S. Lincoln (eds.), *Handbook of Qualitative Research*. 2nd edn. Newbury Park, CA: Sage, pp. 733–767.

Fine, M. (1998). Working the hyphens: Reinventing self and other in qualitative research. In N. Denzin and Y.S. Lincoln (eds.), *The Landscape of Qualitative Research: Theories and Issues*. Thousand Oaks, CA: Sage, pp. 130–155.

Finlay, L. (2012). Five lenses of the reflexive interviewer. In J.F. Gubrium, J.A. Holstein, A.B. Marvasti, and K.D. McKinney (eds.), *The Sage Handbook of Interview Research: The Complexity of the Craft*. 2nd edn. Thousand Oaks, CA: Sage, pp. 317–331.

Freeman, M. (2010). "Even amidst": Rethinking narrative coherence. In M. Hyvärinen, L.-C. Hydén, M. Saarenheimo, and M. Tamboukou (eds.), *Beyond Narrative Coherence*. Amsterdam: John Benjamins, pp. 167–186.

Gee, J.P. (1985). The narrativization of experience in the oral style. *Journal of Education*, 167 (1), pp. 9–35.

Geertz, C. (1973). *The Interpretation of Cultures: Selected Essays*. New York: Basic Books.

Gill, R. (2010). Breaking the silence: The hidden injuries of the neoliberal university. In R. Gill and R. Flood (eds.), *Secrecy and Silence in the Research Process: Feminist Reflections*. London: Routledge, pp. 228–244.

Goffman, E. (1959). *The Presentation of Self in Everyday Life*. New York: Penguin.

Harding, S. (1992). After the neutrality ideal: Science, politics, and "strong objectivity." *Social Research*, 59 (3), pp. 567–587.

Hertz, R. (ed.). (1997). *Reflexivity & Voice*. Thousand Oaks, CA: Sage Publications.

Kaminsky, M. (1992). Introduction. In B. Myerhoff, *Remembered Lives: The Work of Ritual, Storytelling, and Growing Older*. Ann Arbor: University of Michigan Press.

Krieger, S. (1991). *Social Science and the Self: Personal Essays on an Art Form*. New Brunswick, NJ: Rutgers University Press.

Labov, W. (1972). *Language in the Inner City: Studies in the Black English Vernacular*. Philadelphia: University of Pennsylvania Press.

Larner, W. (1995). Theorising difference in Aotearoa / New Zealand. *Gender, Place & Culture*, 2, pp. 177–190.

Luttrell, W. (2003). *Pregnant Bodies, Fertile Minds: Gender, Race and the Schooling of Pregnant Teens*. New York: Routledge.

Luttrell, W. (2010). Introduction. In W. Luttrell (ed.), *Qualitative Educational Research: Readings in Reflexive Methodology and Transformative Practice*. New York: Routledge, pp. 1–22.

Luttrell, W. (2013). Children's counter-narratives of care. *Children and Society*, 27 (4), pp. 295–308.

Martín-Baró, I. (1996). Toward a liberation psychology. In A. Aron and S. Corne (eds.), *Writings for a Liberation Psychology*. Cambridge, MA: Harvard University Press, pp. 17–32.

Michaels, S. (1981). "Sharing time": Children's narrative styles and differential access to literacy. *Language and Society*, 10, pp. 423–442.

Mishler, E.G. (1979). Meaning in context: Is there any other kind? *Harvard Educational Review*, 49 (1), 1–19.

Mishler, E.G. (1984). *The Discourse of Medicine: Dialectics of Medical Interviews*. Norwood, NJ: Ablex.

Mishler, E.G. (1986). *Research Interviewing: Context and Narrative*. Cambridge, MA: Harvard University Press.

Myerhoff, B.G. (1974). *Peyote Hunt: The Sacred Journey of the Huichol Indians*. Ithaca, NY: Cornell University Press.

Myerhoff, B. (1978). *Number Our Days*. New York: Simon and Schuster.

Myerhoff, B. (1992). *Remembered Lives: The Work of Ritual, Storytelling, and Growing Older*. Ann Arbor: University of Michigan Press.

Myerhoff, B., and J. Ruby. (1982). Introduction. In J. Ruby (ed.), *A Crack in the Mirror: Reflexive Perspectives in Anthropology*. Philadelphia: University of Pennsylvania Press, pp. 1–35.

Nagar, R., and S. Geiger. (2007). Reflexivity and positionality in feminist fieldwork revisited. In A. Tickell, E. Sheppard, J. Peck, and T. Barnes (eds.), *Politics and Practice in Economic Geography*. London: Sage Publications, pp. 267–278.

Nagel, T. (1986). *The View from Nowhere*. Oxford: Oxford University Press.

Oakley, A. (1980). *Women Confined: Towards a Sociology of Childbirth*. Oxford: Martin Robertson.

Ortner, S.B. (1996). *Making Gender: The Politics and Erotics of Culture*. Boston, MA: Beacon Press.

Paget, M.A. (1983). Experience and knowledge. *Human Studies*, 6, pp. 67–90.

Plummer, K. (1995). *Telling Sexual Stories: Power, Change, and Social Worlds*. New York: Routledge.

Polanyi, L. (1989). *Telling the American Story: A Structural and Cultural Analysis of Conversational Storytelling*. Cambridge, MA: MIT Press.

Presser, L. (2005). Negotiating power and narrative in research: Implications for feminist methodology. *Signs: Journal of Women in Culture and Society*, 30 (4), pp. 2067–2090.

Rabinow, P. (1977). *Reflections on Fieldwork in Morocco*. Berkeley: University of California Press.

Rabinow, P., and W.M. Sullivan. (1979). *Interpretive Social Science: A Second Look*. Berkeley: University of California Press.

Reinharz, S. (1984). *On Becoming a Social Scientist*. New Brunswick, NJ: Transaction Publishers.

Riessman, C.K. (1987). When gender is not enough: Women interviewing women. *Gender & Society*, 1 (2), pp. 172–207.

Riessman, C.K. (1990). *Divorce Talk: Women and Men Make Sense of Personal Relationships*. New Brunswick, NJ: Rutgers University Press.

Riessman, C.K. (2000). Stigma and everyday resistance practices: Childless women in south India. *Gender & Society*, 14 (1), pp. 111–135.

Riessman, C.K. (2002). Doing justice: Positioning the interpreter in narrative work. In W. Patterson (ed.), *Strategic Narrative: New Perspectives on the Power of Personal and Cultural Storytelling*. Lanham, MD: Lexington Books, pp. 193–214.

Riessman, C.K. (2008). *Narrative Methods for the Human Sciences*. Thousand Oaks, CA: Sage Publications.

Riessman, C.K. (2012). Analysis of personal narratives. In J.F. Gubrium, J.A. Holstein, A.B. Marvasti, and K.D. McKinney (eds.), *The Sage Handbook of Interview Research: The Complexity of the Craft*. 2nd edn. Los Angeles, CA: Sage Publications, pp. 367–379.

Rosaldo, R. (1989). *Culture & Truth: Remaking of Social Analysis*. Boston, MA: Beacon Press.

Rose, G. (1997). Situating knowledges: Positionality, reflexivities and other tactics. *Progress in Human Geography*, 21 (3), pp. 305–320.

Ruby, J. (ed.). (1982). *A Crack in the Mirror: Reflexive Perspectives in Anthropology*. Philadelphia: University of Pennsylvania Press.

Smith, D.E. (1987). *The Everyday World as Problematic*. Boston, MA: Northeastern University Press.

Smith, L.T. (2012). *Decolonizing Methodologies: Research and Indigenous Peoples*. 2nd edn. London: Zed Books.

Stacey, J. (1988). Can there be a feminist ethnography? *Women's Studies International Forum*, 11 (1), pp. 21–27.

Stanley, L., and S. Wise. (1983). *Breaking Out: Feminist Consciousness and Feminist Research*. London: Routledge & Kegan Paul.

Stevens, W. (1990). Description without Place. In *The Collected Poems of Wallace Stevens*. New York: Vintage, pp. 339–346.

Turner, V. (1978). Foreword. In B. Myherhoff, *Number Our Days*. New York: Simon and Schuster, pp. xiii–xvii.

Turner, V. (1980). Social dramas and stories about them. *Critical Inquiry: On Narrative, 7* (1), pp. 141–168.

Turner, V.W., and E.M. Bruner (eds.). (1986). *The Anthropology of Experience*. Urbana: University of Illinois Press.

Wasserfall, R. (1993). Reflexivity, feminism and difference. *Qualitative Sociology*, 16 (1), pp. 23–41.

Whyte, W. (1993). *Street Corner Society: The Social Structure of an Italian Slum*. 4th edn. Chicago, IL: University of Chicago Press.

12 The Role of the Researcher in Interview Narratives

STEF SLEMBROUCK

12.1 Introduction

This chapter focuses on the role of the researcher in interview contexts in which narratives and methodologies of narrative analysis play a role. Such contexts occur widely and, like the paradigm of narrative analysis itself, the role of the researcher within the interview is diversely connected to the disciplinary contexts and considerations on which it is made to bear. For one thing, narrative research has multiple ancestries, and this bears in various ways on its current popularity as a paradigmatic choice in social and cultural analysis. In this, the "narrative turn" sometimes occurs as an ontology, at other times as an epistemology, and very often also as a heuristic strategy or method. This triad can be paraphrased as follows: *ontology*: "social reality is to be understood as essentially organized in narratives" (e.g., Barthes 1982: 251: "narrative is present in every age, in every place, in every society; it begins with the very history of mankind and there nowhere is nor has been a people without narrative"; Fisher 1987); *epistemology*: "narrative analysis provides a better way for understanding how social reality is made sense of, i.e., stories about x are the best way to explain occurrences of x" (e.g., Bruner 1986; Polkinghorne 1988); and *heuristic method*: "the analysis of narratives provides us with active strategies and systematic methodologies for capturing relevant aspects of social representation" (e.g., Riessman 1993; De Fina and Georgakopoulou 2012).

Of course, these are dimensional orientations. Many instances of research can be listed where the differences between these dimensions are far from clear-cut, a result of the inevitable interdependencies in developing them (e.g., the adoption of a narrative epistemology leads one to develop a set of heuristic strategies). For some, the current interest in narrative and narrative analysis originates in literary theory; for others, it is an extension of doing ethnography or it develops out of psychoanalysis. Common threads can nevertheless be detected throughout these lineages. Researchers with diverse disciplinary backgrounds (e.g., in anthropology, sociology, psychology, psychiatry, medicine, social work, criminology, pedagogy, history, knowledge and organization management, etc.) have equally resorted to narratives and consider

The Handbook of Narrative Analysis, First Edition. Edited by Anna De Fina and Alexandra Georgakopoulou.
© 2015 John Wiley & Sons, Inc. Published 2019 by John Wiley & Sons, Inc.

storytelling to be central to doing research in a real-life context of engagement with real people who make sense of the complexities of the world(s) they inhabit.

In some cases, narrative also turns out to be part and parcel of the very stuff they deal with as practitioners of their disciplines – think of social workers, doctors, family therapists, psychiatrists, and lawyers. The point is a general one, applying to doctors who listen to patients' stories, lawyers who listen to clients' accounts and apply the principle of precedent via the analysis of "case stories" (Breeze 2013: 343), etc.

The practitioner perspective has also given rise to explicitly narrative methodologies for practice, particularly in the field of medicine. For instance, Launer's (1999) concept of "talking cures" depends on the ability of giving coherence to a patient's experience of physical or mental illness in ways which enable the construction of a narrative of healing or coping. The method presupposes a patient and a clinician who work together to construct a story that makes sense. For Greenhalgh and Hurwitz (1999), narratives of illness provide a framework for approaching a patient's problems holistically. Comparable developments can be noted in other professions. White and Epston (1990) and Blume (2006) exemplify narrative approaches to family therapy (see Etchison and Kleist 2000 for a research overview). Freeman (2011) advocates a narrative approach to social work, while Baldwin and Estay-Burtt (2012) suggest a reconfiguration of social work ethics rooted in narrative practice.

And further: connections with a postmodernist and/or a constructivist turn in the sciences (e.g., Gergen 1998) are not far off, as the interest in narrative harmonizes with an emphasis on the contextual construction of meaning and the possibility of multiple perspectives on reality, including the idea that relevant truths are grounded in social relations and everyday interaction.

The role of the researcher within this set of possibilities and actualities is diverse and warrants discussion in its own right. As suggested by the title of this chapter, I will be mostly concerned with conditions of narrative and narrative outcomes in the context of a commonly deployed form of data collection, the research interview. How and where do narrative approaches come in, and what role does the researcher play in this context? I will dwell on that role in two senses: the researcher as a (cotemporaneous) interactant with a strategic investment in the unfolding interview and the researcher as a (post hoc) analyst of interview data that has been obtained.

12.2   The Role of the Researcher in Responding to Emerging Narrative Expression

I want to continue by introducing a further preliminary distinction between smaller or larger chunks of narration that emerge in the course of a research interview, and interviews in which the researcher more deliberately seeks to elicit a specific narrative performance. In the former case, we can allude to the common experience of interview talk taking a distinctly narrative turn, a point observed by many qualitative researchers: for instance, a response to a particular question may result in a narrative which continues for some time. Here we can connect with the rather fundamental observation reiterated in various chapters in this volume (e.g., Freeman, chapter 1) that narrative and narrative understanding are primary modes of human thinking that enable human beings to share formulations of cause, effect, and consequence, or, to express this more straightforwardly still: telling each other stories is one way of making sense of what we encounter in the course of our lives (Ochs and Capps 2001; Bruner and Lucariello 1989: 79). The context of a research interview, in which an informant interactively establishes some relevant human, social, professional, institutional, or personal experience, forms no exception to this. Hence, it is almost self-evident that in the course of a series of question-answer exchanges, which are characteristic of the research interview as an activity type, the answer to some questions will constitute an account of what happened on a particular occasion. Such an account may be brief or extended. In fact, one such account may be spread over a number of answering turns, especially when the answer to the interviewer's next question provides the researcher with information which can be interpreted as answering the question: "what happened next?" or "what were the circumstances for this particular action?"

One early example that brought to my attention the capacity for an interview context to be interactionally transformed into what could straightforwardly be recognized as one of narrative performance is captured in the following transcribed excerpt (data recorded in 1989; see Hall, Sarangi, and Slembrouck 1997: 281–285 for a full transcript). The researcher (RI in the transcript below) interviews a social worker (SW) about the then-current policy context of child placement in the United Kingdom, which at the time did not regard residential care as a preferred option. The interviews were conducted in local social work offices and concentrated on the outcomes of particular child protection cases and the reasons for them. The excerpt below comes at the very beginning of the interview. After checking whether the equipment was duly recording (turn 01: *[snaps fingers twice]*), the interviewer begins by checking some of the case details before embarking on a series of questions about the rationale of social work decision-making in the case at hand.

Excerpt 1

(01) RI: start when [snaps fingers twice] (unclear) start when you took it on and I gather from what I could see you took it on in about erm September eighty six

(02) SW: yeah yeah

(03) RI: and the kids were already in care then is that right

(04) SW: well look *I'll* speak to because I can I can speak (unclear)

(05) RI: I'll leave it to you [laughs]

(06) SW: (unclear) I was allocated this case in September nineteen eighty six the case erm had originally been allocated in area five erm for a period of about six weeks prior to me taking it on the circumstances were (.) that erm a child by the name of Catherine erm (.) had been taken to Saint Hugo College Hospital by the child's mother in July nineteen eighty six

The interviewer opens with a series of fact-checking conversational moves, thus establishing a common ground by confirming the case details. The second of these moves (turn 03, "and the kids were already in care then is that right") is responded to with "well look *I'll* speak" – a bid for an extended, more monological turn, in which the case can be presented in its integrity (cf. story-prefaces, Sacks 1967: 82ff.). The social worker's bid for a narrative turn is accompanied by a claim of entitlement (Shuman 1992, see also this volume, chapter 2), that is, a reference to the speaker's authority on the matter. The interviewer cedes the conversational floor and gives permission for the interviewer to state the case in his own terms (turn 05: "I'll leave it to you"). What follows is an uninterrupted narrative that goes on for more than 15 minutes before the research interviewer can return to a set of questions seeking additional information and clarifications.

The point is that the interviewee has succeeded in interrupting the question-answer format, and with this, reallocated roles of narrator and narratee have been established, with the research interviewer now abiding by the topical progression presented by the narrator. The interviewee has taken charge of the interaction, with reallocated roles in discourse as a result: for 15 minutes during the interview, the interviewer has become less of a questioner and more a recipient of a narrative performance. Of course, my analysis of the example rests on a rather rigid distinction between two sets of paired roles, the key point being that the social worker has accomplished a shift from one set to the other: on the one hand, interviewers ask questions and interviewees provide answers (research interviews) while, on the other hand, narrators tell a story and narratees are spectators to such a performance (narrative performance). Narrative expressions in research interviews may also take on less abruptly accomplished forms. For instance, an interviewer's question may result in a very short narrative which forms part of the answer (see also Georgakopoulou 2007 on "small stories," the opposite of a free-standing story); or a more extended narrative can be said to unfold across the various turns of the question-answer sequence. The latter is perhaps to be expected in an interview context which deals with one particular professional case, and indeed it occurred quite commonly in the set of interviews from which my first example has been drawn. The point, then, is that the lines of questioning promote responses that can be easily be heard in terms of "what happened next and why." Successive questions attend to what happened in different stages of the case as well as the justifications for applying diagnostic categories, the motivations behind particular interventions, etc. – ingredients that can be read together as forming a coherent narrative of the particular case that unfolded over a longer period of time. Naturally, the observation that there is a pulse of questioning that pushes forward a stream of narrative performance with various episodes provides a motivation for applying the term "interactively accomplished co-narration."

A second data excerpt derives from the same corpus of UK policy review interviews. (The excerpt is quoted from Hall, Slembrouck, and Sarangi 2006: 37–45, where the case interview is also analyzed at length.) It illustrates a narrative unfolding across a series of question-answer turns through which a social worker justifies how the reception of a family's children into residential care was related to the marital situation of the parents. A particularly dramatic episode occurs in turn 04 of the transcribed interaction below: mother and children have escaped to Canada. What follows is an episode in the case that supports the picture of the mother taking charge of the situation. The episode is announced by the interviewee as inviting heightened attention: "I think the crunch point for the family came in August when …"

Excerpt 2

(01) INT: so this particular at this first reception into care was was very much related to the marital situation [SW: yes yes] and erm (.) at that stage would would any other resources the department had available had prevented that particular reception into care (.) in terms of input into the home or anything

(02) SW: no I can't think of any other resources that would have prevented it (.) cos' we were putting in er a [INT: yes] high amount of resources [INT: right] and failed to prevent it

(03) INT: right (.) so er (.) that was the the June one (.) right (.) and then

(04) SW: I think the crunch point for the family came in August when mother's (.) sister her and sister's husband and his daughter came over from Canada and visited (.) and found (.) I think to their surprise I think (.) and they were just on holiday they intended to be a holiday but to their surprise that things were really quite bad in this household the marriage was in a ropey situation the finances were poor and the husband was drinking and the children were being dragged up rather and they were very concerned and actually persuaded mother that she would be better off taking the children out to Canada separated and started a new life in Canada they were aware that (.) because the children were wards of court there would be legal problems in doing this and they decided to bypass the court system and do it very secretly and no one the father social services the other agencies knew what was happening until we actually had a phone call from Canada to say they were there which is a remarkable feat

(05) INT: that's amazing

(06) SW: yes

(07) INT: this is also a lot of planning [SW: absolutely] to think it through it shows a good of er organization

(08) SW: organization [overlapping] on the part of the relatives 'cos mother couldn't do it on her own

(09) INT: good grief

(10) SW: so that was the crunch point they left early September er but erm the power of the marriage was so great that mother found she could not (.) survive in Canada without her husband and within a day of her arrival she'd started to contact police and social services crisis care organizations to engineer getting back to this country and so (.) it was only a matter of weeks before she actually achieved the return

(11) INT: right [suppressed, understandingly]

(12) SW: and certainly that pushed the marriage into far greater erm difficulties obviously the husband had been extremely upset that he thought he would never see his family again and he was very angry and mother felt when she came back all the father wanted was the children and not her and somehow the marital relationship has never got back on to the same footing since then it's just gone from bad to worse so all the crises since then were sort of linked up

(13) INT: right [almost inaudibly] so that er they

(14) SW: they came back in October

(15) INT: right the children came into care over the weekend

(16) SW: the end of October yes

(17) INT: yes

(18) SW: yes

(19) INT: what was the circumstances of that

During the telling of the "Canadian episode," we can see how the social worker's speech becomes more relaxed. A shared perspective with the research interviewer develops and together they construct an evaluative stance, expressing both surprise and admiration at the mother's unexpected drastic action (see, e.g., turns 05 to 09). So far the mother's personal growth in the problematic family situation has been described as hopeful but nevertheless weak; she is in need of therapeutic support and her actions are set off by the father's increasing alcohol problem and unpredictable behaviors. The escape to Canada marks a short-lived change in the characterization of the mother.

Relevant to our discussion here is the observation that for a number of turns in the interview, the interviewer's role seems to become more backgrounded, with contributions subservient to the goals of narration, including displays of supporting the narrative (rather than facing the social worker with a set of planned questions that interrogate the features of the child protection case). Note that in this particular case, the possibility of the social worker narrating the case had not been anticipated as an expected turn of research events. Narrative elicitation was not explicitly part of the research design. Instead, narrative performance just happened. It became a focus of analytical attention afterwards, as the data had been disclosed for purposes of social scientific research.

12.3   The Role of the Researcher in Encouraging Narrative Forms of Expression

In the two excerpts above, narrative happens during the interview, either because the interviewee successfully bids for an extended narrative turn (excerpt 1) or because a temporal-causal organization of the events talked about develops into a narrative structure and does so particularly at the point where a heightened interest in "what happened next?" becomes defining for the case being discussed (excerpt 2). Both excerpts also underline the role of the researcher in going along with the emerging narrative performance. Let us now turn to the second possibility raised earlier, that of the researcher who consciously seeks to encourage the narration of a particular social experience. S/he does so because this is believed to accord better with particular research goals. In this context, it is worth recalling a study from the early days of sociolinguistics which, though not initially so intended, resulted in a major theoretical breakthrough in the study of oral narrative. The point I'm stressing here is recounted in the opening sentences of Labov (1997: 395; see also Labov 1972: 355).

> The first steps in narrative analysis taken by Joshua Waletzky and myself were a by-product of the sociolinguistic field methods that had been developed in the survey of the Lower East Side (Labov 1966) and in the work that engaged us at the time – the study of African American Vernacular English in South Harlem (Labov, Cohen, Robins and Lewis 1968). We defined the vernacular as the form of language first acquired, perfectly learned, and used only among speakers of the same vernacular. The effort to observe how speakers talked when they were not being observed created the Observer's Paradox. Among the partial solutions to that paradox within the face-to-face interview, the elicitation of narratives of personal experience proved to be the most effective.

Labov's original research motives, which led to the compilation of a corpus of narratives of personal experience, were not intrinsic to the study of narrative: by cueing his informants to tell a story about something that had happened to them on an occasion when their life was in danger, he thought that they would get so immersed in the telling that they would stop paying conscious attention to their speech and thus a corpus of spontaneous speech would become available for sociolinguistic analysis. Of course, Labov is not the only one to have relied on narrative production as a method and as a strategy to be exploited interactionally because it served research goals defined in other terms – in Labov's case, it was a means "to tap the vernacular." One can take a three-decade leap to the Biographical-Narrative Interpretative Method (e.g., Wengraf 2001), in which narrative elicitation has become an almost irreversible norm that qualitative social scientists must orient to. The method prescribes that all interviews must begin with a life-story eliciting question, and two core methodological maxims are: "ask only for narrative" and "never interrupt the response." The problematic assumption lurking in the background here is indeed that unless researchers manage to elicit a life story in an interview, they are somehow perceived as a failure.

12.3.1 Narrative as an involvement-promoting choice offered to the interviewee

There are various ways to elicit a narrative. A narrative form of expression may be offered explicitly as a possibility to the interviewee, who may take it up or decline it. Excerpts 3 and 4 below are examples of such an offer. In both cases, the topic of the interview was parental experiences of a period of residential care for one of their children (Flemish/Belgian data recorded in 2003; see Slembrouck 2011 for a more extensive discussion of the data). At the beginning of the interview, the respondents were offered a choice between a question-answer format and the possibility of just telling the researcher what had happened. Interestingly, such a narrative offer was not always taken up or embraced fully straight away.

Excerpt 3 (original in Dutch; translated into English)

(01) MO: it's rather a lot the story

and I wouldn't know where to begin

perhaps it is better if you ask some questions

then it will happen anyway

and if you think I'm leaving something out just tell me

In excerpt 3, the mother responded to the researcher's question by hinting that there is indeed a story to tell, but she immediately hedged her observation with an expressed uncertainty about how such a narrative, when told in her own terms, would tally with the researcher's expectations. In fact, the interviewee suggests the researcher should proceed by asking questions, but expresses confidence that in the course of answering these, the "bigger" narrative will materialize. This occurrence can be contrasted with excerpt 4 below, in which the mother-interviewee opts more categorically for answers to specific questions, preferring to abide by the authority of the interviewer.

Excerpt 4 (original in Dutch; translated into English)

(01) MO: I prefer you to ask questions

it makes things easy

A more general discussion is warranted here. Hollway and Jefferson (2008) note that face-to-face semi-structured interviews are the most prevalent qualitative research method for finding out about people's experiences in context and the meanings which these hold, but add that, despite efforts to adapt the format to this function,

> the idea that an interviewee can "tell it like it is", that he or she is an incontrovertible expert on his or her own experiences, that respondents are transparent to themselves, still remains the unchallenged starting point for most of this qualitative, interview-based research. This assumption suggests that qualitative researchers believed that the problem they identified in relation to survey-based research would disappear when the "meaning of events for respondents" was taken into account. (2008: 298)

A set of related points must be made here. They have also been articulated elsewhere (e.g., Bauer 1996: 2). Interviewers influence the information which is being exchanged during interviews by selecting theme and topic and by ordering and wording questions in a particular way. Research interviewers are also endowed with expectations: what is the interview really about, what will it include or leave out? Uninterrupted narrative in principle offers an alternative to this, with an agenda and a topical scope that are more open to development, attuned to the respondent's own experiences, and with alternative role definitions for the researcher – being a good listener rather than a questioner – and for the interviewee – acting as a narrator rather than as a respondent.

But does this mean we can take for granted the liberating effects of an ideal narrative performed on the terms of the interviewee? The picture that has emerged so far from these four excerpts is Janus-like, inviting a nuanced understanding of the affordances and constraints of a narrative data methodology. On the one hand, if we go by excerpts 3 and 4, we may (perhaps pessimistically) conclude that research subjects, when offered an opportunity to tell an experiential story in their own terms, do not necessarily embrace this choice. The sobering realization is indeed that the promise of diminished interviewer control over wording and ordering of information in a context of invited narrative performance does not stop the interviewer from holding particular expectations or from assuming a position of judgment over whether the informant's contributions will be sufficient for the purposes of the research. Asymmetries (perceptually grounded or interactionally manifest) cannot be guaranteed to disappear simply because the respondent is offered the choice or because s/he is encouraged to narrate an experience in his/her own terms. Slembrouck (2011) discusses the interview as a situation in which research subjects act as though being "tested." Just as important as the afforded possibilities of selecting and ordering theme, topic, and scope is the research informant's assessment of whether there is a story worth telling in front of a particular (typically academic) audience.

Turning now to the other (more optimistic) side of the coin, excerpts 1 and 2 clearly suggest that a narrative is likely to emerge even when it is not explicitly invited: some research subjects will insist on securing an extended interactional space in which to narrate their experience; or the interaction may just slip into narrative mode because the answer to a specific question comes with heightened conditions of tellability or because a narrative that has been emerging across successive question-answer turns is reaching a climactic point which is defining for the answer to a specific question. Excerpts 1 and 2 also illustrate that the researcher-interviewer may well in practice respond interactionally by accepting the research informant's narrative lead, adopting a listening stance and engaging supportively with the telling (e.g., in excerpt 2: (turn 09) "good grief," (turn 11) "right," and (turn 13) "right [almost inaudibly] so that er they").

12.3.2   Narrative as self-protective distance

From the above discussion, it is clear that the will to tell a story cannot be taken for granted, and while in some cases there may be reluctance on the part of respondents to launch into an uninterrupted telling of their story, one can also easily think of situations where the facts of the narration are too painful or traumatic for direct expression. Trauma and narrative is a theme that has received considerable attention and, in the face of the teller's uncertainty and ambivalences about the telling, the narration of traumatic experiences raises the relevance of interviewing strategies which are quite specific – see, for example, Brown (2013) on "counterviewing questions" (Madigan 2003) that allow for the exploration of dominating discourses that contribute to pathologizing particular traumatic experiences. The domain of fictional narrative may also offer methodological advantages here, as in the following instance of medical anthropological research, which investigates the relevance of social and cultural experiences of illness.

Winskell et al. (2013) present an interesting case drawing on a corpus of 1849 narratives written by youngsters in southeastern Nigeria as part of a 2005 "Scenarios from Africa" scriptwriting contest on the theme of HIV/AIDS. In answering the question how young people navigate available cultural resources to make sense of the pandemic, the authors argue that:

> Fictional narratives make manifest the dialectical relationship between personal experience and the creative imagination on one hand, and cultural norms and shared systems of representation on the other. ... Rich in imagery and emplotment, they reveal the social representations and cultural narratives that undergird this meaning-making process. They are the product of an activity of enjoyment, undertaken at the initiative of the young author, and offer an opportunity to depersonalize sensitive topics through the creation of fictional characters and situations. In comparison with ethnographic interviews or focus group discussions, they represent a relatively non-directive form of enquiry that enables informants to shape the agenda ... without contemporaneous co-construction with the researcher. (2013: 194, 196)

The narrated outcomes are viewed as an encounter between the *homo narrans* (humans as innately disposed to tell stories, e.g., Niles 1999) and the *homo performans* (humans as culture-inventing and self-making creatures, e.g., Turner 1985). In addition to being non-directive, the method of narrative sampling in the case above is also presented as an opportunity to depersonalize sensitive topics, though admittedly it raises issues of entitlement to subsequent use in a research project (cf. this volume, chapter 2 and chapter 11). The fictional nature of the narrative output in particular is presented as a buffer against the kind of personal involvement which might prevent the actual telling. Whereas the opportunity for telling one's own story tends to be more readily thought of as an involvement-promoting condition, here the fictional format enables a relevant telling in a way that artfully maneuvers around the incapacitating effects of personal traumatic experiences and of being too closely involved. This theme is less often dwelt upon in the research literature: fictional narrative as a self-protective distance that may succeed in securing tellership under conditions of painful tellability. There is an affinity here with another elicitation method, the use of vignettes as narrative input during face-to-face interviews or during focus group discussions.

Vignettes, in Finch's definition, are "short stories about hypothetical characters in specified circumstances that researchers can use to elicit participants' values, meanings and beliefs" (1987: 105). Vignettes typically involve a moral/action dilemma that can be narrated and that plays out the tension between the roles of protagonist and evaluator – two roles widely acknowledged as central components of narrative production. Vignettes are also interesting in another respect, which highlights dialogic co-construction: they count both as "pre-narrated" (a narrative input to the research event) and as "to be narrated" (because they are being responded to, endorsed, or rejected, or they may give rise to complementary and alternative accounts by the research subject). Teachman and Gibson (2013), in their discussion of customizable techniques in research with children and youths with disabilities, underline the research subject's capacity to move between the experiences of the self and those projected in the vignette. It is worth citing one of their set of interviewer notes here:

> I had followed through on the idea of getting a little more information ahead of time from the parent to allow me to customize the role-play and other vignette activities, to assist the child to draw from their own experiences and project these onto the characters. This appeared to be very helpful today, as the young girl commented: "Just like me!" on hearing the vignette and when asked, "Do you have any stories like that?" she readily described similar situations that she had experienced. (2013: 266)

Other examples of similar uses of vignettes include Barter and Renold's (2000) study of peer violence among youth in residential children's homes. They note that the participants were better able to engage in discussions of things they had experienced if they could rely on the situations depicted in the vignettes. As indicated by Shuman (this volume, chapter 2), people may claim ownership and entitlement to interpret a story not of their own making when it affects them. Another example is Roels et al. (2013), who motivate the use of vignettes in their study of decision-making about language support strategies in the context of services for immigrants. These vignettes were used as a blame-evasive strategy: when interview subjects were presented with plausible, realistic but fictitious scenarios, they were less likely to read the questions as blaming the organization they represent or their own role in that organization. O'Dell et al. (2012) explore the problem of how to interpret responses when the research participants shift between discussing the vignettes as being about themselves, adopting the perspective of the character in the vignette, and commenting on what "ought" to happen. In their view, a fuller understanding of dialogicity is needed, instead of treating it as an obstacle to overcome. "Voice" is the obvious category here, and its detection requires careful descriptions and elucidations of interactional and linguistic "stance" (Jaffe 2009). Vignettes often consist of preformulated narratives, which have been entextualized beforehand. As a variant of this, particular narrative turns may be deliberately left open for the research subject to entextualize; or, as in the case of Jenkins et al. (2010), the narrative may be organized as a set of hyperlinks (organized in this case as a PowerPoint presentation) in which the choice of the next response item (here: the next slide) is made dependent on the interviewee's reaction to its predecessor. What is partly at stake here is the pursuit of (more) optimal conditions of narration, so that the data can be trusted to contain the sought-after experiential accounts of the respondent.

12.3.3 Monitoring narrative performance as a route to securing more reliable data?

Caution is invited: "leave narrator control to the interviewee and all that is relevant will be told" may sound like an attractive option, but it does not offer a panacea. Some will add here that attention must be paid to the subconscious, the unsaid, and the (nearly) unsayable. These are themes that have been at the forefront of psychoanalytical work on narrative. Hollway and Jefferson's (2008) work on free association narrative in crime studies provides an interesting case of conditions of narrativity being openly embraced while also being monitored very closely in elicitation and interpretation. Interestingly, although their initial critique of classic interviewing embraced the possibility and desirability of an experience-based narrated performance by the research subject, they ultimately did not abandon the question-answer format, but aligned it instead with an interactional methodology in which narrative-eliciting questions play a role alongside other strategies (e.g., the use of open-ended questions, the avoidance of "why"-questions, the use of follow-up on the basis of respondents' orderings and phrasings). Free association plays a central role in the process. In Hollway and Jefferson's view, the research subject is a defended subject for whom threats to the self create anxiety, and defenses against such anxiety are mobilized at the subconscious level. It does not suffice to encourage research subjects to tell what happened to them: if memories of events are anxiety-provoking, they will be forgotten or recalled in a more socially acceptable fashion. This affects the meanings that are available in a particular context and how they are conveyed to the listener. This insight also has implications for how contact with the research subject is conducted. So, while the authors report a stage where they were primarily observing research subjects' failure to concentrate on the details of specific events, they caution against a straightforward move in the direction of a narrative turn: claims for the efficacy and appropriateness of a narrative method for studying experiences and meaning in context are subject to the basic problems of any hermeneutic approach. Their alternative label – the "free association narrative interview" – borrows from psychoanalysis and assumes a defended subject. A model for this was found in the biographical-interpretative method, a particular tradition in life story research first developed by German sociologists producing accounts of holocaust survivors and Nazi soldiers.

> When people are assumed not necessarily to be able to tell it like it is, because their own remembered actions may not be transparent to them on account of defences against anxiety, an approach is needed in which unconscious connections are revealed through the links that people make if they are free to structure their own narratives. This adds a further dimension to the principle of preserving the whole of the account, rather than breaking it down into parts. The "form" or *Gestalt* reveals the unconscious dynamics which structure memory and hence a person's subjective investment in their past actions and experiences. (Hollway and Jefferson 2008: 313–314).

In this case, the conditions of narrative expression are monitored very closely, precisely (and somewhat paradoxically) so that narrative could be engaged in more freely.

12.4   The Role of the Researcher in Detecting Narrativity through Careful Analysis

Finally, we must come to the role of the researcher as a (post hoc) analyst of interview data, the researcher who may consciously adopt a narrative perspective in the analysis of interview data. As Wiles, Rosenberg, and Kearns (2005: 89) note for qualitative research in geography:

> Although interviewing receives widespread attention and is a commonly used qualitative method in human geography, most of the attention is focused on interview structure (i.e. structured, semi-structured and unstructured) and the use of various forms of thematic analysis. Far less attention has been given to alternative strategies for understanding and interpreting interviews.

Hence, the authors' aspiration is to explore the strategies, benefits, and some of the limitations of narrative analysis as an alternative to thematic coding in the analysis of interview talk. Their research topic is the interpretation of "in place" experiences. Narrative analysis occurs here as a strategy for analysis and interpretation, but it is equally assumed that the production of interview data has to be monitored in the direction of narrative performance. The authors go on:

> Narrative analysis is designed to take up the challenge of interpreting and understanding layers of meaning in interview talk and the connections among them. It is a form of interpreting a conversation or story in which attention is paid to the embedded meanings and evaluations of the speaker and their context. Through narrative analysis researchers can understand "the contingent, the local, and the particular". Narrative approaches thus hold great potential for geographers interested in the dynamics of everyday life. (2005: 90)

Similar programmatic statements can be noted for other scientific disciplines: for example, Linde (2001) for knowledge management, Larsson and Sjöblom (2010) for social work, etc. In this respect, it is also worth mentioning how interactional analysis has contributed to the critique of some of the earlier approaches that were more exclusively concerned with narrative representation.

One field of tension here is between those who embrace narrativity as a condition or a configuration of meaning-making to be identified and detected in data, without necessarily advocating formal narrative analysis for the uncovering of its working, and those whose preferred method engages with the micro-dynamics of narrative production – i.e., the detection and explication of layers of narrative expression – as interactionally managed and established. At least three positions on the matter can be detected. (1) Because narrative is generally understood as a widely and readily accessible category of human behavior (cf. the ontological position), the tendency does exist for its interpretation to be treated as unproblematic and transparently readable "off the page." Often, this is done on the assumption that we all know what narrative is and what it entails, and that paraphrase and citation would suffice to explicate the meaning of a particular narrative performance. (2) In contrast, there are those who insist that narrative meaning can only be detected adequately through careful analytical attention paid to its micro aspects of formulation. As Bamberg notes (2012: 78), narrative analysts are required "to lay out the relationship between narrative means and experience that is constituted by such means in order to make transparent and document how they arrive at their interpretive conclusions." But in laboring this point we encounter position (3): the analysis of narrative means of expression cannot really be separated from an elucidation of the dynamics of interaction itself. This position maintains that the telling is not only with the teller; in the case of research interviews, the narrative telling is brought about in the interaction with the researcher and is thus jointly produced. As Atkinson and Delamont (2006) note, if problematic equations are those that equate narrative talk with self-expression and those that confuse narrative content with facts and events, then performativity equally runs the risk of becoming a one-sided dimension, if it is understood only in terms of the narrator's performativity and not in terms of narrative expression inextricably tied up with its conversational context and interactional dynamics.

Advocates of an interactionist approach to narrative/identity analysis include Bamberg (1997), Wortham (2000), Depperman (2013), and De Fina and Georgakopoulou (2012: 163ff.), who also offer a more general discussion of how interactional analysis helps elucidate positioning in narrative tellings. In De Fina and Perrino's (2011: 6–7) view, the "narrative turn" in the social sciences, somewhat paradoxically perhaps, has so far not sufficiently resulted in a widespread engagement with narrative's embeddedness in the interactional context. An old duality also comes into play here: narrative as something which can be understood analytically as a complete textual structure consisting of (in one version) spatially-located and chronologically-ordered action sequences with problem-solving dimensions (as in the Labovian tradition, e.g., Labov 1972) versus narrative as something being accomplished interactively (cf. Sacks's (1967) early work on narrative biddings, Schiffrin's (1984) work on story exits and closings, and subsequent lines of enquiry into further aspects of co-narration, including the adoption of particular social-interactional roles (e.g., problematizer, judge, etc.) that inform individual contributions to interactively accomplished emplotments (e.g., Ochs and Taylor 2001)).

So if our initial point of departure was indeed that the extended narrative often emerges as an apparent departure from a conversational principle of interaction, then we were of course only referring to one of narrative's many different possible manifestations. Now we can come full circle and add that an engagement with the microdynamics of narrative articulation itself, and the multiple windows that it provides on events, experiences, categorizations and identity-bearing positions, requires perhaps most of all a careful analytical understanding of the interactional dynamics through which it is being expressed.

12.5   Conclusion

In conclusion, I want to return to my initial observations, which stress the wide-ranging diversity in the roles of the researcher in the context of narrative data expressions. The narrative perspective on data elicitation, data management and data analysis does not provide a panacea that can once and for all result in more reliable data and, with it, a more reliable interpretation of the social world. Instead, the researcher appears to have little other choice than to actively embrace and heed the contingencies of narrative expression in actual contexts of doing research. Following Carr (1986: 126), stories are "told in being lived and lived in being told." The former stresses the link with experience; the latter that storytelling activity is at all times a social activity. The two dimensions bear on each other directly, and there is no final way to separate them: our fate is to engage methodologically and reflexively with how story-telling *is* social action and experience, while also being *about* social action and experience. We add to this: it is rooted in interaction.

REFERENCES

Atkinson, P., and S. Delamont. (2006). Rescuing narrative from qualitative research. *Narrative Inquiry*, 16 (1), pp. 173–181.

Baldwin, C., and B. Estay-Burtt. (2012). Narrative and the reconfiguration of social work ethics. *Narrative Works: Issues, Investigations, & Interventions*, 2 (2), pp. 1–19.

Bamberg, M. (1997). Positioning between structure and performance. *Journal of Narrative and Life History*, 7 (1), pp. 335–342.

Bamberg, M. (2012). Narrative analysis. In H. Cooper (ed.), *APA Handbook of Research Methods in Psychology*. Vol. 2. *Quantitative, Qualitative, Neuropsychological, and Biological*. Washington, DC: APA Press, pp. 78–94.

Barter, C., and E. Renold. (2000). The use of vignettes in qualitative research. *Social Research Update*, 25 (9), pp. 1–6.

Barthes, R. (1982). Introduction to the structural analysis of narratives. In S. Sontag (ed.), *A Barthes Reader*. New York: Farrar, Straus and Giroux, pp. 251–295.

Bauer, M. (1996). *The Narrative Interview: Comments on a Technique for Qualitative Data Collection*. London: LSE Methodology Institute Papers in Social Research Methods.

Blume, T. (2006). *Becoming a Family Counselor: A Bridge to Family Therapy Theory and Practice*. Hoboken, NJ: John Wiley & Sons, Inc.

Breeze, R. (2013). Traversing legal narrative. In M. Gotti and C. Sancho Guinda (eds.),

Narratives in Academic and Professional Genres. Berlin: Peter Lang, pp. 343–362.

Brown, C. (2013). Women's narratives of trauma: (Re)storying uncertainty, minimization and self-blame. *Narrative Works: Issues, Investigations & Interventions*, 3 (1), pp. 1–30.

Bruner, J. (1986). *Actual Minds, Possible Worlds*. Cambridge, MA: Harvard University Press.

Bruner, J., and J. Lucariello. (1989). Monologue as a narrative recreation of the world. In K. Nelson (ed.), *Narrative from the Crib*. Cambridge, MA: Harvard University Press, pp. 73–97.

Carr, D. (1986). Narrative and the real world: An argument for continuity. *History and Theory*, 25 (2), pp. 117–131.

De Fina, A., and A. Georgakopoulou. (2012). *Analyzing Narrative: Discourse and Sociolinguistic Perspectives*. Cambridge: Cambridge University Press.

De Fina, A., and S. Perrino. (2011). Introduction: Interviews vs. "natural" context: A false dilemma. *Language in Society*, 40, pp. 1–11.

Deppermann, A. (2013). How to get a grip on identities-in-interaction. (What) does "Positioning" offer more than "Membership Categorization"? Evidence from a mock story. *Narrative Inquiry*, 23 (1), pp. 62–88.

Etchison, M., and D.M. Kleist. (2000). Review of narrative therapy: Research and review. *Family Journal*, 8 (1), pp. 61–67.

Finch, J. (1987). The vignette technique in survey research. *Sociology*, 21 (1), pp. 105–114.

Fisher, W. (1987). *Human Communication as Narration: Toward a Philosophy of Reason, Value, and Action*. Columbia: University of South Carolina Press.

Freeman, E. (2011). *Narrative Approaches in Social Work Practice: A Life Span, Culturally Centered, Strengths Perspective*. Springfield, IL: Charles C. Thomas.

Georgakopoulou, A. (2007). *Small Stories, Interaction and Identities*. Amsterdam: John Benjamins.

Gergen, K. (1998). Erzählung, moralische Identität und historisches Bewußtsein: Eine sozialkonstruktivistische Darstellung. In J. Straub (ed.), *Identität und historisches Bewußtsein*. Frankfurt: Suhrkamp, pp. 170–202.

Greenhalgh, T., and B. Hurwitz (1999). Narrative based medicine: Why study narrative? *British Medical Journal*, 318, pp. 48–50.

Hall, C., S. Sarangi, and S. Slembrouck. (1997). Moral construction in social work discourse. In B.L. Gunnarsson, P. Linell, and B. Nordberg (eds.), *The Construction of Professional Discourse*. London: Longman, pp. 265–291.

Hall, C., S. Slembrouck, and S. Sarangi. (2006). *Language Practices in Social Work: Categorisation and Accountability in Child Welfare*. London: Routledge.

Hollway, W., and T. Jefferson. (2008). The free association narrative interview method. In L.M. Given (ed.), *The Sage Encyclopedia of Qualitative Research Methods*. London: Sage, pp. 296–315.

Jaffe, A. (2009). *Stance: Sociolinguistic Perspectives*. Oxford: Oxford University Press.

Jenkins, H., M. Bloor, J. Fischer, L. Berney, and J. Neale. (2010). Putting it in context: The use of vignettes in qualitative interviewing. *Qualitative Research*, 10 (2), pp. 175–198.

Labov, W. (1966). *The Social Stratification of English in New York City*. Washington, DC: Center for Applied Linguistics.

Labov, W. (1972). *Language in the Inner City: Studies in the Black English Vernacular*. Philadelphia: University of Pennsylvania Press.

Labov, W. (1997). Some further steps in narrative analysis. *Journal of Narrative and Life History*, 7, pp. 395–415.

Labov, W., P. Cohen, C. Robins, and J. Lewis. (1968). *A Study of the Non-Standard English of Negro and Puerto Rican Speakers in New York City*. Vol. I: *Phonological and Grammatical Analysis*. New York: Columbia University (Cooperative Research Project No. 3288).

Larsson, S., and Y. Sjöblom. (2010). Perspectives on narrative methods in social work research. *International Journal of Social Welfare*, 19, pp. 272–280.

Launer, J. (1999). A narrative approach to mental health in general practice. *British Medical Journal*, 318, pp. 117–119.

Linde, C. (2001). Narrative and social tacit knowledge. *Journal of Knowledge Management*, 5 (2), pp. 160–170.

Madigan, S. (2003). Counterviewing injurious speech acts: Destabilising eight conversational habits of highly effective problems. *International Journal of Narrative Therapy and Community Work*, 1, pp. 43–59.

Niles, J. (1999). *Homo Narrans: The Poetics and Anthropology of Oral Literature*. Philadelphia: University of Pennsylvania Press.

Ochs, E., and L. Capps. (2001). *Living Narrative: Creating Lives in Everyday Storytelling*. Cambridge, MA: Harvard University Press.

Ochs, E., and C. Taylor. (2001). The "father knows best" dynamic in dinnertime narratives. In A. Duranti (ed.), *Linguistic Anthropology: A Reader*. Oxford: Blackwell, pp. 432–449.

O'Dell, L., S. Crafter, G. de Abreu, and T. Cline. (2012). The problem of interpretation in vignette methodology in research with young people. *Qualitative Research*, 12 (6), pp. 702–714.

Polkinghorne, D. (1988). *Narrative Knowing and the Human Sciences*. Albany, NY: State University of New York Press.

Riessman, C. (1993). *Narrative Analysis*. London: Sage.

Roels, B., M. Seghers, B. De Bisschop, S. Slembrouck, P. Van Avermaet, and M. Van Herreweghe. (2013). *Onderzoek naar de inzet en effecten van sociaal tolken en vertalen* [An Inquiry into the Uses and Effects of Community Interpreting and Translation]. Ghent: University of Ghent Linguistics Department.

Sacks, H. (1967). Mimeo lectures, quoted in M. Coulthard (1997), *An Introduction to Discourse Analysis*. London: Longman.

Schiffrin, D. (1984). How a story says what it means and does. *Text*, 4 (4), pp. 313–346.

Shuman, A. (1992). "Get outa my face": Entitlement and authoritative discourse. In J. Hill and J. Irvine (eds.), *Responsibility and Evidence in Oral Discourse*. Cambridge: Cambridge University Press.

Slembrouck, S. (2011). The research interview as a test: Alignment to boundary, topic, and interactional leeway in parental accounts of a child protection procedure. *Language & Society*, 40, pp. 51–61.

Teachman, G., and B. Gibson. (2013). Children and youth with disabilities: Innovative methods for single qualitative interviews. *Qualitative Health Research*, 23 (2), pp. 264–274.

Turner, V. (1985). *On the Edge of the Bush: Anthropology as Experience*. Tucson: University of Arizona Press.

Wengraf, T. (2001). *Qualitative Research Interviewing*. London: Sage.

White, M., and D. Epston. (1990). *Narrative Means to Therapeutic Ends*. New York: W.W. Norton.

Wiles, J., M. Rosenberg, and R. Kearns. (2005). Narrative analysis as a strategy for understanding interview talk in geographic research. *Area*, 37 (1), pp. 89–99.

Winskell, K., P. Brown, A. Patterson, C. Burkot, and B. Mbakwem. (2013). Making sense of HIV in southeastern Nigeria. *Medical Anthropological Quarterly*, 27 (2), pp. 193–214.

Wortham, S. (2000). Interactional positioning and narrative self-construction. *Narrative Inquiry*, 10 (1), pp. 157–184.

13 Small Stories Research
Methods – Analysis – Outreach

ALEXANDRA GEORGAKOPOULOU

13.1 Introduction

The aim of this chapter is to present the disciplinary points of departure, key assumptions, and analytical tools of small stories research, a paradigm for narrative and identities analysis that has been developed in my own research and, in the early stages, in collaboration with Michael Bamberg (e.g., Bamberg 2006; Georgakopoulou 2006, 2007; Bamberg and Georgakopoulou 2008). As the chapter will show, small stories research at first was put forth as a counter-move to dominant models of narrative studies that: (a) defined narrative restrictively and on the basis of textual criteria; (b) privileged a specific type of narrative, in particular the long, relatively uninterrupted, teller-led accounts of past events or of one's life story, typically elicited in research interview situations. Small stories research has thus made a case for including in conventional narrative analysis:

> a gamut of under-represented and "a-typical" narrative activities, such as tellings of ongoing events, future or hypothetical events, shared (known) events, but also allusions to tellings, deferrals of tellings, and refusals to tell. (Georgakopoulou 2006:130)

To do so, small stories research draws on an eclectic synthesis of frameworks from diverse disciplinary traditions, including sociolinguistics and biographical studies, as I will discuss in section 13.2.

The choice of a term to describe the sorts of stories that have concerned me for much of the past decade was not an easy one. All stories that somehow departed from the canon had up until then been described in negative terms that seemed to exoticize and marginalize them even more – *diffuse stories, disnarrated stories* (Prince 1988), *atypical stories*, etc. My first attempt to discuss stories, which in my empirical study actually emerged as the norm rather than as an aberration, was simply to label them as narratives-in-interaction (Georgakopoulou 2005). However, this term could not articulate the very bias in much of the literature against these kinds of activities. This bias, for the initial stages of the research at least, needed to be expressed in terms that contrasted

The Handbook of Narrative Analysis, First Edition. Edited by Anna De Fina and Alexandra Georgakopoulou.
© 2015 John Wiley & Sons, Inc. Published 2019 by John Wiley & Sons, Inc.

certain privileged narrative activities with the disenfranchised ones that we wished to put on the map.

Thus the term *small stories* was ultimately chosen to make this counter-statement more forceful: if "big stories" had been analyzed extensively, now was the moment to look at the neglected stories, which, in some ways, happened to be literally small too. In the process, however, small stories research went beyond the initial – perhaps somewhat militant – need to articulate in explicit terms what the literature bias was and what had been under-researched as a result. Our intention was not to promote a strict dichotomy between big and small stories. On the contrary, the spirit of small stories research is all about recognizing the pluralism, heterogeneity, and productive coexistence of narrative activities, big and small, in the same event, by the same teller, and so on. Small stories, then, has served as a useful umbrella term – a communication device if you will – for our fellow scholars. Alongside this blanket term, though, there has been a recognition that empirical work needed to be done to add nuance to this label, to bring to the fore the specific genres of small stories that occur in specific contexts and that ought to be brought under the narrative analytic lens. I will show this in the case of a very important genre of small stories, breaking news, in section 13.4.

This empirical work has inadvertently involved developing certain ways of identifying particular discourse activities as small stories. Although the point of departure of small stories research was the need to escape the confines of watertight, all-or-nothing definitional criteria of narrative that automatically excluded a whole range of activities, we were also acutely aware that "anything goes" and "everything is a small story" was not a position we wished to adopt. There is a middle way between posing strict, *etic* (analytical) criteria and not posing any definitional criteria at all: this middle way is about avoiding prescriptions and instead embracing flexibility and relativity in the definitions. More specifically, it is about introducing criteria other than purely analytical ones in the process of identification of an activity as a story, as I discuss further below.

Small stories research has been intended as a *model for*, not a *model of* (Duranti 2005) narrative analysis. Duranti (421ff.) sees *models for* as less constraining, more open-ended frames of inquiry that are not controlled tightly by their proponents and their original assumptions. In this spirit, as I will show below, many of the delights of small stories research have come from imaginative and in many ways utterly unexpected applications and extensions of the model. To use a term in currency, we can claim that small stories research has had *impact* in areas outside of sociolinguistics. As I will argue, much of this impact is based on critical uses of small stories research that help bring to the fore silenced, neglected, and marginalized voices in an array of contexts. In this way, small stories applications are in tune with and infuse new insights into the political edge that narrative research has had in the social sciences since its inception (see this volume, Freeman, chapter 1 and Gabriel, chapter 14). The language-focused, analytical aspects on the one hand and the critical, epistemological aspects of small stories on the other hand need not be or stay separate. The extension of small stories to the study of communication on social media shows this very clearly, as I will discuss in detail below.

13.2   The Context for Small Stories Research

The broader context of small stories research is to be found in anti-essentialist views of self, society, and culture that stress the multiplicity, fragmentation, context-specificity, and performativity of our communication practices (see this volume, De Fina, chapter 18). These views are intimately linked with late/postmodern (viz. poststructuralist) theories. Within sociolinguistics, these views have informed the turn to identities-in-interaction (see this volume, De Fina, chapter 18 and Deppermann, chapter 19), while in literary studies of narrative, they have precipitated a combined focus on the content, the author/narrator, the form, and the readers as active participants (cf. rhetorical narratology). More importantly, though, postmodernist views have relativized the evaluative hierarchies of texts and cultures, problematizing distinctions between high and low, official and unofficial. If we extend this to the study of stories, we can talk about an opening up of the analysis beyond literary stories and certainly beyond stories in research-regulated environments, such as interviews. Sociolinguistics has played a key role since the 1960s in showing that it is worthwhile to study stories in diverse contexts: from friends' conversations, family dinnertimes, and drives to school, to classroom settings, asylum applications, and job interviews.

Small stories research would not have been possible without previous studies of conversational storytelling that provided evidence of an abundance of stories that did not conform to what Labov's (1972) influential study described as a "classic" narrative. In particular, they departed from the format of "an active teller, highly tellable account, relatively detached from surrounding talk and activity, linear temporal and causal organization, and certain, constant moral stance" (Ochs and Capps 2001: 20). Small stories research has therefore been intended as an organized move to put such "non-canonical" or "atypical" stories on the map and to make them a focal part of narrative analysis.

The influences on small stories research have come from the study of narrative both within sociolinguistics and outside of it, such as narrative psychology, sociology, narratology. The framework of small stories research as a result can be described as eclectic. For example, it has drawn insights from conversation analysis, which views stories as talk-in-interaction, as sequential activities that are co-constructed between teller and audiences (see this volume, Goodwin, chapter 10). It has also benefited from the biographical research on stories that stresses the experiential, affective, and subjective ways in which people make sense of their self over time and legitimates the study of lay experience, at the same time as reflecting on the role of the researcher (see this volume, Freeman, chapter 1 and Riessman, chapter 11). Beyond these influences, small stories research has mainly been informed by practice-based approaches to language and identities, which view language as performing specific actions in specific environments and as being part of social practices, shaping and being shaped by them (e.g., Hanks 1996). All narrative meaning making is seen as contextualized but also as having the potential to be lifted from its original context and to be recontextualized – that is, to acquire new meanings in new contexts (see Bauman and Briggs 1990). Narrative thus ceases to be just a single event, and its historicity and circulation become part of the analysis (see this volume, Wortham and Rhodes, chapter 8). In light of this, it does not make sense to talk about narrative as an undifferentiated whole or one homogeneous genre but as many genres closely associated with routine ways of telling stories in different contexts (see this volume, Hyvärinen, chapter 9). The analysis in this respect attempts to capture the regularity of occurrence (iterativity) of narrative genres and the semiotic choices within them (Georgakopoulou 2013a). Ethnographic methods are particularly suited to this task, and they often accompany small stories research.

Useful points of departure as they may be, the above traditions present certain kinds of bias that small stories research has been striving to go beyond: for instance, there has been an emphasis on a story as a single event unfolding in linear sequence, a neatly delineated activity with a clear beginning, middle, and end, when in reality many of our stories are "messy," developing without easily identifiable endpoints and in different environments and media (see section 13.6). At the same time, in narrative-biographical research as well as in classical autobiography, the emphasis has been on the narrative form as a sustained, totalizing project, structured by concerns with time, moral development, and retrospective reflection. So there has been an undeniable bias in telling/writing the self as a process that necessitates self-reflection and a measure of time distance from the events; but as we will see below, breaking news stories, currently proliferating on social media, drastically depart from this idea.

13.2.1   A heuristic for analysis

The eclectic synthesis of different frameworks, as described above, led me to developing a heuristic for the analysis of small stories (Georgakopoulou 2007), which explores the connections of three separable but interrelated levels of analysis: *ways of telling, sites, tellers*. *Ways of telling* refers to the communicative how: the socioculturally shaped and more or less conventionalized semiotic and, in particular, verbal choices of a story. With "ways of telling," I capture iterativity in the types of stories told as recurrent ways of (inter)acting, embedded in recurrent social practices and engendering expectations about the ongoing activity. The stories' plots, the types of events and experiences that they narrate, the ways in which they are interactionally managed during the telling are all important in this respect. So are the intertextual links of the current story with other, previous and anticipated, stories.

Sites refers to the social spaces in which narrative activities take place and captures the conglomerate of situational context factors ranging from physical (e.g., seating) arrangements to mediational tools that the participants may employ. My view of sites is informed by recent approaches to language and space that argue for a dialectic relationship between them and see space not as a monolithic, static entity but as a heterogeneous zone that allows certain language and interaction choices and not others (see this volume, Baynham, chapter 6 and Perrino, chapter 7). Sites allow us to explore the significance of social spaces not just for the here-and-now of the telling activities but also for the taleworlds invoked in the participants' stories.

A study of small stories and identities is incomplete without attention to the actual *tellers*, as participants of a communicative activity and as complex entities: as here-and-now communicators with particular roles of participation; as characters in their tales; as members of social and cultural groups; and last but not least, as individuals with specific biographies, including habits, beliefs, hopes, desires, fears, etc. Following multi-layered approaches to context, I accept that the ways in which the three levels above are connected present contingency (context-specificity) but also durability: some relations become conventional and endure beyond individual contexts of storytelling. Furthermore, ways of telling, sites, and tellers are reconfigured differently in the different recontextualizations of a story across time and space.

13.3   Small Stories Research as a Critique
of the Narrative Canon Definitional Criteria

Small stories research is in tune with other recent approaches to narrative in both sociolinguistics (e.g., Ochs and Capps 2001) and narratology (e.g., Herman 2009) that have moved from all-or-nothing to more-or-less views of what constitutes a story. Specifically, the definitional criteria of narrative widely held to be prototypical, such as the sequencing of events, are seen as necessary but not as sufficient. A longstanding tradition within narratology, for instance, defines narrative on the basis of vital constituents of "narrativity" (i.e., what makes a text narrative). These constituents tend to be distilled in the temporal sequencing of events and the "experientiality" that involves a narrator communicating and in the process making sense of his or her point of view, emotions, thoughts, and (re) actions vis-à-vis the reported events (for a discussion see Fludernik 2009).

Furthermore, there is room for flexibility and versatility within each definitional criterion of a story. For instance, as Herman (2009) suggests, the definitional criteria of narrative, which in his terms include event sequencing, world-disruption, and situatedness of narrated events, should be seen as presenting a continuum of possibilities from more to less prototypical (e.g., from more to less sequenced events, etc.). A comparable case has been made by Ochs and Capps (2001), who stipulate dimensions (tellability, tellership, linearity, moral stance, etc.) that are relevant to a narrative, even if not elaborately manifest. Each dimension establishes a range of possibilities that may or may not be realized in a particular narrative. For example, tellership allows for one main teller but also for multiple co-tellers.

In these attempts, the concept of narrative prototype remains crucial (as stated by Herman 2009), even if the definitions become more fluid. On this basis, there are still certain unresolved issues, such as:

- What happens in cases when tellers *emically* view or refer/orient to an activity as a story?
- How is a narrative prototype defined and by whom, and what is the role of context in this?
- How much of each of the etic criteria, alone and/or in combination, should hold for an activity to qualify as a story?

What small stories research has argued in relation to the above issues is that any definitional criteria should be seen as context-specific and that the full continuum that each allows for should be explored in each case. Accepting the contextual variability and relativity of the norms for types and ways of storytelling precludes any inherent prioritization of prototypical ends. Instead, the assumption should be that in different contexts, different ends of the continua may be foregrounded, different criteria may weigh differently, different "schemas for the organization of experience" (Hymes 1981: 121) may hold. For instance, world-making rather than world-disruption may be more important for some stories in certain contexts. In the same vein, there may be a distinct preference for the sequenced events of a story to be about the future and not about the past in certain contexts (Georgakopoulou 2007). Indeed, the criterion of event sequencing has tended to privilege the temporal ordering of past rather than future or hypothetical events – but this should not preclude the identification of such data as stories or their inclusion in a narrative analysis.

In addition, small stories research argues for the inclusion of *emic* criteria in definitions of narrative as complementing and even overriding *etic* criteria. Emic views can be attested, for example, in participants' reflexive discourses on their activities (Georgakopoulou 2013a, 2014a), their meta pragmatic marking and orientation to an activity as a story. Our ethnographic methods of data collection ensure access to these data too.

In light of the above, small stories that have been documented so far include:

- **Non- or multi-linear unfolding events sequenced in further narrative-making,** not linear sequencing of past events.
- Emphasis on **world-making, i.e., telling of mundane, ordinary, everyday events**, not world-disruption and narration of complications.
- Emphasis on **detachability and recontextualization** of a story, not its situatedness in a specific environment.
- **Co-construction of a story's point, events, and characters between teller and audiences**, rather than sole responsibility resting on the teller. This frequently makes story ownership complicated (see this volume, Shuman, chapter 2).

Beyond the above suggestive ways of identifying an activity as a (small) story, we also urge analysts to pose the question of what difference it makes if an activity is viewed as a story: What will the analysis miss out on if it does not see its target as a story? What is at stake for the analyst, and what is the analyst's investment in embracing the narrative perspective on the study of everyday life discourse activities?

13.4   Small Stories Genres: Breaking News as a Case in Point

Small stories are everywhere, but my own analytical encounter with them happened in two environments of ethnographic study involving social interaction among adolescents: one in Greece (2007), and one in a London school (2008, 2009). Among the many small stories told there, I identified a particular genre of small stories that I have called "breaking news." These are stories of very recent (yesterday) and in some cases evolving (just now) events that, once introduced into a conversation, can be further updated. In my study of a peer-group of female best friends in a small Greek town in the late 1990s, breaking news proved to hold a salient place in the group's communication practices: they filled one another in on events that had happened in the very few hours between school and home study when the friends had not communicated with one another. As a lot of these events literally unfolded in the town's streets, new scenarios arose while the friends were piecing together what had just happened, providing them with more material and opportunities for story plots. In this way, breaking news tended to lead to further narrative-making through updates on the unfolding events and/or projections to the near future.

Similarly, in a project entitled Urban Classroom Culture and Interaction (funded by the ESRC Programme in Identities and Social Action, 2005–2008), in which I and several colleagues studied Year 9 and Year 10 students in a London comprehensive school, breaking news stories were also salient, but in this case they were intimately linked with the pupils' engagements with new media. The aim of this project was to study, mainly through audio-recordings of pupils in classrooms, what kinds of identities they constructed for themselves and others in their daily lives at school. Breaking news abounded in the classroom conversations of the female focal participants. Of those, a student whom I call Nadia was the most prolific storyteller (12 small stories per period), as well as an exceptionally creative communicator who frequently indulged in language play, performative enactments of songs and lines from TV shows and commercials, etc. In a survey of the new media engagements of our focal students, Nadia also emerged as the most prolific student. New media engagements included actual uses of technologies (e.g., texting, talking on a mobile phone), enactments of media events (e.g., singing and dancing as in music videos), and reports of engagement (e.g., talk about a TV series that students had watched). Up to half of such engagements in Nadia's case were in the form of breaking news stories, which reported very recent mediated interactions (e.g., on MSN or Skype). Let us see one such small story below:

Period 1 Math: 8.55–9.40 am
The extract begins five minutes after Nadia has entered the classroom (12.31 minutes from start of recording). Nadia sits at a small table in the back corner of the classroom with her friends Lisa and Shenice (her best friend Laura is not in the lesson). The girls are supposed to be doing their math coursework but Nadia has been talking about her looks, stating that she will never be able to be a model because she is not the correct weight and has a bump on her nose. They then share some snacks as Nadia compares Harry Potter's eyebrows with those of a character from the television program *The OC*. As Mr O'Cain begins the lesson, Nadia launches the following small story about Adam texting her the previous day.

Participants: N: Nadia, L: Lisa, S: Shenice, O: Mr O'Cain

(1) N: ((excited)) oh: Adam text me yesterday   12.31

(2)   d' you know what he said:?=

(3) L: = Re:ally?

(4) N: He was gonna come and see me (.) yesterday

(5) O: Fo:lks you haven't got time to talk

(6) N: and then I says why didn't you?

(7)   he was like (.) cos I got lost

(8)   he said (.) I was gonna come down to your school

(9)   I was like hh ((high pitched))

(10)   and you never come becau:se↑'

(11)   he's like (.) I didn't know where I was going

(12)   >I was like< ((high pitched)) oh::: you're so lovely

(13)   I love you (.) oh my **Go:d**   12.52

(35) N: Anyways yea:h   14.49

(36)   he text me yesterday h-

(37)   oh yeah (.) I didn't forget my phone by the way

(38)   (6.0) ((taking phone out))

(39)   he text me

(40)   I don't know

(41)   (6.0) ((going through messages?))

(42)   Yeah he said (.) ((story continued))

(261) N: Anyways yeah (.) he's like (.)   21.52

(262)   he wants to come and see me

(263)   but I would say yeah you can come Lisa

(264)   but you can't ((story continued))

As I have argued elsewhere (2008, 2011), story snippets such as the above were very common in the classroom data, and the participants tuned in and out of their telling for the duration of the lesson (and beyond). So, a further telling, depending on unfolding events (such as the teller getting a further text-message, as in the case above), remained a possibility and the line of storytelling communication remained open. Normally, a fuller telling was premised on more stuff for storying to come. In this case, when Nadia resumes her telling for the second time (lines 35–42 above), she retrieves the actual text message and quotes from that. In the third relaunching of the telling (line 261 onward), she has received a new text, which allows her both to take the telling further and to involve her friends in this.

If we try to analyze such small stories using some of the conventional means – locating activities with a clear beginning-middle-end, a complicating event and a clear evaluation of the events, for example – we will most likely be frustrated as well as not doing justice to these stories. The stories are being told as the events are unfolding. As the (main) teller is experiencing events very close to the telling, she has literally not had the time to reflect on what the meaning of these events may be. Sharing events as they are happening, then, completely changes the handling of a story's point: the point is not known to the teller (yet), but is emerging through the tellings in collaboration with the audience. In some cases, further events and storying happen collaboratively anyway: the girls, for instance, talk about what text-message Nadia should send somebody, then draft it together, and jointly analyze the response. Clearly, even though such stories report ordinary and mundane events, they have some kind of tellability for the participants, as they are frequently told in a situation in which they are not allowed – a classroom during formal instruction. Their tellability cannot thus be defined outside of their situatedness: where they are told, by whom, with whom, and why. Elsewhere, I have suggested that this has serious implications for how the tellers present themselves and their identities (2009, 2013b): in brief, their identities cannot be presented as settled and reflected upon, as could have been done, for instance, in the context of a life story.

So far, we have singled out two features of breaking news that show how in a small stories approach the study of stories has to be looked at differently: the recentness of events and ongoingness of tellings, and the opportunities that these factors create for the co-construction of tellings. One spinoff from this is that because the tellings are frag-mented and more storying is added as more events unfold, it is neither possible nor appropriate to talk about a full-fledged, sustained narrative performance. Tellability in these cases is all about announcing and jointly assessing events that are part of the everyday routine. Should narrative analysis include such activities within its remit? Even though statistics is never the full answer, it is notable that such storytelling prac-tices are increasingly salient, particularly in new media-rich environments and societies, making them far too common to be ignored. It is no accident that breaking news stories in the data I discussed above were not only about pupils' new media engagements but their tellings were also facilitated by them. Below, I will discuss how stories on social media are currently necessitating a rethinking of some of the mainstay vocabulary of narrative analysis.

13.5   Applications and Outreach

Small stories research has been drawn upon by both sociolinguists and social scientists: despite any differences in the analytical modes employed in these applications, one common thread is the aim to challenge dominant idioms about the self and the life story that are supported by (interview-based) narrative research. In this respect, we can claim that small stories research has been taken up as a critical framework for narrative and identities analysis. This partly involves small stories research applied in service of approaches that (further) interrogate essentialist links between stories and identities. In doing so, small stories research has been effective in bringing to the fore silenced, untold, devalued, and discarded stories in numerous institutional or research-regulated contexts (e.g., interviews). In this way, it has helped make visible big issues (Ryan 2008), "unseen and unheard moments of diversity within prevailing mega-narratives" (Olson and Craig 2009: 549). Small stories then frequently emerge as the *counter-stories*, the stories that are not encouraged or allowed in specific environments, that do not fit expectations of who the tellers should be and what stories they tell. Small stories in these cases introduce contradictions, dilemmas, and tensions on the part of the tellers. In turn, small stories research serves as an epistemology rather than just an analytical toolkit. It becomes an ideological standpoint for the analyst who seeks to "listen" to such counter-stories and make them hearable.

For example, Phoenix and Sparkes (2009) showed, in the case of Fred, a healthy 70-year-old man, that his small stories within the context of an interview presented him as a healthy and physically active man, while the master narratives of aging are about physical decline. As in other studies of small stories, Fred was found to occasion counter-canonical selves through small stories, snapshots of himself that go against what may be expected of his normative categorization as an "older" man. At the same time, the study shows how researchers should not overlook or set aside moments of small stories, even in the context of a research agenda that may dictate a focus on big stories.

Studies of small stories have shown that big stories tend to present deceptively coherent, settled, thought-out lives and selves, while small stories make visible the teller's inconsistencies, the troubled identities, the ambivalent relationships with big issues such as race, gender, ethnicity, etc. (e.g., Georgakopoulou 2009; Ryan 2008). This is the crux of small stories research as an epistemology: it is about the researchers reflecting on their roles and investment in the narrative research process. In the case of a research interview, this means recognizing that interviews are complex communicative encounters, co-constructed between researcher and researched, and they can therefore host different narrative genres – stories both big and small – for different purposes. Paying attention to both big and small stories can help the analyst uncover the complexity of identity processes. It is notable that much of the narrative interview research has been critiqued for being too representational and producing excessively transparent accounts of people's selves (e.g., Atkinson and Delamont 2006). Set against this context, small stories research serves as an approach for uncovering the "messiness," performativity, incompleteness, and fragmentation of people's identities.

A case in point regarding the use of small stories for enhancing researcher reflexivity is Norton and Early's (2011) study of how the researchers impacted the process of educating teachers, as part of a digital literacy project in multilingual Uganda. Norton and Early argued that small stories made visible the complex identities that the researchers enacted throughout the research process, ranging from team member to teacher to international guest. At the same time, small stories were also prominent in the (researched) teachers' telling of their experiences of teaching English as an additional language in a poorly resourced rural school. Overall, a focus on small stories uncovered processes of negotiation of identities between researcher and researched and put the spotlight on the researchers as stakeholders in the research in language education. In this way, in the authors' view, small stories enriched traditional narrative inquiry, both theoretically and methodologically. There have been other studies, too, that have shown the importance of small stories for narrative inquiry in education research, including language teaching in general, TESOL, teacher education, etc. (e.g., Barkhuizen 2010; Simpson 2011; Vasquez 2011; Watson 2007). In these cases, small stories research has emerged as an approach conducive to critical analysis of professional practice. Juswik and Ives (2010), for instance, stress the importance of small stories for capturing the small-scale, interactionally contingent ways in which teacher identities emerge in classrooms.

In tune with the above, small stories have been associated with and documented in cases of the tellers presenting emergent and hybrid identities for themselves, perhaps as part of life transitions – for example, gendered identities in male and female adolescents in different settings and countries, from Greece to Germany (e.g., Spreckels 2008), Scotland (Lawson 2013), Australia and the United States; ethnic identities among immigrants and, more generally, mobile populations in contexts of social transformation, such as post-communist settings (e.g., Galasińska 2009) and intercultural encounters (e.g., Fitzpatrick 2011; Lee 2013). This resonance of small stories is closely related to their salience in social media as part of the communication practices that are becoming prevalent in the era of globalization and mobility (see below for further discussion).

Finally, small stories research has been used to develop flexible models of counseling (e.g., Schuhmann and Sools 2012; Sools 2013) for populations that may find it difficult to have access to a conventional session (e.g., homeless people), or for those who may simply find it very difficult to produce a coherent, extended account of their selves over time, sometimes due to medical conditions that may impair cognitive skills (e.g., Alzheimer's or Parkinson's; see Lenchuk and Swainn 2010). These important and creative applications of small stories research, too, are conducive to professional and research practice reflexivity (in this case, the counselor's) that involves fewer counselor-regulated environments and more transparency in the interactions between counselors and clients. They are also in tune with mobile ethnographic approaches, which are strategically adapted to late modern life conditions, and they offer a response to the call for studying people's identities through diverse stories in diverse everyday life contexts (see, for example, the application of small stories for family identities research in Tovares 2010).

13.6   Small Stories and Social Media

As I suggested above, small stories research was initially developed to address the proliferation of fragmented storytelling phenomena in everyday interactional environments, readily observable in all manner of ordinary social practices. In my latest work, however, I have begun to document a close association of small stories with the explosion of new/social media and their pervasive presence in everyday life, as that is facilitated by the increasing media convergence (Georgakopoulou 2013b, 2013c, 2013d). We saw above how breaking news stories were prevalent in the context of pupils discussing their new media engagements and having new media at their disposal at school via their mobile phones. My study of text-messages, Facebook status updates, Twitter and retweets has in fact shown that breaking news stories abound on those platforms (see Page 2012), as we can see in the examples below.

(1) Dataset of end-of-school text-messages collected in 2011–2012 from Year 7–8 girls in London. The data are part of a larger project on the uses of adolescents' new media, particularly mobile telephony, for the micro-coordination of their everyday lives.

Hey mum had a g day xx c u soon
xx are u picking me up?? Bio thing went SOOOOOO well
we were def the best group we really enjoyed it too.

(2) Data from a Facebook status update:

Susie has got through the day with chocolate brownies!! When was it a good idea to finish a build at the same time the baby is due??

Like 10 Comment 3

(3) Data from a collection of selected celebrity and public figures' Twitter streams and their retweets in lifestyle/gossip columns of two UK newspapers (*The Evening Standard* and *The Mail Online*).

Quote of the day

"Busy day, during which I have finally learnt how to spell 'kaleidoscope'"

Sally Bercow[1] tweets after her husband, Speaker John Bercow, used the word kaleidoscope three times in his speech to the Queen.

(*Evening Standard*, 21/03/12)

This proliferation of small stories on new/ social media platforms is no accident: social media environments afford opportunities for sharing life in miniaturized form at the same time as constraining the ability of users to plunge into full autobiographical mode (e.g., Twitter's constraint of 140 characters). In particular, they offer users the ability to share experience as it is happening with various semiotic (multi-modal) resources, to update it as often as necessary, and to (re)embed it in various social platforms. This prevalence of small stories and the widely held view that social media are endangering more conventional forms of autobiography are making it imperative for narrative analysts to engage with these phenomena with questions that pertain to both what narrative analysis can offer for their scrutiny and how it can respond to the new challenges that they pose. As a result, my primary aim with the use of small stories research on social media is to articulate as fully as possible not only what is distinctive about such new media practices, but also how they draw on or depart from other forms and practices of storytelling. How does this kind of storytelling interweave, mediate, and become consequential for online and offline experience? How do texts get circulated on social media, which ones, and why? How does socially situated meaning-making shift from context to context, and what semiotic modalities are mobilized to do certain things at certain times? Small stories research, having developed tools for examining fragmented and transposable activities, can offer a suitable bridge between narrative analysis, discourse transposition, and social media.

In addition to these questions, the numerous applications and outreach of small stories research discussed above recommend it as a critical micro-perspective on social media engagements, one that can help answer the current key questions in social media research: what is the sociopolitical potential of social media engagements for transformation, and what counter-cultural, hidden, and unofficial practices of meaning-making do social media engender?

There is a lot still to be learnt from how stories are told on social media. Page (this volume, chapter 17) discusses the ways in which tellership and the sequencing of events are produced in different new media platforms. My own research so far (2013c, 2013d, 2014b) has shown how the distribution of small stories across media platforms creates opportunities for multiple tellership and more or less creative reworkings and appropriations of previous stories. I have also shown (2013c) how the smallness of small stories makes them more portable and circulatable than long accounts. It also affords opportunities for the audience to shape the terms of further telling. Finally, the more a story is transposed across online contexts, the more voices and subjectivities become part of its production.

To benefit from the above findings, further studies of small stories on social media ought to have as their initial point of departure that stories produced on social media normally: announce and perform minute-by-minute, often ordinary experience, develop in different media, are embedded into a variety of online and offline environments with different semiotic modes (e.g., verbal, visual), and may be sanctioned and recontextualized in unforeseeable ways and by networked audiences (Marwick and boyd 2011) with processes of like, share, and follow.

13.7   Conclusions

In this chapter, I presented small stories research, a recent model for narrative and identities analysis. I discussed the model's critical engagement with previous research on narrative, its key assumptions, and its eclectic framework. I illustrated the contextualized analysis of small stories research with the example of breaking news stories, which I argued is a prevalent genre in social media-related and social media-afforded environments. In this context, I charted the main directions that the current extension of small stories research into social media is taking. I also showed how small stories research has given rise to creative applications and synergies outside of the immediate analytical concerns of a sociolinguistic study of narrative and identities. These extensions of small stories research have boosted the epistemological aspects of the model as a tool for researcher reflexivity and for uncovering counter-stories and marginalized voices in an array of diverse contexts, including institutional, researcher-led (e.g., interviews), intercultural, etc.

From all the different settings where small stories have been researched, a certain convergence of insights is emerging. The first is the importance in numerous small-story environments and genres – e.g., on social media – of the lack of temporal distance between the tale and the telling. In the context of a longstanding tradition of studying stories of (remote) past events, this deictic proximity between the story and its actual telling has implications for the analysis of narrative, particularly in terms of a story's point or tellability. As I have argued (2013c), tellability in the case of very recent or still unfolding events is premised on *the ability to tell*, to announce and immediately share experience. Conferring meaning on this experience and creating emplotment therefore becomes an inevitably interactional process between teller and audience, where a story's point is not only being negotiated but is also malleable and shifting, as more events and more tellings of them are happening. Closely related to this changing notion of tellability is the abundance of small stories about mundane, ordinary, everyday events rather than about major disruptions. This tendency has reached a peak in social media platforms and is frequently being deplored by commentators as a shallow form of existence in which people spend their time announcing the minutiae of their daily lives. Any aesthetic arguments about these kinds of narrative activities left aside, the point remains that small stories research is in an ideal position to (re)assess narrative analysis priorities and both study and account for this latest advent of ordinary experience telling.

I also argued that the analytical heuristic of small stories research is well suited to exploring relationships between ways of telling, sites and tellers. As small stories research is uncovering conventional associations between social spaces, narrative genres, and specific subjectivities, we are increasingly in a position to find out more about the processes through which certain stories become more legitimate and valued in certain contexts, or more distributed and transposed in others. The implication of this line of inquiry is that it is allowing us to document which specific ways of storytelling in specific sites may foreground and privilege certain aspects of selves and identities, making them more available over time.

Small stories research has often been combined with positioning analysis and, as I discussed above, such identities analysis has shown the frequency and significance of tentative, contradictory, diverse identities that emerge in certain contexts as selves-in-the-making, rather than as settled and reflected-upon projects. An implication of this is that the strong link in much of the conventional narrative analysis between rehearsed/reflected-upon identities and stories has been further problematized.

Since its inception, small stories research has often had to defend its object of inquiry, namely "miniaturized" story instances and fragments, as worthy of analysis. I have already mentioned the frequent aesthetic discontentment of lay commentators with small stories on social media. Painstaking analyses have allowed us to document the redeeming features of small stories and their significance for the people who tell them. In light of the explosion of small stories on social media, we can argue that small stories reflect a process of democratization of a difficult genre, the full mastery of which is not easy to attain, contributing further to the collapse between the high and the low that Web 2.0 environments have encouraged. In fact, small stories present many commonalities with new media literacies, as described, for example, by Jenkins (2006) – in particular their participatory culture (as shown by their multi-authorship properties) and their appropriative elements (as shown by the stories' circulation). The "verbal art" of full-fledged narrative performances may have receded in these cases, but in its place, a portable and distributed multi-modal narrative semiosis has arisen. There is ample evidence that communicative competence in small stories carries a lot of symbolic capital in adolescent peer-groups, serving as a structuring force in peer-group relations, and that successfully interweaving news media experience with everyday experience is a valued attribute, a sign of a "smart" individual (Georgakopoulou 2011, 2014a).

At the same time, further analyses of small stories need a critical agenda that will strike the balance between eulogizing and celebrating small stories on the one hand and being alert to the downsides, too: uncovering biases against them which potentially disadvantage their tellers and interrogating the boundaries that small stories, with their heavy use of allusion and ellipsis, can draw between those who are in the know and those who are not. It is also important, as I suggested from the outset, for small stories not to be painted as the good in a good-evil dichotomy between small and big stories.

To conclude, small stories research has been making strides in uncovering forms of subjectivity through stories in interactional and social media environments. For the future, it is important for a critical mass to be built out of the numerous and diverse explorations of small stories that would bring together insights from the many strands of inquiry but also create alliances with relatable lines of inquiry, where applicable. Crudely speaking, there is a lot that the more analytical lines of inquiry into small stories can learn from the epistemological ones, and vice versa. The critical mass also needs to capitalize on the richness and nuance of contextualized work on small stories in different environments. To continue to operate as a model for narrative analysis, small stories research needs to continue to develop in a pluralized, multi-centric, non-totalizing way: what new points of itinerary will emerge and from where will – and should – remain a productive unpredictability.

NOTE

1   The wife of the Speaker of the House of Commons of the UK Parliament, who has often generated controversy in the UK media with her tweets.

REFERENCES

Atkinson, P., and S. Delamont. (2006). Rescuing narrative from qualitative research. *Narrative Inquiry*, 16 (1), pp. 173–181.

Bamberg, M. (2006). Stories: Big or small: Why do we care? *Narrative Inquiry*, 16 (1), pp. 147–155.

Bamberg, M., and A. Georgakopoulou. (2008). Small stories as a new perspective in narrative and identity analysis. *Text & Talk*, 28, pp. 377–396.

Barkhuizen, G. (2010). An extended positioning of a pre-service teacher's "better life" small story. *Applied Linguistics*, 31, pp. 282–300.

Bauman, R., and C. Briggs. (1990). Poetics and performance as critical perspectives on language and social life. *Annual Review of Anthropology*, 19, pp. 59–88.

Duranti, A. (2005). On theories and models. *Discourse Studies*, 7, pp. 409–429.

Fitzpatrick, M. (2011). Being and becoming Pakeha: A narrative inquiry into children's stories of what it means to be Pakeha. Unpublished PhD thesis. University of Auckland.

Fludernik, M. (2009). *An Introduction to Narratology*. Abingdon, UK: Routledge.

Galasińska, A. (2009). Small stories fight back: Narratives of Polish economic migration on an Internet forum. In A. Galasińska and M. Krzyżanowski (eds.), *Discourse and Transformation in Central and Eastern Europe*. Basingstoke, UK: Palgrave Macmillan, pp. 188–203.

Georgakopoulou, A. (2005). The other side of the story: Towards a narrative analysis of narratives-in-interaction. *Discourse Studies*, 8, pp. 265–287.

Georgakopoulou, A. (2006). Thinking big with small stories in narrative and identity analysis. *Narrative Inquiry*, 16 (1), pp. 129–137.

Georgakopoulou, A. (2007). *Small Stories, Interaction and Identities*. Amsterdam: John Benjamins.

Georgakopoulou, A. (2008). "On MSN with buff boys": Self- and other-identity claims in the context of small stories. *Journal of Sociolinguistics*, 12, pp. 597–626.

Georgakopoulou, A. (2009). Reflection and self-disclosure from the small stories perspective: A study of identity claims in interview and conversational data. In D. Schiffrin, A. De Fina, and A. Nylund (eds.), *Telling Stories: Language, Narrative, and Social Life*. Washington, DC: Georgetown University Press, pp. 226–247.

Georgakopoulou, A. (2011). Teachers, students and ways of telling in classroom sites: A case of out-of-(work)place identities. In J. Angouri and M. Marra (eds.), *Constructing Identities at Work*. Basingstoke, UK: Palgrave Macmillan, pp. 151–174.

Georgakopoulou, A. (2013a). Building iterativity into positioning analysis: A practice-based approach to small stories and self. *Narrative Inquiry*, 23, pp. 89–110.

Georgakopoulou, A. (2013b). Small stories and identities analysis as a framework for the study of im/politeness-in-interaction. *Journal of Politeness Research*, 9, pp. 55–74.

Georgakopoulou, A. (2013c). Storytelling on the go: Breaking news stories as a travelling narrative genre. In M. Hatavara, L.-C. Hydén, and M. Hyvärinen (eds.), *The Travelling Concepts of Narrative*. Amsterdam: John Benjamins, pp. 201–224.

Georgakopoulou, A. (2013d). Small stories research and social media practices: Narrative stancetaking and circulation in a Greek news story. *Sociolinguistica*, 27, pp. 87–100.

Georgakopoulou, A. (2014a). "Girlpower or girl (in) trouble?" Identities and discourses in the media engagements of adolescents' school-based interaction. In J. Androutsopoulos (ed.), *Mediatization and Sociolinguistic Change*. Berlin: De Gruyter Mouton.

Georgakopoulou, A. (2014b). Small stories transposition and social media: A micro-perspective on the "Greek crisis." *Discourse & Society*, 25, pp. 519–539.

Hanks, W. (1996). *Language and Communicative Practices*. Boulder, CO: Westview Press.

Herman, D. (2009). *Basic Elements of Narrative*. Oxford: Wiley-Blackwell.

Hymes, D. (1981). *"In Vain I Tried to Tell You": Essays in Native American Ethnopoetics*. Philadelphia: University of Pennsylvania Press.

Jenkins, H. (2006). *Convergence: Where Old and New Media Collide*. New York: New York University Press.

Juswik, M., and D. Ives. (2010). Small stories as a resource for positioning teller identity: Identity-in-interaction in an urban language classroom. *Narrative Inquiry*, 20, pp. 37–61.

Labov, W. (1972). *Language in the Inner City: Studies in the Black English Vernacular*. Philadelphia: University of Pennsylvania Press.

Lawson, R. (2013). The construction of "tough" masculinity: Negotiation, alignment and rejection. *Gender and Language*, 7, pp. 369–395.

Lee, H. (2013). Telling stories and making social relations: Transnational women's ways of belonging in intercultural contexts. *Applied Linguistics*, Advance Access published December 13, 2013, doi:10.1093/applin/amt038.

Lenchuk, I., and M. Swainn. (2010). Alice's small stories: Indices of identity construction and of resistance to the discourse of cognitive impairment. *Language Policy*, 9, pp. 9–28.

Marwick, A., and d. boyd. (2011). I tweet honestly, I tweet passionately: Twitter users, context collapse and the imagined audience. *New Media and Society*, 13, pp. 114–133.

Norton, B., and M. Early. (2011). Researcher identity, narrative inquiry and language teaching research. *TESOL Quarterly*, 45, pp. 415–439.

Ochs, E., and L. Capps. (2001). *Living Narrative*. Cambridge, MA: Harvard University Press.

Olson, M., and C. Craig. (2009). Small stories and metanarratives: Accountability in balance. *Teachers College Record*, 111, pp. 547–572.

Page, R. (2012). *Stories and Social Media*. New York: Routledge.

Phoenix, C., and A. Sparkes. (2009). Being Fred: Big stories, small stories and the accomplishment of a positive ageing identity. *Qualitative Research*, 9, pp. 209–236.

Prince, G. (1988). The disnarrated. *Style*, 22, pp. 1–8.

Ryan, M. (2008). Small stories, big issues: Tracing complex subjectivtities of high school students in interactional talk. *Critical Discourse Analysis*, 5, pp. 217–229.

Schuhmann, C., and A. Sools. (2012). A small story approach to life stance counselling. Paper presented at the Narrative Matters Conference, American University of Paris, May 28–June 2. http://www.levensverhalenlab.nl/upload/Schuhmann Sools_-_Small_story_approach.pdf

Simpson, J. (2011). Telling tales: Discursive space and narratives in ESOL classrooms. *Linguistics and Education, 22*, pp. 10–22.

Sools, A. (2013). Narrative health research: Exploring big and small stories as analytical tools. *Health*, 17 (1), pp. 93–110.

Spreckels, J. (2008). Identity negotiation in small stories among German adolescent girls. *Narrative Inquiry*, 18, pp. 393–413.

Tovares, A. (2010). All in the family: Small stories and narrative construction of a shared family identity that includes pets. *Narrative Inquiry*, 20, pp. 1–19.

Vasquez, C. (2011). TESOL, teacher identities and the need for small story research. *TESOL Quarterly*, 45, pp. 535–545.

Watson, C. (2007). "Small stories" and the doing of professional identities in learning to teach. *Narrative Inquiry*, 17 (2), pp. 371–389.

Part IV Stories in Social Practices

14 Narratives and Stories in Organizational Life

YIANNIS GABRIEL

14.1 Introduction

Organizing has always been a part of human life, but many scholars approach *organizations* as relatively recent historical figures. They view the rise of organizations as coinciding with the onset of modernity, urbanization, industrialization, and scientific modes of thinking and reasoning. From its origins in Weberian theory of bureaucracy aimed at explaining the growth of organizations and managerial theories aimed at enhancing their efficiency, organizational theory has tended to focus on the rational, impersonal, and structural qualities of organizations. Narratives, stories, and myths[1] had little place in such conceptualizations, which approached organizations essentially as culture-free machines.

The neglect of narrative by organizational scholarship until the 1970s was consistent with the view that modernity, with its emphasis on information, science and facts, had sounded the death-knell for storytelling (Benedict 1931; Benjamin 1968). Equally, however, it was the product of an aversion on the part of researchers to engaging seriously with the messy and unreliable texture of narrative as part of a scientific study of organizations.

This started to change in the 1970s, when a spate of ethnographic studies of organizations indicated that at least some of them had cultures and even folklore, that people told stories, and that these stories expressed profound and frequently shared experiences (see, e.g., Beynon 1973; Pollert 1981). A major realization at that time lay in accepting narratives and stories not simply as mere diversions from the real stuff of working and managing, but rather as essential constituents of organizations themselves. Consistent with social constructionist orientations, an increasing number of scholars have since come to view narrative not as something that happens "inside" a given box called organization, but as something that serves to construct the box itself.

Three other developments have further enhanced interest in organizational narratives and storytelling. The first concerns their embracement by organizational participants, including consultants, managers, and leaders, as an important resource

The Handbook of Narrative Analysis, First Edition. Edited by Anna De Fina and Alexandra Georgakopoulou.
© 2015 John Wiley & Sons, Inc. Published 2019 by John Wiley & Sons, Inc.

for shaping hearts and minds. With the publication of Peters and Waterman's *In Search of Excellence* (1982), which became a major managerial best-seller, the management of organizational culture became a major preoccupation of leadership. Consultants themselves, including Peters and Waterman, started making extensive use of stories and narratives in their practice as a means of advocating particular techniques for effecting organizational change and publicizing particular managerial practices. Since then, the development of managers' ability to recount effective stories has spawned a minor industry with countless workshops and publications (see, e.g., Allan, Gerard, and Barbara 2002; Armstrong 1992; Denning 2005; Simmons 2002).

The second development has been a methodological one and has consisted in overcoming the mistrust of narratives and stories as reliable and valid ways of conducting organizational research. It has now become widely accepted that, even if not accurate or "truthful," stories and narratives open valuable windows into a wide range of organizational phenomena, including culture, politics, knowledge management, group dynamics, and so forth (see, e.g., Rhodes and Brown 2005; Gabriel 1991a; Boje 1991). Thus, *even* researchers adhering to a predominantly positivist paradigm have found ways of identifying, collecting, and analyzing narratives as means of developing their research agendas. Interpretive researchers, for their part, have hugely enlarged their repertoires for working with stories and narratives using the resources of discourse and narrative analysis, which are often imported or translated from other disciplines, including ethnography, psychoanalysis, literary criticism, and media studies.

Related to the increasing acceptance of narrative-based methodologies in organizational research has been a realization that researchers are themselves narrators (Dyer and Wilkins 1991) and that a substantial part of social science research has a narrative character (see Riessman, this volume, chapter 11). Czarniawska (Czarniawska-Joerges 1995, Czarniawska 1999), who has developed this argument furthest, has been able to uncover deep elements of plot and characterization, not just in ethnographic writing, but equally in conventional writing, like Hirschman's (1970) *Exit, Voice, and Loyalty*. The result of these developments has been a general legitimation of narrative in organizational research and its proliferation in a wide range of inquiries. In the rest of this chapter we shall locate the study of organizational stories and narratives in the following partly overlapping areas:

- narratives and stories as vital parts of an individual's and organization's sensemaking apparatus;
- narratives and stories as features of organizational politics representing attempts at control and resistance;
- narratives and stories as elements of individual and group identities;
- narratives and stories as symbolic artefacts expressing deep mythological archetypes;
- narratives and stories as means of sharing, disseminating, and contesting knowledge and learning.

I shall conclude with some reflections on future possibilities in the study of organizational narratives and stories and by indicating some limitations and potential blind-spots of this research.

14.2 Narratives and Sensemaking

Organizations may not, at first sight, appear as natural storytelling or narrative spaces. Unlike pubs, cafés, and other places where people meet to swap stories and experiences, organizations seem too impersonal and formal, too swamped by facts and information, with people too busy and pressured to engage in serious storytelling. All the same, as anyone who has worked in an organization knows, there are plenty of stories told in corridors and offices, hotel lobbies and conference rooms. Increasingly, political leaders and organizational leaders alike can be heard exhorting or inspiring their followers with stories of their own. Furthermore, we are all familiar with narratives that organizations disseminate through their brochures, advertisements, and corporate communiqués. Yet it was not until the 1970s that organizational theorists started to take note of such narratives as important elements of organizational life.

In a visionary early contribution, Mitroff and Kilmann (1975) were the first to explicitly draw attention to organizational storytelling as a feature of organizational life. They opened their article with what must have seemed an outlandish statement to scholars inured in theories of bureaucracy.

> If accounting and finance are the backbone of organizations, then the stories which permeate all organizations of any size are their lifeblood. Stories are so central to organizations that not only do organizations depend on them, but stronger still, they couldn't function without them. (1975:18)

Mitroff and Kilmann noted that stories capture the unique qualities of an organization and serve as repositories of meaning. But they went well beyond this. In an article of scarcely 10 pages, they observed that stories are shared, that they have mythological qualities, that they serve as instruments of organizational socialization, that they offer problem-solving recipes, and that they often express unconscious wishes. They also, more ambitiously, sought to identify the preferred storylines of different psychological characters and highlighted their usefulness as vehicles of learning, *even when not accurate or true*. Above all, Mitroff and Kilmann showed an awareness that stories "construct" specific *events* in organizational life, lying somewhere between fantasy and actuality. Since that article's publication, most of these themes have been taken up, elaborated, or contested within different research agendas.

Writing in 1979, Weick established sensemaking as a core category in the cognitive psychology of organizations, noting that "organizations are often reluctant to admit that a good deal of their activity consists of reconstructing plausible histories after-the-fact to explain where they are now, even though no such history got them to precisely this place" (1979: 5). Weick highlighted the importance of plausibility and the retrospective quality of what he then called "histories" as part of part of the human quest for meaning, but also as a way of organizing experience. As sensemaking devices, narratives and stories do not merely help us infuse events with meaning, but also enable us to mold them to our own needs and desires, to comment on them, and to contest them. As such, they help us process our experiences, communicate them to others, and rearrange them within larger narratives of identity and selfhood.

As scholars of organization turned their attention to organizational culture in the 1980s, stories, myths, rituals, and other cultural features came under scrutiny. Following from Mitroff and Kilmann, several early contributions to the study of stories and narratives in organizations noted how they act as cognitive maps assisting sensemaking (Wilkins 1984) but also how they can be instruments of managerial control over organizational participants (Wilkins and Ouchi 1983). In a contribution that sketched many similarities between organizational and mythological narratives, Martin et al. (1983) argued that a relatively narrow range of plots circulate in most organizations, offering *retrospective* rationalizations for the actions of significant actors by attributing blame and credit. Martin and her colleagues propose a "uniqueness paradox" according to which every organization's narratives carry a claim to uniqueness (the uniqueness of its culture, its leaders, etc.), even though they fall into highly formulaic patterns. Scholars of organization were quick to realize the persuasive qualities of stories, especially as management gurus and consultants were picking them up at around that time (e.g., Peters and Waterman 1982); and there is a distinct managerial emphasis in this research (e.g., McConkie and Boss 1986), the argument being that managers could rely, at least in part, on effective storytelling to disseminate their ideas, initiate change, instill conformity, and overcome resistance.

Against this backdrop, Boje's (1991) contribution broke new ground. Boje argued that an organization could be viewed as "a collective storytelling system in which the performance of stories is a key part of members' sense making and a means to allow them to supplement individual memories with institutional memory" (106). What was original in Boje's research was the view that much of the storytelling in organizations is fragmented, terse, and abbreviated. There is no implicit or explicit "agreed text" (106) to these stories, but only variations and varieties surfacing in unique performances. Stories form part of a noisy, plurivocal, and polysemic universe where they surface, they collide, they are often contested, and they eventually disappear. Many wither away; others are stillborn. Defining a story as "an oral or written performance involving two or more people interpreting past or anticipated experience" (111), Boje emphasizes the multi-authored character of organizational storytelling, where different participants contribute different narrative elements, amplifying some lines and contesting others; at the same time he de-emphasizes the importance of plot. Boje's approach was part of a wider problematizing of "story" in postmodern theorizing that has questioned the centrality of plot and character in narratives and has tended to broaden the concept of story to include many conversational texts that do not necessarily feature beginnings, middles, and ends (e.g., Georgakopoulou 2006a, 2006b, this volume, chapter 13; Kearney 2002).

In subsequent works, Boje developed his postmodern approach to organizational narrative through an exploration of how corporate discourses silence and marginalize some narratives while privileging others (Boje 1995). Concerned about attempts by large corporations to silence stories that they disapprove of, Boje proposed the concept of "antenarrative," a "fragmented, non-linear, incoherent, collective, *unplotted*, and pre-narrative speculation, a bet, ... a wager that a proper narrative can be constituted" (Boje 2001: 1, emphasis added). It is within this antenarrative space that marginalized voices can be found, frequently unable to articulate themselves as full narratives or stories, but capable of doing so under the right circumstances. Boje's later work shows a much keener awareness of the political ramifications of narratives and acts as an important corrective to the "stories-as-sensemaking" approaches that all too frequently overlook power and politics.

Stories as sensemaking has now become orthodoxy in organizational studies. Stories, Weick (1995: 129f.) argues, aid comprehension by drawing connections between causes and effects, by offering mnemonic landmarks of earlier events, and by conveying shared values. What sometimes gets lost in this approach is the politics and depth psychology of storytelling. Why do some stories prove very much more powerful than others? Why do different people mobilize different stories in making sense of the same events? And why is it that sensemaking itself so frequently leaves a deficit of meaning? "You don't have to be mad/crazy to work here but it helps" is a common logo on T-shirts, mugs, and so forth, suggesting that people can make sense of the absurdities, irrationalities and "corporate bullshit" they encounter in their lives as workers and consumers. In a highly original contribution, Pelzer (2004) has argued that sensemaking is a surrogate for meaning rather than a quest for it. When a large part of everyday life is reduced to meaningless routines, when meaning loses its anchors, we turn to sensemaking as its inadequate and doomed surrogate. It is not accidental, then, that bureaucratic senselessness is regularly lampooned in films like *Catch-22*, TV series like *The Office*, and comic strips like *Doonesbury*. It would not be an exaggeration to say that narratives come to the rescue of meaning in organizations when much seems senseless or even perverse.

14.3 Narratives and Politics, Control and Resistance

That narratives play an important part in organizational politics in tangible as well as intangible ways can hardly be seen as an original observation. Anyone who has worked in an organization knows that a very large number of narratives (if indeed not a majority) are *about* politics – about conflicts and alliances, deals and double-deals, victories and losses, and so on. Take politics away and you snuff out much of organizational storytelling.

As instruments of persuasion and even brutalization, narratives carry effective disciplining power – for instance, by warning of the consequences of breaking organizational rules and norms, of insubordination to the dictates of significant players, or of other forms of organizational resistance. The "chastising effect" of comic stories that ridicule particular groups or individuals has been known at least since Hobbes (1651/1962), and Bergson (1980) (for organizational contexts, see, e.g., Collinson 1988; Davies 1988; Linstead 1985). Tragic stories, for their part, demonstrate the wide range of calamities that organizational life can visit on individuals and groups, including humiliation, insult, bullying, oppression, discrimination, demotion, and dismissal, and offer various warnings of what is to be avoided and what is to be emulated. Gabriel (1991a, 1991b) demonstrated how stories related by conscripted soldiers in training camps serve as powerful instruments of organizational socialization and control, generating anxiety and fear and dampening critical and rebellious attitudes. Nor should it be thought that such stories are limited to a few particularly oppressive organizations

(Witten 1993). Theodosius (2008) offers numerous examples of how different cliques of nurses use storytelling as an effective humiliation, bullying, or exclusion device to maintain unofficial hierarchies and privileges. Czarniawska (2008: 1034) has argued that such humiliation, far from being exceptional, is a "standard organizational by-product, considered to be an unavoidable if regrettable effect of power." Sims (2003), for his part, has shown that humiliation is experienced when stories of particular groups are systematically challenged, ignored, or ridiculed.

Stories can then be viewed as part of a potentially brutal disciplinary machinery in many organizations, silencing opposition, instilling conformity, and spreading anxiety and fear. More indirectly, however, as discursive practices that constitute reality, narratives are vehicles for legitimating various organizational regimes by establishing what is regarded as normal, truthful or, indeed, "rational." In this way, as Rhodes and Brown (2005: 174) point out, narratives shield "truth claims from testing and debate, and command attention and memory, often without exciting argumentative challenge." Inspired by Foucault and, more indirectly, Gramsci's theory of hegemony and subaltern theory, some of the theorizing on the power effects of narratives have assumed a rather gloomy metaphysical position: that dominant corporate narratives are always able to snuff out oppositional ones or, as we saw earlier in what Boje (2001) termed antenarrative, to confine them to the space of marginalized voices and frequently unheard voices. Ruling groups, including governments, corporations, NGOs, and so forth, are thus seen as controlling narrative resources every bit as effectively as they control other resources. The "language of organization," argue Westwood and Linstead (2001), finds innumerable ways of normalizing dominant meanings and practices while eliminating alternative ones.

This line of argument is consistent with various discourses that have postulated a decline of employee resistance in organizational life or, more generally, in the political and cultural life world of late capitalism. In a curious way, most of the actual stories discussed in organizational literature tend to be managerial, ultimately serving the interests of managerial control; or pluralist, coexisting often uneasily as different parties seek to legitimate their actions and interests (e.g., Brown 2002). Stories by oppressed or exploited employees are often couched in terms of cynical distancing (e.g., Fleming and Spicer 2003; O'Leary 2003). Possibly less common are stories displaying a rebellious or defiant attitude, challenging managerial prerogatives or ridiculing bureaucratic irrationality and waste. Gabriel (1995) has proposed that such stories are in fact quite common in most organizations, forming part of what he terms the "unmanaged organization," a kind of organizational dreamworld dominated by desires, fantasies, and emotions. This unmanaged organization does not directly challenge the practices of power and management, but involves numerous attempts to side-step or dodge them through spontaneous, uncontrolled activities which may involve clever ruses, privately coded texts, noise, silence, graffiti, cartoons, whispers, nods, smiles, secrets, gossip, and, above all, narratives and stories.

Some of the reasons why narratives lend themselves to such political ends is the plasticity of their material, their tenuous relation to facts, and their ability to select, frame, and connect incidents. The plastic relation of narrative to anything that claims to have a factual foundation goes back to Aristotle (1963) and gives narratives remarkable flexibility in meeting different personal and organizational agendas and giving voice to different interests and experiences. The same incident (for example, an accidental fire) may be narrated in such ways that to some it offers evidence of management neglect, to others it indicates organizational resilience in the face of adversity, to yet others it points to worker cunning, and to others it demonstrates bureaucratic stupidity. It is hardly surprising, then, that different storylines frequently compete for ascendancy or acceptance and may find ways of uncomfortably coexisting with each other in the narrative spaces of organizations (Gabriel 2000). As the resilience of conspiracy theories demonstrates, stories are notoriously resistant to correction by appeal to fact; indeed, virtually any fact can be incorporated in a storyline.

By giving a voice to experience and by valorizing this experience as something that commands automatic respect, contemporary culture has discovered in personal story-telling a new type of authority that can challenge the authority of the scientific, technical, or even bureaucratic expert. *"Thou shalt not deny my experience; thou shalt not silence my voice!"* This emphasis on authority of directly having experienced or lived through something has, in the view of Eagleton (1996: 67), become "one of the commonest forms of postmodernist dogma ... the intuitive appeal to 'experience', which is absolute because it cannot be gainsaid." A result of this has been an argument, implicit or explicit, that *only* he or she who has lived through a certain experience can speak authoritatively about it – thus, only people of color can speak authoritatively about race, only women about gender discrimination, only gay people about sexual marginalization, and only women of color about the combined effects of racism and sexism. In this way, in a generally contested environment where most fragments of discourse are criticized, undermined, and subverted, stories of personal experience offer a shelter from criticism, an oasis of trust, an island of tranquility, where a person can speak with uncontestable authority and expect, if not to be respected, at the very least to have their voice heard (Gabriel 2004b).

Why are personal experience and the narrative forms that it assumes coming to be privileged as a source of knowledge? (See further discussion of this issue in this volume, chapter 1, in relation to Strawson's [2004] well-known objections.) It seems to me that one factor is the rise of consumerism and the cult of the customer, which now dominates the thinking and activities of most organizations (du Gay 1996). Consumers can freely air their voices and tell their stories about particular organizations and their offerings on the Internet and in other forums. Organizations can hardly afford to disregard them. Listening to the stories of their consumers (without asking questions or demanding explanations) is widely seen as vital to organizational success in the profit sector, but increasingly in the public and non-profit sectors, too. The success of a product or an organization today increasingly depends not only on what the pundits say about it, but also on the stories told by users. It would seem, then, that in late modernity, the authority of formal rationality and expertise is being challenged or sidestepped as a source of uncontested knowledge, in much the same way that religion and tradition were. Science has undoubtedly long been guilty of disregarding the voice of personal experience. In fields as diverse as medicine, architecture, history, engineering, to say nothing of the social and psychological sciences, the voice of experience was lost in the midst of the authoritative proclamations of the experts. This is rapidly changing now. It may be more broadly connected with what has been described as a therapeutic culture, or even the "Oprah-ization" of culture, the increasing hegemony of an uncontestable confessional discourse that enables the victim to become a survivor through the magic of finding a voice. When the knowledge of experts is routinely devalued (and often for excellent reasons), when knowledge from introspection, divination, or faith is virtually dismissed, and when facts become infinitely accommodating of diverse interpretations and spin, we are left with knowledge and truth based in authentic personal experience, and the different voices that it takes through narration.

14.4   Narratives and Organizational Identities

In recent times, identity has emerged as something of a "master signifier" in many areas of social and organizational studies (Alvesson, Ashcraft, and Thomas 2008). There are many reasons for this, but it must partly be put down to its ability to mutate and fragment, to grow and shrink, to incorporate and shed elements, and to encompass a terrain rife with crises and struggles. Unlike connate terms like self and subjectivity, identity is not tainted by philosophical assumptions of sovereignty and rationality. It easily accommodates a social component while preserving the fundamental qualities of sameness and uniqueness across time.

Identity and its vicissitudes seem well attuned to the temporary, fluid, and porous qualities of late modernity (Coupland and Brown 2012). In particular, today's organizations make ambiguous and contradictory demands on their employees. They frequently demand that they go beyond "doing a job" by buying into their values, brand, and narratives. At the same time, they fail to offer employees the security of stable employment by constantly looking for opportunities to outsource or go off-shore. The project of identity describes well the plight of the individual who is frequently on the move, often called upon to reinvent him- or herself, free from an obligation of life-long loyalty to an employer (or anyone else, for that matter), but who is also expected to fully identify with his/her employer for indeterminate periods of time. The concept also ties in well with the ways that contemporary capitalism creates disciplined and self-disciplined employees who, in seeking to maintain their identities, go beyond the call of duty (Alvesson 2001; Kärreman and Alvesson 2001).

One of the attractive qualities of the concept of identity has been its easy "narrativization" (Brown and Humphreys 2002) – the readiness with which it can be viewed as the product of different narratives that people tell about their experiences (see, e.g., Ezzy 1998; Holstein and Gubrium 2000; Ibarra and Barbulescu 2010; McAdams, Josselson, and Lieblich 2006; Polkinghorne 1996; Somers 1994). Seminal events in a person's life – academic achievements, job moves, emotional attachments and losses, severe illnesses, and so forth – by themselves do not constitute identity. When, however, such experiences are emplotted in meaningful patterns, with triumphs and reversals, struggles and disappointments, they then become the basis of a narrative identity which people then proceed to "live out" (Sims 2003). There is general acknowledgement that narrative identities are provisional and reflexive. They are provisional in that the story of one's life is constantly being recreated, sometimes in small and sometimes in major ways (Ibarra 1999). What was a success in an early story (e.g., a promising job move) may turn out to be a poisoned chalice in a later one (e.g., a move into a toxic work environment); what seemed like a disaster in an early story (e.g., being fired) may turn out to be an opportunity in a later one (e.g., leading to retraining and vastly enhanced work prospects). They are also reflexive – the author of the story and the story's central character co-create each other. At every moment the storyteller creates a protagonist, whose predicaments redefine the storyteller. In telling the story of our lives, we make sense of past events and create a person living in the present as a continuation of the story. This process, frequently referred to as "storying" (Armstrong 1992; Atkinson 1998; Sims 2003), encapsulates how experience is digested, endowed with meaning, and established as the basis of identity.

Storying work is not easy. Kearney likens it to the work of the midwife who delivers a baby:

> From the Greek discovery of human life (bios) as meaningfully interpreted action (praxis) to the most recent descriptions of existence as narrative temporality, there is an abiding recognition that existence is inherently storied. Life is pregnant with stories. It is a nascent plot in search of midwives. (Kearney 2002: 130)

Organizational scholars have been particularly interested in exploring the intertwining of personal identity narratives and organizational narratives, which may range from full identification, to provisional or ambivalent identification, to total disidentification or distancing (Humphreys and Brown 2002). In a study of British paratroopers, for example, Thornborrow and Brown (2009) found that the identities of these soldiers revolved around an idealized conception of the Regiment. Their stories focused on reminiscences of great and fun times they had had and found their way onto websites, documentaries, and films about the Regiment, sustaining a folklore of paratrooper heroism that reinforced the organizational narrative of the Regiment's elite status. These stories were used to socialize and even "test" new recruits, who seamlessly embedded them into their own newfound identities. Studying a global consultancy firm, on the other hand, Costas and Fleming (2009) found that employees consistently sought to distance themselves from their employer by embracing personal narratives of imaginary authenticity allied with narratives critical of their employer. Yet these employees recognized that their putative "real" identities were paradoxically unreal and foreign to their conformist organizational identities, a paradox explained by revisiting the concept of alienation. Less paradoxical are the numerous studies of organizational life in which employees distance themselves from their employers by celebrating organizational cock-ups and absurdities, regaling one another with tales of the incompetence, arrogance, and hubris of their superiors, and generally constructing their identities through stories that cast them as plucky survivors of organizational bedlam (Gabriel 1999).

Rhodes and Brown (2005: 176) note that an important benefit brought by narrative to the study of identity "rests in a consideration of the many possible identities that organizational members can adopt and the ways in which particular identities strive for dominance." Bringing different life episodes in and out of focus, discovering new meanings in them, juxtaposing them with others, or silencing them altogether allows us to drift or mutate from one identity configuration to another, or to entertain identities that are in conflict with themselves, in crisis or disarray. In this way, individuals can entertain multiple identity narratives, revealing different, contrasting or ambivalent levels of identification with different organizations.

In addition to personal identities, narratives have been viewed as tremendously powerful in fostering and developing organizational and group identities. Such "shared" stories raise organizations above the level of "mere bureaucracies," infusing them with life and meaning and, in the view of some authors, turning them into institutions, that is, objects of value. Just as communities and nations need symbolically charged myths and stories to sustain them, so too do organizations. We have already noted Martin et al.'s (1983) "uniqueness paradox," which describes the narratives through which organizations claim to be singular and unique. In this way, many organizations cultivate "foundation myths," stories that mythologize the organization's origins, for example in a founder's encounter with social injustice (Schwabenland 2006) or an entrepreneur's early experiments in his father's garage. Such stories serve both a legitimating and an inspirational function (Lounsbury and Glynn 2001); indeed, consultants draw upon them extensively in their endeavors to strengthen the collective identities and energize the individual identities of their clients.

14.5   The Mythical Dimension in Narratives – Archetypes and Deep Structures

If organizations can be viewed as cultures, it would follow that at least some of their narratives have mythical qualities. These were among the qualities that brought them to the attention of organizational scholars like Mitroff and Kilmann (1975). They highlighted the epic qualities that characterize many managerial stories, often lionizing the manager as a hero capable of extraordinary deeds and achievements. Indeed, it is these mythical qualities that brought narratives to the attention of management gurus who have made epic stories of managers prevailing against the odds part of their stock in trade (Clark and Salaman 1996; Collins 2007). Several of the early contributions on organizational narratives also displayed a keen interest in myths as "popular untruths" (Bowles 1989; Ingersoll and Adams 1986; Rosen 1984) that cannot be easily corrected by appeal to reason and facts. Since then, there has been a steady growth of scholarship on organizational mythologies, although there has been no general agreement about how a myth may be differentiated from stories and narratives.

The relation between story, narrative, and myth remains a source of substantial disagreement and confusion among scholars. Many have given up seeking to distinguish between narrative and story, treating the two interchangeably, after the example of Polkinghorne (1988). Others, however, believe that there is a useful distinction to be drawn between the two. Culler (1981: 169), for example, preserves a distinction between a story's sequencing of events and their actual telling in narrative, or what Gabriel (1991b) terms "recital." A story, according to this view, may be narrated in different ways. Gabriel (2004c), for his part, opts to view narrative as a generic type of text that involves characters and a plot with beginning, middle, and end, then treats stories and myths as two distinct types of narrative. Czarniawska (1997: 78) likewise prefers to restrict story to plotted texts "comprising causally related episodes that culminate in a solution to a problem. Stories usually contain several stages that contribute to a final solution, albeit in a complex way; for example, via false solutions and the creation of new problems." Both Czarniawska and Gabriel emphasize that the power of stories lies not in the "difference between fact and fiction but in a convincing interpretation [that] is convenient for the negotiation of meaning" (Czarniawska 1999: 15). A myth, on the other hand, embodies larger-than-life, sacral meanings, revolving around unique deeds performed by supernatural heroes and addressing the enduring mysteries of life; as Barthes (1973) suggested, myths lose their historical bearings and become timeless. Stories, by contrast, engage with the realities of mundane everyday life in all their commonplace regularity. Thus while a myth can be seen as part of *mythology* – a system of beliefs and narratives that have a cosmic dimension – a story can be seen more usefully as part of *folklore* (in the sense that accountants, computer programmers, and other professionals develop their own folklores).

The mythological qualities of organizational narratives have not attracted as much attention as their sensemaking, identity, and political aspects, but there has been a steady growth of scholarship, culminating in Gabriel's (2004a) and Kostera's (2008a, 2008b, 2008c) edited compilations of mythological explorations of organizational stories. Bowles (1989, 1990), an early pioneer in this area, argued that as religious worldviews are displaced by scientific and managerial ones, mythology loses its sacral associations and assumes, instead, secular analogues. Thus religious myths are supplanted by, among others, managerial myths; these may revolve around the great achievements of superheroes like Steve Jobs or the wicked deeds of super-villains like Kenneth Lay. Other characters that populate these myths may be shrewd tricksters, rescue objects, sleeping beauties, White Knights (Hirsch 1986), or even holy fools (Kets de Vries 1990). Overall, however, Bowles was of the view that such managerial mythologies generally fail to rise much above routine ideology. As a result they are regularly challenged or contested and their ability to generate powerful and enduring symbolic meanings is limited.

While these myths lose their religious associations, they maintain their relations to unconscious symbolic archetypes, they are immune to "correction" by appeal to actual events, and they have wish-fulfilling qualities. Inspired by Jung's (1968) theory of archetypes, Moxnes (1998, 1999) (whose work remains less known outside of his native Norway than it deserves), has argued that the characters of organizational narratives enact deep unconscious roles drawn from a relatively small cast of 12 archetypal or "deep" roles whose origin lies in the essential family – father, mother, son, and daughter. Each of these roles is available as either a positive or negative version, matching the archetypes of the father as God or devil, the mother as queen or witch, the son as crown prince or black sheep, and the daughter as princess or whore. In addition to these, Moxnes identifies two transcendent roles, the hero and the clown who win or lose battles, and two secondary ones, the material helper and the spiritual helper, who support and advise the other characters. These deep roles recur regularly in organizational mythology and real individuals come to occupy these roles in specific narratives, thus drawing on the symbolic power of the original archetype. A leader can then be experienced, after the father archetype, as benevolent God-like father or, alternatively, as a devil; or he or she may be experienced (and feature in stories) as a prince (hero or clown), or indeed in any of the other deep roles.

Gabriel (1997) has approached the topic of organizational leaders through the eyes of the followers who come face to face with them, and has argued that such encounters trigger powerful fantasies in the followers. These are expressed in narratives in which leaders feature as larger-than-life, mythical figures rooted in early life experiences of the primal mother and primal father. Leaders feature in such narratives as all-powerful, all-caring and all-knowing, or, conversely, as impostors, villains, and tyrants. These archetypally light and dark sides of leadership in organizational narratives have resurfaced recently in work done by Kociatkiewicz and Kostera (2010, 2012), who have demonstrated that the concept of a "good manager" is inevitably drawn toward the shadow of tragedy.

14.6   Narratives, Knowledge, and Learning

Narratives and stories describing the feats of organizational leaders and their relations to followers echo various themes of conventional mythology and have attracted the attention of scholars seeking to study their deep symbolic qualities. A rather different genre of organizational narrative, one dealing with mundane everyday issues and offering solutions to the problems of everyday life, has been the focus of scholars interested in the processes of learning and sharing knowledge. These stories are often viewed as the currency of groups of people referred to as "communities of practice," who share similar problems and have complementary skills and outlooks. These can be occupational groups, like airline managers, computer analysts, and academics, but they can also refer to people sharing hobbies or interests, like plane spotters or amateur gardeners, or people who share particular problems, such as medical conditions or forms of discrimination. Wenger (1998), one of the early adopters of the term, has argued that such communities have histories and develop over time; they often work together, but their members do not have a shared task or agenda; they are not accountable to anyone outside of themselves.

Within communities of practice, the distinction between knowledge and action is diminished. Knowledge becomes inscribed in practices that are not the property of any one individual, and much of this knowledge is not scientific, assuming instead the form of *narrative knowledge*, which includes stories, recipes, and direct accounts of experience. Narrative knowledge was viewed as the product of a distinct form of cognitive functioning by Bruner (1986), who distinguished it from logico-scientific knowledge. Each type of knowledge can be seen as generating its own criteria of truthfulness and validity: where logico-scientific knowledge stresses formal evidence and proof, narrative knowledge stresses the authenticity of experience and the verisimilitude of its narratives.

Orr's (1996) ethnographic research on photocopy repair technicians showed that learning from each other's stories was a crucial feature of participation in the technicians' community. Their stories of machine faults and idiosyncrasies provided a far more coherent and pliable guide and toolbox than what could be found in formal manuals and instructions.

> The circulation of stories among the community of technicians is the principal means by which the technicians stay informed of the developing subtleties of machine behaviour in the field. The telling of these narratives demonstrates and shares the technicians' mastery and so both celebrates and creates the technicians' identities as masters of the black arts of dealing with the machines and of the only somewhat less difficult arts of dealing with customers. (Orr 1996: 2)

Where the chief characters in Orr's study are very clearly the machines, a study undertaken by Patriotta (2003) at a Fiat plant in Italy draws attention to the political dimension of narrative knowledge, emphasizing how problem-solving narratives can be viewed as "detective stories" aimed at sharing social practices on how to deal with formal hierarchies and attributing or shifting blame. In this way, Patriotta's work is very helpful in broadening the scope of narrative knowledge beyond technical problem-solving into cultural knowledge or, more specifically, into *phronesis*, the practical wisdom necessary for handling political situations (Tsoukas and Cummings 1997).

Narrative knowledge, as it emerges from current scholarship in organizational studies, should not to be restricted to a kind of traditional or "folk wisdom" surrogate for scientific knowledge. Instead, it is increasingly understood that it is of vital importance for managers, professionals, and even people working at the cutting edge of scientific discovery (Chia 1998; Czarniawska-Joerges 1995; Orr 1996). In this way, physicians at a conference may announce the latest scientific breakthrough in the treatment of diabetes, but in informal discussions may swap stories about the effects of particular treatments on particular patients. Far from being seen as the enemy of science, narrative knowledge may then emerge as its indispensable corollary (Tsoukas 1998; Tsoukas and Hatch 2001) – knowing the rules of the game is one thing, knowing how to play the game effectively is another.

14.7 Conclusion

Organizational stories and narratives are currently attracting the attention of an increasing number of researchers, who are pursuing some of the research avenues identified above in a wide range of organizations. Currently, much of this attention is focused on the connections between storytelling and organizational identity, the relations between public, formal organizational narratives and private, personal stories, the value of storytelling in knowledge transfer and the building of communities of practice, as well as on the emotional dimensions of different narratives and stories. Another rich area of storytelling studies looks at narratives told by and about leaders as part of the wider management of meaning and emotion, and some of this material has generated practical guidebooks and manuals on how leaders may improve the quality of their stories and use them to inspire their followers. As a feature of research methodology (Czarniawska 2004; Gabriel 1998), the collection, interpretation, and analysis of stories has proven very useful in a wide range of contexts and features regularly in academic publications and doctoral dissertations. While the power of narratives to communicate meanings and experiences is increasingly recognized, a considerable part of organizational literature remains tied to positivist traditions that avoid any field material that cannot be standardized and measured or that requires interpretation rather than statistical analysis to reveal its theoretical potential. This situation is likely to persist.

For researchers who are attracted to narratives and storytelling as important aspects of organizational life and valuable means of research, serious difficulties remain. The absence of an agreed-upon definition of narrative and story would not be much of a problem if not for the confusion that it creates when people with different assumptions and definitions try to communicate with each other. A more important difficulty concerns the as yet unanswered question of whether the concepts of story and narrative must themselves be historicized – whether, in other words, we must recognize the ways in which our culture, with its new communication technologies and its increasingly networked publics, has churned out new forms of storytelling (as well as new forms of art, new forms of work, and new forms of social engagement). These new narrative forms may be shorter, terser, or looser than those known to our grandparents, but in some important respects they occupy the same conceptual space as traditional stories and narratives did in the past. These innovations in storytelling reflect intriguing dimensions of our current context, too, and new considerations of narrative elements may be in order. For instance, would the idea of a plotless story be a contradiction in terms, or would it be an eminently sensible story at a time when people no longer need a plot to make sense of a text?

Another enduring tension, in my view, concerns the relation between narratives and facts. Our times have deeply problematized the notion of the "fact," and some scholars are prepared to give it up altogether. Others, including myself, maintain that facts may be plastic but they are not infinitely malleable, and some of them may indeed be utterly unyielding (Taylor 1971). A narrative may convert a defeat into victory and a hero into a fool, but cannot convert a violent death on the battlefield into a peaceful death in bed.

These tensions, along with the enduring difficulties that interpretation presents for the social sciences, pose serious challenges to social researchers taking up the cause of narratives in their research. But the rewards of narrative-based research – its sudden discoveries and unexpected illuminations, its hidden depths and clarifying powers – amply justify the pursuit.

NOTE

1   The differences between these terms and some of the difficulties in defining them are discussed in later sections of this chapter.

REFERENCES

Allan J., G. Fairtlough, and B. Heinzen (2002). *The Power of Tale: Using Narrative for Organisational Success*. Chichester: John Wiley and Sons, Ltd.

Alvesson, M. (2001). Knowledge work: Ambiguity, image and identity. *Human Relations*, 54 (7), pp. 863–886.

Alvesson, M., K.L. Ashcraft, and R. Thomas. (2008). Identity matters: Reflections on the construction of identity scholarship in organization studies. *Organization*, 15 (1), pp. 5–28.

Aristotle. (1963). *The Poetics*. London: Dent.

Armstrong, D.A. (1992). Managing by Storying Around: A New Method of Leadership. New York: Doubleday.

Atkinson, R. (1998). *The Life Story Interview*. London: Sage.

Barthes, R. (1973). *Mythologies*. London: Paladin Books.

Benedict, R. (1931). Folklore. In *The Encyclopedia of the Social Sciences*. Vol. 6. New York: Longman, pp. 288–293.

Benjamin, W. (1968). The storyteller: Reflections on the works of Nikolai Leskov. In *Walter Benjamin: Illuminations*. Edited by Hanna Arendt. London: Jonathan Cape, pp. 83–109.

Bergson, H. (1980). Laughter. In W. Sypher (ed.), *Comedy*. Baltimore, MD: Johns Hopkins University Press, pp. 59–190.

Beynon, H. (1973). *Working for Ford*. London: Allen Lane.

Boje, D.M. (1991). The storytelling organization: A study of story performance in an office-supply firm. *Administrative Science Quarterly*, 36, pp. 106–126.

Boje, D.M. (1995). Stories of the storytelling organization: A postmodern analysis of Disney as "Tamara Land." *Academy of Management Review*, 38 (4), pp. 997–1035.

Boje, D.M. (2001). *Narrative Methods for Organizational and Communication Research*. London: Sage.

Bowles, M.L. (1989). Myth, meaning and work organization. *Organization Studies*, 10 (3), pp. 405–421.

Bowles, M.L. (1990). Recognizing deep structures in organizations. *Organization Studies*, 11 (3), pp. 395–412.

Brown, A.D. (2002). Narrative, politics and legitimacy in an implementation. *Journal of Management Studies*, 35 (1), pp. 35–58.

Brown, A.D., and M. Humphreys. (2002). Nostalgia and narrativization of identity: A Turkish case study. *British Journal of Management*, 13, pp. 141–159.

Bruner, J.S. (1986). *Actual Minds, Possible Worlds*. Cambridge, MA: Harvard University Press.

Chia, R. (1998). From complexity science to complex thinking: Organization as simple location. *Organization*, 5 (3), pp. 341–369.

Clark, T., and G. Salaman. (1996). Telling tales: Management consultancy as the art of storytelling. In D. Grant and C. Oswick (eds.), *Metaphor and Organizations*. London: Sage, pp. 166–184.

Collins, D. (2007). *Narrating the Management Guru: In Search of Tom Peters*. London: Routledge.

Collinson, D. (1988). "Engineering humour": Masculinity, joking and conflict in shop-floor relations. *Organization Studies*, 9 (2), pp. 181–199.

Costas, J., and P. Fleming. (2009). Beyond dis-identification: A discursive approach to self-alienation in contemporary organizations. *Human Relations*, 62 (3), pp. 353–378.

Coupland, C., and A.D. Brown. (2012). Identities in action: Processes and outcomes. *Scandinavian Journal of Management*, 28 (1), pp. 1–4.

Culler, J. (1981). The Pursuit of Signs: Semiotics, Literature, Deconstruction. London: Routledge.

Czarniawska-Joerges, B. (1995). Narration or science? Collapsing the division in organization studies. *Organization*, 2 (1), pp. 11–33.

Czarniawska, B. (1997). *Narrating the Organization: Dramas of Institutional Identity*. Chicago, IL: University of Chicago Press.

Czarniawska, B. (1999). Writing Management: Organization Theory as a Literary Genre. Oxford: Oxford University Press.

Czarniawska, B. (2004). *Narratives in Social Science Research*. London: Sage.

Czarniawska, B. (2008). Humiliation: A standard organizational product? *Critical Perspectives on Accounting*, 19 (7), pp. 1034–1053.

Davies, C. (1988). Stupidity and rationality: Jokes from the iron cage. In C. Powell and G.E.C. Paton (eds.), *Humour in Society*. London: Macmillan, pp. 1–32.

Denning, S. (2005). The Leader's Guide to Storytelling: Mastering the Art and Discipline of Business Narrative. San Francisco, CA: Jossey-Bass.

du Gay, P. (1996). *Consumption and Identity at Work*. London: Sage.

Dyer, W.G., and A.L. Wilkins. (1991). Better stories, not better constructs, to generate better theory: A rejoinder to Eisenhardt. *Academy of Management Review*, 16 (3), pp. 613–619.

Eagleton, T. (1996). *The Illusions of Postmodernism*. Oxford: Blackwell.

Ezzy, D. (1998). Theorizing narrative identity: Symbolic interactionism and hermeneutics. *Sociological Quarterly*, 39 (2), pp. 239–252.

Fleming, P., and A. Spicer. (2003). Working at a cynical distance: Implications for power, subjectivity and resistance. *Organization*, 10 (1), pp. 157–179.

Gabriel, Y. (1991a). On organizational stories and myths: Why it is easier to slay a dragon than to kill a myth. *International Sociology*, 6 (4), pp. 427–442.

Gabriel, Y. (1991b). Turning facts into stories and stories into facts: A hermeneutic exploration of organizational folklore. *Human Relations*, 44 (8), pp. 857–875.

Gabriel, Y. (1995). The unmanaged organization: Stories, fantasies and subjectivity. *Organization Studies*, 16 (3), pp. 477–501.

Gabriel, Y. (1997). Meeting God: When organizational members come face to face with the supreme leader. *Human Relations*, 50 (4), pp. 315–342.

Gabriel, Y. (1998). The uses of stories. In G. Symon and C. Cassell (eds.), *Qualitative Methods and Analysis in Organizational Research*. London: Sage, pp. 135–160.

Gabriel, Y. (1999). Beyond happy families: A critical re-evaluation of the control-resistance-identity triangle. *Human Relations*, 52 (2), pp. 179–203.

Gabriel, Y. (2000). Storytelling in Organizations: Facts, Fictions, Fantasies. Oxford: Oxford University Press.

Gabriel, Y. (ed.). (2004a). Myths, Stories and Organizations: Premodern Narratives for Our Times. Oxford: Oxford University Press.

Gabriel, Y. (2004b). The narrative veil: Truth and untruths in storytelling. In Y. Gabriel (ed.), *Myths, Stories and Organizations: Premodern Narratives for Our Times*. Oxford: Oxford University Press, pp. 17–31.

Gabriel, Y. (2004c). Narratives, stories, texts. In D. Grant, C. Hardy, C. Oswick, and L.L. Putnam (eds.), *The Sage Handbook of Organizational Discourse*. London: Sage, pp. 61–79.

Georgakopoulou, A. (2006a). The other side of the story: Towards a narrative analysis of narratives-in-interaction. *Discourse Studies*, 8 (2), pp. 235–257.

Georgakopoulou, A. (2006b). Thinking big with small stories in narrative and identity analysis. *Narrative Inquiry*, 16 (1), pp. 122–130.

Hirsch, P.M. (1986). From ambushes to golden parachutes: Corporate takeovers as an instance of cultural framing and institutional integration. *American Journal of Sociology*, 91 (4), pp. 800–837.

Hirschman, A.O. (1970). Exit, Voice, and Loyalty: Responses to Decline in Firms, Organizations, and States. Cambridge, MA: Harvard University Press.

Hobbes, T. (1651/1962). Leviathan: Or the Matter, Forme and Power of a Commonwealth Ecclesiastical and Civil. London: Collier-Macmillan.

Holstein, J.A., and J.F. Gubrium. (2000). *The Self We Live By: Narrative Identity in a Postmodern World*. Oxford: Oxford University Press.

Humphreys, M., and A.D. Brown. (2002). Narratives of organizational identity and identification: A case study of hegemony and resistance. *Organization Studies*, 23 (3), pp. 421–447.

Ibarra, H. (1999). Provisional selves: Experimenting with image and identity in professional adaptation. *Administrative Science Quarterly*, 44, pp. 764–791.

Ibarra, H., and R. Barbulescu. (2010). Identity as narrative: Prevalence, effectiveness, and consequences of narrative identity work in macro work role transitions. *Academy of Management Review*, 35 (1), pp. 135–154.

Ingersoll, V.H., and G.B. Adams. (1986). Beyond the organizational boundaries: Exploring the managerial myth. *Administration and Society*, 18 (3), pp. 105–136.

Jung, C.G. (1968). *The Archetypes and the Collective Unconscious*. Vol. 9. London: Routledge.

Kärreman, D., and M. Alvesson. (2001). Making newsmakers: Conversational identity at work. *Organization Studies*, 22 (1), pp. 59–89.

Kearney, R. (2002). *On Stories*. London: Routledge.

Kets de Vries, M.F.R. (1990). The organizational fool: Balancing a leader's hubris. *Human Relations*, 43 (8), pp. 751–770.

Kociatkiewicz, J., and M. Kostera. (2010). Experiencing the shadow: Organizational exclusion and denial within experience economy. *Organization*, 17 (2), pp. 257–282.

Kociatkiewicz, J., and M. Kostera. (2012). The good manager: An archetypical quest for morally sustainable leadership. *Organization Studies*, 33 (7), pp. 861–878.

Kostera, M. (2008a). *Mythical Inspirations for Organizational Realities*. Basingstoke, UK: Palgrave Macmillan.

Kostera, M. (2008b). *Organizational Epics and Sagas: Tales of Organizations*. Basingstoke, UK: Palgrave Macmillan.

Kostera, M. (2008c). Organizational Olympians: Heroes and Heroines of Organizational Myths. Basingstoke, UK: Palgrave Macmillan.

Linstead, S. (1985). Jokers wild: The importance of humour in the maintenance of organizational culture. *Sociological Review*, 33 (4), pp. 741–767.

Lounsbury, M., and M.A. Glynn. (2001). Cultural entrepreneurship: Stories, legitimacy, and the acquisition of resources. *Strategic Management Journal*, 22 (6–7), pp. 545–564.

Martin, J., M.S. Feldman, M.J. Hatch, and S.B. Sitkin. (1983). The uniqueness paradox in organizational stories. *Administrative Science Quarterly*, 28, pp. 438–453.

McAdams, D.P., R. Josselson, and A. Lieblich. (2006). *Identity and Story: Creating Self in Narrative*. Washington, DC: American Psychological Association.

McConkie, M.L., and R.W. Boss. (1986). Organizational stories: One means of moving the informal organization during change efforts. *Public Administration Quarterly*, 10 (2), pp. 189–205.

Mitroff, I.I., and R.H. Kilmann. (1975). Stories managers tell: A new tool for organizational problem solving. *Management Review*, 67 (7), pp. 18–28.

Moxnes, P. (1998). Fantasies and fairy tales in groups and organizations: Bion's basic assumptions and the deep roles. *European Journal of Work and Organizational Psychology*, 7 (3), pp. 283–298.

Moxnes, P. (1999). Deep roles: Twelve primordial roles of mind and organization. *Human Relations*, 52 (11), pp. 1427–1444.

O'Leary, M. (2003). From paternalism to cynicism: Narratives of a newspaper company. *Human Relations*, 56 (6), pp. 685–704.

Orr, J.E. (1996). *Talking about Machines: An Ethnography of a Modern Job*. Ithaca, NY: ILR Press/Cornell.

Patriotta, G. (2003). Sensemaking on the shop floor: Narratives of knowledge in organizations. *Journal of Management Studies*, 40 (2), pp. 349–375.

Pelzer, P. (2004). The Flying Dutchman and the discontents of modernity. In Y. Gabriel (ed.), *Myths, Stories and Organizations: Premodern Narratives for Our Times*. Oxford: Oxford University Press, pp. 137–150.

Peters, T.S., and R.H. Waterman. (1982). *In Search of Excellence*. New York: Harper and Row.

Polkinghorne, D.E. (1988). *Narrative Knowing and the Human Sciences*. Albany: State University of New York Press.

Polkinghorne, D.E. (1996). Explorations of narrative identity. *Psychological Inquiry*, 7, pp. 363–367.

Pollert, A. (1981). *Girls, Wives, Factory Lives*. London: Macmillan.

Rhodes, C., and A.D. Brown. (2005). Narrative, organizations and research. *International Journal of Management Reviews*, 7 (3), pp. 167–188.

Rosen, M. (1984). Myth and reproduction: The conceptualization of management theory, method and practice. *Journal of Management*, 21 (3), pp. 303–322.

Schwabenland, C. (2006). *Stories, Visions, and Values in Voluntary Organisations*. Aldershot, UK: Ashgate.

Simmons, A. (2002). The Story Factor: Inspiration, Influence, and Persuasion through the Art of Storytelling. London: Perseus.

Sims, D. (2003). Between the millstones: A narrative account of the vulnerability of middle managers' storying. *Human Relations*, 56 (10), pp. 1195–1211.

Somers, M.R. (1994). The narrative constitution of identity: A relational and network approach. *Theory and Society*, 23 (5), pp. 605–649.

Strawson, G. (2004). Against narrativity. *Ratio*, 17 (4), pp. 428–452.

Taylor, C. (1971). Interpretation and the sciences of man. *Review of Metaphysics*, 25 (1), pp. 3–51.

Theodosius, C. (2008). *Emotional Labour in Health Care: The Unmanaged Heart of Nursing*. Abingdon: Routledge.

Thornborrow, T., and A.D. Brown. (2009). "Being regimented": Aspiration, discipline and identity work in the British Parachute Regiment. *Organization Studies*, 30 (4), pp. 355–376.

Tsoukas, H. (1998). Forms of knowledge and forms of life in organized contexts. In R.C. Chia (ed.), *In the Realm of Organization: Essays for Robert Cooper*. London: Routledge, pp. 44–68.

Tsoukas, H., and S. Cummings. (1997). Marginalization and recovery: The emergence of Aristotelian themes in organization studies. *Organization Studies*, 18 (4), pp. 655–683.

Tsoukas, H., and M.J. Hatch. (2001). Complex thinking, complex practice: The case for a narrative approach to organizational complexity. *Human Relations*, 54 (8), pp. 979–1013.

Weick, K.E. (1979). *The Social Psychology of Organizing*. Reading, MA: Addison-Wesley.

Weick, K.E. (1995). *Sensemaking in Organizations*. London: Sage.

Wenger, E. (1998). *Communities of Practice: Learning, Meaning and Identity*. Cambridge: Cambridge University Press.

Westwood, R., and S. Linstead (eds.). (2001). *The Language of Organization*. London: Sage.

Wilkins, A.L. (1984). The creation of company cultures: The role of stories in human resource systems. *Human Resource Management*, 23, pp. 41–60.

Wilkins, A.L., and W.G. Ouchi. (1983). Efficient cultures: Exploring the relationship between culture and organizational performance. *Administrative Science Quarterly*, 28, pp. 468–481.

Witten, M. (1993). Narrative and the culture of obedience at the workplace. In D.K. Mumby (ed.), *Narrative and Social Control: Critical Perspectives*. Newbury Park, CA: Sage, pp. 97–118.

15 Narrative, Institutional Processes, and Gendered Inequalities

SUSAN EHRLICH

15.1 Introduction

Investigations of narrative inequality have typically been conducted in the context of institutions because, as Linde (2001) so eloquently states, "narratives (and narrators) can get mangled at the boundaries of powerful institutions" (520). Here Linde is describing what can happen when individuals interact with institutions and representatives of those institutions: their stories are often altered so that they conform to "institutionally specified form[s]" – forms that correspond to the institution's assessment of what is relevant and meaningful. In doctor–patient interactions, for example, patients may articulate their problems in what Mishler (1984) calls the "voice of the lifeworld" yet doctors will transform these descriptions into technical and medical categories, or what Mishler terms "the voice of medicine." In a similar way, Conley and O'Barr (1990, 2005), in their study of narratives produced in small claims courts, show that the law prefers narratives that conform to the logic of the law: lay litigants who structured their claims for compensation in relation to the violation of legal rules and procedures (in "rule-oriented" accounts) – as opposed to the violation of social norms and obligations (in "relational" accounts) – were more comprehensible to judges and more likely to receive rulings in their favor. According to Conley and O'Barr, judges viewed "relational" litigants as "hard to follow, irrational, and even crazy" and, as a result, they had "a harder time gaining access to justice than [did] their rule-oriented counterparts" (Conley and O'Barr 2005: 73). In Linde's terms, while "relational" litigants may not have had their narratives "mangled," arguably the litigants themselves were "mangled" to the extent that their narratives were viewed as incoherent and their claims for compensation deemed unwarranted.

Conley and O'Barr were not only interested in the linguistic characteristics of institutionally privileged discourse genres, however; they also attempted to determine how social power was implicated in their production. And, in keeping with much other work on narratives in institutions, they argue that the ability to recount

The Handbook of Narrative Analysis, First Edition. Edited by Anna De Fina and Alexandra Georgakopoulou.
© 2015 John Wiley & Sons, Inc. Published 2019 by John Wiley & Sons, Inc.

narratives in institutionally preferred ways is intimately connected to social power. In the context of small claims courts, "the crucial factor associated with this skill" seems to be class-related: familiarity with "the culture of business and law" is a good predictor of people's capacity to make claims for compensation using rule-oriented accounts (Conley and O'Barr 2005: 73). In asylum interviews, Blommaert (2005) and Maryns (2005) have shown how linguistic, cultural, and racial inequalities can have a profound impact on asylum-seekers' ability to produce narratives that meet the standards of truth and reliability required by the institution and necessary for a successful outcome under the Geneva Convention. And in job interviews, Roberts and Campbell (2005) argue that foreign-born interviewees in the United Kingdom are disadvantaged because they lack the linguistic capital to recount "bureaucratically processable" narratives, although, according to the authors, such linguistic skills "may have little bearing on their ability to do the job interviewed for" (68). In this chapter, I am also interested in social inequalities and the production of narratives within institutions; however, here my focus is on *gendered* inequalities as they are reflected and reproduced in *the legal system*.

The courtroom, and legal settings more generally, typically involve a multiplicity of often competing and conflicting narratives told by a multiplicity of tellers (Harris 2001). In the courtroom alone, given the adversarial nature of the Anglo-American common law system, various narratives will emerge as the prosecution and the defense each attempt to put forward an account of the events that will support their own clients' interests. In the legal system as a whole, narratives "travel" (Blommaert 2005: 78), or shift across contexts – for example, when stories told in court move out of the trial and are discussed by juries or represented in the appellate decisions of judges. Crucially, such retellings, as will become evident, inevitably involve changes in meaning. While the investigation of narratives in an institution such as the legal system could, in theory, describe in a somewhat depoliticized manner the variations that exist in such narratives, this is not the way that most research has proceeded. Rather, scholars who approach the law from a "critical" perspective, like Conley and O'Barr, have generally assumed that lay participants in legal settings do not have equal access to discursive and interactional resources, nor do they have the specialized knowledge of the institution that institutional representatives possess. This asymmetry has a number of consequences. First, not all narratives or all narrative styles/genres are considered to have the same value and legitimacy in the eyes of the law (as was discussed above); second, the narratives produced by lay people often do not retain their original meanings as they circulate within legal institutions.

In the remainder of this chapter, I consider work that has pursued the second of these themes in relation to women's accounts of violence told in legal and quasi-legal settings. Specifically, I aim to demonstrate how such narratives can, in Linde's (2001) words, be "mangled": their original meanings can be lost as they are shaped and constrained by institutional and ideological forces and appropriated by authoritative institutional actors. Moreover, I argue that these types of reshapings and appropriations are not innocent acts; rather, as Georgakopoulou (2011: 402) argues, they are informed by and, thus, can "shed … light on … wider social relations of power and control" – in this particular instance, wider patterns of gendered inequalities. Following De Fina and

Georgakopoulou (2012), I have divided the chapter into two major sections. The first considers the recasting and reformulations of "original" narratives in what De Fina and Georgakopoulou (2012: 133) call "their [original] occasions of production" – in this case, courtroom trials. That is, the first section looks at negotiations between lay litigants and lawyers as litigants attempt to tell their stories within the discursive constraints imposed by the courtroom. But the interactional work performed by lawyers is not the only means through which witness narratives can be altered. Once extracted from "their [original] occasions of production," such stories can be reinserted into written documents, quoted and/or summarized by participants not involved in the original speech events, and, in the process, can undergo significant transformations in meaning, "often deeply different from the ones performed in the initial act of communication" (Blommaert 2005: 76). Thus, the second major section of the chapter focuses on the "textual travels" (Heffer, Rock, and Conley 2013) of narratives as they move out of their original speech events and are recontextualized in other settings in the legal system. In keeping with Blommaert's comments above, the emphasis is on the "deeply different" meanings that can accompany such movements.

15.2 Narratives in Their Original Occasions of Production: The Courtroom

Within the adversarial context of the Anglo-American legal system, two parties come together formally, typically with representation (e.g., lawyers), to present their versions of the dispute to a third party (e.g., judge, jury, tribunal) who hears the evidence, applies the appropriate laws or regulations, and determines the guilt or innocence of the parties. Lawyers have as their task, then, that of convincing the adjudicating body that their (i.e., their client's) narrative is the most credible. However, as Atkinson and Drew (1979: 70) note, trial discourse is conducted predominantly through a series of question-answer sequences. In other words, apart from making opening and closing arguments, lawyers use *questions* to elicit witnesses' stories. Such questions are designed to build a credible narrative in support of their own clients' interests, and to challenge, weaken, and/or cast doubt on the opposing parties' version of events.

The turn-taking system characteristic of the courtroom, and of other kinds of institutional settings more generally, has been termed *turn-type pre-allocation* by Atkinson and Drew (1979) in recognition of the fact that the types of turns participants can take, or typically take, are predetermined by their institutional roles. In courtrooms, as noted above, lawyers have the right to initiate and allocate turns by asking questions of witnesses; however, the reverse is not generally true: witnesses are obligated to answer questions or run the risk of being sanctioned by the court. And this question-answer *interactional asymmetry* has been shown to have significant implications for whose formulations of events emerge in these kinds of settings. Drew and Heritage (1992: 49), for example, note that answerers, frequently lay persons, are afforded little opportunity to initiate talk and thus the institutional representatives as questioners are allowed to "gain a measure of control over the introduction of topics and hence of the 'agenda' for the occasion." Referring to legal settings specifically, Atkinson and Drew (1979: 180) have argued that cross-examining lawyers will design their questions so as to repeat some aspects of the cross-examined witnesses' version of events, while "retaining the crucial features" of their clients' own version of events. Indeed, because the narratives that are elicited in trial discourse are shaped to a large extent by the questions lawyers ask of witnesses (e.g., their controlling of topics, their selective reformulating of witnesses' responses, etc.), Cotterill (2002: 149) contends that courtroom narratives are best characterized as "dual-authored texts," "with the emphasis on the voice of the lawyer as the primary and authoritative teller." Cotterill's comments here are significant for what they reveal about the complex production format (Goffman 1981) of trial settings. In Goffman's terms, while lawyers, particularly cross-examining lawyers, may be the "authors" of witnesses' testimony (i.e., they are responsible to a large extent for the formulations of events), it is witnesses who are understood as the "principals" of their testimony (i.e., they are understood as the individuals whose opinions are expressed). That is, in spite of the fact that witness narratives are shaped and altered by lawyers' questions, this mediating role of lawyers is hidden by a linguistic ideology that views witnesses as solely responsible for their testimony – what Trinch (2003: 50) calls "the ideology of narrative ownership." As the work of Harvey Sacks has shown, the right to tell stories is "related to first-hand experience and witness status. Thus, a person who has taken part in an event … is in principle entitled to tell a story about it" (De Fina and Georgakopoulou 2012: 107). And who could be more entitled to recount a narrative of sexual or domestic violence than the victim/survivor of that violence? Complainants in these kinds of legal cases, then, are doubly disadvantaged: they lose control of their narratives, especially in cross-examination, yet the notion that they are the only ones entitled to narrate their experiences of violence obscures the co-constructed nature of their narratives, namely that cross-examining lawyers, in Cotterill's words, are the "primary" tellers of these "dual-authored texts." But what, specifically, is obscured or naturalized when the stories that emerge in these contexts are viewed as the sole product of complainants? As the next section attempts to show, when lawyers, through their questioning, control the way that events come to be constituted in the courtroom, then they also control the ideological frameworks and the "sociocultural inferences" (Matoesian 2013: 705) generated by such frameworks.

15.2.1   *Gendered ideologies: Sexual assault vs. consensual sex*

In spite of widespread reform to sexual assault and rape statutes over the last four decades in Canada and the United States, cultural mythologies surrounding rape continue to inform the adjudication of rape trials (e.g., Coates, Bavelas, and Gibson 1994; Coates and Wade 2004; Ehrlich 2007; Tiersma 2007). Tiersma (2007: 93), for example, makes the point that within the context of rape law, juries and judges must often draw inferences in determining whether a woman has consented to sex or not and these inferences may be based "on questionable or offensive (some would say: patriarchal) assumptions." Indeed, both Ehrlich (2001) and Matoesian (2001) have demonstrated the way that defense lawyers in rape trials can strategically activate these kinds of "questionable or offensive … assumptions" through their questioning, thereby undermining the credibility of complainants. Ehrlich (2001), for instance, argues that the utmost resistance standard – an outdated statutory rule that required a rape victim's "utmost resistance" in order for rape to have occurred – is invoked in excerpt 1 below (and more generally in this trial) when a defense lawyer (Q) questions a complainant, MB, about her efforts to end the sexual aggression of the accused, Matt.

Excerpt 1

(1) MB: And then we got back into bed and Matt immediately started again and

(2)   then I said to Bob, "Bob where do you get these persistent friends?"

(3) Q: Why did you even say that? You wanted to get Bob's attention?

(4) MB: I assumed that Bob talked to Matt in the hallway and told him to knock it

(5)   off.

(6) Q: You assumed?

(7) MB: He was talking to him and came back in and said everything was all right.

(8) Q: Bob said that?

(9) MB: Yes.

(10) Q: But when you made that comment, you wanted someone to know, you

(11)   wanted Bob to know that this was a signal that Matt was doing it again?

(12) MB: Yes.

(13) Q: A mixed signal, ma'am, I suggest?

(14) MB: To whom?

(15) Q: What would you have meant by, "Where do you get these persistent

(16)   friends?"

(17) MB: Meaning Bob he's doing it again, please help me.

(18) Q: Why didn't you say, "Bob, he was doing it again, please help me?"

(19) MB: Because I was afraid Matt would get mad.

In this example, MB recounts one of several incidents in which she attempted to elicit the help of Bob, a friend of the accused, in order to curtail the accused's sexual advances. In line 2, we see that MB reports saying "Bob where do you get these persistent friends?" Not only is this utterance characterized as a "mixed signal" (line 13) by the defense lawyer, it is also problematized when the lawyer poses the question "Why didn't you say 'Bob, he was doing it again, please help me?'" That is, the question asked in line 18 is a negative interrogative, a type of interrogative that Heritage (2002: 1432) argues is often used to "frame negative or critical propositions." This means that the defense lawyer is communicating a negative and/or critical attitude towards the fact that MB did not produce the utterance "He [Matt] is doing it again, please help me" and, in a more general way, is suggesting that MB has not expressed her resistance directly and forcefully enough. What is problematic about the resistance standard invoked by the defense lawyer's questioning in excerpt 1 is the fact that it downplays and obscures the unequal power dynamics that often characterize male–female sexual relations. For example, in line 19, MB explains that her seemingly indirect utterance was motivated by her fear that a more direct approach would have provoked Matt's anger.

Thus, while MB's act of resistance could have been framed as an intelligent and thought-ful response to a man's escalating sexual violence, it instead was characterized as an inadequate act of resistance. This characterization, in turn, has the effect of generating inferences (for the benefit of the judge and/or jury) that the complainant has not resisted "to the utmost" and, correspondingly, that rape has not occurred. In other words, there is an inconsistency established between the complainant's narrative of sexual assault and her behavior, which is (re)framed in the defense lawyer's questioning as lacking in appropriate resistance.

The interactional means by which inconsistency is created in witness testimony is a major theme of Matoesian's (2001) analysis of the William Kennedy Smith rape trial.[1] In Part I of his book, Matoesian focuses on some of the inconsistencies in "logic" imputed to the testimonies of the complainant, Patricia Bowman, and her primary witness, Ann Mercer, during their cross-examination by the defense attorney, Roy Black. While Matoesian notes that the exposing of inconsistencies in witness testimony is a *generic* trial practice designed to undermine the credibility of witnesses, in this particular case he argues that the "logical" standard against which the two women's testimonies were measured – and rendered inconsistent – was not a gender-neutral standard, but rather a male standard of sexuality, what he terms "the patriarchal logic of sexual rationality." In other words, the defense lawyer, Roy Black, activated (patriarchal) cultural frames in his questioning, that, like the utmost resistance standard discussed by Ehrlich, called into question the complainant's, Patricia Bowman's, narrative that William Kennedy Smith had raped her. Consider excerpt 2 below:

Excerpt 2

(1) RB: And you were interested in *him* as a person.

        (0.9)

(2) PB: He seemed like a nice *person.*

        (0.5)

(3) RB: Interested enough that tuh- (0.5) to give him a ride home.

        (0.9)

(4) PB: I saw no-(.) no *problem* with giving him a ride *home* as I stated because it

(5)   was up the street it wasn't out of my *way* (.) he hadn't *tou::ched* me (.) I felt no

(6)   *threats* from him and I assumed that there would be *security* at the *home.*

        (0.5)

(7) RB: You were interested *enough* (.) that you were *ho:::ping* that he would ask

(8)   for your pho::ne *number.*

        (0.7)

(9) PB: That was *later.*

        (0.7)

(10) RB: Interested enough (.) tha:t when he said to come into the *hou::se* you

(11)   went into the *hou::se* with him.

        (1.6)

(12) PB: I (woul-) it wasn't necessarily an interest with *William* (.) it was an

(13)   interest in the *house*.

           (0.6)

(14) RB: Interested enough that uh:: at sometime during that period of time *you*

(15)   *took off your panty hose?*

           (1.2)

(16) PB: I still don't *know* how my panty hose came off.

In this excerpt, Roy Black's questions make available to the jury a number of propositions that are confirmed by Patricia Bowman: that she gave the defendant a ride home, that she went into the house with him, and that she hoped he would ask for her telephone number. (Note that while Bowman acknowledges that her panty hose came off, she doesn't confirm the proposition that she was the one to take them off.) However, it is not just Bowman's acknowledgement of these events that is of interest to Matoesian; of more importance, Matoesian argues, is the semantic connection created among these events through the defense lawyer's use of syntactic parallelism. For example, an element of the main clause of line 1, interested, is incorporated into the syntactic frame, *interested enough* plus complementizer, and then this syntactic frame is repeated four times (in lines 3, 7–8, 10–11, and 14–15), each time with a different complement clause. According to Matoesian, this syntactic repetition "unifies and organizes otherwise disparate particulars of evidence into a coherent, gestalt-like pattern of persuasive parallelism" (2001: 57). That is, events that might otherwise not appear to be connected to each other become linked. And, crucially, the fact that these "linked" events seem more compatible with a narrative of consensual sex than with one of rape amplifies and intensifies the "inconsistency" in Patricia Bowman's testimony. Although acquaintance rape of the type that Kennedy Smith was charged with is much more common than stranger rape (Russell 1982, 1984), Estrich (1987) has argued that the American legal system, and the culture at large, treats sexual violence committed by strangers in singular, random acts much more seriously than sexual violence committed by men women know, men women meet in a bar, and/or men women are intimate with. According to this logic – what Matoesian would no doubt call "the patriarchal logic of sexual rationality" – acknowledging sexual interest in a man, as Patricia Bowman seems to do under the influence of Roy Black's questioning techniques, is tantamount to acknowledging a narrative of consensual sex, not one of rape.

Taken together, the work of Ehrlich and Matoesian demonstrates how defense lawyers in rape trials can strategically exploit cultural ideologies about what constitutes a "genuine" and "legitimate" rape victim and, in so doing, undermine the credibility of complainants who do not appear to conform to these ideas (e.g., victims who do not resist their perpetrators "forcefully enough" or who show an interest in their perpetrators prior to the sexual aggression). And, ultimately, in undermining the credibility of complainants, defense lawyers cast doubt on and call into question the allegations, or narratives, of the complainants – that they have been victims of sexual violence.

The adversarial nature of the Anglo-American common law system means that the narratives and cultural frames mobilized by one side in a courtroom contest can be challenged and resisted by the opposing side. Drew (1992) provides an example of this kind of resistance in a rape trial where he focuses on the rape victim's answers to a cross-examining lawyer's questions. While answerers in courtroom contexts have generally been viewed as lacking in interactional control, Drew's analysis shows how the complainant (i.e., the rape victim) in this particular trial often produced "alternative descriptions" in her answers – descriptions that contested the cross-examining lawyer's version of events. That is, rather than providing "yes" or "no" answers to the cross-examining lawyer's yes-no questions (what Raymond [2003] calls type-conforming answers to questions), the complainant provided competing descriptions that trans-formed the lawyer's damaging characterizations into more benign ones. In excerpt 3 below, for example, the cross-examining lawyer, through the use of declarative ques-tions, attempts to represent the events that preceded the alleged rape as precursors to a consensual sexual interaction. (This is similar to the strategy adopted by Roy Black in excerpt 2.)

Excerpt 3

(1) A: Well yuh had some uh (p) (.) uh fairly lengthy

(2)   conversations with the defendant uh: did'n you?

(3)   (0.7)

(4) A: On that evening uv February fourteenth?

(5)   (1.0)

(6) W: We:ll we were all talkin.

(7)   (0.8)

(8) A: Well *you* kne:w, at that ti:me. that the

(9)   defendant was. *in*:terested (.) in *you* (.)

(10)   did'n you?

(11)   (1.3)

(12) W: *He*: asked me how I'(d) bi*n*: en

(13)   (1.1)

(14) W: J- just stuff like that

Although the lawyer's questions in lines 1–2 and 8–10 suggest that there was a close-ness or intimacy developing between the defendant and the complainant, Drew argues that the complainant provides answers that depict a lack of intimacy between the com-plainant and the defendant, that is, a scene in which there were a number of people who *were all talkin* and in which the defendant issued a greeting that was more friendly than intimate. But why, as Matoesian (2013: 711) says, does the rape victim dispute the lawyer's characterization of the events with her alternative descriptions? In keeping with the findings of Estrich discussed above, the rape victim seems to be rejecting the suggestion that there was any intimacy developing between the two because to do so would be to activate an acquaintance rape scenario or frame for understanding the events under investigation. That is, the complainant seems to orient to the probability that activating such a scenario would be taken as acknowledging her consent to the sexual acts under investigation and, by extension, a narrative of consensual sex.

15.2.2 Determining the "official story": Truth, plausibility, and ideology

Given the presence of competing and contradictory narratives within the courtroom, Cotterill (2003: 25) has argued that "the name often given to the jury in adversarial trial procedure, that of the 'factfinder', is actually something of a misnomer." According to Cotterill, juries do not determine the facts; rather they "adjudicate between more and less plausible narrative accounts." Capps and Ochs (1995: 21) make similar observations about jury members in trials:

> On the basis of divergent versions of events, jury members construct a narrative that is plausible and coherent in their eyes, but the truth is beyond their reach. In this sense, rendering a verdict is analogous not to ascertaining the facts but to determining an official story.

For both Cotterill and Capps and Ochs, then, "the facts" and "the truth" are "beyond the … reach" of juries; rather, plausibility seems to be crucial to the determination of "an official story."

While it is clear that questions of credibility and plausibility are particularly germane to the courtroom, given that adjudicators have to decide among competing narratives, research on oral narratives of personal experience has also been concerned with such issues. Labov (1997), for example, in his revision to the narrative model originally proposed by Labov and Waletzky (1967), claimed that there is an inverse relationship between reportability and credibility. That is, the more reportable an event is (i.e., the more unusual it is), "the more effort the narrator must devote to establishing credibility" (Labov 1997: 407) and, for Labov, this was best achieved through an objective rendering of events. Labov's claims notwithstanding, there is definitely no consensus on the idea that oral narratives of personal experience need to involve objectivity and truth in order to "command the attention … of their audience" (Labov 1997: 415) as Labov believed they did. Ochs and Capps (2001), in their book on everyday storytelling, for example, suggest that a highly tellable story could be one in which a narrator recounts an unusual incident (a reportable event in Labov's terms), but does it in a way "that captures the audience's interest and appreciation and draws them into his or her perspective" (34).

Within the context of the legal system, Capps and Ochs (1995: 20) also point to the power of a narrator's rhetorical skills in the production of successful stories: they suggest that, while the internal consistency and external corroboration of stories told in the courtroom are important to their effectiveness,[2] of equal importance is the "rhetorical prowess" of the witnesses and lawyers who tell the stories. Matoesian's (2001) analysis of Roy Black's "rhetorical prowess" in the William Kennedy Smith trial certainly supports this idea. (Recall that the jury in this trial acquitted Smith of his rape charges.) According to Matoesian (2001: 31), the testimonies of Patricia Bowman and Ann Mercer were not "that inconsistent"; rather, "Black knew how to *create* inconsistency through powerful and affective forms of language, much more so than prosecutor Lasch" (emphasis in original). But Black's success was not solely the result of his impressive oratorical skills. Matoesian argues that "persuasive forms of language" and ideology worked together to create an interpretive lens "through which jurors evaluate[d] legal issues such as consent, coercion, and violence." In particular, when Black successfully created inconsistencies in the testimony of Patricia Bowman and Ann Mercer, Bowman's witness, he did so by measuring their behavior against "the expectations of patriarchal ideology governing victim identity" (Matoesian 2001: 31). For example, through the lens of "patriarchal ideology," the characterization of Patricia Bowman as (initially) sexually interested in William Kennedy Smith (represented in excerpt 2 above) was inconsistent with her claim that she was a victim of rape. Put somewhat differently, Black managed to tap into the jury's "questionable or offensive (some would say: patriarchal) assumptions" (Tiersma 2007: 93) about sexual violence and consent, and Bowman's behavior was then assessed in relation to such assumptions.

The idea that gendered ideologies are at play when adjudicators decide between conflicting stories in the courtroom is also evident in the work of Ehrlich (2007). Ehrlich analyzed both the trial proceedings and the judicial opinions of a 1995 Canadian rape trial, *Her Majesty the Queen v. Ewanchuk*, where two lower courts acquitted the accused of sexual assault, after which the Supreme Court of Canada overturned this acquittal and convicted the accused. The two lower courts acquitted the accused because they claimed that the complainant "implied consent" through her behavior, or what they termed her "conduct." Of special significance was the fact that both lower courts found the complainant credible; in particular, they found her expressions of fear vis-à-vis the accused to be genuine. In spite of finding these expressions of fear credible, however, both courts also commented in their decisions that she did not communicate her fear to the accused. As the trial judge (i.e., the lowest court) said in his ruling, for example, the complainant "was 'frozen' by a fear of force" and "successfully kept all her thoughts, emotions, and speculations deep within herself." Ehrlich points out that the picture emerging from this description of the complainant is one of passivity: that is, a woman who keeps all her thoughts and emotions "deep within herself" and is "frozen" is clearly not initiating sexual activity nor, arguably, is she responding in any active way to the man's sexual advances. However, as indicated above, it was this kind of conduct on the part of the complainant that led the two lower courts to conclude that she "implied consent" to the accused. But what kind of cultural sensemaking framework equates passivity with consent? Ehrlich (2007) argued that culturally normative ideas about women's passive, acquiescing sexuality seemed to be in play when the lower courts ruled that a woman who is emotionless and "frozen" in her demeanor *implies* consent. In other words, the trial judge and the Alberta Court of Appeal judges seemed to view sexual passivity as appropriately feminine and, as a result, what the complainant described as submitting to sex out of fear became intelligible to these courts as consenting to sex, or at the least, implying consent to the perpetrator. While the Supreme Court of Canada ultimately overturned the decisions of the two lower courts, arguing that submission on the part of the complainant did not constitute consent, the kind of ideological assumptions that seemed to underpin the lower courts' decisions are not unusual in the judicial opinions of sexual assault cases more generally (see, e.g., Coates et al. 1994; Coates and Wade 2004; Tiersma 2007) and are revealing of the "logic" that judges can use in deciding among competing narratives in legal cases. As Capps and Ochs (1995: 21) note, "truth is beyond [the] reach" of adjudicators; rather adjudicators seem to determine "official stories" on the basis of other criteria, for example, the rhetorical skills of narrators and/or the plausibility of a story's events, as these events are filtered through the lens of ideologies or cultural sensemaking frameworks.

15.3 Narratives Beyond Their Original Occasions of Production: Text Trajectories

In investigating the different ways that various courts came to narrate the "facts" of a single rape case, Ehrlich's (2007) work illustrates a central feature of communication in the legal system – that of texts moving or traveling across contexts, what Blommaert (2005) has called "text trajectories" and Heffer et al. (2013) have called "textual travels." (See Wortham and Rhodes, this volume, chapter 8 for a more extended analysis of the trajectories of narratives.) As noted above, texts travel in the legal system when courtroom testimony is summarized in the closing arguments of lawyers, discussed by jurors, or represented in the appellate decisions of judges. For Bauman and Briggs (1990: 73–75), what is significant about these kinds of practices – what they call entextualization practices – are their transformative effects. That is, once a stretch of talk is "lifted out of its interactional setting" (i.e., once it is decontextualized) and turned into a "text" (what Bauman and Briggs define as "discourse rendered decontextualizable"), it may bring something from its earlier context, but may also take on different meanings as it is "recentered" in a new context, that is, recontextualized. Moreover, given that participants in the legal system may have unequal access to and/or control over contextualizing spaces, these transformations in meaning can be deeply implicated in larger patterns of social inequality.

One of the features, then, that distinguishes the discussion in this section from that in the previous section is the fact that it does not focus exclusively on the reformulations of narratives in their original "occasions of production" (De Fina and Georgakopoulou 2012: 133); rather, it examines the way that "original" stories can be subject to alterations and modifications as they move into other modes and contexts within the legal system. Bucholtz, following Silverstein and Urban (1996), calls this type of approach to discourse analysis a "natural histories of discourse" approach, and adds:

> If some approaches to discourse analysis emphasize oral discourse, and others focus on written texts, then natural histories of discourse call attention to the interplay between the oral and the written and between earlier and later versions of the "same" oral or written discourse. (2003: 61)

Indeed, it is the "interplay between … earlier and later versions of the 'same' … discourse" that is considered below, and, in particular, how it may be informed by and reproduce wider patterns of gendered inequality.

15.3.1 From oral narratives to affidavits

The first example comes from Trinch's (2003) work on the process by which women obtain protective orders (i.e., restraining orders) that will prohibit their violent partners from making contact with them. In order to secure these protective orders, the US Latina women who were the focus of Trinch's study had to be interviewed about their abuse (i.e., abuse inflicted upon them by their domestic partners) so that the paralegals could produce affidavits for the court. Of interest to Trinch were the discrepancies between the oral narratives of abuse produced by the survivors and the written reports of abuse (i.e., affidavits) produced by the legal authorities. More specifically, as the survivors' narratives traveled in the legal system and were transplanted into written affidavits, Trinch found that their meanings shifted in ways that transformed the representations of the domestic abuse. More specifically, Trinch showed how the cyclical, habitual, and repetitive nature of domestic violence was lost as the survivors' experiences were shaped and molded in order to conform to the structure of the affidavit. For example, the survivors of domestic violence often relayed their experiences in present tense generic narrative-types, which, according to Trinch, "broaden[ed] the scope of their [the survivors'] narration … in order to relate abuse and events in terms of constant and consistent behavior" (2003: 111). By contrast, in keeping with the requirements of the protective order affidavits, the types of narratives that the paralegals attempted to elicit from their clients and ultimately produced in the affidavits were ones that recounted "unique past events, that is, … events that happen once, and will seldom, if ever, be repeated" (2003: 111). Consider the excerpt from an interaction between a paralegal and client, as seen in example (4), and the way it is re-presented in the corresponding affidavit, as seen in example (5).

Excerpt 4

P: Did he make any threats this morning?

C: Um, yeah. He keeps telling me that he's gonna take the kids. That if, if he finds out that I'm doing anything, he just said, any little thing that I do, then he's gonna go over and he's gonna take the kids, he's not gonna let me see them. He, he calls like, ten times a day.

P: And he calls every day?

C: Yeah.

Excerpt 5
On or about ((date)) ((Abuser's name)) called me at home and threatened to take the kids and not let me see them. He called over ten times that day.

In excerpt 4, we see the client representing her partner's actions as ongoing and repetitive ("He keeps telling me …, he's gonna take the kids, he's not gonna let me see them. He, he calls like ten times a day") through the use of present tense denoting habitual events; by contrast, the affidavit reproduces the partner's actions in a Labovian-type narrative where the simple past tense is used to mark the narrative events (e.g., "[He] called me at home and threatened to take the kids … He called over ten times that day"). As a result, the partner's actions are understood as discrete events that occurred on a single occasion. And, as Trinch argued, linear narratives representing violence as single, discrete occurrences are inadequate to capture the recurring and cyclical character of domestic violence.

But what accounted for the various types of omissions and distortions that the survivors' narratives underwent? In part, the reformulation of survivors' narratives produced reports that conformed to legally relevant categories and were "'maximally interpretable' for its [the story's] subsequent recipients" (Trinch 2003: 188). That is, the narratives were constrained by the structure of the affidavit, which required the listing of specific, discrete incidents of abuse that occurred on specific dates, and such constraints, according to Trinch (2003: 188), enabled the district attorney and judge to assess easily and quickly how the elements of the abuse conformed (or not) to the relevant laws.

However, Trinch provides a further explanation for the distortion and erasure of survivors' narratives in the process of institutionalization. While the transformation of the abuse into legally recognizable categories "facilitate[d] the short-term goal of getting women injunctions" (Trinch 2003: 155), Trinch argued that it also kept intact an understanding of violence against women that is consistent with the existing system. Specifically, by representing domestic violence "as singular, unconnected incidents" (274), the paralegals and the affidavits authorized a definition of violence against women that is more consistent with stranger violence than with intimate partner violence. In other words, the transformations in meaning that Trinch documented may have been successful in the short term, but they did nothing to challenge prevailing notions of violence against women. Recall Estrich's work discussed above, which shows that even though violence committed by men women know and are intimate with is much more frequent than that committed by strangers, it is sexual violence committed by strangers in singular, random acts that the law takes seriously.

15.3.2   *From trial testimony to appellate decisions*

Like Trinch's work, the next example also shows how women's accounts of violence can be recast and reframed once they move beyond the context of their "original" telling to other sites in the legal system. This transformation in meaning occurred once the 2004 American rape case *Maouloud Baby v. State of Maryland* (analyzed in Ehrlich 2012, 2013) moved from its trial phase to its appellate decisions. In particular, the case became known as a post-penetration rape case in the appellate decisions, even though it was not framed in these terms in the context of the trial. Post-penetration rape is defined as a situation in which both parties initially consent to sexual intercourse, but at some time during the act of intercourse, one party, typically the woman, withdraws her consent; after this withdrawal of consent, the other party, typically the man, forces the woman to continue intercourse against her will (Davis 2005: 732–733). While this was the characterization of events that became the "official story" of this case, it did not correspond to what transpired during the trial. During the trial, the prosecution in the case argued that the complainant, Jewel Lankford, never consented to the sexual acts initiated by the accused, Maouloud Baby, while the defense argued that she did consent to these acts. Crucially, neither the prosecution nor the defense invoked the categories of pre- vs. post-penetration consent or withdrawal of consent. In fact, the defense argued that the accused was unable to penetrate the complainant. In other words, for the prosecution, there was never consent and, for the defense, there was never penetration.

Given that the appellate courts' post-penetration framing of this case was predicated on the assumption that the complainant at some point consented to sex with the accused, one of the questions addressed by Ehrlich was the means by which the complainant's behavior became construed as consent under this framing. The testimony of the complainant, in both direct and cross examination, revealed that she attempted to resist the accused and his friend, Mike, multiple times, said "no" and "it hurts" multiple times, but finally allowed the accused "to take his turn" as long as he stopped when she told him to and allowed her to go home. Yet, it was this "agreement" that came to be understood as the initial consent issued by the complainant – and then withdrawn – once the case became recontextualized as a post-penetration rape case. Ehrlich argued that both gendered and linguistic ideologies were at play in the recasting of the complainant's submission to sex (i.e., letting the accused "take his turn") as consensual sex.

Research on violence against women has demonstrated that women's submission to sex can, in many circumstances, be a better strategy for surviving violence than physical resistance, given that physical resistance has the potential to escalate and intensify men's violence (Dobash and Dobash 1992). For example, work conducted on rape victim impact statements in the United Kingdom (Woodhams 2008) has shown women to deploy what Woodhams refers to as "offender management strategies" in order to resist their assailants. Such strategies involve women negotiating with their perpetrators in order to minimize the harm inflicted upon them: women may agree to submit to "lesser" forms of sexual assault in exchange for being let go. At the point in the *Baby* case when the complainant allowed the accused "to take his turn," she had already endured much non-consensual sexual activity and indicated that he could take his turn as long as he stopped when she told him to and allowed her to go home. In other words, the complainant could be understood as negotiating with the accused in order to avoid further and more intense sexual violence. But if the complainant's agreement to have sex with the accused was not in fact a signal of consent, but rather a strategy of compliance or submission designed to end the sexual violence sooner rather than later, why was it not understood in this way as the case moved out of its trial phase into the appellate decisions?[3]

Ehrlich located the problem in meta-level understandings of language, or what linguistic anthropologists have termed linguistic ideologies (Schieffelin, Woolard, and Kroskrity 1998; Blommaert 1999). Indeed, a powerful ideology surrounding the interpretation of texts in the West is what has been called a "referentialist" or "textualist" ideology (Collins 1996) – a belief in stable, denotational, and context-free meaning. According to this idea, meaning resides exclusively in linguistic forms and, as a result, words, phrases, or sentences can be extracted from their original interactional and social context and moved to other contexts without any change in meaning. The relevance of this linguistic ideology to the interpretation of the complainant's apparent consent should be clear: her one instance of "agreement" (i.e., allowing the accused "to take his turn") was removed from its context – the series of non-consensual sexual acts that preceded it – and, once decontextualized in this way, it lost its meaning as a strategy of resistance and instead became interpreted as consent.

Interestingly, while the jury found the accused guilty of rape and some other sexually related charges, it was the jury members who first introduced the notion of post-penetration rape into the case via a question they posed to the trial judge during their deliberations: "If a female consents to sex initially and, during the course of the sex act to which she consented, for whatever reason, she changes her mind and the man continues until climax, does the result constitute rape?" (*State of Maryland v. Maouloud*

Baby, Court of Appeals of Maryland, 2007). Although the judge did not answer this question and instead directed the jurors to answer it for themselves based on the legal definitions of rape and of consent provided during jury instructions, this question suggests that at least some of the jurors believed that the complainant's allowing the accused to "take his turn" *was* consent. What ultimately led the jury to find the accused guilty is not known; however, once the notion of post-penetration rape (and the *presupposition* of consent on the part of the complainant) was introduced into the case via the jurors' question, this question then became the basis for the defense's appeal and, by extension, for the transformation of the case into a post-penetration rape case. Appellate courts can only address issues in their opinions that are invoked during appeals; as Mertz (2007: 62) says, "the semiotic frame imposed by … litigants as they [choose] particular issues to appeal" constrains "the issues to which an appellate court may speak." In the *Baby* case, then, what began as an investigation of whether consent was given in the first place evolved, in part because of institutional constraints, into one in which consent was presupposed and the question at issue for the courts was the legal status of post-penetration rape. Put somewhat differently, as the complainant's testimony was recontextualized in various kinds of settings within the legal system, it underwent a fairly radical transformation: a strategy for resisting more extreme and prolonged instances of sexual violence became reconstructed as consensual sex.

15.4   Conclusions

A recurring theme in the work of critical legal scholars, including those who focus on the language of the law, has been the way that lay litigants' narratives are altered and/or rendered unrecognizable –"mangled" in Linde's (2001) words – once they enter the legal system. For example, as this chapter has demonstrated, lawyers' questions in trials – especially in cross-examination – can (re)shape and (re)structure the testimony of witnesses in ways that invoke discriminatory ideologies and ultimately undermine their credibility. As narratives move beyond their original contexts of production into other sites within the legal system, transformative effects are also apparent. Once transplanted into affidavits or appellate decisions, for example, stories are modified so that they conform to institutionally privileged genres and/or categories that are intelligible to the legal system. Indeed, both the discursive constraints of the courtroom and the institutional requirements of other sites in the legal system have been shown to shape women's representations of violence to such an extent that crucial elements of their stories are lost – elements that may have motivated their engagement with the legal system in the first place.

But are the "official stories" that emerge from the legal system unequivocal in their discriminatory qualities? We have seen the way that cross-examining lawyers exploit damaging cultural narratives about rape as a way of undermining the credibility of complainants, but at the same time, given the *adversarial and dynamic* nature of the trial, witnesses' answers and prosecuting lawyers' questions have the potential to produce competing narratives about rape. Drew (1992), as illustrated above, documents the "alternative descriptions" that a complainant provides as a way of blocking the damaging inferences activated by a cross-examining lawyer in a rape trial. Likewise, judges in their rulings have been shown to overturn lower court decisions that rely upon sexist and androcentric ideas (e.g., the Supreme Court of Canada in *Her Majesty the Queen v. Ewanchuk*). Even the ultimate decision in the *Baby* trial from the Maryland Court of Appeals was positive for women in general – arguably, at the expense of the individual complainant in the trial – given its ruling that post-penetration rape was a legal possibility in the state of Maryland. I have argued throughout this chapter that the institutional processes that give rise to narrative transformations and appropriations are informed by wider patterns of social inequality. In the same way, issues surrounding narrative equality in institutions are linked to broader projects of social transformation and resistance.

NOTES

1   William Kennedy Smith (the nephew of the late President John Kennedy, the late Senator Robert Kennedy, and the late Senator Edward Kennedy) was charged with, and subsequently acquitted of, simple battery (unwanted touching) and second-degree sexual battery (rape without the use of a weapon) in the state of Florida in 1991.

2   Early work on this issue (i.e., Bennett and Feldman 1981) concluded that a well-constructed story may be more important to jurors' assessments of plausibility than the existence of evidence.

3   It should be noted that Ehrlich's analysis of the complainant's behavior as compliance or submission, rather than consent, is consistent with the state of Maryland's definition of consent. More specifically, the definition of consent provided by the judge (and reiterated in the judge's answer to the jurors' questions) stipulated that agreement to sex be freely given: that is, consent was defined as "actually agreeing to the sexual act rather than merely submitting as a result of force or threat of force" (*Maouloud Baby v. State of Maryland*, Court of Special Appeals of Maryland, 2005).

REFERENCES

Atkinson, J.M., and P. Drew. (1979). *Order in Court*. Atlantic Highlands, NJ: Humanities Press.

Bauman, R., and C. Briggs (1990). Poetics and performance as critical perspectives on language and social life. *Annual Review of Anthropology*, 19, pp. 59–88.

Bennett W.L., and M. Feldman (1981). *Reconstructing Reality in the Courtroom*. London: Tavistock Publications.

Blommaert, J. (ed.). (1999). *Language Ideological Debates*. Berlin: Mouton de Gruyter.

Blommaert, J. (2005). *Discourse: A Critical Introduction*. Cambridge: Cambridge University Press.

Bucholtz, M. (2003). Theories of discourse as theories of gender: Discourse analysis in language and gender studies. In J. Holmes and M. Meyerhoff (eds.), *The Handbook of Language and Gender*. Oxford: Blackwell, pp. 43–68.

Capps, L., and E. Ochs. (1995). *Constructing Panic: The Discourse of Agoraphobia*. Cambridge, MA: Harvard University Press.

Coates, L., and A. Wade. (2004). Telling it like it isn't: Obscuring perpetrator responsibility for violent crime. *Discourse & Society*, 15, pp. 499–526.

Coates, L., J. Bavelas, and J. Gibson. (1994). Anomalous language in sexual assault trial judgments. *Discourse & Society*, 5, pp. 189–206.

Collins, J. (1996). Socialization to text: Structure and contradiction in schooled literacy. In M. Silverstein and G. Urban (eds.), *Natural Histories of Discourse*. Chicago, IL: University of Chicago Press, pp. 203–228.

Conley, J.M., and W.M. O'Barr. (1990). *Rules versus Relationships*. Chicago, IL: University of Chicago Press.

Conley, J.M., and W.M. O'Barr. (2005). *Just Words: Law, Language and Power*. 2nd edn. Chicago, IL: University of Chicago Press.

Cotterill, J. (2002). "Just one more time…": Aspects of intertextuality in the trials of O.J. Simpson. In J. Cotterill (ed.), *Language in the Legal Process*. Basingstoke, UK: Palgrave Macmillan, pp. 147–161.

Cotterill, J. (2003). *Language and Power in Court: A Linguistic Analysis of the O.J. Simpson Trial*. Basingstoke, UK: Palgrave Macmillan.

Davis, A. (2005). Clarifying the issue of consent: The evolution of post-penetration rape law. *Stetson Law Review*, 34, pp. 729–766.

De Fina, A., and A. Georgakopoulou. (2012). *Analyzing Narrative: Discourse and Sociolinguistic Perspectives*. Cambridge: Cambridge University Press.

Dobash, R.E., and R.P. Dobash. (1992). *Women, Violence and Social Change*. London: Routledge.

Drew, P. (1992). Contested evidence in courtroom examination: The case of a trial for rape. In P. Drew and J. Heritage (eds.), *Talk at Work: Interaction in Institutional Settings*. Cambridge: Cambridge University Press, pp. 470–520.

Drew, P., and J. Heritage. (1992). Analyzing talk at work: An introduction. In P. Drew and J. Heritage (eds.), *Talk at Work: Interaction in Institutional Settings*. Cambridge: Cambridge University Press, pp. 3–65.

Ehrlich, S. (2001). *Representing Rape: Language and Sexual Consent*. London: Routledge.

Ehrlich, S. (2007). Legal discourse and the cultural intelligibility of gendered meanings. *Journal of Sociolinguistics*, 11, pp. 452–477.

Ehrlich, S. (2012). Text trajectories, legal discourse and gendered inequalities. *Applied Linguistics Review*, 3, pp. 47–73.

Ehrlich, S. (2013). Post-penetration rape and the decontextualization of witness testimony. In C. Heffer, F. Rock, and J. Conley (eds.), *Legal–Lay Communication: Textual Travels in the Legal System*. Oxford: Oxford University Press, pp. 189–205.

Estrich, S. (1987). *Real Rape*. Cambridge, MA: Harvard University Press.

Georgakopoulou, A. (2011) Narrative analysis. In R. Wodak, B. Johnstone, and P. Kerswill (eds.), *The Sage Handbook of Sociolinguistics*. London: Sage, pp. 396–411.

Goffman, E. (1981). *Forms of Talk*. Philadelphia: University of Pennsylvania Press.

Harris, Sandra (2001). Fragmented narratives and multiple tellers: Witness and defendant accounts in trials. *Discourse Studies*, 3, pp. 53–74.

Heffer, C., F. Rock, and J. Conley (eds.). (2013). *Lay–Legal Communication: Textual Travels in the Legal System*. Oxford: Oxford University Press.

Heritage, J. (2002). The limits of questioning: Negative interrogatives and hostile question content. *Journal of Pragmatics*, 34, pp. 1427–1446.

Labov, W. (1997). Some further steps in narrative analysis. *Journal of Narrative and Life History*, 7, pp. 395–415.

Labov, W., and J. Waletzky. (1967). Narrative analysis: Oral versions of personal experience. In J. Helm (ed.), *Essays on the Verbal and Visual Arts*. Seattle: University of Washington Press, pp. 12–44.

Linde, C. (2001). Narrative in institutions. In H. Hamilton, D. Schiffrin, and D. Tannen (eds.), *Handbook of Discourse Analysis*. Oxford: Blackwell, pp. 518–535.

Maryns, K. (2005). Displacement and asylum seekers' narratives. In M. Baynham and

A. De Fina (eds.), *Dislocations/Relocations: Narratives of Displacement*. Manchester: St. Jerome Publishing, pp. 174–193.

Matoesian, G. (2001). *Law and the Language of Identity: Discourse in the William Kennedy Smith Rape Trial*. Oxford: Oxford University Press.

Matoesian, G. (2013). Language and law. In R. Bailey and R. Cameron (eds.), *Oxford Handbook of Sociolinguistics*. Oxford: Oxford University Press, pp. 702–719.

Mertz, E. (2007). *The Language of Law School: Learning to Think Like a Lawyer*. Oxford: Oxford University Press.

Mishler, E. (1984). *The Discourse of Medicine: Dialectics of Medical Interviews*. Norwood, NJ: Ablex.

Ochs, E., and L. Capps. (2001). *Living Narrative: Creating Lives in Everyday Storytelling*. Cambridge, MA: Harvard University Press.

Raymond, G. (2003). Grammar and social organization: Yes/no interrogatives and the structure of responding. *American Sociological Review*, 68, pp. 939–966.

Roberts, C., and S. Campbell. (2005). Fitting stories into boxes: Rhetorical and textual constraints on candidates' performances in British job interviews. *International Journal of Applied Linguistics*, 2, pp. 45–74.

Russell, D. (1982). *Rape in Marriage*. New York: Macmillan.

Russell, D. (1984). *Sexual Exploitation: Rape, Child Sexual Abuse, and Workplace Harassment*. Beverly Hills, CA: Sage Publications.

Schieffelin, B., K. Woolard, and P.V. Kroskrity (eds.). (1998). *Language Ideologies: Practice and Theory*. Oxford: Oxford University Press.

Silverstein, M., and G. Urban (eds.). (1996). *Natural Histories of Discourse*. Chicago, IL: University of Chicago Press.

Tiersma, P. (2007). The language of consent in rape law. In J. Cotterill (ed.), *The Language of Sexual Crime*. Basingstoke, UK: Palgrave Macmillan, pp. 83–103.

Trinch, S. (2003). *Latinas' Narratives of Domestic Abuse: Discrepant Versions of Violence*. Amsterdam: John Benjamins.

Woodhams, J. (2008). How victims behave during stranger sexual assaults. Unpublished manuscript.

16 Narratives in Family Contexts

CYNTHIA GORDON

16.1 Introduction

This chapter provides an integrative review of discourse analytic and sociolinguistic studies that investigate narratives in family contexts.[1] I first define the research area, outlining what constitutes both a "narrative" and a "family context"; I also describe data-collection methods and discuss how these methods shape the field of research. Second, I highlight two primary, intertwined functions of narratives in families, which Blum-Kulka (1997) conceptualizes as *socialization*, or the acculturation (of children, especially) into cultural norms of language use and other aspects of social life, and *sociability*, or connecting with others in the family. My review of prior research is supplemented by a sample analysis that demonstrates how the socialization and sociability functions occur moment by moment as narratives unfold; the analysis also shows how narratives work to construct the family itself. In the concluding discussion, I address gaps in the literature and describe how the field's own story is unfolding toward the future.

16.2 Defining "Narrative" in Family Contexts

Because narrative is a prominent discourse form, and the term "narrative" is so widely used in academic and lay discourse alike, defining what "counts" as (a) narrative is not a straightforward task. One confounding factor is that the term is used to refer to the process of storytelling, the stories produced, and the abstract cognitive schemata that shape such stories. Studies of narratives in family contexts suggest that drawing on not only traditional but also newly developed and more flexible narrative definitions is most productive in investigating narratives as part of everyday talk.

The touchstone understanding for most linguists of "narrative" traces back to Labov and Waletzky (1967) and Labov (1972), who elicited narratives in interviews. Labov defines narrative as a stretch of talk, usually produced by an individual, that conveys both a sequence of past events and the teller's perspective on what is reported. It is a textual entity that, in its fully developed form, involves a set of defining structural elements: *abstract, orientation, complicating action, evaluation, resolution,* and *coda.* A Labovian narrative revolves around a "reportable" event, one that is in some way out of the ordinary and presumably engaging to audiences – like Labov's researcher-elicited

The Handbook of Narrative Analysis, First Edition. Edited by Anna De Fina and Alexandra Georgakopoulou.
© 2015 John Wiley & Sons, Inc. Published 2019 by John Wiley & Sons, Inc.

"danger of death" narratives. Many narratives *about families* told in interview situations meet these criteria (see, e.g., Lee 2010; Schiffrin 1996, 2000; Tannen 2008). For instance, Schiffrin (1996) examines Labovian narratives that were told by two women in socio-linguistic interviews. She shows how, through these narratives, the women portray the dynamics of the relationships they have with younger women in their families, and thereby construct their identities as mothers.

In contrast to narratives about families that emerge in interview situations, narratives told *in family contexts* – in the everyday, naturally occurring conversations that family members share, such as during mealtime – often stray from the Labovian prototype in one or more ways, thus problematizing use of a strictly Labovian definition. Numerous studies of narratives in family contexts suggest that, while Labovian insights are impor-tant, a broader definition of narrative more fully captures how narratives emerge as part of everyday family discourse. In fact, seminal research into narratives told in family contexts uses Labov's definition as a starting point, but goes beyond it. For instance, in her study of everyday family dinners among Jewish American and Israeli families, Blum-Kulka (1993: 365) focuses on moments of conversation that "recapitulate past events" – an emphasis highly reminiscent of Labov and Waletzky's (1967: 13) textual definition of narrative (see also Blum-Kulka 1997). However, the highly interactive nature of many of these narratives, especially in the Israeli families, whose members preferred "polyphonic" to "monologic" styles of narration, suggests the limitations of the traditional definition. Blum-Kulka thus focuses not only on the narratives as *tales*, or narratives produced, but additionally as *tellings* – or unfolding (often very collabora-tive) acts of narration – as these are produced by *tellers*. In other words, it is useful to consider narratives in family contexts not as stand-alone texts, but as co-produced *narrative events* (Blum-Kulka 1997: 101; see also Bauman 1986), which means that what is said, how it is said, who says it and to whom, who responds and how, and so on are of interest to analysts. (For more on interactive approaches to narrative, see Goodwin, this volume, chapter 10.)

A recently developed paradigm known as "small stories" (see, e.g., Bamberg 2004; Georgakopoulou 2007, and this volume, chapter 13) readily applies to narratives in family contexts; this paradigm advances an expanded understanding of narrative discourse and advocates investigation into a variety of narrative types, including narratives that are highly collaborative, minimally developed, oriented to the future, in reference to habitual events, or even merely alluded to. Numerous studies of nar-ratives in families – from classic studies in the research area (e.g., Blum-Kulka 1993, 1997; Ochs and Taylor 1992) to those that explicitly take the small stories perspective (e.g., Tovares 2010) – reveal the empirical and theoretical value of rethinking tradi-tional understandings of what constitutes a "narrative": Stories that emerge in and constitute everyday family life take a multitude of forms.

More abstract uses of the term "narrative" also surface in studies of narratives in family contexts, as well as in the aforementioned adjacent area of research that considers how people tell narratives *about families* in interviews and interview-like contexts. Tannen (2008) captures two such abstract senses in identifying three narrative types in data she collected in conversations with women about their sisters. Building on Gee's (1999) distinction between small-d discourse (actual interactions or texts) and big-D

Discourse (ideologies and assumptions), Tannen introduces "small-n narratives" to refer to actual accounts of specific past events (i.e., Labovian or Labovian-like narratives), such as a story one woman conveys about how she and her sister, who lived in distant cities, unknowingly bought identical coats. Tannen uses "big-N Narratives" for themes realized in small-n narratives, such as how sisters who are geographically distant and quite different are actually, on a deeper level, remarkably similar. Finally, her concept of "Master Narratives" refers to cultural ideologies that shape the big-N Narratives; one primary Master Narrative about sisters is that they should be similar and close. Similarly, Bamberg (2004) uses the term "cultural narrative" to refer to assumptions that shape the everyday stories told in a variety of contexts. Austin and Carpenter (2008) reference a parallel idea in their analysis of how women whose children have a developmental disorder tell stories that portray themselves in their maternal roles. They find that these women's stories "trouble" cultural narratives that promote the idea that the good mother is selfless and always available to her children (see, e.g., Hays 1996).

In summary, "narrative" has a number of meanings in studies relating to family discourse. Abstract understandings of "narrative" – as cultural expectations and ideologies about what constitutes a good parent, for example – cut across a number of studies about narratives told about or in family interaction, thereby contextualizing stories told within broader social and cultural worlds of discourse. In studies that focus on how individual people tell narratives about families in interview contexts to construct their identities, a more traditional definition of narrative is often utilized. While this area of research is related to and sometimes intersects with the focus area of this chapter – the study of narratives in family contexts – it is not identical to it: "Family contexts" are typically understood as those situations in which family members interact with one another as part of their everyday lives. Narratives told in interview situations with multiple family members (see, e.g., Petraki 2001; Petraki, Baker, and Emmison 2007) form a sort of middle ground, as do institutional situations that involve more than one family member, such as family therapy sessions (e.g., Aronsson and Cederborg 1994) and parent-teacher-pupil conferences (e.g., Adelswärd and Nilholm 2000). Thus what exactly constitutes "family contexts" is best understood as somewhat fluid.

16.3 Collecting Narratives in Family Contexts

Just as "narrative" has a variety of definitions, ranging from the prototypical to the non-prototypical, from the concrete to the abstract, so too does "family." The field of research exploring "narratives in family contexts" thus is shaped by how individual scholars understand "family," and ultimately by the group of people whose discourse each scholar chooses to investigate. Seminal studies of family narratives, such as those by Blum-Kulka (1993, 1997; Blum-Kulka and Snow 1992) and Ochs and colleagues (e.g., Ochs and Taylor 1992, 1995), involve the audio- and video-recording of dinnertime conversations among nuclear families that are relatively socioculturally "unmarked" or thought to be "ordinary." Such families typically involve a married woman and man and their (biological) children; at times a researcher is present as a guest.

Mealtime is a site of much academic inquiry into family narratives, in part because in many cultures, at the end of the day when family members come together for a meal, talk is expected, as is the holding of extended conversational turns (Snow and Beals 2006: 54). Family dinners have also been privileged as a site because "[a]cross communities and historical time, sharing a meal has constituted an important locus for reifying and structuring social order and for social sense-making" (Ochs et al. 2010). Further, recording dinner conversations is convenient.

Recently, however, work on narratives in family contexts has extended in several directions beyond the "traditional" nuclear family dinner. This includes collecting narratives in situations beyond dinnertime, and being open to nontraditional and evolving senses of the term "family."

Increasingly, scholarly exploration encompasses narratives (and other forms of talk) produced by family members throughout the day and across interactional contexts. For example, as part of their participation in a study of the discourse of dual-income American families in the Washington, DC area, adults in four families carried audio-recorders with them for one week, recording throughout the day (see Tannen, Kendall, and Gordon 2007 for an overview of this project). Conducting a different sort of study that also captures family interactions over time, Beach and Good (2004) and Beach and Lockwood (2003) analyze a series of self-recorded family phone calls pertaining to a family crisis (the mother's cancer diagnosis and prognosis). Studies such as these facilitate exploration of how disparate family conversations are linked together, and demonstrate how narratives interconnect with other discourse activities that make up everyday life experience. For example, Gordon (2006) investigates how non-narrative and narrative interactions are linked together, highlighting intertextual repetition as a resource for identity construction.

These relatively longitudinal studies also demonstrate how narratives are used to create families that extend beyond the nuclear families. For instance, taking a small stories perspective, Tovares (2010) analyzes the short, mundane, and often future-oriented stories told in the everyday interactions among members of one family who participated in Kendall and Tannen's project. Tovares demonstrates how, by including the family's pet dogs in these stories in particular ways, the family's human narrators (and narrative recipients) construct a family identity that not only involves appreciating pets, but also counts them among its members. For example, the mother and four-and-a-half-year-old son construct a "narrative-like hypothetical scenario" wherein one of the family's dogs is able to speak English, and verbally interacts with the son. Tovares demonstrates how members of the family use small stories to construct positive social relationships with pets, and with each other, as family members; they also socialize one another into pet appreciation.

Multi-day video recording in family homes is another recently favored method of data collection for studies of family discourse and narratives. Ochs and colleagues used this method in investigating the everyday talk of 32 families living in Los Angeles (see Ochs and Kremer-Sadlik 2013 for a project overview). This method facilitates research into narratives (and other forms of family discourse) during and outside of mealtime, enables the exploration of both verbal and nonverbal participation in (narrative) activities, and demonstrates how talk is integrated with other activities (see, e.g., Ochs et al. 2010). It also requires the presence of a video crew. Goodwin (2007) draws on this dataset to demonstrate how the activity of "knowledge exploration" – a process through which parents and children unpack meanings of words, events, and concepts – occurs throughout family members' unfolding days, involves narrative and other discourse forms, and is created through both talk and nonverbal means.

In addition, studies have extended not only beyond dinnertime but also beyond narratives of "traditional" families. The field has long showed interest in family diversity through exploring family narratives across cultural or national groups; emblematic of this is Blum-Kulka's (1993, 1997) study of dinners among Jewish American, American Israeli, and Israeli families, and Aukrust's (2002) and Aukrust and Snow's (1998) comparison of American and Norwegian families. While not focused explicitly on family talk, Heath's (1983) ethnographic research compares the language of working-class black and white communities in the Piedmont Carolinas and identifies narrative differences among the groups. Heath suggests that these differences – such as the white families' (but not the black families') emphasis on truthfulness in narrative – may impact children's school achievement.

White and middle-class families tend to be overstudied, though there are exceptions besides Heath (1983). For instance, as part of an ethnographic study, Klein (2009) analyzes narratives drawn from interviews with members of Punjabi Sikh families in Los Angeles; Snow and Beals (2006) focus on dinnertime conversations of lower-income urban families. Some of the families participating in the project conducted by Ochs and colleagues (see, e.g., Ochs and Kremer-Sadlik 2013) were of diverse ethnic origins or featured same-sex parents. Among the "middle-class white families" most commonly studied are North American and European families, although narratives of families in Israel (e.g., Blum-Kulka 1993, 1997), Australia (e.g., Petraki 2001; Petraki et al. 2007), and Japan (e.g., Minami and McCabe 1995) have also been considered, as have narratives of immigrant families, notably Cypriot-Australian (Petraki 2001; Petraki et al. 2007), American Israeli (Blum-Kulka 1993, 1997), and first- and second-generation Sikhs in the United States (Klein 2009). Such studies highlight the diverse narrative forms constructed in family contexts, and illuminate narratives' functions that cut across cultural groups, notably their role in child socialization and family sociability, addressed in more detail in the next section. Despite the richness of these studies, there remains a dearth of discourse analytic research on narratives in family contexts in many parts of the world, such as Africa, the Middle East, and South America.

In sum, collecting "narratives in family contexts" tends to involve audio-recording (and, frequently, simultaneous video-recording) of family mealtimes, though increasingly studies aim to capture family narratives as part of the range of discursive activities in which family members engage throughout their days. While interviews conducted with family members also lend important insights into the roles of narratives in families and how people narrate family relationships, these studies are not central to the research area (narratives in interviews are considered in more depth in Shuman, this volume, chapter 2).

16.4   Functions of Narratives in Family Contexts: Socialization and Sociability

As scholars have repeatedly demonstrated, the functions of narrative discourse are numerous. Narratives construct tellers' identities (see De Fina, this volume, chapter 18), persuade and entertain audiences, create ties between participants, and so on. While narratives in family contexts are similarly multifunctional, they serve two primary functions, following a distinction outlined by Blum-Kulka (1997) in her study of the dinnertime conversations among families in the United States and Israel. As she explains, narratives accomplish "socialization": they acculturate family members, especially children, into family and wider cultural norms (for more on narrative and socialization, see Minami, this volume, chapter 4). In addition, narratives are a means by which family members simultaneously enact "sociability." They talk for the sake of talking and to create relationships with one another (Blum-Kulka 1997). In serving as a resource for both socialization and sociability, narratives construct collective meanings, craft individual and family identities, and (re)create the family as a small group culture.

While socialization and sociability are co-occurring phenomena in interaction, studies of narratives in family contexts often stem from an interest in how children are socialized. Narrative discourse is but one form of family talk that achieves socialization (others include explanations, e.g., Aukrust and Snow 1998; directives, e.g., Blum-Kulka 1997; and referring term use, e.g., Gordon 2007a). However, as Georgakopoulou (2002: 33) explains, due to narrative's prominence in social life and its role in sensemaking (see Bruner 1990), examining family narratives is "an ideal point of entry into the interactive, jointly achieved aspects of the socialization process."

Research has focused on how children are narratively socialized into culturally appropriate language use, including how to tell stories; into family roles and identities; and into culturally shaped ways of thinking and believing. These activities are intertwined and inseparable: Numerous studies show, for instance, how, as children are socialized into culturally preferred narrative practices, they are also socialized into cultural values.

For example, Blum-Kulka (1993, 1997) analyzes the "telling your day" ritual of Jewish American and Israeli families; this ritual involves an exchange of stories about what happened to each family member that day. It reveals the diversity of narrative practices within and across families: Many of the tellings Blum-Kulka examines are highly "polyphonic" – as opposed to "monologic" – especially in the Israeli families. While this mode of telling "is enacted in principle through both co-performance and co-ownership" of the tale (1997: 124), Blum-Kulka uncovers interesting differences across the cultural groups. For instance, "the Jewish American families support monologic performances even when the tales are known to more than one participant, and Israeli narration may unfold highly collaboratively even in cases of unshared tales" (1997: 125). This parallels broader cultural emphases on individualism and collectivity, and thus serves a means of socializing children into cultural mores. "Dialogic" modes of telling, which typically occur in "question-answer format," appear as well in Blum-Kulka's data (1997: 123); this pattern frequently occurs in interactions between parents and young children in many different cultural groups as children learn how to become competent narrators (see, e.g., Gordon 2005; Minami 2001).

In comparing Norwegian and American families' talk, Aukrust and Snow (1998) also found both narrative similarities and differences across groups. Narratives play a role in child socialization; however, the authors found that the Norwegian families produced more narrative discourse, especially about deviations from common social norms, than did American families. American families produced more explanations, especially of events or of individuals' behaviors. Aukrust and Snow suggest that these patterns highlight the contrastive cultural values of Norwegians, who tend to orient to collectivism and homogeneity, and Americans, who tend to highly value individualism and diversity, while also socializing children in each cultural group into these values.

Ochs and colleagues (e.g., Ochs and Taylor 1992, 1995; Ochs et al. 1992) also analyze what can be described as the "telling your day" ritual. However, they focus on the different narrative roles occupied by different participants, and demonstrate how these roles reflect and create a family's social organization. Narrative roles include *introducer* (who begins a narrative or elicits one from someone else), *protagonist* (who is the main character in the story), *primary recipient* (to whom the story is directed), *problematizer* (who judges the actions reported, or how the story is told), and *problematizee* (who is judged). Ochs and Taylor (1992, 1995) focus on how narratives construct (and socialize children into) a family's hierarchical structure and different family-role identities, including those related to gender and generation. In their analysis of 100 narratives collected during the recorded dinnertime conversations of seven American families, they identify a pattern that they call "Father knows best" (Ochs and Taylor 1995). In this pattern (which is not without exception), mother elicits a narrative from child and selects father as primary recipient (e.g., "Tell Daddy what you did at school today"); father subsequently judges the child protagonist. Fathers also frequently problematize mothers. Further, whereas fathers tend to be problematizers (more than problematizees), and children tend to be problematizees (more than problematizers), mothers play the two roles in approximately equal amounts. Thus, narratives and the process by which they are produced "put mothers, fathers, and children into a politics of asymmetry" in the family (Ochs and Taylor 1995: 106).

Tannen (2007a) reanalyzes the pattern identified by Ochs and colleagues in the context of her own earlier theorizing on gendered patterns of interaction (e.g., Tannen 1990), and in consideration of the ambiguity and polysemy of linguistic strategies in terms of power and solidarity (Tannen 1994). Tannen advocates understanding power (or hierarchy) as intertwined and inseparable from solidarity (or connection), including in narrative contexts. She thus suggests that "the mother who initiates a 'telling your day' routine is trying to create closeness and involvement" by facilitating the exchange of "details of daily life" between family members (Tannen 2007a: 33). Indeed, the narrative pattern could be viewed as enacting sociability and connection between family members, while simultaneously affirming and socializing family members into a hierarchical structure.

Erickson (1990) also views narratives as socially organized processes and as creating relationships between family members (and socializing children into these relationships).

He analyzes a series of interconnected stories, told during an American family dinner that was video-recorded. Focusing on the notion of "participation structure" (see Philips 1972), or how speakers and listeners engage with one another and the unfolding talk, he demonstrates how "the conversation as enacted can be seen to be situated in the social organization of the family; an organization that is reflexively manifested in the doing of the talk" (1990: 209). The series of stories, which involves narratives about bike accidents, serves as a means of self-presentation for family members, including reinstantiating each individual's place in the family hierarchy. For instance, the father told the longest story, was the only teller whose story garnered active listening behaviors from all present, and narrated the most impressive story content, involving a motorcycle (rather than bicycle) accident. While the family's sons' bike accident stories were somewhat prominent, the daughter's was not oriented to, and resulted in a narrative fragment. At the same time, all the stories showed thematic and topical connections; all participants contributed to maintaining the discourse coherence of the conversation and the narratives threads that created it.

Georgakopoulou (2002) similarly examines the roles family members play in narrative activities. She analyzes stories involving children as (co-)tellers, addressees, or story characters, with an emphasis on how children are socialized into cultural understandings of narrative tellability and norms of self-presentation, through the narration of familiar, shared stories. These stories were drawn from the discourse of five Greek families who recorded evening conversations (including dinnertime) in their homes. The narratives, in addition to serving to teach children what kinds of stories are worthy of sharing – such as one that highlights siblings' personality differences – also "convey powerful messages for culturally sanctioned roles and obligations for family members," such as proud and attentive mother (Georgakopoulou 2002: 49). In the collaborative telling of shared stories, children additionally learn how to recontextualize them, a skill that has implications for children's developing literacy skills. This harkens back to earlier work on narratives in family contexts by Heath (1983) and Blum-Kulka and Snow (1992), who suggest that family narrative practices may influence children's academic achievement.

Georgakopoulou's (2002) work also connects to research suggesting that family narrative practices acculturate children into thinking and reasoning processes. Ochs et al. (1992) argue that through dinnertime narratives, children are taught how to solve problems and engage in critical thinking skills that they also encounter in formal schooling. As they explain, "narrative 'facts' and ideas are presented, pulled apart, and reinterpreted" during narration, co-narration, and re-narration; children thereby learn to take different perspectives and develop "theories" of what happened (Ochs et al. 1992: 38). Blum-Kulka (2000) demonstrates how narratives that are part of "gossipy events" at family dinners – such as talk about a child's teacher – contribute to creating a family's ethics while also teaching children how to think about and orient to institutional authority.

Related, narratives in family contexts also indicate how children should feel about events and people in the world. This is often explored under the rubric of "morality." For example, Sterponi's (2003) examination of Italian family dinner conversations demonstrates how children use narratives and descriptions to present themselves as moral actors when faced with parents' questioning about their conduct; Perregaard (2010) and Johansen (2011) present compatible analyses focused on children's agency and responsibility through the lens of morality, but in the context of Danish family dinners. Political attitudes and identities are the focus of Gordon (2007a): Analysis of the discourse of one American family identifies storytelling as part of a range of strategies used for political socialization. Taking the perspective that socialization is a mutual, multidirectional process (see Ochs et al. 1992), Gordon demonstrates how, for example, a child's humorous story negatively portraying a Republican US presidential candidate is retold by the mother on multiple occasions, thereby helping to create and socialize family members into their shared Democratic political party affiliation. Simultaneously, it creates connection among family members. Paugh's (2012) examination of dinnertime narratives about parents' workplace experiences in 16 dual-income American families has similar findings: Children are socialized into ideologies about (future) work and workplace practices through narratives. Likewise, Gordon's (2005) analysis of future-oriented hypothetical narratives in one family shows a child's socialization into her quickly approaching new identity of "big sister," and how narratives connect a present family configuration to its future.

Also focused on future-oriented narratives, this time viewing them as part of "trajectories of hope," Sirota's (2010) analysis of the everyday talk of 17 American families that include a child diagnosed with an autism spectrum disorder attends to socialization as well as sociability. In the narratives, which are co-told and feature the children as protagonists, parents and children together construct aspirations, goals, and possible futures for the children. In addition, these stories "scaffold children's involvement in techniques of self-reflection and self-awareness," positioning children as competent co-narrators and moral social actors (Sirota 2010: 558). Thus, narratives create family hope, family togetherness, and positive individual identities for family members.

In summary, scholarly investigations of narratives in family contexts highlight how the narrative process, as well as story content, socialize children into norms of language use (including how to narrate) and ways of thinking, create family relationships, and establish shared family beliefs. Through narrating together, family members connect with one another and construct "who we are," whether that means "Israelis," "members of the Democratic Party," or something more amorphous like "moral people" or "problem-solvers."

In the sample analysis presented next, I demonstrate how sociability and socialization co-occur in the discourse of one family. The analysis also highlights how methods of narrative collection shape analyses, and thereby affect what social groupings scholars understand as "family."

16.5   Sample Analysis: Constructing Family Through Narrative

While it is well established that narratives are resources for sociability and socialization in family discourse, an area of increasing interest is how narratives construct, moment-by-moment, exactly what and who a family is. Norrick (1997: 202) remarks that studies such as Blum-Kulka's highlight that "children sometimes count as full members of the family, but at other times they do not," for example when they are excluded from conversation. Thus what constitutes "family" is, in one meaningful sense, created in unfolding discourse. Mandelbaum (2010), for instance, shows how, through resistance to shared family reminiscing during a holiday mealtime, a family's teenage son demonstrates and tries out his growing autonomy. Her earlier research (Mandelbaum 1987) demonstrating how members of couples construct their coupledom through narrative serves as one source of inspiration for the sample analysis that I present here.

The following narrative extracts are drawn from the discourse of one white, middle-class, dual-income American family whose adult members recorded their own interactions for one week (see Tannen et al. 2007 for a project overview; the analysis presented here is adapted from Gordon 2009: 103–112.). This family consists of mother Janet, father Steve, and their nearly three-year-old daughter, Natalie. While many narratives are produced in the more restricted context of the nuclear family, including for example co-told mother-child narratives (see Gordon 2005), the extracts presented here demonstrate how narrative is used to construct a family that includes an adult from "outside" the family proper: Janet and Steve's close friend, Jill. Specifically, co-narration constructs a family that centers on the child (child-centeredness is typical of many American families; see, e.g., Blum-Kulka 1997; Varenne 1992).

The narrative arises after Janet, Jill, and Natalie had spent the afternoon together at a shopping mall. Natalie was in the process of being toilet-trained; at the mall, with Janet and Jill's assistance and praise, she used a public toilet for the first time. This is a "reportable" event, and it is immediately brought up in conversation when Janet, Jill, and Natalie arrive back at Janet and Steve's house, where Steve has also just arrived. In the first extract, Janet and Jill encourage Natalie to share the story of "tinkles at the mall" ("tinkles" is a familylect term for urination; see Gordon 2009 for others; the childish term for toilet, "potty," is also used). Arrows (⇨) at the front of lines indicate particular analytic importance.[2]

(1a)	(1)	⇨ Janet:	Tell Daddy the news!
	(2)	⇨ Jill:	Tell Daddy.
	(3)	Natalie:	Tinkles!
	(4)	⇨ Janet:	Guess where she made tinkles [Daddy!
	(5)	Steve:	[Where did you- →
	(6)		where did you make tinkles?
	(7)	Natalie:	Tinkles, potty!
	(8)	Steve:	On the potty?
	(9)	⇨ Jill:	Where?
	(10)	⇨ Janet:	At the (.)
	(11)	⇨	(Where.)
	(12)	Jill:	Where were we?
	(13)	Natalie:	Mall!
	(14)	Janet:	At the mall!
	(15)	Steve:	The mall!?

Janet and Jill's collective behavior is highly reminiscent of mothers' roles in "Father knows best" (Ochs and Taylor 1992, 1995): The women collaboratively prompt Natalie to tell the "tinkles" story, also eliciting the pivotal location of the story (lines 9, 11, 12) and designating Steve, the only participant who did not experience the event narrated, as the story recipient. Natalie participates by giving minimal responses to Janet and Jill's repeated prompting (e.g., *Tinkles!*, line 3; *Tinkles, potty!*, line 7; *Mall!*, line 13). The narrative is highly co-constructed. Steve evaluates the child's reported behavior in line 15 through using a voice-quality that indicates surprise and delight (he does not "problematize" her).

As the interaction continues (in lines 16–32, not shown here), Janet and Jill take over narrating what happened; they not only co-narrate the event but also make clear that the two together helped Natalie use the toilet. Thus, Janet and Jill are not only "co-narrators" of the child's experience, but also acted as "co-parents" in the sequence of events described in the tale. This theme of co-parenting continues in excerpt 1b, as Janet expresses appreciation that Jill was with her to deal with the situation, using the kinship term "Auntie" to refer to her (line 33). (In line 53, Jill responds to an earlier indecipherable utterance by Natalie in line 51; Janet however finishes telling Steve the story. "Hover," used in line 35, refers to how Janet wanted to hold Natalie suspended above the toilet so that she would not come into contact with germs.)

(1b)	33	Janet:	Thank God Auntie was there.
	34		[We each went to the bath- ((laughs)) →
	35	Jill:	[Well she thought she was gonna hover,
	36	Janet:	((laughs))
	37		We each went to the bathroom,
	38		and she goes "I have to go,"
	39		or she said [something,
	40	Jill:	[Something like ["I'm gonna go potty".
	41 ⇨	Janet:	[And we were like,
	42		"are you sure?"
	43		And she was like "yes."
	44 ⇨		And we were like "okay,"
	45 ⇨		so we get her in the bathroom,
	46		[and she's-
	47	Steve:	[(? that diaper) looks pretty full right now.
	48	Janet:	Oh, I think it-
	49		Well,
	50		she wouldn't let me change her after [naptime.
	51	Natalie:	[(??)
	52	Steve:	Ah.

53	Jill:	[Dog? That's another new dog. ((to Natalie))
54	Janet:	[So, that's another story.
55		But um, so it was very squishy going.

In co-narrating this story, Janet begins to describe what happened (*We each went to the bath-*, line 34), and Jill overlaps with another detail (*Well she thought she was gonna hover*, line 35). They use repetition cooperatively and to build solidarity (see Tannen 2007b). When Janet uses "constructed dialogue" (Tannen 2007b) to animate what Natalie said (*and she goes "I have to go," or she said something*, lines 38–39), Jill adds her version (*Something like "I'm gonna go potty,"* line 40). Then Janet depicts herself and Jill as cooperating and together taking care of Natalie by using the term "we" to refer to them and by constructing dialogue that creates a conversation wherein Janet and Jill provide one side and Natalie, the other (*And we were like, "are you sure?" And she was like "yes." And we were like "okay,"* lines 41–44).

After Janet summarizes the toilet experience at the shopping mall as somewhat difficult (*But um, so it was very squishy going*, line 55), the topic diverges for several moments before Jill reintroduces the topic by saying that they all are proud of Natalie. Janet and Jill then together tell the story's resolution. They explain that Janet wanted to "hold Natalie over the toilet" (because she perceived it as being dirty) and Jill came up with the idea of putting toilet paper on the seat. They both provide the narrative's coda:

(1c)	98	Jill:	And that worked!
	99	Janet:	And it worked!

This story and how it is told, I suggest, work to construct Jill, Janet, Natalie, and Steve as a family in various ways: Jill and Janet co-elicit a story in which the child is the main protagonist and the father is the primary audience, creating connection between the child and her father. They further build their own relationship by co-narrating the story together, which also displays their shared access to, and cooperation regarding, the sequence of events depicted. In addition, Janet refers to Jill using the kinship term "Auntie," symbolically constructing her as a member of the family. Steve, for his part, positively evaluates the story; Janet and Jill positively evaluate Natalie's behavior as well. This narrative could be considered from multiple perspectives, such as how "Father knows best" occurs; the gendered division of narrative roles in the interaction; how the family constructs itself as "American middle class" through its focus on the child; how co-narration occurs; or how a child is socialized into storytelling and into using the toilet. However, underlying all of these is the idea that the narration, in these conversational moments, creates a family that extends beyond nuclear family boundaries to encompass a family friend.

In sum, while "family" in the context of family narrative research is often identified as a mother, a father, and their children, the analysis presented here adopts a different perspective. As participants accomplish sociability and socialization, family membership is also co-constructed moment-by-moment through talk. The implications of this perspective are elaborated in the next section, in which I critically engage the findings of research on narratives in family contexts and identify directions for future research.

16.6 Concluding Discussion

Research on narratives in family contexts has identified narrative as a primary means of enacting family sociability and accomplishing child socialization, reinforcing narrative's status as an important human sensemaking activity. Study findings have contributed to our understanding of how linguistic and cultural socialization is narratively achieved in families belonging to different cultural groups; how family conversations shape children's (and adults') beliefs and values, along with their language use; and how patterns of narration are used to create and negotiate family relationships. This research contributes to larger goals of scholarship in discourse analysis, pragmatics, sociolinguistics, and related areas. All of these findings illuminate narrative as a social activity, and not just a text; they highlight linguistic and interactional diversity; and they demonstrate that language is constitutive of our social and cultural worlds. They also raise important issues that merit further exploration: the value of different definitions of "narrative," what exactly "counts" as a family, and the various ways in which narratives are told in contemporary life.

First, while many studies of narratives in family contexts use Labov's (1972) definition of narrative as an analytic touchstone, they also reveal that narratives frequently diverge from this definition. This demonstrates the limits of the traditional definition, and highlights the value of engaging with new narrative understandings, such as those offered by the small stories perspective. This finding should press researchers to continue to investigate the many discourse activities that make up family interactions, and how these are woven together in everyday talk. Extant research reveals that narratives intersect with other discourse activities in family contexts, such as explaining (e.g., Aukrust and Snow 1998), accounting (e.g., Sterponi 2003), gossiping (e.g., Blum-Kulka 2000), and parent-child pretend play (e.g., Gordon 2006). Yet how these activities relate to, and may at times interactionally fade into or out of, the "underrepresented narrative activities" (Georgakopoulou 2007: 148) that small stories encompass is ripe for further exploration in family contexts and beyond.

Second, despite the relative prominence of comparative perspectives on family discourse and narrative, and some ongoing efforts to diversify the ethnic, cultural, and socioeconomic backgrounds of families whose narratives are considered, most studies minimize diversity within the individual family structure, focusing on traditional nuclear families. At present, there is an increased interest in the discourse of a fuller diversity of family forms. For instance, Varenne (1992) and Gordon (2003) investigate the conversations among members of blended families (though the concept of "narrative" does not figure prominently). Davies (2010) analyzes the discourse of senior co-habitating sisters and their nephew, focusing on how the participants' co-narratives create a shared family ethos. As part of her ethnographic, discourse analytic study of families headed by gay male co-parents, Pash (2008) analyzes the first-person narratives male co-parents tell, lending insights into their experiences and perspectives, including the importance of networks they develop with female kin. Sirota's (2010) analysis of the discourse of families that include a child diagnosed with a developmental disorder reveals how, through co-narration, children with high-functioning autism and Asperger's syndrome are socialized into narrative telling practices. Gordon (2007b) analyses an interaction in which the uncle of a pre-school age child narrates to the parents how their child misbehaved while he babysat, focusing on how the mother's narrative response strategies work to construct her maternal identity. Al Zidjaly (2006, 2007), in her analysis of the everyday communication of a quadriplegic man and his caregivers, provides a rare glimpse into the discourse and narrative practices of a family in the Middle Eastern country of Oman.

Despite this breadth of studies, there remains much to be learned about the narratives of families across the globe and of diverse ethnic and religious backgrounds. Further, how exactly the view of family as constructed through discourse and narrative meshes with more common understandings of family – as two parents and their children, or as a group of people related through marriage and adoption – merits further exploration.

Third, research on narratives in family contexts has, to date, largely focused on narratives that emerge in conversations. Accompanying this body of research are studies of narratives about families told in interviews, such as Schiffrin's (1996, 2000) analyses of narrativized mother-daughter relationships; Lee's (2010) analysis of interview narratives of Korean women who live overseas with their children; Tannen's (2008) analysis of women's stories about their sisters; and Petraki's (2001) and Petraki et al.'s (2007) examination of narratives told collaboratively in interviews conducted with multiple family members. However, scholars have increasingly begun to acknowledge that family narratives are constructed in many other contexts. For instance, Nylund (2008) examines online discussion boards where family relationships are a topic. Gordon (2011, 2013) investigates family discourse as presented on a reality television show, noting how the program's editing constructs a particular narrative for audiences. Al Zidjaly's (2006, 2007) analyses reveal how creative Microsoft PowerPoint slide presentations tell stories that shape family discourse and trajectories of action. Such studies offer exciting new venues for family narrative research, extending it into the numerous digital contexts that now make up everyday family life.

In conclusion, investigations into narratives in family contexts should continue to expand, diversify, and refine (and sometimes redefine) concepts and ideas. Revisiting terms like "narrative" and "family" has served to enrich the research area. Future research will lend further insights into how family narratives impact multiple aspects of everyday family experience – from learning and understanding to connecting and being – as well as lending important insights into narrative itself.

NOTES

1   I thank Najma Al Zidjaly and the editors of this volume for their insightful comments on earlier versions of this chapter.
2   Each line represents an intonation unit. An arrow (→) indicates that the intonation unit continues onto the next line. When words or question marks are enclosed in single parentheses, this indicates uncertain transcription.

REFERENCES

Adelswärd, V., and C. Nilholm. (2000). Who is Cindy? Aspects of identity work in a teacher-parent-pupil talk at a special school. *Text*, 20 (4), pp. 545–568.

Al Zidjaly, N. (2006). Disability and anticipatory discourse: The interconnectedness of local and global aspects of talk. *Communication & Medicine*, 3 (2), pp. 101–112.

Al Zidjaly, N. (2007). Alleviating disability through Microsoft PowerPoint: The story of one quadriplegic man in Oman. *Visual Communication*, 6 (1), pp. 73–93.

Aronsson, K., and A.-C. Cederborg. (1994). Conarration and voice in family therapy: Voicing, devoicing and orchestration. *Text*, 14 (3), pp. 345–370.

Aukrust, V. (2002). "What did you do in school today?" Speech genres and tellability in multiparty family mealtime conversations in two cultures. In S. Blum-Kulka and C.E. Snow (eds.), *Talking to Adults: The Contribution of Multiparty Discourse to Language Acquisition*. Mahwah, NJ: Lawrence Erlbaum, pp. 55–83.

Aukrust, V.G., and C.E. Snow. (1998). Narratives and explanations during mealtime conversations in Norway and the U.S. *Language in Society*, 27 (2), pp. 221–246.

Austin, H., and L. Carpenter. (2008). Troubled, troublesome, troubling mothers: The dilemma of difference in women's personal motherhood narratives. *Narrative Inquiry*, 18 (2), pp. 378–392.

Bamberg, M. (2004). Considering counter narratives. In M. Bamberg and M. Andrews (eds.), *Considering Counter Narratives: Narrating, Resisting, Making Sense*. Amsterdam: John Benjamins, pp. 351–372.

Bauman, R. (1986). *Story, Performance and Event*. Cambridge: Cambridge University Press.

Beach, W.A., and J.S. Good. (2004). Uncertain family trajectories: Interactional consequences of cancer diagnosis, treatment, and prognosis. *Journal of Social and Personal Relationships*, 21 (1), pp. 8–32.

Beach, W.A., and A.S. Lockwood. (2003). Making the case for airline compassion fares: The serial organization of problem narratives during a family crisis. *Research on Language and Social Interaction*, 36 (4), pp. 351–393.

Blum-Kulka, S. (1993). "You gotta know how to tell a story": Telling, tales, and tellers in American and Israeli narrative events at dinner. *Language in Society*, 22 (3), pp. 361–402.

Blum-Kulka, S. (1997). *Dinner Talk: Cultural Patterns of Sociability and Socialization in Family Discourse*. Mahwah, NJ: Lawrence Erlbaum.

Blum-Kulka, S. (2000). Gossipy events at family dinners: Negotiating sociability, presence and the moral order. In J. Coupland (ed.), *Small Talk*. London: Longman/Pearson Education, pp. 213–240.

Blum-Kulka, S., and Snow, C.E. (1992). Developing autonomy for tellers, tales and telling in family narrative-events. *Journal of Narrative and Life History*, 2 (3), pp. 187–217.

Bruner, J. (1990). *Acts of Meaning*. Cambridge, MA: Harvard University Press.

Davies, C.E. (2010). "We had a wonderful time": Individual sibling voices and the joint construction of a family ethos through narrative performance. *Narrative Inquiry*, 20 (1), pp. 20–36.

Erickson, F. (1990). The social construction of discourse coherence in a family dinner table conversation. In B. Dorval (ed.), *Conversational Organization and Its Development*. Norwood, NJ: Ablex, pp. 207–238.

Gee, J.P. (1999). *Social Linguistics and Literacies: Ideology in Discourse*. 2nd edn. London: Taylor & Francis.

Georgakopoulou, A. (2002). Greek children and familiar narratives in family contexts: En route to cultural performances. In S. Blum-Kulka and C.E. Snow (eds.), *Talking to Adults: The Contribution of Multiparty*

Discourse to Language Acquisition. Mahwah, NJ: Lawrence Erlbaum, pp. 33–54.

Georgakopoulou, A. (2007). *Small Stories, Interaction and Identities.* Amsterdam: John Benjamins.

Goodwin, M.H. (2007). Occasioned knowledge exploration in family interaction. *Discourse & Society,* 18 (1), pp. 93–110.

Gordon, C. (2003). Aligning as a team: Forms of conjoined participation in (stepfamily) interaction. *Research on Language and Social Interaction,* 36 (4), pp. 395–431.

Gordon, C. (2005). Hypothetical narratives and "trying on" the identity of "big sister" in parent–child discourse. In A. Tyler, M. Takada, Y. Kim, and D. Marinova (eds.), *Language in Use: Cognitive and Discourse Perspectives on Language and Language Learning.* Washington, DC: Georgetown University Press, pp. 191–201.

Gordon, C. (2006). Reshaping prior text, reshaping identities. *Text & Talk,* 26 (4–5), pp. 545–571.

Gordon, C. (2007a). "Al Gore's our guy": Linguistically constructing a family political identity. In D. Tannen, S. Kendall, and C. Gordon (eds.), *Family Talk: Discourse and Identity in Four American Families.* Oxford: Oxford University Press, pp. 233–262. (Originally printed in *Discourse & Society,* 15 (4), 2004, pp. 607–631.)

Gordon, Cynthia (2007b). "I just feel horribly embarrassed when she does that": Constituting a mother's identity. In D. Tannen, S. Kendall, and C. Gordon (eds.), *Family Talk: Discourse and Identity in Four American Families.* Oxford: Oxford University Press, pp. 71–101.

Gordon, C. (2009). *Making Meanings, Creating Family: Intertextuality and Framing in Family Interaction.* Oxford: Oxford University Press.

Gordon, C. (2011). Impression management on reality TV: Emotion in parental accounts. *Journal of Pragmatics,* 43 (14), pp. 3551–3564.

Gordon, C. (2013). "You are killing your kids": Framing and impoliteness in a health makeover reality TV show. In N. Lorenzo-Dus and P. Garcés-Conejos Blitvich (eds.), *Real Talk: Reality Television and Discourse Analysis in*

Action. Basingstoke, UK: Palgrave Macmillan, pp. 245–265.

Hays, S. (1996). *Cultural Contradictions of Motherhood.* New Haven, CT: Yale University Press.

Heath, S.B. (1983). *Ways with Words: Language, Life, and Work in Communities and Classrooms.* Cambridge: Cambridge University Press.

Johansen, M. (2011). Agency and responsibility in reported speech. *Journal of Pragmatics,* 43 (11), pp. 2845–2860.

Klein, W.L. (2009). Turban narratives: Discourses of identification and difference among Punjabi Sikh families in Los Angeles. In A. Reyes and A. Lo (eds.), *Beyond Yellow English: Toward a Linguistic Anthropology of Asian Pacific America.* Oxford: Oxford University Press, pp. 111–130.

Labov, W. (1972). *Language in the Inner City: Studies in the Black English Vernacular.* Philadelphia: University of Pennsylvania Press.

Labov, W., and Waletzky, J. (1967). Narrative analysis: Oral versions of personal experience. In J. Helm (ed.), *Essays on the Verbal and Visual Arts: Proceedings of the 1966 Annual Spring Meeting of the American Ethnological Society.* Seattle: University of Washington Press, pp. 21–44.

Lee, H. (2010). "I am a *Kirogi* mother": Education exodus and life transformation among Korean transnational women. *Journal of Language, Identity, and Education,* 9 (4), pp. 250–264.

Mandelbaum, J. (1987). Couples sharing stories. *Communication Quarterly,* 35 (2), pp. 144–170.

Mandelbaum, J. (2010). Concurrent and intervening actions during storytelling in family "ceremonial" dinners. In D. Schiffrin, A. De Fina, and A. Nylund (eds.), *Telling Stories: Language, Narrative, and Social Life.* Washington, DC: Georgetown University Press, pp. 161–173.

Minami, M. (2001). Maternal styles of narrative elicitation and the development of children's narrative skill: A study of parental scaffolding. *Narrative Inquiry,* 11 (1), pp. 55–80.

Minami, M., and A. McCabe. (1995). Rice balls and bear hunts: Japanese and North American family narrative patterns. *Journal of Child Language*, 22 (2), pp. 423–445.

Norrick, N.R. (1997). Twice-told tales: Collaborative narration of familiar stories. *Language in Society*, 26 (2), pp. 199–220.

Nylund, A. (2008). "We are a lot closer now, thank goodness!": Structure and the role of "closeness" in online stories of sibling experience. *eVox*, 2 (1), pp. 51–66.

Ochs, E., and T. Kremer-Sadlik. (2013). *Fast-Forward Family: Home, Work, and Relationships in Middle-Class America.* Berkeley and Los Angeles: University of California Press.

Ochs, E., and C. Taylor. (1992). Family narrative as political activity. *Discourse & Society*, 3 (3), pp. 301–340.

Ochs, E., and C. Taylor. (1995). The "father knows best" dynamic in family dinner narratives. In K. Hall and M. Bucholtz (eds.), *Gender Articulated: Language and the Socially Constructed Self.* New York: Routledge, pp. 97–120.

Ochs, E., M. Shohet, B. Campos, and M. Beck. (2010). Coming together at dinner: A study of working families. In K. Christensen and B. Schneider (eds.), *Workplace Flexibility: Realigning 20th-Century Jobs for a 21st-Century Workforce.* Ithaca, NY: Cornell University Press, pp. 57–70.

Ochs, E., C. Taylor, D. Rudolph, and R. Smith. (1992). Storytelling as a theory-building activity. *Discourse Processes*, 15 (1), pp. 37–72.

Pash, D.M. (2008). The lived worlds of gay co-father families: Narratives of family, community, and cultural life. Doctoral dissertation, University of California, Los Angeles.

Paugh, A. (2012). Speculating about work: Dinnertime narratives among dual-earner American families. *Text & Talk*, 32 (5), pp. 615–636.

Petraki, E. (2001). The play of identities in Cypriot-Australian family storytelling. *Narrative Inquiry*, 11 (2), pp. 335–362.

Petraki, E., C. Baker, and M. Emmison. (2007). Moral versions of motherhood and daughterhood in Greek-Australian family narratives. In M. Bamberg, A. De Fina, and D. Schiffrin (eds.), *Selves and Identities in Narrative and Discourse.* Amsterdam: John Benjamins, pp. 107–132.

Perregaard, B. (2010). "Luckily it was only for 10 minutes": Ideology, discursive positions, and language socialization in family interaction. *Journal of Sociolinguistics*, 14 (3), pp. 370–398.

Philips, S.U. (1972). Participant structures and communicative competence: Warm Springs children in community and classroom. In C.B. Cazden, V.P. John, and D. Hymes (eds.), *Functions of Language in the Classroom.* New York: Columbia Teachers Press, pp. 370–394.

Schiffrin, D. (1996). Narrative as self-portrait: Sociolinguistic constructions of identity. *Language in Society*, 25 (2), pp. 167–203.

Schiffrin, D. (2000). Mother/daughter discourse in a Holocaust oral history: "Because then you admit that you're guilty." *Narrative Inquiry*, 10 (1), pp. 1–44.

Sirota, K.G. (2010). Narratives of transformation: Family discourse, autism and trajectories of hope. *Discourse & Society*, 21 (5), pp. 544–564.

Snow, C.E., and D.E. Beals. (2006). Mealtime talk that supports literacy development. *New Directions for Child and Adolescent Development*, 111, pp. 51–66.

Sterponi, L. (2003). Account episodes in family discourse: The making of morality in everyday interaction. *Discourse Studies*, 5 (1), pp. 79–100.

Tannen, D. (1990). *You Just Don't Understand: Women and Men in Conversation.* New York: Quill.

Tannen, D. (1994). The relativity of linguistic strategies: Rethinking power and solidarity in gender and dominance. In *Gender and Discourse.* Oxford: Oxford University Press, pp. 19–52.

Tannen, D. (2007a). Power maneuvers and connection maneuvers in family interaction. In D. Tannen, S. Kendall, and C. Gordon (eds.), *Family Talk: Discourse and Identity in Four American Families.* Oxford: Oxford University Press, pp. 27–48.

Tannen, D. (2007b). *Talking Voices: Repetition, Dialogue, and Imagery in Conversational Discourse*. 2nd edn. Cambridge: Cambridge University Press.

Tannen, D. (2008). "We've never been close, we're very different": Three narrative types in sister discourse. *Narrative Inquiry*, 18 (2), pp. 206–229.

Tannen, D., S. Kendall, and C. Gordon (eds.). (2007). *Family Talk: Discourse and Identity in Four American Families*. Oxford: Oxford University Press.

Tovares, A. (2010). All in the family: Small stories and narrative construction of a shared family identity that includes pets. *Narrative Inquiry*, 20 (1), pp. 1–19.

Varenne, H. (1992). *Ambiguous Harmony: Family Talk in America*. With the collaboration of C. Hill and P. Byers. Norwood, NJ: Ablex.

17 The Narrative Dimensions of Social Media Storytelling

Options for Linearity and Tellership

RUTH PAGE

17.1 Social Media Storytelling: Contexts for Analysis

This chapter examines the narrative dimensions of stories that are told in social media contexts. The stories published on blogs, social network sites, and wikis are important resources that exemplify the increasing range and diversity of storytelling practices employed at the turn of the twenty-first century, providing case studies against which scholars can test existing definitions and frameworks for narrative analysis. The discussion of the stories told in social media contexts is informed by several fields of research. First, the focus on the distinctive affordances of social media (as compared with print or face-to-face contexts for narration) places the analysis in the context of transmedial narratology (Ryan 2004), multimodal narrative analysis (Page 2010), and intermedial narrative studies (Grisakova and Ryan 2011). The need for a media-sensitive approach can be understood as part of the expansion of post-classical narratology (Herman 1997). The particular stream of transmedial narrative analysis that has examined the stories produced and consumed with the use of digital technology (which would in its broadest sense also include the social media stories told via digital devices like computers and smart phones) has for the most part been taken up within narrative criticism with a focus on digitally enabled forms of fictional narrative, such as hypertext fiction (Bell 2010); literary gaming (Ensslin 2014), and fan fiction (Thomas 2011); see also Ryan (2006) for an overview.

The focus on digitally enabled modes of narration has also influenced discourse-analytic and sociolinguistic narrative research. Rather than focusing on texts that purport to be fictional, sociolinguists, anthropologists, and media scholars have begun to examine examples of personal storytelling told online in public contexts, including those posted to discussion forums (McLellan 1997; Harrison and Barlow 2009), on reviewing sites (Vasquez 2014), in live Internet commentaries (Jucker 2010), in private online interactions like e-mail (Georgakopoulou 2004, 2007), and in the life

The Handbook of Narrative Analysis, First Edition. Edited by Anna De Fina and Alexandra Georgakopoulou.
© 2015 John Wiley & Sons, Inc. Published 2019 by John Wiley & Sons, Inc.

writing gathered in public memorial archives of different kinds (Rak and Poletti 2013). This research has considered the extent to which narrative patterns found in earlier, offline contexts of storytelling (such as conversational storytelling or written forms of autobiography and oral history accounts) also occur in online contexts, but might be reshaped by the asynchronous, written interactions which are specific to the sites under consideration. The focus on digitally enabled narration in online contexts for interaction should also be understood within the broader field of computer-mediated communication (see Androutsopoulos 2006 and Herring 2007 for useful introductory overviews). In this chapter, I focus on the forms of narration found in one particular form of computer-mediated communication: the online platforms developed in the mid-1990s that are brought together under the umbrella term "social media." Often associated with the similar term "web 2.0" (Kaplan and Haenlein 2009), social media sites are many and varied (including blogs, wikis, and social network sites) and have begun to form a particular area of interest within studies of computer-mediated communication more generally (Barton and Lee 2013; Thurlow and Mroczek 2011) and in studies of storytelling in particular (Georgakopoulou 2013; Page 2012).

Like other computer-mediated discourse, social media genres are highly intertextual and multimodal, exhibiting the networked convergence of information streams and interactions that typify contemporary Internet use. However, social media genres are characterized by their distinctive collaborative potential (the opportunity for narrators to interact with a networked audience), their episodic formats (the distribution of textual fragments as posts or updates within an archive), and their tendency to prioritize recency over retrospection (through the use of timelines and reverse-chronological ordering). The episodic and collaborative affordances of social media formats present opportunities for people to tell stories in ways that might at first appear novel and qualitatively distinct from offline modes of narration. But as Heyd (2009) reminds us, complete innovation in communicative practices is relatively rare. More often, apparently novel forms of computer-mediated discourse may have antecedents in earlier examples. The social media genres I describe in this chapter are in a state of constant evolution, and may not appear "new" at all, depending on the perspective from which they are viewed. In order to distinguish between the more or less innovative storytelling practices as shaped by social media contexts, I draw on Herring's (2011) useful description of types of change as familiar, reconfigured, and emergent. The need to distinguish between more or less familiar genres is not limited to narrative analysis, and has generated considerable interest in relation to computer-mediated discourse more generally. As Giltrow and Stein (2009) point out, the use of the term "genre" (here understood as recognizable and regular patterns of communication) is not bound to a single semiotic mode or production medium, nor is it confined to a single discipline or research tradition; hence it might be readily applied to elucidate the hybridity and convergence (Jenkins 2006) that characterize social media interactions. Herring's distinctions between familiar, reconfigured, and emergent genres can thus draw diachronic comparisons between examples of computer-mediated discourse (including those found in social media sites) and their formal and functional antecedents in different modes of communication (such as print, film, face-to-face interaction, and earlier digital formats).

Familiar genres are those that are reproduced from earlier formats with minimal change marked by transferring the story to its new social media context. Examples of familiar narrative genres include uploading existing narrative content (such as news broadcasts) to the video-sharing site YouTube. Although publishing a broadcast in YouTube may enable comments to be posted, these comments will not change the content of the broadcast itself. Other examples (outside social media sites) might include uploading an unmodified written narrative to a digitized format (such as the archived texts in Project Gutenberg or other free e-book sites). In contrast, reconfigured genres are those that have antecedents in existing practices, but that have been influenced by the formats in which they are produced or consumed. Examples of reconfigured genres might include the relationship between diaries and the new format of personal blogs, which enables the public creation of a previously private form of life writing. The interactive affordances of blog writing, such as linking, commenting, and embedding content from other sites, can in turn impact the qualities of the story genres that emerge in and across blog posts (see Page 2012 on blogs and illness narratives and Walker Rettberg 2008 on the narrative potential of blogs more generally). Finally, emergent genres are those that are entirely innovative, and qualitatively distinct from their predecessors. Examples of emergent narrative practices in social media contexts include the use of wiki software to enable multiple contributors who are geographically and temporally remote from each other to add, edit, or delete a developing story's content, and to archive that process so that previous versions of the narrative are also available alongside the most recent revision of a narrative account. As these examples suggest, Herring's distinctions highlight the extent to which a particular genre is more or less comparable with an earlier form. That being the case, there might be close comparisons between social media examples and earlier genres in one mode (such as conversation) that seem quite distinct from another (say a print-based model of narrative production). In a similar principle, it might seem that only one aspect of the social media storytelling in a particular example has been reconfigured, while other aspects of the narration appear to be familiar and unchanged from the antecedent genre in question.

Distinguishing between the familiar, reconfigured, and emergent examples of social media storytelling is useful as a means of sketching out the variation in the forms of storytelling currently proliferating in social media contexts, and also as a means of reflecting on the nature of narrative itself. It is thus useful to return to key definitions and frameworks for narrative. The widespread use of the term "narrative" across different disciplines is well documented, along with ongoing debates about what that term might actually mean (Ryan 2004, 2006). In this chapter, I will use "narrative" to refer to a particular kind of textual genre, rather than broader uses of the term that refer to culturally constructed modes of interpretation for social phenomena, such as Lyotard's (1984) "grand narratives." Literary-critical and discourse-analytic traditions of narrative research have put forward text-centered definitions of narrative in similar but distinctive terms. From a literary-critical tradition, Prince defined narrative as "the representation of at least one event, one change in a state of affairs" (1999: 43). In this definition, eventhood and change are the minimum criteria for a text to be deemed a narrative. From a sociolinguistic perspective, Labov defined narrative as "one method of recapitulating past experience by matching a verbal sequence of clauses to the sequence of events which (it is inferred) actually occurred" (Labov 1972: 359–360). Like Prince, Labov's definition emphasizes events (as opposed to description) that are reported in a sequence, but that are sequenced so as to iconically match "real world" events. A full survey of the ways in which these minimal, criterial definitions of narrative have been critiqued and refined is beyond the scope of this essay (but see Herman 2009 and Ryan 2007 for overviews).

Put broadly, both traditions of narrative research have moved away from "all or nothing" attempts to classify narratives (where a text is either classified as a narrative or it is not), to a more flexible, relativist recognition of the diverse forms and functions of narrative, sometimes framed within debates about narrativity (a scalar concept where a text can be more or less like prototypical examples of narrative). The move towards narrativity has gone hand-in-hand with a move away from considering what Herman (2009: 34) described as "set piece" narratives (such as the self-contained literary artifacts that dominated structuralist narratology and the elicited narratives that informed the early sociolinguistic development of the Labovian paradigm) towards a wider range of storytelling practices, such as those described as small stories (Georgakopoulou 2007, and this volume, chapter 13). But determining which aspects of a text might give rise to perceptions of narrativity is no easy task; these features are many and varied, belonging to an open-ended, "fuzzy set" (Ryan 2007: 28). From a literary-critical perspective, perceptions of narrativity are associated with textual features, such as tense and aspect (Herman 1997); structural elements, such as the logical connections evoked between reported events, where there is a preference for causality above temporality alone (Onega and Landa 1996); and the extent to which the sequenced events are combined in regular patterns that resemble a "plot" revolving around the resolution of a problem with a clearly marked beginning, middle, and end (Ryan 2007).

In discourse-analytic traditions, a multilayered approach to comparisons between narratives in different social and modal contexts has gained traction particularly in response to Ochs and Capps's (2001) elegant description of narrative dimensions. Ochs and Capps's dimensional framework outlines the different structural and contextualized aspects of narrative and is well suited to the analysis of social media storytelling, which must take account of both the narrative product and the narration process. The dimensions of narrative are summarized in Table 17.1.

A full discussion of how the dimensions of narrative are reworked in social media contexts can be found in Page (2012). Given that the distinctive features of social media sites are their episodic formats and architectures emphasizing recency, and their capacity for enabling reconfigured forms of interaction among multiple participants (illustrated through metaphors like "a network of contacts" or the rhetoric of "crowd sourcing" for collaborative endeavors), I concentrate in this chapter on how these affordances influence two interrelated narrative dimensions: first, the ways in which the formal features of social media storytelling are positioned within the spectrums of linearity; and second, the opportunities for tellership that are enabled through social media's interactive capacities.

In order to provide a coherent focus for the analysis, the illustrative examples chosen for discussion all center on social media responses to and retellings of the same event: the Hillsborough disaster of 1989. The Hillsborough disaster was a human stampede on April 15, 1989 at a domestic football match in Sheffield, United Kingdom, which resulted

Table 17.1 Narrative dimensions and possibilities.

Dimension	Possibilities
Tellership	Whether the story is told by a single teller, or multiple tellers
Tellability	The value of a story as highly worth telling, or seemingly irrelevant
Embeddedness	The extent to which as story can be detached from or embedded in its context
Linearity	The structural qualities of a story as closed, temporal sequence, or open-ended and multi-linear
Moral Stance	The narrator's attitude towards reported events, which may be certain or fluctuating

Adapted from Ochs and Capps 2001: 20.

in 96 deaths and several hundred injuries. The disaster has been described as one of the worst sporting tragedies of the twentieth century, and its legacy continues for the victims' families and football fans in the United Kingdom to the present day. That legacy has included an ongoing quest for justice, with a particular focus on the need to attribute blame appropriately for the events that took place, and therefore to investigate and appropriately remedy the faults which led to the tragedy.

The events of the Hillsborough disaster thus include both the accounts of the crush itself and the aftermath. The subsequent quest for justice remains unresolved (at least at the time of writing), and has over the years included reports of key events such as the initial inquiry in 1990, which resulted in the Taylor Report, but which was found to be unsatisfactory as an explanation and remediation for the faults that gave rise to the crush and the subsequent loss of life. The later publication of the Hillsborough Independent Panel's report in September 2012 documented failure on the part of the South Yorkshire police force, the emergency services, and certain media outlets for their response to the disaster. In December 2012, the verdicts of accidental death for the 96 fans were then quashed by the High Court and a new criminal inquiry reopened. In this sense, the events that constitute the story of the Hillsborough disaster are still ongoing, and continue to attract high-level commentary in both mainstream and social media channels for the charitable fundraising associated with the cause, its impact on British football communities, and the politicized critique of public services within the United Kingdom.

17.2 Linearity and Social Media Storytelling

The dimension of linearity concerns the options that a narrator might take up when organizing reported events in a narrated sequence. As Ochs and Capps point out, there are different ways in which those events might be sequenced. They present the alternatives for organizing an event sequence in binary terms: "The dimension of linearity concerns the extent to which narratives of personal experience depict events as transpiring in a single, closed, temporal, and causal path or, alternatively, in diverse, open, uncertain paths" (2001: 41).

This description is a useful starting point, but as Ochs and Capps go on to argue (2001: 56–57), while much is known about the characteristics of prototypical linearity, once we move beyond conventional examples of storytelling (for example, those told in narrative interviews), alternative forms of linearity remain relatively unexplored and may not fall into the simple binary contrast suggested by Ochs and Capps's description. In moving towards description of less conventional examples of storytelling (such as the social media examples in this chapter), it is useful to separate the different aspects of linearity glossed by Ochs and Capps by drawing on narratological discussions about the features that give rise to narrativity. In this case, I begin by differentiating the "temporal" aspects of linearity (as indicated through the textual resources of tense choices) and the contrast between "open" and "closed" paths (the ways in which events can be combined in sequences that invoke longer, recognized patterns with defined outcomes).

17.2.1   Linearity and the representation of time

Early narrative definitions (such as Labov's given earlier in this chapter) presuppose a retrospective, single temporal sequence of prototypical linearity, where a linear model of chronological time (Carr 1990) is mapped onto the textual realization of the narrative. But narrators need not recount events in the past tense, and may imply the temporal orientation of events in various forms. Narration can include syntactic options of tense and aspect to indicate whether events are represented as taking place in the past, in the present, or in future projections, and whether the events are completed or continuous. Compare examples 1–3 below from different social media sites (my italics).

(1)   The ensuing influx of supporters *caused* crushing and some fans *climbed* over side fences or *were lifted* by fellow supporters onto the stand above to escape the crush. (Wikipedia article, "Hillsborough Disaster," November 12, 2014)

(2)   The families of the 96 people who died at Hillsborough, very emotional, *are leaving* the court now. (@David_Conn, December 19, 2012)

(3)   Hillsborough inquests: Video link facilities *have been arranged* to Liverpool Civil and Family Courts in Vernon St, Lpool city centre. You *will be able to follow* the court proceedings in London. Approximate time is from 10.30 am tomorrow (Wednesday 19th December). Let's *hope* the judges *do* the right thing and *quash* the accidental death verdicts.
(Official Hillsborough Justice Campaign, Facebook group post, December 18, 2012)

The narrative examples each report a series of events in a "single sequence." But the temporal orientation of the events varies, from simple past tense verbs ("caused" and "crushed"), which report completed events in the retrospective account in the Wikipedia article, to present continuous constructions ("are leaving"), which present events as if they are being reported in real time in the Twitter update by newspaper reporter David Conn, to the projections of future outcomes using modal auxiliaries ("will be able to follow") and non-finite forms ("hope," "do," and "quash").

Although options to represent events in the past, present, or future are available for stories told in social media, the conventions for updating tend to favor recency over retrospection (see Page 2010 on the frequency of "breaking news" stories on social network sites in particular; see also Georgakopoulou 2007, and this volume, chapter 13). The examples considered in this chapter are too small to permit a generalized, quantitative comparison, but a study of the temporal adverbs found in a larger study of social media narratives found that language that reflects the present moment (as indicated through adverbs like "now" or "tomorrow") occurred more often in updates posted to Twitter and Facebook than in offline contexts, with other social media genres like blogs falling midway between the two (Page 2012: 192). The range of options for representing linear time thus includes retrospective accounts of events located in the distant past, but also makes use of present tense and non-finite forms, particularly exploited by the real-time reporting favored by social media sites like Twitter, which describes itself as the place to "find out what's happening, right now" (Twitter homepage).

17.2.2   *Linearity and predictable patterns*

But the temporal orientation of events is only one textual device that might give rise to the interpretation of linearity as more or less canonical. As Herman (1997: 1053), suggests, the grammatical structures (tense forms) that lead the audience to infer actions carried out by participants is perhaps only a minimal cue for narrativity. In addition, "narrative also depends on how the form of a sequence is anchored in – or triggers a recipient to activate – knowledge about the world" (1997: 1048). This cognitive approach to narrativity frames "knowledge about the world" in terms of psychological models of "scripts" and "schemas." The extent to which schemas might help explain how the open or closed dimensions of linearity are interpreted can be assessed through Hoey's (2001) categorization of particular schemas as predictable patterns. Like Giltrow and Stein's (2009) discussion of genre, Hoey's model of predictable patterns suggests that the audience's recognition of the pattern is in part generated by features "in" the text (particular content or lexical choices) but also argues that these textual features are contextually interpreted by audiences; linearity is thus in part signaled by textual features, but is also activated as a cognitive, contextual process on the part of the audience.

Specifically, Hoey's (2001) description of the Problem-Solution pattern as a textual schema associated with prototypical narrative suggests that the perception of a final outcome as a resolution to the narrative's complication or "trouble" often rests on the presence and position of an evaluated outcome. For a narrative to be complete, the outcome must be positively evaluated as a satisfactory solution, or negatively evaluated as beyond remediation. Following Labov, the narrator's indications of evaluation are thus a crucial element in determining the outline of a "fully formed" (1972: 362–363), rather than partially completed, narrative. A narrator may then mark the closure of the narrative sequence by including events that resolve a previous problem, or by providing an evaluative comment or punchline. The extent to which the linearity of a story might be interpreted as open-ended thus depends on whether a predictable pattern (like the Problem-Solution pattern) is evoked or not, and the extent to which the elements of the pattern are represented completely within the narrative sequence or not (i.e., whether there is an evaluative end point or not).

The events of the Hillsborough disaster necessarily invoke a problematic scenario, both in the nature of the localized tragedy and in the broader need for justice. On the basis of the story content, the reports of the events in the Hillsborough disaster may be interpreted as activating a Problem-Solution pattern. But the extent to which the reported events complete the Problem-Solution pattern (that is, provide a response and evaluated outcome) can vary from instance to instance. The account of the Hillsborough disaster and its aftermath given in the Wikipedia article of that name is lengthy (over 14,000 words), with a summarized account of events given in the opening stub (the introductory section that appears in all Wikipedia articles). In the version of the article available on November 12, 2014 (example 4), the stub closed with the following paragraph:

(4)   In September 2012, the Hillsborough Independent Panel concluded that up to 41 of the 96 fatalities might have been saved had they received prompt medical treatment. The report revealed "multiple failures" by other emergency services and public bodies which contributed to the death toll. In response to the panel's report, the Attorney General for England and Wales, Dominic Grieve MP, confirmed he would consider all the new evidence to evaluate whether the original inquest verdicts of accidental death could be overturned.

At the time of writing this version of the Wikipedia article, the narrative resolution to the quest for justice was incomplete: the new inquest starting in March 2014 was still hearing evidence and was not expected to give its verdict until 2015, nor had remediation for the injustices been carried out satisfactorily. Although the narrative sequence indicated a series of problems (the fatalities that "might have been saved" and the "multiple failures" of public services), the schema lacked a resolution or evaluation. Without a final outcome, the quest for justice was ongoing; thus the schematic outline of the Problem-Solution pattern at this point can be considered incomplete and the linearity of the path "open".

In contrast, once the news broke that the verdicts of accidental death had been quashed by the High Court of England, resolutions to the narrative and positive evaluations began to be posted to social network sites. Quoting the Lord Chief Justice, news reporter David Conn tweeted a projected positive outcome to the inquiry:

(5)   The families of those who died will be vindicated and the memory of those who died will be respected. (@David_Conn, December 19, 2012)

And on Facebook, supporters of "The Official Hillsborough Justice Group" posted evaluative comments indicating that the current episode in the Hillsborough aftermath had come to an end:

(6)   At last they get what they deserve
(7)   Brilliant news, justice at last.

The options of whether or not to invoke predictable patterns that employ a sense of closure are by no means limited to social media, and can be found in other online narratives (such as digital fiction), and in conversational and print forms of unfinished stories, such as incomplete trauma narratives or stories which are revised selectively as the narrator's ongoing life history (Linde 1993). However, the option to defer a final outcome or evaluation is well suited to the episodic, ongoing nature of narration in social media formats, which evolves as events unfold – for example through revisions to a Wikipedia article, or updates posted to a Twitter timeline. It is these episodic formats that draw attention to the third and final aspect of linearity: the modes of production employed by narrators.

17.2.3   Linearity and modes of production

Ochs and Capps's (2001) insights about linearity were derived from a specific sub-corpus of narrative material: conversational stories. These conversational stories included forms of open-ended linearity that were distinguished on the basis of narrative logic (the predictable patterns activated) and the orientation of the narrative content to temporal frames of reference (past, present, or future projection). Further forms of open-ended linearity are enabled by the modes of narrative production and reception that dominate social media. In this respect, there is a contrast between social media modes of production where the narrative sequence is published within a single textual unit (such as a single blog post), and modes of production where the narrative sequence is distributed across multiple textual units (such as blog posts and comments). Although examples of narrative sequences published as self-contained artifacts within a single unit can be found in social media (such as online news reports of the Hillsborough disaster, or uploads of television documentaries to YouTube), these examples are overshadowed by the increasing number of episodic formats that have emerged from social media contexts (such as a series of updates and comments, or repeated revisions to wiki pages), which are well suited to open-ended forms of narrative linearity. The social media alternatives to the turn-by-turn or page-by-page examples of canonical linearity are many and varied. The first distinction between episodic arrangements of narrative material in social media formats is based on how the individual narrative episodes are arranged within a framing archive.

The episodic publication of textual segments (such as posts or updates) can be arranged within the archived architectures of different social media platforms in sequences that mirror the sequential reporting of events over time, or which use other kinds of non-chronological ordering principles. For example, some archives use chronological order to store material (for example, presenting posts in a timeline), but that chronology need not be standard and may use reverse-chronological order (that is, presenting the most recent material first). Other archives (like YouTube or the more recent joke-sharing site 9GAG) may instead use rankings to determine which position within the archive an individual post occupies, or may employ other database systems to categorize and make material searchable. As the convergence of shared materials across multiple networked sites continues to increase, it is possible for the episodes of a particular story to be published in multiple, interlinked archives. For example, a person who is a member of sites like Tumblr, Instagram, Facebook, and Twitter may choose to share a post simultaneously across multiple networks. When this happens, an individual episode may be archived within timelines across multiple sites: the open-ended nature of the linearity is thus extended to distribution within multiple networks, not within a single network.

As this brief overview suggests, the many and varied aspects of narrative design implied by linearity can be combined in multiple patterns that render a simple, binary contrast between canonical and open-ended sequences too simplistic. Instead, we might use these factors to help us map out the ways in which particular instances of storytelling in social media rework this narrative dimension in more or less innovative ways. The various possibilities for linearity (dependent on temporal orientation, narrative schemas and mode of production) are open to further variation when they are combined with the options single or multiple narrators can draw upon when they (co-)construct stories from social media materials.

17.3   Tellership and Social Media Narration

The narrative dimension of tellership concerns the extent to which a narrative is produced by a single teller for a relatively passive audience, as compared with multiple participants who actively co-construct the shape of the story. The possibility for many tellers to collaborate occurs in different media, including the conversational storytelling considered by Ochs and Capps (2001) and others (Goodwin 2007, and this volume, chapter 10; Norrick 2008). In this chapter, tellership is approached in textual terms, for example in the options for narrators to share the distribution of narrative content between different tellers, who post their contributions episodically in social media formats like forum threads, updates, or comments in a fashion similar to the ways in which narration can be distributed across multiple turns. Other social aspects of what might be broadly construed as tellership are taken up in other contributions to this volume (for more on entitlement claims, see, e.g., Shuman 2005, and this volume, chapter 2).

As discussed in more detail in Page (2012: 196–200), the distinctive options for co-tellership in social media can be distinguished on the basis of whether control of the narration is shared equally between participants, or is retained by particular individuals. These options for control are not just determined by the floor-holding strategies familiar from face-to-face contexts of narration, but are structured according to the affordances of the particular textual formats that each social media genre uses (for example, within Facebook, a profile owner has more options for authoring text within the space of their profile than do the members of their Friend list). The options for social media tellership are also differentiated according to whether the contributions from multiple tellers are distributed across separate textual units (for example, a blog post by one teller and a comment made by a second teller), or whether the contributions are additions made to a single textual unit (such as a wiki page). In addition to these distinctions, we might also distinguish co-tellership derived from direct interactions between the narrative participants from co-tellership generated primarily by the algorithms of search engines (such as a Twitter search for a keyword or hashtag), which aggregate material that may not entail interactional coherence between the participants.

Like the narrative dimension of linearity, the social media options for generating new formats for co-tellership are varied, and range from familiar to more innovative examples. At the more familiar end of the spectrum, co-tellership patterns reminiscent of those in conversational narration can be found in the turn-by-turn, post-by-post exchanges made on discussion forums, or within comments appended to updates in sites like Facebook. But the options to combine those separate contributions within single textual units can lead to reconfigured textual patterns, such as modified retweets, where the second turn is placed before the initiating narrative content. In example 8, the original tweet posted by journalist David Conn appears in an abbreviated form to the right of the abbreviation MT (for "Modified Tweet"), while the second participant has added the deictic pointer "That →" to draw attention to the outcome.

(8)   That→MT @david_conn inquest into the 96 people who died in the Hillsborough disaster has been quashed (@Hallymark 19 December, 2012)

More extensive examples of co-tellership, in which multiple authors contribute to an emerging narrative told within a single textual unit, include the collaborative efforts of creating wiki pages, such as Wikipedia articles. For example, the Hillsborough Disaster Wikipedia article was edited by over 1500 contributors between 2002 and 2012. Unlike offline examples of collaborative textual production, the co-tellership of Wikipedia pages makes its processes of collaboration transparent and accessible in the archives of page histories, allowing the audience to identify which parts of the narrative were added, edited or deleted by which contributors over time.

Perhaps the most innovative example of co-tellership in social media is enabled by the algorithms and architectures of search engines on particular sites, which aggregate the posts made by many contributors about a particular topic. Here co-tellership does not originate from the interactional contributions generated within the coherence of a conversational exchange, but rather as a result of the archived organization of material generated by a search engine. Not all search engines return results in a way that uses a temporal sequence to organize material (the returns of a Google search cannot be said to constitute a narrative, for example), but the architectures of sites like Twitter and Facebook, which use a reverse-chronological timeline in their news feeds, can enable the co-tellership of ongoing narratives about particular topics to emerge as the search engine draws together posts published by many different members of the site in question. The extent to which these computer-generated timelines function to enable co-tellership is varied. As Herring (1999) suggests, the extent to which interactional coherence is possible can vary according to the architectures of particular sites. The same is true of the narrative coherence created through co-tellership. Just because a timeline or a forum thread is created by posts from multiple tellers over time does not mean it will yield a coherent narrative. Even within sites where the interaction on threads enables sequential or interactional coherence, the development of a single thread as posts are added over time can sometimes be disrupted as new tellers join the discussion and shift the topic or stance in new directions (Georgakopoulou 2013).

The affordances (Hutchby 2001) of the microblogging site Twitter would seem to offer particular but constrained potential for coherence between the updates posted to the site about a particular topic. On the one hand, site members can mark their posts as contributing to a topic by using a hashtag, which in turn can be retrieved by searching for that term in the "discover" tab. Thus the results of a search for a particular topic, such as "Hillsborough," will return all the updates posted to Twitter containing that word and present them in reverse-chronological sequence relative to the time of the post's publication. On the other hand, Twitter is a "noisy," fast-paced, ephemeral environment where posts rapidly disappear from view, and where participants often talk about the same topic without directly interacting with each other.

The topic-centered talk on Twitter has been described as a form of ambient affiliation (Zappavigna 2011), where participants might be broadly aware that their commentary on and conversation about particular topics of interest (such as a political election, national sports event, or television show) is a way of marking their membership within a broader social category (such as fans of a particular celebrity, political affiliation, or nationality). Ambient affiliation is characterized by a constellation of talk about a topic, not by direct exchanges between individual members of Twitter. Thus while the hundreds of Twitter members who post updates about the ongoing legal battles and charitable fundraising associated with the quest for justice following the Hillsborough disaster show affiliation with the topic by using the hashtag #JFT96 (an abbreviation of "Justice for the 96," referring to the fans who were killed in the crush), they do not necessarily respond to each other's posts. As such, the co-tellership of the aggregated posts found in a search for "Hillsborough" appears to be generated by the algorithms of the search engine, not by a collaborative design on the part of the Twitter members.

17.4   Linearity and Tellership Combined

Linearity and tellership are separable but interrelated dimensions that can be visualized as intersecting parameters that compare and contrast the qualities of different narrative examples. The four possible options for combining familiar or innovative dimensions of linearity and tellership are represented in Table 17.2. The impact of each combination of the dimensions on storytelling practices is discussed in turn in the subsections below.

Table 17.2   Combinations of linearity and tellership.

Familiar linearity and single teller Example: Television news flash uploaded to YouTube	*Innovative linearity and single teller* Example: News feed of a single Twitter member
Familiar linearity and multiple tellers Example: Wikipedia article	*Innovative linearity and multiple tellers* Example: Aggregated search results for a keyword or hashtag in Twitter

17.4.1　Familiar linearity – single teller

The video-sharing site YouTube contains over 2500 uploads that focus on the Hillsborough disaster. These videos are of many kinds, including tribute videos, music videos, copies of dramatizations of the events (such as McGovern's 1996 television drama), and copies of news footage relating to the events and its aftermath. Unlike episodic formats, which allow the narrator to update a narrative timeline with new material or to respond to comments made by the audience, when preexisting narrative material is posted to YouTube, the narrative dimensions of the original content are preserved even when the text is remediated (see also Burgess and Green 2009 for a more detailed introduction to YouTube). For example, the script read by the news-reader during the BBC news flash which reported the Hillsborough disaster immediately following the events on the afternoon of April 15, 1989 narrated the details of the crush in a past-tense chronological sequence that matched the order of the report with that of the actual events shown in footage, as follows.

(9)　Fans tried to escape up into the stands from the crush at the Liverpool end and over the spiked crowd barriers at the front. An ambulance appeared as the scale of the disaster became clear. The first casualties were stretchered away, fans and soccer officials helping the rescue workers. Desperate attempts were made to revive victims where they lay as firemen and police struggled to reach those trapped behind security barriers. The Prime Minister has called for an urgent report on the disaster.

The BBC news report itself was first aired in 1989, and was posted to YouTube in 2008. Although comments continue to be appended to the channel years afterwards, these comments do not influence the event line in the news report: they cannot add to the video itself, which remains a self-contained artifact.

17.4.2　Innovative linearity – single teller

Open-ended forms of linearity in social media depart from the textual markers found in past-tense reports, and from modes of production that use standard chronological sequence as an ordering principle. One production alternative is to use reverse chronological archiving principles. For example, when a reader views a Twitter news feed, and they read in a conventional pattern from the top of the screen downwards, they are presented with the most recently posted update first. The conventions of updating in Twitter are that the time of posting is assumed to match the time of the reported event, so if a reader wishes to recover the start point of a narrative retrospectively, they must scroll down through the archive and read from the bottom of the page upwards. In order to accommodate the constantly updated content that appears at the top of a Twitter news feed, the verb forms found in this form of real-time reporting often favor non-finite particles and present or present continuous tense, which create an ongoing sense of "now-ness." The combination of reverse chronological ordering and real-time reporting are illustrated in the following examples, which are taken from the news feed of a journalist who live-tweeted the events of the Hillsborough hearing at the

High Court on December 19, 2012 (my italics). Due to the absence of past-tense verbs, the sense of narrative sequence is contributed primarily by the formats of social media, in this case the timestamp of the update and its position within the timeline of the news feed relative to other posts.

(10)   The Attorney-General *accepts* there is a possibility of a different Hillsborough verdict, such as unlawful killing, if there are new inquests (@David_Conn, 19 December 2012, 10:29)

   The Attorney-General *is applying* himself for the inquest to be quashed, mainly due to medical evidence discrediting coroner and 3:15 cut-off (@David_Conn, 19 December 2012, 10:26)

   Sitting in court 5 *waiting* for the Hillsborough hearing to start, family members *filling* the public gallery, three rows of lawyers in front (@David_Conn, 19 December 2012, 10:23)

17.4.3   Familiar linearity – innovative tellership

Wikipedia has attracted considerable attention as a large-scale collaborative writing project (Myers 2010). In order to maintain consistency across this collaborative enterprise, the Wikipedia community has established a series of key principles, including Neutral Point of View, No Original Research, and Verifiability. Although not every article in Wikipedia is a narrative, the structural guidelines for achieving Neutral Point of View point to the importance of chronological sequence as key principle for ordering the event line within individual articles. Wikipedia's guidelines (2014) suggest that contributors should

(11)   follow the chronological order of events when possible. People remember pieces of information better when they are connected. Chronological order is universally understood. For each individual event, explain "who did what when why," with possible explanations of special challenges, techniques, resources or consequences.

The article for the "Hillsborough Disaster" is structured according to these principles so that each section follows in chronological order, beginning with a description of problems before the events of April 1989, the crush itself, the three investigations of the disaster to date (the Taylor Inquiry, the Stuart-Smith Inquiry, and the Hillsborough Independent Panel), and ongoing legacies (memorials and controversies). Within each subsection of the article, material is consistently organized by chronological sequence, with past tense reports of events that had taken place in the past and so could be verified. For example, the section "Disaster" is further subdivided into subsections: Build-up, The crush, Reactions, Disaster appeal fund, and Effects on survivors.

But Wikipedia articles are not static artifacts. They are in a state of continuous evolution and never regarded as complete. The familiar linearity of the front page is only the most recent iteration of the article, and the archived revision history reveals a more complex process of narration. Perhaps the most radical innovation for co-tellership enabled by wiki software is the capacity for another teller to alter or delete the contributions made by someone else. In Wikipedia, these changes are usually negotiated between contributors on the surrounding forums known as "Talk Pages." In the case of the Hillsborough Disaster article, debates included whether comparisons with other football tragedies should be deleted (which they were) and which later inquiries should be included (or not). Hence the arrangement of events given on the front page is only one aspect of the linearity that typifies Wikipedia. Other, more incomplete or alternative versions of the page can be restored, which points to the unstable, open-ended processes of narration that lie behind the most recent update.

17.4.4   *Innovative linearity – multiple tellers*

The final example of social media storytelling returns to the microblogging site Twitter, but rather than examining a news feed authored by a single person, it considers the narrative potential of a news feed that aggregates the posts written by many people about the same topic (Hillsborough) into a single timeline. As I argued earlier, the linearity of Twitter is far removed from the canonical narratives and their past tense reports, and instead is characterized by events reported in real time without the retrospective point of evaluative closure that marks the completion of a predictable pattern. In both respects, the textual marking of time (through non-finite verb forms) and the abrupt shift from topic to topic make the linearity of stories posted to Twitter seem "open" – all the more so because of the modes of production where reverse chronological archiving structures yield a default view of the Twitter feed with the most recently posted examples first. The ambient affiliation that characterizes Twitter also creates weak interactional coherence between the updates posted to the sites. Not only are the contributions posted by multiple tellers asynchronous (and therefore subject to non-adjacent positioning within a fast-moving archive of the news feed), the contributions are seldom framed as interactions with another individual Twitter member. The multiple tellers whose posts are brought together in an aggregated news feed are not necessarily responding to posts written by each other, they are only marking their contributions as concerned with the same topic (for example, through the use of a hashtag).

The potential for interpreting sequenced posts from an aggregated Twitter timeline as a narrative therefore seems somewhat strained. But, on the surface, the news feed for the search term "Hillsborough" sometimes results in a sequence of events which are reported in real time. Because the updates in Twitter tend to be reported in near synchrony with the time of events, it is thus possible for consecutive posts to seem like a story, as in example 12, taken from the news feed for the search term "Hillsborough" in the Twitter timeline on December 19, 2012.

(12)   Hillsborough Inquests Set to be Quashed – Yahoo! News UK
Via @YahooNewsUK
@huffygit 19 December 2012

Hillsborough families begin to arrive and the Royal Courts of Justice lockerz. com/s/270120028
@Jennyhulse 19 December 2012

Hillsborough at the High Court – follow live updates from 10am liverpoolecho.co. uk/2012/12/19.
@topaunty 19 December 2012

These sequenced posts seem to meet the minimal definitions of narrative given by Prince (1999) and Labov (1972): they report events which unfold over time (the anticipated and actual start of the verdict given at the High Court). However, longer stretches from the aggregated timeline suggest that there is only topical coherence between the posts (generated by the search term). The extent of the temporal connections between reported events is limited to isolated pairs of posts, and it is more typical to find that the aggregated timeline for the search term "Hillsborough" is characterized by repetition and disparate opinions. The following examples are taken from the timeline immediately prior to example 12.

(13) Hillsborough Verdict Set To be Quashed: High Court to be asked to quash original accidental death verdicts after … http://bit.ly/YjvZw2
@NetSecUK

The Hillsborough disaster was terrible but I don't see where this is heading, #timetomoveon
@creationtv

Did people think through "He Ain't Heavy" being the #hillsboroughdisaster charity single? Didn't people die when a stand collapsed?!
@ian_mannly

Sick of hearing about the Hillsborough tragedy! It happened 22 years ago & if the fans were behaving it wouldn't of happened #DealWithIt
@Pat_Duggan25

Hillsborough Inquests Set to be Quashed – Yahoo! News UK uk.news.yahoo.com/ Hillsborough via @YahooNewsUK
@huffygit

This longer sequence of posts taken from the Twitter timeline is typical of the timeline as a whole. Without the clear textual cues of verb tense or temporal adverbs to invoke linearity, and without interactional coherence of a conversational frame between the tellers, the result is a simply a list of "breaking news" and "shared stories" (Georgakopoulou 2007) that are published in time, not a single coherent narrative.

17.5 Conclusion

The episodic and collaborative affordances of social media sites influence the narrative dimensions of linearity and tellership in different ways. Although familiar chronological sequence can be found in some examples (like the past-tense reports found in Wikipedia articles and uploaded YouTube footage), often social network sites exploit real-time reporting and prioritize recency over retrospection. Likewise, while single tellership is possible, there are many forms of co-tellership that reconfigure conversational interactions through social media's architectures and algorithms. The analysis of the social media storytelling examples thus point to the ongoing value of a multidimensional narrative analysis that can examine different aspects of the narrative and narration (its structure and style) and the contexts of production (here the number of tellers and the ways their participation is framed through interactions on different sites). In this chapter, I have dealt only with linearity and tellership, but other narrative dimensions are important for social media storytelling (not least embeddedness).

The variation indicated even in the small selection of social media contexts examined in this chapter also lends strength to the call in narrative analysis for greater attention to the fragmentary stories that occur in interactional contexts, often brought together under the heading of "small stories." As the interactional affordances of social media sites continue to develop and intersect with conversational interactions taking place in face-to-face contexts, there will, no doubt, be further work to refine the ways in which small stories are positioned in increasingly convergent interactional practices across virtual and physical locations. Lastly, the discussions in this chapter focused only on the verbal content of the stories (and on a single language variety: English). While stories published to social media sites by no means do away with the written word, they often exploit multimodal resources (such as image, video, and so on) and take place within a varied, multilingual context. As work on social media storytelling continues to develop, it will need to broaden its horizons to take into account recent trends in computer-mediated communication, such as the analysis of resemiotization (Iedema 2003) and the complex networked practices of multilingual narrators (Androutsopoulos 2013).

REFERENCES

Androutsopoulos, J. (2006). Introduction: Sociolinguistics and computer-mediated communication. *Journal of Sociolinguistics*, 10 (4), pp. 419–438.

Androutsopoulos, J. (2013). Networked multilingualism: Some language practices on Facebook and their implications. *International Journal of Bilingualism*, published online June 11, 2013, doi: 10.1177/1367006913489198.

Barton, D., and C. Lee. (2013). *Language Online: Investigating Digital Texts and Practices*. London: Routledge.

Bell, A. (2010). *The Possible Worlds of Hypertext Fiction*. Basingstoke, UK: Palgrave Macmillan.

Burgess, J., and J. Green. (2009). *YouTube: Online Video and Participatory Culture*. Cambridge: Polity.

Carr, D. (1990). *Time, Narrative and History*. Bloomington: Indiana University Press.

Ensslin, A. (2014). *Literary Gaming*. Cambridge, MA: MIT Press.

Georgakopoulou, A. (2004). To tell or not to tell? Email stories between on- and offline interactions. *Language@Internet*, 1, http://www.languageatinternet.org/articles/2004/36, accessed October 30, 2014.

Georgakopoulou, A. (2007). *Small Stories, Interaction and Identities*. Amsterdam: John Benjamins.

Georgakopoulou, A. (2013). Small stories research and social media: The role of narrative stance-taking in the circulation of a Greek news story. King's College London, Working Papers in Urban Language and Literacies, 100, http://www.kcl.ac.uk/sspp/departments/education/research/ldc/publications/workingpapers/the-papers/WP100.pdf, accessed October 30, 2014.

Giltrow, J., and D. Stein. (2009). *Genres in the Internet: Issues in the Theory of Genre*. Amsterdam: John Benjamins.

Goodwin, C. (2007). Interactive footing. In E. Holt and R. Clift (eds.), *Reporting Talk:*

Reported Speech in Interaction. Cambridge: Cambridge University Press, pp. 16–46.

Grisakova, M., and M.L. Ryan. (2010). *Intermedial Storytelling.* Amsterdam: John Benjamins.

Harrison, S., and J. Barlow. (2009). Politeness strategies and advice-giving in an online arthritis workshop. *Journal of Politeness Research*, 5, pp. 93–111.

Herman, D. (1997). Scripts, sequences, and stories: Elements of a postclassical narratology. *Publications of the Modern Language Association*, 112 (5), pp. 1046–1059.

Herman, D. (2009). *Basic Elements of Narrative.* Oxford: Wiley-Blackwell.

Herring, S. (1999). Interactional coherence in CMC. *Journal of Computer-Mediated Communication*, 4 (4), accessed October 30, 2014, doi: 10.1111/j.1083-6101.1999. tb00106.x.

Herring, S. (2007). A faceted classification scheme for computer-mediated discourse. *Language@Internet*, 4, http://www. languageatInternet.org/articles/2007/761, accessed October 30, 2014.

Herring, S. (2011). Discourse in web 2.0: Familiar, reconfigured, and emergent. Paper presented at Georgetown University Round Table on Languages and Linguistics: Language and New Media: Discourse 2.0. Washington, DC, March 10–13.

Heyd, T. (2009). A model for describing "new" and "old" properties of CMC genres: The case of digital folklore. In J. Giltrow and D. Stein (eds.), *Genres in the Internet: Issues in the Theory of Genre.* Amsterdam: John Benjamins, pp. 239–262.

Hoey, M. (2001). *Textual Interaction: An Introduction to Written Discourse.* London and New York: Routledge.

Hutchby, I. (2001). Technology, texts and affordances. *Sociology*, 35 (2), pp. 441–456.

Iedema, R. (2003). Multimodality, resemiotization: Extending the analysis of discourse as multi-semiotic practice. *Visual Communication*, 2 (1), pp. 29–57.

Jenkins, H. (2006). *Convergence Culture: Where Old and New Media Collide.* New York: New York University Press.

Jucker, A.H. (2010). "Audacious, brilliant!! What a strike!" Live text commentaries on the Internet as real-time narratives. In C.R. Hoffmann (ed.), *Narrative Revisited: Telling a Story in the Age of New Media.* Amsterdam: John Benjamins, pp. 57–78.

Kaplan, A., and M. Haenlein. (2009). Users of the world unite! The challenges and opportunities of social media. *Business Horizons*, 53, pp. 59–68.

Labov, W. (1972). *Language in the Inner City: Studies in the Black English Vernacular.* Philadelphia: University of Pennsylvania Press.

Linde, C. (1993). *Life Stories: The Creation of Coherence.* Oxford: Oxford University Press.

Lyotard, F. (1984). *The Postmodern Condition: A Report on Knowledge.* Translated by G. Bennington and B. Massumi. Minneapolis: University of Minnesota Press.

McLellan, F. (1997). "A whole other story": The electronic narrative of illness. *Literature and Medicine*, 16 (1), pp. 88–107.

Myers, G. (2010). *The Discourse of Blogs and Wikis.* London: Continuum.

Norrick, N. (2008). Negotiating the reception of stories in conversation: Teller strategies for modulating response. *Narrative Inquiry*, 18, pp. 131–151.

Ochs, E., and L. Capps. (2001). *Living Narrative: Creating Lives in Everyday Storytelling.* Cambridge, MA: Harvard University Press.

Onega, S., and J.A.G. Landa. (1996). *Narratology: An Introduction.* London: Longman.

Page, R. (2010). Revisiting narrativity: Small stories in status updates. *Text and Talk*, 30 (4), pp. 423–444.

Page, R. (2012). *Stories and Social Media: Identities and Interaction.* New York: Routledge.

Prince, G. (1999). Revisiting narrativity. In W. Grünzweig and A. Solbach (eds.), *Transcending Boundaries: Narratology in Context.* Tübingen: Gunter Narr Verlag, pp. 53–51.

Rak, J., and A. Poletti. (2013). *Identity Technologies: Constructing the Self Online.* Madison: University of Wisconsin Press.

Ryan, M. (2004). *Narrative Across Media: The Languages of Storytelling*. Lincoln: University of Nebraska Press.

Ryan, M. (2006). *Avatars of Story*. Minneapolis: University of Minnesota Press.

Ryan, M. (2007). Toward a Definition of Narrative. In D. Herman (ed.), *The Cambridge Companion to Narrative*. Cambridge: Cambridge University Press, pp. 22–35.

Shuman, A. (2005). *Other People's Stories: Entitlement Claims and the Critique of Empathy*. Urbana and Chicago: University of Illinois Press.

Thomas, B. (2011). What is fanfiction and why are people saying such nice things about it? *StoryWorlds: A Journal of Narrative Studies*, 3, pp. 1–24.

Thurlow, C., and K. Mroczek. (2011). *Digital Discourse: Language in the New Media*. Oxford: Oxford University Press.

Vasquez, C. (2014). *The Discourse of Online Reviews*. London: Continuum.

Walker Rettberg, J. (2008). *Blogging*. Cambridge: Polity Press.

Wikipedia contributors. Hillsborough disaster, http://en.wikipedia.org/w/index.php?title=Hillsborough_disaster&oldid=528877181, accessed October 30, 2014.

Wikipedia contributors. How to structure the content, http://en.wikipedia.org/w/index.php?title=Wikipedia:How_to_structure_the_content&oldid=412862647, accessed October 30, 2014.

Zappavigna, M. (2011). Ambient affiliation: A linguistic perspective on Twitter. *New Media and Society*, 13 (5), pp. 788–806.

Part V Performing Self, Positioning Others

18 Narrative and Identities

ANNA DE FINA

18.1 Introduction

Narrative and identity are often regarded as closely connected. Narratives are seen as the prime vehicle for expressing identity and narrative analysts have gone so far as to argue that the stories we tell mold us into what we are. This is the spirit of Bruner's famous quote according to which "in the end, we become the autobiographical narratives by which we 'tell about' our lives" (1994: 53). However, research on the connections between narrative and identity is relatively recent, as the most important contributions to the field date back to the 1990s when the so-called "narrative turn" (Bruner 1990) started to gain strength as a movement in the social sciences. The field has grown into a vast interdisciplinary area comprising research from disciplines as diverse as social psychology, linguistics, anthropology, and history, just to name a few. Because of this, narrative-based studies of identity belong to different traditions and employ widely dissimilar methodologies. In this chapter I will focus on main trends in ways of theorizing the connections between narrative and identity, and I will discuss only the approaches and concepts that have been most influential in discourse-oriented narrative investigations.

There is little disagreement on the fact that narratives are often used to express and negotiate both individual and collective identities. There is also a large degree of consensus among narrative analysts on some fundamental principles that have been popularized by poststructuralist thinkers. These can be subsumed under the general idea that identities are not sets of characteristics that can be ascribed to individuals or manifestations of individual essences, but emerge through semiotic processes in which people construct images of themselves and others (see De Fina, Schiffrin, and Bamberg 2006 for a discussion). Social constructionist thinkers such as Stuart Hall and Anthony Giddens have profoundly influenced the field of identity studies in general with their anti-essentialist stance. Stuart Hall, for example, talked about the need for a battle against the "self-sustaining subject at the center of post-Cartesian Western metaphysics" (1996: 15), a subject conceptualized as singular, mental, rational, and unitary. He encouraged scholars to shift their focus toward the discursive practices through which subjects are constituted. Also underlying Giddens's ideas about the postmodern self is the constructionist view of "the self as a reflexive project"

The Handbook of Narrative Analysis, First Edition. Edited by Anna De Fina and Alexandra Georgakopoulou.
© 2015 John Wiley & Sons, Inc. Published 2019 by John Wiley & Sons, Inc.

(1991: 75) in which self-understanding is seen as the product of a process of "building/ rebuilding a coherent and rewarding sense of identity" (ibid.). Finally, social constructionists also stress the plurality and polyphonic (Barrett 1999) nature of identities and therefore also the fact that different and contradictory identities may coexist within the same individual. These authors propose, in sum, that the self is not the essential expression of an individual but a historical and interactional construction subject to constant work and revision.

18.2   Two Paradigms: Biographical and Interactionally Oriented Approaches

These common starting points notwithstanding, there are still deep divisions among narrative analysts in the ways in which identity is studied and theorized. A broad dividing line can be traced between biographical and interactionally oriented studies (see De Fina and Georgakopoulou 2012 for a discussion) – that is, between approaches that regard the life story and the individual narrator as the source of data and target of analysis, and approaches that center on the interactional process of storytelling as the focus of attention. The distinction runs deep in that research belonging to these different fields asks different kinds of questions and employs largely dissimilar methodologies. Biographically oriented studies (McAdams 1988; McIntyre 1984; Freeman this volume, chapter 1) are often based on the premises that the process of identity building has as its objective the production of a coherent self, and that the ability to create that coherence afforded by narrative has itself a positive effect on self-identity. Although theorists agree that people may hold different and sometimes conflicting images of themselves, biographical approaches still tend to see the process of life-storytelling as achieving integration through different mechanisms. According to Gregg (2011: 319–320), for example, in one approach unity is achieved through the process of constructing a "life story" (McAdams 1988), while in a different approach, proposed by the author himself, it is obtained through a combination of key symbols and metaphors into different but coherent self-presentations. Within this theoretical frame, the study of autobiographical stories has significant cognitive and psychological implications given that storytelling is seen as a fundamental mechanism for self-development (Gregg 2011: 319), as a device to enhance a positive sense of self (Smorti 2011), and even as a tool for coping with difficult life events (Bohlmeijer et al. 2007; Fivush and Sales 2006).

Interactionally oriented approaches start from completely different premises and are oriented to different research questions. For interactionists the issues of interest are not whether narrative contributes to a positive self-construction (for a critique of this principle see Strawson 2004), or whether subjects do in fact achieve coherent self-presentations. What they focus on is the process of identity construction itself – the strategies used by narrators, co-narrators, and their audience to achieve, contest, or reaffirm specific identities. Cognitive and psychological issues are not at stake here, because most interactionists tend to concentrate on the social rather than mental aspects of all semiotic processes since they believe that it is through such social constructions that ideas and images are created and circulated. Identity therefore is literally in the doing, rather than in the thinking, and it is this doing that is amenable to observation for discourse analysts. These premises reveal the clear links that connect interactionally oriented trends in narrative studies with ethnomethodological (see Garfinkel 1984) and ethnographic traditions in that the focus is on close observation of participants' local interactions and the ways in which they manage discursive categories. Identity studies in the interactionist perspective have also been greatly influenced by work in conversational analysis (see Antaki and Widdicombe 1998). The latter has paved the way for a recognition of the situated nature of identity claims – that is, the local occasioning of identity categories as they emerge within specific sequences of talk – and of the importance of participation frameworks (Goodwin 1986 and this volume, chapter 10; Goodwin 1990) for the way identities are proposed and negotiated in storytelling on the other. With respect to local occasioning, particularly important is the reference to work by proponents of the Membership Categorization Analysis (henceforth MCA) movement (see, e.g., Hester and Eglin 1997; Antaki and Widdicombe 1998). MCA researchers have developed ideas on categorization first introduced by Sacks (1992/1966) to explain how interactants create and use "membership categories" and routinely link certain activities to them. For MCA proponents, the investigation of the way identities are generated and negotiated must always start with the observation of the local level of interaction rather than with presuppositions about how participants' transportable identities (such as gender or class) may affect their talk. Thus, to give a concrete example, investigating police interrogations and reconstructions of events, Stokoe (2009) found that when policemen wanted to create affiliative relations with suspects, they temporarily made relevant identities that they had in common with their interlocutors, such as that of heterosexual men, as opposed to their local identities as police/suspect. In that sense, the MCA movement stresses ways in which tellers resort to certain identity categories (for example gender or professional categories) to accomplish concrete social actions rather than simply looking at how people present themselves as certain kinds of people.

Besides recognizing the importance of categorization phenomena for identity analysis, narrative scholars have also started to pay a great deal of attention to indexicality. The concept refers to ways in which linguistic constructs "index" (Silverstein 1976), or point to, elements of the social context without explicitly evoking them. Through indexicality, associations are created between specific sounds, words, discourse constructions or styles, and social characteristics or identities. Thus interactionally oriented narrative studies have shown, for example, how accents, words, styles, and other linguistic constructs may be manipulated to indicate affiliation or distancing with respect to specific groups defined by ethnicity (Bucholtz 1999) or gender (Kiesling 2006). And indexical processes are the source of much of the identity work that is done explicitly by narrators and interpreted by audiences.

18.3   Interactionally Oriented Approaches: An Illustration

In order to illustrate how identities are analyzed within an interactionally oriented framework and to contrast this with the biographical approach, I am going to discuss a narrative told by a young woman in a conversation with a group of friends.[1]

Excerpt 1: Mean Girls
Setting: Meredith's kitchen. Amelia (Am), Matt (M), Angie (A), Rose (R), and Meredith (Me) are seated around the kitchen table.

(1) Am: Angie, did you ruin someone's LIfe?

(2) M: [Yeah, whose key-

(3) R: [Yeah, Angie was a life ruiner I'm just a key stealer.

(4) M: [Wh- whose key did you steal?

(5)   [@@@

(6) R: [She didn't steal- she stole someone's key to their soul

(7) A: [Speaking of keys

(8) A: @@@It was like, it's really bad. It's like,

(9) R: It's really bad.

(10) A: It's – As ashamed as she is of her key story, I'm that ashamed times twelve.

(11) Am: [What did you do?

(12) M: [Well now what'd you do?

(13) A: Okay, when I was younger ((crashing noise)) woops! I had this friend named Megan.

(14)   and (.) ((crashing noise)) well I think before I even go into this I have to tell you

(15)   the type of child I was.

(16)   I: preferred books to talking to anybody the friends I had had up to this point I hated.

(17)   and it was just like kinda like a social means to an end cuz I didn't want my teachers like

(18)   *ta*lking about me.
          ((a few lines deleted))

(19)   Um (.) a:nd so like I clearly don't have a great concept of like loyalty to friends or

(20)   anything because I just- hadn't developed them.

(21) R: Friends (.) not the loyalties.

(22)   ((All laugh))

(23) A: Umm a:nd @@

(24) R: Nervous laugh.

(25) A: O(h)hh it's sO bad every time I hate telling it but it needs to happen (.)

(26)   alright um so eventually I had this friend named Megan and she was really nice and

(27)   really sweet →

(28)   and like I think her parents like fought a lot →

(29)   and like (.) you know so she didn't come from a great home situation- →

(30)   um but she was like really smart and bright and like always did the right thing in school=

(31) M: =So she already had it rough [a:nd was still a nice person

(32) R: [Yeah and dot dot dot

(33) M: Okay no go on so what did you do to her?

(34) Me: So she was resilient,

(35) R: At this point she was,

(36) Me: @@At this point (....).

(37) A: Um a:nd I was kind of like, I guess (.) I(h) I was like Regina in *Mean Girls* of my tiny=

(38) Me: Oh my God!

(39) =friend group basicall(h)y,

(40) A: Except a lot less fashionable and maybe twice as mean (.) Um=

(41) M: =Oh my God.

(42) A: And just one day for literally *no* reason I can fathom I have *no* reason why this

(43) happened (.)

(44) I was just like, I don't want to be friends with her any more.

(45) I don't like her, and I don't want MY friends to be friends with her.

(46) M: hhhhhhhh I don't want my friends to be friends with her.

(47) ((all laugh))

(48) R: DAMN.

(49) A: So in addition to myself I turned her other friends against her.

(50) a:nd-

(51) Me: How did you turn your friends against her?

(52) A: Cause I just like bitched about her

(53) and was like, oh God she like such a goody two shoes, I can't stand her,

(54) and blah da dah,

(55) and like (.) < they followed suit>

(56) R: Hhhhhh Regina!

(57) A: Cause children are [the evilest of beings.

(58) Me: [Oh Regina!

(59) R: Yes they are.

(60) ((all laugh))

(61) Am: Especially the smart ones,

(62) Me: Yeah.

(63) R: I would *never* steal anybody's key (.) now!

(64) A: Um a:nd it like went on for a really long time,

(65) and like she would like cry and stuff

(66) and she like eventually

(67) ((all laugh))

(68) R: OH MY GOD.

(69) She would cry? How old were you?

(70) A: I think, I think, wait, I think at this point her parents like actually started going

(71) A: [through the process of divorce too

(72) R: [=OH MY GOD Angie!

(73) M: [OH MY GOD!

(74) yeah (.) I was in fifth grade.

(75) M: hhh Fifth grade!

(76) R: [Fifth is worse than kindergarten!

(77) Me: [Oh(hh)h that's=

(78) M: =Yeah fifth grade versus five(.)

(79)   li@ke (.)

(80)   yea:h hhhhh

(81) Me: Yea:h=

(82) R: =Um at least you've grown as a human being,

(83) Me: You have. a:nd=

(84) M: =Then again like fifth grade is starting that's like that ti(h)me < when like > =

(85) Me: =You don't know who you are and you need to find yourself,

(86) M: Everyone's=

(87) R: =your hormones are raging

(88) M: [<Yeah so you know it's not necessarily>

(89) Am: [Yeah it's a really awkward time,

(90) A: Bu:t so I did that and that was terrible.

(91) M: but still (.) terrible.

(92) A: And that's like the worst thing, ever.

The fragment reproduced here clearly illustrates how narratives that are occasioned by talk about identity do not always represent moments of positive self-construction and are also not necessarily initiated by the narrator as self-serving examples. Indeed, in this case it is the narrator's friends Amelia and Matt who drag her into the story-telling by eliciting a comparison between something bad that the previous narrator (Rose) had admitted to doing (which is described as "ruining someone's life" in line 3) and something that Angie might have done (lines 1 and 3). We also notice that the identity categories which are regarded as relevant to the identity that is being developed here are also introduced by these friends: the first category being "life ruiner," and the second being "key stealer" (line 3). While Matt continues with the possible attribution of the category of "key stealer" to Angie, Rose again intervenes to project a new identity onto Angie. She modifies the basic idea of a material key stealer into that of a "stealer of keys to someone's soul" (line 6). At this point Angie reacts by qualifying her own behavior as "really bad" and declaring that she is ashamed of it (lines 8 and 10). Rose echoes such self- presentation by repeating her negative assessment of Angie's behavior (line 9). This negative foreshadowing has an important interactional function as it creates suspense and interest and therefore works as a story preface (Sacks 1992/1970), as demonstrated by the interlocutors' encouragement for her to tell the story (lines 11–12).

Angie's story opening focuses on depicting her personality as a child (lines 13–18), a self-presentation which is again fairly negative. She proposes a series of orientation details (Labov 1972): she preferred books to people, she had no liking for her friends, and she just used them to be more acceptable to her teachers. Angie's description is interrupted by a joking comment by Rose, who is acting to a certain extent as a co-teller (line 21) but also trying to relieve the seriousness that seems to characterize Angie's talk. She indeed manages to get the other friends to laugh (line 22) and continues to punctuate Angie's storytelling with her own light-hearted comments (line 24). In line 25 Angie comments on how every time the story is told it makes her look terrible, but also on how she cannot avoid telling it, which points to the fact that this is a rehearsed story that has been told before at least once in the presence of Rose.

Lines 26–30 are devoted to another orientation, this time about the story's other protagonist, Megan. It is interesting how Angie uses this orientation to contrast all the negative traits that she has attributed to herself as a child with the positive traits that characterize her antagonist. Megan is presented as "nice" and "sweet," "smart" and "bright" even though she had a difficult situation at home with her parents close to divorce (lines 26–30). This positive depiction and its contrast with herself as a child is intensified by the use of "really" in front of adjectives like "nice" and "sweet." Both Matt and Meredith participate in the construction of Megan's identity, paraphrasing in explicit terms what Angie had hinted at ("So she already had it rough and was still a nice person," line 31 and "So she was resilient," line 34). While Rose prods her to go on telling the story, she also responds to Meredith's remark by again underlining Angie's responsibility in creating difficulties for Megan since she notes that "at that point" Meagan was resilient, thus implying that she had had to endure obstacles to her wellbeing that had been posed by Angie (see lines 34–35). In line 37, Angie proposes another explicitly negative self-presentation in which she compares herself to a well-known character in youth culture, the protagonist of a popular teen comedy film featuring a clique of bad girls who she leads: a young woman called Regina (line 37–40). Here, not only does Angie compare herself to the worst girl in the show, but her comparison favors Regina: Angie declares that she herself was "a lot less fashionable and twice as mean."

One thing to notice is that this long orientation about the protagonists of the story, besides having the effect of creating specific identities for the narrator and the characters, also has the effect of stirring interest for the story and setting the stage for the complicating action. Indeed, what follows immediately after is the main complicating action, where Angie is presented as deciding that she does not want to have anything to do with Megan and does not want her friends to have anything to do with her (lines 42–45). The complicating action is presented in the form of an internal dialogue, which gets then partly repeated by Matt as a form of appreciation (line 46), as shown by subsequent laughter and commentary by Rose (line 48). It is noticeable that Angie continues with her self-deprecation even in the complicating action as she underscores that her decision was completely unmotivated (line 42–45) and adds that she proceeded to turn all her friends against Megan (line 49). This statement is followed by a question by Meredith, who asks her how she achieved that, and Angie again reproduces her own speech (this time probably addressed to her circle of friends at the time) against Megan's personality (line 52–55). Rose's reaction is one of reprobation expressed indexically through the long in-breath and the scolding tone in which she pronounces her friend's newly acquired name, "Regina" (line 56), and the same technique is employed by Meredith. Here Angie offers an evaluation of her behavior, describing it as typical of children. Notice how this exemplifies the way Membership Categorization is used: Regina was a bad child, but "being bad" with other children is connected to children as a typical behavioral characteristic in this utterance. So if a child is being bad there is nothing surprising about it. In a way, it seems that Angie has provided a safety net for herself: by declaring that children tend to be bad, she could be seen as excusing herself for having acted so viciously. And indeed, both Rose (line 59) and Amelia take up the idea in their own turns. Amelia also proposes the first positive characterization of Angie's identity: she was bad because she was a smart child (line 61). Notice this new Membership Categorization involving smart children: smart children are worse than less smart children. Rose also provides a further opportunity for Angie to contrast her present self with her past self by declaring that she herself would never steal today (line 63). But Angie seems to have no intention of saving face, and she continues depicting her bad behavior and how she made Megan cry (line 64–66) and adding further aggravating circumstances to her actions (line 70–71), which leads to a new slate of negative evaluations of her personality by the other participants (lines 68, 72, 73) and questions about her age at the time. When Angie responds that she was in fifth grade (line 74), Rose, Meredith, and Matt take another opportunity to save her face as they argue that fifth grade represents a bad moment for all children (lines 76–81). Rose also tries to provide a positive contrast for Angie between her past story-world self and her present self (line 82), and this observation starts a new cycle of justifications of Angie's behavior by the audience based on the fact that children at that age are confused and angry (lines 84–89). But Angie does not take any opportunity to redeem her past self or to contrast it with her present self and simply restates the gravity of what she did and how horrible it was (lines 90–93).

The analysis of this narrative clearly exemplifies the contrast between an interactionally and a biographically-based account of identity. In the first place, it shows how autobiographical talk can be triggered by others who are not the storyteller and can actually be resisted by narrators. It also exemplifies how categories of belonging may be proposed, opposed, taken up, or modified by all participants and how they get introduced and develop in connection with ongoing talk. Finally, it connects identity displays with the concrete context in which they happen without making any claims about the essential nature of the storyteller's identity. In this case, for example, we see that the narrator focuses her identity presentation on her past self, that this presentation is essentially negative, and that by declaring shame over the way she was as a child, the narrator is also hinting at the fact that she is not the same person today. But we also saw that there is no emphasis on this contrast and therefore no attempt at insisting on a positive self-presentation by Angie, even with her friends' attempts at saving her face. In sum, this is fundamentally a self-deprecating story. Of course we could attempt to provide a psychological explanation for why self-deprecation may have a function in the identity presentation of narrators. But – and this observation is far more concrete as it can be backed up with discourse data – what we have observed is that this negative self-presentation has an important interactional function in that it increases the drama and interest of the story told by Angie. Indeed, one could go one step further and propose that self-deprecation may have a sociability function for members of closely-knit groups. It has also been proposed that stories based on self-deprecation are common among girls (see Branner 2005). A final point is that we have seen that identity work is done both through open categorization and through indexical processes. For example, the reference to *Mean Girls* allows participants to make clear inferences about how Angie was as a child by inviting associations between her and this popular character's main traits.

18.4   Identity Types, Contexts, and Their Interactions

It is widely accepted by identity analysts that besides being plural and potentially multi-voiced, identities can also be of different kinds and can pertain to different contexts. For example, identities may be analyzed in personal or collective terms (see Van De Mieroop, this volume, chapter 21) in that people may claim that they are specific kinds of persons, and/or they may claim membership in certain categories to which others belong as well. Zimmerman (1998: 90–91) also noted how identities can differ in terms of the context that they relate to. He talked about three kinds of identities: *discourse*, *situational*, and *transportable*. Discourse identities are related to people's roles as speakers and refer to discourse positions such as storyteller or audience member. Situational identities, such as "doctor" or "patient," are made relevant by specific social situations and activities. Transportable identities, in turn, are potentially independent from particular contexts as they refer to more permanent characteristics or affiliations of individuals and groups, such as gender, social class, ethnicity, and so forth. The relationships between different kinds of identities like those proposed by Zimmerman and their relative relevance in different contexts is one of the main points of debate among narrative analysts, as we will see. But narratives also pose the need to recognize yet another distinction: the one between narrator's identities and character's identity, a differentiation that is unique to storytelling. Indeed, when storytellers tell a story, particularly one in which they were participants, they are simultaneously building their own and others' identities in the story world and their identity in the storytelling world. For example, in the narrative that we analyzed above, we saw that Angie was constructing an identity as a mean child in the story world, and an identity as a moral person in the storytelling world. The existence and interaction of these two planes was discussed in very clear terms by Deborah Schiffrin (1996) in her seminal paper "Narrative as Self-Portrait: Sociolinguistic Constructions of Identity," where she noted that narrators may manipulate two kinds of self-presentation: an epistemic and an agentive self. While the epistemic self represents a projection of the narrator's beliefs and convictions, and therefore a projection of her moral self, the agentive self is the one that is presented as an acting person in the story world. Schiffrin analyzed how, in stories told by Jewish women about their children's partners, the women tended to embrace in the storytelling world a certain epistemic self that was not compatible with their self as acting figures in the story world. It was through the analysis of the relationships between such self-presentations that Schiffrin was able to propose an interpretation of the process of identity construction of these women in interaction and of the more general significance of such identity displays in relation to social issues, such as the role of women within the family and mainstream ideologies supporting it.

The interaction between the storytelling self and the story world self is at the center of one of the most important theories about narrative identity: positioning theory. Positioning was initially proposed by Davies and Harré (1990: 48) for discourse in general, not for narrative in particular. The authors regarded it as "the discursive process whereby selves are located in conversations as observably and subjectively coherent participants in jointly produced story lines." Thus, they saw it as tightly connected to ongoing interaction. The framework was developed in connection with storytelling by Bamberg (1997) and then by Wortham (2011), among others (see also Deppermann, this volume, chapter 19). Bamberg introduced the idea that the narrator can position herself at three levels: vis-à-vis other characters in the world of the story, vis-à-vis interlocutors in the storytelling world, and vis-à-vis herself. At the first level, narrators convey images of themselves and other characters in the story world, creating protagonists and antagonists, expressing evaluations of such characters' actions, distributing responsibilities, and so forth. At the second level, the narrator positions herself to the audience, in the sense that she uses the story to say something about her present self in relation to it. For example, the narrator may be constructing her past actions as a model behavior or as a justified reaction to an aggression, soliciting solidarity on the part of the audience. In sum, the second level of positioning is firmly anchored to the story-telling event as it is unfolding. According to Bamberg, positioning at the third level responds to the question "who am I?" and invites investigation of how the narrator wants to be seen beyond the local level of interaction, in more general and permanent terms. Wortham (2001) refined Bamberg's model, identifying "positioning cues" that may be used to convey such images. Positioning cues are linguistic elements and discourse constructions that are instrumental to achieving particular identities, such as certain words used to describe characters, constructed dialogue (Tannen 1989) attributed to characters, or "meta-pragmatic" verbs, verbs that reflect a particular point of view on events and story world figures.

Even though positioning has proven to be a very productive tool for analyzing identities – not only in terms of story representation but also in terms of the dynamics between such representation and participants' action – this kind of analysis also poses problems that are not easily solved (see Deppermann, this volume, chapter 19). Indeed, the distinction between the different levels is not straightforward in concrete analysis. For example, the distinction between second- and third-level positioning is particularly challenging in that part of the effectiveness of interactional positioning derives from narrators' ability to represent themselves as certain kinds of persons beyond the limits of the current interaction, and therefore their interactional identities are often related to broad social categories of belonging.

Besides the orientation to local interactional dynamics in storytelling and the conception of identity processes as positioning, a third theoretical and methodological approach has contributed to a view of identity that is not reduced to a description of story world representations. That is the view of storytelling as practice (see De Fina and Georgakopoulou 2008 and 2012) – that is, an attempt to capture the embedding of narrative within different contexts beyond conversation and interviews. In this perspective, the identities negotiated within storytelling events are closely related to the rights, obligations, and particular tasks that are indexed by specific social activities.

The recognition of such embedding leads to a reconsideration of how issues of power, habitus, specialized knowledge, and institutional involvement may affect the ways identities are conveyed and negotiated. Indeed, research has shown, for example, that narrators who tell stories in institutional activities such as asylum-seeking interviews (see Maryns and Blommaert 2001) or legal encounters (see Trinch and Berk-Seligson 2002; Carranza, this volume, chapter 3) need to learn how to manage their situational identities and also how to encode institutionally acceptable identities in their stories in order to be successful. This view of narrative as practice also underlies the stress on the need to analyze interview narratives as interactional encounters in their own right (see De Fina 2009 and papers in De Fina and Perrino 2011) and therefore not to overlook the role of the interviewer in the co-construction of meanings in general and identities in particular. Indeed, interviewers can propose identity categories that are then taken up by respondents, share presuppositions about indexical associations related to categories, and participate in many other ways in identity constructions. De Fina and King (2011) showed, for example, that in sociolinguistic interviews with Latin American women which were centered on their language experiences, interviewers shared with their interviewees and participated in reproducing an ideology in which language conflict was related to ethnicity in a rather direct way. In other words, in the narratives and in questions and evaluations by interviewers, being perceived/recognized as Latino was presented as the source of conflicts with members of other ethnicities. Looking at narrative as practice therefore also involves considering the participation and role of all parties in a specific storytelling event and the way such participation and their relations (institutional or of other sorts) may affect the type of identities made relevant and negotiated.

18.5   The Dilemma of Local versus Transportable Identities

Among the most important issues raised by the analysis of identity in storytelling (but also in other kinds of discourse events) is in what way the identity processes that take place in specific interactional occasions relate to processes at different levels and even at different scales. For example, one may ask whether the identities conveyed by narrators on particular occasions are coherent or conflicting with identities conveyed on different occasions, or whether the categories of belonging chosen by a person during a specific interaction may reflect and help constitute views of social events and relations that are shared by other individuals belonging to the same group. Proposing and interpreting those kinds of connections involves taking a more general stance about the relations between discursive and social phenomena. The debate on these issues has seen a sharp divide between Conversation Analysts and researchers in other fields such as sociolinguistics or discursive psychology. Indeed, conversation analysts have criticized the tendency of many discourse analysts to ascribe categories of belonging to speakers based on their transportable or other presupposed identities, rather than looking at the identities that are actually made relevant by participants (see Schegloff 1997 on this point). They describe the method as "ascribing theorised labels" (Benwell and Stokoe

2006: 158) to stretches of talk, and argue that most of the time such labels are invoked by the analyst but not oriented to by participants. Referring to the study of categorization in discourse, Stokoe (2012: 47) summarizes the debate in the following terms:

> A persistent issue for MCA is how far it is possible, for any category, for analysts to "assert" what the relevant activities, predicates, and so on are, such that the analysis does not become "wild and promiscuous" (see Schegloff, 1992, 2007). That is, how far can one claim the relevance of categorial phenomena that are not formulated explicitly and unambiguously by speakers? And what is left to analyse if everything is made explicit? The issue remains rather fuzzy because, according to Sacks, categories are "inference-rich." This means that categories store "a great deal of the knowledge that members of a society have about the society." (Sacks 1992: 40–41)

Indeed, as forcefully argued by Wetherell (1998) in her well-known exchange with Schegloff (1997) about the respective merits and shortcomings of Conversation Analysis and Critical Discourse Analysis, even the most literal description of a conversational exchange involves selection and interpretation; thus, the answer to the dilemma between staying very close to participants' explicit orientation to identity categories and proposing connections with more general social categories does not lie in interpretive asceticism. While it is true that past research may have been too ready to make generalizations about "culture" being the source of differences in the way identities are presented in discourse by individuals and groups, more recent work has been firmly grounded in the close analysis of the local level of interaction and has invoked the support of ethnographic observation as a basis for making generalizations. Ethnography involves a prolonged exposure to and observation of the practices of a community and significant interaction with its members in order to understand what kind of semiotic resources they use and how they deploy them. Through such observation the analyst can grasp not only what is going on between the participants in a specific interaction, but also which categories and processes appear to have a more general significance (beyond the local context) through the analysis of semiotic patterns. In the case of storytelling and identity, for example, repetition of storytelling roles, actions, positions, and other elements across storytellers and stories points to the possibility of significance beyond the level of particular interactions. Research on gender identity, for instance, has shown the existence of persistent indexical associations between gender categories, roles, behaviors, and local identity claims. Georgakopoulou (2006) demonstrated, for example, that in a close-knit group of female teenagers, storytelling roles such as "initiator" or "evaluator" of story-world events in particular instances closely corresponded with members' identity in terms of power and leadership within the group, and also that such standings were influenced by more general models about female roles in society. Associations between gender roles and storytelling identities have also been found in terms of types of stories told. Branner (2005) illustrates, for instance, how the adolescent girls she studied had a marked preference for presenting themselves as protagonists of disaster rather than success stories, thus again contributing to perpetuating socially shared gender norms that value solidarity over competitiveness in women's relations.

Generalizations about the social significance of storytelling identities may also be made when analyzing patterns in terms of roles and scenarios in the stories that members of particular communities tell. Thus, for example, Wortham and Rhodes (2011), who investigated a recent Mexican immigrant community in Pennsylvania, argued that "payday mugging narratives" are commonly exchanged among members of this community. In these narratives, Mexicans are regularly portrayed as victims of attacks by black people who want to steal their pay. I have found similar commonalities in narratives told by immigrants about being mistreated and harassed in encounters with members of out-groups based on their "looking" different (see De Fina 2003, 2006, 2014). In these narratives there were both ethnic categorizations (protagonists described themselves as "Hispanic" rather than Mexican) and patterns of actions by protagonists and reactions by antagonists that were similar such that they could be described as presenting a sort of common schema. Narrators also conveyed certain ideas about implicit characteristics related to their ethnic categorizations. In particular, they presented being Hispanic as closely linked with being black and implied the existence of ethnicity scales in which Hispanics and blacks were seen as similar in terms of power and social standing. I argued that these patterns point to the existence of collective representations and inventories, which in turn can be connected with wide social processes such as economic and cultural struggles.

These studies show that there are many ways in which local identity displays and negotiations may be connected to and make relevant different kinds of contexts. Identities constructed in storytelling may help reproduce, confirm, and perpetuate in different ways roles that participants in a community play outside the storytelling events under analysis, pointing to more permanent relations between members of a group. They may also reproduce and recirculate generally shared representations about self and others, and indexical associations between categories and characteristics or behaviors that are dictated by habitus – the "set of dispositions" or implicit views that, according to Bourdieu (1979: 72), underlies commonsense constructions about social relationships and identities.

Having said that, it is important to note that the dilemma between focusing on local contexts and the significance of identity work in the creation and interpretation of such contexts on the one hand, and looking for connections with multiple contexts and for the generalizability of identity processes beyond those local levels on the other, is not a false one in that it points to opposite directions in research. One direction privileges the here and now and tends to minimize the researcher's interpretive work, while the other privileges the generation of multiple connections and relies much more heavily on the researcher's own process of interpretation of data. Although these two ways of looking at the study of identities are quite different, they do not need to be in contradiction with each other. As I have argued, a bridge connecting these approaches can be provided by ethnography and by specific attention to the local level as the starting point for any kind of generalization. Recent work on interdiscursivity (see Agha 2007; Wortham and Rhodes 2013) problematizes the idea that the complex interactions between identities and contexts can be reduced to a binary opposition between micro and macro, pointing to the fact that indexicalities are sustained and built through time and across contexts. Indeed, processes related to the formation of identities take place across speech events and are the product of sedimentation of narrative practices, roles, and linguistic usage. Identities are also sensitive to historical time as processes of enregisterment (Agha 2007) contribute to the fixation of both identity repertoires and the characteristics attributed to identities. Finally, globalization processes also make different scales potentially relevant to the interpretation of identities, especially in the case of migrant and displaced populations (see Baynham and De Fina 2005).

18.6 Identity and Narratives in Computer-Mediated Contexts

The technological revolution that has accompanied globalization has brought about a plethora of new contexts for storytelling practices and therefore also a variety of new issues and dilemmas for narrative analysts. While the study of computer-mediated communication is a well-established field (see Herring 2001), analyses of stories in such context are still scarce at the moment of my writing (but see Georgakopoulou 2013 for a review). Computer-mediated environments and particularly social media (see Georgakopoulou 2014; Page 2012 and this volume, chapter 17) offer a terrain for the interplay of contradictory forces in terms of identity. Indeed, it is widely accepted (Jäkälä and Berki 2013; Code 2013) that the participatory culture that permeates social media such as Twitter, Facebook, personal blogs, discussion forums, and all kinds of interest groups pushes participants in online communities to engage in self-disclosure and in emotional, intimate talk much more than in other more traditional communicative environments. Thus, storytelling seems to be intimately connected with "authentic" identity performances. And indeed, some studies of storytelling in Internet communities claim that access to social media allows members of minorities and oppressed groups to explore and convey to others who they really are because they provide them with opportunities to get out of their isolated physical spaces (see for example Gray 2009 on coming out stories). On the other hand, however, scholars who have studied storytelling and other kinds of discourse in social media note that the communicative practices that underlie the use of particular media also set stringent rules on the kinds of identities that are acceptable and relevant in concrete instances. Amaral and Monteiro (2002) talk, for example, of "technological identities" as being dictated by online communities. Relevant identities are also governed by local practices. For example, in a study of Twitter stories Arthur (2013: 9) shows how users tailor their descriptions of who they are to the storytelling activity at hand. She discusses, for example, how in a series of posts about multiracial families, a user in her Twitter profile biography self-identifies as "writer, creative consultant, psychotherapist, clinical supervisor, transracially adoptive parent, New Yorker."

These delimitations become very clear when one looks at Facebook posts and stories. Because social media expose the teller to continuous scrutiny (Facebook participants are, in a sense, always online), people often carefully choose what kind of identity they want to present and put a stress on the performative elements of such presentation. In addition, there are a variety of formats of online identity that can lead to very different relations between tellers and stories. Jäkälä and Berki (2013: 5) distinguish, for example, between eponymity, when one is associated with an official name and other descriptors; nonymiti, when the identity is not declared and cannot be detected; and polynymity, which has to do with different identities related to different communities. All these aspects of the way identities are presented online have an impact on storytelling but also underscore one of the central tenets of this chapter, that identities are always embedded and conveyed within specific storytelling practices which are constituted by concrete participation frameworks, rules of engagement, and interactional routines. Thus, studying storytelling as practice will also lead to a deeper understanding of identity processes.

18.7 Conclusions and Directions for Future Research

In this chapter I have argued for an interactionally oriented and practice-based approach to the study of identities in and through narratives. I have illustrated how identities are not essentialized within this paradigm, but are seen as firmly grounded in specific interactional processes and narrative practices and therefore cannot be divorced from the storytelling events in which they are produced. I have argued that this type of approach is also closely linked with ethnographic methods and the investigation of participant orientations and understandings.

The study of the interconnections between identities and narrative is destined to grow and diversify, both because of the healthy interdisciplinarity that characterizes this field and because of the widening range of contexts offered by online communication. Even though narrative analysis has been slow to catch up in these environments, I expect important developments to take place in the analysis of issues that are at the core of research on identity. Among them are questions of authorship, tellership, and responsibility online, and new forms of self-presentation in the media. On the other hand it is likely that the increasing influence of practice-based research in storytelling will open up new territories for the study of the construction of identities through storytelling in a variety of institutional and everyday contexts of communication.

NOTES

1   This narrative is part of a corpus of conversational narratives collected by students for a course on narrative analysis at Georgetown University. The narrative was collected and transcribed by Alice Maglio, to whom I am grateful for making it available to me.

REFERENCES

Agha, A. (2007). *Language and Social Relations.* Cambridge: Cambridge University Press.

Amaral, M., and M. Monteiro. (2002). To be without being seen: Computer-mediated communication and social identity management. *Small Group Research,* 33 (5), pp. 575–589.

Antaki, C., and S. Widdicombe (eds.). (1998). *Identities in Talk.* Thousand Oaks, CA: Sage.

Arthur, P. (2013). Narrative Genres in Online Interaction: The Telling of Accounts on Twitter. Paper presented at the 13th Annual Meeting of the AAA, Washington D.C. December, 7, 2014.

Bamberg, M. (1997). Positioning between structure and performance. *Journal of Narrative and Life History,* 7 (1–4), pp. 335–342.

Baynham, M., and A. De Fina. (2005). *Dislocations, Relocations, Narratives of Migration.* Manchester: St Jerome Publishing.

Barrett, R. (1999). Indexing polyphonous identity in the speech of African American drag queens. In M. Bucholtz, A. Liang, and L. Sutton (eds.), *Reinventing Identities.* Oxford: Oxford University Press, pp. 313–332.

Benwell, B., and E. Stokoe. (2006). *Discourse and Identity.* Edinburgh: Edinburgh University Press.

Bohlmeijer, E., M. Roemer, P. Cuijpers, and F. Smit. (2007). The effects of reminiscence on psychological well-being in older adults: A meta-analysis. *Aging and Mental Health,* 11 (3), pp. 291–300.

Bourdieu, P. (1979). *Outline of a Theory of Practice.* Cambridge: Cambridge University Press.

Branner, R. (2005). Humorous disaster and success stories among female adolescents in Germany. In U. Quasthoff and T. Becker (eds.), *Narrative Interaction.* Amsterdam: John Benjamins, pp. 113–147.

Bruner, J. (1990). *Acts of Meaning.* Cambridge MA: Harvard University Press.

Bruner, J. (1994). Life as narrative. *Social Research,* 54 (1), pp. 11–32.

Bucholtz, M. (1999). You da man: Narrating the racial other in the production of white masculinity. *Journal of Sociolinguistics,* 3 (4), pp. 443–460.

Code, J. (2013). Agency and identity in social media. In S. Warburton and S. Hatzipangos (eds.), *Digital Identity and Social Media.* Hershey, PA: Information Science Reference, pp. 37–57.

Davies, C., and R. Harré. (1990). Positioning: The discursive construction of selves. *Journal for the Theory of Social Behavior,* 20, pp. 43–63.

De Fina, A. (2003). *Identity in Narrative: A Study of Immigrant Discourse.* Amsterdam: John Benjamins.

De Fina, A. (2006). Group identity, narrative and self-representations. In A. De Fina, D. Schiffrin, and M. Bamberg (eds.), *Discourse and Identity.* Cambridge: Cambridge University Press, pp. 351–375.

De Fina, A. (2009). Narratives in interview – The case of accounts: For an interactional approach to narrative genres. *Narrative Inquiry,* 19 (2), pp. 233–258.

De Fina, A. (2014). Positioning level 3: Connecting local identity displays to macro social processes. *Narrative Inquiry,* 23 (1), pp. 40–61.

De Fina, A., and A. Georgakopoulou. (2008). Analysing narratives as practices. *Qualitative Research,* 8 (3), pp. 379–387.

De Fina, A., and A. Georgakopoulou. (2012). *Analyzing Narrative: Discourse and Sociolinguistic Perspectives.* Cambridge: Cambridge University Press.

De Fina, A., and K. King. (2011). Language problem or language conflict? Narratives of immigrant women's experiences in the US. *Discourse Studies,* 13 (2), pp. 163–188.

De Fina, A., and S. Perrino (eds.). (2011). Narratives in interviews, interviews in narrative studies. Special Issue, *Language in Society,* 40.

De Fina, A., D. Schiffrin, and M. Bamberg. (2006). *Discourse and Identity*. Cambridge: Cambridge University Press.

Fivush, R., and J.M. Sales. (2006). Coping, attachment, and mother-child narratives of stressful events. *Merrill-Palmer Quarterly*, 52 (1), pp. 125–150.

Garfinkel, H. (1984). *Studies in Ethnomethodology*. Cambridge and Oxford: Polity Press with Blackwell Publishers.

Georgakopoulou, A. (2006). Small and large identities in narrative (inter)action. In A. De Fina, D. Schiffrin, and M. Bamberg (eds.), *Discourse and Identity*. Cambridge: Cambridge University Press, pp. 83–102.

Georgakopoulou, A. (2013). Narrative and computer-mediated communication. In S. Herring, D. Stein, and T. Virtanen (eds.), *Pragmatics of Computer-Mediated Communication*. Berlin: Mouton de Gruyter, pp. 687–708.

Georgakopoulou, A. (2014). Small stories transposition and social media: A micro-perspective on the "Greek crisis." Special Issue, *Discourse & Society*, 25 (4), pp. 519–539.

Giddens, A. (1991). *Modernity and Self-identity: Self and Society in the Late Modern Age*. Stanford, CA: Stanford University Press.

Goodwin, C. (1986). Audience diversity, participation and interpretation. *Text*, 6 (3), pp. 283–316.

Goodwin, M.H. (1990). *He-Said-She-Said: Talk as Social Organization among Black Children*. Bloomington: Indiana University Press.

Gray, M. (2009). Negotiating identities/queering desires: Coming out online and the remediation of the coming-out story. *Journal of Computer-Mediated Communication*, 14 (4), pp. 1162–1189.

Gregg, G. (2011). Identity in life narratives. *Narrative Inquiry*, 21 (2), pp. 318–328.

Hall, S. (1996). Introduction: Who needs identity? In S. Hall and P. du Gay (eds.), *Questions of Cultural Identity*. London: Sage, pp. 1–17.

Herring, S. (2001). Computer-mediated discourse. In D. Schiffrin, D. Tannen, and H. Hamilton (eds.), *The Handboook of Discourse Analysis*. Oxford: Blackwell, pp. 612–634.

Hester, S., and P. Eglin. (1997). *Culture in Action: Studies in Membership Categorization Analysis*. Washington, DC: International Institute of Studies in Ethnomethodology and Conversation Analysis / University Press of America.

Jäkälä, M., and E. Berki. (2013). Communities, communication and online identities. In S. Warburton and S. Hatzipangos (eds.), *Digital Identity and Social Media*. Hershey, PA: Information Science Reference, pp. 1–13.

Kiesling, S. (2006). Hegemonic identity-making in narrative. In A. De Fina, D. Schiffrin, and M. Bamberg (eds.), *Discourse and Identity*. Cambridge: Cambridge University Press, pp. 261–287.

Labov, W. (1972). The transformation of experience in narrative syntax. In W. Labov (ed.), *Language in the Inner City: Studies in the Black English Vernacular*. Philadelphia: University of Pennsylvania Press, pp. 354–396.

Maryns, K., and J. Blommaert. (2001). Stylistic and thematic shifting as a narrative resource. *Multilingua*, 20 (1), pp. 61–84.

McAdams, D.P. (1988). *Power, Intimacy and the Life Story: Personological Inquiries into Identity*. New York: Guilford.

McIntyre, A. (1984). *After Virtue*. 2nd edn. Notre Dame, IN: University of Notre Dame Press.

Page, R.E. (2012). *Stories and Social Media: Identities and Interaction*. New York: Routledge.

Sacks, H. (1992a/1966). "We"; Category-bound activities. In G. Jefferson (ed.), *Harvey Sacks: Lectures on Conversation*. Vol. 2. Oxford: Blackwell, pp. 333–340.

Sacks, H. (1992b/1970). Stories take more than one utterance: Story prefaces. In G. Jefferson (ed.), *Harvey Sacks: Lectures on Conversation*. Vol. 2. Oxford: Blackwell, pp. 222–238.

Sacks, H. (1992c). *Harvey Sacks: Lectures on Conversation*. Vols. 1 and 2. Edited by G. Jefferson. Oxford: Blackwell.

Schegloff, E.A. (1992). Introduction. In G. Jefferson (ed.), *Harvey Sacks: Lectures on Conversation*. Vol. 1. Oxford: Blackwell, pp. ix–xii.

Schegloff, E.A. (1997). Whose text? Whose context? *Discourse & Society*, 8, pp. 165–187.

Schegloff, E.A. (2007). A tutorial on membership categorization. *Journal of Pragmatics*, 39, pp. 462–482.

Schiffrin, D. (1996). Narrative as self portrait: sociolinguistic constructions of identity. *Language in Society*, pp. 167–203.

Silverstein, M. (1976). Shifters, linguistic categories, and cultural description. In K. Basso and A. H. Selby (eds.), *Meaning in Anthropology*. Albuquerque: University of New Mexico, pp. 11–55.

Smorti, A. (2011). Autobiographical memory and autobiographical narrative: What is the relationship? *Narrative Inquiry*, 21 (2), pp. 303–310.

Stokoe, E. (2009). "I've got a girlfriend": Police officers doing "self-disclosure" in their interrogations of suspects. *Narrative Inquiry*, 19 (1), pp. 154–182.

Stokoe, E. (2012). Moving forward with membership categorization analysis: Methods for systematic analysis. *Discourse Studies*, 14 (3), pp. 277–303.

Strawson, G. (2004). Against narrativity. *Ratio*, 17 (4), pp. 428–452.

Tannen, D. (1989). *Talking Voices: Repetition, Dialogue, and Imagery in Conversational Discourse*. Cambridge: Cambridge University Press.

Trinch, S., and S. Berk-Seligson. (2002). Narrating in protective order interviews: A source of interactional trouble. *Language in Society*, 31 (3), pp. 383–418.

Wetherell, M. (1998). Positioning and interpretive repertoires. *Discourse & Society*, pp. 387–412.

Wortham, S. (2001). *Narratives in Action*. New York: Teachers College Press.

Wortham, S., and C. Rhodes. (2011). Interactional positioning and narrative self-construction. *Narrative Inquiry*, 10 (1), pp. 157–184.

Wortham, S., and C. Rhodes. (2013). Life as a chord: Heterogeneous resources in the social identification of one migrant girl. Special Issue of *Applied Linguistics*, 34 (5), pp. 536–553.

Zimmerman, D. (1998). Identity, context and interaction. In C. Antaki and S. Widdicombe (eds.), *Identities in Talk*. Thousand Oaks, CA: Sage, pp. 87–106.

19 Positioning

ARNULF DEPPERMANN

Over the last two decades, "positioning" has become an established concept used to elucidate how identities are deployed and negotiated in narratives. This chapter first locates positioning in the larger field of research on identities and discourse. Commonalities and differences in conceptions of positioning are highlighted. In the following, the historical development of theoretical approaches to positioning and their methodological implications are reviewed in more detail. The article closes by taking up two current lines of debate concerning the future development of the concept of positioning.

19.1 Positioning as an Approach to Identity and Discourse

Both classic psychological and sociological theories (Erikson 1959; Mead 1934) and narrative approaches (Bruner 1990: 99–139; Ricoeur 1990: 137–198) view identity as an overarching, abstract, non-empirical, reflexive structure that integrates the experiences of a person and organizes his/her actions. "Identity" in these approaches is importantly characterized by normative notions of coherence and consistency, which refer to ideas of a "good life" (cf. Freeman 2010).

"Positioning" is designed as an alternative to studying the subject in terms of an overarching identity. Theories of positioning take issue with the conception of "identity" sketched above in several respects (cf. De Fina and Georgakopoulou 2012, ch. 6).

- They insist that people's actions and their conceptions of self are not self-contained psychological entities, but tied to social discourse. It is therefore inadequate to isolate subjects' identities from the context of the discourses in which they are embedded. Positioning theories, instead, approach facets of identity in the way they are accomplished in and by discourse.
- Positioning is a non-essentialist and practice-bound concept. Positions are accomplished by social practice (De Fina and Georgakopoulou 2008). Practices are routine,

The Handbook of Narrative Analysis, First Edition. Edited by Anna De Fina and Alexandra Georgakopoulou.
© 2015 John Wiley & Sons, Inc. Published 2019 by John Wiley & Sons, Inc.

habitual ways of speaking and interacting, which are sensitive to situational contingencies. They are organized in genres and tied to certain temporal and local occasions in a community of practice. Positions are meaningful, semiotically structured ascriptions. A positioning view on self and identity thus is opposed to a monadic, static, and essentialist view of identity in terms of personality as defined by (essentially biologically based) traits and dispositions. It equally rejects an individualized conception of the self as being a private, reflexive, representational, cognitive structure, that is, the self-concept. Positioning theory does not locate identity in some abstract, integrated structure "behind" discursive practice, but in what people observably do. Positions are tied to the social actions by which they are made relevant. Studies on positioning in narratives therefore allow us to deal empirically with how people accomplish situated identities.

- Theories of positioning neither theoretically claim nor normatively presume that identities be integrated, coherent entities. Rather, positions are situated achievements, which do not sum up to a coherent self. Positions give evidence of multiple facets of personal identity. They are potentially contradictory, and they may be fleeting and contested.

While different approaches to positioning agree on the above points, major theoretical and methodological differences concern the role discourse plays in processes of positioning. When introducing the concept of "subject positions" in discourses, Foucault's original idea was to reject the notion of an agentive, teleological subject, who deliberately fashions and controls social behavior and the changes of knowledge formations (Foucault 1969). Rather, he saw discourses as the institutional infrastructure of distributions of power and knowledge, which provide opportunities and constraints for individual action and cognition. In Foucault's structuralist thinking, historical subjectivity comes into being and is shaped by societal discourses. Gee calls them D-discourses and defines them as "a socially accepted association among ways of using language, other symbolic expressions, and artifacts, of thinking, feeling, believing, valuing and acting that can be used to identify oneself as a member of a socially meaningful group or 'social network'" (1996: 131). Later developments of positioning have increasingly questioned and both rejected discursive determinism and the usefulness of the concept "D-discourses." More recent interactional approaches to positioning inspired by narrative research, conversation analysis, and ethnography stress that participants actively project and negotiate positions (Bamberg 1997a; Bamberg and Georgakopoulou 2008). Positions are locally occasioned and designed, they are temporally and situationally flexible, and they are multifaceted – that is, different facets of identity are relevant in different discursive contexts. The interactional approach underscores that discourse does not determine subject positions by itself. Rather, people interacting with each other co-construct positions by their actions. A matter of dispute, though, is whether participants are only able to choose among competing, available discourses (or story lines) which are predefined (Hollway 1984; Davies and Harré 1990), or whether discursive positions themselves are subject to participants' construction and perspectival interpretation as well (Wortham 2001; Lucius-Hoene and Deppermann 2004a, 2004b).

Researchers also differ in terms of whether they regard positions as brought about by individual, strategic acts (Harré and van Langenhove 1999) or as emerging from interactional co-construction. This difference also resonates with methodological choices. In biographic interviews, opportunities for overt reciprocal interactional positioning are scarce, while rich opportunities for multifaceted self-positioning of the teller are offered (Lucius-Hoene and Deppermann 2004a). Interactional studies, in contrast, are more likely to discover how positions depend on interactional contingencies and practical concerns that participants deal with through their talk (Georgakopoulou 2007, 2008).

19.2 Theoretical Approaches of Positioning

19.2.1 Foucault

The term "positioning" has its origin in Foucault's notion of "subject position" (Foucault 1969). Foucault was interested in the history of discursive formations. He argued that recourse to the agency of individual subjects cannot account for the becoming and change of discursive practices. Instead, researchers have to analyze the "dispositifs" in which discourses are embedded, that is, the whole bodily, technical, architectural, legal, etc. apparatus that organizes a field of social practice, and the topical, syntactic, and genre-related structures of the discourse. Discourses position subjects in terms of status, power, legitimate knowledge, and practices they are allowed to and ought to perform (Foucault 1969: ch. 4). Discourses are defined by the kinds of statements they consist of and license as knowledge, thereby determining the interpretation of self, (social) world, and others (Foucault 1969: chs. 2 and 5).

19.2.2 Hollway

Bringing Foucault's historic approach to bear on synchronic social psychology, Wendy Hollway (1984: 235) uses positioning as an analytical tool to capture how people conceive of themselves in terms of gendered subjectivities. "Discourses make available positions for subjects to take up. [...] women and men are placed in relation to each other through the meanings which a particular discourse makes available." According to Hollway, discourses determine available positions. Although Hollway admits that adopting positions from hegemonic discourses is preferred for legitimizing actions, she rejects any discursive (or other, biological, social, psychological) determinism. Rather, people are able to choose among positions, because there are "several coexisting and potentially contradictory discourses concerning sexuality [that] make available different positions and different powers for men and women" (1984: 230). Hollway stresses that discourses and the positions they imply do not exist independently of their being permanently reproduced by discursive practices enacting the positions which the discourses afford. She insists that a theory of discourse must be accountable for the issue of historical change; however, she does not discuss mechanisms of change. Hollway mentions three discourses about gendered relationships (the male sexual drive, the have/ hold, and the permissive discourse). Each discourse provides complementary positions for men and women that confer meaning and value on people's actions and feelings and that imply different distributions of power, status, and agency (in terms of being the subject vs. object of the discourse). In Hollway's approach, choice of positions is motivated both by people's prior biographical positionings and by their psychodynamic "investments" (*Besetzungen*, cf. Laplanche and Pontalis 1972: 92–96) – in other words, which powers they seek and which desires and fears (e.g., to be emotionally dependent and vulnerable) are suppressed. Psychodynamic defense mechanisms like repression, exclusion, and projection of desires via other-positioning are seen to be operative in taking up discursive positions, thus being eminently consequential socially and politically. Although the empirical basis of her study consists of biographical interviews about heterosexual relationships, Hollway does not use analytic tools from narratology, nor does she link positioning specifically to narrative or interactional practices.

19.2.3 Harré et al.

Davies and Harré (1990) were the first to bring positioning to bear on interactive exchanges and to relate it to narratives. They regard positioning activities as the primary locus of the discursive production of selves, "whereby selves are located in conversations as observably and subjectively coherent participants in jointly produced story lines" (1990: 48). According to them, positioning is the basic mechanism by which a self and identities are acquired in social interaction in terms of practical, emotional, and epistemic commitment to identity-categories and associated discursive practices. Therefore, they insist on an immanentist understanding of selves as part and parcel of discursive practices.

Ever since, Harré and his disciples have elaborated on various facets of positioning. The basic constituents of Harré's conception are represented by the "positioning triangle" (Davies and Harré 1990; Harré et al. 2009):

- Story lines are taken to be the paramount organizational structure of discourses used by people to make sense of their experience. Harré et al. (2009: 8) claim that "life unfolds as a narrative, with multiple, contemporaneous, interlinking story lines." Story lines provide positions of categorically defined actors related to each other within a sequence of acts and events. Story lines are embodied in discursive practices, which people have to acquire in order to develop "our own sense and how the world is to be interpreted from the perspective of who we take ourselves to be" (Davies and Harré 1990: 47). Story lines of past experience are autobiographical fragments used to interpret interactional episodes.
- Social acts are defined by their illocutionary force in the sense of Speech Act Theory (Austin 1962; Searle 1969). However, Harré underscores that single actions in isolation do not have a determinate social force. In contrast to Searle, it is neither the individual's intention nor the conformity of linguistic action with conventions operating on the level of single utterances, which define their meaning. Rather, it is only on behalf of their being embedded in jointly produced story lines that speech-actions become socially determinate speech-acts. A major part of illocutionary force resides in positionings accomplished by linguistic action.

- Positions are constitutive of story lines. They are defined by the rights and duties they imply for the actors they are assigned to. Positions are mostly complementarily organized in terms of dual or triple socio-categorial relationships, such as "doctor/nurse/patient," "mother/father/child," "leader/disciples," etc. Positions are reflexively related to social acts: While people are positioned by social acts, the meaning of social action itself may heavily depend on how its producer is taken to be positioned, that is, which rights and entitlements to action s/he is being perceived to have.

Slocum-Bradley (2009) proposes to extend the triangle to a "positioning diamond" by adding another dimension, "identities." While "positioning" refers to rights and duties attributed to an actor, "identities" refers to personal, moral, and social attributes (but see Harré and van Langenhove 1991: 397f. on "moral" vs. "personal positioning"). Identities may be ascribed according to how persons use their rights and perform their duties: Disregarding duties may lead to the ascription of a personal moral property like being "corrupt" or "dishonest," people who abuse their rights may be called "ruthless," and those who observe their duties and respect limits of entitlements may be perceived as being "honest." Inversely, moral identities imply positions conferring specific rights and duties to their incumbents. Slocum-Bradley (2008) shows this for identity-categories like "worker," "illegal alien," and "human being" in competing discourses about illegal immigration from Mexico into the United States. Each of these identities implies different ascriptions of motives, characterizations of actions (e.g., as justifiable or blameworthy), and assignments of moral rights to people so categorized, and each warrants different kinds of political responses.

Harré and van Langenhove (1991) distinguish between self- and other-positioning. They assume that both actions are almost always performed in the same act by implication, because positions are mostly complementary to one another. People do not only position themselves actively, but they are also positioned by others' acts of other-positioning. They may react to this (and also to others' self-positioning) by second-order positioning, for example, by questioning, resisting, or affiliating with previously ascribed positions. "Third order positioning" is a term used for the retrospective discussion of previous acts of positioning. Harré and van Langenhove (1991: 398–404) underscore that positioning can be intentional or tacit, unforced or forced – the latter being the case when people who are entitled to demand positionings from others make good on those entitlements (as in institutional situations, for example).

Davies and Harré (1990: 49–58) stress that acts of positioning may be multilayered and ambiguous, because acts can be seen to project several positions at once and may be interpreted differently by various actors. Interpretation depends on the story lines, their associated moral orders, and the available positions and normative expectations considered to be in play. Positions are thus dynamic, emergent, and possibly subject to change over the course of an interactional episode, which Davies and Harré (1990: 53) equate to an "unfolding narrative."

Harré and his disciples have mainly applied positioning to the study of conflicts between social groups, organizations, and nations (e.g., Harré and Moghaddam 2003; Harré and Slocum 2003; Slocum-Bradley 2008, 2009, 2010). The classic example from

Davies and Harré (1990) is a (made-up) conflict between a man and a sick woman. While the man called "Sano" treats the woman called "Enfermada" with commiseration and courtesy, positioning himself as nurse, Enfermada rejects this as condescension and resists being positioned as a dependent, helpless woman. In her response, she projects her insistence on being positioned as equal, while Sano understands this move to be positioning him as a chauvinist, a position which he likewise protests.

Harré and Davies (1990) claim that positioning not only avoids the pitfalls of essentialist psychological theories of identity and personality, but that it is also more apt to do justice to the flexible, self-determined, and interpretive character of individual action than the more static and ritualistic notion of "role," which tends to imply a socio-structural determinism shaping individual action. Moreover, "role" does not capture facets of identity having to do with psychological, biographical, and moral characteristics. Still, Harré's emphasis on rights is rooted in macro-social orders that transcend the individual instance of conversation, and in this sense it is very much akin to the concept of role.

19.2.4   Bamberg

Michael Bamberg (1997a) offers a refinement of the notion of positioning based on research on narratives in interaction. Bamberg (1997a: 337) distinguishes three levels of positioning.

Level 1. Positioning on the level of the story: "How are the characters positioned in relation to one another within the reported events?" Level 1 positioning operates on the referential plane of the story world. It also includes relational positioning of characters in the story vis-à-vis each other (Bamberg and Georgakopoulou 2008: 386). This level of positioning is specific to narrative and other descriptive practices.

Level 2. Positioning on the level of the interaction: "How does the speaker position him- or herself to the audience?" Level 2 positioning operates on the interactional plane, involving turn-generated discourse identities (e.g., positioning oneself as someone who has a story to tell); situational identities[1] (e.g., positioning as participants in a research interview); and management of relationships in terms of responsibility (e.g., via operations on production formats; see Goffman 1981), emotional stance, and expectations towards co-participants (Bamberg and Georgakopoulou 2008).

Level 3. Positioning with respect to the "Who am I?" question: "How do narrators position themselves to themselves?" Later formulations of level 3 positioning make clear that Bamberg intends to describe more general and more enduring, "portable" aspects of self and identity, which transcend the ephemeral, local interactional moment and its action-related contingencies (see also De Fina 2013). Bamberg and Georgakopoulou (2008) add that level 3 positioning has to do with "how the speaker/narrator positions a sense of self/identity with regards to dominant discourses or master narratives" (385), by which the teller "establishes himself as 'a particular kind of person'" (391). In Bamberg and Georgakopoulou (2008), level 3 positioning concerns discourses about masculinity, gender-relationships, and associated issues of responsibility, commitment, desire, and heterosexual interest. In their data, an adolescent boy positions himself with regard to wider public media discourse by borrowing song lines from the pop-star

Shaggy, thus positioning himself as a male who shows sexual interest in girls while at once displaying a non-committing, nonchalant stance.

Bamberg's interest in positioning developed from empirical observations on evaluation and the display of emotional stance (like anger) in stories (Bamberg 1997b). He takes issue with Labov and Waletzky's (1967) claim that evaluation is a segmental component of narrative structure. Instead, Bamberg argues, actions are implicitly evaluated throughout the story by the way categorizations, deixis, and descriptions are used in order to characterize actors and to ascribe agency in terms of initiative, responsibility, and knowledge. Agency involves two "directions of fit" (Bamberg 2011). Active agency implies a subject-to-world direction of fit, while passive agency implies a world-to-subject direction of fit. Much of the narrator's moral work in storytelling lies in positioning characters and oneself as a teller by attributing different kinds of agency. The narrator can thereby convey his/her perspective and evaluative stance and call for empathy and affiliation without necessarily producing overt assessments.

Interactive, level 2 positioning has gained importance in Bamberg's approach since his turn to small stories in everyday interaction (see Georgakopoulou 2007, and this volume, chapter 13) and focus groups (Bamberg 2004; Korobov and Bamberg 2007), as opposed to big stories elicited in the context of autobiographical research interviewing (cf. Bamberg 2007; Georgakopoulou 2006). Small stories are stories embedded in the flow of conversational interaction. They are occasioned by situated discursive concerns, such as justifying actions, blaming, advice-seeking, and advice-giving. In these contexts, interactional positioning becomes the prime motivation for storytelling because it is the means by which storytellers position themselves and others. Small stories make it plain that a performative approach to narrative and positioning is needed. Still, although it may be harder to see at a superficial glance, performative and pragmatic aspects matter equally in the production of big autographical accounts in research interviews, because they are also informed by situated, hearer-oriented concerns that impinge on narrative design and function.

19.2.5   *Wortham*

Wortham (2000, 2001) and Lucius-Hoene and Deppermann (2004a, 2004b) have elaborated further on the concept of "narrative as (inter-)action." They argue that autobiographical narratives must not be analyzed solely as representations of the tellers' past experiences that mirror historical reality (cf. Schütze 1981, 1984). Wortham (2000, 2001) distinguishes between representational and interactive functions of narratives. Whereas the former relate to the descriptions in a story, the latter are tied to narrative as action: "autobiographical narrators *act* like particular types of people while they tell their stories and they relate to their audiences in characteristic ways as they tell those stories" (Wortham 2001, xi, italics in the original). Although Wortham does not refer to Bamberg, this distinction clearly resonates with Bamberg's positioning levels 1 and 2. Viewing narrative as action, Wortham (2000) is interested in the ways in which storytelling can transform selves and relationships by enacting transitions from one position to another. Interactional positioning is achieved through the functions and effects of the represented characters on the positions of the interactional participants, for example, being an active and assertive person vs. being a passive and vulnerable person (Wortham 2001: ch. 4). Drawing on Bakhtin (1981), Wortham uses the concept of "voice" in order to refer to the different positions that tellers enact locally: People use ways of speaking that index social positions, contexts, assessments, and ideological stances, which have become associated with linguistic choices through previous social usage. Because of this socio-indexical property of language, narrators do not need to "explicitly represent their points, but instead they adopt positions by juxtaposing and inflecting the voices of various characters" (Wortham 2001: 63). Through double-voicing and ventriloquation, narrators take up the words of others (e.g., by quoting, paraphrasing, mimicking) and inflect them using intonational and other framing cues. The result is a layering of two often divergent intentions in one utterance, that is, the speaker takes a stance on the intention attributed to the person quoted (see Rampton 1995; Deppermann 2007). Irony, mockery, and sarcasm are prime examples of double-voicing. Wortham (2001: 15) insists that positioning analysis needs to be advanced by answering the question: "How do linguistic and paralinguistic cues position the narrator and the audience interactionally?"

Wortham (2001: 70–75) mentions five types of cues that index voices and enable interactional positioning:

- Reference and predication concerns the way persons, objects, events, and actions are categorized. Thus, for example, *my neighbor, doctor, deceiver* may possibly be used to refer to the same person, but they position the person very differently in terms of moral characteristics and relevant facets of identity.
- Meta pragmatic descriptors are verbs of saying used to categorize linguistic actions (e.g., *scolding, arguing, blaming*), suggesting different motives and assessments of the agent.
- Quotation is used to position the quoted person by the use of intonation, voice qualities, and code-switching. These means convey stances towards the credibility or motives of the quoted person (Bakhtin 1981; Günthner 1999).
- Evaluative indexicals are descriptions which position persons morally with respect to shared normative expectations and social types. For example, Wortham (2000) discusses a narrator's description of her early years at boarding school, where she reports that "'you were allowed to visit with your mother on Sundays only'" (173). The evaluative indexical here relies on presuppositions about reasonable (and unreasonable) limits of discipline, and positions the characters accordingly. Thus the child is positioned as a victim, while her teachers are positioned as being excessively severe and cruel.
- Epistemic modalization is accomplished by mental verbs (*guess, think*), adverbs (*of course, possibly*) and discourse markers (*I dunno, y'know*). These means convey (un)certainty, evidentiality, subjective vs. objective perspective, and common ground. They may work, for example, to decline commitment to positions, to presuppose that they are intersubjectively shared, or to index that the speaker does not expect recipients to align with him/her.

Drawing on interactional sociolinguistics and conversation analysis, Wortham (2001: chs. 2–3) conceives of the relationship between linguistic cues and positionings in terms of indexical mediation and emergence. Linguistic forms do not code positions directly.

Rather, they are used to cue relevant features of context indexically – that is, they are associated with certain social groups, ways of speaking, moral, evaluative, and epistemic stances, and interpretive repertoires and are used to construct locally relevant positions. Certain contexts often become available only if other contexts are presupposed to hold. The process of contextualization is indeterminate (Silverstein 1992), because it is specifiable, defeasible, and negotiable in subsequent narration and interaction. Therefore, positionings are not accomplished on the spot, but it is by their interactional consequences and in the light of the whole emerging story that they solidify and become sufficiently determinate for interactional purposes (see this volume, chapter 8).

19.2.6   *Lucius-Hoene and Deppermann*

Lucius-Hoene and Deppermann (2000, 2004a, 2004b) deal with positioning in autobiographic research interviews, which are studied to gain access to the narrative identity of a person. Like Wortham (2001: ch. 5), they insist that narrative identity does not only encompass the narrated self, but also performative aspects of identity having to do with self-presentation and interactional negotiation. The autobiographical interview involves communicative tasks and opportunities different from other conversational and institutional occasions of storytelling. Interviewees are required to produce a "coherent biographical grand story" (Lucius-Hoene and Deppermann 2000: 204, 2004a: ch. 4) with only minimal intervention and stance-taking by the interviewer. Occasioned by the need to relate a series of events to each other and to adopt a life-span perspective, which the teller may never have done before, s/he may discover new orders of coherence between actions and events, reappraise biographical causalities, and reinterpret both past and present in the light of other biographical phases. Autobiographic storytelling thus does not simply express a preexisting identity. The act of telling can cause autoepistemic effects by the communicative setup of the research setting.

Lucius-Hoene and Deppermann (2000, 2004b) propose a communicative model of autobiographical research interviewing that captures the various temporal levels of positioning in play in this setting. They underscore that the narrative interview itself is preceded by preparations, preconceptions, and possibly also prior encounters of interviewer and interviewee, which pre-position both participants reciprocally in terms of pragmatic, epistemic, normative, and topical expectations, competencies, goals, and emotional stances. Narration in the interview setting is also surrounded by non-narrative talk (greetings, talk about the research project, privacy regulations, etc.) in which positions are negotiated. These cognitive, pragmatic, and interactive frames impinge on the way stories are told and on the positions in play. Methodologically, they need to be taken into account – for example, by including field notes and recordings of non-narrative stretches of interaction in the study of autobiographic narratives.

Building on Bamberg's positioning levels 1 and 2, Lucius-Hoene and Deppermann (2004b) deal in more detail with the temporal and interactive sources of positioning in autobiographical narration (see Figure 19.1).

19.2.6.1   (1a) Level 1: Positioning of story characters vis-à-vis each other   On the story-level, the former self and other characters in the story world position each other, for example,

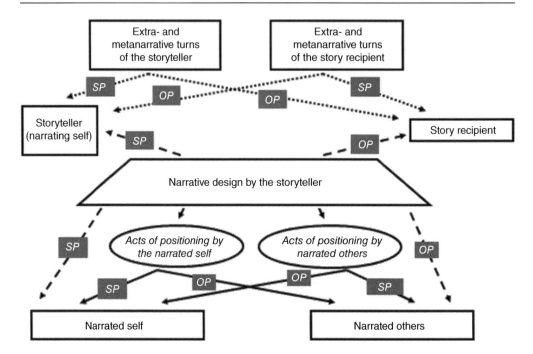

Figure 19.1   Sources of positioning in the autobiographical research interview
(SP = self-positioning, OP = other-positioning). Adapted from Lucius-Hoene and Deppermann
2004b, with kind permission from Springer Science and Business Media.

they blame each other. This is most prominently done by enacting reported dialogues
(see Schiffrin 1996; Tannen 1989), in which characters react to and thus position each
other. The narrator acts as an animator (Goffman 1981): S/he lends his/her voice to the
characters, indexing to render what others have said. Formulation, content, and intentions of the reported actions are presented as belonging to the characters.

19.2.6.2   (1b) Level 1: Positioning of story characters by narrative design   Characters' acts
of positioning are not uninterested renderings, but they are strategically designed by
the narrator from his/her present point of view. This becomes obvious when double-
voicing (for instance through prosodic design; see Günthner 1999) or verbs of saying
(Silverstein 1993) are used to convey that the narrator's own positioning of the characters is not identical to how the characters understand their positions in the story world
(e.g., the narrator lets on that one of the characters is pretentious, incredible, more
blameworthy than the other). Instead of being mere animators, narrators actively design
the story by linguistic and narrative means, which they employ to position the story
characters in often implicit ways for the listener to interpret:

- Social categorization and the description of category-bound actions and attributes
  (Sacks 1992);

- expressions and ways of speaking (formulae, code-choice, etc.) associated with the style of particular social groups and registers (Coupland 2007; "evaluative indexicals," Wortham 2001: 72);
- selection, choice of the granularity of representation, and linearization of actions and events reported convey relevance and relationships of causation and intention;
- cohesive links (Linde 1993) establish causality, concession, contrast, and instrumentality;
- management of information in orientation and background segments suggests or rules out certain motives and causes.

19.2.6.3 *(2a) Level 2: Self-positioning of the teller by extra- and meta narrative self-reflexive activities* Tellers may explicitly take a stance toward past events and their past selves through meta narrative retrospective comments, argumentations, and evaluations from the present point of view. Such activities do not only position the narrated self (level 1); the teller simultaneously positions his/her current self as someone who, for example, has matured, is honest with him/herself, or has converted to a morally more valuable stance. The double temporal indexicality of autobiographical storytelling and the double indexicality of the self arising from it offer manifold and sometimes very intricate ways of distinguishing and displaying facets of self and identity. The two temporal planes of storytelling allow for representing biographical change, expressing different subjective perspectives on the same events from different biographical vantage points, and indexing self-reflexive stances and emotions, accounts and evaluations. Tellers can equally reflect on their present self, the biographical events that have shaped it, and the prospects for its future.

19.2.6.4 *(2b) Level 2: Interactional positioning by narrative design* Tellers performatively position themselves towards the listener through their story design. It conveys the subjective perspective of the teller's present self, his/her evaluation, normative and epistemic stances, and co-membership and solidarity with characters as opposed to distance and critique. It may be more or less recognizably designed with respect to the particular recipient. Narrative strategies, such as humor, irony, the expression of emotional, moral, and evaluative stances, choices of codes, lexis, formulae, and constructions indexing group membership, project performative claims to locally relevant identities – a skilled entertainer, a deplorable victim, an incorruptible judge. Interactional other-positioning of the listener is the other side of interactional self-positioning. The teller can project a shared identity or, to the contrary, s/he can position him/herself as someone who is to be admired, who distances him/herself from the hearer, or who needs the recipient's support.

19.2.6.5 *(2c) Level 2: Interactional positioning by meta narrative activities of the teller* Meta narrative activities include formulating assumptions or asking about the recipient's knowledge and evaluative stance, laughing, seeking agreement, and explaining to the interviewer. The methodological guidelines of biographical narrative research interviews (see Wengraf 2001) require the interviewer to restrict him/herself to asking open questions and producing response tokens that align with and support the teller's story. The interviewer is not to openly affiliate or argue with the narrator or to reciprocate with stories of his/her own experiences. Therefore, the recipient remains much more elusive for the narrator than in conversations and in other institutional interactions, where participants' expectations include the reception of determinate (affiliative) responses, the accomplishment of shared meanings, and, often, reciprocal self-disclosures. In the absence of these interactional expectations, the narrator can position him/herself much more in line with self-presentational and auto-epistemic desires and position the researcher as a largely imaginary representative of significant others, rivalling inner voices, authorities, or an idealized companion (Lucius-Hoene and Deppermann 2000: 213–215), by importing routine interactional patterns into the interview – a process not unlike what is theorized by psychoanalysts in terms of transference (cf. McAdams 2011; Crapanzano 1992).

19.2.6.6   (2d) Level 2: Interactional positioning by the story recipient   Although the narrator's ideas about the recipient play an important role in the narrative research interview, the researcher's factual activities equally contribute to shaping the teller's positioning. The interviewer's questions make certain topics and genres of representation relevant (cf. Van De Mieroop and Bruyninckx 2009) and s/he may be heard to suggest preferential ways of responding. By responses to the story (e.g., continuers, acknowledgements, agreement tokens, emotional stance markers, repair initiation, follow-up questions, etc.), the listener becomes a co-author and takes part in negotiating positionings of both participants.

Temporality, the representational and performative design, and the interactivity of storytelling are the systematic sources for the manifold potentials of positioning in narratives. By attending methodically to the different levels of positioning and their interplay, facets of the self can be identified that might otherwise remain unnoticed. Explicit, representational positionings in the story (e.g., being a victim) may be at odds with positions enacted on the interactive plane (e.g., having indisputable epistemic authority over one's biography).

19.2.7   *Wetherell*

Margaret Wetherell's approach to positioning builds on discursive psychology (Potter and Wetherell 1987), which set out to root psychological topics in the interpretive practices of both public and private discourse. She aims to integrate a conversation analytic take on social interaction with a poststructuralist approach to subject positions (e.g., Mouffe 1992) in order to overcome what she sees as the limitations and problems of the two approaches. Wetherell praises the technical precision of CA and its emphasis on recovering the meanings that interactional episodes have for the participants themselves (Schegloff 1997). Still, she reproaches CA for focusing too narrowly and exclusively on sequential context and for not considering "ideological dilemmas" and "broader interpretive repertoires" (Wetherell 1998: 400), which provide for the "institutionalized intelligibility" (Wetherell 1998: 394) of discursively constructed positions. This is where the poststructural notion of "subject positions" proffered by societal discourses comes in. However, Wetherell rejects discursive determinism and criticizes poststructuralist approaches for failing to deal with situated practices of positioning in sufficient detail and for not attending to how accountability of positions is accomplished in discourse (see also Korobov 2001). Wetherell (2003, 2011) argues for an approach to positioning that integrates psychoanalytic concepts with narrative and critical discourse analysis, drawing both on micro and macro aspects of discursive practice and including ethnographic knowledge.

19.3　Currents Debates in Positioning Research

19.3.1　The micro-macro problem: The relationship between positioning and D-discourses

Theorizing about positioning was sparked by the idea that societal discourses provide positions that individuals inhabit in social practice. It soon became evident that dominant discourses do not automatically determine the position subjects adopt. In media discourse, for example, the famous encoding/decoding model by Hall (1973) distinguishes between the hegemonic, negotiated (i.e., what holds generally vs. for particular cases) and oppositional positions that recipients of media products may inhabit, leading to different interpretations of media products. But even in many of the approaches to positioning discussed above (e.g., Foucault, Hollway, Harré et al.), discourses – and story lines – are treated as socially given and culturally shared, providing for possible positions from which subjects may choose. According to this view, positions themselves cannot be understood without recourse to D-discourses (Foucault 1969; Gee 1996) and rights and duties tied to characters in story lines (e.g., Davies and Harré 1990; Harré and van Langenhove 1991; Harré and Moghaddam 2003). This view of positioning and discourse has come under increasing criticism for various reasons:

(1) The identification of D-discourses is all but self-evident: What statements and assumptions does a D-discourse consist of? Who participates in the discourse? Where does it take place? While early discourse theorists tended to take for granted that these issues could be settled by drawing on their knowledge as members of a culture and their theoretical knowledge as social scientists, the methodological foundations of the notion of "D-discourse" have become an issue in their own right.

(2) Postmodern theorists have shown that discourses are fragmentary, self-contradictory, and subject to conflicting interpretations. This is increasingly so given the dynamics of social change, and the processes of individualization, pluralization, and globalization in modern societies yield various counter-discourses and counter-narratives that challenge the notion of monolithic, hegemonic discourses and master narratives (Bamberg and Andrews 2004). Thus, neither the unity of D-discourse nor the question of whether one discourse is really dominant, obligatory, or more powerful than alternative discourses can be said to be a settled issue independent of empirical investigation.

(3) Even if it can be methodically demonstrated that some discourse matters more in some segments of society (e.g., certain media sources), it does not necessarily follow that actors in some field – tellers of a given story, for example, or, more precisely, participants in some stretch of interaction under study – orient to this discourse.

Conversation analysts argue that researchers must attend to how participants themselves observably appeal to D-discourses and display that they are relevant for their talk (Stokoe 2005). The "display" requirement includes showing in the data at hand that the discourse invoked is procedurally consequential for how the interaction (or the narrative) develops (Schegloff 1997). In this way, the macro context "D-discourse" has to be shown to be oriented to by the participants, that is, that it is "talked into being" (Heritage and Clayman 2010: 20–33) by local action. This theoretical stance is linked to the inductive (or abductive) methodology of conversation analysis. It rejects starting the analysis with theoretical assumptions about social structure, identity, and ideologies in mind. Such assumptions may lead to attending selectively to the phenomena in the data and subsuming observations to theoretical preconceptions, resulting in premature interpretations and/or circular analyses. A related problem is the tendency of critical discourse analysts to assume that societal power relations and power-sensitive identity categories such as gender, race, class, and ethnicity invariably and ubiquitously matter in discourse (Benwell and Stokoe 2006: ch. 2). Bamberg and Georgakopoulou (2008) have shown how this conversation analytic approach to societal discourse can be used to analyze level 3 positioning by discussing how (in their data) media discourse is explicitly invoked for local acts of positioning. Still, it is to be questioned whether the problem of identifying discourses and relevant positions can always be sufficiently and unambiguously solved by exclusively attending to the actions to be analyzed. This topic will be taken up in the next section.

19.3.2   *Positioning and membership categorization*

The interactional understanding of positioning is closely related to the conversation analytic approach to "identities in talk" (Antaki and Widdicombe 1998). It also views positions as local accomplishments in interactional practice and as participants' resources for performing social actions (Widdicombe 1998; Korobov 2013). The conversation analytic approach to identities in talk relies on the concept of "membership categorization" (Sacks 1972, 1992; Schegloff 2007; Stokoe 2012). It deals with how members categorize persons and how this is used as a resource for ascribing properties, explaining and evaluating actions, attributing responsibility, and engendering inferences and expectations regarding the actions of category-members. Membership categorization owes much of its inferential and moral power to the association of categories with category-bound activities and predicates (Sacks 1972). These allow for implicit assessments and adumbrations of category membership, properties, or actions to be expected of people so categorized. Kitzinger and Wilkinson (2003) identify a conversation analytic approach to positioning with membership categorization analysis. While it is beyond doubt that explicit categorization and ascription of actions and properties are basic and pervasive positioning maneuvers, membership categorization does not exhaust practices of positioning (Deppermann 2013; see also Day and Kjaerbeck 2013).

Particularly in narratives, people use practices of positioning in addition to membership categorization when projecting identities in talk in at least three ways:

- The double temporal indexicality of narratives (telling vs. tale) allows for the deployment of multiple positions concerning the telling self and the told self.
- Narratives can have a biographical scope (thus speaking to the dimension of constancy and change; see Bamberg, De Fina, and Schiffrin 2011), and narrative trajectories can index kinds of identities that develop only over extended stretches of events and actions. In this way, narratives allow for displaying more complex identities than categorization and action-description (Deppermann 2013).
- Membership categorization focuses almost exclusively on explicit positioning by referential practices and categorization (Schegloff 1997, 2007; Stokoe 2012). The hallmark of positioning, however, is to recover how positions are invoked by more implicit, indexical practices.

Using socio-phonetic cues (Eckert 2008), adumbrating by innuendo, double-voicing (Bakhtin 1981) (e.g., irony through echoic mention), and stylistic choices of register and code (Coupland 2007) are cases in point. Such indexical practices require specific knowledge and familiarity with routines and histories of a community of practice in order to recognize indexical cues as such and to recover the contexts indexed (Gumperz 1982). To some extent, indexicality is built into all practices of social action. Therefore, unlike Bamberg (1997a), Lucius-Hoene and Deppermann (2004a, 2004b) do not conceive of reference to discourses as a level of positioning of its own. Rather, practices of positioning on levels 1 and 2 may to some degree index the cultural discourses needed to make sense of local action.

Methodologically, indexical displays often cannot simply be read off the interactional surface by just any methodologically skilled analyst. Even if bits of relevant contexts can be identified by attending closely to interactional data, much remains implicit that is relevant for participants in terms of associative inference and evaluation and that informs their responses in a way that may be opaque to an outsider-analyst. There may be participant displays that speak only to those who possess relevant ethnographic background knowledge (Deppermann 2000). Of course, invoking ethnographic background has to be methodologically restrained. Ethnographic considerations must not be introduced prematurely as a substitution for close data analysis. The analyst's task is to show that they add to an understanding of phenomena that remained unnoticed or uncomprehensible in detailed sequential analyses of audio and video-recordings and transcripts. Ethnographic knowledge contributes to analytical insight if it increases the overall coherence of the understanding of participants' actions and stories (Deppermann 2000). In sum, ethnographic research should complement a conversation analytic approach to positioning in order to accurately discern how local action connects with wider contexts of social structure (De Fina 2008, and this volume, chapter 18), because such knowledge is needed to grasp more subtle and indirect ramifications of the positions accomplished in situ (De Fina 2013). One ethnographically-based methodology that seems to be particularly promising is to attend to iterative patterns of action and interpretation that recur throughout a community of practice or across the actions of an individual speaker. In this way, the more stable, overarching social discourses that people orient to may be recovered from interactional data (Georgakopoulou 2013), enabling us to take a further step across the gap between so-called "micro" and "macro" concerns.

NOTES

1   For the distinctions between "discourse," "situational," and "transportable identities," see Zimmerman (1998).

REFERENCES

Antaki, C., and S. Widdicombe (eds.). (1998). *Identities in Talk*. London: Sage.

Austin, J.L. (1962). *How to Do Things with Words*. Oxford: Clarendon Press.

Bakhtin, M.M. (1981). Discourse in the novel. In M.M. Bakhtin, *The Dialogic Imagination: Four Essays*. Edited by Michael Holquist. Austin: University of Texas Press, pp. 259–422.

Bamberg, M. (1997a). Positioning between structure and performance. *Journal of Narrative and Life History*, 7, pp. 335–342.

Bamberg, M. (1997b). Emotion talk(s): The role of perspective in the construction of emotions. In S. Niemeier and R. Dirven (eds.), *The Language of Emotions*. Amsterdam: John Benjamins, pp. 209–225.

Bamberg, M. (2004). Form and functions of "slut-bashing" in male identity constructions in 15-year-olds. *Human Development*, 47, pp. 331–353.

Bamberg, M. (2007). Stories: Big or small: Why do we care? Special issue, *Narrative Inquiry*, 16 (1), pp. 139–147.

Bamberg, M. (2011). Who am I? Narration and its contribution to self and identity. *Theory and Psychology*, 21 (1), pp. 3–24.

Bamberg, M., and M. Andrews (eds.). (2004). *Considering Counter-Narratives: Narrating, Resisting, Making Sense*. Amsterdam: John Benjamins.

Bamberg, M., and A. Georgakopoulou. (2008). Small stories as a new perspective in narrative and identity analysis. *Text and Talk*, 28 (3), pp. 377–396.

Bamberg, M., A. De Fina, and D. Schiffrin. (2011). Discourse and identity construction. In K. Luyckx, S. Schwartz, and V. Vignoles (eds.), *Handbook of Identity Theory and Research*. Berlin: Springer, pp. 177–199.

Benwell, B., and E. Stokoe. (2006). *Discourse and Identity*. Oxford: Blackwell.

Bruner, J.S. (1990). *Acts of Meaning*. Cambridge, MA: Harvard University Press.

Coupland, N. (2007). *Style*. Cambridge: Cambridge University Press.

Crapanzano, V. (1992). *Hermes' Dilemma & Hamlet's Desire: On the Epistemology of Interpretation*. Cambridge, MA: Harvard University Press.

Davies, B., and R. Harré. (1990). Positioning: The discursive production of selves. *Journal for the Theory of Social Behaviour*, 20 (1), pp. 43–63.

Day, D., and S. Kjaerbeck. (2013). "Positioning" in the conversation-analytic approach. *Narrative Inquiry*, 23 (1), pp. 16–39.

De Fina, A. (2008). Who tells the story and why? Micro and macro contexts in narrative. *Text & Talk*, 28 (3), pp. 421–442.

De Fina, A. (2013). Positioning level 3: Connecting local identity displays to macro social processes. *Narrative Inquiry*, 23 (1), pp. 40–61.

De Fina, A., and A. Georgakopoulou. (2008). Analysing narratives as practices. *Qualitative Research*, 8 (3), pp. 379–387.

De Fina, A., and A. Georgakopoulou. (2012). *Analyzing Narrative*. Cambridge: Cambridge University Press.

Deppermann, A. (2000). Ethnographische Gesprächsanalyse: Zu Nutzen und Notwendigkeit von Ethnographie für die Konversationsanalyse. *Gesprächsforschung*, 1, pp. 96–124, http://www.gespraechsforschung-ozs.de/fileadmin/dateien/heft2000/ga-deppermann.pdf, accessed January 6, 2015.

Deppermann, A. (2007). Playing with the voice of the other: Stylized "Kanaksprak" in conversations among German adolescents. In P. Auer (ed.), *Style and Social Identities*. Berlin: Mouton de Gruyter, pp. 325–360.

Deppermann, A. (2013). How to get a grip on identities-in-interaction: (What) Does "Positioning" offer more than "Membership Categorization"? Evidence from a mock story. *Narrative Inquiry*, 23 (1), pp. 62–88.

Eckert, P. (2008). Variation and the indexical field. *Journal of Sociolinguistics*, 12 (4), pp. 453–476.

Erikson, E.H. (1959). *Identity and the Life Cycle*. New York: International Universities Press.

Foucault, M. (1969). *L'Archéologie du savoir*. Paris: Gallimard.

Freeman, M. (2010). *Hindsight: The Promise and Peril of Looking Backward*. Oxford: Oxford University Press.

Gee, J.P. (1996). *Social Linguistics and Literacies: Ideology in Discourses*. 2nd edn. London: Taylor & Francis.

Georgakopoulou, A. (2006). Small and large identities in narrative (inter)-action. In M. Bamberg, A. De Fina, and D. Schiffrin (eds.), *Discourse and Identity*. Cambridge: Cambridge University Press, pp. 83–102.

Georgakopoulou, A. (2007). *Small Stories, Interaction and Identities*. Amsterdam: John Benjamins.

Georgakopoulou, A. (2008). "On MSN with buff boys": Self- and other-identity claims in the context of small stories. *Journal of Sociolinguistics*, 12, pp. 597–626.

Georgakopoulou, A. (2013). Building iterativity into positioning analysis: A practice-based approach to small stories and self. *Narrative Inquiry*, 23 (1), pp. 89–110.

Goffman, E. (1981). Footing. In E. Goffman, *Forms of Talk*. Oxford: Blackwell, pp. 124–159.

Gumperz, J.J. (1982). *Discourse Strategies*. Cambridge: Cambridge University Press.

Günthner, S. (1999). Polyphony and the "layering of voices" in reported dialogues: An analysis of the use of prosodic devices in everyday reported speech. *Journal of Pragmatics*, 31, pp. 685–708.

Hall, S. (1973). *Encoding and Decoding in the Television Discourse*. Birmingham: University of Birmingham, Centre for Cultural Studies, pp. 507–517.

Harré, R., and F.M. Moghaddam (eds.). (2003). *The Self and Others: Positioning Individuals and Groups in Personal, Political, and Cultural Contexts*. Westport, CT: Praeger.

Harré, R., and N. Slocum. (2003). Disputes as complex social events: On the uses of positioning theory. In R. Harré and F. Moghaddam (eds.), *The Self and the Others*. Westport, CT: Praeger, pp. 123–136.

Harré, R., and L. van Langenhove. (1991). Varieties of positioning. *Journal for the Theory of Social Behaviour*, 21 (4), pp. 393–407.

Harré, R., and L. van Langenhove (eds.). (1999). *Positioning Theory*. Oxford: Blackwell.

Harré, R., F.M. Moghaddam, T.P. Cairnie, D. Rothbart, and S.R. Sabat. (2009). Recent advances in positioning theory. *Theory & Psychology*, 19 (1), pp. 5–31.

Heritage, J., and S. Clayman. (2010). *Talk in Action: Interactions, Identities, and Institutions*. Oxford: Wiley-Blackwell.

Hollway, W. (1984). Gender difference and the production of subjectivity. In J. Henriques, W. Hollway, C. Venn, and V. Walkerdine (eds.), *Changing the Subject*. London: Methuen, pp. 227–263.

Kitzinger, C., and S. Wilkinson. (2003). Constructing identities: A feminist conversation analytic approach to positioning in interaction. In R. Harré and F. Moghaddam (eds.), *The Self and Others*. Westport, CT: Praeger, pp. 157–180.

Korobov, N. (2001). Reconciling theory with method: From conversation analysis and critical discourse analysis to positioning analysis. *Forum: Qualitative Social Research*, 2 (3), http://www.qualitative-research.net/fqs-texte/3-01/3-01korobov-e.htm, accessed October 30, 2014.

Korobov, N. (2013). Positioning identities: A discursive approach to the negotiation of gendered categories. *Narrative Inquiry*, 23 (1), pp. 111–131.

Korobov, N., and M. Bamberg. (2004). Positioning a "mature" self in interactive practices: How adolescent males negotiate "physical attraction" in group talk. *British Journal of Developmental Psychology*, 22 (4), pp. 471–492.

Korobov, N., and M. Bamberg. (2007). "Strip Poker! They don't show nothing": Positioning identities in adolescent male talk about a television game show. In A. De Fina, M. Bamberg, and D. Schiffrin (eds.), *Selves and Identities in Narrative and Discourse*. Amsterdam: John Benjamins, pp. 253–272.

Labov, W., and J. Waletzky (1967). Narrative analysis: Oral versions of personal experience. In J. Helm (ed.), *Essays on the Verbal and Visual Arts*. Seattle: University of Washington Press, pp. 12–44.

Laplanche, J., and J.-B. Pontalis. (1972). *Das Vokabular der Psychoanalyse*. Frankfurt am Main: Suhrkamp.

Linde, C. (1993). *Life Stories: The Creation of Coherence*. Oxford: Oxford University Press.

Lucius-Hoene, G., and A. Deppermann. (2000). Narrative identity empiricized: A dialogical and positioning approach to autobiographical research interviews. *Narrative Inquiry*, 10 (1), pp. 199–222.

Lucius-Hoene, G., and A. Deppermann. (2004a). Narrative Identität und Positionierung. *Gesprächsforschung*, 5, pp. 166–183, http://www.gespraechsforschung-ozs.de/fileadmin/dateien/heft2004/ga-lucius.pdf, accessed January 5, 2015.

Lucius-Hoene, G., and A. Deppermann. (2004b). *Rekonstruktion narrativer Identität: Ein Arbeitsbuch zur Analyse narrativer Interviews*. Wiesbaden: VS.

McAdams, D.P. (2011). Narrative identity. In S.J. Schwartz, K. Luyckx, and V.L. Vignoles (eds.), *Handbook of Identity Theory and Research*. Vol. 1. New York: Springer, pp. 99–115.

Mead, G.H. (1934). *Mind, Self and Society from the Standpoint of a Social Behaviorist*. Edited by C.W. Morris. Chicago, IL: University of Chicago Press.

Mouffe, C. (1992). Feminism, citizenship and radical democratic politics. In J. Butler and J.W. Scott (eds.), *Feminists Theorize the Political*. New York: Routledge, pp. 369–385.

Potter, D., and M. Wetherell. (1987). *Discourse and Social Psychology*. London: Sage.

Rampton, Ben (1995). *Crossing: Language and Ethnicity among Adolescents*. London: Longman.

Ricoeur, P. (1990). *Soi-même comme un autre*. Paris: Seuil.

Sacks, H. (1972). On the analyzability of stories by children. In J. Gumperz and D. Hymes (eds.), *Directions in Sociolinguistics: The Ethnography of Speaking*. New York: Holt, Rinehart and Winston, pp. 325–345.

Sacks, H. (1992). *Lectures on Conversation*. 2 Vols. Oxford: Blackwell.

Schegloff, E.A. (1997). Whose text? Whose context? *Discourse and Society*, 8, pp. 165–187.

Schegloff, E.A. (2007). A tutorial on membership categorization. *Journal of Pragmatics*, 39 (3), pp. 462–482.

Schiffrin, D. (1996). Narrative as self-portrait: The sociolinguistic construction of identity. *Language in Society*, 25 (2), pp. 167–204.

Searle, J.R. (1969). *Speech Acts: An Essay in the Philosophy of Language*. Cambridge: Cambridge University Press.

Schütze, F. (1981). Prozeßstrukturen des Lebenslaufs. In J. Matthes, A. Pfeifenberger, and M. Stosberg (eds.), *Biographie in handlungswissenschaftlicher Perspektive*. Nürnberg: Nürnberger Forschungsvereinigung, pp. 67–156.

Schütze, F. (1984). Kognitive Figuren des autobiographischen Stegreiferzählens. In M. Kohli and G. Robert (eds.), *Biographie und soziale Wirklichkeit*. Stuttgart: Metzlersche Verlagsbuchhandlung, pp. 78–117.

Silverstein, M. (1992). The indeterminacy of contextualization: When is enough enough? In P. Auer and A. di Luzio (eds.), *The Contextualization of Language*. Amsterdam: John Benjamins, pp. 55–76.

Silverstein, M. (1993). Metapragmatic discourse and metapragmatic function. In J. Lucy (ed.), *Reflexive Language: Reported Speech and Metapragmatics*. Cambridge: Cambridge University Press, pp. 33–58.

Slocum-Bradley, N. (2008). The positioning diamond: Conceptualizing identity constructions at the US-Mexico border. In N. Slocum-Bradley, *Promoting Conflict or Peace through Identity*. Aldershot, UK: Ashgate, pp. 103–138.

Slocum-Bradley, N. (2009). The positioning diamond: A trans-disciplinary framework for discourse analysis. *Journal for the Theory of Social Behaviour*, 40 (1), pp. 1–29.

Slocum-Bradley, N. (2010). Identity construction in Europe: A discursive approach. *Identity*, 10 (1), pp. 50–68.

Stokoe, E.H. (2005). Analysing gender and language. *Journal of Sociolinguistics*, 9 (1), pp. 118–133.

Stokoe, E. (2012). Moving forward with membership categorization analysis: Methods for systematic analysis. *Discourse Studies*, 14 (3), pp. 277–303.

Tannen, D. (1989). *Talking Voices*. Cambridge: Cambridge University Press.

Van De Mieroop, D., and K. Bruyninckx. (2009). The influence of the interviewing style and the historical context on positioning shifts in the narrative of a Second World War resistance member. *Journal of Sociolinguistics*, 13 (2), pp. 169–194.

Wengraf, T. 2001. *Qualitative Research Interviewing: Biographic Narrative and Semi-Structured Method*. London: Sage.

Wetherell, M. (1998). Positioning and interpretive repertoires. Conversation analysis and post-structuralism in dialogue. *Discourse and Society*, 9, pp. 387–412.

Wetherell, M. (2003): Paranoia, ambivalence, and discursive practices: Concepts of position and positioning in psychoanalysis and discursive psychology. In R. Harré and F.M. Moghaddam (eds.), *The Self and Others: Positioning Individuals in Personal, Political, and Cultural Contexts*. Westport, CT: Praeger, pp. 99–120.

Wetherell, M. (2011). A step too far: Discursive psychology, linguistic ethnography and questions of identity. *Journal of Sociolinguistics*, 11 (5), pp. 661–681.

Widdicombe, S. (1998). Uses of identity as an analysts' and a participants' tool. In C. Antaki and S. Widdicombe (eds.), *Identities in Talk*. London: Sage, pp. 191–206.

Wortham, S. (2000). Interactional positioning and narrative self-construction. *Narrative Inquiry*, 10 (1), pp. 157–198.

Wortham, S. (2001). *Narratives in Action*. New York: Teachers College Press.

Zimmerman, D.H. (1998). Identity, context and interaction. In C. Antaki and S. Widdicombe (eds.), *Identities in Talk*. London: Sage, pp. 87–106.

20 Narrative and Cultural Identities

Performing and Aligning with Figures of Personhood

MICHELE KOVEN

20.1 Introduction

In this chapter, I analyze how people summon up, perform, and evaluate recognizable "cultural identities" in storytelling interactions. When people tell stories, they do not simply reflect their cultural identities as static, monolithic entities, describable by single demographic (e.g., ethnic, national, etc.) labels. Instead, with the perspectives of Goffman's (1979) notion of footing and Bakhtin's (1981) notion of heteroglossia, one can treat "cultural identities" in narrative as multivoiced productions. This multivoicedness results from participants' coordinated presentations, evaluations, and enactments of multiple images of selves and others, across here-and-now narrating and there-and-then narrated events (Mannheim 1998; Wortham 2001; Bakhtin 1981; Bamberg 1997; Hill 1995; Keane 2011; Koven 2002, 2007, 2013a). In particular, I draw from recent scholarship that treats such images as voices or figures of personhood (Inoue 2006; Agha 2007; Wortham, Mortimer, and Allard 2011). These figures are thus "typifiable speaking personae" (Agha 2005b: 39), or "image[s] ... performable through a semiotic display" (Agha 2006: 177), that if widely distributed across different segments of a population, may be described as "enregistered" (Agha 2006). "Cultural identities" in narrative therefore emerge through participants' recognition of, performance of, and alignments toward such recurrent figures.

To illustrate this approach, I analyze how French Luso-descendant women, daughters of Portuguese migrants raised in France, tell each other stories in which they perform and comment upon dialogues between locally recognized figures of personhood. In these storytelling interactions, participants try to establish like-mindedness as fellow Luso-descendants. They do this by inviting shared alignment from each other in their here-and-now interaction, in relation to there-and-then narrated interactions. Participants do this through multivocal performances and evaluations of two recurring

The Handbook of Narrative Analysis, First Edition. Edited by Anna De Fina and Alexandra Georgakopoulou.
© 2015 John Wiley & Sons, Inc. Published 2019 by John Wiley & Sons, Inc.

figures: the modern, youthful, urban French adolescent and the old-fashioned, chronologically old, rural Portuguese kinswoman. They alternatively inhabit, perform, and evaluate these two figures in the narrating interaction with each other, and in the narrated interaction as characters. Narrating and narrated participants may then transiently embody the two figures, presented as both specific individuals and general types. Participants' sense of each other as having particular "cultural identities" emerges through their previous experiences with, joint constructions of, and alignments toward these figures.

I conclude by arguing that future research should investigate how particular figures and participants' alignments toward them "travel" beyond the individual storytelling (see Wortham and Rhodes, this volume, chapter 8). This will help illuminate how the identities salient to a particular individual or to a given group may appear to stabilize or become "enregistered" across contexts, over space and time.

20.2 Previous Work on Narrative and Cultural Identity: A Focused Review

Narrative scholars have offered many perspectives on cultural identity. Some have treated the relationship between narrative and cultural identity as a psychological question (Hammack 2008), using the terms "identity" and "self" interchangeably. Addressing the range of scholarship that has sought to define identity is beyond the scope of this discussion (see this volume, De Fina, chapter 18 and Van De Mieroop, chapter 21). In this chapter, I adopt the perspective often evident in sociolinguistics, sociology, and linguistic anthropology, where identities are understood to be interactionally emergent within and across communicative events (Goffman 1959; Bucholtz and Hall 2004; Agha 2006) as the semiotically displayed and inferred images of personhood to which social actors may be recruited and linked.

20.2.1 Group-specific narrative styles and "cultural identities"

As noted by De Fina and Georgakopoulou (2012), there is a tradition of sociolinguistically informed work documenting the existence of variation in narrative styles across (researcher-determined) groups, often defined by nationality, class, race/ethnicity, and/or region (Blum-Kulka 1993; Heath 1983; Labov 1972; Linde 1993; Michaels 1981; Miller, Fung, and Mintz 1996, Miller et al. 1997; Miller et al. 2012; Polanyi 1989; Tannen 1984, 1986). Some of this scholarship involves intergroup comparisons. For example, in a large comparative corpus, Labov (1972) compared the formally identifiable strategies of narrative evaluation used by working-class African Americans and middle-class European Americans. He found that his white participants generally engaged in more "external" evaluation compared to the African American participants, whose stories were more "internally" evaluated. Concretely, this meant that working-class African American narrators' stories were more likely to be dramatically performed than those told by middle-class European Americans. Miller and her colleagues have found similar phenomena when participants were compared by social class (Miller and Sperry 2012; Miller, Cho, and Bracey 2005; Cho and Miller 2004). By examining narrative strategies associated with dramatic performance, they showed that their working-class participants were consistently "better" storytellers than their middle-class participants. Although not explicitly comparative, Marjorie Harness Goodwin (1990) demonstrated the great verbal and interpersonal skill that a group of African American children deploy to participate in a variety of narrative-based social practices. Countering widespread notions of verbal deprivation of participants whose discourse is often stigmatized in a wider sociolinguistic order, this scholarship shows the richness, complexity, and specificity of narrative strategies associated with different demographically identifiable groups. Such work demonstrates and valorizes the virtuosity in narrative ways of speaking that may not otherwise be socially valued (Miller, Koven, and Lin 2011).

Scholars have also done comparative work outside the United States, documenting systematic group-differences in multiple dimensions of storytelling of relevance to the study of cultural identity (Blum-Kulka 1993; Miller et al. 2012, Miller et al. 1996; see De Fina and Georgakopoulou 2012 for a review). In a number of publications, Miller and her colleagues have compared how middle-class European Americans and middle-class Taiwanese co-narrate personal experiences with young children (Miller et al. 1996, 1997, 2012). In particular, they have noted differences in how children's narrated misbehavior is presented in the context of a current interaction. In stories of children's transgressions, Taiwanese parents were more likely to cast the child's previous narrated misdeeds as justifying current scolding and as an opportunity for current moral teaching. European American participants were more likely to cast the child's previous narrated misdeeds in a way that presented the child as cute in the present interaction. The authors link these differences to different developmental outcomes and cultural values in the United States and Taiwan. For example, in avoiding current criticism of a past transgression, American parents are socializing "self-esteem," a phenomenon best understood as specific to a particular time and place, rather than a universal psychological good. Taiwanese parents, on the other hand, treat children's transgressions and their subsequent narrations of them as didactic opportunities. Miller and colleagues describe how through routinized interactions, these divergent practices socialize children to local cultural models of self. Such work documents the variability of narrative practices and their connection to other cultural phenomena, such as the socialization of group-specific values and images of self.

While such comparative scholarship has compellingly demonstrated the local variability of narrative practices, it has focused less on how participants *themselves* interpret their own and others' narrative styles as signs of group-specific identities. As such, some comparative work on narrative styles has been critiqued for providing an overly "etic" account of group-specific narrative performances based on analysts' correlations of narrative style with demographic groups rather than attending more directly to participants' perceptions of narrative styles (De Fina and Georgakopoulou 2012). These authors argue instead for an emic approach to narrative and cultural difference.

What might an "emic" approach to narrative and cultural identity look like? One might ask how particular ways of telling a story come to signal identities *to participants themselves*, investigating how participants recognize images of selves and others as types through narrative. We see the beginnings of such an approach in scholarship that is not only comparative, but also *intercultural or intergroup*, that is, the researcher examines storytelling encounters *between* people from different sociolinguistic backgrounds (Blommaert 2001; Heath 1983; Jacquemet 2008; Maryns 2006; Michaels 1981; Tannen 1984). Although this work may not explicitly engage questions of "identity," it does so implicitly, insofar as participants may infer particular images of one another as a result of an awkward interaction (Goffman 1959). These scholars showed interactional awkwardness that emerged when participants' ways of launching, telling, and responding to stories differed. Michaels (1981) and Heath (1983) noted the effects of mismatched narrative styles in the institutional setting of school, where minority children's narrative practices learned at home often did not match those valued and validated in mainstream classrooms (see Miller et al. 2011 for a review). In an educational context, such interactional awkwardness had serious consequences for minority children's performance in school, as teachers "misrecognized" children's group-specific ways of telling as deficits. Similarly, more recent scholarship has examined mismatches in narrative performance and interpretation in the power-laden institutional settings of asylum hearings (Blommaert 2001; Jacquemet 2008; Maryns 2006). Following Gumperz's (1982) tradition of interactional sociolinguistics, in such institutional contexts, awkward intercultural encounters among people with different narrative practices may result in those who do not master the most valued narrative styles being denied critical material and semiotic resources (Heller 2010; Gal 1989; Irvine 1989). Differently positioned participants may then interpret one another's narrative behavior as evidence that each belongs to more or less stigmatized social types, a process of direct relevance to questions of "identity": Such narrative-based encounters may thus contribute to and reinforce more widely circulating negatively evaluated images of speakers from particular groups.

Without focusing on misunderstandings as such, I extend this approach by directly addressing how participants summon up and display recognition of such images through narrative. As noted by Silverstein (2003) and Johnstone and Kiesling (2008), for participants to understand a way of speaking as an index of group identity (i.e., as associated with particular figures of personhood), participants must recognize it as *distinct* from alternate ways of speaking. Through indexically ordered language ideologies (Silverstein 2003), participants may then interpret someone's use of one among several available ways of speaking as signaling particular dimensions of context, including participants' identities, as particular sociocultural types. The analyst can then observe how participants reflexively display their recognition of the "meanings" of different ways of speaking and associated personas through the ways they implicitly and explicitly orient to, evaluate, and perform them. The research focus then shifts from analyst-identified differences in how people from different backgrounds tell stories, to participant-identified differences. This offers a better perspective from which to observe how participants themselves use narrative to infer, enact, and evaluate a range of culturally recognizable types. A priority for analysis, then, is to demonstrate the "emic" salience of particular figures and the stakes of being identified with them. In this chapter I do this by analyzing how participants invite one another to recognize and align with different locally recognized figures.

20.3   Bakhtinian Perspectives

Sociolinguistic and linguistic anthropological research has highlighted that social actors' "identities" are multiple. Through multiple ways of speaking, speakers can lay claim to or have ascribed to them different personae (Agha 2006; Bailey 2000; Koven 2007). This is unsurprising, insofar as all people may have multiple context-reflecting and context-creating ways of speaking.

Like "identity," "context" is rarely single or static (Goffman 1979; Gumperz 1982; Duranti and Goodwin 1992). A multiplicity of interconnected "identities" and "contexts" is particularly evident in narrative, as there are multiple, embedded communicative contexts or events at stake. Narrative interaction involves, minimally, a narrated and a narrating context or event (Goffman 1979; Jakobson 1957; Bauman 1986; Silverstein 1993; Wortham 2001; Koven 2002, 2007, 2011; Bakhtin 1981). As participants establish and infer "identities" for one another in the immediate narrating context, *and* for characters in the narrated context (Goffman 1979; Bakhtin 1981; Agha 2005b), story-telling participants perform and comment upon multiple socially and spatiotemporally (here-and-now, there-and-then) locatable images of selves and others.

Interactants must also "calibrate" the links between participants in the current narrating interaction and participants in the narrated events (Silverstein 1993). More generally, calibration designates how participants relate a current narrating event to other speech events. In narrative, participants negotiate the relationship between the space, time, and personnel of a current interaction and the space, time, and personnel in a distinct there-and-then speech event (i.e., characters). There are different ways of accomplishing this. Sometimes, in what Silverstein (1993) calls "reportive calibration," people calibrate a one-time narrated event between particular narrated characters (e.g., a friend, brother, customer) at a specific place (e.g., the bus stop) and time (e.g., last summer). Participants may also negotiate the relationship between the current interaction and a separate narrated "timeless" realm, often invoked in proverbs that assert general truths, or narrated events that are presented as generalized and typical, in what (Silverstein 1993) calls "nomic calibration." Both types of calibration may be at issue in a given storytelling event, and participants may alternate among them, for example by linking specific narrated characters and their one-time actions with enduring social types and habitual or timeless activities. If the analyst attends to how participants explicitly or implicitly link specific participants with general types, he/she may learn how participants themselves infer and attribute generalized "cultural identity" types to current and narrated participants.

Another key dimension of narrative calibration involves how participants make the narrated world focal in the here-and-now narrating event. Elsewhere, I have discussed the different ways storytellers may calibrate a narrating and narrated event when telling a story (Koven 2002, 2007, 2011). For example, someone may tell a story primarily from the perspective of the here-and-now interaction, with minimal performance of narrated characters. In this type of calibration, the story-world events and characters may appear relatively muted. This may happen, for example, if a storyteller relates events primarily in indirect rather than direct quotation. On the other hand, participants may perform a narrated character in such a way that the boundary between narrating and narrated events appears to vanish, as if the "there-and-then" narrated character comes to life in the "here-and-now." When participants fuse their roles as participants in the here-and-now interaction with the speech of a there-and-then character, it may sometimes even be indeterminate whether participants are speaking as a character, or speaking as "themselves" in the immediate interaction, or speaking as both simultaneously. Such moments of ambiguity/simultaneity/coincidence of narrated and narrating events are often particularly powerful and even transformative for participants (Wortham 2001; Silverstein 2003; Koven 2013a; Eisenlohr 2006). During such moments, current participants may even seem to inhabit or actually *become like* the narrated figures of personhood (i.e., "identities"). These are often moments when "cultural identities" become the most salient to participants, as narrated and narrating participants are most likely to be identified with each other and with particular figures of personhood. Below, I present excerpts from an interaction that demonstrate how the Luso-descendant participants I studied speak simultaneously as enacted characters and as current conversationalists.

20.3.1 Figures of selves and others

What are the figures at issue? From a Bakhtinian perspective, narrators routinely summon up a range of socially recognizable types whom they voice and ventriloquate (Hill 1995; Wortham 2001). In the following discussion, I address both participants' alignments and disalignments with such types. I then also speculate about the question of "social recognizability," that is, the emergence, enregisterment, and "circulation" of particular types for particular social actors.

Participants need not align with the figures of personhood that they evoke. Evoked figures may not (re)present narrators' "own identity"/"selves," but may be figures of "otherness," from which current participants distance themselves (Hastings and Manning 2004). "Crossing" (Rampton 1995), when people perform out-group ways of speaking, often involves precisely such enactments of figures of otherness. We also see this in Basso's (1979) discussion of Apache "Portraits of the Whiteman," in Hill's (1995) discussion of Don Gabriel and his evocation of Spanish-speaking otherness, and in Bucholtz's (1999) discussion of Brand One, a Euro-American adolescent who evokes racialized others as targets of both alignment and dissociation. We also observe this in Chun's (2009) discussion of how the comedian Margaret Cho stylizes her immigrant mother's speech, distinct from Cho's "normal" voice. In past work, I have similarly shown how daughters of Portuguese emigrants perform figures of socially stigmatized types, the "bad ostentatious emigrant" (Koven 2013a) and the "backward racist" (Koven 2013b). In this chapter, I will describe how Portuguese migrants' daughters perform figures of otherness, presented as nonmodern, older, rural Portuguese women.

However, figures of personhood do not occur in isolation, but usually come in contrastive sets (see Irvine 2001). One or more figures in the set may be more or less implicit or unmarked (Bucholtz and Hall 2004). The discourse I present below is representative of a pattern in which the figure of the nonmodern other appears in explicit or implicit dialogue with the figure of the young, modern, urban French person. It is the dialogic interaction among figures that is often most central in storytelling events.

Finally, one can ask how people come to recognize and jointly interpret particular semiotic displays as signaling given figures of personhood. What are the more or less local "scales" from which people "find" figures (see Keane 2011)? People may discover relevant figures in multiple, often interconnected sites, including schools (Eckert 2001; Wortham 2005, 2006), peer groups (Eckert 2001; Bucholtz 1999; Mendoza-Denton 2008), and families, all of which are part of larger sociohistorically grounded hierarchies (Wortham 2005; Eckert 2001). This approach then treats any given "cultural identity" dynamically, as presupposable and emergent for particular actors in particular contexts.

20.4   Figures of Personhood and Alignment to Them in Portuguese Emigrants' Daughters' Narratives

Here, I discuss how the daughters of Portuguese migrants raised in France perform and align with two recurring figures of personhood in narrative, who always appear in dialogue with each other across narrating and narrated events. The examples shown below come from a long-term study of language and storytelling among bilingual adult daughters of Portuguese emigrants, raised in France. My participants' parents emigrated from rural, impoverished Portugal to urban France during the 1960s and 1970s for economic reasons. Given the relative proximity between Portugal and France, even though the parents spend much of the year working in France and the children attend French schools, the families return at least annually to the parents' village of origin, where many have built homes, and they maintain relationships with local family and friends.

As I have discussed at greater length elsewhere (Koven 2007, 2013b), when my participants tell each other stories about experiences with their parents and people they have encountered in rural Portugal and urban France, they often fashion such others into narrated figures who take on patterned resemblances to recurring, chronotopically framed figures of personhood. My participants regularly animate figures of others, imaginatively situated in the backward time and space of rural Portugal, and figures of self, imaginatively situated in the modern time and space of urban France.

Participants encounter these two recurrent figures of personhood in multiple sites through experiences of socialization in family, peer, and institutional settings of both rural Portugal and urban France. The figures therefore emerge and converge from lived personal experiences and from participants' access to more broadly circulating contrasting cultural images of France and Portugal. These images can be understood as cultural chronotopes, the recurrent social visions interlinking space, time, and person that participants presuppose and establish in written and oral discourse (Agha 2007; Bakhtin 1981; Dick 2010; Gal 2006; Koven 2013b; Koven and Marques in press; Perrino, this volume, chapter 7). As such, they add a spatiotemporal dimension to any notion of personhood.

My participants draw from a set of cultural chronotopes that construct and contrast Portugal as less modern than France (see Dick 2010; Koven and Marques in press). Such a chronotope shaped their emigrant parents' decision to leave the poverty of rural Portugal in the 1960s and 1970s for the more "evolved" and affluent urban France. As their offspring, my participants draw from a somewhat different version of a modernist chronotope that circulates in urban French contexts through which Portugal and Portuguese migrants may be perceived as relatively nonmodern. In this version of the modernist chronotope, "France" (as imagined place, people, and time) has an ongoing civilizing mission, not only in relation to its former colonies, but also to current immigrants on French soil (Schnapper 1991; Blanchard et al. 2013; Silverstein 2005). These parallel chronotopic visions of French and Portuguese relative (non)modernity are not mere abstractions to my participants, but mediate their everyday encounters. These chronotopes provide lenses through which participants understand their lived transnational experiences and apprehend selves and others.

Participants thus present many narrated Portuguese characters from the perspective of a French modernist chronotope. We will see this below in participants' enactments of older female kin as unreasonably old-fashioned and conservative. These then become figures of otherness, which participants present as fundamentally unlike themselves, both in the narrated and narrating events. These figures of old-fashioned Portuguese otherness appear quite often in stories concerning gendered norms of courtship, dress, and outings, where the participants discuss their encounters with their families' vs. their peers' expectations about what young unmarried women should wear, how they should date, and whether they should go out. Indeed, they often quote such characters in Portuguese, thus associating language with this persona, whom they situate in a place that is presented as outdated and peripheral. In contrast, they present their own narrated selves as characters as reasonable, youthful, modern, and affiliating with urban French norms and rebelling against the "old-fashioned" Portuguese elders. Their current narrating and past narrated selves are shown identifying with this youthful, modern, urban, and implicitly French figure. Often the youthful, modern characters are made to speak adolescent/ "young" French when in dialogue with the other figure.

What emerges throughout these narratives is a confrontational dialogue between the two recurrent figures, both as general types and as the specific characters who embody them. Participants sometimes treat these two recurrent types (older, conservative, restrictive female kin from rural Portugal vs. younger, progressive, liberal modern youth in urban France) as exemplars of "Portuguese" vs. "French" people in general. (Indeed, nonmigrant Portuguese from urban areas may find such constructions of these categories reductionist, critiquing Luso-descendants for confusing their families' experiences in the village with Portugal writ large). In what follows, we will see how participants entextualize these two types as characters, and how they align with and enact them in a current narrating interaction. This approach will show how the participants themselves come to understand "French" vs. "Portuguese" cultural identities in narrative.

To analyze participants' performance and alignment toward these figures, I systematically examine how participants evoke and perform narrated characters' speech (Bakhtin 1981; Bauman 1986; Hill 1995; Koven 2001; Silverstein 1993), while also attending to how participants position themselves in the here-and-now relative to each other and to the narrated world and personas within it. Specifically, participants use a variety of indexical strategies to do this: deictics of time, such as verb tense and temporal adverbs (Dick 2010; Hanks 1990, 1992; Silverstein 1976); ways of indexing person, such as pronouns (Benveniste 1971; Brown and Gilman 1960; De Fina 2003; O'Connor 1994; Silverstein 1976); ways of evoking place, such as spatial adverbs (Davidson 2007; Hanks 1990; Modan 2007; Schegloff 1972); and language variation in the form of style-shifting (Eckert and Rickford 2001) and code-switching (Auer 1998; Gumperz 1982; Woolard 2004). With attention to these strategies, I will show how the young women usually inhabit the figure of the modern, urban, French-speaking youth, aligning with each other as immediate interactants and as narrated characters. Sometimes current story-telling participants align so fully with the "youthful" French character that some of their utterances simultaneously enact the figure as a character, and as current interlocutory storytelling participant. They then evoke and perform figures of "old-fashioned" Portuguese others in a humorous confrontation with the young, modern figures. The old-fashioned figure is presented as ridiculous.

Bold text here indicates Portuguese

(1) J: ... <u>toutes</u> les vacances, on se la <u>paie</u>. P'tain, et puis c'était comme ↑ci fais pas ↑ci fais pas↑ça, t'habille pas comm' ci, t'habille pas comm' ↑ça.

J: ... <u>every</u> vacation, we have to <u>deal</u> with her. <u>Fuck</u>, and then it was like ↑this, don't do ↑this don't do t↑hat, don't dress like this, don't dress like ↑that.

(2) Putain.

Fuck.

(3) un ↑coup, ((inspiration)) oh je euh c'était euh, y a y a 2 ans quand chuis partie avec mon frère. donc euh j'étais euh chez ma cou↑sine. et y a eu **a São Memede, sozinha à pé**. j'allais faire chais pas quoi, bon, je pouvais y aller à pied, bon.

↑Once ((breath)) Oh, I uh it was uh, it was it was two years ago when I went with my brother. So I was at my cousin's. and there was to **São Memede, alone on foot**. I was gonna do, I dunno what, okay, I could go there on foot, okay.

(4) et et alors j'mets mon <u>walkman</u>, t'sais j'étais en salopette et tout, tee shirt t' sais euh, okay,=
V: =ouais
J: =sac à dos [(unclear)
S: [(unclear)

and and so I put on my <u>walkman</u>, y'know, I was in overalls and everything, t-shirt, y'know=
okay=
V: =yeah=
J: =backpack [(unclear)
S: [(unclear)

(5) J: et tout,

J: and everything,

(6) e' m' fait euh (.) **"vais com isso nas orelhas p'a p'ra rua,"**

and she's like uh (.) **"you're going out into into the street with that in your ears?"**

(7) j'fais, "ben oui (.)"

I'm like, "well, yeah (.)"

(8) S: ((giggle))

S: ((giggle))

(9) J: t'sais, je la r'garde =
V: =ben et alors

J: y'know, I look at her=
V: =well, so what

(10) J: (unclear) e' m'fait ↑**"AH mas isso não se ↑FAZ.,"**

J: (unclear) she's like, ↑**"AH but one doesn't do THAT."**

(11) j'fais euh (.) "ça va <u>pas</u> ↑là?"
V: [hhhh
J: et ↑<u>toc toc</u> hein? =
V: =[hhhh

I'm like, "What's <u>wrong</u> with you?"
V: [hhhhhh
J: and ↑<u>hello</u>, eh=
V: =[hhhhh

(12) J: e' fait, **"Ah isso não é bem"**

J: she's like, **"Oh, that's not good."**

(13) j' fais **"Ah, esteja calada."** chuis partie.

I'm like **"Oh be quiet."** I left.

(14) el' m'a poussé la main.
e' me fait, "**já sabes, atu- tua mãe de de- a minha mãe, a tua mãe ainda está no- nos tempos antigos.**"

she pushed my hand.
she's like, "**you know your your mother- my mother, your mother is still in the olden days.**"

(15) je fais, "mais attends, **diz-me lá onde 'stá o mal. Tu não escutas, sabes que ? já é ?** (unclear)"
V: =Ben ouais

I'm like, "but wait. **Tell me what the problem is. You don't listen, do you know that ? it's ? (unclear)**"
V: =well, yeah

(16) J: mais elle elle a un problème celle-là (.)

J: but that one's got a real problem (.)

(17) V: i'sont arriérés

V: they're backwards

((next excerpt is taken from several minutes later in the conversation))

(18) V: C'est du style euh ouais "**vem ela, antes de vir pra'qui e lá, vais a ver como é que ela se veste, vais a ver.**"

V: It's like, uh, yeah, "**here she comes, before coming here and there, look at how she's dressed. you're going to see.**"

(19) S: Ah ça (unclear)
V: Ouai(h)s
J: Vous l'avez pas entendu ça déjà? (.)

S: For sure (unclear)
V: Yea(h)
J: You guys haven't heard that before? (.)

(20) Ma mère, (.) [t'sais, l'autre jour
V: [ouais
J: j've j'vais à, j' voyais un short, ah je fais, "ah, il est mignon le short." en jean et tout (.)

My mother (.) [y'know, the other day
V: [yeah.
J: I g- I go to-, I saw a pair of shorts, oh, I'm like, "Oh those shorts are cute." in denim and everything(.)

(21) "**vais meter isso depois de 'tares casado?**"

"**you're going to wear those after you get married?**"

(22) je dis, "ben, alors?"=
S: =[hhhhh
J: à ton choix (.)

I say, "yeah, and so?"=
S: =[hhhhh
J: your choice (.)

(23) "**Ah mas depois de 'tares casado não podes.**"

"**Oh but after you're married, you can't.**"

(24) j'fais, "mais arrête!"

I'm like, "stop it!"

(25) S: Une fois, mais. c'est ça. une fois qu't'es mariée
J: Faut plus t'habiller [comm' avant
S: [tu dois, va ranger tes minijupes,

S: Once , but. that's it. once you're married
J: can't dress anymore [like before
S: [you have to, go put away your miniskirts,

(26) J: j'fais à ma mère, j'fais,
S: = [(unclear) genoux
M: [c'est quoi le problème

J: I go to my mother, I'm like
S: = [(unclear) knees
M: [what's the problem

(27) J: "**Ah, mas vais 'tar com os panos (unclear)**"

J: "**Oh, but you'll have to wear rags (unclear).**"

(28) j'fais, "non mais t'es tarrée toi . ça va pas la tête."

I'm like, "No, but you're retarded. what's wrong with you."

This transcript, also discussed in Koven (2007: ch. 3), was taken from a recording of a casual conversation between me and three young female friends, all daughters of Portuguese migrants raised in France. In these two excerpts, the participants summon up narrated events that include interactions between *others* who are old-fashioned,

Portuguese, elder female kin, rooted in the village, and *selves* who are modern, young, urban, and French-speaking. The older Portuguese women believe women should dress conservatively, while the younger daughters raised in France believe these norms are unreasonably restrictive and old-fashioned. Across these two excerpts – and indeed, across the larger set of data – we see recurrent struggles between these two enacted figures, as the immediate participants side with each other against the first figure in favor of the second. I will now discuss in detail how participants align with each other and with the performed figures throughout these excerpts.

In lines 1–2, J complains about always having to tolerate a particular Portuguese elder's sartorial restrictions during summer trips in Portugal. She offers a recurring/ habitual scene (shown with nomic/tenseless verb "have to deal with her"/*se la paie*, and the use of "every"/*toutes*). Narrated and narrating events briefly coincide through J's use of the expletive interjection, "Fuck"/*Putain*, which simultaneously evokes and fuses her current and past negative reactions toward this character and the type she embodies. J subsequently offers a stylized parody of this elder Portuguese female character's words showing J's distance from this figure. In both narrating and narrated events, J inhabits the persona of someone who both opposed and opposes those who promote such sartorial interdictions.

From her shift from the imperfect past (*imparfait*) to the simple past (*passé composé*), we see that J then transitions in line 3 from a generalized habitual narrative of something that happens regularly to a narrative of a one-time past experience, which occurred during a summer trip to her family's rural Portuguese home. In line 4, she dramatically highlights her act of dressing by shifting briefly to the historical present (Wolfson 1978) – "I put on my walkman"/"*je mets mon walkman*." She then describes the rest of her outfit (overalls, t-shirt, backpack), while interspersing multiple discourse markers, *t'sais, okay, et tout*. As noted by numerous scholars (see Schiffrin 1987), such discourse markers often serve interactional rather than referential functions. That is, speakers do not use them to advance plot, so much as to negotiate stance and alignment. I argue that J uses these discourse markers to invite the other co-present participants to side with her, that is, to get them to agree that she was indeed appropriately dressed in the narrated event. And indeed, V shows her alignment with J through responsive back channels. J has obtained her fellow conversationalists' implicit agreement that in the narrated event, it was she, not her older relative, who was in the right.

J then quotes the first of several similar exchanges between old-fashioned and modern figures in line 6. She first quotes the elder female Portuguese character in Portuguese, questioning her wearing of "that"/*isso* (her Walkman) on the street. In line 7, J then quotatively performs herself as a youthful, French influenced character in French. This performed character fails to see the problem the elder character has identified ("well, yeah"/*ben oui*). S then giggles at the performance of the two contrasting types.

Throughout the telling, the other participants consistently align with J. At moments, they even co-perform the contrasting figures in this story, so that narrated and narrating events appear to overlap and blend. For example, V's "well, so what" is almost identical to J's quoted response to her Portuguese relative. V sides with J in the here-and-now (line 9) of their recorded conversation, while simultaneously speaking as if she were also quoting a similar "youthful" retort directly to the older figure.

J re-performs the Portuguese-speaking elder female figure, who again issues sartorial proscriptions (line 10). She then enacts the French-speaking younger figure who critiques and mocks the first figure, to the laughter of her co-present conversational partners (line 11). When J quotes herself talking to her cousin (line 15), in half French, half Portuguese, she repeats her lack of understanding about the proscriptions. In line 16, J's words simultaneously address her cousin and her fellow conversationalists. V chimes in again, speaking from both inside the story as a fellow character and outside it as a fellow evaluator. In line 17, when V says *ils*/they, she links J's performance of a specific character (*elle*/she) to a general *"arriéré"* / "backward" type. V aligns with J in favor of the young, modern figure and type over the older, old-fashioned one.

In line 18, V also offers up another generic stylized performance of the words of the local critical Portuguese-speaking type who criticizes emigrants' daughters' manner of dress. As with the earlier segments, S, V, and J all orient to this performance, showing that they indeed recognize the type (line 19).

We move again from a narration of a nomically calibrated event with routine actions of generic types to a reportively calibrated past-tense narrative of a one-time past incident involving shopping with a specific figure (J's mother) in line 20. As in the earlier example, there is an exchange between an enacted French-speaking figure (who expresses admiration for a pair of shorts), and a disapproving Portuguese-speaking figure (who asks whether she intends to wear "that" after marriage, line 21). The two figures use constructions parallel to those used in the earlier narrative, where the Portuguese figure asks *"vais ... isso ...?"* and the French figure answers in French, *"ben, alors."* This again elicits laughter from all present (line 22). In line 24, the French-speaking figure says to the Portuguese-speaking figure "stop it!" The other participants consistently recognize the old-fashioned elder Portuguese female figure as a type assigned to specific individual characters as in line 25. S and J then jointly articulate the broader principles J's narrative has enacted, that is, that married women do not dress "like before." They articulate these as generalized principles for a nonspecific *tu*/you (O'Connor 1994), in a tenseless present of the verbs *falloir/devoir* "to have to." J concludes the excerpt with another quoted exchange between the two figures (lines 27 and 28), in which the elder Portuguese-speaking figure insists that married women normatively wear rags, and the younger French-speaking figure accuses the elder of being "retarded" and "not well in the head."

In these excerpts, the young women summon up, enact, and evaluate cultural types, toward which they show common orientations. They use language to construct individual characters and to link them to socioculturally identifiable types that talk/act in characteristic ways. One can also see how participants make these figures relevant in a current interaction. There are different ways they may establish relevance of the figures. These may range from such full identification with a figure that participants transiently become and speak "like" the figure, to the quoted performance of a figure as a sympathetic "there-and-then" character, to the quoted performance of a parodied other.

20.5   Conclusions

What have these materials illustrated? I briefly summarize the key points of this chapter here, followed by some remaining issues for future research.

(1) "Cultural identity" is too coarse of a notion to capture how people present, inhabit, and align with recurrent figures of personhood in narrative. With this approach, I have shown how storytelling participants entextualize sets of figures in narrative, with and for each other. As noted by Hill (1995), if a storyteller's self/identity appears coherent, such coherence only emerges through his/her through complex alignments toward multiple, often "kaleidoscopically" presented voices. In keeping with Goffman's notion of footing (1979) and Bakhtin's notion of heteroglossia (1981), attention to how people dynamically perform and align with figures of personhood in narrative allows the analyst to bypass earlier problematic notions of "culture" and "identity" as static, monolithic, and singular.

(2) Recurrent figures and dialogues among them are of particular interest. In the data presented here, we did not just see a single enactment of the dialogue between old-fashioned/old and modern/young types, but multiple iterations of it across stories told in this extended interaction. And beyond the excerpts shown here, I can attest that dialogue between these two figures recurs across a larger corpus of naturally occurring and elicited materials.

(3) These figures come in sets. As we saw in the excerpts above, there was not only one figure at issue, but rather a contrastive display of exchanges between the old-fashioned Portuguese rural elder and the young, modern Parisian urbanite. It is conceivable that sometimes a particular figure may be relatively unmarked (Bucholtz and Hall 2004), hence less visible, and less a focus of stylized performance. For example, Inoue (2006) talks about the dialogue between the figures of bourgeois nineteenth-century Japanese male and the vulgar Japanese schoolgirl. In this case, the narrator may inhabit the backgrounded male figure, who then quotes the performed female figure. In the discourse presented in this chapter, the voice of the youthful figure may appear relatively unmarked relative to the voice of the old-fashioned figure. Although multiple figures are at issue, people may notice the marked figure who is parodied more than the unmarked figure who parodies (Koven and Marques in press).

(4) We must document not only the figures of personhood, but also current partic-ipants' alignments with them (Agha 2007; Voloshinov 1976; Bakhtin 1981), from complete identification to distancing parody. Others may make complex inferences about figure types and participants' alignments with or dissociations from them, assigning narrated and/or narrating personnel to distinct types. For example, in other work (Koven 2007), I showed how listeners may judge performed characters separately from how they judge the current narrator, that is, they may dislike a character, but like the storyteller; similarly they may sympathize with a character, but criticize the storyteller. In other words, storytelling involves complex positionings relative to these figures, across narrating and narrated events.

(5) We should examine cultural "identities" as figures/types signaled *to* and recognized *by* someone in some respect (Peirce 1940; Kockelman 2005). As such, one should be wary of claims that people "perform cultural identities" in narrative, without demonstrating how participants indeed infer social types from storytellings, however implicitly. With a more "emic" approach, one can note how participants themselves reflexively display their orientations to particular figures in the interaction.

20.5.1 Remaining questions

I conclude with several remaining issues for future research about narrative, figures of personhood, and people's relationships to them across communicative contexts.

20.5.1.1 Moving beyond isolated communicative events: individuals and groups Much work from a Bakhtinian perspective has focused on narrative performances of recognizable identities in single events. Following a long tradition in linguistic anthropology and sociolinguistics, scholars have tended to focus on the communicative event as the unit of analysis (Jakobson 1960; Hymes 1972). However, there is growing recognition that scholars should also address how particular performances of types are habitualized across events (Agha 2005a, 2006; Bourdieu 1977; Carr 2011; Haviland 2005; Mehan 1996; Miller et al. 2012; Wortham 2006; see also Wortham and Rhodes, this volume, chapter 8). By looking across events, one can then observe how particular figures (and people's alignments with them) appear to circulate and/or perdure.

To the extent that narrative is a privileged medium through which people's identifications with types are stabilized, one can address these questions both at the level of an individual social actor and at the level of a group. Individuals may find their alignments toward recurrent figures transported and even habitualized across a series of interactions, so that something like (the experience and/or appearance of) a "self" is socialized into being (Haviland 2005; Wortham 2001; Miller et al. 1996; Koven 2007). This can be treated as a developmental problem of language socialization (Wortham 2001), or even a psychotherapeutic problem (Wortham 2001). One may then also move "up" in scale, beyond the individual, to also ask how recurrent figures and alignments toward them become enregistered, so that they are recognizable and habitualized within particular communities of practice, and/or more broadly defined populations (Agha 2006).

20.5.1.2 The sources and trajectories of figures of personhood A further multiscale question is less about the actual social actors, and more about the figures themselves. How/where do these figures of personhood originate, and how do they then "travel" across communicative events? This may also include "mass mediated" figures of personhood and people's alignments toward them over longer periods of time (Inoue 2006; Bucholtz and Lopez 2011; Carr 2011; Wortham et al. 2011).

For example, in the data explored here, I speculated about the relationships among the various sources and trajectories for the figure of the backward Portuguese elder. As discussed above and elsewhere (Koven 2004, 2013a; Koven and Marques in press), this figure is situated in broader international hierarchies, so that my participants' notions of "modernity" are connected to more widely circulating French notions that have treated immigrants as "uncivilized" until assimilated into "French culture." Similarly, from a widely circulating Portugal-centric perspective, my participants may evoke particular images of rural Portugal, linked to the time and place of their families' emigration from peripheral regions in the 1960s and 1970s, during the Salazarist regime. As such, their images of Portugal display little influence of the country's rapid "modernization" (democratization, urbanization, Europeanization) in the 1980s and 1990s. On the other hand, although they are connected to these broader historically situated scales, these figures also take on meaning in the contexts of participants' personal encounters with people. They then interpret such encounters through cultural chronotopes that have greater and lesser degrees of local resonance.

In earlier scholarship, scholars referred to this as the "micro-macro" problem, that is, how broad social, cultural, political, and economic orders are both reflected in and accomplished in individual encounters. Scholars have more recently critiqued such a binary approach to the complexity of social phenomena, arguing that one must empirically discover the multiple relevant time scales (Wortham 2005, 2012; Wortham et al. 2011) that inform trajectories (sources and effects) of meanings of different figures of personhood as these emerge across multiple sites. Future scholarship should continue to explore the circulation of particular figures of personhood and people's alignments toward them. Such figures rarely emerge *de novo* in a given encounter, nor are they deterministically imposed upon unwitting interactants. A historically grounded, trajectory-sensitive approach necessarily complicates any understanding of specific "cultural identities" as overly static, merely local, or overly homogeneous.

20.5.1.3   Narrative and figures of personhood in power-laden context   Finally, research should also examine the different kinds of symmetrical and asymmetrical narrative interactions in which participants find themselves and others recruited to different figures of personhood. From the perspective of socialization, one can study these processes during and beyond childhood, with different types of co-participants. Socialization to recognize, perform, and align with particular figures may sometimes happen in solidary contexts, as with the Portuguese migrants' daughters who jointly summoned up shared images of types and orientations to them. However, there is no rule that narrative negotiation of participants' alignments with figures of personhood must be collaborative or shared, or happen in contexts where participants are peers. As discussed above in reference to students from minority backgrounds and asylum seekers, narrative performances of and alignments with figures of personhood may unfold in situation where participants occupy unequal status, such as various institutional settings (legal, medical, educational, etc.) in which the stakes for non-shared alignment are not the same for all. For instance, a participant may perform a figure type that others do not recognize; participants may recognize the type, but not share alignment toward it. Carr (2011) explored how participants came to recognize, perform, and align with the figure of the "addict." Their performance and alignment was then taken up and "stabilized" (recontextualized) by the social worker who had the authority to transfer an image of the participant-as-addict in a case file. In this way, the original participant's "career" as a particular social type would further congeal, as it was made to travel from one context to the next (Bauman and Briggs 1990; Silverstein and Urban 1996). Future work should further investigate narrative and figures of personhood in such power-laden settings, where differently positioned participants' performances of, alignments with, and *sometimes coercive recruitments to* particular figures of personhood may have different potential consequences for differently positioned participants.

REFERENCES

Agha, A. (2005a). Semiosis across events. *Journal of Linguistic Anthropology*, 15 (1), pp. 1–5.

Agha, A. (2005b). Voice, footing, enregisterment. *Journal of Linguistic Anthropology*, 15 (1), pp. 38–59.

Agha, A. (2006). *Language and Social Relations*. Cambridge: Cambridge University Press.

Agha, A. (2007). Recombinant selves in mass mediated spacetime. *Language and Communication*, 27, pp. 320–335.

Auer, P. (1998). *Code-Switching in Conversation*. London: Routledge.

Bailey, B. (2000). The language of multiple identities among Dominican Americans. *Journal of Linguistic Anthropology*, 10 (2), pp. 190–223.

Bakhtin, M. (1981). *The Dialogic Imagination: Four Essays*. Austin: University of Texas Press.

Bamberg, M. (1997). Positioning between structure and performance. *Journal of Narrative and Life History*, 7 (1–4), pp. 335–342.

Basso, K.H. (1979). *Portraits of the Whiteman: Linguistic Play and Cultural Symbols among the Western Apache*. Cambridge: Cambridge University Press.

Bauman, R. (1986). *Story, Performance, and Event: Contextual Studies of Oral Narrative*. Cambridge: Cambridge University Press.

Bauman, R., and C.L. Briggs. (1990). Poetics and performance as critical perspectives on language and social life. *Annual Review of Anthropology*, 19, pp. 59–88.

Benveniste, É. (1971). *Problems in General Linguistics*. Coral Gables, FL: University of Miami Press.

Blanchard, P., S. Lemaire, N. Bancel, and D. Thomas. (2013). *Colonial Culture in France since the Revolution*. Bloomington: Indiana University Press.

Blommaert, J. (2001). Context is/as critique. *Critique of Anthropology*, 21 (1), pp. 13–32.

Blum-Kulka, S. (1993). "You gotta know how to tell a story": Telling tales and tellers in American and Israeli narrative events at dinner. *Language in Society*, 22 (3), pp. 361–402.

Bourdieu, P. (1977). *Outline of a Theory of Practice*. Cambridge: Cambridge University Press.

Brown, R., and A. Gilman. (1960). The pronouns of power and solidarity. In T.A. Sebeok (ed.), *Style in Language*. Cambridge, MA: MIT Press, pp. 253–276.

Bucholtz, M. (1999). You da man: Narrating the racial other in the production of white masculinity. *Journal of Sociolinguistics*, 3 (4), pp. 443–460.

Bucholtz, M., and K. Hall (2004). Language and identity. In A. Duranti (ed.), *Companion to Linguistic Anthropology*. Oxford: Blackwell, pp. 369–394.

Bucholtz, M., and Q. Lopez (2011). Performing blackness, forming whiteness: Linguistic minstrelsy in Hollywood film. *Language and Communication*, 15 (5), pp. 680–706.

Carr, S. (2011). *Scripting Addiction*. Princeton, NJ: Princeton University Press.

Cho, G.E., and P.J. Miller. (2004). Personal storytelling: Working-class and middle-class mothers in comparative perspective. In M. Farr (ed.), *Ethnolinguistic Chicago: Language and Literacy in Chicago's Neighborhoods*. Mahwah, NJ: Lawrence Erlbaum, pp. 79–101.

Chun, E. (2009). Ideologies of legitimate mockery: Margaret Cho's revoicings of mock Asian. In A. Reyes and A. Lo (eds.), *Beyond Yellow English: Towards a Linguistic Anthropology of Asian Pacific America*. Oxford: Oxford University Press, pp. 261–287.

Davidson, D. (2007). East spaces in west times: Deictic reference and political self-positioning in a post-socialist East German chronotope. *Language and Communication*, 27 (3), pp. 216–226.

De Fina, A. (2003). *Identity in Narrative: A Study of Immigrant Discourse*. Amsterdam: John Benjamins.

De Fina, A., and A. Georgakopoulou. (2012). *Analyzing Narrative: Discourse and Sociolinguistic Perspectives*. Cambridge: Cambridge University Press.

Dick, H. (2010). Imagined lives and modernist chronotopes in Mexican nonmigrant discourse. *American Ethnologist*, 37 (2), pp. 275–290.

Duranti, A., and C. Goodwin. (1992). *Rethinking Context: Language as an Interactive Phenomenon*. Cambridge: Cambridge University Press.

Eckert, P. (2001). *Linguistic Variation as Social Practice*. Oxford: Blackwell.

Eckert, P., and J. Rickford. (2001). *Style and Sociolinguistic Variation*. Cambridge: Cambridge University Press.

Eisenlohr, P. (2006). *Little India: Diaspora, Time, and Ethnolinguistic Belonging in Hindu Mauritius*. Berkeley: University of California Press.

Gal, S. (1989). Language and political economy. *Annual Review of Anthropology*, 18, pp. 345–367.

Gal, S. (2006). Contradictions of standard language in Europe: Implications for the study of practices and publics. *Social Anthropology*, 14 (2), pp. 163–181.

Goffman, E. (1959). *The Presentation of Self in Everyday Life*. New York: Doubleday.

Goffman, E. (1979). Footing. In *Forms of Talk*. Philadelphia: University of Pennsylvania Press, pp. 124–159.

Goodwin, M.H. (1990). *He-Said-She-Said: Talk as Social Organization among Black Children*. Bloomington: Indiana University Press.

Gumperz, J. (1982). *Discourse Strategies*. Cambridge: Cambridge University Press.

Hammack, P.L. (2008). Narrative and the cultural psychology of identity. *Personality and Social Psychology Review*, 12 (3), pp. 22–47.

Hanks, W. (1990). *Referential Practice: Language and Lived Space among the Maya*. Chicago, IL: University of Chicago Press.

Hanks, W. (1992). The indexical ground of deictic reference. In A. Duranti and C. Goodwin (eds.), *Rethinking Context: Language as an Interactive Phenomenon*. Cambridge: Cambridge University Press, pp. 43–77.

Hastings, A., and P. Manning. (2004). Introduction: Acts of alterity. *Language and Communication*, 24 (4), pp. 291–301.

Haviland, J. (2005). "Whorish old man" and "One (animal) gentleman": The intertextual construction of enemies and selves. *Journal of Linguistic Anthropology*, 15 (1), pp. 81–94.

Heath, S.B. (1983). *Ways with Words*. Cambridge: Cambridge University Press.

Heller, M. (2010). The commodification of language. *Annual Review of Anthropology*, 39, pp. 101–114.

Hill, J. (1995). The voices of Don Gabriel: Responsibility and self in a modern Mexicano narrative. In D. Tedlock (ed.), *The Dialogic Emergence of Culture*. Chicago, IL: University of Illinois Press, pp. 97–147.

Hymes, D. (1972). Towards ethnographies of communication: The analysis of communicative events. In P. Giglioli (ed.), *Language and Social Context*. New York: Penguin Books, pp. 21–44.

Inoue, M. (2006). *Vicarious Language: Gender and Linguistic Modernity in Japan*. Berkeley: University of California Press.

Irvine, J. (1989). When talk isn't cheap: Language and political economy. *American Ethnologist*, 16 (2), pp. 248–267.

Irvine, J. (2001). Style as distinctiveness: The culture and ideology of linguistic differentiation. In P. Eckert and J. Rickford (eds.), *Style and Sociolinguistic Variation*. Cambridge: Cambridge University Press, pp. 21–43.

Jacquemet, M. (2008). Crosstalk 2.0: Asylum and communicative breakdowns. *Text & Talk*, 31 (4), pp. 475–498.

Jakobson, R. (1957). *Shifters, Verbal Categories, and the Russian Verb.* Cambridge, MA: Department of Slavic Languages and Literatures, Harvard University.

Jakobson, R. (1960). Closing statement: Linguistics and poetics. In T.A. Sebeok (ed.), *Style in Language.* Cambridge, MA: MIT Press, pp. 350–377.

Johnstone, B., and S. Kiesling. (2008). Indexicality and experience: Variation and identity in Pittsburgh. *Journal of Sociolinguistics*, 12 (1), pp. 5–33.

Keane, W. (2011). Indexing voice: A morality tale. *Journal of Linguistic Anthropology*, 21 (1), pp. 166–178.

Kockelman, P. (2005). The semiotic stance. *Semiotica*, 157, pp. 233–304.

Koven, M. (2001). Comparing bilinguals' quoted performances of self and others in tellings of the same experience in two languages. *Language in Society*, 30 (4), pp. 513–558.

Koven, M. (2002). An analysis of speaker role inhabitance in narratives of personal experience. *Journal of Pragmatics*, 34 (2), pp. 167–217.

Koven, M. (2007). *Selves in Two Languages: French-Portuguese Bilinguals' Enactments of Identity in Two Languages.* Amsterdam: John Benjamins.

Koven, M. (2011). Speaker roles in personal narratives. In J. Holstein and J. Gubrium (eds.), *Varieties of Narrative Analysis.* Thousand Oaks, CA: Sage, pp. 151–180.

Koven, M. (2013a). Speaking French in Portugal: An analysis of contested models of emigrant personhood in narratives about return migration and language use. *Journal of Sociolinguistics*, 17 (3), pp. 324–354.

Koven, M. (2013b). Antiracist, modern selves and racist, unmodern others: Chronotopes of modernity in Luso-descendants' race talk. *Language and Communication*, 33 (4), pp. 544–558.

Koven, M., and I.S. Marques. (in press). Performing and evaluating Portuguese migrant figures of personhood on YouTube: The Case of Ro et Cut's Antonio de Carglouch. *Language in Society*.

Labov, W. (1972). *Language in the Inner City: Studies in the Black English Vernacular.* Philadelphia: University of Pennsylvania Press.

Linde, C. (1993). *Life Stories: The Creation of Coherence.* Oxford: Oxford University Press.

Mannheim, B. (1998). The dialogics of southern Quechua narrative. *American Anthropologist*, 100 (2), pp. 326–346.

Maryns, K. (2006). *The Asylum Speaker: Language in the Belgian Asylum Procedure.* Manchester: St. Jerome Publishing.

Mehan, H. (1996). The construction of an LD student: A case study in the politics of representation. In M. Silverstein and G. Urban (eds.), *Natural Histories of Discourse.* Chicago, IL: University of Chicago Press, pp. 253–276.

Mendoza-Denton, N. (2008). *Homegirls: Language and Cultural Practice among Latina Youth Gangs.* Oxford: Blackwell.

Michaels, S. (1981) "Sharing time": Children's narrative styles and differential access to literacy. *Language and Society*, 10, pp. 423–442.

Miller, P.J. (1994). Narrative practices: Their role in socialization and self-construction. In U. Neisser and R. Fivush (eds.), *The Remembering Self: Construction and Accuracy in the Self-Narrative.* Cambridge: Cambridge University Press, pp. 158–179.

Miller, P.J., and D.E. Sperry. (2012). Déjà vu: The continuing misrecognition of low-income children's verbal abilities. In S.T. Fiske and H.R. Markus (eds.), *Facing Social Class: How Societal Rank Influences Interaction.* New York: Russell Sage, pp. 109–130.

Miller, P.J., G.E. Cho, and J. Bracey. (2005). Working-class children's experience through the prism of personal storytelling. *Human Development*, 48 (3), pp. 115–135.

Miller, P.J., H. Fung, and M. Koven. (2007). Narrative reverberations: How participation in narrative practices co-creates persons and cultures. In S. Kitayama and D. Cohen (eds.), *The Handbook of Cultural Psychology.* New York: Guilford Press, pp. 595–614.

Miller, P., H. Fung, and J. Mintz. (1990). Narrative practices and the social construction of self. *American Ethnologist*, 17 (2), pp. 292–311.

Miller, P., H. Fung, and J. Mintz. (1996). Self-construction through narrative practices: A Chinese and American comparison of early socialization. *Ethos*, 24 (2), pp. 237–280.

Miller, P.J., M. Koven, and S. Lin. (2011). Language socialization and narrative. In A. Duranti, E. Ochs, and B. Schieffelin (eds.), *The Handbook of Language Socialization*. Oxford: Blackwell, pp. 190–208.

Miller, P.J., A.R. Wiley, H. Fung, and C.-H. Liang. (1997). Personal storytelling as a medium of socialization in Chinese and American families. *Child Development*, 68, pp. 1557–1568.

Miller, P.J., H. Fung, S. Lin, E.C.-H. Chen, and B.R. Boldt. (2012). *How Socialization Happens on the Ground: Narrative Practices as Alternate Socializing Pathways in Taiwanese and European-American Families*. Oxford: Wiley-Blackwell.

Modan, G. (2007). *Turf Wars: Discourse, Diversity, and the Politics of Place*. Oxford: Blackwell.

O'Connor, P. (1994). "You could feel it through your skin": Agency and positioning in prisoners' stabbing stories. *Text*, 14 (1), pp. 45–75.

Peirce, C.S. (1940). Logic as semiotic: The theory of signs. In J. Buchler (ed.), *The Philosophy of Peirce: Selected Writings*. New York: Harcourt, Brace and Company, pp. 98–119.

Polanyi, L. (1989). *Telling the American Story: A Structural and Cultural Analysis of Conversational Storytelling*. Cambridge, MA: MIT Press.

Rampton, B. (1995). *Crossing: Language and Ethnicity among Adolescents*. New York: Longman.

Schegloff, E. (1972). Notes on a conversational practice: Formulating place. In D.N. Sudnow (ed.), *Studies in Social Interaction*. New York: MacMillan, pp. 75–119.

Schiffrin, D. (1987). *Discourse Markers*. Cambridge: Cambridge University Press.

Schnapper, D. (1991). *La France de l'intégration: Sociologie de la nation*. Paris: Gallimard.

Silverstein, M. (1976/1995). Shifters, linguistic categories, and cultural description. In B. Blount (ed.), *Language, Culture, and Society: A Book of Readings*. Prospect Heights, IL: Waveland Press, pp. 187–221.

Silverstein, M. (1993). Metapragmatic discourse and metapragmatic function. In J. Lucy (ed.), *Reflexive Language: Reported Speech and Metapragmatics*. Cambridge: Cambridge University Press, pp. 33–58.

Silverstein, M. (2003). Indexical order and the dialectics of sociolinguistic life. *Language and Communication*, 23 (3–4), pp. 193–229.

Silverstein, P. (2005). Immigrant racialization and the new savage slot: Race, migration, and immigration in the New Europe. *Annual Review of Anthropology*, 34, pp. 363–384.

Silverstein, M., and G. Urban. (1996). *Natural Histories of Discourse*. Chicago, IL: University of Chicago Press.

Tannen, D. (1984). *Conversational Style: Analyzing Talk among Friends*. Westport, CT: Ablex.

Tannen, D. (1986). Introducing constructed dialogue in Greek and American conversational and literary narratives. In F. Coulmas (ed.), *Direct and Indirect Speech*. Berlin: Mouton de Gruyter, pp. 311–322.

Voloshinov, V. (1976). *Marxism and the Philosophy of Language*. New York: Academic Press.

Wolfson, N. (1978). A feature of performed narrative: The conversational historical present. *Language in Society*, 7, pp. 215–237.

Woolard, K. (2004). Code-switching. In A. Duranti (ed.), *Companion to Linguistic Anthropology*. Oxford: Blackwell, pp. 73–94.

Wortham, S. (2001). *Narratives in Action*. New York: Teachers College Press.

Wortham, S. (2005). Socialization beyond the speech event: Intertextuality and interdiscursivity in social life. *Journal of Linguistic Anthropology*, 15 (1), pp. 95–112.

Wortham, S. (2006). *Learning Identity: The Joint Emergence of Social Identification and Academic Learning*. Cambridge: Cambridge University Press.

Wortham, S. (2012). Beyond macro and micro in the linguistic anthropology of education. *Anthropology and Education Quarterly*, 43 (2), pp. 127–234.

Wortham, S., S. Mortimer, and K. Allard. (2011). Homies in the New Latino diaspora. *Language and Communication*, 31 (3), pp. 191–202.

21 Social Identity Theory and the Discursive Analysis of Collective Identities in Narratives

DORIEN VAN DE MIEROOP

Studies on collective identities typically refer to Tajfel's definition of social identity and its relation to social groups and intergroup comparison. On the one hand, the insights from social identity theory regarding group membership and a person's collective identities are indeed very useful and relevant, as I discuss in the first part of this chapter; but on the other hand, the fact that social psychologists consider these social groups as continuously, though often only latently, present, is untenable from a social constructionist angle. I briefly go into these issues before moving to the discussion of a discursive approach to collective identities and their role in narratives. In the analytical part of this chapter, excerpts from one lengthy story are scrutinized and particular attention is paid to the integration of the insights of social identity theory into the analysis, which is further commented on in the last section of this chapter.

21.1 Social Identity Theory

Social psychologists have devoted a great deal of attention to identity and its relation to social groups. According to this theory, social identity is defined as: "that *part* of the individuals' self-concept which derives from their knowledge of their membership of a social group (or groups) together with the value and emotional significance attached to that membership" (Tajfel 1982a: 2, italics in the original). As the italics indicate, this is only a partial description of social identity, which, according to Tajfel (1982a: 2), also consists of the way individuals perceive themselves in relation to the surrounding social and physical world. Nevertheless, group memberships are considered to be crucial, and social categorization is viewed as "a system of orientation which helps to create and define the individual's place in society" (Tajfel 1981: 255).

It is implied in this definition that every individual can be a member of a number of different social groups. These groups are the result of an individual's segmentation of the social world into categories on the basis of variables such as similarity, common

The Handbook of Narrative Analysis, First Edition. Edited by Anna De Fina and Alexandra Georgakopoulou.
© 2015 John Wiley & Sons, Inc. Published 2019 by John Wiley & Sons, Inc.

fate, and proximity. These variables should not be regarded as static, but rather as active processes that evolve over time and in relation to their – inherently dynamic – social contexts. This means that individuals, if they see it to their advantage, may leave their own groups and seek membership in new groups (Tajfel 1981: 256). The meaning of an individual's group membership is further defined by comparing these groups to relevant outgroups. This comparative intergroup perspective tends to highlight the ingroup qualities as opposed to the attributes of the outgroup, thus resulting in a positive social identity. This positive ingroup identity implies that its members perceive themselves as being "better" than the members of the outgroup, who are often characterized reductively to the extent that they become flat characters.

Furthermore, these diverse groups are characterized by a difference in salience for individual members. This is related to the level of members' awareness of their membership in the group (cognitive component), the degree to which they attribute a positive connotation to this membership (evaluative component), and the extent to which this membership is accompanied by emotions towards their own and other groups (emotional component) (Tajfel 1981: 229). This salience is also regarded as fluid, since it is closely related to the particular social contexts in which individuals function (Tajfel 1982a: 2–3), thus presenting groups as dynamic "processes" rather than static "things" (Tajfel 1982b: 485). For example, Tajfel explains that there are "*some* social situations which will force most individuals involved, however weak and unimportant to them may have been their *initial* group identifications, to act in terms of their group membership" (Tajfel 1981: 239, italics in the original). The persistence of such situations will consequently have an influence on the general significance that is attributed to this group membership. Such a growing significance, in turn, is reflected in the individual members' increasing orientation to ingroup uniformity – and a decreasing orientation to variability – when interacting with members of the outgroup (Tajfel 1981: 243). Outgroup members are often perceived in terms of stereotypes, and interactions with them are viewed as inter*group* rather than as inter*personal* exchanges.

On the one hand, this demonstrates the fluid and dynamic nature of individuals' orientations to their group memberships, and their potentially corresponding behavior in relation to different social contexts. On the other hand, it highlights the fact that social psychology considers groups and categories to be entities that reside in individuals and are always latently present, although they are not continuously activated. Further, many of these findings are derived from studies that use an experimental approach, thus occurring in a social vacuum. And although the importance of the effects of the sociocultural context on the data are emphasized as well (see, e.g., Tajfel 1981: 22), such laboratory experiments never come close to duplicating the different levels of complexity so typical of "real life," in which a myriad of interactions between local and global contextual elements form the backdrop of – and potentially influence – every social encounter. Also, in studies of more naturalistic situations, social psychologists tend to take an etic perspective, imposing their own frame of reference onto the observations. Furthermore, the interest in the role of discourse and communication has always been fairly limited in social psychology (Van Dijk 2009: 30). It is thus not surprising that from a discursive perspective, some of the assumptions of social identity theory are criticized, for example its reductionism (Wodak and Reisigl 2001: 375) and its tendency to posit an a priori ingroup-outgroup opposition, which is problematic when studying relativized and frequently shifting social identities in real life (Coupland 2010: 256). Many of these criticisms are related to the general, cognitive nature of this approach, which stipulates the pre-discursive existence of group memberships (e.g., based on gender or ethnicity). This view is of course contrary to the widely accepted social constructionist perspective on identity in discourse analytical studies (see, e.g., De Fina, Schiffrin, and Bamberg 2006: 2; De Fina, this volume, chapter 18), which emphasizes the central role of language in the process of *creating* identities, instead of *uncovering* a priori categories to which individuals belong and which define their ingroup identities. Identity is thus viewed as a discursive accomplishment and a product of social interaction. But in spite of the essentialist views of social identity theory, some of these insights can be incorporated in a meaningful way into the discursive analysis of identity in relation to social groups (see Van Dijk 2009: 71). However, this necessarily implies a shift from an etic perspective to an emic perspective, which means that instead of applying researchers' pre-established categories to social identity claims, as social psychologists tend to do, discourse analysts focus on how participants themselves orient to these claims in interactions and how they interactively draw on the kinds of distinctions identified in social identity theory – for example, the polarization between positive ingroup and negative outgroup evaluations, or the simplification of outgroup characteristics. Before discussing this in more detail, I first go into the way collective identities are dealt with discursively and from a social constructionist point of view, which describes a variety of approaches that "share in common an emphasis on the multiple ways that social identities are constructed" (Widdicombe 1998: 197). Then I will discuss what makes collective identities a particularly interesting topic for a social constructionist analysis of narratives, with its particular focus on the local discursive construction and negotiation of identities.

21.2   Discursive Approaches to Collective Identities

From a discursive perspective, the fluid nature of collective identity is emphasized, which means that every individual shifts in and out of diverse memberships in a multitude of social groups, resulting in a wide variety of potential collective identities that are each interactively constructed and negotiated. The collectivities in which people can discursively establish their membership range from relatively tangible entities, such as institutions or professional organizations, through abstract ones such as nation-states; they include groups constructed on the basis of similar features at a macro level, such as ethnicity, class, and gender, and those predicated on the basis of shared roles, such as "parent," "child," "teacher," as well as groups based on – often highly fleeting – features at a micro level.

On the one hand, at the micro end of the continuum, conversation analysis (CA) tends to bypass the theoretical aspects of the concept of self and takes an action orientation by scrutinizing "in rich technical detail how identities are mobilized in actual instances of interaction" (Widdicombe 1998: 203). This approach thus focuses on the collectivities that are constructed ad hoc by an interlocutor in relation to the local context at hand and specifically for the other interlocutors who are co-present at that particular time. For example, Antaki, Condor, and Levine (1996) discuss the way the identity "hotrodder" that was discussed by Sacks (1992) is "indifferent to any watching analysts' more abstract categorization" and functions in contrast with other locally constructed categories (Antaki et al. 1996: 475). Many studies have adopted these viewpoints, and instead of applying "the traditional vocabulary of the social scientist" (1996: 475) to expected categories in their data, researchers have focused on identity practices that participants – often collaboratively – make up in the course of an interaction, and which can disappear again just as quickly as they have emerged, thus illustrating the transience of their existence. Such volatile categories would never come up in studies in social identity theory, simply because they can only *emerge* in moment-to-moment interaction, unfolding in front of the observing analyst's eye, and cannot be *tallied* on a score sheet with pre-established categories.

On the other hand, researchers in the field of critical discourse analysis (CDA) aim to combine the micro, interactional level with the macro, societal level, which are considered to be "mutual requisites" for the analysis of discursive practice (Fairclough 1992: 85). Hence, the way group membership is made relevant on a micro level is related to its ideological implications on a macro level. From this perspective as well, the interaction between different collective identities and the interplay between them and an individual's personal identities are especially interesting. The latter are, as Triandafyllidou and Wodak argue, closely intertwined and mutually constituted (2003: 211). Naturally, such a complex interplay hardly ever results in the construction of monolithic identities; instead, individuals typically shift in and out of a number of identities that are in constant dialogue with each other, with the other interlocutors and with their contexts. This dialogue continuously causes changes in the identities that are talked into being at a particular point in time, resulting in an ever-changing, ephemeral constellation of identities for each interlocutor. So from this perspective, reproducible as well as ad hoc categories may emerge, just as in CA studies. However, the focus of CDA is not only on the complexity of these ever-shifting categories within the local, interactional context, but also, and especially, on the interaction between these locally emergent categories and their global, societal context.

21.3   Collective Identities in Narratives

The interplay, and sometimes the tension, between the individual and the collective level of identity construction is at stake in a number of different contexts and genres, but this is especially the case in narratives, as scholars of autobiographical studies have demonstrated. This can be related to the two "why tell" functions of autobiographical narratives, as identified by the narrative psychologist Bruner: "Not only must a narrative be about a sequence of events over time, structured comprehensibly in terms of cultural canonicality, it must also contain something that endows it with exceptionality" (Bruner 1991: 71). So on the one hand, a story must be comprehensible to its audience, who have canonical expectations regarding stories in familiar cultural contexts. This relates to the collective identities of both narrator and audience, for example as members of a particular culture. As such, people invoke in their stories what is typical of this particular group according to the "folk psychology" intrinsic to the interlocutors' culture (Bruner 1991: 71). However, narrators often counter canonical expectations, as such making their stories new – and worth listening to – thus meeting the demand of reportability or tellability (Labov 2006). This reportability is closely related to the social contexts in which these stories occur, since some violations of canonicity transcend the upper boundary of tellability because they are "too personal, too embarrassing or obscene" (Norrick 2005: 323), while other violations may be culturally incomprehensible, meaning that a successful breach of canonicity "must be a violation … that is itself canonical" (Bruner 1991: 72). Such breaches endow the story with exceptionality, enabling the narrator to construct his or her identity as an individual who does not always act the way he or she is expected to. As such, the narrator avoids the attribution of group features, and this may function as a way to negotiate the membership of a stigmatized group identity, for example. For instance, in a previous study (Van De Mieroop 2012a) in which I analyzed an interview with a poor, unemployed Belgian man, the interviewee described his busy "career" while referring to his work as a volunteer. He thus precludes any imputation of laziness from his listener – a feature that sociological research has demonstrated to be an important Belgian poverty stereotype ("poor people are lazy"). As such, one of the canonical expectations regarding poor people is breached, and this, among other things, allows the interviewee to construct an alternative identity that challenges the stigma of this particular group membership potentially projected onto him by the interviewer. Of course, there are various means to construct exceptional twists in stories: they may comprise the constructions of alternative group identities, or they may be presented as the result of a collective action that further contributes to and enforces a previously constructed collective identity.

So there are many different ways in which interlocutors can manage the dual function of autobiographical narratives. In addition, the canonical nature of the backdrop against which potentially exceptional stories are sketched functions as a benchmark for the audience, and an implicit appeal is often made to sharedness and collectivity based on membership in the same culture. On the basis of this shared cultural background, the audience can at least detect and begin to understand the meaning of the breaches in canonicity. For example, in a story about two acquaintances meeting each other again after a long time, it would be considered a breach in canonicity for some audiences if the narrator describes that during this encounter, there was not a minimal form of physical contact (e.g., a handshake, a hug, or a kiss on the cheek). For other audiences, however, this may seem "normal" behavior and no exceptionality would be detected. Thus if narrators and their audiences do not share a cultural canonical backdrop, stories may become "culturally incomprehensible" unless explicit disambiguations are added.

Given the interactional nature of storytelling (see also Goodwin, this volume, chapter 10), much also depends on the way the narrator constructs ingroup/outgroup boundaries with the other participants and vice versa, since the audience should not be regarded as passive recipients, but rather as full participants who can project ingroup/outgroup memberships upon the teller as well. As such, an interlocutor can draw on locally occasioned group memberships that could be regarded as having their own micro-cultural canonicity and may be shared by some, but perhaps not all, participants. To give a rather simple example, a conversation between colleagues may appeal to a shared professional ingroup, and this may imply a number of canonical expectations related to specific workplace norms. In certain cases, only members of a given workplace can detect and understand the implications of certain breaches of these norms, and the story would totally miss its point if related to outgroup members, simply because the latter have no "folk psychological" knowledge of these ingroup norms. So canonicity and exceptionality are relative, since they should always be regarded not only in relation to their global contexts, but also within their local, interactional contexts.

Moreover, it is important to focus on which memberships are made relevant by the participants in the interaction and how these memberships serve a specific communicative function, or, as is often the case, a combination of such functions. For example, in a study of personal anecdotes in the workplace, Holmes (2006) demonstrates how these off-record stories contribute to the "construction of complex personal, professional and social identities for workplace participants" (186) within their communities of practice. Such a story may construct the interlocutor's identity as a competent professional, but it may at the same time foreground his/her gender identity, and this construction of membership in a group based on gender criteria is not at all monolithic, as Holmes demonstrates (174–176). Thus these anecdotes allow the interlocutors to "emphasize particular facets of their social identities and different dimensions of social meaning – professional status, team solidarity, authority responsibilities, gender category, group affiliations, distinctive workplace culture, and so on" (Holmes 2006: 186; see also Ehrlich, this volume, chapter 15 regarding institutional constraints on identity work).

21.4   Analytical Tools for the Discursive Analysis of Collective Identities

As always with the discursive study of identity, its analysis is characterized by the absence of hard and fast rules for how identity should be mapped analytically. Indeed, this is just as it should be. Rather than applying established categories based on the research subjects' demographic characteristics as social psychologists often do, discourse analysts follow a data-driven approach and scrutinize interactional data in order to find participants' orientations to any kind of locally occasioned – and often swiftly shifting – identities. While some of these orientations may be quite explicitly formulated in language, others may be fairly implicit. In order to integrate these different types of orientations in their analyses, discourse analysts draw on different research traditions. First, the principle of indexicality is central. This concept is derived from linguistic anthropology and it "connects utterances to extra-linguistic reality via the ability of linguistic signs to point to aspects of the social context" (De Fina et al. 2006: 4). This means that any aspect of language at any linguistic level – ranging from phonological features (e.g., Kiesling 2006) to switches between particular linguistic codes (e.g., De Fina 2007) to performance features and genre characteristics of narratives (e.g., Baynham 2006) – may invoke or counter group membership. The most obvious example of linguistic elements reflecting the relationship between language and context is, of course, deixis. In linguistic studies of collective identities, many researchers have devoted attention to the analysis of person deictics, particularly the first person plural pronoun "we," whose volatile inclusive or exclusive reference often – but not always – invokes group memberships. This is especially the case when the pronominal construction of an ingroup is opposed to that of an outgroup through the creation of an "us-them" opposition, highlighting the fact that the relational nature of collective identity involves "as much what we are not as what we are" (Baynham 2006: 395). Given the extreme variety of resources that may function as indexicals for speakers to interactively construct their membership in social groups, indexical relationships should be regarded as "never given," but as being "continuously negotiated and recreated by speakers because of the infinite possibilities inherent in the association of signs with meanings" (De Fina et al. 2006: 15).

Second, collective identities are often constructed by the interactive creation and use of "membership categories," which was inspired by Sacks's (1992) work and has been developed in Membership Categorization Analysis (MCA). Originating in ethnomethodology and now employed selectively within conversation analytical studies, this approach focuses on the study of how interactants label themselves and others and what characteristics are discursively attributed to these categories. MCA explicitly distances itself from a priori categories, but rather focuses on locally occasioned categories that are linked to a number of category-bound features. These categories are made relevant by the interlocutors themselves and their force lies in their interactional consequentiality, which is investigated on a turn-by-turn basis (see Antaki and Widdicombe 1998; see also Deppermann, this volume, chapter 19). Although this categorization can take the form of explicit category use, it may also be the result of category-implicative descriptions and other naming practices (Stokoe 2009: 93). Given its link to conversation analysis, it is not surprising that this approach has a strictly anti-cognitivist nature, and this orientation may be problematic when studying the construction of collective identities in narratives. This is mainly because narrative studies often relate the local to the more global context, working, for example, with notions such as socially shared discourses (see also De Fina 2006: 354–355) that form the backdrop of an interaction. From this perspective, MCA may on the one hand be too restrictive for some researchers because of its explicitly local interactional orientation; on the other hand, it is often appreciated and drawn upon in narrative analyses because of its focus on category work as an interactional achievement.

21.5   Applying This Variety of Insights

In the discussion below, I present a discursive analysis of the construction of collective and related individual identities in an autobiographical narrative obtained through a research interview. I aim to particularly highlight the fluid nature of identities as they are talked into being in the narrative, thus taking a clearly social constructionist perspective on these data. Even though this story can be characterized as a big story, containing relatively more stable identities than the ones we typically come across in mundane interactions (Georgakopoulou 2006), the following analyses demonstrate that this narrator frequently shifts in and out of locally constructed and quickly changing collective identities while these are being negotiated with the interviewer. These changes in identity lead to a complex interplay between individual and collective identities. The analyses integrate analytical tools provided by the different research traditions sketched above, and special attention is paid to the way collective identities are discursively invoked by referring to insights from social identity theory and also by making use of the observations of autobiographical studies. Before going into the analysis, I first describe the data from which this story was excerpted.

21.5.1   The data

The story is part of a corpus of semi-structured, one-on-one research interviews regarding people's lives and careers. A small subset of this corpus consists of interviews that took place in 2009 between a young female interviewer and a number of women of Moroccan descent in their late 20s or early 30s living in Antwerp, Belgium, who have degrees from Belgian universities and who have fairly high-ranking jobs. A few of these interviews were already discussed in Van De Mieroop (2012b). I particularly chose these data because of the fact that in Belgium, people of Moroccan descent are still regarded as a separate group by many people. This group is typically contrasted with that of the "native Belgians" by labeling them as *allochtonen* ("the allochthonous," or "those who originate from another country"), which is then opposed to *autochtonen* ("the autochthonous," or so-called "native Belgians"). In 2012, these terms figured in a highly publicized media debate when the Flemish newspaper *De Morgen* proposed to abolish *allochtonen* because of its inaccuracy[1] and because of its polarizing contribution to the construction of an ingroup-outgroup dichotomy and the stigmatization of the group it purports to describe. Furthermore, the educational attainment and employment rate of this group is significantly lower than that of the "native Belgians" and the women in this group score especially low in this respect because they tend to marry earlier than Flemish women (for a more detailed description, see Van De Mieroop 2012b).

   Hence, the "allochthonous" interviewees in this data set are quite exceptional members of this ethno-cultural group because of their successes – especially as women – in education and professional life; and this may result in the creation of alternative, but potentially intersecting, group memberships. Finally, this complex ethno-cultural group membership is of course just one tiny aspect of the vast diversity of other groups in which these interviewees can construct their memberships. As mentioned before, such groups can be based on a wide array of features, ranging from general demographic characteristics such as age and class, through professional, occupational, or personal roles (e.g., as women in the workplace or as wives), to ad hoc categories that are interactively talked into being on the spot by interactional participants (e.g., "non-headscarf-wearers" or "shy students," as we shall see below).

21.6   Analysis

In this section, I discuss excerpts from a lengthy story that occurred in one of these interviews and, while focusing on the turn-by-turn construction of collective identities, I also pay specific attention to the interlocutors' orientation to the ingroup-outgroup distinctions described by social identity theory. By adopting such an emic perspective, I aim to integrate these findings in a discursive analysis of identity construction.

In the story, the interlocutors are talking about racist incidents that Hafida,[2] the interviewee, encountered during her university years. Hafida has a Master's degree in Communication Sciences, and at the time of the interview she is still studying in order to obtain a Master's in Comparative and European Politics. At the same time, she is the managing partner of a consultancy firm that is involved in engineering diversity and recruitment. Throughout the interview, she tends to discuss the topics from a fairly detached point of view and limits personal involvement in her stories (see also interview 3 in Van De Mieroop 2012b). However, during the discussion of life at university in general, and the lack of fellow students of foreign descent in particular, a few probes by the interviewer incite Hafida to produce a personal narrative containing a concrete example of an encounter with racism. The final prompt by the interviewer occurs in line 1 of the fragment, after which Hafida embarks on a fairly lengthy story of 61 lines in which she relates a particular incident that occurred while she was studying at the university.

I discuss the most relevant excerpts from this story for the purpose of this chapter. Each excerpt is dealt with in a subsection focusing on one of the points raised in the theoretical discussion of collective identities sketched above. The excerpts follow chronologically on one another, and in order for the reader to understand which part of the story the excerpts occur in, I draw on Labov and Waletzky's structural analyses of narratives (1967). They identified six phases that can, but do not always, occur in typical narratives. In parentheses, the lines of every section in the story under discussion are mentioned:

- Abstract: a summary of the upcoming story (line 2, elliptic abstract only).
- Orientation: a section orienting the listener in respect to person, place, time, and behavioral situation (lines 3–9, with occasional orientational additions in the next phase).
- Complicating action: the main body of narrative clauses which usually comprises a series of events (lines 10–43).
- Resolution: the result of these events (lines 44–46 and 48–51).
- Coda: a device for returning the verbal perspective to the present moment (lines 57–61).
- Evaluation: the point of the story (line 47 and lines 52–55).

In the course of the analyses, I situate the excerpts (in English translation) within this prototypical story structure to clarify the main line and structure of Hafida's story for readers (the Dutch original can also be read in the appendix to this chapter).

21.6.1   *Volatile identity categories: Shifting in and out of collective identities*

The first excerpt consists of the first part of the story, containing the (elliptic) abstract (line 2) and orientation phase of the story (line 3–9):

Excerpt 1

(1) I   Uhu (.) Can you give an example of that?

(2) H   < Erm. For example. A professor who erm > .

(3)   Yes so, >a lot of courses were communal with the people

(4)   who erm studied poli- political sciences and sociology<

(5)   And: >one of these communal courses was philoso↑phy<

(6)   and we were sitting in the front, so a number of erm (.)

(7)   erm ladies of Moroccan descent. E:rm

(8)   You could deduce that from the fact that they were wearing, erm,

(9)   a headscarf. The professor deduced it like that.[3]

In line 2, Hafida initially orients her response to one of the preceding prompts by the interviewer, who probed for the agents of racist acts ([*Did you get racist remarks*] *from professors or other students?*), but then she self-repairs and embarks on the orientation phase of her story, in which she sketches the course setup (lines 3–5) and implicitly asserts the large number of students present in the particular course where the events of the story took place. In line 6, then, Hafida introduces the protagonists of the story by means of the deictic we-form, thus invoking an ingroup that still needs to be defined. First, she localizes them in the auditorium (line 6), which implicitly qualifies them as committed students who can typically be found in the front rows during courses. Then, she solves the referential ambiguity of the deictic first person plural pronoun *we* by explicitly disambiguating its referent, identifying the ingroup as *ladies of Moroccan descent* (line 7). So this disambiguation demonstrates that the collectivity to which the we-form refers is based on ethnic descent and gender, thus invoking these two variables as criteria for group membership. Furthermore, she adds another feature that visually marks this ingroup's similarity, namely, the presence of a headscarf (lines 8–9). The latter criterion is then framed as the factual reason why the antagonist (i.e., the professor) knew of the ladies' Moroccan descent (line 9), which thus implicitly asserts the lack of any prior knowledge of or any preceding contact between the protagonists and the antagonist, thus anticipating any potential alternative interpretations of her story.

Interestingly, after the initial disambiguation of the we-form in line 6, Hafida shifts to the third person plural form ("zij," *they*, line 8) when discussing the presence of the headscarf. Since Hafida does not wear a headscarf at the time of the interview and has never worn one, as she states elsewhere in the interaction, it is of course fairly logical that she does not use an inclusive we-form here. However, since the headscarf is framed as the discerning factor for the antagonist (i.e., the professor) to construct an ingroup-outgroup opposition (line 9), and since Hafida herself was the victim of the story, as will be discussed, this pronominal shift from *we* to *they* may also be interpreted as a disaffiliation from the group of women who wear explicit religious symbols such as headscarves. This potential disaffiliation from the initial ingroup, as was marked by the we-form in line 6, is not further explored, however, as Hafida then picks up the thread of the story again in line 10. So this already shows the ease with which people shift in and out of collective identities – even if they have just been constructed a few lines earlier, without clearly demarcating the groups to which they refer and without making explicit the way these group memberships function in the argumentative setup of the story.

21.6.2   *Shifting from an interpersonal to an intergroup exchange*

In line 10, Hafida moves into the complicating action phase of the story, in which she shifts back to an individual perspective as marked by the first person pronoun, and in which she quite factually narrates what happened in lines 10–12.

Excerpt 2

(10) H   And at a certain point (.) erm •hh I wanted

(11)   to take something out of a bag, a plastic bag and that made

(12)   quite a lot of noise. And, erm, that professor, instead of saying

(13)   "Yes, stop making noise".

(14)   That's an auditorium in which erm about a thousand people fit ↑hey.

(15)   So you can already imagine, if you get a remark there, that (.)

(16) I   °yes°

(17) H   And, erm (.) he says,

(18)   erm yes he orders us t- to be quiet, says then (o-) of "yes, erm

(19)   >could it be a little more quiet, because I am actually not used to that<

(20)   of- (.) ladies like ↑you (.) we are rather used to the sub*servi*ent." (.)

(21)   And erm, yes that is thus an allusion to the fact that you of:

(22)   have an Islamic background [hey.

(23) I   [°mm°

In line 13, she continues by formulating a potential reaction of the professor by means of direct reported speech, which is a seemingly literal report of the words of other interlocutors, or of oneself at another point in time. This direct quote, however, is anticipatorily framed as counterfactual (line 12) and it indicates the reasonableness of a remark about the noise, thus demonstrating that the point of Hafida's story is not about *what* happened, but rather about *how* it happened, or, more accurately, about the formulation of the professor's comment. Research has demonstrated that interlocutors typically use direct reported speech for this, because it suggests that the words are literally repeated and replayed in front of the audience's eyes, thus adding "a tone of authenticity and veracity" (Schiffrin 2003: 549) to the narrative and, in particular, to the accuracy of the formulation, which is extremely important for the point of Hafida's story.

Before contrasting the counterfactual quote with the actual quote, Hafida shifts back to the orientation phase of the story in the following lines. After closing this second orientation phase, Hafida continues by relating the complicating action in line 17. Before voicing the direct quote (already implicitly announced in line 13), she breaks off after the quotative in line 17 and gives a brief abstract of the point of the story in line 18. When she then finally replays the direct quote, she first voices a fairly neutral evaluation of the situation in line 19 by means of a rush-through, after which she formulates the racist statement that forms the focal point of this story. Crucial in this statement is the shift from the personal perspective in Hafida's description of the events to the collective perspective in the professor's response, which is addressed to the initially constructed ingroup of "ladies of Moroccan descent." This demonstrates the antagonist's orientation to the perception of the situation from a collective rather than an individual point of view, thus framing it as an inter*group* rather than as an inter*personal* exchange. This, following social identity theory, is an indication of the significance that is attached to group membership, and in this case, the professor's shift from a personal to a group identity projection clearly already marks his statement as racist. This is further corroborated by the attribution of the feature of subservience to this group. Both elements – the relevance of group membership and the projection of a distinctive feature to this group – are prosodically marked, namely by the rising pitch of the second person plural pronoun ("↑jullie," ↑*you*) and the intonational stress on the group feature ("sub*serv*ient"). Hafida then continues to account for the choice of this feature by framing it in terms of religion, thus yet again constructing an alternative group membership, namely that of "people with an Islamic background." Interestingly, in this case she uses the second person pronominal form "ge" (*you*, line 21), which can be used both for plural and singular referents and which has a generic meaning here. As such, she avoids aligning with a collective identity on the basis of religious criteria and she resists the antagonist's projection of a group identity related to religion and subservience.

21.6.3 Downplaying ingroup variability: Blurring the boundary between individual and collective identities

After a short detour in lines 24–29, Hafida picks up the thread of her story again in line 30. She starts relating the second part of the complicating action in which the professor is confronted with his behavior and is forced to account for his racist remark in a relatively long reported exchange (Buttny 1997) consisting of sequences of direct reported speech, of which we see the first part here.

Excerpt 3

(24) H   And, yes, during the break stepped up to him. And just.

(25)   Ah sorry, that was not philosophy, that was political science.

(26) I   °mm°

(27) H   Political science.

(28)   Oh, when I even think of it now. Bastard.

(29) I   @@@

(30) H   Stepped up to him and, erm, said of: "Well yes,

(31)   What do you mean actually with the:: remark of, erm, subservi[ent?"

(32) I   [°yes°

(33) H   And you thus saw him change color completely.

Interestingly, the initiator of the confrontation is quite vague in the beginning, since Hafida deletes the subject and simply uses past participles instead of full verb forms ("gegaan," *stepped*, "gezegd," *said*, line 30), resulting in an ungrammatical and overtly agentless sentence that introduces the first direct quote. When she describes the non-verbal reaction of the antagonist (line 33), Hafida also uses the generic second person pronominal form "ge" (*you*), which, as mentioned before, can have both plural and singular referents. As such, the collective or individual nature of this reference is blurred in the initial lines of this part of the complicating action. Hafida is thus downplaying a potential claim of ingroup variability, in which she would stand out from the rest of the ingroup as more assertive than the average group member, which – according to the professor's reductionist outgroup characterization – was precisely that feature deemed most important for this ingroup (subservience instead of assertiveness).

21.6.4 Challenging reductive characterizations and intergroup comparisons

Hafida then continues to relate the interaction between herself and the professor. She shifts back to an interpersonal perspective in this final part of the complicating action, hence clarifying the vagueness discussed in the previous section:

Excerpt 4

(34) H He did not know very well what to re- how to react. He says

(35)   "Yes look, that, I knew that that would go down the wrong way,

(36)   but I actually didn't mean anything with it.

(37)   I have taught for a ve:ry long time in America and I see that

(38)   for example (.) American students are very assertive and and

(39)   Flemish student timid."

(40)   I say "Ah okay, so American students asse:rtive,

(41)   Flemish students erm, more, erm, timid and

(42)   the Moroccan ones are subservient then?"

(43)   He like "No no no." I say "Sir, we are going to leave it at this."

The antagonist's initial reaction is first described in non-verbal terms, namely as showing signs of surprise (line 33: change of color, line 34: not knowing how to react), and then his response is voiced by direct reported speech. In this utterance, the professor first downplays his remarks (lines 35–36) and then invokes his identity as a university teacher who is familiar with working in different cultures (lines 37–38: working in America) and who attributes a stereotypical feature to each nationality. As social identity theory specifies, stereotyping simplifies the features of a certain group and constructs it as homogeneous, in this case regarding its members' behavior in the classroom. So this direct quote sets up an ingroup-outgroup distinction between the professor and his students, and within the latter group, a further division is made on the basis of membership of different nationalities. As in the initial remark of the antagonist in line 20, he thus again invokes a collective perspective on an interpersonal incident (between Hafida and the professor), but now he not only makes explicit that nationality is the distinctive feature of group segmentation; he also assumes an intergroup perspective, which is in line with the importance that social identity theory attaches to this comparative element in the definition of one's social identity. Interestingly, in this direct quote, the antagonist changes the membership criteria in operation (from religion to nationality) and defuses the situation by not referring to the ethnic descent of the protagonist.

In response to the professor's answer, Hafida presents another direct quote which, this time, is explicitly attributed to herself ("I," line 40). This quote mirrors the professor's words, but it expands the intergroup perspective so that it now includes her own ingroup, making her roots relevant ("Moroccans," line 42). The stereotypical feature that is attributed to this group is subservience (line 42) and she thus refers back to the antagonist's initial remark, as such resisting the use of alternative – and fairly neutral – membership criteria of the preceding quote. This is refuted by the professor through a thrice-repeated negative particle (line 43), and then Hafida inserts a final direct quote, attributed to herself again, in which she closes the topic. The formulation of this topic-closing sentence at the end of 43 is quite different from the previous direct reported speech, since it contains an explicit polite term of address ("meneer," *sir*, line 43) and an inclusive we-from, referring to the two interlocutors (the professor and Hafida). The interviewee thus sets up an interactional ingroup that transcends the group boundaries sketched by both interlocutors earlier (e.g., Moroccans versus Belgians). Hafida thus makes the intergroup comparative perspective irrelevant here by orienting to the local interactional level of the conversation at hand. Also, since she is the one who tells him what to do, Hafida presents herself as an assertive student who does not fit into the reductive characterization projected upon her by the professor (namely that of the subservient Moroccan student).

21.6.5   *Constructing an ingroup-outgroup polarization*

After relating the resolution phase of the story (lines 44–46), Hafida moves into the story evaluation, which is complementary to the previous, relatively implicitly formulated parts of the story, in that it now explicitly refutes the relevance of the feature of subservience that the professor focused on in his remark. Hafida's evaluation of this remark as senseless is not only explicit (line 47), but the prosodic stress on the negative adverb "↑nergens" (*n't … ↑any*, line 47) further emphasizes her strong negative point of view.

Excerpt 5

(44)   And never gone back to that course again. S[o taken that exam,

(45) I   [°yes°

(46) H   succeeded, but not gone back anymore.

(47) H   So that's such a remark that doesn't make ↑*any* sense.

(48)   And that, erm, I have heard from somebody later

(49)   on from teaching administration that fellow students of ours,

(50)   so autochthonous ones, went to tell it because

(51)   even they thought it that, erm, that it really went too far.

In line 48, she briefly returns to another aspect of the resolution, in which she talks about the support for this matter they received from "autochthonous" students – referring to students with Belgian roots (line 50). Interestingly, even though all the students are presented as clearly in agreement regarding the unacceptable nature of the professor's remark, Hafida does not construct an ingroup of all the students here. Instead, she sets up an us-them opposition between the interviewee's small ingroup ("ons," *ours*, line 49) and the "autochthonous" students ("zij," *they*, line 51), who are explicitly labeled (line 50) and whose disagreement with racist remarks is presented as surprising, as the presence of the adverb "zelfs" (*even*, line 51) indicates (see De Fina 2006: 367–368). This formulation polarizes these two groups, in spite of their agreement regarding the acceptability of racist remarks, and this construction of an ingroup-outgroup opposition further underscores the extreme nature of this incident (see line 51, when *even* students with Belgian roots think it was an inappropriate comment).

21.6.6   Drawing on shared micro-cultural canonical expectations

The story then moves back to the evaluation, which was already introduced in line 47 and which is rephrased and expanded in lines 52–55.

Excerpt 6

(52) H   Yes, really such stupid remarks that that are neither here nor there,

(53)   but tha:t are quite confronting for young students

(54)   who just (.) get started at erm, at the university. And in any case

(55)   already (.) have to contend somehow with disadvantages.=

(56) I   = °yes°=

(57) H   = So, that is the last thing that you want to hear then

(58)   [hey, such stupid remarks.

(59) I   [°yes° ( )

(60)   (.)

(61) H   But yes, you have to accept that.

In this rephrasing of the evaluation, a more general angle is taken, widening its scope to stupid remarks (line 52) in general. Furthermore, Hafida now frames the remarks as oriented to young, inexperienced, and disadvantaged students (line 53–55). So in this case, the division into social groups is based on age, experience, and (dis)advantage, which are of course quite different factors from the initial criteria of gender and ethnicity as they were made relevant by the interviewee in excerpt 1. This construction of a new intergroup perspective is further confirmed in the coda (lines 57–61), in which Hafida addresses the interviewer by using the second person singular form "je" (*you*, line 57) and the tag "he" (*hey*, line 58), thereby implicitly appealing to the interviewer's status as a student and to shared "folk psychological" knowledge regarding student matters. The interviewer confirms this and after a brief pause, Hafida closes the story by providing a general affirmative response, as marked by the generic nonstandard second person pronominal clitic form "-e" (translated as *you*, line 61), as such linking up to the initial question again (regarding whether she encountered any forms of racism at university).

So Hafida constructs yet another group membership here, namely the ingroup of young students, and thus renders ethnic descent irrelevant, though this variable was used just a few lines earlier as the main criterion for setting up an ingroup-outgroup polarization between the students without and with Belgian roots (see previous subsection). This again highlights the volatile nature of identity categories and the importance of analyzing their function in their local interactional context. In this case, setting up this collective identity enables Hafida to draw on canonical expectations shared by the ingroup of young students, of which the interviewer is also a member. These fluid realignments clearly illustrate the importance of the interactive negotiation of collective identities in narratives.

21.7   Discussion and Conclusion

As we have seen demonstrated in the six analyses above, many distinctions identified by social identity theory (Tajfel 1981) are explicitly talked into being by the characters in Hafida's storyworld. The most important are: (a) the shift from an interpersonal to an intergroup perspective on the incident that makes the criteria of ethnicity and gender relevant in the construction of an ingroup-outgroup dichotomy; (b) the intergroup comparative perspective on social identities; (c) downplaying ingroup variability; and (d) the projection of a homogeneous and simplified identity upon members of the outgroup through stereotyping. These distinctions are all clearly present in this narrative as they are made relevant by the narrator.

At the same time, the analyses refrained from applying any pre-established categories to the story, as social psychologists tend to do, and instead took a data-driven approach. As mentioned before, a social constructionist perspective emphasizes the identities that locally emerge through the interlocutors' talk. This social constructionist lens typically allows the researcher to zoom in on the many nuances and subtle – sometimes even contradictory – shifts in social groups that are constructed in the course of a story. The analyses here also highlighted the fluidity of the social groups as they are under constant interactional negotiation, and their basis on ever-shifting criteria for group membership (in Hafida's case: ethnicity, gender, religion, age, experience, social disadvantage, the presence of a headscarf, her status as a student, and so on). Furthermore, by means of this bottom-up approach, the ambivalent position of the narrator in relation to these different social groups could also be brought to the surface.

Hafida's shifting position regarding her membership in the group of female students with Moroccan roots is interesting. Her ambivalence may seem a bit unexpected at first, given the fact that this story can be considered to be a counter-narrative in which socially shared discourses on the subservient nature of Islamic women and on the limited educational attainment of students with non-Belgian roots are tackled. When refuting such prejudices, one could on the one hand expect the narrator to carve out a unique place for herself against the backdrop of canonical stories about subservient, uneducated women with Moroccan roots, thus meeting both the demands of canonicity and exceptionality identified by Bruner (1991). On the other hand, following insights from social identity theory, the intergroup perspective could be expected to be consistently constructed, thus firmly positioning Hafida within the ingroup under attack by the professor, which could be qualified as one of those situations in which it is inevitable to think and react in terms of group membership (see Tajfel 1981). However, her story is characterized by a discursive oscillation between the individual and the collective level of identity construction, as occurs quite frequently in narratives (see, e.g., De Fina 2003: 70–79). In this case, these levels are closely intertwined, especially because the repeated agentless formulations endow the story with vagueness regarding the perspective that is talked into being. Since it is reasonable to assume that Hafida was the one who stepped up to the professor, as she explicitly quotes herself twice in the reported exchange, one could frame the absence of a consistent shift to an individual perspective as a way to share the ownership of her story with others. Given the many and highly diverse collective identities that are being constructed in the course of this story, it is impossible to state that Hafida constructs her identity as the spokesperson of one particular social group (e.g., Islamic female students), which would have been a likely conclusion if the analyses had taken pre-discursive "big identities" (Georgakopoulou 2007: 615) based on demographic features as a starting point.

To conclude, these analyses emphasized that taking an intergroup comparative approach glosses over the many nuances that interlocutors talk into being in terms of their fluid memberships in collective identities and the relation between these and their individual identities, and it leaves hardly any room to fully explore the negotiation of collective identities on a micro level. However, I also argued that the insights from social identity theory can be meaningfully integrated into a discursive analysis of collective identities. I aimed to demonstrate that the analyst may be more attentive to interlocutors' subtle displays of orientation to group membership when keeping relevant insights from the social identity framework in mind. Importantly, though, special care must be taken to analyze the interactional data from an emic viewpoint, rather than applying this social identity framework etically, lest one fall into the trap posed by pre-discursively expected categories. So in this case, by scrutinizing the data concerning participants' own orientations to group memberships, it became clear from the early story phases onwards that the narrator constructs and negotiates the racist nature of this remark. Because of the insights from social identity theory, the analyst's attention is particularly drawn to, for instance, the shift back and forth between the interpersonal and the intergroup perspective and the discursive negotiation of the two, such as when the boundaries between individual and collective identities are blurred. As such, these insights also have an explanatory force that can contribute to structuring and giving meaning to the analyst's observations of highly fluid identity constructions, projections, and interactive negotiations. Thus, this chapter aimed to illustrate that interlocutors' references to distinctions central to social identity theory may serve as important markers highlighting their orientation to collectivities, and that this is an interesting topic for further exploration when discursively analyzing a narrator's flexible orientation to ad hoc individual and collective identities.

NOTES

1   "Allochthonous" people are born in Belgium and hence they can scarcely be considered as foreigners.
2   This name is fictitious in order to guarantee the interviewee's anonymity.
3   Any awkward phrasings in the English translation are based on atypical, unfinished or ungrammatical sentences in the Dutch original.

REFERENCES

Antaki, C., and S. Widdicombe. (1998). *Identities in Talk*. London: Sage.

Antaki, C., S. Condor, and M. Levine. (1996). Social identities in talk: Speakers' own orientations. *British Journal of Social Psychology*, 35, pp. 473–492.

Baynham, M. (2006). Performing self, narrative and commuity in Moroccan narratives of migration and settlement. In A. De Fina, D. Schiffrin, and M. Bamberg (eds.), *Discourse and Identity*. Cambridge: Cambridge University Press, pp. 376–397.

Bruner, J.S. (1991). Self-making and world-making. *Journal of Aesthetic Education*, 25 (1), pp. 67–78.

Buttny, R. (1997). Reported speech in talking race on campus. *Human Communication Research*, 23 (4), pp. 477–506.

Coupland, N. (2010). "Other" representation. In J. Jaspers, J. Verschueren, and J.-O. Ostman (eds.), *Society and Language Use*. Amsterdam: John Benjamins, pp. 241–260.

De Fina, A. (2003). *Identity in Narrative: A study of Immigrant Discourse*. Amsterdam: John Benjamins.

De Fina, A. (2006). Group identity, narrative and self-presentations. In A. De Fina, D. Schiffrin, and M. Bamberg (eds.),

Discourse and Identity. Cambridge: Cambridge University Press, pp. 351–375.

De Fina, A. (2007). Code-switching and the construction of ethnic identity in a community of practice. *Language in Society*, 36 (3), pp. 371–392.

De Fina, A., D. Schiffrin, and M. Bamberg. (2006). Introduction. In A. De Fina, D. Schiffrin, and M. Bamberg (eds.), *Discourse and Identity*. Cambridge: Cambridge University Press, pp. 1–23.

Fairclough, N. (1992). *Discourse and Social Change*. Cambridge: Polity Press.

Georgakopoulou, A. (2006). Thinking big with small stories in narrative and identity analysis. *Narrative Inquiry*, 16 (1), pp. 122–130.

Georgakopoulou, A. (2007). "On MSN with buff boys": Self- and other-identity claims in the context of small stories. *Journal of Sociolinguistics*, 12 (5), pp. 597–526.

Holmes, J. (2006). Workplace narratives, professional identity and relational practice. In A. De Fina, D. Schiffrin, and M. Bamberg (eds.), *Discourse and Identity*. Cambridge: Cambridge University Press, pp. 166–187.

Kiesling, S.F. (2006). Hegemonic identity-making in narrative. In A. De Fina, D. Schiffrin, and M. Bamberg (eds.),

Discourse and Identity. Cambridge: Cambridge University Press, pp. 261–287.

Labov, W. (2006). Narrative pre-construction. *Narrative Inquiry*, 16 (1), pp. 37–45.

Labov, W., and J. Waletzky. (1967). Narrative Analysis: Oral versions of personal experience. In J. Helm (ed.), *Essays on the Verbal and Visual Arts.* Seattle: University of Washington Press, pp. 12–44.

Norrick, N.R. (2005). The dark side of tellability. *Narrative Inquiry*, 15 (2), pp. 323–343.

Sacks, H. (1992). *Lectures on Conversation.* Oxford: Blackwell.

Schiffrin, D. (2003). We knew that's it: Retelling the turning point of a narrative. *Discourse Studies*, 5 (4), pp. 535–561.

Stokoe, E. (2009). Doing actions with identity categories: Complaints and denials in neighbor disputes. *Text & Talk*, 29 (1), pp. 75–97.

Tajfel, H. (1981). *Human Groups and Social Categories.* Cambridge: Cambridge University Press.

Tajfel, H. (1982a). Introduction. In H. Tajfel (ed.), *Social Identity and Intergroup Relations.* Cambridge: Cambridge University Press, pp. 1–11.

Tajfel, H. (1982b). Instrumentality, identity and social comparisons. In H. Tajfel (ed.), *Social*

Identity and Intergroup Relations. Cambridge: Cambridge University Press, pp. 483–507.

Triandafyllidou, A., and R. Wodak. (2003). Conceptual and methodological questions in the study of collective identities: An introduction. *Journal of Language and Politics*, 2 (2), pp. 205–223.

Van De Mieroop, D. (2012a). Maneuvering between the individual and the social dimensions of narratives in a poor man's discursive negotiation of stigma. *Narrative Inquiry*, 22 (1), pp. 122–145.

Van De Mieroop, D. (2012b). The discursive construction of gender, ethnicity and the workplace in second generation immigrants' narratives: The case of Moroccan women in Belgium. *Pragmatics*, 22 (2), pp. 301–325.

Van Dijk, T.A. (2009). *Society and Discourse: How Social Contexts Influence Text and Talk.* Cambridge: Cambridge University Press.

Widdicombe, S. (1998). Identity as an analysts' and a participants' resource. In C. Antaki and S. Widdicombe (eds.), *Identities in Talk.* London: Sage, pp. 191–206.

Wodak, R., and M. Reisigl. (2001). Discourse and racism. In D. Schiffrin, D. Tannen, and H. Hamilton (eds.), *The Handbook of Discourse Analysis.* Oxford: Blackwell, pp. 372–397.

APPENDIX

Original fragment in Dutch

(1) I   Uhu (.) Kunt u daar een voorbeeld van geven?

(2) H   <Euhm. Bijvoorbeeld. Een professor die euh>.

(3)   Ja dus, >veel vakken waren gemeenschappelijk met de mensen

(4)   die poli- politieke wetenschappen en sociologie euh studeerden<

(5)   En: >een van die gemeenschappelijke vakken was filoso↑fie<

(6)   en wij zaten vanvoor, dus verschillende euh (.)

(7)   euh dames van Marokkaanse origine. Eu:hm

(8)   Da kon je afleiden door het feit dat zij een hoofddoek, euh,

(9)   droegen. Zo heeft de professor het afgeleid.

(10)   En op een gegeven ogenblik (.) euhm •hh wilde ik

(11)   iets uit een zak halen, een plastieken zak en da maakte

(12)   nogal lawaai. En, euh, die professor, in plaats van te zeggen van

(13)   "Ja, stoppen me lawaai maken". Dus da 's een giga*n*tische aula ↑he.

(14)   Da 's een aula waar euh iets van duizend personen in kan ↑he.

(15)   Dus je kan je al inbeelden, als je daar een opmerking krijgt, dat (.)

(16) I   °ja°

(17) H   Iedereen daar staat te staren. En, euh (.) hij zegt,

(18)   euh ja die maant ons aan t- tot rust, zegt dan (v-) van "ja, euh

(19)   >zou het eens wa stiller kunnen, want da ben ik eigenlijk ni gewoon<

(20)   van- (.) dames zoals ↑jullie (.) zijn we eerder het onder*da*nige gewoon." (.)

(21)   En euh, ja da 's dus een alludering naar het feit da ge van:

(22)   islamitische background [hebt he.

(23) I   [°mm°

(24) H   En, ja, tijdens de pauze derop afgestapt. En het gewoon.

(25)   Ah sorry, da was ni filosofie, da was politicologie.

(26) I   °mm°

(27) H   Politicologie.

(28)   Oh, als ik er nu nog aan denk. Smeerlap.

(29) I   @@@

(30) H   Er naartoe gegaan en, euh, gezegd van: "Ja zeg,

(31)   wa bedoelt u eigenlijk met de:: opmerking van, euh, onderdan[ig?"

(32) I   [°ja°

(33) H   En ge zag die dus helemaal van kleur veranderen.

(34)   Hij wist ni goe wat te re- hoe te reageren. Zegt 'em

(35)   "Ja kijk, da, ik wist dat da in 't verkeerde keelgat ging schieten,

(36)   maar ik bedoelde der eigenlijk niks mee.

(37)   Ik heb hee:l lang les gegeven in Amerika en ik zie dat

(38)   bijvoorbeeld (.) Amerikaanse studenten heel assertief zijn en en

(39)   Vlaamse student dan weer timide."

(40)   Ik zeg van "Ah oké, dus Amerikaanse studenten assertie:f,

(41)   Vlaamse studenten euh, meer, euh, timide en

(42)   de Marokkaanse zijn dan onderdanig?"

(43)   Die zo "Nee nee nee." Ik zeg "Meneer, we gaan het hierbij laten."

(44)   En nooit meer teruggegaan naar die les. Du[s da examen afgelegd,

(45) I   [°ja°

(46) H   geslaagd, maar ni meer teruggegaan.

(47)   Dus da's zo'n opmerking die ↑nergens op slaat.

(48)   En da, euh, ik heb daarna van iemand gehoord

(49)   van onderwijsadministratie dat medestudenten van ons,

(50)   dus autochtonen, het zijn gaan vertellen omdat

(51)   zelfs zij het vonden dat, euh, dat 't er echt over was.

(52)   Ja, echt zo stomme opmerkingen die kant noch wal raken,

(53)   maar die: wel confronterend zijn voor jonge studenten

(54)   die pas (.) beginnen op euh, aan de unif. En sowieso

(55)   al (.) te kampen hebben met ergens een een achterstand.=

(56) I   = °ja°=

(57) H   =Dus, dat is het laatste da je dan wil horen

(58)   [he, zo'n stomme opmerkingen.

(59) I   [°ja° ( )

(60)   (.)

(61) H   Maar ja, da moete erbij nemen.

22   Narrative Bodies, Embodied Narratives

EMILY HEAVEY

22.1   Introduction

The relationship(s) between narrative and identity are long established (and debated); chapters in this volume demonstrate the extraordinary diversity within narrative identity research, and the analytic and theoretical dilemmas that this diversity can create (see Freeman, chapter 1; De Fina, chapter 18; Van De Mieroop, chapter 21). Narratives that construct lives and identities affected by illness and other bodily crises have been a particular area of interest for narrative analysts, medical sociologists, clinicians, and patients themselves. Scholars of identity have found such narratives to be a rich source of data, in part because of the variety of identities that different narrators (or even the same narrator) can construct in response to a changing body, and because of the variety of analytic approaches to such storytelling. Some analysts have argued, for example, that bodily crises are experienced as disruptions to a person's life and sense of self, and that that person might attempt to *repair* that disruption through telling stories of how the bodily crisis came to be, how it affected (or did not affect) their lives, and/or how it was or will be resolved (e.g., Frank 1995; Riessman 2003; Smith 2008).

Recently, there has been a turn to the importance of the body itself in narrative, with analysts asking questions about how the fleshy reality of the body affects the narratives we tell, and how we use the body, and are constrained by it, as we tell them (e.g., Langellier 2001; Sparkes and Smith 2011). This turn is particularly relevant to the view of narrative as performance. Langellier and Peterson (2004), for example, argue that all storytelling involves performance – a *taking* of one's (embodied) experience and a *making* it into (embodied) experience for one's audience. All storytelling, then, is embodied:

> Performing narrative is not a cognitive or reflective process for which the body is a container. The body of the storyteller is not a film or video screen upon which or through which stories may be projected. Before performing narrative is conceived or represented, it is lived through the body as meaningful. (2004: 9)

Further, storytelling takes place in the context of bodily comprehension and understandings of bodily practices that are shared (at least to an extent) by the audience. Storytelling

The Handbook of Narrative Analysis, First Edition. Edited by Anna De Fina and Alexandra Georgakopoulou.
© 2015 John Wiley & Sons, Inc. Published 2019 by John Wiley & Sons, Inc.

(and being the audience to a story) involve bodily participation to the extent that stories always "come out of" bodies, and stories and storytelling are based on the lived, embodied experience of narrators, and interpreted through the filter of the lived, embodied experience of the audience. This is even so, Langellier and Peterson argue, when the storyteller and audience are not physically co-present, as in digital or online forms of storytelling: "A person can read or write a weblog only to the extent that he or she is bodily capable of doing so" (2004: 166).

However, even those analyses that emphasize the embodiedness of storytelling tend to remain driven by a focus on narrative *identity* construction. In this chapter, I will argue for a complementary, but not contradictory, focus on narrative *body* construction, which I define as the process of constructing, performing, and making meaningful one's own body in the narratives one tells about it. While I will consider plot structure and linguistic choices of participants' narratives, aspects of narrative that can be analyzed outside of the performance frame, I approach the narratives told as performative exchanges between the interlocutors, and exchanges which draw on their lived, embodied experiences.

I will begin by addressing some of the existing literature on bodies and identities, and then the literature on narrative and the body, before outlining my own theory of narrative body construction. I will illustrate this theory by analyzing the narratives of two people who were interviewed as part of a larger study, who I call Lily and Matt. Lily had undergone a mastectomy at the time of the interview, and Matt a below-knee amputation. Both narratives deal with the (real or imagined) event of the narrator's prosthesis becoming detached in public. I will show in the analysis that, through the performance of their narratives, the narrators construct their own bodies and prostheses in quite different ways, even as they narrate ostensibly similar events. At the same time, both narratives are affected by, and reliant on, the narrators' materially real bodies.

22.2   Bodies and Identities

It has been said that Western thought, and particularly Western medicine, is dominated by Cartesian dualism (Hacking 2007), which views consciousness and selfhood as "entirely and truly distinct from [the] body" (Descartes 2008: 115). In this view, the body is merely a vehicle for the self, rather than *being* (a part of) the self. The phenomenological tradition opposes this dualistic view, and argues that the body is a condition of selfhood, that it governs our perception of the world and our experience of self and others, and that most people, under most circumstances, experience themselves as being a unified body-self (Leder 1990; Merleau-Ponty 1962). Charon succinctly summarizes the view: "'This,' said as one firmly pounds one's chest with the flat of one's hands, 'is me'" (2006: 87).

Some arguments within social constructionism, which has roots in phenomenology (McNeill 1990: 120), also emphasize the links between body and self, and the relevance of embodied performances of the self. Goffman's (1959, 1966) work on the performance and social construction of the self argues that the body is the site of self-presentation, and that a person's performances in public, and in particular his or her "bodily idioms," "convey information about the actor's social attributes, and about his conception of himself" (1966: 34). The individual's intentional presentation of particular bodily idioms (for example, style of dress or certain kinds of body language) and interlocutors' interpretations of those (and other, unintentional) idioms, are based on conventionalized discourses *about* bodily idioms, and how they relate to particular social identities. In turn, we perpetuate such discourses through our presentation and interpretation of our own and one another's bodies and selves. In particular, Goffman argues that certain forms of bodily presentation, such as the intended or unintended exposure of a non-normative body or body part, will lead to the body and hence the person being stigmatized and "disqualified from full social acceptance" (1968: 9); these social responses are based on conventionalized discourses about what it means to be "normal" and "normal-bodied."

Both phenomenology and social constructionism are relevant to narrative identity analysis, although neither *constitutes* narrative identity analysis (phenomenological analysis is often based on the presentation of stories as representative, rather than constructive, of experience). Langellier and Peterson's (2004) approach to narrative as performance occurring in fields of bodily practice has roots in the phenomenology of Merleau-Ponty, and even those forms of narrative (performance) analysis with less of an emphasis on embodiment emphasize the subjective nature of narrated experience (e.g., Georgakopoulou 2007). Narrative identity analysis as a whole has a basis in constructionism, and Riessman (2003) credits Goffman's notion of performance as the originator of the view of narratives as performances of identity. Many analyses specifically emphasize social constructionist ideas, asking how individuals' stories draw on, repeat, and perhaps disrupt master narratives or shared discourses about, for instance, masculinity and disability (Riessman 2003; Sparkes and Smith 2002). In this chapter, I adopt a narrative constructionist approach, in that I consider how storytellers *construct* their embodied experiences, and their bodies themselves, in the narratives they tell in interaction with their interlocutor(s), rather than claiming to report exactly what storytellers' experiences (or bodies) "are." At the same time, I incorporate the phenomenological understanding of one's self and one's lived experiences *as* embodied. The storytelling too, is an embodied process.

22.3 Narrative Embodiedness

> The stories that ill people tell come out of their bodies. The body sets in motion the need for new stories when its disease disrupts the old stories. The body, whether still diseased or recovered, is simultaneously cause, topic, and instrument of whatever new stories are told. (Frank 1995: 2)

In recent years, there has been an increasing emphasis on the relevance of narrators' bodies to their narratives, particularly – although not exclusively – when those narratives focus on bodily crises such as illness and acquired disability. Since Frank's (1995) seminal work, *The Wounded Storyteller*, argued for the importance of recognizing illness narratives as being told *with*, *through*, and *because of* bodies, his argument has been parsed and expanded in various ways. I will now discuss two aspects of what I will call *narrative embodiedness*, that is, (spoken) narratives as produced and affected by physically real and present bodies. I will then turn to the ways in which such narrative embodiedness is relevant to, but does not entirely dictate, the narrative construction of the body that produces that narrative. While Langellier and Peterson (2004) have argued that narrative embodiedness is relevant to all forms of storytelling, including online forms, I will limit my argument and my analysis to face-to-face storytelling.

The first relevant aspect of narrative embodiedness is the material body as the *source* and *topic* of a narrator's stories. Bodily crises are often also life crises, and even identity crises, as they present the individual with a new set of (embodied) circumstances, and perhaps a new set of daily routines, social interactions, and expectations for the future. A common response to such crises is storytelling; people may tell stories that make sense of their lives and selves *now* in terms of their lives and selves *then*, and such stories may highlight similarities or differences. In a seminal example of the former, Riessman (1990, 2003) shows how Burt, a man with multiple sclerosis, told selected stories in order to construct and perform coherent masculine identities, as a good father, husband, and worker, despite the changes to his body that his illness caused, and the subsequent breakdown of his marriage and loss of his job. In this case, Burt's disability – and the changed self his audience might assume it to have wrought – prompted him to tell particular stories *negating* such expectations. For example, Burt's stories show his audience how the changes to his body did not stop him from being a good husband; rather, his marital problems were the result of his wife's moral failings, and Burt remained a good husband to the end of his marriage. Conversely, Langellier (2001) showed how Rhea's breast cancer narratives work to perform a self that *has* been altered by the embodied changes brought about by cancer; Rhea's multiple, fragmented identities include the passive patient who is tattooed for medical reasons and the agentive survivor who chooses to have her mastectomy site tattooed, and to expose and take pride in that latter tattoo. Whether presenting and performing identities that are unchanged or identities that have radically changed after illness, the narrators' illnesses and changing bodies *prompt* them to tell these particular stories of who they take themselves to be, and are crucial *foci* of the stories.

When the body is the source and topic of stories, even if it is presented as only a tangential topic, it is crucial to acknowledge that that body is *more than* those stories. We permanently live with our bodies, and these bodies inevitably shape our lives and the stories we tell about those lives (Eakin 1999). More than simply a construction, the individual's body is an *object* in Hacking's sense of the term. It is "'in the world' in a commonsensical, not fancy, meaning of that phrase" (Hacking 1999: 21), regardless of how we story it. That is, the body – Burt's multiple sclerosis, Rhea's cancer, mastectomy, and tattoos – is not *only* constructed in stories, but exists beyond those stories as both fleshy object and subjective experience; in turn, this material reality, which I call the individual's *object body*, shapes the stories that the individual tells about it. Smith and Sparkes (2008) demonstrate this phenomenon in their analysis of Jamie's narratives. Jamie was paralyzed by spinal cord injury (SCI) and Smith and Sparkes argue that, while he is initially drawn to tell a restitution narrative (Frank 1995) and present his injured body as fixable, eventually the physical reality and severity of his injuries obscures his ability to tell this narrative. Jamie's narratives become chaotic and he rejects the possibility of a restorable body-self; crucially, this is "partly due to the obdurate reality of Jamie's body and what it could and could not do given the level of his SCI" (Smith and Sparkes 2008: 223). That is, Jamie's narrative is shaped – although not entirely dictated – by the physical reality of the body that he has and is. It is not simply the case that any narrative can be told by anybody (or any body); as source and topic of the narrative, the storyteller's body *constrains* the narrative.

The second relevant aspect of narrative embodiedness is the body as the *instrument* with which the narrative is performed. When storytellers tell stories in face-to-face interaction, they are doing so to, for, and with an audience. The storyteller and audience see and hear one another, and the bodies present in the room will form and influence the story told. As Langellier and Peterson put it, storytelling "requires bodily participation: hearing and voicing, gesturing, seeing and being seen" (2004: 8). Particularly when the stories told are *about* the storyteller's body (whether in the past, or in some imagined scenario), the storyteller can use his or her storytelling body – the body that the audience can see and that constitutes the deictic centre of the telling – to make, emphasize, and illustrate the story's claims or point(s). Various analysts have emphasized the importance of non-verbal performance in storytelling; Heath (2002), for example, shows how a patient tells her doctor the story of her recent headache experiences, physically performing her symptoms and gesturing to the location of the pain as she does so. Such gestures "render visible what would otherwise remain hidden and unavailable for inspection" (Heath 2002: 615), and invite the doctor to be convinced of and empathize with the patient's problem. That is, the patient uses her storytelling body to make claims about her storied body (the body that has recently suffered headaches). Her embodied actions form part of the story that she tells through, with, and about her body.

To summarize, when people tell stories about their own bodies, the physically real and present body of the storyteller produces, affects, and performs those stories. As source, topic, and instrument of their stories, storytellers' object bodies are what Langellier and Peterson call "constraints" to narrative performance, where a constraint is a "boundary that defines the conditions of what is possible. A constraint is not merely a constriction or an obstruction. … constraints both facilitate and restrict possibilities for expression and perception" (2004: 14). A storyteller's object body will influence him to tell certain stories in certain ways, and restrict him from telling other stories (as Jamie's body did). A storyteller's body will also *facilitate* her telling certain stories in certain ways, particularly through allowing her to produce physical performances (as the headache patient's body did). I will now turn to the ways in which these aspects of narrative embodiedness are relevant to the narrative construction of bodies.

22.4 Narrative Body Construction

Just as we can apply the idea of narrative constructedness to less tangible aspects of selfhood (such as Burt's masculinity or Rhea's agency), we can also apply it to that physical basis of selfhood: the individual's body. In analyzing narrative body constructions, I argue that, as people tell stories that are explicitly or implicitly about their bodies, they are also constructing and performing versions of those bodies. However, unlike agentive or masculine identities, the body will exist as a material reality whether or not narratives are being told about it. In turn, storytellers' narrative body constructions are anchored to and affected by their physically real bodies, even as they are not simply neutral descriptions of what is physically present. The material reality of the storyteller's body will be relevant to his or her narrative body constructions in (at least) the two ways discussed in the previous section.

The interaction between an individual's narrative body construction and that individual's object body can be illustrated with a brief example, taken from an interview with "Adam." Adam told a long story about how, following an accident that left his leg severely damaged, he chose to have the leg amputated, to allow him the best possible mobility. He ended the story:

> So I made the decision to have the amputation, because in my mind the leg that I had wasn't doing its job. So they weren't cutting my leg off, they were taking away a useless piece of flesh that wasn't fulfilling its function and replacing it with something made of plastic and metal that did. [*gestures at prosthetic leg*] OK not quite as well, but certainly better than being on crutches.

Adam's narrative works to construct his leg as irreparably damaged following the accident, to the point that it no longer "counted" as a body part, but was instead "a useless piece of flesh." In this sense, he is constructing an amputated part of his object body as non-body, even *before* it was physically removed through amputation. He is also constructing his prosthetic leg in a positive way, as something that allows him to return to the state of physical function that he had lost ("something made of plastic and metal that did [fulfil the function of a leg]"). Crucially, Adam could have told this story differently, constructing his damaged biological leg as a vital part of his body despite its damage, and lamenting its loss, and/or constructing his new prosthetic leg as a poor substitute for the biological one, an unnatural and alien addition to his body. By telling the story he tells and rejecting alternative tellings, Adam makes his body meaningful in particular ways: his narrative *constructs* his body in these particular ways and not in others.

At the same time, this narrative body construction is anchored to and constrained by Adam's physically real object body in the ways discussed. First, as the source and topic of Adam's narrative, there are certain obdurate facts about Adam's body with which his narrative must engage: he has had his right biological leg amputated below the knee, he now uses a prosthetic leg, and there are *some* things that are more physically difficult for Adam to do with a prosthetic leg than with an undamaged biological one ("OK, not quite as well"). Although Adam could have *constructed* his amputated leg and his prosthetic leg quite differently in the narrative, he cannot tell an amputation story (or at least not a credible one) in which these obdurate *facts* about his body are ignored or changed. He must acknowledge and interpret these facts in the story told. Second, Adam draws attention to his body as the topic of his narrative, gesturing at the prosthetic leg of which he speaks and inviting me to *see* "something made of plastic and metal." Here, we see

Adam's object body as the instrument that facilitates the telling of his narrative, just as the patient's headache performance facilitated hers (Heath 2002). In this example, we can see how a storyteller's narrative addresses and accounts for the physical reality of his object body and uses that body in the telling, even as the narrative constructs his body as *more* than its own materiality.

People might narratively construct their own bodies with regards to various aspects of those bodies; narrative body constructions may focus around the body as an entity in *interaction* with other people, or in *comparison* with other people's bodies, for example. In this chapter, I will focus on one particular aspect: the narrative construction of prosthetic parts in relation to the rest of the body, and specifically the construction of those parts as body parts or as non-body.

22.5 Narrative Incorporation and Exclusion of Prosthetic Parts

"It's not my *bad* leg, it's just my other leg." (Matt, interviewee)

In her "Cyborg Manifesto," Haraway argues that we should reject such binaries as animal and machine, natural and artificial, and asks, "Why should our bodies end at the skin?" (1991: 178). The phenomenological tradition has a particular concern with how people experience and perceive their own bodies, and prosthetic additions to those bodies. Since Merleau-Ponty's suggestion that a blind man who habitually uses a cane can eventually incorporate that cane as "a bodily auxiliary, an extension of the bodily synthesis" (1962: 153), other analysts interested in the phenomenological experience of the body have used interviews and stories of their own experience to demonstrate prosthesis-users' integration (or lack thereof) of their prostheses into their bodies.

Rawdon Wilson writes of experiencing his own prosthetic knee as "anomalous, even (in dark moments) as personal slime" (1995: 250). He extrapolates his own experiences to other prosthesis-users, and argues that prosthetic parts are never truly incorporated into one's body, but always "grumble unnervingly in a new tongue" (239). In particular, he suggests that prostheses' ability to detach and otherwise fail makes them non-body, and that "any consideration of prostheses has to take into account their potential failure and, even, the conditions under which they might go wrong or turn against their users" (242). Similarly, Crompvoets points to the daily task of removing and replacing a prosthetic breast as a "constant interruption to the seamlessness of the whole body" (2012: 111), and a reason that the prosthesis cannot replace a woman's experience of her own breast, and cannot be experienced *as* a breast. Conversely, other analysts have argued that prostheses *can* be incorporated into one's body, while recognizing that this incorporation may not happen for everyone, and that it may not be a permanent state. Murray's (2004) analysis of interviews with amputees found that many came to experience their prostheses as being part of their bodies, while some saw their prostheses as tools – useful for, but distinct from, the body. Speaking of their own and other amputees' experiences, Kurzman (2001) and Sobchack (2007) acknowledge that a malfunctioning prosthesis can lead to an inability to see that prosthesis as part of one's body; in such moments, as Sobchack puts it, the prosthesis "becomes an absolute other" (2007: 27). However, unlike Rawdon Wilson, both Kurzman and Sobchack argue that the prosthesis can be experienced as part of one's lived body *despite* these moments of "otherness." Sobchack (2007) claims that as she "lives" her own prosthetic leg, it becomes interchangeable with her biological leg.

Such analyses use stories – the analyst's own or other people's – to make their arguments about prostheses being perceived and experienced as body parts or as non-body. However, they do not address how the storytellers *construct* their prostheses in these ways, *through* these stories, but rather present the stories as *reflections* of bodily experience. In this chapter, I will show how two narrators construct prostheses as a part of the storyteller's body or as *not* a part of the storyteller's body. That is, I ask how storytellers incorporate (or do not incorporate) prostheses into their bodies in the stories they tell, rather than asking whether or not they habitually *experience* their prostheses as part of their bodies. It is possible, even likely, that the same person may consistently tell stories that include or exclude a prosthesis as a body part, and that such constructions may be shaped by – and shape – that person's perception of their own body. However, this analysis does not seek to prove such perceptions, but instead to show how storytellers "do" inclusion or exclusion in their stories, thus producing particular narrative body constructions.

In my analysis, I will consider how the two storytellers construct the prostheses as body or as non-body by presenting those prostheses as meaningfully similar and proximal to or meaningfully different and distant from the rest of the storyteller's body. In particular, I will focus on the structure, language, and non-verbal performance of the two stories, and how these aspects work to construct the prostheses in these ways. How does the plot of a narrative work to associate the prosthesis with the narrator's body, or dissociate it from that body? How do the lexico-grammatical choices used to name or describe the prosthesis, including detailed images or descriptions, work to associate or dissociate the prosthesis? How do storytellers' iconic and deictic gestures work within the story to portray the prosthesis as body or as non-body? As discussed, storytellers' narrative body constructions, including their constructions of prosthetic parts, are anchored to and constrained by their physically real object bodies. In the analysis of Lily and Matt's stories, I will draw attention to the ways in which their bodies and, to an extent, my own act as constraints to the stories told.

22.6   Lily: Narrative Exclusion of a Prosthetic Part

Lily had a mastectomy after diagnosis with breast cancer, and later underwent a surgical reconstruction. She wore a prosthetic breast while she awaited the reconstruction, and described the idea of continuing to wear a prosthesis as "a horrible thought." In extract 1, Lily presents a narrative of past experiences and a hypothetical narrative of wearing the breast prosthesis, depicting the possibility of the prosthesis accidentally slipping out of her bra and coming away from her body. Through her emplotment of the hypothetical narrative, as well as the terms and images she uses to describe the prosthesis, and the gestures she uses to perform it, she depicts the prosthesis as something distinct from her body, and distant from it in a literal and metaphorical sense. In excluding the prosthesis from her narrative body construction, she implicitly *justifies* her decision to have a surgical reconstruction rather than continuing to wear the prosthesis; that is, Lily's story accounts for and explains the body she has now. Non-lexical sounds ("um," "mm") have not been reproduced in the transcript.

Extract 1

(1) Emily: So, when you said the prosthesis is a horrible thought,

what was it about wearing the prosthesis that was horrible?

Lily: Well, *interestingly*, I'd had a trauma twice when I was younger,

and a lady had asked-

(5) Just sort of put her hands either side of my waist,

to <u>move me over slightly</u>, very kindly, gently.

[miming]

I was out with my mother.

When I looked down, <u>she had no hands</u>.

(10) [curling hands]

And I had nightmares about that for *years*.

And then, on my way to school,

I used to pass a house and there was always a little boy outside,

he was a thalidomide child.

(15) And I think because he'd been tormented, he used to tease me.

And because I reacted,

he was like I'm gonna *get* you!

You know, he was really *deformed*,

he had an artificial *leg*, <u>and half a leg on the other, or-</u>

(20) [gesturing at legs]

You know, and <u>a funny hand</u>, and a-

[holding hand up, curled over]

You know, <u>half an arm.</u>

[waving curled arm]

(25) And he used to *come* at me,

and it really played a big part.

And then my cousin lost his leg,

and his sister said to me,

you wouldn't *notice* he's got an artificial leg,

(30) apart from when he sits down it *clicks*. (1.0)

So I had this really sort of [exhales] *unnatural*, if you like (1.0)

feeling about, you know, *amputees* and things like that.

So this to me was like an amputation.

[gesturing with both hands at chest]

(35)   And this was something that was in that *department*.

You know, of *artificial limbs*, and *prosthesis*, and-

It was just *horrible*,

and it was also the *embarrassment* of (1.0)

losing it, or it being *seen* or something?

(40)   Because believe it or not, it was only (1.0)

about six, seven years ago,

that Marks and Spencers brought out a <u>proper mastectomy bra</u>

                              [gesturing in front of chest]

where you could put the implant inside a <u>pocket</u>?

(45)   [miming putting prosthesis in]

So you were really quite <u>secure</u>.

                    [gesturing under bust]

Up to then it'd just been a bra where you could <u>pop it in</u>.

                              [miming]

(50)   Against your *skin*,

which meant there was a (<u>1.0</u>)

[two hands flat in front of chest, sliding over each other]

a higher <u>risk of that coming away</u>.

[moves hands away from chest in slight arc]

(55)   So yeah, and it was *horrible*.

It was just like a big piece of <u>fleshy fat</u>.

[mimes holding hemisphere shape in both hands]

The extract contains two distinct narratives, which both contribute to the construction of the prosthesis as non-body. To answer my question, Lily launches a narrative of experiences in her past, long before the mastectomy (ll. 3–30), in which three temporally disparate events are thematically linked to contextualize the horror that she felt toward the prosthesis. Lily goes on to tell a hypothetical narrative (ll. 40–55), which presents the imagined events of wearing the prosthesis and having it slip out of her bra; this latter narrative will be my main focus here.

Turning first to Lily's lexico-grammatical choices, we can see that nowhere in the extract does she describe the prosthesis using any body-part nouns (for example, *breast*, *boob*). It is "the implant" (l. 44), "that" (l. 53) or, more frequently, "it" (ll. 37, 39, 48, 55, 56). As Johnstone observes, "[d]eciding what to call something can constitute a claim about it" (2008: 58). That is, Lily's naming choices do not simply reflect an objective reality about the prosthesis, but they constitute an implicit claim that it is *not* a breast (as we shall see in Matt's narrative, prosthetic parts can equally be named *as* body parts). In Lily's naming choices, too, we see a lack of possessive grammar; not only is the prosthesis not a "breast," it is specifically not *"my* breast" (or even *"my* implant"). Again, this linguistic choice constitutes a claim; Fleischman notes that, when people discuss their own diseases,

> Distancing is ... achieved by use of a definite article or neuter pronoun "it" with diseases and afflicted body parts (*the leg doesn't feel right; make it* [a tumour in the patient's right breast] *go away!*) rather than the personal "I" or "my." (2001: 492; original emphases)

We can see this same distancing in relation to a prosthetic part, in Lily's uses of "it," "the," and "that," her grammatical choices denoting non-ownership and distance from that prosthesis. As she ends the narrative, Lily offers a more detailed description of the prosthesis: "It was just like a big piece of *fleshy fat."* Unlike her other descriptions of the prosthesis, this image is evocative of flesh; however it is evocative of *disembodied* flesh, flesh that has been separated from a body, like packaged meat. Lily's final description explicitly presents the prosthesis as something different and physically separate from a living body: different and separate from *her* body.

The structure and non-verbal performance of Lily's hypothetical narrative enforce this presentation of the prosthesis as non-body. Lines 31–39 work to evaluate the narrative of her traumatic past experiences, and act as something of an abstract (Labov 1972) to the narrative of her own prosthesis slipping, linking the two narratives. She relates her mastectomy (which was "like an amputation," l. 33) and prosthesis to these negative earlier experiences of "amputees and things like that" (l. 32), setting up the hypothetical narrative of prosthesis-use as a narrative of negative experience, specifically a narrative about a body that is in some way *"unnatural"* (l. 31) and may reveal itself as such to other people (ll. 38–39). Lily goes on to present a particular (hypothetical) incident representing a particular concern she had about wearing the prosthesis: the insecurely fastened prosthesis "coming away" (l. 53) and slipping out of her bra. This hypothetical slippage is the type of "potential failure" that Rawdon Wilson (1995: 242) suggested prevents prostheses from ever being fully embodied. While this is not the experience of all prosthesis-users, in Lily's hypothetical narrative she *constructs* the prosthesis as non-body – as a source of unnatural horror – by *making relevant* its impermanence and potential to fail.

The slippage incident can be seen as a type of complicating action (Labov 1972) or narrative trouble, and as she narrates the incident, Lily uses her hands to indicate the slipping of the prosthesis (l. 52), sliding one hand in front of the other, to indicate a gap between her body ("your skin") and the prosthesis ("it"). Crucially, even as her hands briefly touch, they are two separate objects, and constantly in motion, constantly at risk of separating. Lily enforces the metaphorical and literal distance that occurs (or *could* occur) between the prosthesis and her body in l. 54; as she moves her hand away from her chest, the prosthesis that she has non-verbally constructed moves away from her chest too, her gesture vivifying its separateness from her body. Crucially too, neither Lily's words nor her non-verbal performance offer any *resolution* to the narrative trouble of the slipping prosthesis. She does not mention or mime putting the prosthesis back into her bra, which would be the most likely next event in this hypothetical scenario. Instead, she mimes holding it in her hands (l. 57), away from her chest. The gesture (and the elision of the event of reattachment) again constructs the prosthesis as an object that is separate – and *remains* separate – from her body.

Lily's body is a physically real object – one that was two-breasted, underwent a mastectomy, was one-breasted for a time, and has now undergone a surgical reconstruction. For a time, too, her body was adorned with a prosthesis that horrified her. Her mastectomy, her reconstruction, and her experience of wearing the prosthesis, as well as my opening question in the extract, set into motion her stories about her body, and her stories acknowledge and account for these physical realities, negatively evaluating the mastectomy and prosthesis, and implicitly justifying the reconstruction. Further, Lily explicitly uses the body from which her stories emerge, and for which they account. She repeatedly touches and gestures at her chest as the site of her mastectomy, emphasizing that it is *her* body and *her* mastectomy that she narrates, and later gestures away from her body to indicate the physical and metaphorical distance of the prosthesis from that deictic centre. Crucially too, as a non-prosthesis-user, *I* embody a naïve outsider to the problems that prostheses can present; Lily represents an authority on such problems, and her story explains them to me. It is not too high an inference to suggest that, were I a prosthesis-user, Lily may have told her story in a different way; in this sense, my body, as well as Lily's, informs the story she tells. Yet even as our object bodies are crucial to Lily's hypothetical narrative of the prosthesis slipping, the narrative also *constructs* her body and her prosthesis. In constructing the latter as non-body, she is constructing her body itself as something whose boundaries end at its own skin, and did so even at a time when she wore a prosthesis.

Lily's construction of the prosthesis she used to wear as being non-body is not merely a reflection of the fact that the prosthesis was impermanent or strange-looking; as we will see in Matt's narrative, differing appearance, even removability, can be mentioned and emphasized in stories that construct prostheses as body parts.

22.7   Matt: Narrative Inclusion of a Prosthetic Part

Matt had his left leg amputated below the knee six years before the interview took place, following a motorbike accident. He now wears a prosthetic leg. Extract 2 follows me asking if he still rides a motorbike; Matt replied that he does, and explained some of the adaptations that he has had made to his bike. He explained that the adaptations mean that he does not need to use his left leg to change gears, so "there's nothing for my left leg to do." At this point, he begins his narrative. In contrast to Lily's narrative, the language, performance, and emplotment of Matt's narrative work to present his prosthesis *as* a body part, both in the events narrated and in the moment of narrating; *like* Lily's narrative, then, Matt's narrative justifies and accounts for the body he now has: a body that continues to wear a prosthesis.

Extract 2

(1) Matt: Although, *funnily* enough,
            The kind of leg I've got has got a kind of <u>push button release</u>,
                              [touching index fingertips together]
            it's got a ratchet-

(5)   a pin and a ratchet, so a push button release,
and I went out on the bike the other week,
and I stopped at a set of traffic lights,
and it was <u>my old leg I had on</u>.
      [touches leg]

(10)   And, for some reason <u>the button</u>-
         [touching index fingers together]
I don't know why-
The button's usually on <u>the outside</u>,
        [gestures at leg]

(15)   but it was on the inside,
and I stopped at a pedestrian crossing,
and put my feet down,
and cos your legs <u>kind of straddle the bike</u>, (1.0)
      [straddling motion with arms]

(20)   or the scooter, and it touches the bodywork.
And what it does, <u>it pressed against the pin</u>.
       [reaching down to touch leg]
And as I moved my leg, my leg started coming off? (<u>1.0</u>)
         [smiles]

(25)   So, and I'm- (<u>1.0</u>)
[miming holding handlebars]
But I'm okay, I'm on my oth- I'm on my right leg,
so I had to <u>call out to someone</u>,
      [miming as if holding handlebars]

(30)   <u>Scuse me, can you help me? Scuse me</u>-
[looking over shoulder and calling out]
Cos I'm kind of <u>balancing</u>, my leg was coming off,
      [miming handlebars]
[laughs]

(35)   and the bike was gonna fall over.
So I had to get them to hold the bike,
so then I could adjust my leg and get that back on,
<u>and then drive off</u>
[reaching down, miming pushing the leg back on]

(40)   [laughs]

Like Lily's hypothetical story, Matt's narrative of past experience presents an incident of a prosthesis accidentally detaching. In his case, as in hers, the material reality of his body, specifically the impermanence of his prosthesis, was the source and topic of his story. However, where Lily used her story to explain to a non-prosthesis-user the *insurmountable* problems with prostheses (that is, the possibility of detachment), Matt uses his to explain how he *managed* one such incident. Further, in contrast to Lily's painful story of the fear of humiliation, Matt presents the incident as humorous and entertaining, introducing the narrative with "funnily enough" and laughing throughout. These differences work to present the potential failure of his prosthesis (even the potential *public* failure) as "no big deal." Indeed, in Matt's story, the detachment of the prosthesis is little different from any other temporary lapse of bodily control, some minor "dys-appearance" that briefly brings one's own body to one's attention as dys-functional or problematic (Leder 1990). Just as a stumble or a trip is soon righted and does not render one's feet "non-body," Matt's prosthetic failure does not render his prosthetic leg non-body in the story as he tells it. He constructs his prosthetic leg *as* his leg – his body – through the structure, non-verbal performance, and lexico-grammatical choices of his story.

In contrast to Lily's narrative, Matt refers to his prosthetic leg as "my leg" throughout his narrative (ll. 8, 23, 32, 37). (He refers to "the kind of leg I've got" in l. 2, but this is to distinguish his leg from the other types of prosthetic legs available.) Indeed, Matt's leg remains "my leg" even as it malfunctions and begins to *detach* from the rest of his body (ll. 23, 32). Further, he does not *distinguish* between his left (prosthetic) leg and his right (biological) leg in his lexico-grammatical choices. In l. 17, Matt states that "[I] put my feet down." The feet are not separated as "my foot" and "my/the prosthesis." They are spoken together as simply "my feet." Similarly, at l. 27, Matt is "on my oth- I'm on my right leg," not "on my leg" or "on my real leg": in this story, they are *both* his legs. In arguing that she experiences her prosthetic leg as incorporated into her body, Sobchack states that her biological and prosthetic legs are "to a great degree, *reversible* each with the other" (2007: 26). In Matt's lexico-grammatical choices, we can see the *narrative construction* of such reversibility, and the prosthetic leg being constructed as a body part, alongside his biological leg.

Although his prosthetic leg is simply referred to as "my leg" throughout the narrative, and his two legs are treated as reversible at a linguistic level, Matt does draw attention to the mechanical details that distinguish his right leg from his left leg. However, where Rawdon Wilson (1995) and Crompvoets (2012) drew attention to the distinguishing features of prostheses (their material difference, their impermanence) as reasons that they are experienced as non-body, in the context of Matt's narrative, the mechanical features of his prosthesis do not work to exclude it from his body. His left (prosthetic) leg is still presented as his leg, even as it materially differs from his right (biological) leg. The distinguishing details are not introduced *merely* to distinguish his legs from one another, but are what Johnstone (1990) calls "thematic" details, in that they directly contribute to the plot of the narrative. Specifically, the details contribute to a plot that presents his prosthetic failure as a simple, unexceptional, and rectifiable lapse of bodily control. Matt's initial description of the "push button release" and "pin and ratchet" system that allow him to remove the leg (ll. 2, 4–5) form part of the narrative's orientation (Labov 1972), which Matt picks up on later in the narrative. Having explained the mechanics of how his leg is usually removed, Matt describes how the position of his leg accidentally engaged the push-button release and caused the leg to detach in the particular incident narrated (ll. 10–15, 20–23). In this story, the prosthesis is not some untrustworthy or unpredictable "other" that "turns against" the user (Rawdon Wilson 1995: 242); rather, Matt's own actions – indeed, his own *body* movements – cause the prosthesis to detach. The details work to remove the potential mystery and otherness of the prosthesis, and logically account for the malfunction as a perfectly explicable bodily lapse, like the stumble caused by not lifting one's own foot high enough to reach a curb.

Where the orientation of Matt's narrative *explains* his prosthetic failure, the resolution of his narrative presents its *repair*. Both Matt's and Lily's narratives include the complicating action of the prosthesis detaching, but in contrast to Lily's, Matt's story includes the resolution of the leg being *reattached* (ll. 36–39). Indeed, Matt non-verbally performs this aspect of his narrative, miming the reattachment of the leg (l. 39) and inviting me to witness the leg being drawn back to the deictic centre of his body. This is in striking contrast to Lily's deictic gesture *away from* her body, and the iconic gesture that ended her narrative. Her prosthesis separated from her body, and her story ended as she mimed holding it in her hands, still separated; Matt's leg separated from his body and is reattached, returning to its appropriate place as part of his body as his story ends. Matt's mime visually renders the narrative one of a rectified bodily lapse, and not of the betrayal of his body by a non-body object. Lily's prosthesis detaching was a humiliating and unresolved/unresolvable problem, and therefore a reason not to use a prosthesis; Matt's leg detaching is a temporary – and *embodied* – problem that he fixes.

This particular mime, and Matt's gestures at his leg throughout (ll. 9, 14, 22), also work to link the narrated prosthetic leg of the motorbike incident with the (different) prosthetic leg he wears as he tells me his story, implying an equivalence between the two. That is, Matt's gestures make his *present* leg a focus of our interaction, even as he discusses his *past* leg. By relating his past and present prosthetic legs, Matt is suggesting a certain degree of interchangeability, suggesting that, just as he managed the failure of the prosthesis in the events narrated, he *could* manage the failure of the prosthesis he wears as he tells the story. So, where Lily's construction of the prosthesis as non-body in the events narrated also worked to explain why she does not wear a prosthesis in the moment of storytelling, Matt's construction of his leg as a body part in the events narrated works to explain why he is happy to wear a prosthesis now, as he tells the story, or at least why he is not *afraid* to do so. Although their stories construct their prostheses in very different ways, both Matt and Lily's narratives are anchored to the bodies that they *have had*, and to the bodies that they *have*, as they tell their stories.

It is an objective fact of bodies with external prostheses that those prostheses can be detached from the rest of the body; however, the ways in which incidences of such detachment are *narrated* can constitute the construction of those prostheses as body parts or as non-body, and in turn, can constitute one particular form of narrative body construction. While in Lily's narrative, her body begins and ends with her own flesh, in Matt's narrative, we have seen that storytellers can narrate instances of prosthetic detachment and *still* construct their prostheses as body parts. The fact that prostheses are impermanent does not mean that they are never integrated into the "whole" or "seamless" body. Rather, through the stories the prosthesis-user tells, the body itself might be constructed as something that is not necessarily seamless, and something that goes beyond one's own flesh.

22.8 Discussion

Starting from the assumption that narratives are performances that are constructive of individual experience, this chapter has argued for the need to understand that individuals construct versions of their own bodies in the stories that they tell.

Specifically, I have shown how people who use prostheses, or who have done so in the past, narratively construct those prostheses as part of their bodies or as something separate and distinct from their bodies. Crucially, even as this chapter argues for the recognition of narrators' ability to construct versions of their bodies, it also recognizes the essential material reality of narrators' bodies and prostheses, and the effects of this materiality on the stories told about and through the body. The story cannot change the physical realities of the storyteller's body (or prosthesis), but it acknowledges, accounts for, and exploits these realities in its telling and in its physical performance; at the same time, the story bears on the physical body, by making meaningful its physical realities.

This chapter offers two key contributions to the understanding of the body and the study of narrative. First, it presents an argument for the recognition of narrative body constructions in the stories people tell about their bodies. While there has been much focus on the narrative construction of self in the face of illness and other bodily crises, there has so far been no such study of the narrative construction of the body itself. Equally, while there has been a specific focus on prosthesis-users' experiences of their prostheses as body or non-body, these studies tend to examine narratives as *reflective* of narrators' embodied experiences, rather than as *constructive* of their bodies. Lily and Matt's narratives may or may not reflect consistently held feelings or attitudes toward their bodies and their prostheses; what they certainly *do* do is produce versions of those bodies and prostheses. Lily constructs her prosthesis as non-body, and hence constructs her body as ending at the boundaries of her skin, by performing her narrative in a particular way, while Matt constructs his prosthesis as a body part, and hence his body as extending beyond his own flesh, by performing a very different kind of narrative. To understand bodies in terms of narrative construction is to open up new possibilities for exploring the multiple, flexible, and diverse meanings of the individual body and avoid the simplistic idea that every individual's body can be defined as no more than a fleshy object that begins and ends at the boundaries of that individual's skin. To understand narratives in terms of their construction of bodies is to open up new possibilities for narrative research, a point I will return to shortly.

The second contribution that this chapter makes is to offer a systematic way of approaching this particular type of narrative body construction, through the examination of the presentation of plots, the employment of naming and descriptive choices, and the performance of non-verbal gestures. While there may be many other aspects of narrative which work to construct the storyteller's body in some way, the analysis of these key aspects offers an accessible starting point for the examination of the narratively constructed body.

The chapter, as well as the concept of narrative body construction that it describes, also offers new directions for narrative research. Once the concept of narrative body construction is recognized, we can ask *what* other forms of narrative body construction take place, and *how* they take place. We might, for example, ask how storytellers like Matt and Lily construct their bodies in terms of other people's bodies, as opposed to asking how they construct the boundaries of their own bodies. We might ask, too, how storytellers' narratives draw on, and perhaps subvert, shared narratives about bodies in general: narratives of disability, femininity, even pollution and deterioration.

Further, while the concept of narrative body construction seeks to expand narrative analysis *beyond* the analysis of narrative identity construction, the two forms of analysis are not at odds with one another. Indeed, the embodiedness of the self means that narrative body construction will always be relevant to narrative identity construction, and vice versa. When people talk about their bodies, they are necessarily and inevitably talking about themselves: body stories *are* self stories. To return briefly to Matt's narrative, just as we can see the construction of his prosthesis as part of his body, so too can we see the construction of narrative identities, with the two modes of construction thoroughly interdependent on one another. In narrating his reaction to the prosthesis's detachment, Matt is presenting a resourceful, strategic, and agentive self who reacts quickly to resolve a potentially dangerous situation. He took control of the incident (note how he directed the actions of his unnamed assistant), and of his own body, rather than allowing the incident to become a disaster. In his jovial *performance* of the narrative, Matt is also presenting himself as carefree and self-assured, free from embarrassment or fear of such incidents of prosthetic failure. These self-constructions enforce and are enforced by Matt's narrative body construction. The jovial, agentive self in control of and unperturbed by the bodily dys-appearance only makes sense in the context of a story in which Matt's body (specifically, his prosthesis) *can be* controlled, and is not an inevitable source of alarm or disgust. In Matt's story, his construction of his own agency and joviality is contingent on the construction of his prosthesis as something over which Matt has sovereignty, and with which he has some affinity, in contrast to the prosthesis being that unruly and frightening "other" described by Rawdon Wilson and constructed by Lily.

Analyses of people's stories, including stories of bodily crises, have tended to neglect the idea that the body can be seen as a narrative construction, even where the narrative construction of the body has clear and definite implications *for* the narrative construction of the self. Narrative body construction should not simply be seen as a conduit to narrative identity construction, and should be considered in its own right. However, storytellers' narrative constructions of their bodies and selves can build on and reinforce one another. As well as representing a new field for narrative analysis, then, the analysis of narrative body construction also offers an expansion of the existing field of narrative identity analysis.

REFERENCES

Charon, R. (2006). *Narrative Medicine: Honoring the Stories of Illness*. Oxford: Oxford University Press.

Crompvoets, S. (2012). Prosthetic fantasies: Loss, recovery, and the marketing of wholeness after breast cancer. *Social Semiotics*, 22 (1), pp. 107–120.

Descartes, R. (2008). *Discourse on the Method and the Meditations*. Translated by J. Veitch. New York: Cosimo Inc.

Eakin, P. (1999). *How Lives Become Stories: Making Selves*. Ithaca, NY: Cornell University Press.

Fleischman, S. (2001). Language and medicine. In D. Schiffrin, D. Tannen, and H.E. Hamilton (eds.), *The Handbook of Discourse Analysis*. Oxford: Blackwell, pp. 470–502.

Frank, A. (1995). *The Wounded Storyteller: Body, Illness & Ethics.* Chicago, IL: University of Chicago Press.

Georgakopoulou, A. (2007). *Small Stories, Interaction and Identities.* Amsterdam: John Benjamins.

Goffman, E. (1959). *The Presentation of Self in Everyday Life.* New York: Doubleday.

Goffman, E. (1966). *Behaviour in Public Places: Notes on the Social Organization of Gatherings.* New York: The Free Press.

Goffman, E. (1968). *Stigma: Notes on the Management of Spoiled Identity.* London: Penguin.

Hacking, I. (1999). *The Social Construction of What?* Cambridge, MA: Harvard University Press.

Hacking, I. (2007). Our neo-Cartesian bodies in parts. *Critical Inquiry,* 3, pp. 78–105.

Haraway, D. (1991). A cyborg manifesto. In *Simians, Cyborgs and Women: The Reinvention of Nature.* New York: Routledge, pp. 149–182.

Heath, C. (2002). Demonstrative suffering: The gestural (re)embodiment of symptoms. *Journal of Communication,* 52 (3), pp. 597–616.

Johnstone, B. (1990). *Stories, Community and Place.* Bloomington: Indiana University Press.

Johnstone, B. (2008). *Discourse Analysis.* 2nd edn. Oxford: Wiley-Blackwell.

Kurzman, S.L. (2001). Presence and prosthesis: A response to Nelson and Wright. *Cultural Anthropology,* 16 (3), pp. 374–387.

Labov, W. (1972). *Language in the Inner City: Studies in the Black English Vernacular.* Philadelphia: University of Pennsylvania Press.

Langellier, K.M. (2001). "You're marked": Breast cancer, tattoo, and the narrative performance of identity. In J. Brockmeier and D. Carbaugh (eds.), *Narrative and Identity.* Amsterdam: John Benjamins, pp. 145–184.

Langellier, K.M., and E.E. Peterson. (2004). *Storytelling in Daily Life: Performing Narrative.* Philadelphia, PA: Temple University Press.

Leder, D. (1990). *The Absent Body.* Chicago, IL: University of Chicago Press.

McNeill, P. (1990). *Research Methods.* 2nd edn. London: Routledge.

Merleau-Ponty, M. (1962). *The Phenomenology of Perception.* London: Routledge and Kegan Paul.

Murray, C.D. (2004). An interpretative phenomenological analysis of the embodiment of artificial limbs. *Disability and Rehabilitation,* 26 (16), pp. 963–973.

Rawdon Wilson, R. (1995). Cyber(body)parts: Prosthetic consciousness. In M. Featherstone and R. Burrows (eds.), *Cyberspace/Cyberbodies/Cyberpunk: Cultures of Technological Embodiment.* London: Sage, pp. 239–259.

Riessman, C.K. (1990). Strategic uses of narrative in the presentation of self and illness: A research note. *Social Science and Medicine,* 30 (11), pp. 1195–1200.

Riessman, C.K. (2003). Performing identities in illness narrative: Masculinity and multiple sclerosis. *Qualitative Research,* 3 (1), pp. 5–33.

Smith, B. (2008). Disabled bodies and storied selves: An example of qualitative research and narrative inquiry. *European Journal of Adapted Physical Activity,* 1 (1), pp. 23–34.

Smith, B., and A.C. Sparkes. (2008). Changing bodies, changing narratives and the consequences of tellability: A case study of becoming disabled through sport. *Sociology of Health & Illness,* 30 (2), pp. 217–236.

Sobchack, V. (2007). A leg to stand on: Prosthetics, metaphor, and materiality. In J. Morra (ed.), *The Prosthetic Impulse: From a Posthuman Present to a Biocultural Future.* Cambridge, MA: MIT Press, pp. 17–42.

Sparkes, A.C., and B. Smith. (2002). Sport, spinal cord injuries, embodied masculinities, and the dilemmas of narrative identity. *Men and Masculinities,* 4 (3), pp. 258–285.

Sparkes, A.C., and B. Smith. (2011). Inhabiting different bodies over time: Narrative and pedagogical challenges. *Sport, Education and Society,* 16 (3), pp. 357–370.

Index

The Handbook of Narrative Analysis, First Edition. Edited by Anna De Fina and Alexandra Georgakopoulou.
© 2015 John Wiley & Sons, Inc. Published 2019 by John Wiley & Sons, Inc.

Printed and bound by CPI Group (UK) Ltd, Croydon, CR0 4YY